Thou Shalt Not Kill

MARY S. RYZUK

POPULAR LIBRARY

An Imprint of Warner Books, Inc.

Any similarity between the fictitious names I have created to maintain privacy and those of living persons is coincidental.

POPULAR LIBRARY EDITION

Copyright © 1990 by Mary S. Ryzuk

Popular Library® and the fanciful P design are registered trademarks of Warner Books, Inc.

Popular Library Books are published by
Warner Books, Inc.
666 Fifth Avenue
New York, N.Y. 10103

 A Warner Communications Company

Printed in the United States of America

First Printing: July, 1990

10 9 8 7 6 5 4 3 2 1

"I'M SURE MANY WILL SAY 'HOW COULD ANYONE DO SUCH A HORRIBLE THING.' MY ONLY ANSWER IS IT ISN'T EASY AND WAS ONLY DONE AFTER MUCH THOUGHT."

After the kill, John List wrote these chilling words in a written confession to the pastor of his church. The following is a photocopy of the letter's shocking ending:

John got hurt more because he seemed to struggle longer. The rest were immediately out of their pain. John probably didn't consciously feel anything either.

Please remember me in your prayers I will need them whether or not the government does its duty as it see it. I'm only concerned with making my peace with God + of this I am assured because of Christ dying even for me.—

P.S. Mother is in the hallway in the attic – 3rd floor. She was too heavy to move.

John.

CONTENTS

PART I—THE KILL

PART II—BEFORE THE KILL

PART III—AFTER THE KILL

A NOTE
TO THE READER

Thou Shalt Not Kill is a novelized version of a true crime. Although many people are involved, it is essentially John Emil List's story.

On June 1, 1989 Robert P. Clark was arrested by the FBI in Richmond, Virginia for the 1971 murders of John Emil List's mother, wife and three teenage children in Westfield, New Jersey. The FBI contended that the two, Clark and List, were one and the same man.

During the entire time I spent researching this book, Robert P. Clark insisted that he was not the fugitive John Emil List. This book was based upon my conviction that John Emil List and Robert P. Clark were one and the same man. Vindication for my convictions came on February 15, 1990, when Elijah Miller, Jr., Robert P. Clark's defense attorney, filed a series of motions in Union County, N.J.'s superior Court, one of which finally conceded that Robert P. Clark was, indeed, John Emil List.

The crime has been carefully reconstructed according to all physical evidence. Every event is based on fact as taken directly from many hours of interviews with persons who were directly concerned, as well as from police files, fire reports, newspaper photographs, police photographs, trial transcripts, magazine articles, and extensive local and national newspaper articles (See Bibliography) for example, the brilliant reportorial coverage of the case in *The New York Newsday* by columnist Carole Agus, in *The Philadelphia Inquirer* by Inga Safrrom, Stacey Burling and Carol Horner and a series of articles for New Jersey's *Courier News* which appeared daily from 8/13/89–8/21/89, by Mary

Romano and Jill Vejnoska. The same research and care went into assembling the mountains of material for this book that would have occurred had I chosen to give a strict reportorial accounting of the facts.

In addition, I have tried, with the aid of psychological experts, to delve into the minds of the participants. It was an area in which I was deeply interested. Understandably, John List's attorney, Elijah Miller, Jr., would not let his client speak with me since, at the time of this writing, he was on trial for mass murder in Union County, New Jersey. And, of course, I could not speak with the victims, Helen List, Alma List, Patricia List, John List, Jr. and Frederick List.

Since I am a creative writer, not a journalist, I chose to dramatize the facts of the story while recreating the chronology of events with as much accuracy as possible, always allowing for the possibility of errors in research through the distortion of time and memory. In reconstructing 64 years of a man's life, there were, unavoidably, some gaps that had to be bridged. Certain scenes had to be dramatically reconstructed in order to portray more effectively the personalities of the direct participants. Although dramatic license has been taken, particularly in the creation of dialogue, not one incident, as depicted, did not have the authenticity of events as remembered by people who lived them and knew the Lists personally.

In choosing to novelize a true story, I must make the following point very clear: It is in the recreation of the private moments of all of the public figures in this case, both alive and deceased—most particularly with dramatically imagined and recreated dialogue within the family structures of the Lists, Morrises, Syferts and Clarks—that I claim the most dramatic license to have been taken and in which errors of word and interpretation might have been made. But since the dialogue was created to fill gaps in the narrative as well as to capture the essential flavor of the events and to help in understanding the characters as intimately as possible, I beg indulgence.

My feelings kept changing as I took an emotionally charged journey through 64 years of John List's life.

I have done my best to mirror faithfully what happened. In doing so, it has not been my purpose either to condemn or forgive. What I have tried to do is give this tragic story the dignity of understanding. I have no "conclusions." I leave them to those of you who take the journey with me. I leave the legal judgments to the Union County, New Jersey judicial system. And the final judgments to John List's own God.

Mary S. Ryzuk
May, 1990

CAST OF CHARACTERS

John Emil List	confessed murderer
Robert Peter Clark	alias for John List

Helen Morris Taylor List	John List's 45-year-old wife	murdered
Alma M. List	his 85-year-old mother	murdered
Patricia Marie List	his 16-year-old daughter	murdered
John Frederick List (John junior)	his 15-year-old son	murdered
Frederick Michael List	his 13-year-old son	murdered

Family Members

Delores Miller Clark	Robert P. Clark's wife
Brenda Taylor List Herndon De Young	Helen List's daughter by first marriage
Harold List	John List's cousin
Reverend and Mrs. Herbert J. Meyer	Alma List's sister (Aunt Lydia)
Edward Morris	Helen List's brother
Eva Morris	Helen List's mother
Fred H. Morris	Helen List's brother
James W. Morris	Helen List's brother
Betty Jean Syfert	Helen List's sister
Gene Syfert	Jean Syfert's husband
Marvin Everett Taylor	Helen List's first husband

Pastors who have served the List/Clark family

Reverend Louis Grother	Zion Lutheran Church, Kalamazoo, Michigan
Reverend Herbert A. Mayer	Zion Lutheran Church, Bay City, Michigan
Reverend Edward Saresky	Faith Lutheran Church, Rochester, N.Y.
Reverend Alfred T. Scheips	Univ. of Michigan Chaplain
Reverend Eugene A. Rehwinkel	Lutheran Church of the Redeemer, Westfield, NJ
Reverend Joseph Vought	Lutheran Church of Our Savior, Richmond, Va.
Reverend Robert West	St. Paul's Lutheran Church, Denver, Colo.

Helen List's Doctors

Dr. Brady
Dr. Maxilind
Dr. Arnold Rose
Dr. Vitalli

Dr. Eugene Loeser
Dr. Mueller
Dr. Richard Taylor
Dr. Zazanis

Westfield Police Department

Lieut. Det. Robert Bell
Investigator John Connelly
Officer Stanley J. Cyran
Sergeant Charles Haller
Desk Sergeant Floyd Hewitt
Officer Robert Kenny
Captain John Lintott
Sergeant Earl Lambert
Lieutenant Bernard Marmalo
Chief of Police James A. Moran (at time of murders)
Sergeant William Muth
Lieutenant Glenn Owens
Officer William Roeben
Chief of Police Anthony Scutti (at time of List's capture)
Captain Richard Tidey
Lieutenant Det. Bernard "Barney" Tracy
Captain Alfred Vardalis
Captain Robert Ward
Detective Yanusz
Sergeant George Zhelesnik

Westfield Fire Department

Deputy Chief G. Breitfeller
Fireman J. Brennan
Fireman R. Gary
Fireman Larkin
Fireman Charles Pfefer
Captain Walter Ridge
Chief Norman Ruerup

Union County, N.J.

Karl Asch	Assistant Union County Prosecutor
Judge Edward W. Beglin, Jr.	Union County Superior Court
Deputy Sheriff Peter Campanelli	Union County Deputy Sheriff
Eleanor Clark	Assistant Union County Prosecutor
Brian D. Gillet	Assistant Union County Prosecutor
Dr. Bernard Ehrenberg	Union County Medical Examiner
Sheriff Ralph Froehlich	Union County Sheriff
Judge Bryant W. Griffin	Union County Superior Court
Roger Halpern	Union County Clerk
David Hancock	Union County Prosecutor's office
Sergeant Jeffrey Hummel	Union County Prosecutor's office
Deputy Sheriff William Malcolm, Jr.	Union County Sheriff's office, Fugitive Squad
Deputy Sheriff William Malcolm	Union County Sheriff's office, Fugitive Squad
Captain Frank Marranca	Union County Prosecutor's office

Sergeant William Mello	Union County Prosecutor's office
Elijah Miller, Jr.	Union County Public Defender
Michael Mitzner	Assistant Union County Prosecutor
Andrew Nardelli	N. J. forensic scientist
Sheriff Ralph Oriscella	Union County Sheriff's office
Dr. Maximilian Schoss	Union County Medical Examiner
Sergeant Joseph Simmons	Union County Prosecutor's office
Sergeant Joan Spano	Union County security
John Stamler	Union County Prosecutor
Judge Jerome Switzer	Union County Superior Court
Judge William L'E. Wertheimer	Union County Superior Court

Westfield, N.J.

Herbert Argast	Milkman
Barbara and David Baeder	Neighbors and fellow church congregants
Rick and David Baeder	their sons
John Bakke	First Fidelity Trust
Ellen Scott Brandt	Associate Editor—*The Westfield Leader*
Jack J. Camillo	Westfield resident
Bob Compton	Westfield student—classmate
Dr. and Mrs. William Cunnick	Neighbors
Kitty Duncan	Owner—Jarvis Pharmacy
Lorraine Eisenbach	Westfield Home Newspaper Service
Kathleen L. Gardner	Editor—*The Westfield Leader*
Eileen Gilmartin (Jones)	KVM Assoc.
Carol Hollstein	Suburban Trust Bank
Edwin Illiano	Westfield Recreation—drama teacher
Gay Jacobus	KVM Assoc.
Susan Jacobus	Roosevelt Jr. H.S. teacher
Robin Kampf	Resident and researcher for this book
Jane Kemp	Neighbor
Margaret Koleszar	KVM Assoc.
Mildred Kreger	Westfield schools attendance officer
Lamperty Brothers	Donors of tombstone to List family at cost
Dr. L. E. Law	Westfield Superintendent of Schools
Marvin Marr	Roosevelt Jr. H.S. teacher
David J. Meeker	Attorney for Mr. Poppy of Gray's Funeral Home
Patricia Mozaki	Westfield student—classmate
Mr. Charles Frederick Poppy	Gray's Funeral Home
William Praesel	Duke's Sub Shop
Robert L. Scully	Suburban Trust Bank
Ann Sales	Roosevelt Jr. H.S. secretary
Barbara Sheridan	Westfield Recreation drama teacher assistant

Warren T. Vliet	President, KVM Assoc.
John Wittke	Neighbor

Federal Bureau of Investigation

Kevin M. August	Glen Henelright
J. Wallace LaPrade	Barry Martino
Joseph C. McGinley	Kevin O'Hara
John Stattler	Drucilla Wells

Denver, Colorado

Wanda Flanery	Robert and Delores Clark's neighbor
Randy and Eva Flanery Mitchell	Wanda Flanery's daughter and son-in-law
Mr. Morrow	President of All-Packaging Co., Aurora, Colo.
Jim Roberto	Roberto Distributing Co.

Richmond, Virginia

Gerald Bailles	Governor of Virginia
David P. Baugh	Robert Clark's second defense attorney
M. H. Bruce	Virginia State Police
Joel G. Clarke	Robert Clark's first defense attorney
Mr. and Mrs. Pat Ferguson	Robert and Delores Clark's neighbors
Christopher Ferguson	their 11-year-old son
Judge Al Harris	Henrico County
Charles S. Joyner	Maddrea, Joyner, Kirkham & Woody
Judge David G. Lowe	Henrico County
Ross Mise	Henrico County investigator
Sandra Silbermann	Secretary—Maddrea, Joyner, Kirkham & Woody
Les Wingfield	C.P.A.—Maddrea, Joyner, Kirkham & Woody

Others

Kurt C. Bauer	bought List's property
Frank Bender	Philadelphia forensic artist
Benjamin Bontempo	bid on List's property
Mr. Calzone	bid on List's property
Edward Dross	Social security administrator
Richard Eittreim	Attorney—State Mutual Life Assurance Co.
Ronald Fain	Jury foreman
Burton Goldstein	State Mutual Life Assurance Co.
Irving J. Johnston	Attorney from First National Savings & Loan
Thomas Kean	Governor of New Jersey
Michael Lindner	*America's Most Wanted*—TV

Colleen O'Connor	National Director-ACLU
Randall Pinkston	CNN-Cable TV
Benjamin Peterson	State Mutual Life Assurance Co.
Margaret Roberts	*America's Most Wanted*—TV
Richard D. Walter	Criminal psychologist
Bob Wismer	John List's ROTC buddy

Pseudonyms

The following list represents two categories:
1. Real people who were interviewed and preferred to have their names withheld.
2. Real people who, for purposes of clarification, have been drawn into composites.

Connie Anderson	Mrs. Karen Peter
Katie and Neil Anderson	Mrs. Putnam
Mr. and Mrs. Bennett	Mr. and Mrs. Jack Raeder
Ed Benson	Mr. and Mrs. Michael Ryan
Howard Birdson	Bill Sauter
Bob Canfield	Edward Schneider
Mr. and Mrs. Joseph Davidson	Geraldine Schneider
Mr. and Mrs. Emerson	Peter Schneider
Jonah Folger	Dr. Schumann
Gerhard Herrmann	Richard Severeid
Mrs. Hollister	Cindy Taylor
Paula Hudson	Sheldon Thorn
Terry Henderson Lewis	Richard Tobias
Alfred Logan	George Candem
Rose Linden	Mr. and Mrs. Vandermere
Frank Moreland	Mitch, Pam and Mary Vandermere
Mr. and Mrs. Bill Murray	Christina Worman
Jake O'Hara	
Mr. and Mrs. Hank O'Malley	

Specialists consulted
J. T. Francisco, Psy.D.
Vincent L. DeChiaro, Ed.D., A.C.S.W.
Louis Schlesinger, Psy.D.
Reverend John Rieker, pastor of the Lutheran Church of the Holy Spirit, Montville, N.J.

ACKNOWLEDGMENTS

Special thanks to:
Warner Books editor, **Fredda Isaacson**, for her encouragement, patience and red pencil....to **Gene Light** for his "introduction"....to my friend and agent **Bertha Klausner** for her belief in me....to my colleague and researcher, **Shellie Sclan**, for her intuitiveness and enthusiasm for travel....to **Franziska Ryzuk** for her help with the German portions of this book. ...to **Pamela Ryzuk** for her extraordinary secretarial skills.... to **Sam Sayegh** of WJDM Radio Elizabeth and WINS, New York for establishing the accuracy of the trial and courtroom proceedings....to **Richard and Diane Cappel** who have taught me the meaning of true friendship through their loyalty and support....and to **Robin Kampf** whose candor with her own personal recollections, hard work and investigative diligence were essential in helping to tell the List story with truthfulness and accuracy.

Very special thanks go to my sons, **Regan** and **Mitchell**, for all of their support....and most particularly to my lifetime companion and love, **Ony**.

PART I | THE KILL

1 | The Lights Go Out

Westfield, New Jersey—December 7, 1971

It was rainy and getting colder. "Cloudy skies with periods of rain are expected today for northern and central Jersey," the radio weatherman announced in his measured deep bass voice. "Temperatures in the mid-fifties dropping into the low thirties tonight. Winds gusting . . ."

Mrs. Bennett, checking to see that the windows of her house on Hillside Avenue were tightly closed against the cold, could no longer ignore the conflicting anxieties she was experiencing as she looked out at the neighboring List house. On one hand, she had always prided herself on being the kind of neighbor who had the good sense to mind her own business; on the other, she could not get over the nagging apprehension that something was wrong.

The lights on all three floors of the formal, nineteen-room Victorian house—so stately and grand that it was always referred to as a "mansion"—had been blazing throughout the nights for most of the past month. They streamed through the huge double-hung, wood-laced windows of the main-floor dining room, through the smaller windows of the back laundry room and the kitchen, and through the pastel curtains of the second-floor bedroom of John List and his wife, Helen. Night and day for the past month the light over the beautiful heavy-paneled double front door had shone on the five broadly spaced entry steps leading to the imposing white-columned portico. The soft glow, captured under the stiffly squared roof, spilled across the wrought-iron gate at the steps, onto the long circular driveway that graced the entrance.

Mrs. Bennett knew that the List family was away on vacation and that the lights had been left burning for normal security reasons; nothing at all surprising about that. It was a common practice in the area to leave lights on in order to discourage potential burglars. Westfield was an affluent bedroom community, populated largely by upper-middle-class executives who commuted the fifteen miles to and from New York City in order to afford their families the

3

peace and quiet of suburban life. Usually, nothing more serious than teen speeding disturbed Westfield's inherent serenity, yet families realized that leaving a house unattended for prolonged periods of time offered a temptation to anyone looking for an opportunity to break and enter.

But the early part of last week the lights in the List house had started to flicker and go out. First the upstairs bedroom light went out. Then the dining room windows suddenly went dark. While driving by, Mrs. Bennett saw the overhead portico light bulb snap off, throwing the front porch into black shadows, and she could not get over the feeling that something was definitely wrong.

"It's so strange. Shouldn't we do something?" she asked her husband later as she stared out of her window at the List house.

"What do you want to do?" he asked.

"Well . . . I don't know. . . . Look. . . ."

Mr. Bennett moved next to her and peered across the nearly frozen green lawns.

An air of mystery had always seemed to surround that house, he thought, right from the first day the Lists moved in five years ago. The neighbors had given a welcoming party for the family, but it had not set the expected tone for shared neighborliness. Shortly after moving in, Helen List had gone into seclusion within the walls of the rambling mansion. She had not been seen again since the night of that welcoming party. Rumor had it that she had suffered some sort of nervous breakdown. Now the List mansion, standing silent and smoky white in the fog of the December night, looked deserted, eerie.

"Even if nothing is wrong . . ." Mrs. Bennett continued tentatively.

Mr. Bennett looked closer. The house suddenly seemed to take on an even deeper cloak of gloom; and when he asked, "What could be wrong?" he found himself whispering.

"I don't know," she said. "Nothing, I guess. But even so, if the lights are burning out and they aren't back from vacation yet, that's going to leave the house vulnerable. Don't you think so? I mean, if it all goes black."

"How long has it been since you've seen the Lists, anyway?" Mr. Bennett asked.

"I can't remember exactly, but weeks. Way before Thanksgiving."

"Didn't they say anything to you when they left? Like 'Look after the place' or 'Keep an eye out' or anything like that?"

"Since when do they ever talk to anyone!" she exclaimed.

He nodded, knowing what she meant.

"Besides," she continued, "I never saw them before they left."

"Me neither. And the car's been gone."

Mrs. Bennett was starting to get that same uneasy feeling she had experienced a week ago when she'd noticed the first light go out. "One day they were just gone and the lights were burning night and day. Now . . ." She hesitated. "What if someone is turning them off?"

"Who?" he asked skeptically.

She shrugged lightly. "I don't know."

Mr. Bennett became very thoughtful. "I don't like to start trouble."

"Well neither do I, but. . . ."

"But maybe we should inform the police. You know, tell them that the lights are being turned off and the family's still not back."

"Yes," she said, and moved toward the telephone, realizing that all she had needed was a little encouragement. She picked up her phone and dialed 411.

"Information. Can I help you?" The operator's voice broke the silence.

"Listing, please, for the Westfield Police."

A short beat. "Westfield 9–4000."

"Thank you." Mrs. Bennett pressed the disconnect button with her thumb, released it, waited for the dial tone, and dialed Westfield 9 . . . But suddenly a feeling of foolishness began to dispel her sense of foreboding, and she quickly hung up.

"It's probably nothing," she said sheepishly to her husband.

He shook his head at her indecisiveness.

Several of their neighbors also were harboring the same suspicions. Dr. William Cunnick and his wife, Shirley, lived across the street. The List children had excitedly told Shirley they were going to North Carolina for Thanksgiving and that their grandmother, Alma List, who lived on the third floor, was going to Michigan at the same time. Alma had even asked if Shirley would have her shoes fixed while she was away. Now the Cunnicks also had become apprehensive when they noticed the lights going out after the third week. The children never came to tell about their trip. Alma never came to pick up her shoes. When Shirley had knocked on the door there had been no answer. Now Dr. Cunnick thought the house had an increasingly sinister appearance, an abandoned aspect. He didn't expect a family tragedy, but he did know that the family had been under a great deal of stress lately, that the wife was ill, and that John List had recently suffered a disastrous change of employment.

Other neighbors such as the Ryans and the O'Malleys had also noticed the growing air of desertion and had begun to express concern, but nobody felt close enough to the Lists to take action. Like the Bennetts, they watched and wondered.

2 | Discovery of a Dead Family

On that same foggy December day, Ed Illiano was also thinking about the List family. He was sixteen-year-old Patty's drama coach at the Westfield Recreation Group. He knew she was in North Carolina visiting relatives, but even when she went away for a weekend, she usually sent him a postcard. It wasn't like her not to write, especially when the drama group was in rehearsals and so close to opening night. True, she was only understudying the role of Blanche DuBois in Tennessee Williams's *Streetcar Named Desire*, but she was now supposed to be trying out for a part in *Arsenic and Old Lace*. She had been so excited at the prospect when he had last spoken with her, yet she had not written to tell him when she was returning or, indeed, if she would be back in time for the production at all.

Although Ed had a genuine interest in all the youngsters in the theater group, he was especially fond of Patty. Perhaps it was because she seemed to need the emotional outlet acting provided; her home life was not a very happy one, he'd heard. He'd driven past her house on a couple of evenings, even ventured into the driveway and found no one there. It was very strange. Maybe the police knew something. He checked his watch—only 4:30—why not call his friend, Al Vardalis, who had been on the force for twenty years, and see if he thought this was something worth investigating?

Captain Vardalis listened to Ed's concerns. This inquiry was the first indication he'd had that anything might be wrong.

"I'll do what I can," he promised, and assigned an officer to contact the Westfield High School and inquire about Patty.

"No problem," the officer reported back an hour later. "They went on vacation."

"How do you know?"

"Mr. List himself notified the school authorities that his family would be away." But Vardalis hadn't been completely satisfied himself. At 7:30 P.M., with a few moments on his hands, he took it one step further. Pulling out his "Polk" directory, which lists addresses first, he contacted several neighbors on Hillside Avenue. No one seemed to know anything definite. When he called Mrs. Cunnick and asked her if she noticed anything peculiar regarding the Lists' residence, she told him about the burning lights going out one by one and that each night for about a week, a white Pontiac had driven up into the driveway, parked for a few minutes, and then left.

"Next time you see that car," Vardalis said, "I'd appreciate it if you would call me immediately."

It was 9:30 in the evening and still drizzling as Ed and Barbara Sheridan, the assistant drama coach, got into his car.

"Thanks, Barbara," Ed said, "for coming along with me tonight. I know we may be on a fool's errand, but I just have this feeling. . . . You know, Patty and her brothers seemed so scared of their father. I called Al this afternoon, and he said he would investigate, but I wanted to take another look at the house myself."

The drive to 431 Hillside Avenue took only a few minutes. As they approached, Barbara sighed, "I've always admired this house."

It was a stately old Victorian home with Colonial influences built at the turn of the century on a full acre on a broad and grassy hill. Painted white with greenish shutters, it belonged on this street where the neighboring homes were valued between $75,000 and $100,000. It even had a thirty-seven foot ballroom in the rear.

Ed and Barbara pulled into the sweeping circular driveway and parked just past the main entrance. It's really something, Barbara thought, even though she could see that the frame structure was beginning to reveal the kind of external decay and disrepair that accompany prolonged neglect. It had been decades since the peeling paint had been scraped away and replaced with a freshening coat. Every surface of the huge, multisided house needed attention. She knew the interior wasn't much better. Walls were cracked. Ceilings were crumbling, and in some places paint was peeling in huge splintered chunks from the plaster walls.

The front porch was dark as they walked up the wide steps, but they could see light in some of the windows.

"Look at that," Ed said. There were fewer lights burning now than the first time he had driven up to the house just a few days ago. "It's darker."

Ed knocked on the front door. There was no answer. He moved to one of the long windows flanking the door and looked inside. Aided by lights spilling through the door of the kitchen deep in the backround, he could see the darkened outlines of the long main hallway within and the austere shadows of the wide central staircase, but little else. They stepped off the porch and moved to the right of the house. As they pushed their way through the space between the tall evergreen shrubbery, they were both beginning to feel uneasy. They peered into the first-floor window in front. The room inside, empty of furniture, looked deserted.

"Let's go round to the back," Ed suggested.

Mrs. Cunnick across the street dialed Westfield 9–4000. It was 9:50 P.M.

"Westfield Police Sergeant Floyd Hewitt speaking."

"I'd like to speak to Captain Vardalis," she said.

"One minute," said the desk officer.

She waited until she heard the familiar voice pick up a connecting line. "Captain Vardalis here."

"This is Mrs. Cunnick up on Hillside Avenue."

"Yes, hello."

"That car is back," she found herself whispering. "The white Pontiac."

Ed and Barbara made their way to the back of the house, past a flower garden that even in the dark they could see was overgrown with dead weeds that had not been pulled during the growing season.

They opened the screen door and knocked on the top portion of the Dutch door. Through the smudged panes of glass they could see that no one was in the back hallway. Angling sharply to their right, they were able to see part of the deserted kitchen through the darkened laundry. Dishes were piled up in the drain board next to the kitchen sink.

They walked around to the ballroom and peered into the windows. The windowsills were too high. They could not see inside. They circled the house. "Something's wrong," Barbara said. "Let's call Vardalis."

Ed thought a moment, stood back and studied the apparently deserted house with lights still blazing in some of the upstairs windows, and nodded.

"Let's go."

Patrolmen Charles Haller and George Zhelesnik were on Rahway Avenue near the high school at 9:55 P.M. when they received the call from Desk Sergeant Floyd Hewitt to proceed to 431 Hillside Avenue to investigate a neighbor's suspicions regarding a house that had been vacant for a month. "A possible burglary," Zhelesnik told his partner.

"I know the place," Haller said as he turned the patrol car in the direction of Hillside Avenue. "I remember when we got the notice to watch that house while the family's away. On vacation or something."

"Wasn't that a while ago?"

"Yeah."

At 10:03 P.M. the lone patrol car pulled up in front of the house, coming to a quiet stop directly near a short flat rail fence that bordered an unlit lamppost at the edge of the property. "Leave it here," Zhelesnik said. Haller could see in the headlight beams that the rocky driveway was muddy. They parked, got out, and began the long walk up to the front entrance where a white Pontiac was parked.

As Ed and Barbara started toward their car to find a telephone, they saw the police car pull up at the curb.

"Is that your car?" Zhelesnik asked.

"Yes," Ed said. "We're glad you're here. We were just going to call you."

"Do you live here?"

"No, I'm Ed Illiano. I teach drama at the municipal building. . . ."

"Oh, yeah," Haller said, recognizing him. "I think I've seen you around."

Barbara and Ed quickly told them their worries about the silent house, about contacting Captain Vardalis, and about their growing suspicions. The two patrolmen knocked on the front door, but there was no response from within. "It might be easier to break in at the back," Ed suggested.

"Break in?"

"These people haven't been seen in weeks."

"No, wait," Haller said. They walked around the porch to the east side of the house. The window was unlatched. He lifted it open and crawled into the room next to four oversize fish tanks. He could see a container of fish food sitting on top and the silent gleam of a couple of fish moving slowly about in the murky water in one of the tanks. He was immediately struck by the stale smell and the sound of music. The room was dark. He turned on his flashlight.

"Wait here," Zhelesnik said before following Haller inside. But Illiano wasn't about to wait. He climbed in behind them. What he would later describe as "churchlike music" was playing softly throughout the house on an intercom.

"Hello?" Zhelesnik called loudly into the interior of the house. "Anyone here?"

"Patty?" Illiano called.

None of them really expected a response. And none came.

Barbara saw the beam of flashlights within the house. Suddenly frightened at being left alone on the porch, she lifted herself into the house through the window just as she heard Zhelesnik say, "These people must have moved. There's no furniture."

"No," Barbara said as she shivered in the bone-chilling cold of the deserted house. It's colder inside than outside, she thought. "There wasn't much the last time I was here, either."

Even in its barrenness, the house struck them as beautiful and rich as they moved to the first room on the right to start their search. They headed through the empty dining room and butler's pantry, drawn to the back kitchen where a small light still burned. In the spillage of light they saw stains on the wall in the pantry. They weren't immediately identifiable as blood to Barbara and Ed, but the two patrolmen glanced at each other and quietly unlatched their side arms. It was purely a precautionary action; the rooms had the stale, frigid feel of a house that had been unoccupied for a prolonged period of time. On the checkerboard tiled floor of the empty kitchen, they saw crumpled newspapers on a small rug. The floor was streaked with dark stains, as were the walls and woodwork next to the door.

"I don't like this," Barbara murmured apprehensively.

"We'll look around. You stay here."

"No," she said quickly. "I'll come with you."

From the kitchen they moved into the rear hallway that led through the interior of the house back toward the front door. The liturgical music followed them softly, but it was the smell that made the greatest impact. It was an odor that would haunt Ed forever. Barbara was particularly sensitive to odors, and she tried not to inhale too deeply. Now they could see that the floor in the hallway was smeared with long thin streaks of a ruddy-brown substance that looked like dried blood even to Ed and Barbara. Drag marks.

Going down on one knee, Haller inspected the floor more closely. The dark brown blood was brittle to the scrape of his fingernail.

Oh, God, something terrible's happened. They looked at each other anxiously. No one wanted to speculate.

The streaks covered a broad section of the floor, thinning out in spots as though unsuccessful attempts had been made to wipe the floor clean.

"This way. . . ."

Standing near the kitchen door, they began to follow the line of the stain . . . back through the hallway. . . . The stains turned right into the parlor and seemed to lead toward the back of the house, where Barbara and Ed knew there was a huge room, sometimes referred to as a ballroom. Ed pulled aside the heavy gray curtain that was obstructing the entrance. The music and the dank odor coming from the cold, thirty-seven-foot room seemed to be stronger beyond the curtain.

With the cloak of darkness minimizing its peeling disrepair, the room impressed the two patrolmen with its beauty and elegance. The intricacy of the high ceilings designed with detailed moldings could be discerned in the shafts of night light coming from the huge skylight overhead. The stained-glass ceiling, dark against the night sky, was rich with colors. The walls were deep oak paneling with English-style cut molding. The windows were stained glass and the wood floor was intricately designed parquet. On top of the mantel of the tall, ornately carved Italian green marble fireplace sat a soda can and a glass, leftovers from a recent Halloween party.

They looked down and saw what appeared to be mounds of clothes stacked like laundry that had been sorted out and separated in the middle of the floor next to the fireplace. It took a moment for them to accept the evidence of their own eyes, to realize that the mounds of "clothing" were four bodies placed side by side just to the left of the marble fireplace. Trails of blood still marked the route along which the bodies had been dragged from the place of their murders to the ballroom, which had been turned into a neatly rowed family mortuary.

Ed tried to pull Barbara back as she began to shake, but she was rooted to the spot. She saw the witch's hat in the corner and realized that it too was a macabre leftover from the Halloween party Patricia had thrown a month earlier.

"Are these the people you were looking for?" Haller asked quietly.

Ed nodded. He didn't have to look closely at the bodies. He knew who they were. They had found the bodies of Helen List and her three children: Patricia Marie, age sixteen: John Frederick, Jr., age fifteen: and Frederick Michael, age thirteen.

They were still exactly as their killer had left them one month earlier, with rags of toweling over their faces serving as their only shrouds. The three children were placed side by side on bloodied sleeping bags. Their mother, also on a sleeping bag stiff with blood, lay at a T angle beyond their heads.

Patrolman Haller touched the woman to feel for a pulse, but it was like squeezing a piece of wood. The arm was hard and stiff. She was obviously dead.

Ed finally managed to pull Barbara away and into the dining room. Officer Zhelesnik remained behind with them as Officer Haller now hurried down the long driveway and pulled open the door of the patrol car. "My God, you'd better send help out here," he radioed into headquarters. "There's been a mass murder. There's bodies all over the place." Then he started the engine and drove up to the front of the house, his tires spinning on the muddy rocks beneath.

"We'd better check the rest of the house," Zhelesnik told Haller when he returned. "You two stay here." Ed nodded.

The first room the two officers came to on the second floor obviously belonged to the dead woman. They felt like intruders as they looked into the privacy of her bedroom. On the nightstand next to the unmade bed were a pack of Raleigh cigarettes, a Zippo lighter, and a glass ashtray. The bed had been slept in; the chenille bedspread and blankets were pulled down and in disarray.

"Look. . . ." They noticed a few stains of dried blood on the sheets of the bed, no more than three or four small splotches.

"There isn't enough blood for her to have been killed here," Zhelesnik said.

"The killer must have sat here afterward," Haller agreed. "On the bed. Maybe he had some blood on his clothes."

The next bedroom they entered obviously belonged to one of the boys: metal desk, unmade double bed, small mahogany harp table acting as a nightstand, a radio built into the headboard of the bed, no curtains on the windows, wood walls, nothing much on the bed, a couple of socks, no blankets. It was John junior's room.

Then they came to Freddie's room. In it were an antique-looking, mahogany bed with a tall Ethan Allen–style headboard and an old wooden rocking chair in the corner. There were no curtains on the windows, just drawn window shades. A small worn rug was on the floor; an unframed landscape print hung over the bed. The room looked just as bare as the others. "Doesn't seem like a kid lived here. . . ."

They moved to the next bedroom. "This has to be the girl's room. Looks like she smoked Marlboros," Haller said, noting the pack on top of a dull white dresser. There was a bare box spring and sheeted mattress. A book, an empty glass, tissues, another book, two wall posters tacked up on the raggedy walls, an old lamp. "The kind you buy at J. C. Penney," Zhelesnik thought. Again no curtains on any of the windows. The blanket was tossed aside on the unmade bed.

"Looks like they just got up to go to school. . . ."

After surveying the last bedroom, the policemen went up the flight of steps to the third story, which seemed to be a private apartment. They could hear the music playing through a wall intercom in one of the rooms. As they hit the upper landing, they immediately noticed a sharp difference in maintenance and care. To the right was a woman's pretty bedroom. It had the sharply slanted ceiling of an attic roof tapering over the bed, which was perfectly made up with a pretty, fresh chenille bedspread. The room was in perfect order. Even the two large-size floral-colored slippers were aligned symmetrically close to the bed on the twist rug covering the floor. Crisp, white princess curtains were crisscrossed over the windows.

As they followed the source of the music, the telltale stench of decaying flesh became powerful again. The two policemen looked at each other grimly. They knew they were in for another grisly discovery. All they had to do was follow the odor. They went into the kitchen, which had a light burning. It was white. Spotless. Scrubbed. All items—canister sets, kitchen utensils, hand towels, pot holders—were precisely placed in neat, orderly rows. The intercom was on the wall over the stove. It was Officer Zhelesnik who opened the door to the large storage area off the kitchen. The stench in the enclosed area was stomach-wrenching.

Although the face was covered with a dish towel, it was obvious that they had discovered the body of a large, heavy-boned woman wearing a print housedress with a short apron tied about her waist. Her position was extremely awkward. She was lying on her back just a few feet away from her white stove and white cabinets. Her knees were spread wide apart, while the calves of her legs were positioned underneath her as though she had collapsed to her knees and fallen onto her haunches with her head thrown backward.

Haller bent to lift the towel from her face. Removing the covering revealed an old woman with her mouth agape and her eyes wide open, staring wildly at the ceiling behind her. They recoiled at the sight of the old lady stiff and unnatural in her grossly undignified position with an expression of utter horror on her face. Time had taken a heavy toll. Her cheeks had caved in, and her short white hair, discolored with the residue of her own blood, was standing almost on end. Her left hand was raised up toward her head and splattered with blood, her right was over her lower stomach, stiff, blackened, very bony, and thin, as though the flesh had withered away under the skin. The fingers were stretched wide apart and pointing rigidly toward the door where her killer had stood. She had been shot just above her left eye.

Next door, Mr. and Mrs. Bennett sat comfortably ensconced for the evening watching their favorite television program, when they became aware of the flashing red lights in the street. The silent night had suddenly exploded with activity. Hillside Avenue was jammed with patrol cars parked in the street directly outside at crazy angles; some even pulled up on the dark frozen lawn next door. The List mansion was swarming with police.

Something *was* wrong.

Hastily erected police barricades seemed to materialize out of nowhere to hold back the growing crowd of curious neighbors attracted from their homes by the abnormal activity. The breath from their excited conversations was visible in short bursts of steam punctuating the cold night air. No one knew what was going on. The reason for the commotion. They shivered in the December night and pulled their coats tighter about themselves.

Shadows of policemen could be seen moving through the List home.

A dark car pulled up. Chief of Police James Moran and Lieutenant Detective Robert Bell emerged from the car and entered the house with a brief nod to those who made room for them to pass. The mournful organ music still played softly throughout the house as they looked at the four bodies lying on the ballroom floor.

"Where's that coming from?" Moran demanded.

"A record player in a hall closet. It's been playing all this time, and—"

"Well, turn the damn thing off!" The scene was eerie enough without adding the accompaniment of the kind of background music straight out of a grade-B horror movie. There was a sense of relief when the music was finally silenced.

In the ballroom, Chief Moran ordered, "Let's get some light in here." And as police trained large flashlights on the bodies, they could begin to draw conclusions about what had happened.

Helen List had been shot in the left side of the head. It was easily surmised from the trail of bloodstains that the killer had dragged her body by the feet from the kitchen to the ballroom. Her arms, sprawled above her head and heavily streaked with blood, must have trailed behind and gathered the leaking spillage of her own blood from her head wound. Her nightgown had ridden up above her thighs, leaving her legs, also smeared with blood, completely exposed and slightly apart, with both toes pointing outward toward the fireplace. Her left eye was closed, but her right was wide open and glaring. She had no eyelid left. Her mouth was misshapen and twisted as though grotesquely startled by the violence of sudden death. With her hair flattened to her head by massive blood loss, her head appeared skull-like. The position in which the killer had dragged her was the manner in which he'd left her. He had not even bothered to cover up her nakedness.

Swallowing hard, the investigators turned to Patty List.

The young girl lay on her left side just under a miniature pool table on which was a tipped over vase of artificial flowers. She was wearing a winter parka, jeans, and sneakers as though she had just come home when surprised by her killer. Her body, with her hands hidden beneath her, was in a loose fetal position. It appeared that she had also been dragged by her feet and probably rolled onto the sleeping blanket only inches away from her mother. Her left cheek was pressed so deeply into the bloodied little flower designs of the sleeping blanket that her face was not visible. Her long hair, partially hidden by the shoulders of her jacket, was parted down the middle. She had been shot in the head.

"Aw, Jesus," Lieutenant Detective Bell said softly, looking at the next body. "This one here's just a little kid."

Lying on his stomach, the boy didn't look more than ten or eleven years old. Freddie had also been shot in the head. He, too, had on a winter jacket, dark corduroy pants, and shoes. His right cheek was pressed down. His right arm was bent and extended slightly with the hand up to his shoulder. His left arm was beneath him. He had been placed to the girl's right . . . close to her . . . facing her. They were covered up enough in their heavy winter clothing so that, except for the pools of blood under both their heads that had deep-ened the red color of the sleeping bags, they appeared to be sleeping.

There was no peace in the repose of the young man next to them. He lay flat on his back with his winter jacket unzipped and spread wide apart, and the savagery of his slaughter was obvious to the observers. He had been shot repeatedly by his murderer. His right hand, lying across his stomach, still wore a bloodied woolen glove. His bullet-battered head, with bushy hair messed and matted with blood, was turned so sharply to his right that his chin almost touched his right shoulder. His face was covered with so much blood, it masked the decomposition of the flesh beneath. The color of his shirt was unrecognizable because of the amount of blood that had gushed from all the chest wounds. "He's just a kid, too," Chief Moran said quietly, "Big, but not a man yet. . . ."

Captain Vardalis took his own patrol car up to the house as soon as he heard about the grim discovery and joined Chief James Moran, Lieutenant Detective Robert Bell, Haller, Zhelesnik, Sergeant Detective William Muth, Sergeant William Kenny, Patrolman Robert Kenny, and Patrolman William Roeben. Members of the Union County Detective Department, led by Captain R. Ward and by Dr. Maximilian Schoss, the Union County medical examiner, arrived soon after.

Throughout the rooms where the killings had taken place, walls and woodwork were streaked with caked blood where efforts had been made to wipe them clean. Besides the paper bag in the ballroom full of the towels now browned and hardened with dried blood, police found two more bags in the kitchen crammed with paper towels and newspapers that had been used by the killer in the cleanup attempt.

One rookie patrolman came out of the front door and stood silently in the middle of the lawn directly in front of the portico. He leaned against the wrought-iron railing, took off his cap, and rubbed his eyes. Even in the dim evening light, he looked as though he were going to be ill. But he took out a crumpled handkerchief, blew his nose, and reentered the house, pausing only long enough to exchange a few mumbled words with another patrolman who was stationed at the front door. This was Westfield's first murder in eight years. Things like this weren't supposed to happen here. None of the Westfield policemen had ever before seen anything like the carnage discovered within the walls of the beautiful house.

Barbara Sheridan and Ed Illiano stood in the dining room on the first floor looking at the four tropical fish tanks. In three of the tanks, the fish floated at the surface of the murky icy water, discolored in death, even beginning to disintegrate. But in one of the tanks, several fish were alive, still swimming about slowly despite the fact that their water, icy cold in the heatless house, hadn't been changed in a month and that they had long since run out of food. Barbara reached for the little container of food left on top of one of the tanks and slowly poured some into the tank. The tiny fish, the only life that still survived in this house of death, lunged at the food. Ed put his arm about Barbara, and he led her out onto the front porch. The crisp night air seemed fresh and clean even as it cut into their lungs like icicles.

Dr. Ehrenberg, another Union County medical examiner, arrived. Looking down at the body of John junior with Chief Moran at his side, he shook his head. "I think this one put up a fight."

Chief Moran was deeply affected by the killings—the sheer *numbers*—but he was affected most particularly by the bullet-mutilated body of John junior. "How could someone shoot a kid like that?"

"Eight, nine times, maybe more," said Dr. Ehrenberg.

Chief Moran turned around at a shadow in the doorway. "Who's this guy?" he demanded as he saw a man standing in the doorway next to an officer.

"Dr. Cunnick," he was told. "To identify the bodies. He lives across the street."

"Okay, let him in."

Dr. Cunnick approached the bodies on the floor tentatively. "Let me make it clear," he said softly. "I did not know the family very well. Mostly they kept to themselves. I've never even been inside this house before tonight."

"Would you know them if you saw them?"

"I think so," said the doctor. Looking down at the corpses of his neighbors was a horrible confirmation of all the suspicions that had been building that something awful had happened. The whole scene was eerie. The corners of the room were dark; there were no lights left in this part of the house. The identification had to be made with the aid of large, bright flashlights. Despite the cold temperature the bodies had started to decompose. There was a disintegration of the fingertips and toes, small maggots on the bodies. The bodies were bloated, which suggested to the doctor that they had been there for some time: but they were easily recognizable. He named them one at a time. "This one is Helen List, the mother. This one is Patty, sixteen years old. This is Freddie. Thirteen, I think. And this is John. Fifteen."

The bodies now had names.

"Thanks," said Chief Moran quietly. He nodded to one of the officers to escort him out and get his signed statement of identification. "Wait a minute."

The man turned around.

"Do you know who the old lady on the third floor is?"

"That would have to be the grandmother," Dr. Cunnick said.

"We found her upstairs."

"Dead?"

"Yes."

Unreal, Dr. Cunnick thought. He didn't feel like going upstairs to identify her. There was no doubt in his mind who the old lady was.

"Anybody else live here?" Moran continued.

"Well . . . there's her son."

"Their father?" he asked, nodding toward the children.

"Yes."

"Know where he is?"

"I don't know. I thought they were all on vacation. That's what he said."

"Who?"

"John List."

That was the first time Chief James Moran had heard the name.

"Is he dead, too?" Cunnick asked.

"He doesn't seem to be around."

"Oh. . . ."

"Okay, thanks for all your help."

Dr. Cunnick was eager to leave. There was nothing else he could do, but he looked back once more before leaving. The bodies were laid out methodically just like an accountant would do it, he thought. "In a line."

When the police had entered the home that night, they hadn't known anything about John List. Someone would have to tell him that his whole family's been wiped out. "Do we know the guy?" Moran asked.

"Not much to know. Just your average citizen," answered Captain Vardalis.

"We have anything on him?"

"Pretty clean," said Vardalis. "I've already checked him out."

"Okay. Fill me in. . . ."

* * *

John Emil List was six feet one inch tall, of medium build, 180 pounds, bespectacled, and very quiet. His complexion was light, and his hair, which he wore long and combed straight back, was dark brown. He was forty-six years old.

He held B.A. and M.A. degrees in business administration from the University of Michigan, where he was graduated in 1950. Although an accountant by profession, he sold insurance and mutual funds out of the front-room office of his home in Westfield, New Jersey. He was studious, meticulous of habit, and conservative of dress. Neighbors always thought of him as a family man. A bit taciturn, a bit introverted, but definitely a man whose family and church were the main focus of his life.

List was often seen doing the family shopping. He frequently performed services for the Lutheran Church of the Redeemer on Cowperthwaite and Clark streets, leading the church's Boy Scout troop and teaching Sunday school to the parishioners' children. He was considered a church leader by his pastor and fellow congregants.

Here was a man who was the quintessential soul of respectability.

"However," said Vardalis, "There's more."

"I'm listening."

"On October 14, 1971, he came into the station and applied for a gun permit."

"Is that a fact?"

"Police Sergeant William Muth fingerprinted him."

"Bill, huh. Interesting."

"Routine."

"I know."

"Chief . . ." another voice called from behind him.

Moran turned around to Lieutenant Detective Robert Bell, who had entered and listened to the last of Vardalis's background check on John List.

"What?" the chief said.

"We got some more interesting stuff up front. In his office."

Chief Moran whistled quietly at what had been found in John List's office in the front living room. "Will you look at this!"

An astonishing directory of little notes was taped to the filing cabinet. Out of his own stationery headed "A Few words from John E. List—Career Builder, 55 Washington Street, Suite 209, East Orange, N.J. 07017. Tel: 676-4100," List had made labels for each of the filing cabinet drawers—a precise directory of where everything could be found: "To the Finder." "Note to Jean." "Note to Mother Morris." "Note to Lydia Meyer." "Letter to Reverend Rehwinkel."

"On his own stationery," Bell said.

"Considerate of the guy," Moran said appreciatively, reading the first note. A few officers in the room chuckled, grateful at the little respite in the stiff horror surrounding them.

To the finder:
Number 1. Please contact the proper authorities.
Number 2. The key to this desk is in an envelope addressed to myself. The keys to the file are in the desk.

J. List.

"We found a special delivery notice about the key on the floor under the front door."

The top drawer was labeled "Guns and Ammo." Two weapons and unused ammunition were placed within. There were about twenty bullets left. The guns, a nine-mm Steyr automatic pistol and a tiny .22-caliber American Colt revolver, were immediately impounded as possible murder weapons. They were given to Captain Vardalis to "make sure they were safe" and would not discharge while being examined as evidence. Then they were tagged and sent for ballistics identification.

Inside the desk they had found a large unsealed, unstamped manila envelope with an open flap marked "Pastor Eugene A. Rehwinkel, Redeemer Lutheran Church." Inside were checkbooks, bank books, tax records, and insurance policies. They also found the man's "Budget Book" in his own handwriting. It was a meticulous documentation of accumulating, as well as long-standing, debts that chronicled a family history of severe financial straits.

Inside the envelope there were also five notes and one long letter to Reverend Rehwinkel.

One by one, they read the chilling words of the killer, written in his own hand on the night of the murders, as he had coolly said his "good-byes," expressed his "sympathy and condolences" to family members, offered business tips to associates, and made final "arrangements" for the burial of his slaughtered family:

To the principal—Nov 9, 1971

"November 9." They had a date.

Westfield High School
Our daughter Patricia is a student in the 11th grade at
Westfield High.
She will be out a few days next week since we had to
make an emergency trip to North Carolina. We left after the
school was closed so I'm sending this letter to you to
explain her absence.

John E. List
431 Hillside Ave.
Westfield.

It was in neat handwriting on a folded sheet of yellow paper torn off a pad. The same concise little note was written to the principal of Roosevelt Junior High School regarding John junior and Freddie.

There was another note to KVM Real Estate, where Patricia and Freddie worked after school part-time. This he put on his own stationery with the heading "A Few Words from John E. List— Career Builder:"

KVM Associates
Mrs. Dawson,
Patricia and Frederick will be absent for several days as we
had to make an emergency trip to NC (North Carolina)
during the night. I'm sorry for the inconvenience.
John E. List.

Next, a quick note to his neighbor, John Wittke, thanking him for a book that he had lent him, and another note with a few tips to his boss, Burt Goldstein of State Mutual Assurance Co. of America, in Jericho Long Island. "A Few Words from John E. List— Career Builder:"

Hello Burt,
I'm sorry that it all had to end this way but with so little
income I just couldn't go on keeping the family together.
And I didn't want them to experience poverty.
I want to thank you for everything that you did for me.
You treated me better than any associate I've ever dealt
with and I'm sorry that I have to repay you this way.
The files are marked so that they can be turned over to
you.
Maybe Paul Greenberg can follow up on some.
The best prospects for a quick sale are:

> *Douglas Moe*
> *Edward Varga*
> *Odendahl*
> *Also be sure to contact Charles Jacobson CPA. I worked with him on the Swokenden thing and that worked real good.*
> *Also don't fail to follow up with Harvey. He may be just about ready.*
>
> > *Best wishes,*
> > *John*

"Hey, why lose a sale?" Moran cracked, but he was shaking his head. It was incongruous that a guy who apparently had just murdered his wife, his mother, and his kids was thoughtfully giving insurance tips to his boss.

The letter to Mrs. Eva Morris, mother and grandmother to four of the victims, was terse and "explanatory" in nature. It also passed on the responsibility for any needed help to his pastor, who would "add a few thoughts" on the matter for her comfort.

> *Mrs. Morris*
> *By now you no doubt know what has happened to Helen and the children. I'm very sorry that it had to happen. But because of a number of reasons I couldn't see any other solution.*
> *I just couldn't support them anymore and I didn't want them to go into poverty. Also, at this time I know that they were all Christians. I couldn't be sure of that in the future as the children grow up.*
> *Pastor Rehwinkel may add a few more thoughts.*
> *With my sincere sympathy,*
>
> > *John E. List*

By the time he wrote notes to his mother's sister, Lydia Meyers, and to Helen's sister, Jean Syfert, List seemed to have run out of explanations. They were curt, brief, and formal, more like notes from a stranger than from a nephew and a brother-in-law of twenty years.

> *Mrs. Lydia Meyer*
> *By now you no doubt know what has happened to Mother and the rest of the family. For a number of reasons this was the only solution that I could see for the family.*

And to save Mother untold anguish over that result I felt it best that she be relieved from this vale of tears.
   Please accept my sincere condolences.

                                                                    John

Mrs. Jean Syfert
   By now you have heard of what happened to Helen and the children. I'm sorry that it had to go that way but when I couldn't support them I couldn't let them go on welfare etc.
   Please accept my sincere sympathy.

                                                                    John

And finally, they found the most important letter of all: the five-page confessionary letter to his pastor, Reverend Eugene Rehwinkel of the Redeemer Lutheran Church in town. It was written in List's neat longhand on five pages torn from a standard-size pad of yellow paper with light blue lines. This was the most damning piece of evidence against the missing man of the house. It outlined the entire grisly story of his "righteous" motives for murdering his family. The careful explanation of why it had been necessary was told in a precise, rational, and unemotional manner. He spoke of a very sick wife who was deliberately turning away from God, of a daughter who was also slipping away from God, albeit surreptitiously, through her activities with the theater. "Now that Patricia is going into acting, who can say whether she will continue to be Christian? . . . ." he wrote. He spoke of how he had prayed to the Lord for guidance about his situation and how the Lord had obviously chosen not to answer his prayers. He spoke of serious financial troubles and asserted that the conditions of the world were not conducive to the Christian manner in which he wanted his children to grow.

I can think of no other way. . . . I don't want things to get to the point where welfare is the only way.

He went on to say that although it looked horrible, he took special care to make sure it wasn't painful. He said they never saw it coming. That was why he shot them in the back of the head. He said that even though John put up a struggle and it appeared that he suffered, he didn't think he suffered for very long. He wrote:

I got down on my knees and prayed after each one.

List gave detailed instructions to the reverend for their burials. Cremation. He wanted services for each. He wanted them to go straight to heaven. It was a very rational statement of fact and a grocery list of instructions. He gave no indication of remorse. It was not a soul-searching letter, full of emotion, begging for forgiveness. It was a letter from a man who had been absolutely determined to do what had to be done, from a man who never wavered for one moment from the strong, righteous position that what he had done was the right thing. It was too bad if some people did not understand. What mattered was that he had saved his family. "Now at least they died as Christians."

Then he added a postscript:

P.S. Mother is in the attic. She was too heavy to move.

There was a long silence after they had finished reading the letter. Then Chief Moran said, "Okay. You can show it to the reverend."

Michael Mitzner, from the Union County Prosecutor's Office, took the letter. Reverend Rehwinkel was on his way.

"Then," Moran continued, "I want it sealed. No one is to know the contents of that letter until we catch the guy!"

Mitzner nodded.

"What else?" Moran asked.

"From what we can determine right now," Lieutenant Detective Bell said "everyone was shot once in the head except for John. However, it's too soon to tell." The evidence showed how many times each person had been hit, not how many times he had been shot at. "They may all have been hit more than once, too," Bell continued. "But we'll have to wait for autopsies. And we've located other shell casings."

"Where?"

"We found some bullet holes in the kitchen walls, and we already pulled two slugs out of the wall in the storage room behind the old lady. I'm pretty sure he fired at her more than once, and maybe more than twice."

"What else?"

"Looks like we got something like seventeen shells from the nine mm and seven discharged from the twenty-two," Bell continued.

"So we're talking twenty-four shots and five people," Moran said, making a quick calculation. "Looks like our Mister Accountant was shooting all over the place."

* * *

Reverend Rehwinkel, to whom John List's confessionary letter had been addressed, was brought in to confirm the identities of his former congregants. He was a heavy-set man with thick bushy brown hair streaked with gray. Usually open and friendly, with a deep rich resonant voice, he was more talkative than Dr. Cunnick had been and more overtly traumatized by the mass killings of his parishioners by his friend and Sunday-school teacher, John.

The reverend brushed his hands over his eyes. "I can't believe this," he said, choking a bit on his own words. Only a few days ago, on December 5, he had stopped by the house and left his own personal calling card. While he had stood on the porch scribbling on the back, "Hello; Haven't seen you folks for a while. Fred missing in confirmation class. Give me a jingle, please. Paster R," they were all inside lying on the floor, dead.

"The Lists were a beautiful family," he heard himself saying. "They were devout churchgoers. Not the wife. Not Helen. She hasn't been well lately. And not always the mother. She was getting on in years. But John and the three children came to services every Sunday. Always dressed neatly. Never missed. The children—" His voice cracked. "And John . . . This is truly tragic. He was a church leader. He . . . taught Sunday school." To the reverend, they were a wonderful family, and the tragedy was incomprehensible. "This is more tragic than words can describe or a human mind can comprehend." Again and again, he said, "It was a wonderful family, a very fine family. They weren't only devout. They were active churchgoers, and the children all took part in youth groups, including one that put on plays."

Chief Moran did not want to hurt the reverend's feelings. The man was obviously and understandably distressed. But the chief was not in the mood to hear about John List's "fine qualities." The man was missing, and his family had been butchered. He had seen a great deal in all of his years on the force. But this one, this crime, this horror, would stay with him obsessively for a long time. He stared down at the bodies again, not realizing that already, this early in the stages of investigation, he was making a moral commitment never to rest until the perpetrator was caught and brought to justice. "No one should get away with this," he said. "No one should just walk away after doing something like this. That guy is on my list!"

He showed Reverend Rehwinkel the letter List had written to him. As Moran would say later to the press, it was "revelatory." Not only did it give detailed explanations and instructions, but the tenor of the letter clearly demonstrated that List had been feeling a great deal of pressure both financial and personal for a prolonged period of time. Ironically, despite the specificity of List's instructions, the implied determination in his recitation of the absolute necessity of his act, the righteous confidence behind his motives, and his passionate certainty that he would be ultimately forgiven by God, List's letter indicated that he himself had every intention of remaining alive.

The pastor took the letter into the privacy of another room within the huge, cold house and read it several times through eyes blurred with emotion.

Michael Mitzner from the Union County Prosecutor's Office was standing next to him when he finally rejoined the police in the front room and returned the letter into the waiting hands of Chief Moran. "You'll have to keep the contents of the letter confidential," Mitzner told the pastor.

"Of course," Reverend Rehwinkel said.

"We'll have to keep it as evidence. Only the murderer knows what's in it. We don't want it to get out to the press," Mitzner added.

"I want to cooperate," Reverend Rehwinkel assured him. Then he turned to Chief Moran. "But . . ."

"Yeah?"

"Please use discretion."

"Sure."

The letter to Reverend Rehwinkel was then sealed by the authorities as "evidence" to be presented when the killer was ultimately brought to trial. "And he will be," vowed Chief Moran. "If I have anything to do with it. He will be!"

At 10:10 the case had been classified as a homicide. By precisely 11:05 P.M., within a short hour of the onset of their investigation, they had already put out a Teletype alarm for "John Emil List— Wanted in connection with a mass murder." The search quickly spread not only across the fifty states of the nation, but well beyond the national boundaries as well.

"I'll make the necessary phone calls to the family," Reverend Rehwinkel offered solemnly.

Finally, after thirty-one days on the floor, the bodies were taken away to the County Medical Examiner's Office for autopsy. The old lady's legs cracked when they tried to straighten her out for removal. It was a sound long remembered by those present.

At 3:00 A.M. Jean and Gene Syfert woke to the ringing of the telephone in their home half a continent away in Midwest City, Oklahoma. Jean picked up the phone, groggily noticed the time, and immediately became uneasy. Phone calls in the middle of the night usually meant bad news and she knew from her aunt Cora that her mother was ill in North Carolina.

"This is Reverend Rehwinkel."

"Who?" she asked blankly.

"Reverend Eugene Rehwinkel, pastor of Redeemer Lutheran Church in Westfield, New Jersey."

"Oh. Hello. Is something wrong?"

"Is this Mrs. Jean Syfert?"

"Yes."

"Sister to Helen List?"

"Yes. What is it?"

"I'm afraid I have terrible news."

"What's happened? My sister . . . ? Please . . ."

Jean's husband, Gene, became completely alert at the alarm in her voice and joined her at her side. And as Reverend Rehwinkel told the woman that her sister had been murdered as well as her niece, her two nephews, and the mother of the man suspected of the killings, she almost collapsed. "All of them?" she gasped in horror. "All?"

"Yes."

"John?" she cried incredulously. "John did it? I don't believe it. No! I don't believe any of it. . . ."

The pastor tried to give scriptural words of comfort, but Jean Syfert was not Lutheran and was not having any of it. The shock was overwhelming. Gene Syfert took the receiver out of his wife's hand and continued the conversation with the pastor, trying to get as many details about the situation as possible while Jean paced in the background and sobbed and kept mumbling, "No, I don't believe it. . . . No. . . ."

The Syferts had tried to call Helen only the past Thanksgiving Day when they saw a Nebraska football player on television with the name of List playing in the Oklahoma-Nebraska game. They had realized they hadn't heard from Helen in a while despite the two letters Jean had recently written to her. The phone in Westfield rang and rang, and no one had answered. "They could all be dead," Gene had joked, "and no one would even know about it."

"Should we call the police?" Jean had asked her husband.

But in thinking it over, they both thought it would be silly. Maybe the family had gone out for Thanksgiving, although that would be unusual for them since Helen was never really well enough or even willing to go out. . . . Still, the Syferts had decided to do nothing. And now here they were with the horrendous realization that Gene's offhand remark had been no joke.

Somehow, Gene was not really surprised. He couldn't immediately understand why he wasn't. Then he remembered the unusual conversations he'd had with his brother-in-law, John, the last time he had seen him. He and Jean were about to leave for a two-year air force stint in Germany and had visited the family in Westfield sometime back in May of 1968 before leaving for Europe. Gene remembered standing in John's office on the main floor of the house where John had a great many books on the subject of how to commit a murder without getting caught. Sort of "how-to" books, Gene had thought. The perfect crime . . . getting away with it. He also remembered how John had pointed out the rows of accounting files he had accumulated on clients.

"Do you have any idea how easy it would be to come up with a new identity?" John had said. "A new Social Security number?"

"I suppose," Gene had said thoughtfully.

"Especially for someone like me," John had continued. "An accountant with access to so many files and so many people. . . ."

And Gene remembered John's taking him down to the basement, a rather gloomy and scary place sectioned off into many dark, dank little rooms. "You know how easy it would be for someone to live down here for a long time and never be found?" John had continued.

"What for?"

"To disappear."

"Why?"

"It's just interesting to think how easy it would be to become another person," John had said. "Or to disappear."

Gene remembered the strange conversation, but he didn't think it would be appropriate to bring it up to Jean at this moment. They would share many thoughts and feelings later. But now they must get past the shock, do all the necessary things people did at times like this, keep busy. Phone calls would have to be made to Jean's three brothers, spread so far apart, soon to be united in tragedy: Fred in Arizona, Ed in Nevada, and Jimmy in Ohio.

They must call Helen's mother, Eva Morris, in Elkin, North Carolina. How would they tell her that she had just lost her first daughter and her three beautiful grandchildren? That they had apparently been murdered by the son-in-law they all thought was so quiet, so gentle, so passive? That they had been dead on the floor of their own home for weeks? That her son-in-law was missing?

No, it was all too much.

And then there were funeral arrangements to be made. My God! For five people. John had killed his own mother as well. That was almost more difficult to believe than his killing his own children. John and his mother had always been so close.

"And we have to call Brenda," Jean sobbed. "In Kalamazoo. . . ."

Brenda De Young in Kalamazoo, Michigan, was Helen List's twenty-nine-year-old daughter by her previous marriage to Marvin Taylor. When told that her mother, half sister, two half brothers, and stepgrandmother had all been murdered, she collapsed. Not only was she hospitalized because of the severity of the emotional trauma, but Kalamazoo police put an instant guard on her to protect her in the event her stepfather might try to kill her too. But it wasn't necessary. Too much time had passed. Her stepfather wasn't going to seek her out in Kalamazoo.

John List had simply walked away from the life he'd led in Westfield, New Jersey, leaving others to deal with the tragedy he'd left behind. It fell to family and friends to make the funeral arrangements, clean out the house, and try to survive the stunning aftermath.

3 | The Morning After

Wednesday—December 8, 1971

The next morning, when the police went through the backlogged mail that had been held at the post office "until further notice," they found mail addressed to various members of the List family. Among the usual advertisements and junk mail was a preponderance of unpaid bills. Included were two unanswered letters from Helen's sister, Jean Syfert, written several weeks earlier.

On Hillside Avenue, the usually quiet, well-to-do neighborhood was still bustling with activity. Police blockades still cordoned off the "crime scene" on Hillside Avenue as the investigation continued. In the light of day, the water tank in the storage area on the third floor was emptied in case there were more bodies hidden. The garage was searched, as were the woods behind the house. Policemen, both on and off duty, who had volunteered their services in response to the tragedy, swarmed through the woods in an inch-by-inch search for additional evidence.

Susan Jacobus was twenty-two, fresh, and eager in her new position as a teacher at Roosevelt Jr. High School. She heard the news on the radio even before she got to school. Of the three children, John junior was the one she remembered. He had been in her homeroom in late November of 1970 when she first began her teaching career. She hadn't seen him in a while, and as she drove to school, she tried to picture the boy. She remembered him as big compared with some of the other kids. He wore glasses, so he usually sat fairly close to the front. She was always conscious of his long legs hanging out from the one-piece sled desk that was too small for him. Good-looking boy, personable, but he kept very much to himself. He seemed to be less energetic than the other students, but very polite. It sort of didn't go together, she thought. So big and so polite. She remembered that quietness about him.

Once she got to school that morning, she stopped to talk to Ann Sales, the school secretary, who knew just about everybody and everything that went on in school. Ann Sales's eyes were red. "I had John in my homeroom class last year," Miss Jacobus told her after Miss Sales sadly confirmed the story.

"And Freddie," Miss Sales continued. "He was such an imp. Remember him?"

"No, I didn't know him."

"Only thirteen. . . ." They looked at each other. "This sort of thing just isn't supposed to happen," Miss Sales found herself saying. "A town like this . . ."

"It's not just that," Miss Jacobus insisted. "When you're in education, children are your business. To lose any one of them, in any way, is a blow. But like this. To think that these kids are just gone," she continued, "just like that. So senseless."

"And that a parent could do it."

"That's the worst part," Miss Jacobus agreed. Such a betrayal of parental trust was beyond even her most malevolent imaginings. "Do the children in school know?" she asked the secretary.

"Buzzing all over the place."

"They'll need help," she said, moving on.

Even before the start of classes on the morning of December 8, the story had spread very quickly. There was hardly a student at either Westfield High or Roosevelt Junior High who had not already heard of the murders when they came to school the morning after. The fever brought on by the discovery of the murders was hashed and rehashed within the halls of both schools. The killings created a great deal of fear among the youngsters who had known the List children. If their father could actually put a gun to their heads and kill them—the utterly unthinkable—could their own fathers do something like that to them, too? Fundamental trusts had been shaken.

Fifteen-year-old Bob Compton was one of the few who hadn't heard about it until he arrived at school. He looked in disbelief at the empty seat next to him in Spanish class where John junior used to sit next to him. "He was killed with a hammer!" he exclaimed. "Johnny List?"

"Yeah, his father did it," another classmate told him. "With a hammer!"

"Wow. . . ." They'd had a lot of classes together. And they played together on the baseball team.

"His kid brother, too. Remember him?"

"No."

"He had big ears, too. Sticking way out."

"Oh, yeah, yeah. I remember him," Compton said. "Played baseball with his brother. Quiet kid just like Johnny."

"His father killed him, too."

"With a hammer?"

"Yeah. And their sister, too."

Compton remembered Patty. She was like his older sister, Terry. Always dressed real cool, like a hippie. Totally different from John and Freddie, though. "Why'd he kill them?"

"I don't know. I hear the kids were into devil worship or something."

"That's bull!" Bob Compton said flatly.

The story on the first day was augmented and distorted to the point where everyone had to wait until they got home from school to hear on the TV news the truth of how the murders actually occurred.

Even before daybreak the morning after, newsmen from major national television and press had gathered at the scene of the crime, at police headquarters, at the schools, anywhere they felt they might be able to piece together the "sensational" puzzle of what had actually happened on that fateful day one month earlier when the killings had taken place. But the authorities weren't talking much. The superintendent of Westfield schools, Dr. L. E. Law, gave no information to the press other than that Patricia List had attended Westfield High School on Dorian Road and that John List, Jr., and Frederick List had attended Roosevelt Junior High on Clark Street. Part of the restraint was due to a protective reticence in not wanting to add further sensationalism, part was due to the "lid" having been put on by the authorities handling the case. Even neighbors who lived near or next to the dead family were ordered by the Union County Prosecutor's Office not to comment on the case to anyone until the investigation was completed, particularly to the very active, visible, and demanding press.

Mrs. Bennett felt a bit put out by the order. She, like most who were directly involved, had a desperate need to talk about it. But she realized the necessity of silence under the circumstances and decided to restrict her discussions to those she shared with her husband within the confines of her own home. With no outside restrictions to put a lid on their emotions, they talked and talked and talked about the murders, as did most everyone whose lives had been touched by those of the Lists, even superficially.

Next-door neighbor Mike Ryan was at home recuperating from a serious operation. His wife, Diana, went up to his room and told him, "Hank O'Malley just called. A terrible thing has happened. Our neighbor has murdered his family."

As Diana told him about it, she remembered another conversation at Thanksgiving. Her son, Brian, was home for the holiday from the Pennsylvania Academy of Fine Arts. When they told him that the List house had been lit up for weeks and that the lights were burning out one by one, he had said, "Those people are weird. I bet I know what's going on. They're all dead in there." It was a macabre joke at the time. They'd actually laughed.

The next day's headlines emblazoned the story in bold black print:

HUSBAND HUNTED IN MASS SLAYING
(*The Star Ledger*—12/9/71)

5 IN JERSEY FAMILY SLAIN: HUSBAND SOUGHT
(*The New York Times*—12/9/71)

But headlines rarely speak to the emotional aftermath of shock and grief left in the wake of such tragedy. Not only had Westfield been a quiet community suddenly made infamous and forced to undergo the penetrating scrutiny of a nation's eyes turned in its direction because of the acts of one of its residents, but the nature of the crime itself was formidable. The impact of the complete revelation of what had occurred within the private walls of the house on Hillside Avenue was overwhelming. It was the stuff of which nightmares are made. Thus it was far more than curiosity that made neighbors step out of their homes in the frosty December morning air and huddle together talking about the tragedy, exchanging stories about the List family, whispering, staring, sighing, even crying. They had to go over it, talk about it, rehash distant unimportant incidents that suddenly popped out of stored memory banks they had long thought closed to access. They simply could not bring themselves to accept the horror.

"He was so meticulous," said one elderly, retired gentleman with tears streaming out of fading eyes.

But "I knew something was wrong," said another close neighbor with the crystal clarity of hindsight. "You just don't pick up your family in the middle of the school year and go on vacation."

The killing of the children was the most shocking aspect of the murders. Even civilized men can often rationalize the killing of a spouse; it is common enough in the annals of violent crime not to attract much attention. Even matricide is not that uncommon. But that a man could kill his own children . . . ! "All three?" was the question asked again with painful awe. "Not all three?"

"I saw them taking the bodies out." Tears suddenly running down cheeks. "In plastic body bags."

"Dear God. But he was a deeply religious man, wasn't he?"

"Yes. The quiet type," spoken with unrestricted irony.

Caught up in the macabre excitement of the morning activities, sixteen-year-old Pam Vandermere and her seventeen-year-old brother Mitch were already late for Westfield High School, where they had shared classes with Patricia List. "We both knew Patty."

"Did she ever say anything?"

"Patty? Never," Pam said. "She would never talk about her family. We got the feeling right off the bat with Patty not to ask any questions about her family."

"She was very bright, though," Pam's mother added. She and her husband, Ralph, with their seven children lived across the street from the Lists. "I always thought she was a very normal teenager. Friendly."

It wasn't long before newspaper reporters intruded into the neighborhood groping for any nugget of sensational information that they, as neighbors, might have. The newsmen wanted their insights and even their speculations as to possible motive for the murders. For the question on everyone's mind was, "Why?"

"We hardly knew the Lists," said Hank O'Malley, backing away a bit.

"Sure we feel sad. It's a real horror that such a tragedy could happen to a family," his wife, Joyce, added. "But we didn't know them. What do you want us to say? They were not the kind of people that anyone in the neighborhood could get to know well."

"Anything you can remember at all," they were pressed, playing upon the very real psychological need to sift through the weight of overburdened feelings. "It doesn't matter how unimportant you may think it is. . . ." The newsmen could tell the neighbors were slowly giving in, their need to talk superseding the resentment they felt at the persistence of journalistic prying.

"Do you remember the welcoming party we threw for them the week they moved in?" Hank O'Malley suddenly asked aloud.

"Sure I do," said Diana Ryan.

"Tell us about it," urged the man with the little tape recorder in his hand, pointing the microphone in the direction of the speaker.

"There's really nothing to tell," Diana said hesitantly. "They seemed appreciative, I guess. But no one ever saw much of them after that. Especially her. Helen List."

"She never returned the social call," added Hank O'Malley's wife, Joyce.

"Patty was friendly, though," said young Pam Vandermere quickly, as though the murdered girl had to be defended against unkind speculations of any kind. "She had really come into her own this past year. You could see the change," she insisted with an unconscious sense of identification with the murdered girl. "In tune with the times. Usually casually dressed in hippie fashion. She was really okay."

"But Mrs. List, she disappeared," said Joyce O'Malley. "They came from Rochester, you know. I remember him saying that. Rochester, New York. And then they went into seclusion. Almost immediately. And he was not very friendly, if you ask me. I know he went to church a lot and that he taught Sunday school . . ." She turned to her neighbor, Ralph Vandermere, who was standing with a deep frown on his face, reliving his own memories. "Why don't you tell them, Ralph," she urged him, wanting to hear as much as the newsmen. "You probably knew him better than anyone else around here."

"No, I didn't," Vandermere said reticently. He didn't want to talk about it. He was already late for work. But pressing—always pressing—the newsmen managed to get a brief statement out of the man who remembered List well enough, although he made a definite disclaimer prior to his statement. "I really didn't know him at all," he said firmly. "It was never more than a casual acquaintance. We'd wave to each other across the street when we were both busy working on our grounds."

"Did you ever strike up a lengthy conversation?"

"Lengthy? Not even short!" he exclaimed. "Pretty soon he wouldn't even wave back." It seemed to him that the more internal problems the family had, the more reclusive they became. He remembered looking up from his pruning as he saw John List across the street behind his lawn mower. Vandermere tried not to shake his head, but there he was again, mowing his lawn all dressed up in a suit and tie. His shirt was buttoned up to his Adam's apple. He waved when he thought he perceived that List had glanced his way. But List did not wave back. He kept his attention riveted to the task at hand as he bent over the lawn mower he was pushing. Vandermere shrugged. No use in forcing oneself upon a neighbor who insisted on remaining a loner. Odd, though. He had never before seen anyone mowing a lawn all dressed up in a suit and tie. In fact, he couldn't remember ever seeing John List dressed casually.

The newsmen pressed on. . . .

"No one knew them well," Vandermere's wife added, coming to his rescue. "You've got to believe that. Hardly anyone had seen Helen List in the past five years, believe it or not."

Mrs. Vandermere remembered that she had walked across the street when the Lists first moved in, just to be neighborly, merely to say hello. "But we heard eventually, through neighborhood talk mostly, that she'd had a nervous breakdown or something. Something serious that kept her in bed most of the time. Like an invalid. After a while, I didn't even bother paying attention anymore. They weren't what you would call good neighbors, in the sense of being friendly or anything."

And the children? The newsmen were insistent. . . .

"Hardly ever saw them playing around the house," Hank O'Malley said. "This street is full of kids. They were hardly ever around." He knew about kids. He and Joyce had six of their own. "And when they came out they just watched. I used to see the boys over there, sitting on the steps watching all the kids play baseball on the lawns.''

Pam was shaking her head now as though suddenly wanting to sever the connection with the dead girl. ''Patty was a lot different from me. Mitch knew her better. I really didn't hang around with her at all.''

''How do you feel now that this has come out?'' The microphone turned to her brother.

''I don't know,'' Mitch hedged. ''They were weird.''

Just as suddenly, Pam's feelings swung back to a defensive mode. ''I liked her,'' she murmured, not recognizing the turmoil reflected by her emotional shifts. ''Patty was probably the best known of the three kids because of her activities with the drama group at the Westfield Recreation Center. She was really okay.'' She hesitated again. ''I just didn't know her *that* well.''

Of course there were the curiosity seekers, too, who added to the nightmare by driving by in great numbers. In addition, there was an environmental program given by the Rack & Hoe Garden Club at the time of the murders. Between the traffic created by the Rack & Hoe Club and the voyeurs driving along Hillside Avenue, the quiet streets of Westfield became virtually impassable at times.

But there were a great many who had a deep personal investment in the tragedy. Karen Peter, a resident from St. Marks Place, only blocks away, heard about the killings. She was one of the few who refused to go up to Hillside Avenue to ''look.'' She didn't want to see the death house, as it was already wildly being called. But from the moment she heard about the murders of the Lists, she kept envisioning Patty's face. How clearly she remembered the day the past September, shortly after moving to Westfield, when, with moving crates still spread out over her parlor floor, she'd answered a knock on her front door. There was Patty List standing on her doorstep.

''Hi,'' she had greeted the teenager.

''I understand you recently moved here and that you give piano lessons.''

''Yes, I do.'' Mrs. Peter looked beyond the girl.

''Could you give me lessons?'' Patty asked quietly. ''Piano lessons?''

''Of course,'' Mrs. Peter answered, noting that the child had come alone as she would in the remaining months of her life. No doting parent ever came with her. No questions were ever asked about her potential, or even her talent. Most parents displayed some interest in their children's musical progress.

"I play the guitar," the girl had said, "but I'd like to study piano, too."

She had been such a pretty girl, long oval face, deep almond-shaped brown eyes, shoulder-length dark hair. An expression of hope . . . vulnerability . . .

4 | The Killer's Trail

Thursday—December 9, 1971

On December 9, John List's missing car, a 1963 blue Chevrolet Impala with the New Jersey license plate KBN 813, was found. It was discovered by security at Kennedy International Airport in the long-term parking area after the Westfield Police Department sent telegrams to all the major airports to be on the lookout for the missing vehicle. Although the parking voucher on the windshield was dated November 10, the car had not attracted any notice. It was impounded and brought back to Westfield, where it was photographed and searched. Finding the car was a step forward in the hunt for the killer. The contents made it clear that List was relinquishing not only his car, but his identity as well. Besides the keys to the car, there was a University of Michigan ID card, an Alumni Association card, an American Forestry card, and two New Jersey State Board Accounting IDs dated 12/31/69 and 12/31/71. No one by the name of John List was recorded as having taken a flight, and it would have been virtually impossible to track all the people who flew out of Kennedy Airport on November 9 and 10 to determine if any had used assumed names. There was also the strong possibility that part of List's strategy was to plan an alternate avenue of escape and leave the car at Kennedy to throw the authorities off his trail. He could have taken a bus or taxi from the airport or had another car waiting for him. The trail that started at Kennedy Airport with the discovery of List's car ended there as well. It was ice cold. Since the car was found at an international airport, however, the presumption could be made that he had fled over state lines and perhaps over national boundaries. It was, therefore, legally possible to call the Federal Bureau of Investigation into the hunt, a factor the killer might not have taken into account at the time he planted the car at the airport.

A federal warrant giving the FBI jurisdiction in the case was issued in Newark, New Jersey, charging John Emil List with "unlawful flight to avoid prosecution." A second legal move, five murder indictments, was taken against the fugitive. Assistant Union County Prosecutor Michael Mitzner presented the case to the grand jury on Thursday, the morning of December 9, 1971. By early afternoon the Union County grand jury had indicted the fugitive on five counts of murder, committed "willfully, feloniously, and with his malice aforethought."

Now the police became very cooperative with the press. At a major news conference held in Newark, members of the Westfield Police Department, Union County Prosecutor's Office, and the Federal Bureau of Investigation were willing to answer just about any questions put to them by the media. Except for List's confessional letter to Reverend Rehwinkel, much of the pieced-together details of the murders were revealed in the hope that extensive media coverage would aid in the hasty apprehension of the lone suspect in the murders. The questioning, handled mostly by Chief of Police James Moran, Chief Inspector Robert Bell, and Michael Mitzner from the prosecutor's office, was fast, furious, and thorough.

"What kinds of guns were used?" asked one of the reporters.

"One was a twenty-two-caliber revolver and the other a nine-mm pistol. A Steyr. German make."

"Have you determined yet which guns were used on which members of the family?"

"Not until autopsy reports."

"Who will perform the autopsies?"

"County Medical Examiner Dr. Bernard Ehrenberg."

"When?"

"They're under way now."

"Do you know where List got the guns?" asked another one of the reporters, changing the direction of the questions.

"We believe they were bought out of state," Moran said.

"But the guns were very old," Bell added.

"Were they registered in New Jersey?"

"Neither gun is registered under New Jersey law," the chief continued. "Although I've been informed that List did apply for gun permits at the Westfield Police Station recently. He even allowed himself to be fingerprinted." He grinned. "Any little thing List does, any misdemeanor, anything that gets him fingerprinted, and we've got him."

"What else was in the desk besides the murder weapons?"

"We don't know for certain yet that the two guns found were the murder weapons," said Moran with characteristic professional caution.

"What about ballistics testing?"

"Both guns are now in West Trenton," Inspector Bell answered.

"Where?"

"At the state police ballistics laboratories," he answered patiently. "Undergoing ballistics testing."

"What about his safety-deposit box?"

Michael Mitzner stepped in. "We had it opened. It contained only several pieces of jewelry. Nothing significant to the case."

"Which bank was it?"

"Suburban Trust Company of Westfield."

"And the key to his desk?"

"Found in the special delivery letter on the floor under the front door addressed to himself. But we didn't need it. We busted the desk open the night the bodies were discovered," Moran said.

"Why do you think he did it, Chief?"

"Your guess is as good as mine," Moran answered.

"C'mon. Whattaya think?"

"I'll leave the speculation to you guys at this point. All we want to do is get him. Your write-ups can help spread the word. I want to get this guy. Bad. No one should be able to do something like that and walk away from it. To find five bodies like that isn't common. The numbers. And to see the boy he shot nine, ten times. It just isn't right that he should walk away from it."

"You must have some idea as to why."

"Records show that he'd only earned five thousand dollars so far this year selling insurance," Investigator Bell offered, "and he was behind in everything. Five thousand dollars is a big drop from the twenty-four thousand a year he earned as vice-president of First National Bank in Jersey City when he moved his family to Westfield five years ago."

"So he sold insurance?"

"Not very successfully. He worked by phone from his house," Bell continued. "Sometimes selling. Sometimes setting up 'financial investment plans' for some of his clients. But there's no indication in his records that he ever received remuneration for his services."

"And you're saying he was in financial trouble at the time of the killings?"

"Up to his eyeballs," Moran said.

Chief Inspector Bell pulled out a sheet of paper and leaned forward. "Okay, here it is. Right out of his own 'Budget Book,' which we found in the cabinet in his study."

"With the weapons?"

"Yes."

"Does *he* call it 'Budget Book'?"

"Yes."

"What is it?"

Everyone leaned forward almost involuntarily at the first piece of solid evidentiary material being brought forth by the authorities.

"It's a meticulous collection of receipts for all his household and business expenses, including food," Bell said, with his eyes on the numbers in front of him. "Right down to the last penny. It tells a pretty grim story of his financial downfall, all written in his own neat script. A record of all the unpaid bills that were accumulating. Everything is recorded. The supermarket," he said, ticking them off one by one. "The cleaning bills. It shows that he's in debt by several thousands of dollars. He had an outstanding fuel bill of well over a thousand dollars. He was behind on his mortgage payment. That's another thousand. And it shows that he bought the house—"

"When did he buy it?" a reporter interrupted.

"In 1966."

"Where'd he get the money?"

"He bought it with ten thousand dollars given to him by Mrs. Alma List."

"The woman he killed on the third floor?"

"Yes. His mother."

"The house was assessed for $80,000 when he bought it—worth $100,000 today...."

"And I thought I was overextended on my new $16,000 split," one reporter murmured to another.

"Shhh."

"But he got it for $50,000," Bell continued. "So he had a $40,000 mortgage. Then, a couple of years ago—October of 1969, to be exact—he got a second mortgage of $7,000 and paid off an outstanding $4,000 personal loan at the same time. Last year he took out mortgage number three, this one for $1,800. He only had about $1,000 worth of equity in the house, and one of the letters we picked up at the post office was—"

"How many letters were there?" another interruption.

Bell answered always with great patience "Precisely one hundred sixty-two pieces. One of the letters was from the bank that held the mortgages on the house. It was a notification that foreclosure proceedings had already been started against him.''

"When?''

"Three months ago. In August.''

"So he was gonna lose the house?''

"Seems that way. And that, according to his letter, he might have to apply for public assistance—apparently, for him, a fate worse than death.''

"What about his old lady? Couldn't she help him out?''

"Mrs. List's money was gone.''

"Did he take it?''

"Looks like it,'' Moran said dryly. "He had her power of attorney, and it looks like he's been siphoning off her money for a long time.''

"How much did she have?''

"It could have been somewhere in the neighborhood of $200,000. We're not sure.''

There were numerous whistles and murmurs of appreciation at the unexpectedly large amount of cash the elderly Mrs. List had amassed.

"But it was mostly gone,'' Mitzner said.

"When his mother moved to Westfield,'' Bell continued, "she had him deposit $10,000 in stocks and bonds with the Westfield branch of Wood Walker and Co., a Wall Street brokerage firm. She also had a large checking account at a Michigan bank. But that was all gone, too. All that was left in her account was a balance of $7.94.''

5 | The Funeral

Friday, December 10, 1971

Meanwhile there was a mass funeral to arrange.

At 10:00 A.M. the next morning, C. Frederick Poppy was in the pastor's office talking to his old friend. Fred Poppy was in his mid-forties. He was a large man, six feet tall, and heavy-set. Intelligent and caring by nature, he was a great asset to Gray Funeral Home as its vice-president and manager. Married for sixteen years, he and his wife lived with their five children in nearby Mountainside.

"I may be calling on you," the pastor said to him after telling him of the situation.

"I'll wait to hear from you."

Poppy went back to his office at Gray's. Later that afternoon they touched base again, and Reverend Rehwinkel asked him, "Fred, will you take care of these folks?"

"Yes."

"At this point there's only one relative that I know of," Rehwinkel told him. "Mrs. List's sister, Jean Syfert. She and her husband will be here this afternoon at four o'clock."

"The pastor has asked me to assist in making arrangements for the funerals," Poppy told the grieving sister and her husband.

"I'm afraid there's a problem—" Gene Syfert began, and broke off.

"Money's a problem," Reverend Rehwinkel filled in gently.

"There is none in the estate," Gene continued, "and the five funerals. Well . . . there just isn't any money."

"Why don't you let me make all the arrangements," Mr. Poppy said.

"But the money . . ."

"I'll take care of it."

Jean and Gene looked at each other, not quite understanding the implications of what Mr. Poppy had said.

"Am I to understand . . . Who will pay for the funerals?" Gene asked, a bit bewildered.

"Perhaps we'll be able to get payment out of the estate itself."

"Let me be perfectly candid," Gene said honestly. "I have no idea what kind of condition the estate is in or if there's any money at all."

"Mr. Syfert," Reverend Rehwinkel offered, "let's not make that the first priority. They have to be buried."

"I don't want any viewing," Jean said suddenly.

"I agree," Mr. Poppy said.

"No one looking at them. Please. They're making such a circus of it."

"Leave everything in my hands."

"Mrs. Syfert," Reverend Rehwinkel added, "rest assured that

Mr. Poppy and I will do everything in our power to handle the entire proceedings with the utmost taste and delicacy.''

"Thank you," she murmured tearfully.

"Just a simple service within the confines of the church."

"And the coffins?" she asked.

"A coffin is a shaper," Mr. Poppy corrected gently. "We'll use caskets. They will be placed in metal caskets."

"Oh . . . yes," she agreed numbly, not inquiring as to the technical difference. Both Mr. and Mrs. Syfert were so shaken by the tragedy that they were constantly drifting off into private solemn reveries as though they were suffering from mini–memory lapses and constantly had to be brought back to the reality of the present.

"And the funeral itself?" Gene finally continued. "How will we proceed?"

"Pastor and I will take care of everything," Mr. Poppy reassured them again.

"No viewing," Jean reiterated. But then she added slowly, "But I want to see them."

They all looked at her.

Poppy thought quickly. They would not be able to get the remains yet. Of course they would prepare them the best they could under the circumstances, but it was not a wise request. This was Mrs. List's sister, Poppy thought. How close they were he didn't know, but the condition of the remains . . . there *had* been decomposition.

"Mrs. Syfert," he said gently, "my humble opinion is that I would like you to remember your sister and her children as they were before this. If I permit you to see her and them, you will never be able to erase that final vision from your memory. You have the right . . . if you insist . . . but if you would listen to a bit of advice and forgo a visitation . . . ,"

Jean looked at her husband. She could tell he wanted her to agree.

"Remember them the way they were," he urged his wife.

She wiped her eyes, sighed softly . . . and agreed.

Rehwinkel and Poppy glanced at each other in relief.

"Is that the thing to do?" Rehwinkel asked Poppy when they were alone. "Metal caskets?"

"It's not the best," Poppy said candidly, "but the cost situation here . . . Believe me, Gene, it will be more than acceptable."

"You make the selections," Rehwinkel said.

* * *

The bodies were taken out of the home by the morgue keeper late
on the night of December 7 and brought to the Union County Medical
Examiner's Office for autopsies.

Gray Funeral Home picked them up from the morgue almost
twenty-four hours after their initial discovery. It was at 9:30 on the
night of the eighth, a dark moonless night. Nobody saw anything,
Poppy thought with satisfaction. We made sure of that.

The media kept coming to the funeral home, asking if there would
be visitation or a wake, and the answer was a definite "No."

The New Jersey Star Ledger's death notices announced the formal
obituary:

LIST—Mrs. Helen (née Morris), Mrs. Alma (née List), Miss
Patricia M., John F., and Frederick M. List of 431 Hillside
Ave., Westfield, N.J. Memorial services will be held on
Saturday, December 11, at 10 A.M. at the Redeemer Lu-
theran Church, 229 Cowperthwaite Pl., Westfield. The Rev.
Eugene A. Rehwinkel officiating. Interment Fairview Cem-
etery, Westfield, N.J. . . . in lieu of flowers, please make
contributions to Redeemer Lutheran Church Youth Me-
morial Fund. Arrangements by the GRAY FUNERAL
HOME, 318 E. Broad St., Westfield.

"Gene," Poppy said to Reverend Rehwinkel, "I think the best
time for us to bring the caskets to the church would be around four-
thirty in the afternoon. We'll come in the back of the church through
the churchyard. We'll bring them in through the back door so that
the public won't see anything. At four-forty, five o'clock, everybody
is rushing home to eat."

Rehwinkel agreed. There had been so much attention already,
they were anxious not to attract more.

While Poppy remained waiting with the pastor at the church five
blocks away from Gray Funeral Home, the caskets were brought
over one at a time in the only hearse Gray owned. Five round trips
were made. It took an hour and a half to get them all into the church.
The first one into the sanctuary, over in the farthest corner, was
Grandma. Poppy did that for a purpose. He knew who was in each.

casket, and he had it set up accordingly since Grandma wasn't going to Fairview Cemetery.

Oh, yes, Poppy thought to himself. He still had to call the funeral home in Michigan to tell them which flight to meet. Alma List's body was to be taken there for interment.

Five palls were needed to cover the caskets at the altar. Redeemer Lutheran didn't have enough. Rehwinkel had to borrow several from neighboring churches. They placed the five caskets in the sanctuary facing the altar. Then they locked up the sanctuary for the night. No one could get in. The dead family spent its last night together placed in a row before the altar of the darkened church.

Helen's mother, Mrs. Eva Morris, flew in from Elkin, North Carolina, on Friday night, the night before the funeral. The stricken woman, still suffering in the aftermath of the recent serious kidney ailment that had kept her out of touch with her daughter for a month, was accompanied and assisted by relatives. Upon her arrival in Westfield, she was greeted by Reverend Rehwinkel, who tried to console her as best he could.

Chief Moran, keeping a tight watch on those in attendance, was aware that Helen's sole remaining child, Brenda, had come, too. Strange girl, he thought. He didn't want to think unkindly about the distraught young woman, but he couldn't help noticing that she came to the funeral in a station wagon loaded with what seemed to be all of her belongings. Most of it appeared secondhand garbage. And then he felt bad for thinking such disparaging thoughts. He knew the young woman had broken down completely upon hearing the news of the murders. She was going through a bad time.

Lieutenant Detective Bell told him that Brenda had asked for the two TVs from the house. Well, why not? he thought. They belong to her after all. . . .

From the List side of the family, attendance was sparse. Mr. and Mrs. Fred List, John's nephew, son of his half brother, William G. List, attended the funeral. They represented the stunned family that waited in Frankenmuth, Michigan, for the arrival of the body of Alma List.

By 9:30 A.M. on Saturday, December 11, a crisp, sunny day, Reverend Rehwinkel, who was to conduct the services for the murdered family, could see that the number of people waiting outside for the funeral to begin was already reaching into the hundreds. He could also discern evidence of the Westfield police quietly on the job: plainclothesmen playing the role of curiosity seekers standing nearby and across the street, sitting in as mourners in one of the back pews, hiding in an unmarked car far up the street. He knew they were already waiting, dressed unobtrusively as ground attendants, in a far corner of Fairview Cemetery in the remote possibility that John List might show up.

Also in evidence was the press.

Reverend Rehwinkel could not avoid the press as he stood in the vestibule of his church awaiting the arrival of the grieving family members.

"How long have you known them, Reverend?" was one of the first questions thrown at him.

"The family?"

"Yeah."

"About three and a half years."

"Did you know them well?" came another voice.

"I thought I did. I had spent a great deal of time with the family at various times. Usually on Friday night."

"Every Friday night?"

"No, not—"

"What were they like?"

"A beautiful family."

"What were the kids like?"

"Regular kids."

"We understand that only the children had been visible in the neighborhood."

"Yes. Through their school and community activities. Particularly Patty. But John played soccer on the Roosevelt Junior High School team. I understand he was an up-and-coming athlete. And the younger one, Freddie, why, he was just a real regular little guy," he said. "The parents may have been quiet and reserved, but the children certainly were not. They had great relationships in the community and in the church."

"What was she like?"

"Helen List?"

"Yes."

The pastor measured his words carefully before responding. "I can only confirm reports that have already been given to you, to the effect that Helen List had suffered a nervous breakdown shortly after the family moved from Rochester to Westfield nearly five years ago."

"And him? List?"

The reverend shook his head slowly. "Mr. List played both the role of mother and father during these years. . . ."

One reporter quietly noted in a pad with a cynical grin, "And then the roles of judge, jury, and executioner . . . or was it the role of God?"

No one asked about John's mother, Alma List.

The dark limousines began to appear at the sidewalk in front of the red brick church. "Gentlemen, please," the pastor said, pulling away. "The family is arriving. Later. . . ."

The focus turned from him to the handful of mourners slowly getting out of the black cars parked at the curb. Necks craned as people strained to see the faces of the family. Photographers began their positioning dance, trying to get the perfect Pulitzer Prize–winning photograph.

Eva Morris arrived at the church, pale and drawn. She was sobbing audibly as she was helped into the pew by relatives.

On October 6, 1971, Mrs. Morris had sent her daughter, Helen, a brief letter telling them that she loved them all and asking if she could come to Westfield to visit the family for the Thanksgiving Day holiday:

> *If John doesn't care, tell him I'll give him $30 a month while I'm there. That is what I'm paying here [in North Carolina]. . . .*

But Eva Morris had been ill. Her illness, diagnosed as a severe toxic kidney ailment, wouldn't permit her to travel. By the end of October Helen had received another note, this time a very brief one, from her aunt Cora Yarbourgh in North Carolina, telling her that her mother was very ill in Elkin Hospital. "Love to you all," she added.

The service lasted an hour. Throughout, Mrs. Morris was plagued with the thought that if she hadn't been sick, if she had been able to come north as she had wanted to do, the tragedy might have been averted. If she had not been preoccupied with the severity of her own illness, she might have wondered more actively why she hadn't heard from her daughter, why Helen had not responded to Aunt Cora's letter. If . . . if . . . if . . . So many recriminations were tangled in with the grief. They might not have had to lie there for a month. Alone. So cold. It never occurred to her that she might have been a victim herself had she been visiting at the time of the murders.

Reverend Rehwinkel spoke. "We are not concerned here this morning about explaining the illogical, irrational, and bizarre behavior of a son, a father, a parishioner, and a friend." Oddly enough he did not include "husband."

His words reached past the crowded pews, through the hastily set up PA system, and out to the curious who hadn't been able to get inside the church.

"We have all been leveled," the pastor continued, "but God will lift us up. Let us look at the prophet Isaiah, who said, 'All mankind is grass; they last no longer than a flower in a field.' "

At the conclusion of the service, Reverend Rehwinkel and Mr. Poppy accompanied each casket separately from the sanctuary of the church to the five waiting hearses lined up in a dark row at the curb outside. The family members, all visibly shaken, entered the black limousines.

Grandma was the first in church, and Grandma was the last one out, Poppy thought. She went into the fifth hearse.

Barbara Baeder, a fellow parishioner of the Lists, who had driven John junior home from school to his awaiting death at the hands of his father, was inconsolable. It was the most difficult funeral she had ever attended. Her husband, Donald, and her two sons, Rick and David, who had been friends of the two slain boys, were pallbearers.

Jane Kemp, who lived around the corner from the church, did not know the List family personally. But she was drawn to the occasion by the weight of the tragedy and all the attention it evoked. The five hearses pulling up to the church and lining up at the curb one after another was a sight she would never forget. One by one the caskets were carried out of the church to the waiting hearses with their back doors ajar. Some of the pallbearers, those who carried the caskets of the children, were children themselves—students . . . classmates . . . solemn and pale, sobered by the senseless horror. Ms. Kemp, who watched the cortege slowly take shape as each casket was placed within, and then watched the somber procession as it moved off in the direction of Fairview Cemetery, summed it up quite aptly to one of the ever-ready reporters at hand. "It was a loss of innocence," she said, "and in such an awful way." And then she added the fervent hope of everyone present: "I hope they catch him."

About a hundred onlookers stood in the bright morning sunshine across the street from the red brick church. As the cars left, scores of mourners remained. It was as though no one wanted to leave. To leave was to close the incident, to end it. It was too painful to put away so soon. A great deal of catharsis was needed. Many of the weeping young friends of the three slain teenagers remained

behind trying to console one another. So many feelings to ponder.
So many fears to sort out. So many unanswered questions.

"They were always off by themselves."

"They were such goody-two shoes."

"Don't say that! Patty wasn't."

"Well, the guys were always alone. I never even saw John or
Freddie even eating lunch with anyone else."

"Why didn't we try to include them more? Maybe they were just
shy."

"Why would their father want to kill them?"

"Why didn't they share their problems with us?"

"Could we have helped?"

The cortege proceeded on to the cemetery. Fairview was on North
Broad Street. When it passed Gray's Funeral Home, also located
on Broad Street, the fifth hearse quietly left the cortege and pulled
into the funeral home parking lot. That afternoon, mother Alma was
taken to Newark Airport to be flown back to Frankenmuth, Michigan, her place of birth, for burial. One of six children, two boys
and four girls, she was survived by a lone sister, Lydia. She was
to be interred in a family plot next to her older sister and close
confidante, Augusta. The burial site had one remaining plot, one
that had been reserved long ago for her beloved son, John Emil.
She made the solitary flight back home. The plane flew right over
Bay City, where she had raised her son with such care and devotion,
where they had spent so many beautiful days and evenings together,
where memories of their simple lives, filled with caring and Bible
reading, still hovered about like gentle ghosts.

Meanwhile, the slow-moving funeral cortege to the cemetery was
flanked on both sides by quiet people the entire route. Some stared,
some wept, some bowed their heads in prayer. Finally the cortege
turned through the huge wrought-iron gates into Fairview Cemetery,
no more than eight or nine blocks away from the church where final
services had been held. At Fairview more people were waiting.
There was an embankment across from the burial site, a lovely
grassy hill. Unbelievable, Poppy thought, shaking his head. It was
littered with hundreds of people. The police had to help to control
the crowd. He had never seen anything like it. At the gravesite,
many of the people flanking the caskets were strangers.

The ground where the mother and her three children were to be
buried was gently sloped. The setting would someday be quiet,
serene, and pastoral. But the dignity of the solemn occasion began
to erode as people pushed for better positioning. Photographers
actually stood on top of nearby headstones in order to get a better

view for their incessant photographs. Others gawked openly at the grief of the family. It was like a reenactment of a bad film. Resentment at the intrusion was beginning to run deep in the hearts of family and close friends.

Conducting the last rites at the gravesite, where the caskets waited in masked suspension over multiple openings in the ground, Reverend Rehwinkel tried to ignore some of the surrounding commotion and spoke to the gathering softly in order to restore a sense of dignity. The more softly he spoke, the more quiet and attentive the gathering became. "None of us know," he said in his final words, forcing the gathering to lean forward to hear, "but if John is living, give him the grace that his heavy soul may have communion with you, Helen, Patricia, John, and Frederick."

His picture was snapped by a photographer balanced precariously on top of a headstone two gravesites away.

A sixteen-year-old girl who had shared an English class with Patty List burst into renewed sobs next to her parents as she saw the circuslike atmosphere surrounding her friend in the final moments before Patty disappeared forever into the earth. Her mother gently put a hand to her shoulder. The girl was close enough to see the immediate family trying desperately to escape the seeking eye of the cameras clicking away furiously, gathering "bites" for the six o'clock news. The girl would never forget Helen List's mother, Eva Morris, as a family member tried to shield her from the camera's prying lens. The media was exploiting the grief, the young girl thought angrily, for the benefit of sensational headlines that would emblazon newspapers all over the nation. She looked about, thinking how horrible it all was. Her little town had become infamous. Thanks, Mr. List, she thought bitterly.

At the conclusion of the committal service, Poppy saw to it that everybody was quietly and quickly ushered back to their cars and on their way.

Now Rehwinkel agreed to continue the news conference that had begun before the services.

"Reverend, can you tell us about the letter?"

"Is it true that John List wrote a confession to you?"

"Are you going to reveal the contents of the letter at this time?"

"Where is the letter now?"

The questions from the newsmen again were fast, direct, and outrageous in their expectations since they knew the letter was to be held in evidence for the trial when the fugitive was apprehended. But the reverend waited patiently for the onslaught to die down before speaking. "I cannot reveal any matters of a confidential or confessional nature," he said.

He could sense the disappointment as feet shuffled and soft murmurs stirred throughout the crowd of people present; many onlookers had joined the interview.

"With reference to notes and letters," he continued, "I have no comment."

"Did he write you a confession?" one reporter persisted. "Can you at least tell us that?"

The pastor shook his head. "I cannot. But I do have something to say."

A murmur of expectancy stirred through the thickly clustered group. And then it became clear why the pastor had agreed to the news conference, despite the fact that he had no intention of answering any of the pointed questions that had been directed at him. There was a deep silence as he made an impassioned public appeal for his congregant and friend, John List, to return.

"John," he said in a deep, resonant voice, "as your pastor, I am still very much your friend who will always support you, stand by you, and help you. The Lord God, whom you know and believe in, will not forsake you in these most agonizing times. Please contact me."

One anxious reporter broke in, "Do you think he will, Reverend?"

"My message to John List is a very personal pastoral appeal," the clergyman said patiently. "Please let me finish. . . . John," he continued, "if you are prevented by other circumstances at this time, wait, pray, and contact me when you can, any time, day or night."

He never did.

Union County Prosecutor Karl Asch said, "As of this morning it is believed that Mr. List is still alive, and that he may well indeed turn himself in."

He never did.

Helen List's daughter, Brenda, could not believe any of it. She was still in a state of deep shock. Murdered? All of them? And her stepfather missing? Her stepfather the prime suspect in murdering her entire family? It was a nightmare she could not accept. At this particular moment in her desperate grief, it probably did not occur to her that had she still been living at home, she might have been another one of the victims. All she wanted now was to reach out to the only member of her family who might still be alive. She had to talk to her stepfather, and she, too, sent out a despondent appeal to him. "Daddy," she cried out through the accommodating press, "you are all I have left. Please call me," she begged.

He never did. But her plea made a wonderful headline.

On Sunday, the skies turned cloudy. It was windy and colder than it had been on the morning of the funeral. The temperatures were raw, in the low thirties. The headlines in the local papers over the story of the burial read: MURDERED LIST FAMILY BURIED; SEARCH STILL ON.

And while the search continued, Westfield suffered the consequences of infamy and notoriety. Already the curiosity seekers were driving back and forth in front of the "death house" on Hillside Avenue, keeping the tragedy vividly alive. They stopped. They stared. They whispered. They got out of their cars. They took pictures. It wasn't long before the numbers of the house, 431, were stripped off a fencepost and stolen. Next, the mailbox was ripped out of its mooring and disappeared, taken by souvenir hunters. Even pieces of the dirty gray-white house siding were torn off and carried away.

Mr. Poppy, who had served the family well in its funeral arrangements at Gray Funeral Home, was also made administrator of the estate by the family when they had returned to their homes in other states. He quickly went about selling what little furnishings there were and then had the house tightly boarded up, trying to dispel the intrusion of curiosity seekers. Every window was nailed shut with planks of plywood. The beautiful house looked even seedier in its abandonment.

But the abandonment wasn't total. The attraction of the death house was too great. Not only did it serve as a constant tourist attraction, but local teenagers began daring each other to go "close" to the house. First they would race up to the porch and race back down. Then they would dare each other to touch the front door. Then just getting close to the house wasn't enough of a challenge. They had to get inside.

Soon they discovered that they could climb up a heavy vine on the side of the house and slip in through a broken skylight. Once within, the bold game designed to test mettle began in earnest.

Shouting into the empty, echoing rooms.

Writing "devil stuff" on the walls.

Scaring each other.

Recklessly running through the haunted hallways.

Trying to "raise the ghosts" of the dead.

Determining who had the most courage.

One fearless youth even managed to lie down on the deeply stained floor of the dark ballroom, where the corpses had been found. It was crazy, rash, foolish, exhilarating, and frightening. Unable to retrace their steps and climb up out of the skylight, they found a small window in the basement out of which to crawl. No one spent very much time in the basement. The dark, dank, sectioned-off little rooms with their multishadowed corners were too frightening for even the most audacious to explore. Playing "Psycho" was not a game for the faint of heart. Surely, at night in the darkened privacy of their own bedrooms, nightmares often followed.

And they weren't the only ones who suffered nightmares. Even the less audacious were pulling bedsheets up tight under their chins. After all, the List children could never, in their wildest dreams, have imagined that their own father—moral, righteous, churchgoing, so very proper—would ever point a gun at their heads and pull the trigger.

But he had.

So the "impossible" *could* indeed happen.

Could it happen to them?

Robin Kampf, who lived in Mountainside, was only fourteen years old when she woke up and first read about the Lists on the front page of *The Star Ledger*. Even at fourteen she had always had a strong urge to read the news rather than watch it on television, and she devoured the frightening article. The young, imaginative child did not know it at the time, but John List was to become an obsession with her.

Her best friend, Kathy, had cousins who lived in Colonia, a town next to Westfield, and, after finding out about the tragedy, they were all extremely nervous about it because, as Robin reported in her diary:

*This man fled, and he's somewhere, out there! And we
didn't know where, and that scares all of us. We talk about
it all the time.*

Another entry read:

*I'm really afraid to be alone, be in the dark, going to sleep
at night in my room. I keep checking behind the doors in
my closet, underneath the bed before I go to sleep. Mom
thinks I'm crazy. But a lot of us kids share the same
feelings. Me and Kathy were talking with her cousins, and
all sorts of rumors are still flying around. You know, like, I
knew them. Or, my cousin's cousin knew them, you know
all this stuff. They're probably making a lot of it up. To
scare us.*

Another entry:

*I was talking to Kathy today about it. She told me that
every time she goes to her cousin's house, they'd drive past
the house. I have a curiosity about doing it too but I can't
bring myself to do it. No way. You're not going to believe
this, but it's becoming so everybody goes down there. They
load up in cars and drive down there past the house. They
keep saying, you want to come? I had the chance, but I
won't go. It's just like the Chester Ghost. The same
category. The Chester Ghost on the Chester railroad tracks
and kids are always piling into carloads of caravans and
riding up there and daring each other to go and cross the
railroad tracks outside of the car. Last time I did it, we all
shivered in the car from fear. Scary! That's how I feel
about John List. He's in the same category as the Chester
Ghost.*

While Jean Syfert went through the family's belongs in January
of 1972, she came across the handwritten lyrics of a song Patty had
written in which she kept repeating that she didn't want to be left
alone. In it she said that she had given her heart to the person to
whom the lyrics were directed, begged him not to leave or to say
good-bye, and asked why "they" couldn't see that they had to be
together and begged for "notice."

Jean cried when she read the lyrics of her niece's song. To her
it showed how lonely the girl was. Yet it also indicated that she

had the normal feelings of most adolescents who perhaps had experienced their first feelings of love. She should have had the chance to live, the opportunity to grow, to feel, to explore, to make mistakes, to learn. To live. So should they all have. And Helen. Poor Helen, so sick, so alone, removed from her entire family. So ill that she often could barely move. She should have been taken care of instead of murdered. And those boys. Who had the right to decide they should not grow to manhood!

PART II | BEFORE THE KILL

6 | The Mystery of John Emil List

Piecing together the deadly, mysterious puzzle of John List and re-creating the path that led to murder is no easy task. Who is this man who spent a lifetime devoted to Christian duty? This man who appears sincere in his religious beliefs and yet can savagely murder his entire family in such a cold-blooded, premeditated manner?

The puzzle that is John List is a confusion of conflicting theoretical assumptions. Everyone who knew him saw him differently. Since he did not appear to be an intimately involved friend or neighbor, most perceptions were developed from a distance, but there may be truth in each one. As a personality, he was interpreted by his friends and neighbors as everything from a retiring, reserved, and taciturn milquetoast who was devoted to his family to an arrogant, unfriendly, and even intimidating man who aggressively chased children away from his property. In business, the closer, day-to-day observations were also a symphony of opposites: associates categorized him as everything from a brilliant, excellent worker to a sloppy, inept plodder. He had descended in his career from the vice-presidency of a bank to selling mutual funds out of his home, from successful executive to financial failure, and in his personal life from active "church leader" to mass murderer. Now the FBI's vastly circulated poster described him as **"armed and dangerous."**

Who, then, is John Emil List? When did the murderous thoughts start? Where did the deadly drives begin? What would motivate him to slaughter his wife, his mother, his own children? Were the reasons buried in List's background? Did his actions stem from his relationship with his overprotective, domineering mother? A desperately unhappy marriage? Rebellious children adding to his already heavy anxieties? Did he believe himself the instrument of a righteous God meting out punishment for the sins of disobedience and saving his straying family from further iniquity? Had the despair of personal failure and certain financial ruin overwhelmed his judgment? Was he delusional? Paranoid? There were more questions than answers.

One of the most pathetic theories was that of List's own step-daughter, Brenda De Young. She didn't believe he had done it at all. She thought perhaps, through his accounting services, he had become involved with the Mafia in some way. That perhaps he had borrowed or even taken money from them and was unable to pay it back, and the Mafia had retaliated by killing his entire family. The idea that her "daddy," as she thought of him, could have done this was obviously too wrenching to tolerate.

And where had he gone?

"Brazil. Or Argentina. . . . Sure—he'd blend in with all the German expatriates down there left over from World War II. Or maybe to Germany. Don't forget they found his car at Kennedy International. He could have flown out."

Both theories were logical. List spoke German so fluently, it was said the Nazis released him after his capture during World War II because they thought he was "one of them." This story was believed by his mother, Alma, who had heard it from John himself. She had repeated it proudly to one of her lady friends in Bay City, Michigan.

One of the most romantic notions was that he had assumed the adventurous cloak of a skyjacker; that using the name of D. B. Cooper, he had skyjacked a Northwest Airlines plane under the threat of exploding a bomb in flight and, after negotiating for four parachutes and a $200,000 ransom, had daringly leapt from the airplane, disappearing into a raging snowstorm over the Rockies in southwest Washington. There is a great deal of romance in this kind of yarn. D. B. Cooper was already becoming legendary as the perpetrator of the only unsolved skyjacking episode in the nation. Since there was a vague similarity in the descriptions of the two men, and since the skyjacking happened on Thanksgiving eve only fifteen days after the killings in Westfield, N.J., the possibility of a connection between the two fugitives was seriously considered and checked out by the FBI. But could John List and D. B. Cooper be one and the same? It wasn't likely. Cooper's pattern of behavior was inconsistent with everything that was known about List. Jumping out of an airplane is a very adventurous and dangerous thing to do. John List would worry about hurting himself.

The theories and assumptions surrounding the crime itself, and John List personally, were boundless. It was obvious that he was also beginning to develop mythic proportions in his new role as a fugitive. But who was he? And where was he? Those who had a religious bent believed that the only course he could have taken after the murders was to kill himself. And they were, therefore, certain where he was: he had gone straight to hell.

* * *

In lifting the veil of time, the List family can be traced to Bavaria as far back as the seventeenth century. The first generation of Lists recorded in the Mittel Franken region of Bavaria dates back to 1690 with the birth of Leonhard List. Four generations later, John's paternal great-grandfather, Johann George List, born in 1784, married Kunigarda Biertein. They had ten children, two of whom were destined to emigrate to the New World. That's where the story of John Emil List really began and where the beginning of his strict religious upbringing had its roots. Religion was a deeply ingrained part of life in the new colony in Michigan. It was a hardworking, tightly knit German Lutheran community that had its daily life deeply rooted in its Christian faith.

Reverend Frederick Schmid, a Lutheran missionary, had gone to America in 1833 from Mittel Franken and established in Frankenmuth, Michigan, a new Bavarian missionary colony. It was to be exclusively German Lutheran. Only German would be spoken in the homes, schools, shops, and church.

Two brothers from Bavaria, Johann Adam List (1814) and Johann List (1816), came to Frankenmuth in 1845. Although moved by the missionary spirit, Adam and Johann, aged twenty-nine and thirty-one, were more interested in serving the mercantile needs of their expatriated brethren who they felt were just as much in need of material solace as they were of spiritual comfort. Together they began the hazardous adventure of a more than four-thousand-mile voyage across the Atlantic Ocean to upstate New York and from there to Michigan. They brought with them all the values of their rigid Bavarian heritage—values that had served them well in withstanding the difficulties of traveling across ocean, rail, and bumpy dirt road.

Once in Frankenmuth, they were warmly welcomed by those who had preceded them from Bavaria. Staying close to the German community helped dispel much of the loneliness inherent in their permanent expatriation. They quickly settled in and originated the List dynasty on the western side of the Atlantic Ocean.

There is a bronze plaque on St. Lorenz Church on Tuscola Road commemorating its founders: on the plaque are the names of Johann Adam List, whose granddaughter Alma became John List's mother, and Johann List, whose son became John List's father.

In 1882 history repeated itself. Just as Adam and Johann had left Bavaria to seek new opportunities in America, Johann's sons, J. F.

and John Adam, left their home in Frankenmuth to seek new opportunities in nearby Bay City. They were attracted by the business opportunities in a city that was twenty times the size of Frankenmuth in population and flourishing with the logging boom of eastern Michigan's greatest natural industry.

The German Lutheran exclusivity, so successful in Frankenmuth, was attempted in Bay City by the church elders, but with less success. There were too many external influences forcing their way into the seclusion. It is little wonder, though, that the German section of town was nicknamed "Salzburg."

J. F. and John Adam bought a piece of property on Salzburg Avenue, the center of West Bay City before the turn of the century. Both excellent carpenters, they constructed a clapboard building with an imposing brick front to create a series of shops numbering from 212 to 216. They etched the name *List* into the front of the building to mark their place in time and opened what they knew was greatly needed in the community, a dry-goods store at 212–214 Salzburg. They were two healthy, vibrant young men who were ambitious and industrious, one of the constant trademarks of the List family. It was hardly surprising that they would quickly expand their operations to three general stores.

In time J. F. moved his wife, Anna Marie Hubinger, into the house he'd built around the corner at 1808 South Wenona Avenue. He carefully etched "J. F. List" on the glass portion of the front door to his home. J. F. and Anna Marie had one son. They named him William G. List. William G. eventually opened a grocery store at 216 Salzburg Avenue next door to his father's dry-goods store, thereby keeping up the tradition of family shopkeepers.

Business prospered.

Close by on Salzburg Avenue was a little hat shop owned and operated by Augusta List, J. F.'s spinster cousin once removed. She was the daughter of his first cousin, Michael Johann. It was not as prosperous a business as the dry-goods or grocery stores of her relatives, but it had a steady clientele, enough to warrant having her younger sister, Alma, come from Frankenmuth to help out in the store.

As a young girl, John Emil's mother, Alma, had worked with Augusta in the little hat shop while studying nursing. It was unusual for a woman to study for a career, but Alma knew that, like her sister, Augusta, she would probably end up a spinster. The thought of spinsterhood did not bother her too deeply, but she knew that without a husband and children to care for, she had to keep busy, and she did not want to be a merchant all her life. The nursing profession fit very well into her idea of how a woman should spend her life—in service to others.

The cousins, J. F., John Adam, Augusta, and Alma List, ran into each other often.

By the time J. F.'s wife, Anna Marie, became seriously ill, Alma was in her late thirties and a full-fledged registered nurse. Everyone knew the terminal nature of Anna Marie's illness—cancer. She was at home, and it became obvious that J. F. needed help. Alma, who had the necessary training and skills, was asked to help him in this terrible time of crisis and need.

Alma discussed the arrangements of cousin J. F.'s needs with her sister, Augusta, and agreed to do whatever she could to help him.

"How could you refuse?" Augusta had asked. "It's a family duty to help in times like these."

Alma agreed to use all her nursing skills to help make Anna Marie's last weeks on earth as comfortable as possible. She went to live with John Frederick and his ailing wife in his house on South Wenona Avenue just around the corner from the shops.

"You should make yourself at home here," J. F. said when she entered his home carrying one bag of luggage.

"Thank you."

"These are difficult times. . . ."

"Yes. . . ."

"And I want to make sure you are as comfortable as possible."

"You are not to worry about me," she had said. "We have other things to think about."

And she immediately went to Anna Marie's room and sat by the bed. Holding her cousin's frail hand within the palm of her own firm, steady one, she knew the end was not far off.

"Alma," the dying woman said from her pillow when her tall young cousin walked into the sickroom, "I'm happy you are here. . . ."

"And I will stay as long as you need me."

At almost thirty-seven years of age, Alma List was what everyone described as a "lovely woman," tall, straight, almost regal in her bearing, with a generous, easy smile. Her nurturing instincts added greatly to her nursing skills. J. F. could tell immediately that Anna Marie was now in good hands. Alma cooked and cleaned and scrubbed. Professionally she consulted with the doctor and took over completely every aspect of the care of J. F.'s dying wife. Every night without fail, she sat and read the Bible—sometimes in the living room, sometimes in the privacy of her own room, sometimes aloud at Anna Marie's bedside, in soft-spoken German.

J. F. was impressed with his cousin's dedication to her job and her industrious ways. It was obvious that they shared the same values and the same deep devotion to church, community, and their common heritage. The kitchen once again took on the aroma of hearty German meals, for not only did Alma administer to Anna Marie, but she made sure that the husband was taken care of as well during these trying times.

She, in turn, was impressed with J. F.'s stature, his religiosity, and his continuing industry, as well as his success. Now his face was a bit red all the time, and he had put on the weight of age, but even at sixty he was still broad-shouldered, muscular, and, she thought, handsome, with his deep-set eyes, full head of wavy graying hair parted on the left side, and the full mustache that in Alma's mind gave him the appearance of a German baron who should be riding through the Black Forest rather than tending shop.

Alma was twenty-three years J. F.'s junior.

Dying was difficult. Pain was a constant—the crying out, the retching, the cleaning up, the loss of bodily functions, the cleaning up again, and again, the administering of drugs to ease the pain, the sickly odor of ether and morphine, the perennial smell of the sickroom no matter how much Alma scrubbed. She must console the father, console the son, play hostess to the quiet flow of relatives who came to visit. The more difficult the situation became, the more devoted Alma became. Prayers were never far from the lips of either the nurse or the husband.

In November of 1923, when the trees of Bay City had taken on the radiance of autumnal colors, Anna Marie Hubinger List finally succumbed to the ravaging disease and passed away quietly in her sleep.

Alma comforted J. F. and William. She helped in the preparations for the funeral. She cooked for all the grieving relatives who visited. Her behavior was exemplary.

Finally, all funeral duties completed, the tired Alma prepared to leave. "I will go now," she said to J. F.

"The burial is over," said the grieving man, anticipating the loneliness ahead. "Now begins the hard part."

"There is strength in prayer," she said. "And your family is never far off."

"How can I express my appreciation?" he asked solemnly.

"Please," she begged. "Anna Marie was my cousin, too. Thank God I could do what little I did."

"I shall miss you," he said sincerely.

She lowered her eyes.

"You have been very deeply valued here," he continued.

"Thank you."

They kissed lightly on the cheeks, and Alma left the home of her cousin, John Frederick.

She went back home to Frankenmuth, where whispered stories of her sacrificing dedication followed wherever she went. J. F. and his son, William, were very grateful. J. F. knew he would have to wait a decent interval before approaching this woman again. He did not like the idea of living alone, and although Alma was much younger, did it matter? He had a fine home to offer her and the comfort of a certain amount of wealth. They were cousins once removed. That certainly didn't matter, either.

This was in the days before genetic experts began to discourage the practice of intermarriage, and it was very common. Not only had the colonists often married just before embarking on the hazardous journey to America, but intermarriage was common in any close-knit family community that kept to itself rather than open its door to outsiders, to diversity, and to a possible breaking down of the very carefully structured way of life that had been brought intact from the old country. Suspicion of strangers was very keen, not only because of difference in language and religion, but because differences often brought about the danger of physical assaults. Ethnic prejudice was a given.

The List family was no different from any other family that had settled in the region, whether Irish, French-Canadian, or Polish. They all wanted to keep to themselves. The List family tree demonstrated the long generational history of cousins marrying cousins. Alma's own brother, Emil A., had married Caroline Hubinger, who was related to Anna Marie Hubinger List, the woman who had just passed away.

J. F. didn't necessarily want any more children, and there was some question in his mind as to whether Alma had passed the point of childbearing years anyway, but that didn't really matter, either. He wanted a companion to share his home and take over its duties. If God wanted them to have a child, it would be His will.

Of all her family, Alma was closest to her sister, Augusta, who was older by four years and in whom she had always confided. When, one year later, J. F. asked her to marry him, Alma sat in the hat shop carefully sewing a veil onto the brim of a dark blue hat and discussed his proposal with Augusta.

"Why not?" Augusta said. "He's a fine figure of a man. Devoted to the church."

"I don't think I love him."

"Does that matter?"

"Not really."

"At your age?" Augusta scoffed lightly.

"No, it doesn't." Alma smiled.

"More important, do you *like* him? You stayed in his house for a long time. You should be able to tell by now."

"Yes, I like him."

"And he is a respected member of the community, Alma," Augusta urged. There was no doubt in her mind that her sister should marry. "He will make a good husband. You will be taken care of for the rest of your life. You won't have to die a spinster."

In her heart Alma knew that she would accept J. F.'s proposal even before she had told Augusta about it, but she wanted to talk it out with her sister, to think it out carefully, logically, to hear aloud all the reasons why she should.

"After all," Augusta pointed out reasonably, "for me at forty-two there is not much prospect of a marriage. You're almost thirty-eight now. This may be your only opportunity to have a home of your own. Maybe even a family."

Alma stopped her sewing for a moment to think of such a prospect. She yearned for a child. If God would only grant her a child. The only objection to the marriage was her cousin's age. But as Augusta pointed out, he was still a fine figure of a man. Perhaps it was not too late for either of them. She would pray very hard to be blessed with a child.

When she accepted J. F.'s proposal of marriage, he smiled. "You have made me very happy, Mumma." That's what everyone called Alma: "Mumma."

In December of 1924, almost exactly one year after the death of Anna Marie, John Frederick List and Alma M. List married. William G. List, J. F.'s adult son, acted as best man at the ceremony. He was pleased for his father. He liked his cousin Alma, who was the same age as he. On her wedding day Alma was nearly thirty-eight years old and her new husband sixty. Alma List did not even have to change her name. Theirs was to be a marriage based on mutual respect, sharing, caring, and fulfilling the more mundane needs of life. Within the parameters of its expectations, it would turn out to be a very successful union.

Ten months later Alma's fervent prayers were answered. On September 17, 1925 Alma gave birth to her only child, a son. She was almost thirty-nine at the time of his birth. J. F. was sixty-one. Following in the List tradition of naming their male offspring Johann or John, they baptized their son John Emil List.

7 | Young John at Mama's Knee

John Emil was born in "Salzburg," at 1808 South Wenona St., around the corner from Salzburg Avenue where his father and uncle had prospered as merchants and his adult half brother, William G., ran the local grocery store. In a house constructed in the Victorian style with Greek revival influence in the columns that supported its squared portico roof, young John Emil List grew up.

The first floor had only one bedroom, which was occupied by J. F. and Alma. Young John slept in the front room, which overlooked the porch and was situated across the hall from the living room. It had no door. From childhood to adolescence to his teenage years, privacy would not be a component in his life.

Practically the entire back portion of the house was given over to the kitchen. It was here that his mother spent so much of her time cooking robust German fare. It was the child's favorite room. But as he grew, his favorite place increasingly became the privacy of his own thoughts.

His half brother, William, lived only four blocks away on Raymond Avenue with his wife, Pauline. Their children, Louis, Florence, Erwin, Richard, Fred, and Ruth, John Emil's own cousins, were also his half nieces and nephews. Intermarriage was so frequent that the relationships could become very confusing to sort out even within the family.

None of it mattered to young John. Few of them were factors in his life. When he was growing up, his world consisted of a ten-block section in West Bay City, bordered on one end by the Zion Lutheran Church across the railroad tracks on Salzburg Avenue, where he not only went to services but also attended school, and on the other end by South Wenona Street, where he lived alone with his parents. The area was still called "Salzburg" by the locals. Its ambiance was extremely conservative and just as cliquish as its ethnic counterparts within other parts of town.

Only German was spoken at home. It was John's first language. The family didn't own a radio. Necessary information was obtained through newspapers and verbal exchanges with relatives and friends. Frugality was a mutually ingrained component in family management between J. F. and Alma. John learned early the value of careful budgeting and planning. Outside of one Sunday dress and her nursing uniforms, Alma's entire wardrobe consisted of housedresses frequently washed and ironed; she always looked clean and neat. The heat in the house was kept so low that in the harsh Michigan winter months the Lists compensated by wearing heavy one-piece woolen undergarments known as union suits.

Alma scrubbed and cleaned and cooked with the enthusiasm born of the deeply industrious tradition that was her heritage. J. F. had little to do with his young son. He had already raised one son. He was in his sixties when John Emil was born, and he was beginning to slow down. He left the care of the boy in the hands of his very capable wife. She couldn't have been happier.

Right from the very beginning of his existence, Alma kept John Emil close to her side, fussing tenderly and busily over her only child. She had waited so long for a child of her own. In the summer he was not permitted to run barefoot as so many of the other children in Bay City did. Even on the hottest days, he was scrubbed and neatly combed and dressed in a hat and dark sensible clothes, which he was always gently reminded to keep clean. In the winter he was heavily scarved, gloved, hatted, and booted. A sneeze was blown way out of proportion, a runny nose was cause for chest rubs and a towel being wrapped around his head as he leaned over a boiling pot of water steaming with an aroma of Vicks. A fever was cause for doctors and nighttime vigils. He was virtually smothered with nurturing and mothering; but it was the only existence he knew, and the bond between mother and son grew very strong. At her side he acquired the custom of nightly readings from the Bible. He loved the comfort of familiar routines.

Once in a while Alma would have occasion to cross one of the drawbridges over the river into East Bay City. At these times John was combed and polished and dressed in his best Sunday clothes. He could sense his mother's pride as she walked with him holding onto his hand while he gazed in awe at the palatial City Hall and the magnificent library and at all of the logger-baron mansions that composed so much of East Bay City's architecture; their size and stature impressed him greatly. Mansions, he thought.

Alma was a contemporary of her stepson, William G., and his wife, Pauline. They always got along very well. The same could not be said for the younger generation of Lists. William's children spent very little time with his much younger half brother, John Emil. Not only was there an age disparity, but they thought the boy was a little peculiar. He rarely spoke to them. He rarely smiled. Even at the age of five, he looked and behaved more like a little old man than a child.

One spring there was a family gathering in Frankenmuth, where it began to be apparent to the rest of the family how differently little John Emil behaved from the other children present. It was a festive occasion. Children's games were in progress. Before long his cousins began to look in John's direction encouragingly. He pretended not to notice. He listened instead to the music.

John would never forget the music. He had never heard so much all at one time. Uncles and cousins of his were playing German songs on accordians. There was a boisterous camaraderie that struck young John as odd. He had never seen adults laugh so heartily. He had never seen so much drinking of beer. He had never seen a man backslap another in such good fellowship. His father remained a bit aloof from all the gaiety. He sat in a far corner of the room deep in discussion with some of the other old men in the room. He heard someone call his father "Fritz," and he actually seemed relaxed with his feet crossed and stretched before him, his stomach bulging in front of him. Then, incredibly, John saw his father burst out laughing. He looked up at his mother. She too was joking and laughing. He had never seen her like that, either. She was delightfully outgoing and friendly surrounded by many close relatives who lived too far away for her to visit often. She seemed happy and at home. John felt a surge of excitement at the sense of pleasure he perceived all about him.

Venturing a move alone, he walked over to the table where the food was spread out across what seemed to him like three full-size dining room tables. The food was rich, deliciously aromatic, and plentiful. He began to reach.

Alma was at his side immediately. She smiled down at him brightly and fixed a dish for him of *knoedel*. She cut the food into bite-size morsels, then she carried the plate for him to a side chair, where she patiently sat next to him while he ate. But not before they had said grace. One of the boys stopped his game to stare at them while they prayed over the dish in John's lap. John didn't seem to notice as he began eating.

"*Gut?*" Alma asked.

"*Ja Mutter.*"

"*Iss langsom, liebling.*"

When he could eat no more, she gently urged a few more bites before getting up to take his plate away.

Sitting alone, he solemnly watched the other children playing at the gathering. Their game, running in and out around the adults, tagging, giggling, crawling under the tables, was becoming boisterous enough to attract a few casual admonishments from nearby adults. Nobody really seemed to mind. Children's games were an inherent part of family festivities when all the cousins got together.

One little boy, a distant cousin whose name John did not even know, suddenly stopped in front of him. He was breathing heavily and was sweating from running about. His shirttail was hanging out of the back of his pants. There was an impish, mischievous look in his eyes. "C'mon!" he said to his cousin.

His mother was at his side immediately. "That's all right, darling," she said to the little boy. "John has just finished eating. He can't play right now. You run along."

The boy looked up at her as she smiled down at him from her full height, and then he scampered off.

John said nothing as she sat next to him again. He watched the game they played from across the room. He saw them run. One fell. He looked at *Mutter* sitting tall and erect by his side. He could tell she didn't approve. She looked down at him, smiled gently, and patted his hand. "That's all right. There are other things to do besides run around and get dirty." He looked back at the children. She could not tell whether he wanted to play with them or not. There was little expression on the child's face. "You don't want to get hurt, do you?" she asked.

He shook his head. He did not seem to object to being left out. She brushed back his straight hair even though not a strand was out of place.

Eventually the children ignored their younger cousin.

The pattern would continue. Even when he had reached the age when most boys broke away from parents, he still stayed by his mother's side at family gatherings.

"Don't bother with him," said one young cousin to another. "He only does what his mother tells him to do."

It was an image that would be carried deep into the future, the one thing many family members would always remember about young John Emil. By the age of thirteen he had already adopted the attitudes, values, and behavior patterns of one of the church elders;

and although most of the younger generation went to church regularly, few took it as seriously as John.

"He ought to be a preacher," one cousin whispered to the giggles of another.

"Who cares?"

"Aw, leave him alone."

And they did.

Young John began his school days at Zion Lutheran Elementary School, which he attended from grades one through eight. The school was located on the grounds of the Zion Lutheran Church, which had been founded in 1901. He had heard many stories from his mother of how both his father and his uncle Johann Adam had been on the founding committees and had helped in the actual construction when they were young men.

All the children were taught to read and write in German. Part of the curriculum was also a daily class in religion. It was here that John memorized Martin Luther's Small Catechism, studied the Ten Commandments with all the other parish children, and learned that the head of the family was responsible for teaching the commandments to his family by deed and example as well as by word. There was something very comforting to him in the early religious training and the strict regimen of the school curriculum—its precision, its explicitness, its categorizing of all human emotions and desires into a strict set of precepts, a punctilious basis for behavior.

The pastor preached civic duty from the pulpit.

His mother preached control, stoicism, devotion to God and the Bible.

His father preached the work ethic, an honest day's work for an honest day's pay.

They all preached against the sins of greed, and lust, and idleness, and godlessness, but his mother and father went even further. They placed many natural and socially acceptable behaviors under the category of "sin"—drinking a little too much, dancing, going to the theater, even speeding a car and racing a horse. All human weakness fell under this condemnation. They left little room for maneuvering, little room for deviation from the exaggerated maxims they set down for their son. For John Emil List it seemed natural, normal, the ways things were, the way things should be. It was a structure into which he had been born, weaned, rigidly trained. He knew no other way. It shaped his life. Deviation from these standards was to become anathema to him throughout his life.

There was strictness involved in the actions of the church elders as well. His father made sure the boy would "know" and "learn" the consequences of breaking the rules. For seven terms J. F. acted as both treasurer of the church and a member of its board of trustees. Young John remembered accompanying his father to a "private" meeting to settle the delicate issue of one of its female parishioners. He sat outside the closed doors while the board of elders sat in judgment. He glanced about. The hallway was dark and a bit foreboding, but not as frightening as the momentous decisions that were going on behind the heavy door. Occasionally a voice would be raised enough for him to hear a few words: "not possible..." "divorce..." and "must leave the church..." Such a prospect seemed to deepen the shadows in the hallway.

He was jolted to rigid attention when the heavy door opened and the young woman who had been the subject of the meeting came out crying softly.

Young John caught her eyes as she walked out. His heart immediately went out to her. She seemed so desolate, so sorry. Was there no recourse other than to be asked to leave the church, to be stricken from the membership rolls? That was probably the worst thing that could happen. It made him shudder to think of the righteous morality behind the action, but he believed in the authority of the council and quietly accepted the harsh inevitability of its decision.

There was nothing to question.

Not staying within the laws of the community was a sin. Still, if she were sorry enough, if she confessed... Anything could be forgiven under confession. He remembered that very clearly, that the "Office of the Keys and Confession" said

We receive absolution or forgiveness from the pastor as from God himself, and firmly believe that by it our sins are forgiven before God in heaven.

But what was there for her to confess? he wondered. The deed had been done. A civil divorce had been granted. There was no recourse but to remove her from the church's rolls. It was harsh punishment, but necessary. He said a silent prayer for her imperiled soul and waited for his father. Someday he, too, would serve on the church board, he thought. Someday he, too, would follow in the familiar pattern of so many of his male relatives. Like his father, his uncle Johann Adam in Frankenmuth had served as treasurer and clerk for years. He had also collected subscriptions for St. Lorenz's church support. It was a family tradition, John thought. Particularly, he liked dealing with figures. Perhaps someday he too could become a church leader. Down deep there was a part of him that liked the idea of making the kinds of momentous decisions that deeply affected people's lives. There was a subtle sense of power in the thought. But he would be kind, he thought.

His father exited the meeting room. Several of the other church elders were with him. They whispered a few words to each other before J. F. nodded to his son. "Come," he said in German. "I told your mother I would have you home in time for readings."

On the walk home his father continued the never-ending process of indoctrination as he carefully explained what had just happened and why the young woman had been forced out of the religious community. She had committed the unpardonable. She had been married under God's law and had obtained a civil divorce because of "personal reasons" without taking into consideration that God's laws cannot be broken without consequence. He embellished the story with all the fearful consequences of reprisals for immorality. It was a hellfire-and-brimstone approach to morality out of the darkest pages of the Old Testament. There was no forgiveness. Just like there was no forgiveness for certain sins a foolish young boy might commit.

John never thought that the strict religious upbringing might be casting long shadows over his life. Even as an adolescent, without playmates or close friends, the Scriptures and the regimentation of his life were not only a comfort, but an absolute necessity in order to deal with and explain the social deprivations he felt only on a subconscious, even primitive level. Somewhere down deep, he always felt the outsider. But he never rebelled. It never even occurred to him that he might be lonely. Nor did it occur to him that an environment was being created in which an obsessive-compulsive personality would flourish.

One crisp autumn afternoon at the Zion Lutheran Church schoolyard ten-year-old John, tightly buttoned up in a heavy winter coat, stood and watched as a group of students played football after school under the eyes of one of the teachers.

Edward Schneider, who taught fifth and sixth grade, looked at the tall, thin boy with the wire-rimmed glasses at the periphery of the group. He was so bashful, he was all by himself again. If there were only something Schneider could do to ease the boy's shyness.

It was almost too painful to witness. "Why don't you invite John into the game," he suggested to one of the leaders of the group.

"Him? He can't play football."

"How do you know if you don't ask him?"

"He never plays anything," the boy said reluctantly.

"I would appreciate it if you would just ask him."

The boy looked at John distastefully but walked over at the teacher's insistent suggestion.

"We could use another guy," he said sullenly to John. "Would you like to fill in?"

John's face turned pink. "I can't. Thank you, but no," he said politely.

The boy hurried back to the game with relief and tossed the football to a friend who had been watching the scene impatiently with his hands on his hips.

Mr. Schneider walked over to young John. "John," he said, "why did you say no?"

"My mother told me not to play football."

"Your mother?"

"Yes, sir."

"I'm sure she would be very happy if you would join in with the other boys."

The boy shook his head solemnly. "She said I would catch cold if I took my coat off." There didn't seem to be any resentment as he made the statement.

From May of 1938 until 1941, Christina Worman and her husband moved into the upstairs apartment at the List home. They were young marrieds who were looking for a rental until they could afford to settle into a home of their own. She was a teacher, and they both went to work daily. They were neat, they were clean, they were not noisy, they were perfect tenants. Alma List liked the younger woman immediately, and the two developed a warm friendship. Christina found the elderly Mr. List to be pleasant but formidable in his austerity, yet she found herself liking him, too.

"Ah," she said pleasantly to J. F. when introduced to young John, who was not yet thirteen. "Is this your grandson?"

Alma laughed. But J. F. just said, "My son."

"Oh, I'm sorry," she said quickly, embarrassed by her error.

"That's all right. That's all right," Alma reassured her in her lightly accented English. "It's an understandable mistake." After all, J. F. was seventy-four now.

And as the weeks went by, Christina felt more and more at home.

Living upstairs in the List home was warm and comfortable. There was a quiet, a serenity, even a sense of deep peace, about the home. Often after work, Christina found herself sitting on the porch next to her landlady. Mrs. List's hands would always be busy knitting, crocheting, or darning.

"It is so lovely being here, Mrs. List," she said. "So peaceful and quiet."

"Thank you, Mrs. *Vor*man," Alma said warmly. She always called her "Mrs. Worman" even though Christina was much younger and had told her she could call her "Christina" if she liked. But there was a charm in Mrs. List's formality, and Christina smiled at the slight German lilt Mrs. List gave her name: "Mrs. *Vor*man."

"Do you know," Christina continued, "I was just telling my husband the other day that I don't think I've ever heard a cross word or a voice so much as raised in this house."

"Raised voice." Alma laughed. "Now why should there be? When everything is as it should be, there is no reason for harsh words."

On Halloween night it was bitterly cold, but despite the slashing north wind coming from the bay, the "trick-or-treaters" were out in carnival numbers.

From her upstairs window, Christina could see one noisy group approaching the house—sheeted ghosts and masked, horned devils carrying their bags, hoping for another tasty handout. Christina smiled as they stomped across the lawn toward the front steps and moved back into her kitchen to gather the treats she had prepared for the occasion, little white bags stuffed with popcorn and tied at the top with thin colorful ribbons.

Downstairs, young John also watched from the window of the front room, where he was already in bed. It seemed silly to him. All those kids dressed up like devils. And yet his eyes were shiny. Their bags looked as though they were stuffed with candies.

Christina had her apron filled with the little bags of popcorn when she suddenly heard screams and shrieks of fear from the front lawn. She dropped the treats and rushed to the window in time to see J. F. angrily chasing away the small band of goblins. He shouted after them in German and shook his fist. One little boy tripped in his anxiety to flee and fell heavily on the front lawn. The contents of his bag spilled wildly—apples and cookies and fudge and candies. The jolt of his fall was frightening and painful, and he began to scream loudly. Tears ran down his reddened cheeks. J. F. stopped in his tracks. But he shouted again, *"Geht weg! Geht fort!"*

The boy's crying echoed in the night as he managed to pick himself off the ground and limp toward his friends, who had been waiting for him at a safe distance.

Alma quietly observed the scene from the living room window as J. F. retreated within the house again, went into his bedroom, and shut the door.

John watched as the children crept back and silently scrambled to retrieve the scattered contents of the injured boy's bag. Then he felt his mother by his side. "If those children were in bed where they belong at this time of night, this wouldn't have happened," she said firmly as she helped him back into bed.

Upstairs, Christina sat down at her kitchen table thoughtfully. She was troubled by Mr. List's hostility as he chased the children away and also by the fact that he did not try to find out how badly the little boy was hurt. Why would he be so intolerant? After all, they were just children. She found herself thinking of young John.

There was a price to pay for the incident.

It was not uncommon for disputes within the congregation to be handled through pastoral intervention. Several of J. F.'s fellow congregants complained bitterly to the pastor of Zion Lutheran Church, Reverend Herman A. Mayer. The father of the boy who fell was particularly irate. "What is the matter with him!" he said. "As an elder of the congregation, he does something like that to one of the parish children?"

"He's an old man," Pastor Mayer said appeasingly to the angry father.

"That doesn't matter. My son was injured."

"Seriously?"

"That's not the point," said another parent.

"His entire arm is black and blue, and he scraped his knee," the father continued. "And what is he to think when an adult treats the children so harshly for no reason? It was Halloween, and they were only doing what all children do on Halloween."

"Mr. List can't understand the ways of young people anymore," said the pastor.

"He has a son himself. He *should* understand."

"I will speak to him. Now try not to dwell on this. Mr. List is a good man in many ways. We all know that. But I will speak to him. I promise."

Later Reverend Herman A. Mayer sat alone in his study and thought about it. He didn't think talking to J. F. would do much good. Mayer was a tall man of moderate attitudes. He kept his mustaches tightly trimmed and his dark, receding hair brushed straight back over a high forehead. He took off his wire-rimmed glasses and cleaned them slowly with the white cotton handkerchief from his breast pocket.

No, there would be no changing J. F., he felt sure. He was too set in his ways. Not only was he approaching his seventy-fifth birthday, but he was an "old" seventy-five, deeply entrenched in old-fashioned attitudes and scriptural dogma. Almost excessively so, the pastor found himself thinking to his own surprise. The once vibrant, ambitious, industrious young man who had blazed trails in Salzburg in 1882 during the rough early days of Bay City had become an old fuddy-duddy with a much younger wife whose attitude about the modern world seemed to be even more archaic than his.

Reverend Mayer shook his head. He was a bit surprised at Alma List. She never seemed to question J. F.'s authority or his decisions. She had been brought up to respect her elders, but still, didn't she, at least, realize that they were hurting their son? The pastor sensed an isolation in the boy that he felt was not entirely the boy's own doing. This incident would not help his standing with the parish children. Mayer knew how cruel children could be, how they would take their anger at John's father out on him. They already ridiculed him because his father was so old-fashioned, so "different." He had seen it himself. Young John never fought back. Several times the pastor had had to intervene.

He shook his head a bit sadly.

The boy was a loner. Whether by choice or because he was pushed out, the minister wasn't certain, but he was sure that he spent most of his time alone. It was probably a combination, he thought. He was sure that, down deep, John wanted very much to be a part of his peer group since it was obvious to all that he was not a part of his family/cousin group. There were times when John spoke to him, always hesitantly and never really completing a conversation. But at these times the pastor felt that John was pursued by the nagging dictates driven into his consciousness by his parents and equally plagued by his own conviction that obeying his parents was an absolute maxim by which to live. The boy was not aware that many of their admonitions were contrary to the accepted behavior of normal youngsters growing through the different stages of their development. And even when the pastor tried to tell him so—in essence to "loosen up" a bit—the boy resisted. But despite some astute observations, the pastor was never fully aware of the long history of repression that had been imposed on John under the guise of duty and religiosity. The boy always gave the pastor the impression of being too mature for his age. He never seemed to go through the dirty-up-and-tear-your-pants stage. Or the climbing-trees stage. Or the athletic stage. Or the hunting-and-fishing stage. Or even the interest-in-girls stage. What he had were books and an avid interest in reading. It was through the world of books that young John experienced the adventures he was denied in life. But not too much. He himself put restrictions on his reading. The book he read most avidly was the Bible.

Reverend Mayer knew that the Halloween incident would have an effect on young John. And it did. His world got even smaller. He resorted more and more to the comfort he found in the afterlife of Heaven that was promised to everyone of good faith.

The next night, the List home on South Wenona Street was quiet. Christina Worman sat in Alma List's warm kitchen. She wanted to talk to Mrs. List about what had happened on Halloween night, but Alma was busily chatting away about the Ladies Aid Society, and Christina thought perhaps she had better not bring it up. The Ladies Aid Society met at Zion Lutheran School. "The first Thursday of each month," Alma said as though she really looked forward to the occasion. It was the only outside activity she had besides Sunday services.

Mrs. List's kitchen was permeated with the glorious aroma of specially prepared German fare for the meeting. Each of the women brought home-cooked dishes for their dinners. "Everybody tries to outdo everyone else." Alma laughed. "It becomes like a competition."

"I'll bet you win," Christina said, breathing in the aromas emanating from the oven.

"You must take some upstairs for your husband," Alma said. "There is plenty."

There were problems at the Lists, Christina found herself thinking, but there were compensations as well. Mostly, it was a home. A happy, thoughtful home. The one all-inclusive word for it would have to be "secure." Even she felt the security, she insisted to herself. On cold autumn afternoons Christina often sat in the Lists' kitchen while Mrs. List kept herself busy cooking or baking or scrubbing—always something—while young John was outside raking.

"Good evening," he said to the woman in the kitchen as he came in after his work. He was just like the men in the neighborhood, Christina thought, men who raked leaves, shoveled snow, or swept the sidewalks on Sundays, sometimes even getting down on their hands and knees to trim their grass.

"John, come and have a tall glass of milk for *enerchee*," Alma called out to her industrious young son. He came into the kitchen before going to the front room, to have his glass of milk for energy. Here at home he would always be protected, Christina thought. Here he would always be secure.

"He's such a good boy," Christina said after John had gone to his room.

"Yes," said Mrs. List proudly. "You must come to his confirmation party."

"Why, yes, we'd love to."

"It's also Mr. List's seventy-fifth birthday. We'll have a double celebration."

It was too bad the boy couldn't have the celebration all to himself, Christina thought. More and more she noticed his isolation and felt a little sorry for him. There were all those hot summer days when she could see many of the neighborhood children running about barefoot. But John always wore shoes and a hat because his parents said he should.

She liked the Lists very much and felt guilty thinking any negative thoughts about how they were raising their son. She found herself blaming the problem on their age. Even Mrs. List seemed so much older than she actually was—not in appearance, certainly, but in attitude. The boy *had* to feel stifled by the overprotective environment. Domination would be more appropriate, she thought. It made John seem peculiar to the other children. He probably wasn't really very likable to them, Christina thought sadly, and he was such a nice boy. She could imagine that he never had much to say to them, that he always remained on the periphery of their groups. It was as though he had come from another planet, as though he didn't belong in the world into which he had been thrust.

Once Christina came home after work and saw the three of them sitting on the davenport on the porch. Mr. List on one side, Mrs. List on the other, and the boy nestled in between them. The three of them had their heads bowed as they quietly read the Bible. She paused for a moment to look at the family and thought, I'm wrong.

I'm making too much of it. She looked at them seated together. There was something very beautiful about their attachment to one another.

"Good evening," Christina said as she reached the first of the six steps leading up to the porch.

Mr. List nodded. The boy raised his head and smiled. It was Mrs. List who returned her greeting in her warm slightly accented voice. "Ah, Mrs. *Vor*man," she said pleasantly. "A nice night for walking, *ja*?"

"Oh, *ja*," Christina agreed.

J. F. got up to go into the house. "Don't be too late."

"We won't," Mrs. List said pleasantly.

"Good night," he said.

"Good night, Mr. List."

After J. F. had disappeared within the house, John put aside the book he had been reading. He moved to the upper step of the porch and sat facing the street. She looked at his back darkened by the shadows of the porch.

Another time, when they were seated on the porch alone, he looked up from a book he was reading. As she sat crocheting, the boy talked softly to her. He trusted her. She was aware he was telling her "things," confiding. But her thoughts wandered off. She barely heard the boy until he said to her, "Sometimes I think I'd like to go hunting."

"That would be nice," Christina said a bit absently.

Once John mentioned to his mother that he'd heard a boy at school tell how he had gone hunting with his father early one morning and had "bagged a deer."

"I just mention it," young John said. "He said the sky was pretty."

"You can see the sky anytime," she sniffed, feeling compelled to discourage what she considered would be a very dangerous venture for young John. "You don't have to kill to see a sky." Most important, Alma didn't approve of guns.

"What do you think?" the boy asked Christina.

"What?"

"Hunting."

"Why don't you go hunting with your brother?"

"Half brother."

"Your mother told me he goes hunting all the time."

John looked out across the porch at a house similar to their own on the other side of South Wenona. "He goes with his own sons."

"You could go fishing alone," she suggested, looking up. "Couldn't you?"

"Yes," he said. "I could."

But she knew he wouldn't. She stopped crocheting and looked closely at the boy, who had gone back to his book. "Doesn't your brother have something to do with bowling?" she asked. The boy looked up again. "I'm pretty sure I heard your mother say something like that," she said.

"At school." He nodded.

"School?"

"In the basement. There's a bowling alley in the school basement."

"Really," she said cheerfully. "Well, now that's nice."

"He sponsors a team."

"Why don't you go sometime?"

"It's for teams."

"Surely he would let you throw a few balls or something."

"I guess he would."

His eyes went back down to his book. She knew that John would not go.

Both Christina and her husband thought the confirmation party for John was a wonderfully warm occasion. The food was abundant and delicious. But Christina noticed that there there were no children at the party. Only adults.

The boy smiled proudly when everyone sang "Happy Birthday" to his father on the occasion of his seventy-fifth year.

8 | School Days— The Loner

John noticed the brilliantly colored flaring skirts of the young girls in school as he walked down the hall of Bay City Central High School. He could sense the playfulness of the boys as they experimentally "horsed around" with them in joyful adolescent fervor.

No one was aware that he watched them as he passed. He thought about what it would be like to join in on the antics. Even as a teenager, aside from the church affairs that he attended with his parents, he was never seen attending a school dance, a party, a pep assembly, or any of the football games. Once again no one asked him, and no one missed him. In fact, no one seemed to notice him even when he was there except that he did look different. "Peculiar" was the word that was often used to describe him. And as an adolescent, he *was* a bit peculiar. He was always dressed in dark, sensible colors, which, as usual, made him appear older than he really was. While the other boys in school wore colorful sweaters and brightly colored open-collared shirts, sometimes covered with sleeveless vests, he wore long-sleeved formal shirts. His sweaters were deep brown, or gray, or black over the white shirts, and he always wore a tie. While the other boys mostly adopted the current fashion of saddle shoes, he wore dark dress formal shoes, often covered with galoshes. Even now he always wore a hat and gloves and scarf in the wintertime. With his plain-rimmed old-fashioned spectacles and his protruding ears, he was the picture of a very conservative young man completely out of step with his generation. If he was aware of the snickering as he passed the others on his way to the school library, it didn't show. Did he hear the soft "pantywaist" or "Mama's boy" thrown in his direction? No one ever knew. He certainly gave no indication of having heard. He displayed no outward reactions to the deliberately derisive epithets. Was it an act? Was it a stony resolve not to be bothered by the jeers of his classmates? The truth might have been that John List was more alone than anyone ever realized.

At home he continued to work around the house. His father was nearly eighty, and had lost much of his vigor, but that wasn't the reason John did all the chores. He *liked* working around the house. From the time he was a boy, he had seen how the men tended the lawns and gardens of their homes. Everything had to be taken care of: leaves raked, grass cut, hedges trimmed, house painted. Everything was kept up beautifully, neatly, so that the neighborhood had the appearance of precision, care, beauty, and perfection. It was a treat to walk down the street and see all the trim and tidy houses. He loved it all. He absorbed the role of caretaker of the house from these early days of observation and fell into fulfilling it long before he was a man.

When her stepson, William G., asked Alma if she would like the boy to work in his grocery store after school as his own children did when they became teenagers, she rejected the idea in favor of his staying home to study. William G. did not argue with Mumma. Neither did John.

During John's years at Bay City Central High School, Christina Worman still was aware that he didn't have friends, but by now she was used to it. She no longer wondered at the potential harm in having his activities focused only within the narrow boundaries of the ten-block section of Salzburg between school and church.

He appeared content. He studied long hours and made the National High School Honor Society. Alma was very proud. He did not object when his mother met him after school many afternoons and walked home with him. "There goes John List and his girl," said Geraldine Schneider, giggling. And then she found herself swallowing hard, her heart suddenly going out to him. It's nice to be close to your mother, she thought to herself on a more compassionate level, but *that* close?

He did not object when Alma led him into church services by the hand. He did not seem to notice that others in the congregation rolled their eyes to heaven at the sight. When one of the elders— a fellow congregant, a friend—tried to talk to J. F. about the spectacle of his teenage son being led into church by the hand, J. F. took immediate offense. And the discussion was aborted before it began. J. F. did not think that Alma was being overprotective at all. For him, protecting John Emil was a necessity. Times had changed. The neighborhood was growing, Bay City was modernizing. It was totally different from what it had been in the early days when he and Johann Adam had first made their way here. The population had more than tripled. The Poles were now the dominant nationality. By the time John Emil was in high school, German was no longer the only language spoken in the stores. It was becoming more necessary than ever before to close ranks and keep tightly knit. Hostility was even being felt against his German heritage because of the war in Europe. Even Zion Lutheran School had stopped teaching German because of these outside pressures. J. F. thought that was incredibly stupid, but his son was already fifteen and in Bay City Central High, and it no longer affected him personally. He knew that everyone was talking about "stopping the Nazis." What he didn't know was that young John was no different in this respect. After Pearl Harbor there was a burning desire to "join up." Every boy in high school wanted to go "fight the Nazis and the Japs." They could scarcely wait for graduation to enlist. John could feel himself being caught up in the fever of enlistment: the daring, the adventure, the freedom . . . It was like something out of books.

He never mentioned his feelings at home.

One day John became aware that a young classmate of his came to school at least one hour early every morning in order to "get in shape" for the army. He was a handsome young man with a lithe body and a quick smile. Young John watched him running up and down the steps in the high school football stadium. John would have liked to join him in the exercise of the run. He knew he could keep up physically, but he was intimidated at the thought of making a spectacle of himself, running up and down the steps in the stadium, perhaps having to go into class perspired . . . overheated . . .

Instead he watched Robert J. Clark from a distance.

When he graduated from Bay City Central High School's class of 1943, all that the class yearbook could say about John was; "John List is in the Quartermaster Corps."

Many of the young men of John List's 1943 graduating class did not wait for graduation before they enlisted. So many of them had already joined the army that the ranks of the class were thinned out a good deal on graduation day. John was one of the students who received his rolled-up diploma in the palm of his left hand, shook hands with the principal with his other, and walked off the platform knowing that now he would have to follow through with the decision made long ago in the quiet of his thoughts.

He had a desperate need to get away, but he certainly didn't think of it as such. He was merely doing his patriotic duty under the circumstances of the war that had impacted the lives of the entire nation. Being of German descent, he felt more keenly than most, perhaps, the need to prove his patriotism under the weight of ever-growing tensions as the war progressed into its second full year. He was not going to wait to be drafted.

He signed up and then informed his parents that on June 14, Flag Day, he had joined the army. Alma cried softly. His father summoned up all of his stoicism and nodded briefly to his son. John Emil was eighteen years old. J. F., too, had left home when he was eighteen years old. John Emil had had a good, solid German Lutheran upbringing, he thought. He was well equipped to deal with the outside world.

John left home with echoes of all the past admonitions ringing in his ears: "Don't forget to wear your boots" and "Cover up," so reminiscent of "Don't play with the boys, you'll get dirty,"

"Don't play football, you'll have to take your jacket off and you might catch cold."

9 | Into a Modern World

John liked the army. He liked the regimentation, the discipline, the authority, the compartmentalizing of all thoughts and activities. He had been trained well during his formative years always to accept an authority higher than his own—parent, minister, God. He had developed the perfect attitude to make the perfect soldier. He was shipped immediately to Louisiana for basic training and then began his active army duty on December 15, 1943. He enjoyed being away from home, although he didn't look at it quite that way. He thought of it more in terms of enjoying the fact that he was doing his duty as a soldier and as an American.

He belonged.

No one could point a finger at him now and giggle. The uniform gave him a distinction he had never before felt. Now his clothes conformed to those around him. He didn't stand out as the oddball. He was obedient, courteous, straight, erect. He was also an excellent marksman—"a sharpshooter." He enjoyed intensely the power of hitting the bull's-eye again and again. He could even rationalize, in the name of God, the idea of killing another human being as necessary in defense of his country.

J. F. died on August 30, 1943. He was seventy-nine years old.

Young John was stationed in Louisiana when he received word of his father's death and was granted a short emergency leave so that he could attend the funeral.

The day after John returned home, Alma asked Christina Worman to visit. "Spend the day with us," Mrs. List said to her over the phone. "Share our sorrow."

Christina could not say no, even though she knew that Mr. List would be laid out in a coffin in the living room in view of the doorless front room in which young John had spent the first eighteen years of his life. She was glad she and her husband no longer lived on South Wenona Street. The idea of Mr. List's coffin in the house didn't sit too well with her.

Alma offered to let John come pick Christina up where she now lived on Central Avenue. She was waiting on the porch for him with her baby in her arms when the young soldier drove up. He smiled brightly at her when he got out of the car. "Mrs. Worman, how nice to see you." He still tilted his head slightly to the side, she thought warmly.

"How wonderful you look in your uniform, John."

He smiled. "Just like all the other guys are wearing."

He was such a nice boy, she found herself thinking again. He seemed genuinely happy to see her and to "meet" her new baby. There didn't seem to be any signs of grief over the death of his father, even as they drove back to South Wenona St. He told her about basic training, about the climate in Louisiana, and about how much he liked the army.

Mrs. List greeted her with the same usual warm smile as she dutifully "oohed" and "aahed" over the baby. She too seemed genuinely happy to see Christina.

Together they went into the living room so that Christina could pay her respects to the late Mr. List, and then they sat nearby and spent the day visiting, just like old times.

"We have to go on," Mrs. List said. "He lived a long life."

John nodded.

For a moment Christina thought they were putting on a splendid act to cover their grief. Then she realized that there was no act. They *would* go on. As though nothing had happened. J. F. was buried at Elm Lawn Cemetery close to his first wife, Anna Marie Hubinger List.

After John left home again to go back to camp, Alma, alone and lonely, returned to work as a nurse.

"Do you like it?" Christina asked.

"Working? Oh, yes," Alma said enthusiastically. "I love it. You know," she confided to her friend over the phone, "some of the other nurses don't like that I clean and mend for my patients, but I don't mind what they say. Let them criticize. I like to keep busy, and I do it when my patients are asleep. I surprise them." She laughed warmly. "*They* don't criticize."

"Do you still work for the Ladies Aid Society at the church?" Christina asked.

"Of course."

"I don't know how you do it," Christina said, shaking her head in approving disbelief.

"I have to keep busy."

"I know."

"Especially with John away so much now." She sighed. "He's going overseas, you know. Europe."

"I worry so about that," Christina said earnestly.

"You don't have to. That's a lack of faith, Mrs. *Vor*man," Alma reproved her gently. "God will look after my boy. I know that."

John spent exactly eleven months and twenty-five days overseas as a medical technician.

"My John is a private first class," Alma told Mrs. *Vor*man and Mrs. Hollister and all her lady friends at the Ladies Aid Society at Zion Lutheran Church.

"How proud you must be. . . ."

"Proud!" she scoffed at such an obvious understatement, and she would readily go into the memorized litany of achievements her son wrote her about. He was awarded the Combat Infantryman's Badge, the Good Conduct Medal, and the Bronze Star for "exemplary conduct" against the armed enemy. There was the European-African-Middle Theatre service Medal, the Asiatic-Pacific Theatre Service Medal, a sharpshooter's badge, infantry service medals, and a certificate of merit for conspicuous bravery "in an heroic attempt to evacuate wounded comrades," Alma said proudly. She told the story of how John had been captured by the Germans during combat, but they released him because his German was so fluent they mistook him for "one of them." She laughed heartily even though she was deeply frightened as well as impressed that he had gone through such an experience. She never questioned whether or not the story was true. It would never occur to her to question the honesty of anything John said or did. All to whom she spoke nodded pleasantly but privately found it difficult to believe that the John they knew could become involved in such heroic acts of conduct. None, however, voiced this skepticism to the proud mother.

When John was discharged from the service at McCoy Base in Wisconsin, on April 22, 1946, he still held the rank of private first class.

The war was over.

Alma expected him to come home and stay with her for good, but John immediately enrolled at the University of Michigan, where he joined the Reserve Officers Training Corps. He remained in Bay City with his mother only until he had to leave for college. She was disappointed, but she was happy he wanted to continue his education.

Things were certainly different now, John thought while he waited at home to begin school. His father's death left a great void in the small family. His father's place at the table seemed like a vacuum. Even more alien was his mother's working.

"Do you like it?" he asked as they sat over dinner.

"Oh, yes."

He also knew that she was very proud of her nursing profession. Still, he persisted. "But *Mutter*," he said softly, "don't you get tired?"

"*Nein, nein*. Is good." She smiled.

"But full-time? Why not a part-time job if you feel you have to work?"

"I only work in the afternoon." She was pleased at his genuine concern for her welfare. But she was a very healthy fifty-seven years old, and she really enjoyed her work. She had switched to taking care of private patients in their homes in much the same manner as she had done when J. F.'s first wife, Anna Marie, had been ill over twenty years earlier. Alma had always been, and still was, the type of woman who had to keep busy. "And with you going to college in the fall . . . not that I'm complaining," she added quickly. "What am I supposed to do with myself all day? I have so much *enerchee*."

"Are we all right with money, *Mutter*? You're not working because you have to?"

"*Nein, nein*," she reassured him. "You know Papa left half the store to me and the other half equally divided between you and William."

"Yes, I know, *Mutter*, but—"

"And there is money in the bank besides the store. Your father was a frugal man."

He felt better. "I just don't want to think of you working because you have to, that's all."

She patted his hand gently. "There is something else, too. We must talk of it, John."

"Yes, *Mutter*?"

"William wants to buy out our shares in the store."

"Oh."

"Do you think you will ever want to work in the store?"

"No."

"I didn't think so. I'm glad. You must finish school. Then you must decide what to tell William."

"Tell him . . . he can buy out our shares."

"A good decision," she said with a deep nod of her graying head. "There will be even more money in the bank now. A very comfortable amount. You must have whatever you need for school, and there will be much left over. You have made a good decision." She smiled proudly at her son.

With his father gone, John was now the "head of the house." Alma deferred to him. For the first time in his life, patriarchal responsibilities were his. Not knowing exactly what was expected of him now that the important decision to sell their shares in the store had been made, he immediately fell into old patterns.

He took out the Bible and sat at her side. Together he and his mother resumed the familiar practice of reading the Bible nightly.

10 | "Boola, Boola" and Repeated Patterns

At twenty, tall, slender, fresh from the experiences of the overseas combat that he never discussed in any detail, not even with his mother, John left Alma again in Bay City to begin at the University of Michigan. Through the G.I. Bill he had the opportunity to pursue his studies in business administration. For in-state residents, tuition was only $70 per semester, and veterans received $65 a month subsistence pay. Down deep, Alma heartily approved his decision to take advantage of the government's offer to returning veterans. Besides, the university was in Ann Arbor, only ninety miles south of Bay City. Her son would not be so far away that she could not visit him.

The University of Michigan has long been referred to as the "Harvard of the West." In academic circles it is usually rated as one of the "top five" in the country. Its business administration school is rated as highly as its medical, law, and engineering schools. It pleased John greatly that the university had such a fine academic reputation. A business administration degree from the University of Michigan would be prestigious and would stand him in good stead in the job market when the appropriate time came.

Getting a "good" job would become one of the major preoccupations of his life.

The weather came from Canada and moved with gusto through the town, contributing to its nickname, "Ann Arbor Grey." Somebody once said, "There are twenty-five storm centers in the United States, and twenty-four of them pass over Ann Arbor." John liked the cold weather. It didn't bother him that the temperatures constantly hovered in the low twenty's. Cold, gusty, windy. Worse in January and February. And snow! Once it snowed, the campus remained white all through the winter. The thaw wouldn't begin until the middle of March at the earliest. Just like Bay City. Nice.

There were three categories of students: young men right out of high school, young women out of high school, and mature young men returning from the armed services. Veterans were usually highly motivated; they were older than the usual eighteen-year-old freshmen. John fit the veteran's pattern. All his training in his most formative years had to do with the work ethic and a rigid adherence to the principles of devotion to duty.

John was housed at one of the resident dormitories, Wenley House, where he would eat and sleep until he graduated. The architecture was English Tudor derivative. The rooms were small: one or two roommates were indiscriminately assigned to each, and there was only one bathroom for a prescribed number of people. A "section" leader was assigned to stop any hell raising that went on. Banging on the doors of noisy students was their prerogative and pleasure. Women were not allowed.

It didn't bother John that life at Wenley House was very restrictive. The austerity of the dormitories was reminiscent of barracks-style living. Although radios were acceptable, there was always someone studying, so the volume had to be kept low. Any complaints from the studious, and the section leader could insist that the radio be turned off entirely. To watch television one had to go down to the Michigan Union, where there was a communal set. The Michigan Union also had a dayroom where the students could relax over a game of Ping-Pong or pool. The more socially minded dorm student was fortunate that Wenley was attached to Michigan Union. It was the pulse center of campus—not geographically, but "where the action was." It served as a center for everybody, alumni, students, and visitors alike.

There were about thirty fraternity houses on campus. A few were honor fraternities and societies, but most of them were social. One didn't have to eat at his fraternity house; one didn't even have to live there in order to belong. The important thing was simply to *belong*. But before one could belong, one had to be accepted. Not being accepted was perceived as worse than banishment. There was a great deal of social pressure as the young hopefuls went from fraternity house to fraternity house during "rush week." Dress was important. What one said was important. The least little thing out of line and you were "finished."

As in high school, John had maintained a low profile. It wasn't long, particularly during "rush week," before he had begun to think that the emphasis was on the wrong things.

"Are you going to rush?" he was asked by Howard Birdson, one of the eighteen-year-old freshmen on his floor at Wenley House. He was small, impish, and energetic.

"Rush?"

"For a frat?"

"Oh," he said. "No. I don't think so. I've already joined the Gamma Delta Society."

"What's that?"

"A Lutheran student organization."

"Do you have to be pledged to get into that?"

"No. And it's not restricted to people of the Lutheran faith exclusively. It's open to everybody."

"But it's not the same, is it?"

"As a social fraternity? No, it's not. It's a religious organi—"

"If you're not in a frat, you're nowhere," Howard said over his shoulder as he hurriedly left to start his "rush."

John shook his head. He had no intention of "rushing." The pattern of his life would not change because of the social pressures of college. Religion had always been and still was the centerpiece of his existence. As Alma had always given his life direction, his faith had always given his soul direction.

He introduced himself to Reverend and Mrs. Scheips and attended services at the campus Lutheran chapel every Sunday. Every Sunday evening he went to the Gamma Delta Society's building on Washtenaw Avenue for their 5:30 P.M. suppers, which were always followed by a religious program. There were usually ninety to one hundred fellow Lutherans present. Although he felt at home in this environment, John kept as low a profile here as he did in his other activities on campus.

After the Sunday program, the pastor made the announcement to the students. "We're going to need help with the supper committee to help set up for next Sunday's supper."

A murmur of dissent went through the room, coupled with a bit of chuckling. No offering hand went up.

The chaplain smiled. "You don't have to volunteer right now...."

"Or at all!" came a deep-voiced quip from the back of the room.

Reverend Scheips good-naturedly put his palm up to the general laughter. "There will be a sign-up chart outside," he announced.

The next day, the first name signed on the list was John E. List.

Not only did he sign up, but he came early and helped, first to set up the tables, then to set the tables with tableware, silverware, and glassware. Except to ask what had to be done, he spoke little to the reverend's wife, who was in charge of the committee. Mrs. Scheips watched him out of the corner of her eye as he worked. She took an immediate liking to the quiet young man with the beautiful warm brown eyes.

After he had completed setting the last teaspoon in place, he asked, "Do you need anyone to help serve the food?"

"Yes, as a matter of fact," Mrs. Scheips said. "We can always use help in that department."

"I'll be glad to," he said.

"Thank you, John." She smiled. "That's very good of you."

He looked embarrassed. "What time do you want me to be here?"

"About five?"

"Fine."

"You won't forget now?" she joked. "I'm counting on you." Mrs. Scheips looked after his tall, retreating figure fondly and realized that John would never forget. If she wasn't mistaken, he would arrive early. He never disappointed anybody.

He arrived at 4:00 P.M.

"You can't get angry at him like you do with some of the other boys who're always full of promises and always so forgetful," she had said to her husband. "Johnny-on-the-spot, that's him." She liked the young man. She knew that to many in the society, John was the proverbial invisible man, but to Mrs. Scheips he was kind and helpful, one of the few consistently reliable ones. His shyness would soften once he got to know everyone better, she thought. She imagined him to be quite lonely. But she could be mistaken.

She often found him sitting at Gamma Delta reading. "John,"

she said to him one day, "you shouldn't spend so much of your time alone. You're a beautiful young man. You have many gifts. You're too much of a loner, I think."

"I'm not lonely."

"Everybody feels lonely in the beginning, but you've been here long enough to have made friends."

"I have friends," he said. "Here at Gamma Delta. You and Pastor."

She loved when he smiled at her with his head tilted to the left, but she pursued her point. "You have to create your own friends and your own neighborhood. But you must also reach out to people beyond your neighborhood. And you must meet girls, and—"

"There's plenty of time for that," he said with some embarrassment.

Men had a way of rating girls. A lot of that sort of thing went on in the army; it wasn't always kind. He'd heard that the girls rated the men on campus, too, particularly the G.I.'s who were supposed to have had the most experience and therefore were the most sought after by girls looking to expand their experiences.

He wondered what they'd say about him.

"Him?" he imagined. "That guy never takes his glasses off."

"I'll bet he sleeps in a suit and tie."

"I think he's nice. Kind of gentle. And he has soft eyes."

"What a bore."

"There are a lot of attractive girls here, and there are a lot of girls with money, too," Mrs. Scheips continued. She could tell he was embarrassed by the way he looked away, but she pressed on. Sometimes a boy had to be pushed by an older woman in matters like these, like a mother would do. "Because of Detroit," she continued. "The auto business. There are a lot of young women from Grosse Point, Bloomfield Hills. Those are expensive towns."

He didn't answer.

"John," she said, and he turned to look at her with the warm eyes she liked so much. "There is a tremendous opportunity to participate in a million different things here at school without having to give up any of the things you're already comfortable with. Often the students in our society go to the Michigan's Children Institute to entertain handicapped children, or we'll take a trip to the mental institution near Ypsilanto to conduct Bingo games for the patients. We even bring little prizes for them if they win."

He smiled and lowered his eyes.

"If you don't like that sort of thing," she said gently, "there are a great many cultural activities right here on campus all the time. . . ."

"I've gone to the concerts."

"Good, good. What about intramural sports?"

"I don't play."

"Be a spectator, then," she encouraged. "Football. Have you been to any of the football games?"

"No."

"All the students seem to like it. And I always see bunches of young people walking down the street to go to a movie." She smiled. "Or how about joining a bridge tournament, or participating at one of the university papers, like *The Michigan Daily*? In other words, anything so you won't be so alone all the time."

No one had ever spoken to him like that before.

"I don't seem to have the ability to get involved in any of them," he suddenly confided to the woman.

"Try," she urged softly. "Try, John."

He looked away, and she wondered if her words had had any effect.

"By the way," he said. "My mother is coming up again this weekend."

"She is very loyal, John, isn't she?"

"Oh, yes. She visits at least once a month. We'll be coming to Sunday services together again."

"I'm always happy to see your mother," Mrs. Scheips said. "She is a charming woman."

"Thank you."

Treu hersig, she thought. He has such a true heart.

Walking back to Wenley House, John thought about what Mrs. Scheips had said. The girls did seem to like the older G.I.'s. He'd noticed that. But the girls should be careful of them, he thought. Most of the vets had been overseas, and all they were looking for was sex. It wasn't right outside of marriage. He was sure of that.

He could see the girls across the campus grounds in their bobby socks and saddle shoes and tan polo coats with the belts in the back. If they only knew what most men thought about all the time, they would guard themselves a little more carefully! The war had certainly loosened some of the moral fiber of America's youth and with the same, corrupting lame excuse: "Live today, for tomorrow you may die. Life is so uncertain in this nuclear age." There was always a great deal of socializing between the G.I.'s and the girls. Too much, he thought. And too much drinking. Michigan wasn't dry. It was a controlled state. The vets were old enough to walk into any one of the state-owned liquor stores and buy over the counter. Several times John was asked by younger students to go out of the county to buy liquor for one of their parties.

He usually refused. But he did do it. Once. For one of the girls. It was a special night, she had said, an important occasion. Somehow, he couldn't refuse her. She was pretty.

Back in the dayroom of Michigan Union, he sat reading a book while listening to the chatter of some of the other gathered students. He already had the reputation of being a bookworm, so no one paid much attention to him. They were talking about football again, about the "big game" on Saturday.

Suddenly John decided that he would go see what all the fuss was about. Then he realized he wouldn't be able to go. The games were on Saturday, and Alma would already be here by game time. But maybe next weekend, he thought. "Is there another game next Saturday, too?" he asked one of the students who was enthusiastically spouting off scores.

"Are you kidding!" He stared as though John had just landed from Pluto.

"Is there?"

"Of course!"

The following Saturday, true to his decision, John found himself seated in the 98,000-seat stadium. He had no idea how difficult it would be to get a ticket and had been a bit sorry he had given away the ones he'd received from the school. It seemed that Michigan's football team had become a powerhouse to be reckoned with on a national scale. Everyone was excited about it. John didn't realize that he was witnessing Michigan's "golden era" of football. They had already won twenty-four straight games and were practically on the way to the Rose Bowl to play the winner of the Pacific Coast Conference. But despite the tremendous demand, he'd managed to get a ticket.

"Rose Bowl! Rose Bowl! Rose Bowl!" The spectators chanted. Michigan was in the "Big 10," and the winner of the "Big 10" always went to the Rose Bowl. The chanting was intended to propel the team to the culmination of its championship season. Some ebullient fans started shout-singing " *California, Here I Come*."

There were parties both before the game and during. John presumed the festivities would continue well into the night after the game as well. Many of the grads had come back for the game. The stadium was packed.

"Here we are, honey! Here we are!" a cheerer shouted to his female companion. They were seated in the row in front of John. "What'd I tell you! A football game in Ann Arbor! Sitting here under a perfectly blue sky with a hundred thousand people yelling, listening to the band play '*Hail to the Victors*.' Wow!" He turned to his female companion and said, "We're very lucky to be experiencing this! It's something we'll never forget." She smiled and waved a pennant with just as much enthusiasm. The team was winning again, although it was a very rough game with a great deal of crunching and groaning; but the excitement in the air was electric and contagious. John found himself pulling for his school team despite his antipathy for all of the violence.

Then, at half-time, the cheering intensified as the University of Michigan's Marching Band strutted onto the field. "This is the greatest marching band in the country," the young man in the row in front of him shouted to his girl over the din.

And then time was running out on the clock, and Michigan was pulling for the touchdown that would bring the winning streak to "twenty-five wins, no losses."

The stadium erupted in a wild chant of "Go Blue!" One-half of the stadium shouted, "Go!" and the other half shouted, "Blue!" louder and louder until the din of almost one hundred thousand people was awesome in its ear-splitting intensity. The air was charged. The stadium rumbled on its girders.

Suddenly John pulled back and became very quiet. He looked at the raw, windblown, flushed faces about him. It was almost as though they were having a religious experience, pushing each other on to a greater and greater frenzy of abandoned participation. "Go! Blue! Go! Blue!" Something inside of John told him it was excessive. It was only a game. He couldn't seem to get caught up in the excitement anymore. The game was taking the place of something much more important. All of this energy could be better spent elsewhere, he thought.

When Michigan won its twenty-sixth straight game and went to California to play the University of Southern California in the Rose Bowl, some of the wealthier students made the trip to watch the game in person. On campus, in the dorms, in the frat houses, in all the communal areas, it seemed that everyone in school had his ear glued to the radio. The accompanying roots, hoots, and encouragement were boisterous and pervasive throughout the campus.

The final score was 49–0. Michigan "literally destroyed them," as the loyal student body would brag for weeks to come.

"They're incredible."

"Go! Blue! Go! Blue! Go! Blue!"

John List did not have his ear glued to the radio. He was aware of what happened, that Michigan had won the "battle of brute force," as he had quietly come to think of it, but he was not deeply involved. It didn't matter to him one way or the other.

"You're absolutely right," Alma reassured him when she visited during Homecoming. "There are other things besides football."

"Would you like to see the library?"

"*Ja*," she said pleasantly. "Thank God I have such a sensible son. The important thing, John, is to get your education," she encouraged softly, as she had always encouraged him. "This isn't the time to play games. Keep that always in mind. And you'll never go wrong."

"I know."

"How are your grades?"

"Straight B's."

"*Sehr gut*," she said, pleased.

Weeks passed for John in study and work and homework and library and the Gamma Delta Society, his home away from home. Mrs. Scheips continued to encourage his participation in social activities. he began to find it quaint. She tried to act like a mother to him, but she wasn't like a mother at all, he thought. He could even interpret some of the the things she encouraged—girls, for instance—as sinful, if he hadn't been kindly disposed toward her.

At the cafeteria, Ed Benson sat next to him. John remembered him from one of his literature classes. He looked pale and ill. "You're Grover, aren't you?" he mumbled.

"No."

"Do I know you?"

"John List. We've shared a class in English lit."

"Oh."

"What's the matter with you?" John asked, noticing the white thin line encircling Benson's clenched mouth. "Are you ill?"

"Ever been to a purple Jesus party?"

"A purple . . . what?" He couldn't believe his ears.

"A purple Jesus party." He was still slurring his words. "You know, where they get medical alcohol, put it in a large urn, put grape juice in it, and everybody lays around in togas and sips this stuff from a straw." Benson rubbed his head painfully. "A three-day drunk. That's what they should call it. Ever been?"

"No," John said. "And I think you should change the name."

"Oh, I didn't make it up. That's what they've always called it. Purple Jesus parties. Am I sick!"

"I'm not surprised," John said thinly.

"What's your frat?"

"I don't belong to a frat." John's words were clipped.

"You don't?" he asked with surprise. "Why not?"

"Because I don't believe in them!" For some reason he couldn't quite explain, he was very angry. "Because I think the fraternity and sorority system has too much power!" he raged. His voice became deep and powerful in its bass-toned intensity. "Too much emphasis on being in a fraternity or sorority. That's a bunch of garbage, but you people believe it! It becomes more important than classwork. These are supposed to be the golden years of football, but they're also the golden years of social snobbery!"

"Hey, look," Benson stammered under the unexpected verbal assault, "forget it . . . okay?"

"It's affecting the classwork of a lot of students. And so many of you—"

"Hey, listen, I'm sorry I brought it up."

"The immature ones. They really think they're better than the average person who lives in the residence house. The average outsider . . ."

"Hey, fuck off, creep," Benson said over his shoulder.

John was left alone. He was a bit surprised at himself. He couldn't remember the last time he had actually lost his temper like that. He calmed his fury and silently begged forgiveness.

In his senior year in 1949, John finally pledged to a fraternity house. He rationalized his change of heart by telling himself that *Delta Sigma Pi* was not a social fraternity but a professional one, a business administration organization. About fifty or sixty business administration majors were members. Belonging to it would be beneficial to his future. Important contacts could be made. Pretty soon he would be in the job market. He even let himself smile through the necessary "rush period," actually a six-to-eight-week pledge education program in which he learned the history and rules of the "secret" organization, was let in on its "secret" handshake, and even went to several of the *Delta Sigma Pi* private parties.

Delta Sigma Pi hosted interesting events—not only meetings revolving around careers and professional development, but very often functions that sponsored important after-dinner guest speakers, one of which was the brother of the shah of Iran. There was also a social side to *Delta Sigma Pi's* activities. The fraternity held their biannual buffet dinner dances in May and December, usually after the football games with Navy, Army or Minnesota—always football, he sighed with a little more indulgence than usual. Now John found himself participating socially. He even permitted a few dates to be arranged for him when it would be inappropriate to attend these functions alone. He struck everyone at the fraternity as quiet, sweet, unobtrusive, and a gentleman.

But he never abandoned the Gamma Delta Society. Twice each semester Reverend Scheips called for volunteers to "clean house" while keeping costs down.

"Work Holiday This Weekend"
Bi-Annual General Clean-Up Time
We need volunteers to help rake leaves and sweep up
SIGN-UP SHEET IS POSTED.
PLEASE JOIN US.

Without fail, even in his senior year, John List's name was one of the first on the posted sign-up sheet. Without fail, he would show up.

Yet the sad irony is that when Reverend and Mrs. Scheips were asked years later by journalists Jill Vejnoska and Mary Romano from the *New Jersey Courier News* to reminisce about the young man who worked for them so diligently during his days with the Lutheran Society, they could not quite place him. Not even Mrs. Scheips. They had to look through old albums. They searched through the faded, grainy black-and-white photographs until they found one of John List. There it was, an old photo taken at a luncheon before a football game. It had been reprinted in the December 1950 alumni newsletter. In the photo some twenty-five to thirty young men and women were smiling and laughing with their arms wrapped around each other. In the back row, standing, as usual, a little apart from the others, was John Emil List, a slight smile on his mouth.

Now Mrs. Scheips remembered. He was the one who was always alone, a little apart from the others, joining in only at a discreet distance, watching, smiling with his beautiful eyes, never intimately belonging to any particular group.

* * *

Throughout his four years at the University of Michigan, despite all of the self-imposed restrictions, John developed a secret but avid curiosity about how the other students lived and behaved.

He had one college classmate, a handsome all-American-looking young man with fair hair, a friendly disposition, and a quick grin who lived in the West Quad. His major was in aeronautics and electrical engineering. His name was Robert N. Clark. John remembered the young boy at high school, Robert J. Clark, who used to run up and down the stadium steps to get in shape to fight the Nazis. They looked alike to him. Same type. Same sense of freedom. He wondered if they were related.

There was such a sense of freedom in everyone's attitude, he thought. He watched intently as the young men and women dated and seemed so natural together. He had never felt comfortable with young people. He still didn't really understand their behavior or what motivated the lack of discipline or the need for "a good time" all the time. Where was their sense of duty?

And yet . . .

By staying on the outside he could see a great deal more. He saw how they held hands and "necked" on benches and on the quiet spots on campus. He saw how they piled into cars and sped away to cavort in town. He saw how they behaved when they were drunk . . . loud, disorderly, undisciplined. And he saw how little attention they seemed to pay to their eternal souls.

That was the part, perhaps, that he understood the least. Didn't they realize how they jeopardized their souls with all the excesses of their behavior?

And yet . . .

There was a dull ache in the young man. With a profound, though unidentified, sense of envy, he watched the ease with which they sped through life.

In his loneliness, he turned with even more fervor to God.

11 | Helen

When the Korean War broke out John immediately joined the Reserve Officers Training Corps at the University of Michigan. As a combat veteran of World War II, he was able to apply his military service record toward undergraduate credits at Michigan, which enabled him to skip the first two years of the ROTC program.

In the ROTC, John gravitated toward Bob Wismer. They had certain characteristics in common. Both were shy. They went to Lutheran services together. They both wore steel-rimmed glasses. Their ties were neatly tucked between the third and fourth buttons of their shirts in the prescribed military fashion. In 1949 they had a photo taken together for their ROTC yearbook. The caption had been fashioned by their platoon mates. It indicated that the two young men spent much of their free time together and were best remembered for the "Wismer waddle." Hands at their sides, standing almost at military attention, they looked stiff and awkward. In the photo John had a slight smile on his lips, but it had been Bob Wismer's "waddle walk" that would attract attention. Even in the caption John was ignored as an individual. It said that both were "injected with the true Transportation Corps spirit."

During the 1949 summer break of their last year at college, they were sent to begin their T.C. studies at the Transportation Corps Camp in Ft. Eustis, Virginia. That was the first time John ever set foot in Virginia. It would not be the last.

When he graduated from the University of Michigan in June of 1950, John was commissioned as a second lieutenant. Alma attended the ceremonies.

"*Du bist ein sehr guter junger Mann*." she said, holding her head high.

She was proud, even though he would not be returning home to Bay City. On November 4 he would begin his active duty in the army. Underneath the pride she felt at her handsome son's graduation from the prestigious University of Michigan, a List family first, was a quiet but palpable anxiety at the thought of his going through another war. He had been lucky during World War II. God had sent him home unhurt. Now he was returning to war. The news reports from Korea were not good. The fighting was fierce and constant. The casualty rates were growing in frightening numbers. But Alma did not reprimand him for reenlisting. Even when he told her, she said again, "*Du bist ein sehr guter junger Mann.*" She put her trust in the faith that had always sustained them both. Before taking leave, she opened her Bible and said to her beloved son, "*Sollen wir jetst susammen in der Bibel lesen?*"

He readily agreed. "*Ja, Mutter.*"

"*Sets dich su mir,*" she said, patting the seat beside her. And he sat next to her, and they read the Bible together one more time before parting.

Before entering the military again, John first took an internship position at Ernst & Ernst, a major organized national accounting firm in Detroit. Getting the position was not as difficult as he had thought it would be. Companies had come to the university during senior year looking for recruits, and John's grades were high enough to command respect.

He looked at the personnel form for the accounting position and wondered why they wanted to know what his "hobbies" were. What possible relevance could that have to his abilities as an accountant? Hobbies . . . what were his hobbies? He had never given it much thought before. After a moment he wrote down, "Going to plays and listening to classical music." He did like to listen to classical music. He wasn't sure why he wrote, "Going to plays," except that seemed to be an acceptable kind of hobby.

Once again he bade farewell to his mother and moved to Detroit to accept his first paying accounting position. As an auditor for Ernst & Ernst, he earned a handsome $225 a week.

Alma sighed at yet another separation, but Detroit was not as far away as where the army would probably send him. She needn't have worried. He would not set foot on foreign soil again. This time John fought only paperwork. He was stationed at various military bases around the country. One was Ft. Benjamin Harrison in Indiana, where he continued his education at the army's expense by going to Ft. Harrison's finance school. Ft. Harrison had been closed after World War II, but with the the construction of the Army Finance Center at the base, making it the headquarters for the army's finance and accounting business, it had been reopened on April 1, 1951.

Unbeknownst to John, a soldier named Marvin Taylor was killed in action in Korea the same month he began finance school at Ft. Harrison.

The army returned John, along with a number of other reserve officers to Ft. Eustis, Virginia. The base was having some difficulty getting experienced military and civilian personnel. His background qualified him for its transportation school, which taught twelve separate courses in aviation, truck, rail, and water transportation. He studied the fundamentals of the army's payment and accounting system. He was one of 233 lieutenants stationed at Ft. Eustis and was one of the 1,028 graduates.

His transfer to Fort Eustis had been in September of 1951, but this time when he set foot in Ft. Eustis, his life would change.

The month List was graduated was the same month that Marvin Taylor's body was returned to the States from Korea, a full six months after he was killed in action.

For social activities, Ft. Eustis offered a movie theater, an officers' gymnasium, and an officers' club. Although he availed himself of the officers' club, every Sunday at 10:00 A.M., John attended Lutheran services as always, in a temporary building on base that served as a chapel.

Helen Morris Taylor sat in her mother's kitchen on Washington Avenue in Newport News, Virginia, disconsolately sipping a cup of after-dinner coffee. She lived in her mother's house with her sister, Jean Seyfert, whose husband, Gene—was a career military man. She was not feeling well. It had only been a few days since she had buried her own husband, Marvin Taylor. He had finally been returned home from Korea six months after being killed in action. The family had come for the funeral, and Jean had stayed on since Gene was away and her sister, Helen, still couldn't seem to grasp the reality that her husband, Marvin, was never coming back. Even when his body had been returned, even after the family had buried him, the depression lingered on.

There were hundreds of soldiers in Newport News these days, all from Ft. Eustis, wandering about, some on the prowl, some just alone and lonely. Maybe it would be good for Helen to get out, to start seeing people again.

Marvin had been Helen's first love. She was still grieving deeply over her loss. "Oh, Jean, no, please," Helen protested. "I don't feel like it."

"You've got to fight it, Helen."

"I'm not up to it yet."

Jean was about to suggest a film. Then she shook her head. She knew Helen would merely use the darkness of the theater to go into her shell of memories. The only thing she knew for certain was that her sister needed a diversion.

"You've got to try, Helen," she insisted. "Let's go bowling."

Helen agreed reluctantly.

Gerhard Herrmann was one of John's buddies in the T.C. classes. He was a gregarious sort, and John often tagged along with him as he led the way through awkward social situations by virtue of bravado alone. Gerhard, in turn, liked having John along. He was so shy that Gerhard seemed expansive and important by contrast.

"I pass on the officers' club tonight," he said, standing over John and pushing down the newspaper he was reading. "I'm going into Newport News."

"What's in Newport News?"

"Whatever it is, it's more than here," Gerry said, pulling the newspaper out of John's hands and throwing it aside jauntily. "Come on. It's only fifteen miles, and I'm bored around here. They're throwing some kind of an officers' bowling party. Let's go. Stretch the muscles. Maybe find us some girls."

John agreed willingly.

What might have happened to the hapless Helen Taylor had she not permitted herself to be persuaded to go to that bowling alley on that particular night in October, and had not met either John List or Gerhard Herrmann? Might she have ultimately met another man whom she could have loved as she had loved Marvin? Perhaps if more time had passed, if the grieving period had been allowed to run its full course, or if she had met someone when her mind was more at peace with itself, she might have made a more suitable selection in a husband; but fate had set the inevitable in motion.

* * *

Jean and Helen found Gerry amusing. He was a little playful, a little frisky, and a little loud, but full of life and a lot of fun. The other fellow stood just a bit out of view, tall, lanky, his hands dangling awkwardly at his sides. He didn't seem comfortable. He didn't have the cocky air of a serviceman on the make. He had a funny little grin on his face.

"What did you say your name was?" Jean asked him.

"Lieutenant John List."

"Oh."

She hadn't even remembered his name when Gerry introduced him to the girls, and she didn't like him much. Lieutenant, she thought. Few soldiers referred to themselves by rank in a social scene. He seemed kind of standoffish to her. A bit odd. Standing back and not making a move except when it was his turn to bowl. Even then he seemed very self-conscious about himself and his bowling. But it didn't matter; Jean saw that Helen was actually smiling at something Gerry had said. This is just the diversion she needs, Jean thought. "Listen, fellas," she said. "I'm married. To a great big soldier. So don't go getting any ideas about me. But my sister's single."

"Is that so?" Gerry said, beaming.

Helen tried to give her the sign to be quiet, but Jean was irrepressible in her earnest desire to console her sister.

John thought that Helen was the most beautiful creature he had ever seen. He glanced at her every chance he could when he was sure no one was looking. She was delicate, he thought. Such soft-looking, smooth skin. And her hair. Rich, thick, warm, brown. Her mouth, lightly painted, was sad, he thought. Vulnerable. It bothered him that amid the clatter of bowling pins, Gerry kept trying to make a date with her. Why couldn't he be like Gerry? Why couldn't *he* make a move? Never before had he wished so fervently to be a little more outgoing. How did one talk to a girl like Helen?

"How about it?" he heard Gerry say to her.

"What?"

"We don't have to go someplace like this. We can go to a nice place. Quiet-like. Not bowling."

John watched as his friend made his pitch.

"Just us," he said, winking at John. "We don't have to have anyone tag along."

Jean looked at Helen. She knew it was really too soon for Helen to "date" someone, but she was smiling at the young lieutenant's boyish antics, and that was encouraging. In between each throw of the ball, he looked back at Helen and either laughed, passed a comment, or groaned with the failure of his throw. At one point, Helen actually laughed aloud.

John waited to see what the girl's response to Gerry's invitation would be.

Helen shrugged and answered diffidently, "I don't know."

"C'mon. What you holding out for? A better offer? You're not going to get much better than me," he teased, and Helen laughed again.

On the way home Helen expressed an interest in the handsome young man. He *was* fun. It had been a long time since anything had actually made her laugh. Maybe it *would* be good for her to start dating again.

"I guess it couldn't hurt to go out with him." Jean smiled.

And Helen proceeded to date him. Over the next few weeks she invited him to her house more often than they went out. Several times he brought his buddy John List with him. He was very quiet and seemed content merely to listen to Gerry and look at Helen. She introduced them to her parents and to her nine-year-old daughter, Brenda.

Helen began to look forward to their visits, which distracted her from thoughts of Marvin. On the nights Gerry and John were there, time went by without pain.

Then one night in early October, Gerry sought out John at the mess hall. He seemed a bit beside himself. "You have to help me out," he said.

"Has something happened?"

"You bet it has! Ellen's coming down. I just heard. She wants to 'surprise' me. Wants me to pick her up on the ten-ten bus."

"Who's Ellen?" John asked.

"My wife."

John was shocked. "Your wife? But . . . you never mentioned you had a wife. . . ."

"You don't talk about things like that when you're on base, boy." Gerry shook his head once again, always surprised at his buddy's naiveté. "You can't get anywhere if everyone knows you're married."

"That's dishonest!" John said with surprising sternness.

"So it's dishonest. So what!" Gerry said defensively. "It's just for fun. Hell, I get lonely. Don't you?"

"Not lonely enough to lie to a girl. Especially a recent widow."

"You don't have to come," Gerry said, annoyed at being reprimanded.

"I'll come," John said firmly.

That night when Gerry knocked on the front door of the Morris home on Washington Avenue, Helen opened the door. The light behind her from inside the house gave her hair a luminous halo. She looks so lovely, John thought again. Her little girl, Brenda, stood behind her.

"Hi," Helen said, standing aside in the doorway to allow them to enter past Brenda.

"No, we can't come in," Gerry said a bit awkwardly.

"What's the matter?"

"I have to tell you something."

"You're not shipping out, are you?" she asked, genuinely concerned for them. So many of the boys were shipping out to Korea. So many would not return.

"No, nothing like that. It's just that I can't stay. I . . . my wife's coming in tonight."

"Your wife." She looked at him strangely for a long moment. Then she looked past him to John. "Did you bring him along for protection?"

"No . . . my buddy . . ."

"What did you think I was going to do?"

"He wanted to come," Gerry said defensively.

"To hold your hand?" she snapped.

"No need to get nasty. . . ."

"Why don't you just go!" she said. "You should have told me. I'm not looking for anything special, but you shouldn't have lied to me. I don't go out with married men."

"We were just having a little fun. What's the harm in that?"

John touched his arm. "Go," he said.

"Well . . ." He hesitated. "Ain't you coming?"

"No."

Helen looked at John closely for the first time.

Gerry backed off and finally slipped away into the darkness.

"I didn't think what he did was right," John said suddenly with a force that came out of a very deep righteous anger at Jerry's behavior. "I didn't know he was married. He never told me. It's not right."

It was the most Helen had ever heard John say at one time.

Jerry's lie hadn't broken Helen's heart. She was certainly not in love with him. He was fun, and that was about all. "He lied to me," she said. "And he wasn't even man enough to tell me alone. He had to bring you along to break the news."

"I wanted to come anyway."

"I can't tolerate a man who doesn't have the courage to act like a *man* !" she said with a conviction he would come to know all too well.

"I wouldn't lie to you."

She didn't want to close the door in his face. She politely waited for him to leave. He didn't. He seemed more distressed at what had happened than she was.

"Come on in," she sighed. "I'll make you a cup of coffee."

The Morrises were very casual, simple, and warm-hearted people. They accepted him willingly enough even though he was not very outgoing. Gene Syfert, Jean's husband, thought John was strange when he was first introduced to the lanky lieutenant who rarely had anything to say and who seemed to be just hanging around. "He looks different," he said to his wife. His tone suggested that by "different" he meant unpleasantly so.

"Oh, he's okay," Jean said. "At least he's not married."

"Yeah, but he's like a little kid happy to get whatever's left over."

"Helen seems to like him."

Gene made a face. But Jean thought. It's been tough for Helen after Marvin's death. For the first time she seems to be coming out of it.

"And she's lonely," she said, concluding her thoughts aloud. "I think that may have a lot to do with her letting him come around."

What they didn't know was that John had encouraged Helen to talk about Marvin, to tell him all of her feelings. Not only was he intensely interested, but it was a way of avoiding having to initiate conversation. Listening also meant he didn't have to talk as much about himself. And he could sense that it was a strengthening bond to be her confidant and friend. He wanted the bond to strengthen. He was falling in love.

"I wasn't even sixteen when I married him," she said. "I was just a kid."

"Why did your parents let you marry so young?" he asked.

"Oh, they couldn't stop us. Marvin was twenty-three and a man. Once he made up his mind, that was it," she said softly, masking the tenacity of her own will. "I went from my father's house to my husband's house. From playing with Dionne Quintuplet and Shirley Temple paper dolls to playing with a real baby. I had Brenda less than a year after we married."

"You were so young, to have so much responsibility," he said sympathetically.

"Marvin helped. He was wonderful. But I kept getting pregnant," she said sadly. "My second child, Kenneth Everett, died when he was only six months old." Tears suddenly filled her eyes. He had been so tiny. So helpless. He would have been Marvin's only son. "And then . . . and then there were two stillbirths."

She's only twenty-five, John thought, and she's already been through so much. He'd led such a sheltered life in comparison; nothing like the tragedies that Helen experienced had ever touched him, and he was a year older than she.

"It had something to do with the Rh negative factor," she was saying evasively, "but I never knew for sure. The doctors weren't even sure."

It was very hard. One tragedy after another. One death after another. He felt a little uncomfortable about the casual way she spoke of pregnancy and childbirth: "my water broke . . ." and "they kept telling me to bear down . . ." He had been raised to believe that those kinds of things should be kept within the doctor and patient relationship and discussed only with great delicacy in social situations. Perhaps it was because she was grieving that she had to talk about such sensitive matters so openly, he decided, too caught up in her aura to be critical of her candor.

"I've never been alone," she said as they walked across the lawn of Ft. Eustis. "I was a New Year's Day baby."

"Oh, but that's good luck," he said with a gentle smile. He loved the sound of her southern accent. To him it seemed so ladylike.

"My parents had five children. I was the third, so I've never been alone, my whole life. I'm still not, but now I feel . . . alone."

"You don't have to be," he said shyly.

She smiled.

He cleared his throat. "What's your mother's name?"

"Eva."

"And your father's?"

"Edward," she answered, thinking that he seemed so genuinely interested in every detail no matter how unimportant. He was a wonderful listener.

The coffee shop in Newport News was bustling with single servicemen and girls and waitresses hurrying orders across the counter and down the aisles between booths. John and Helen sat off in a quiet corner at the farthest end of the shop, leaning toward each other. He couldn't stop looking at her. The closer he got to her, the more enthralled he became. Helen was slim, lovely. Her eyes, spaced wide apart, were a deep warm brown. She held herself erect in a way that reminded him of Alma. Her hair, cropped short and feathered lightly, ended at the very base of her skull and accentuated her long, slender, "swanlike" neck. She wore little makeup: her skin was soft, with the smoothness of alabaster, and her smile seemed more mysterious and wistful even than when he'd first seen her at the bowling alley.

"I remember the five of us, growing up," Helen continued in her soft drawl as he urged her on. "Jean and my brothers Bill, Fred, and Jimmie."

"Where was that?"

"Greensboro, North Carolina. And you? Where did you grow up?"

"Bay City."

"Is that around here?"

"North. In Michigan."

"Oh. Do you have any brothers or sisters?"

"No."

"How sad."

"It was all right. Go on."

"Everything was wonderful when we were growing up," she said with a melancholy little smile at the loss of childhood.

"Tell me about your father."

"Dad?" She smiled. "He was like everyone else around Greensboro. Everybody was middle class. Everybody worked in the cotton mills. It was very comfortable."

"And your religion?"

"Baptist."

She didn't notice him frown at that as she finished her coffee. "Papa and Mama worked at Cone's Factory," she continued. "All it made was denim. I don't know how they weren't bored out of their minds. 'Specially since Papa studied music when he was a boy. In Roanoke. That was his great love, music. He used to play the fiddle at auctions and land sales," she reminisced affectionately. "It was fun to listen to. Auctioning off land and possessions to the sound of his fiddle."

"Would you like something else?" he asked as she sipped the last of her coffee.

She shook her head.

"A piece of cherry pie?"

She smiled. "No, thanks."

He was afraid that she was going to say it was time to take her home. He quickly waved to the waitress for more coffee. "What did he do at the factory?" he asked.

"Dad? At Cone's? He repaired the loom and shuttles."

"And your mother? She worked there, too? With five children? Isn't that unusual?"

"Not around Greensboro. Everybody worked. She used to work on the line watching for breaks and tears in the denim."

They paused as the waitress poured steaming coffee into their heavy porcelain, green-rimmed white cups.

"And then, when the war started—not the Korean War, the other one . . ."

"World War Two."

"Yes."

John started to say that he had joined the army right after high school and had served in the war; but she continued, and he listened as he prepared her coffee with sugar and cream the way he had seen her do it. She let him.

"My two brothers, Fred and Bill, I remember it as being wonderful when we were growing up. They were older. They went off to fight. Jimmie didn't like being left behind with Jean and me, but he had to go to school like us. I remember Jean liked to roller-skate. I loved to read. And we waited for them to come home safely. . . ."

She paused a long time. He waited painfully as she slowly backed into her memories.

"I married Marvin in 1941. He was twenty-three years old and in the military. Then my parents moved to Newport News in 1943, two years after I got married, and I went to stay with them while we waited for the men to come back home. They did. He came back safely, too." She turned and looked at the young man whose eyes were so intently riveted on her as she spoke. "Are you sure you want to hear all this?" she asked quietly.

"Tell me about Marvin," he answered.

She looked off into the distance of her memories and began again; this time tears came to her eyes. She still couldn't believe that her brash young childhood sweetheart was not coming back. She expected at any moment that he would be there, grabbing her hand, pulling her onto the bed with him.

"We were married ten years," she began slowly. "It always seemed to get better."

Ten years, John found himself thinking despite his growing love for the young woman. That was a long time to be with another man. "I went to Korea with him, you know," she said.

He was surprised.

"To be with him. We didn't want to be separated again like in the first war."

And that struck him as terribly devoted. A wonderful quality in a woman.

"We had spent a few years traveling all around the country to different army bases. We were kids, and we were very much in love. We had great times. It was wonderful and exciting and different from anything I had grown up with." Words poured out of her as never before. The lonely young widow, who was usually shy, was telling of the torment of losing her husband as though she were speaking to a father confessor. Once she began, the floodgates of repressed anguish opened and she couldn't stop. It suddenly became just as important to her to tell this sweet young man of her pain as it seemed to be for him to know it. He wanted to know. She wanted him to know. She trusted him as she hadn't trusted anyone in a very long time.

"Brenda was getting to be a real little army brat. Then when the Korean War broke out . . . in the summer of 1950," she remembered, "my mother wanted me to come home. But instead we all went to Japan. That's the way he was. 'You two are gonna stay with me,' he said."

She smiled at the memory of his fearless determination not to be separated again, and then her eyes filled up with tears once more. "We . . . we had this little house near the army base." She took a napkin out of the little black metal container in a corner of the table and wiped her eyes. "Brenda was nearly eight and 'Daddy's little girl.' They adored each other. She loved his uniform. Brenda and I stayed home and played house while Marv went to shoot at the enemy in Korea. It all seemed so make-believe, so unreal. I was pregnant and my water broke and I went into labor and it was awful. He was away when they took me to the military hospital. They botched it all up. They even spilled ether in my right eye, and I was blinded. And the baby . . . the baby was stillborn."

She stopped as she cried softly into the napkin. Was she crying for the baby? For Marvin? For herself? He couldn't tell. It didn't matter. She was getting it out.

"Blind?"

"Yes, in my right eye. From the ether," she lied. She couldn't bring herself to tell him the truth about that. Unaware of the lie, John waited patiently for her to go on. Instinctively he reached his hand forward at the sight of so much grief. He stopped. But Helen clasped it. The shock of warmth running through his body at the touch of her was almost unbearable. He shakily covered her hand with his other one.

"Then it kept getting worse," she cried softly. "I became very ill with jaundice, and they insisted on sending me back to the States to Walter Reed Army Hospital. Marvin didn't want me to go, but the army insisted. They couldn't take care of me in Japan. I didn't want to leave. I keep thinking that if I stayed there, nothing would have happened to him. . . . Of course, that's silly, but that's how I felt. . . ."

She pulled her hand away in order to sip her coffee almost convulsively as she approached the hardest part of her story. John felt abandoned. But she reached for him again, and they clasped hands once more.

"Then on April 16"—she was crying steadily now, her voice barely audible—"while saving twelve other soldiers during a battle, he . . . led his troop up a hill. I never got the complete story straight. Except that they walked right into a barrage of enemy fire that killed him. . . . He won a battlefield promotion to first lieutenant and a Silver Star. . . . They waited six whole months before they sent him back to me. Six whole months lying there in stacked-up boxes like so much forgotten waste. All I have left now is the flag that covered his casket." She looked up at him. She seemed so pathetic. "I haven't been able to forget, John."

He wanted to put his arms around her.

"Jean tells me I dwell on it too much, but I can't . . . I haven't been able to forget."

She clung to his hands. He sat quietly until the tears were spent . . . until she calmed a bit. He shook his head slowly, grieved for her and indignant at the injustices of war. Why couldn't they at least have shipped him home sooner? The six months of waiting must have been torturous for her, he thought. Prolonged the grief. Didn't give her a chance to put her heart at rest.

In the taxi ride home, she put her head on his shoulder and slept. With his arm finally around her, he knew he would have to take care of her for the rest of her life.

From that evening on, he became a nightly visitor in the close-knit Morris home. To Helen he was "Mr. Nice," "Mr. Clean." He had overcome her natural shyness by encouraging her to speak so candidly about herself and her grief at a moment when she was in desperate need to do so. To the grieving widow, he was a good-looking officer and the most understanding man she had met in a long time. And he was. Love seemed to have softened many of the sterner aspects of his personality.

John was spellbound with Helen and with her family. He had never met a family with such a genuinely casual enjoyment of daily living. They were far removed from his own rigid German Lutheran upbringing. They, in turn, found him a bit eccentric with his before-and after-meal prayers. It was unusual to find a genuinely religious soldier. But they wholeheartedly accepted him for Helen's sake. She seemed to like him. She found him charming and quaint.

But she was worlds apart from him in terms of experience.

At twenty-six he was a beginner. The few dates he had had in college had all been arranged by acquaintances who knew how naïve he was about women. From the first moment they met, Helen brought big changes in his life. They hesitantly began to discuss the possibility of marrying.

Helen's mother, Eva, looked at him as he sat in her living room waiting for her daughter. She had tried to start a conversation with him, but he was so shy that it was painful to persist. His face became blotchy with rushing blushes. She handed him the evening's newspaper, thinking that reading might take some of the pressure off any necessity for small talk. Then without his realizing it, she watched him out of the corner of her eye as she busied herself tidying up the other side of the living room.

"He stacked the papers up," she later told her daughter Jean with a light shake of her head.

"What do you mean?"

"Stacked them up. Neat. He wants to be so neat. He sat in the recliner and went through the whole newspaper, from beginning to end. When he started, the papers were lying on the floor stacked up to his left, and by the time he was through they were stacked up on the floor on his right-hand side in a neat pile. Can you imagine what his toilet training must have been like?"

They broke into quiet peals of laughter, but Jean couldn't get over feeling uneasy at the suggested compulsiveness of the young man's behavior. She was used to seeing her brothers toss newspapers around, leaving them lying every which way when they were finished with them.

At first John ignored Helen's young daughter, Brenda. He paid little or no attention to the child who came into the room and sat with him as he visited. It was not that he didn't like her, but because he really didn't know what to say to her. He had never had to deal with a little girl before. She was like a foreigner to him.

As he sat on the easy chair waiting for her mother, she looked at him. She liked his uniform. It was like her daddy's uniform. She wanted to say something to him. She wished he would talk to her; but he glanced at her sideways, once, and then began to read the newspapers that had been lying nearby. It was as though she'd ceased to exist for him. She sat quietly and watched him as he read. He was very aware of her eyes on him. His cheeks grew a light shade of crimson, but he kept his eyes glued to the newsprint.

When Helen entered the living room, she looked lovely in the soft pink cashmere sweater and inexpensive pearls dotting the tips of her ears and also looped in a long string above her breasts. Pink was a good color for her. It accentuated the clearness of her skin and the brightness of her eyes.

"Mommy, you look pretty," Brenda said appreciatively, getting up and hugging her. It had been a long time since her mother had appeared happy.

John flushed with pleasure as he got up. To him she was not just pretty, she was beautiful.

Although she was a year younger than John, Helen was worlds older in seasoning. Having been married ten years, she was quite expert in the ways of man-woman behavior, whereas John, who had been sheltered and set apart all of his life, was still inexperienced. She thought it charming. She didn't know there were any young men around who were as unworldly as John.

Helen was the gentle aggressor in the relationship.

It was the most exciting experience of his life. For the first time, he ignored the rigid rules that had dominated his every waking moment since his mother first read him the Bible and walked him by the hand into a Lutheran church.

Helen leaned into him to be kissed in the most natural manner. He wouldn't have known how to say "no" even if he had been so disposed. But he was eager for this moment to happen. He had thought about it often enough when he had seen all the other students in college behaving so "naturally." Helen awakened turbulent feelings in him that he had usually repressed. He wanted to take care of her, to protect her. It was the first love of his life, his first passion, his first experience. There was no question in his mind that their union had to be sanctified by marriage.

Helen seemed content at the prospect of marrying John List, not that she ever spoke about him excitedly the way she used to about Marvin. But, of course, she was a woman now and probably beyond that stage of girlish gushiness. The Morrises raised no objections. Only Jean and her husband, Gene, worried. They felt John and Helen were worlds apart in just about everything: experience, religion, life-style. The odds for a happy life together were against them, Jean thought pessimistically. She knew they would try to make their marriage a success, but she also thought that the very trying would soon become difficult, since it would require so much effort to bridge the gaps between them. He was from the north—she was from the south. He was a strictly raised, practicing Lutheran—she was a once-in-a-while Baptist. He had led a very sheltered, overprotected life—she had married at sixteen and begun an adventurous army life. He had advanced degrees in school—she had never completed high school. He was an only child—she came from a family of five. . . .

Eva Morris tried to take the positive approach. Actually John might be good for Helen, she thought. He certainly was devoted to her, and he wasn't the type who would fool around with women. He was handsome in his uniform. He was a college graduate and had a bright future ahead of him in business. He would probably be able to support Helen in a style Marvin, as a military man, would never have been able to afford. And they believed John, an only child, came from a wealthy family in Michigan.

The bottom line was that they seemed to be in love.

And yet, Jean observed, one week "it's yes" with Helen, the next week "it's no."

"I don't think she wants to get married," Jean said to her husband. Helen certainly hadn't taken so long to make up her mind when she'd decided that Marvin was the one for her. *No* one would have been able to talk her out of it. But this time? "I don't think she's ready to get married again."

Jean shared her doubts with her mother over a cup of coffee. "I'm glad Helen has found someone to help her get over Marvin," she said, "but I don't know. It's too soon, for one thing, and he's so different."

"In what way?" Eva Morris asked. She had been worried about Helen for a long time, and now she seemed more in control.

Jean hesitated a moment and then decided to forge ahead. "I think he's sissified."

"Oh, come on," Eva scoffed. "A soldier?"

"And a mama's boy. I hear he calls his mother all the time, long distance. About everything."

"It's nice that a boy is close to his mother. A man who treats his mother good will treat his wife good."

"Even Gene says he would never have picked someone like John for Helen," Jean continued doubtfully.

"Are they in love, Jean?"

"I guess so. They act like they are."

"Isn't that all that matters?"

"I suppose. . . ."

"And Helen's been so alone and unhappy."

"But they're so opposite, Mom," Jean insisted. "She was more of a team with Marvin. They were able to work together. Someone has to tell John what to do every step of the way. Helen leads him around by the nose, Mom. Gene says that's probably a holdover."

"From what?"

"From his mother's influence. Gene thinks he was probably overprotected. And that's one of the reasons John does so well in the military. Because all decisions are basically made for you there, and he was trained in the obedience mold."

"Gene's in the military."

"Gene's different. And so was Marvin. He knew how to manage money. More important, he knew how to manage Helen and everything else about their lives. He was really a wonderful man."

"He's gone, Jean."

"I know. . . ."

Then Helen realized that she was pregnant. She was not happy about it. Pregnancies had never been easy for her, and now, here she was, unmarried and pregnant again. The first one she told about it was Jean.

Her sister was almost more unhappy about it than Helen was. It seemed to "cinch" things somehow. "Are you going to tell John?"

"I guess I'll have to."

"How do you feel about it?"

"I'm not sure."

Helen knew how much John cared for her.

It was very soothing to have someone so devoted, so caring, so understanding of her needs as a widow. When she told him about Marvin, he understood. When she told him of her loneliness, he said he would pray for her. She had never met anyone like him before. At first she thought he was joking, but he was serious. He actually *would* pray for her. It made her feel secure and comfortable and suddenly not so alone anymore.

When she told John she was pregnant, the indecision he was feeling himself about marrying Helen because of her religion ceased to exist. To him it seemed as though the "decision" had definitely been taken out of his hands. He abandoned the meticulous, careful planning he had always considered so important in the past in favor of his newly found passions. He asked her to convert to the Lutheran faith and to marry him immediately. Converting was not an issue of great import to Helen, and she agreed without giving it a second thought. Baptist, Lutheran, what difference did it make? It seemed to matter so much to John.

He called Alma to share his news, but she was not overjoyed, despite the enthusiasm he could not hide in his voice.

"*Sei vorsichtig*," she warned. "*Sei vorsichtig*."

"I *am* being careful, Mother," he reassured her. "There's nothing to worry about. You'll see when you meet her."

"And her name?"

"Helen Taylor."

"Is she Lutheran?"

He hesitated. "No, but she's Christian, and she's going to convert."

"Tell me about her, *mein Lieber*. . . ."

And in his enthusiasm and innocence, he told her everything Helen had confided to him.

Afterward Alma shared her serious concerns with her friend Mrs. Hollister as the two women sat on the porch and spoke quietly.

"She's very young." Alma explained. "Only twenty-four, I think. And already she has an eight-year-old daughter. Nine years old, maybe. I'm not sure exactly."

"I understand they marry young in the South," Mrs. Hollister offered helpfully.

"And her husband was killed in the war."

"Oh."

"And there is something about her . . . about what he told me about her . . ."

"What?"

"I don't think she is right for John."

"Alma," Mrs. Hollister said gently, "would anybody be right for John in your eyes?"

"Oh, yes. Someone from here. Someone like us. I just don't think she's right for him. I want nothing more than for John to be happy, but I understand the girl is very quiet, like John. And she's not Lutheran."

"What is she?"

"Presbyterian or maybe Methodist. Of course she will convert. . . ."

"Well, that's something, anyway."

"And they will marry in a Lutheran church. We wouldn't have it any other way. And any children will be brought up as Lutherans, of course. That's very important to us. But . . ." She stopped with a hesitancy brought about by a very deep rooted displeasure. "She's only twenty-four years old, and she has a nine-year-old daughter."

"Yes? . . ."

"And she's had two miscarriages, one stillborn child, and one child dead at the age of six months due to illness. That's five pregnancies in all."

"Five. Dear God. That many."

"She began very young," Alma said distastefully.

Mrs. Hollister nodded and understood.

Then Helen found out she wasn't pregnant after all.

John was at the base, and her mother, Eva, was at work when Helen sat at the Morris kitchen table on Washington Avenue over a light drink and told her sister, Jean.

"I don't think he wants to marry you just because he thought you were pregnant," Jean said, misunderstanding Helen's depression.

"No. But that's the main reason *I* started thinking about it."

"But not him. That's not why," Jean persisted, still not wanting to interpret the surge of foreboding she felt.

"I know," Helen said.

"I think he really loves you."

Helen didn't answer right away. Then she said, "No matter what you might think, he was vacillating more than me about getting married, till he found out I was pregnant."

"Why?"

"Because I'm not Lutheran," she said with a light shrug.

"But he really cares for you. I always thought so," Jean said. "Right from the beginning I always thought so. You could tell by the way he looks at you. Even now. So . . .'' Jean hesitated. "Does it really matter?"

Helen didn't answer immediately.

Jean looked at her sister carefully. "Does it?"

"I don't know."

"You can start all over with John, Helen," Jean tried to rationalize. "He's intelligent, and he's kind enough to Brenda."

Helen finished her drink. "He hardly pays her no mind."

"I thought you really loved him," Jean said. "That's what we all thought."

Helen looked off into her still very active memories. "He's so . . . different," she said slowly. And Jean knew that Helen had already begun to make the fatal comparison between Marvin and John.

"So what are you going to do?"

Helen shrugged lightly. "I know I don't like being alone. . . ."

On December 1, 1951, Jean and Gene Syfert were witnesses at the quiet wedding ceremony performed in a Lutheran church in Baltimore, Maryland. John, at twenty-six, looked handsome in his army uniform. Helen, at twenty-five, looked lovely in a pale-colored wool suit. Alma remained in Bay City. No one questioned Helen's odd insistence that the marriage had to take place in Maryland. And when, the night before the wedding, Helen happily informed John she wasn't pregnant afterall, he felt only a slight tug of hesitation about proceeding with their hastily made plans.

John had never before been inside a supper club, but on the night of the wedding, the four dined, drank, and danced the night away at a smart supper club.

John preferred to sit and hold Helen's hand rather than dance. Helen thought nothing of it as they watched Jean and Gene dance past their table.

"This is really a lovely evening," Jean said breathlessly when they sat down. "I'm having a lot of fun. How about you two?"

"Of course," John answered. "We're really celebrating." He turned to his bride. "Right?"

"Yes," Helen said.

Gene raised his glass and made toasts throughout the evening. John joined in with a broad smile and drank. The drinking loosened him up to the point where he actually found himself toasting his own bride and himself as well. In German.

"Ich trinke auf meine Braut, die ich immer lieben werde."

"What does that mean?" Jean asked.

John blushed.

They laughed.

"C'mon, tell us," Jean persisted playfully.

"It's private," he insisted.

The waiter brought over the bill and handed it to John. Gene immediately reached forward and took it out of John's hand.

"Wait. No, really," he protested.

"On me," Gene said grandly.

"No, please."

"Let him," Jean said. "We want to."

"Sure. A little wedding present," Gene said.

"Besides,—" Jean laughed. "Gene's drunk. Now's the time to take advantage. You don't think he'd do this if he was sober, do you?"

They laughed some more.

John looked at Helen for approval. She nodded. "Let him if he wants. It's okay."

And John let himself be talked into it.

"Seventy-one dollars!" Gene exclaimed.

"We could share," John began nervously.

Helen touched his arm to stop him.

"It's okay." Gene reassured him. "It's only money."

"Only money, did he say? He's drunker than I thought," Jean said in a loud stage whisper.

They laughed again. The mood of celebration lay joyously and lightly in the air. Nothing could dispel the gaiety.

"You're not gonna believe this," Jean said later to her husband when they were alone that night in their hotel.

"What the hell," Gene Syfert had answered when she told him they had been invited to join the newlyweds on their honeymoon in Washington, D.C. "They're still shy with each other. And he never seems to know what to say. So we'll leave them alone, and we'll do some sight-seeing in the capital!"

But Gene did think it demonstrated a certain eccentricity on John's part to invite them along on his honeymoon. *He* certainly hadn't wanted anyone around on his. And again he thought that there was something about John that had struck him as peculiar. But when, after a moment's thought, he mentioned it again to Jean, she reassured him that if it wasn't "meant to be," it wouldn't have happened.

"They'll be fine!" she said, this time deliberately suppressing her own misgivings, Helen and John were married now. It would have to work out somehow.

And so the Lists and the Syferts spent John and Helen's honeymoon week together in Washington, D.C.

Jean still had misgivings, but Gene's doubts were beginning to dispel. Although the Lists spent most of the time in their room while the Syferts went sightseeing, Gene observed that when the four were together, Helen and John seemed happy. They were always holding hands, always kissing, and apparently intended to work very hard at making this marriage work. Helen had found herself a nice enough young man who was obviously madly in love with her and who would take care of her for the rest of her life. She was probably lucky to have found him.

From Washington, D.C., Jean and Gene went back south, and John took his bride north to Bay City to meet *Mutter*.

12 | *Mutter*

As she took her new daughter-in-law's hand in her large warm grasp, Alma smiled broadly. John looks a lot like her, Helen thought. Tall, straight, large-boned. Helen didn't mind when John and his mother spent half their time speaking in German. It gave her the opportunity to look about the scene of his childhood at leisure. She knew at once that Mother List was a demon housekeeper. The house was immaculate and neat, not a cup out of place in the china closet, not a doily one inch off center on the couches and armchairs. Even her well-stocked kitchen pantry closet was packed with a precision that suggested great care and attention to the positioning of every can, every box, every jar. John better not be like that, Helen thought with a smile.

The smell of German cooking hung thickly in the air. John beamed at the hearty culinary preparations for his homecoming with his new bride and tried to teach her how to say the dishes in German.

"This is *Paprikahuñer*."

"What's that?"

"Chicken with a paprika and sour cream sauce," he said. "And

Bratwurst in Ale and *Krauspätsle oder-nudeln*. That's Swabian sauerkraut noodles.''

She tried to pronounce it after him.

"And *Rheinische Mohrrüben*,'' he said, laughing.

"It looks like plain old carrots to me,'' she said.

Alma had even baked an *Apfelstrudel*. "And a *Brauner Kirsch-kuchen* for dessert. That's a chocolate cherry cake,'' he explained.

"*Brau . . . ner Kirsch-kuc-hen*,'' Helen tried. He found it very humorous to hear her repeat the German words with her gentle southern drawl. John seemed more in control here, Helen thought. More sure of himself and of his place. He seemed even a bit un-bending in the way "things should be done,'' as though there were some kind of written rule for everything. She thought it amusing.

Helen liked Bay City, but it was already thickly white with snow and very cold. She had been warned that it was cold here all the time, and once the snows came the city wouldn't thaw out completely until at least April, when the smell of spring had already been in the air for weeks down south. The wind never stopped rushing through the streets and rattling against the windows. To Helen it seemed to blast off the Saginaw River with bitter impact, almost like physical blows.

Although John's mother was extremely polite and smiled readily at her, Helen sensed early on that the older woman did not quite approve of her. John didn't seem to notice. But the disapproval was subtly present in little things like the manner in which she said, "You sit. Don't move. I'll clear the table.'' She was always polite, but with a subtle edge. "Don't bother with the dishes, I'll do them.''

Even the way she tried to make the "skinny'' girl eat, to "put some meat on her bones,'' held an implied criticism. The tone she adopted, and the grammatical use of the third person in her presence, smacked of disapproval. She would pile Helen's plate with *Nieren* and potatoes. Helen didn't like kidneys no matter how they were prepared.

Alma would start cooking in the morning. There was always a smell of cooking in the house that made Helen feel queasy.

Mother List separated John's laundry from hers and washed and pressed everything to perfection, as though she were trying to dem-onstrate how it should be done, how he should be taken care of. Helen saw her examining her own clothing hanging in the closet next to John's as she pushed her pieces aside to pull out a jacket of her son's that had to be brushed.

The couple slept in John's boyhood room. There was no door

and no privacy. From the moment they arrived in Bay City, their honeymoon was over.

Although the List family had been established in Bay City for decades, Helen noted that Alma and John did not seem to have a social life. They didn't go anywhere except to church. That was one of the first places they went to introduce Helen to the pastor and to the congregation. She was treated kindly by the parishioners, but it wasn't long before she began to feel very confined by the rigidity of the way of life here, even though she and John would not have to remain at Mother List's house long. Fortunately John's leave was soon over, and the couple returned to the base in Newport News. Helen did not tell John how relieved she was to be returning to Virginia.

"Well," said Alma's friend Mrs. Hollister after Sunday service, once the couple had gone. "She seems nice enough"—referring to the new Mrs. List—"but what is she really like?"

"We'll see," Alma said, reserving open judgment.

Mother List took to calling the newly married couple almost nightly, just to see see how they were getting along and to chat with her son.

Helen could hear them speaking on the phone in German. She felt shut out but tried not to resent it. The army was reassigning John anyway. He would not be going into active combat in Korea. They already knew they would be moving to Ft. Ord in San Francisco soon. It would be too expensive to keep up the long-distance telephone calls on a steady basis once they were stationed almost a continent away.

In January of 1952 John wrote to a fellow accountant who had shared space with him at Ernst & Ernst in Detroit:

I spent three months at Fort Eustis, Va., attending transportation school. That is also where I met my wife. We were married before I left Virginia. I feel very well adjusted to the army regiment.

Even though he had already been married a month by the time he wrote the letter, he enclosed a wedding invitation.

* * *

"It doesn't make sense," Eva Morris confided in shock to her daughter, Jean. "They're transferring out to Ft. Ord in California."

"So that's definite, then." Jean nodded happily. "What's the matter, Mom? That's good news. It means no combat duty."

"But they want to leave Brenda with me."

Jean didn't know how to respond. "Well, I guess maybe they want to be alone at first so they can get to know each other. . . ."

"They're taking his mother with them!"

"What?"

"His mother, for heaven's sake."

"I don't believe it."

"How are they going to get to know each other with her around?"

"Now that really doesn't make sense." Jean found herself repeating her mother's words. "And it doesn't sound like Helen, either."

"And you know how much I love Brenda," Eva began almost defensively.

"That's not the point." Jean was truly stunned at the news. What could Helen be thinking of to agree to such an arrangement?

"But what with my job all day long," Eva continued unhappily, "how can I give Brenda the attention she needs, and—"

They both broke off and looked at each other.

"It has to be his idea," Jean said. "Or the mother's. I know Helen certainly would never suggest it."

Nine-year-old Brenda had not been happy about her mother's remarriage. The child was still grieving over the abandonment she felt after the death of her father. She couldn't find it in her heart to accept John List as her new "daddy." It didn't become easier when her mother left her back in Newport News with her grandmother and took off for California. It was only natural that she would feel a great sense of rejection. She'd lost her father, and now she'd lost her mother, too. She missed her terribly. But it was obvious to her that her mother had chosen John List over her.

13 | Helen and *Mutter* Together

The final months of John's Korean enlistment in California were not happy ones. Alma's move with them to San Francisco placed a strain on the new marriage from which it would never fully recover. It was hardly an auspicious way for John and Helen to begin married life. The tension created by Alma's ubiquitous presence was to prove to be the first step in the eventual disintegration of the Lists' relationship. Helen couldn't know that this pattern of mother-son involvement was merely a continuation of the patterns begun when John was a child and even perpetuated into the years when he went to the University of Michigan, where Alma had visited him with regularity every month; if she could have, Alma probably would have stayed with him during his entire attendance at school.

It was Helen who was made to feel the intruder. She was the one who was standing in between their close relationship, and she was smothered with what was gently presented to her as Alma's superior wisdom. John often sided with his mother.

Helen thought she would go crazy.

There was no way she could accept Alma's rigid German ways. Now Helen was beginning to appreciate the differences in heritage, religion, upbringing, housekeeping, even the differences inherent in regionality. She began to tell John, in no uncertain terms, how much she resented his *mutter*'s presence.

When John found out his service tenure was ending and he was going to be separated from the army on April 19, 1952, he had a private conversation with mother—one that he dreaded.

"*Mutter*," he began, "it would be better if . . ." It was difficult to say.

"Tell me, John."

"I don't want you to feel bad. . . ."

"You are going to take the job in Detroit."

"Yes. I've been offered my old job back at Ernst & Ernst. It's a good company. One of the 'Big Eight' accounting firms. . . ."

"And why not?" said Alma. "They were impressed that you

126

earned two business degrees. They know that just to be accepted into the University of Michigan means you are very smart. They are lucky to have you, a straight B student. They were impressed with you. That's why they want you to return."

"So I'm going back there," he said, coming to the hard part.

"And you don't think it would be a good idea if I went with you," she said for him.

John looked down. It was a very difficult moment for him. He was terribly torn between his mother and his wife.

"I understand, John," she said, and smiled at him. "I don't think it would be a good idea, either. And I miss home. I will go back to Bay City."

"You mustn't feel bad."

She touched his hand gently and smiled again. She loved him so dearly. He was everything to her. She could see that he was deeply distressed at having to tell her she could not stay with them any longer.

Alma was tired, too. It had not been a happy stay with her son and his wife. Helen's angry "Do you have to talk in German all the time?" still resonated for her. She needed to get away from the constant tension for a while. "What do you have to say to each other all the time, anyway?" Helen seemed to lose her shyness when she became angry. John's cheeks would blotch with embarrassment and anger at her lack of respect for his mother. Alma would leave the room.

"We will keep in touch," she reassured her son. "We will never let anything separate us. Nothing and no one could ever do that."

"*Nein Mutter.*"

He was relieved that his mother had been so understanding. It was going to be difficult enough to start a family life together for the first time once they picked up Brenda in Virginia, without also having to worry about whether Helen and his mother were getting along.

When Alma had resettled herself into her home in Bay City, Christina Worman came to pay a welcome-home visit. It was good to be home, wonderful to see her young friend again, so relaxing and free of stress to sit on the familiar porch on South Wenona Street in the cool April evening, buttoned up in wool sweaters and tasting the rejuvenating freshness of the oncoming spring already in the night air.

Significantly, Alma said nothing about John and his new wife even though Christina knew she had lived with them in San Francisco. However, after exhausting all of the hometown news and gossip, Christina finally asked the question that was on both their minds. "So, my friend . . . how are they?"

Alma shook her head slowly. "I was right. It is not a good marriage. She is very bad for my John. I don't see good things ahead for them," she said more prophetically than she realized. "Only trouble. I pray for them every day."

Christina realized sadly that the two women in John List's life had not "hit it off." In fact, they disliked each other intensely. Having them together in the same house was a situation that was doomed to failure. They had nothing in common but John. Any mutual understanding between the two women was an impossibility. It had been difficult to keep up appearances even for John's sake, but Christina sensed that, of the two, it was always Alma who had backed off for the sake of her son.

John's tour of duty ended in April 1952. Now he and Helen returned to Virginia to pick up Brenda before moving north to Highland Park, approximately five miles north of Detroit, Michigan. They rented half of a duplex house at 3409 Coy Avenue.

Once again John was put on the books as a staff accountant at Ernst & Ernst. He was happy to be back. And Helen was happy to be reunited with her daughter and to be alone with her husband at last. Brenda was happy to be with them. She found it very cold in Michigan, accustomed as she was to the more temperate climate of North Carolina, but she was so thankful to be a part of the family that she never complained of the rawness of the temperatures. Now John began to be more friendly and attentive to the little girl who had been left behind. He even adopted her. She was thrilled to be a "legal" part of her mother's new family, as though with the adoption she had finally become a part of her mother's remarriage. She still wasn't sure about her new "daddy," despite the adoption, but eventually he would win her over. He was kind and understanding to her, and she was beginning to feel that she could depend on him.

John and Helen were still virtual newlyweds. They had never been alone yet. They had spent their honeymoon in Washington, D.C., with Jean and Gene; they had gone to Fort Ord with Alma; and now they were in Highland Park with Brenda. John didn't mind having Brenda around. In some ways it was easier to deal with the child than to deal with Helen, who became pregnant—no false alarm this time—and was beginning to feel ill and severely out of sorts. Actually, except for the pregnancy, which was taking its toll on Helen's health again, John's separation from the service initiated a fairly good period for the new family.

Right from the first day, Helen List rubbed Janet Murray the wrong way. Janet and her husband, Bill, lived next door to the family home on Coy Avenue in Highland Park where John and Helen set up housekeeping. She had tried to be neighborly, making it a point to welcome the new family, stopping to chat with Helen at every opportunity, but Helen never returned a phone call and rarely accepted or returned an invitation.

Once, John and Helen had accepted an invitation to stop by for a New Year's Eve drink. When they arrived they both stood off to one side, hardly participating in the evening's growing gaiety. Janet noticed that John never left Helen's side. Helen seemed already to have had a few drinks by the time they arrived, even though she had told Janet that she was going to have a baby.

"Maybe you shouldn't," Janet said when Helen reached for a refill. "Because of the baby, I mean."

"It's okay," Helen snapped a bit defensively. "I know what I'm doing."

Janet realized that the drink was to ease the social uneasiness she was experiencing among strangers.

"What a pair!" Janet said later to Bill. "He's seems nice enough, but neither one is great shakes socially. He never has anything to say, and I think she drinks." She felt a little guilty about her appraisal when she heard a few weeks later that Helen had miscarried. When she paid a call to offer her sympathies, she was introduced to John's mother, Alma List.

"Well, come in, come in," Alma said warmly. "How generous of you to take the time to call."

"How's Helen?"

"Not well," she whispered.

"Can I see her?"

"Oh, not now, she's resting." The older woman sighed. "I'm afraid she's depressed, poor thing. She has recurring bouts with malaria, you know, and she doesn't carry well. She's already lost

. . . let me see—three others. No, four. I lose count," she whispered confidentially with a sad shake of her head.

"That's terrible. I had no idea. Helen never told me."

"I'm not surprised. My son's wife usually keeps to herself. She's very shy."

"Yes, I know. If there's anything I can do . . ."

"How kind," Alma said, and smiled warmly. "No. We'll manage. But thank you, Mrs. Murray. . . ." And as she poured Janet a cup of hot coffee, she told her how her son had called her in Bay City to come down to help take care of things while his wife recuperated. "I'm a nurse," she explained. "All those pregnancies," she said again, shaking her head from side to side. "It's terrible, isn't it."

Later that night Janet told Bill what a charming woman John List's mother was. So outgoing and hospitable and friendly, with the warmest smile imaginable. Now *she* would make a wonderful neighbor.

Helen was beginning to demonstrate signs of hostility toward John. The source of some of the friction may have been the fact that Alma visited frequently. Detroit was not far from Bay City, but far enough that a visit always involved overnight stays. Helen was never consulted. It was always a *fait accompli* by the time she found out. "Mother's coming this weekend," John would inform her, and that was that.

Another source of dissension with John was the anxiety over yet another unwanted pregnancy, which culminated in another miscarriage: her sixth loss, with all the accompanying trips to the doctor's office, the hospital stays, the D&C's, the pain, the depression, and *Mutter*'s visits to console her son.

Helen was despondent over the two miscarriages. She was also physically very frail. It took months for her hormone level, which was severely off balance again, to stabilize. And she was drinking a little more than usual to try to dissipate the postpregnancy depression and the loneliness that overcame her when her mother-in-law visited. John tried to be supportive, but he didn't really understand the depth of Helen's feelings. He knew that his mother was sincerely trying to help. And she was. Alma even talked to John about trying to avoid any more pregnancies, even though it was not easy to discuss such matters. Instead they prayed together and asked God to help them in these times of trial.

* * *

"John's mother thinks you're just *von*derful," Helen told Janet Murray when they met in front of the building. "Just *von*derful," she said, imitating the older woman's accent.

"How nice."

"Is it?" She was surprised. She couldn't believe anyone would like hearing that. Being "wonderful" in Alma's eyes meant you were different from her daughter-in-law, whom Alma did not think was so "*von*derful."

"Oh, by the way," Helen said. "We're moving."

That took Janet by surprise. Helen hadn't given the slightest indication. "When?"

"Soon."

"Where will you be going?"

"Not far enough away from Bay City."

Janet Murray wished she could bring herself to say she'd miss them, but the truth was that she wouldn't.

They rented an upstairs apartment in a two-family house on Parkwood Avenue in Inkster, a suburb about ten miles west of Detroit.

Helen began to feel better physically. She even stopped her occasional drinking. She liked the apartment well enough to want to fix it up. John was delighted at her sudden enthusiasm for housekeeping. They painted the apartment and decorated it. They planted flowers that matured into peonies that were so huge and topheavy, they seemed to have been made of crepe paper; but even though she liked the flowers, Helen didn't care much for gardening. The work involved was too physical for her; and eventually whatever gardening needs there were were taken over exclusively by John, who was used to doing all the necessary chores that went into maintaining the grounds.

In April of 1954 Helen became pregnant again. This time she was disconsolate at the news. She did not want another pregnancy, even though, since she was being carefully monitored to prevent further mishaps, it seemed that she might hold this baby to term. She wouldn't tell anyone about her greatest fears, not her mother, not Jean, certainly not John. She *had* to tell her doctor for the extra preventive measures needed under the circumstances, but she swore him to secrecy and then worried about the baby anyway. She blamed

John for not being careful, for not wanting to use contraceptives. The fact that John was so "fuddy-duddy" about it when she began to show her pregnancy made it worse. She was on a very tight stress level. Arguments began to spring up like leaks in a rusty pipe.

"I don't think you should go out like that," he began tentatively.

"Like what?"

"You look . . . pregnant."

"I am!" she screamed.

"There's no need to advertise it," he said, trying to be as gentle about it as possible. He couldn't get away from the rigidity of his background, where these matters were kept discreetly within the family.

"John! Go back to the nineteenth century!" she told him angrily. "I'm going for a walk. I need air. I can't breathe in here!"

"It's cold."

"I don't care. I don't care. I don't *care*!"

As she waited for the birth of this child, her eighth pregnancy, Helen was filled with understandable anxiety. John had to be careful with her. He had to treat her with sympathy and kindness. He backed off.

Then on January 8, 1955, exactly one week past her own twenty-ninth birthday, Helen gave birth to her second daughter and John's first child, Patricia Marie, a beautiful baby girl. Helen breathed a sigh of relief; the baby was healthy.

Brenda was delighted. Now she had a half sister she could call her own. Once Mom got back on her feet again and they had settled and had adjusted to the new baby, they would begin behaving like all young families with children to tend to and entertain. But soon the adventure of the new baby settled into a normal routine and eventually into daily chores. Helen didn't recuperate quickly. In order to combat the distress of severe postpartum blues and to ease her growing loneliness, she quietly began taking a few pep pills during the day, two or three sleeping pills at night, and an occasional Scotch in the afternoon. It fell to Brenda, at the age of thirteen, to assume more and more of the care of her little sister when Daddy wasn't home. When he returned from work, he relieved her of many of the tasks.

Finally . . . slowly . . . Helen began to feel better again.

When she did, the family took interesting excursions in and around Detroit. Brenda loved the trips to the zoo: passing by the cages and feeding the animals; the petting zoo was her favorite. Daddy even took them to the circus, which, Brenda could tell, Mom enjoyed a great deal. And then there was the time they took a day-long trip to Detroit to visit the Henry Ford Museum. That was Daddy's favorite.

On the Saturday nights when Daddy made pizza for the family, even the prayers were fun to the little girl. "Bless us, O Lord . . ." before the pizza, and "Bless us, O Lord . . ." after the pizza. She had never had such disciplined behavior imposed upon her before. There seemed to be a real caring implicit in the regimentation. She loved the Sunday mornings when they attended church together: she, Daddy, Mommy, and little Patty, all dressed up in their Sunday-best clothes. Mom didn't always come, but when she did she looked so lovely. Daddy bought her such pretty clothes. Mom was beginning to accumulate a wonderful collection of the most beautiful sweaters imaginable. Brenda loved to feel them when her mother would let her. Wools, nylons, even cashmeres priced at $40 to $45 apiece. She didn't know that John was overspending extravagantly in order to please her mother—to try to make her smile, to try to alleviate her debilitating depressions.

There were times when she went shopping alone with her mother, leaving Patty with Daddy. He was very good with the baby: dressing her, feeding her, changing diapers, and even bathing her. He was very attentive and caring. He even had his private conversations with the infant in German. It never occurred to Brenda on their shopping expeditions that her mother was spending inordinate amounts of money—more than John's salary could ever cover.

Sometimes Brenda would go out with her daddy alone. The best times were when he took her ice fishing. On these quiet outings it seemed to her that he was all hers. She talked. He listened.

He was always there for her. They were becoming very close. The memory of Marvin had begun to slip away. The quick furloughs in North Carolina, the adventurous days in the army, even his death—these memories seemed very distant to the girl, who was now almost fourteen years old. She had grown to love her new daddy very much and to depend on him for all of her emotional needs. Especially since Mom was beginning to get a bit distant.

More and more, Mom was pulling away from them, so slowly at first that it was almost imperceptible. The child was not even consciously aware that she was feeling a lack of daily family participation on her mother's part.

One weekend they drove up to Bay City, Michigan, where Mother List still lived in the lovely old frame house on South Wenona Avenue where John had been born. Brenda did not understand the sudden tension she sensed the moment they walked into the house. When Daddy took her across the Saginaw River to show her the baronial mansions left over from the Saginaw Valley's great logging days, she wished Mommy could see them, too; but Mommy remained at home with Patty, who had a slight cold. Although Mother List had offered to take care of the baby while she went "sight-seeing," Helen had chosen not to leave the baby.

That night John quizzed Brenda on her catechism, as was his habit at home. But this time he quizzed her under the watchful eye of Mother List, who nodded in approval.

"You must not forget Patricia's religious education, too, when she grows up, John," she said.

Brenda did not understand why her mother became so annoyed. To the child the sudden annoyance was irrational and a bit frightening.

In February of 1956, when Patty was eleven months old, Helen became pregnant again. It was her ninth pregnancy. She was distraught. The last thing she wanted was another baby. She couldn't stop throwing up. She couldn't stop crying for days. By the time she called her sister, Jean, she was desperate and irrational.

"I don't want this baby!" she cried hysterically into the phone.

Jean tried to console her. "Helen . . . don't—"

"I don't want it! I don't want it!"

"Please calm down. Oh, honey . . ."

"I can't go through this again," she sobbed pathetically. "Jean . . . I can't . . . Oh, Jean, help me, please!"

Jean was furious. "What the hell's the matter with John! Doesn't he have a brain in his head!"

"He doesn't believe in birth control. He prays!" she said viciously. "That's what he does, and he reads the Bible. Oh, Jean, Jean. I'm not going to make it this time."

"Yes, you will."

"No . . ."

"You will. Don't say that. Please . . ."

Helen cried into the phone uncontrollably.

She hated the doctor. This time she didn't tell him a *thing*. She knew what to do on her own from the last pregnancy with Patty. She knew what medicines to take. But she was nervous nonetheless. The tensions increased, not only because of another unwanted pregnancy, but because Helen made it very clear that she was not the mothering type. And didn't want to be! She became demanding and irrational. It was easier for John to let the care of Patty fall to him and Brenda than to argue with her.

Brenda was beginning to slip away from home every opportunity she could find, and John spent a great deal of time on the phone with his mother, until it finally came again. "Mother's coming."

Helen took to her bed.

John took photos of his mother taking Patty for a walk in her stroller along Parkland Avenue. The baby looked pretty. Alma smiled broadly into the camera. At night when they spoke quietly together, she sympathized with John and offered consoling words and prayers to help lessen the burdens brought on by the obvious disintegration of his personal life.

John had to find another job. He needed more money to support his growing family and what were turning out to be his and Helen's excessive expenditures. He couldn't seem to control her spending whenever she felt well enough to leave the house. He knew that buying things was some kind of a comfort to her, some kind of compensation for the nervous tension she suffered, but it was destroying the delicate balance of their finances. Everything in his Budget Book pointed to financial ruin unless he could augment his income.

John knew another job might mean another move for the family, but he had no way of knowing that moving again could be very dangerous for Helen. Her irrational behavior was more than likely chemically oriented and not merely situationally motivated. Not only had her hormone level been in constant flux over the past several years, but her alcohol intake seemed to have affected her. Dr. Schumann had even carefully suggested doing some preliminary neurological testing. Helen was terrified at the idea. She immediately rejected his counsel.

"I don't like that doctor," she cried softly to John later that evening. "I'm pregnant, and *he* wants to test my *head*. He doesn't know anything. I want another doctor. Please . . . why can't we go to another doctor, one who isn't German?"

But the doctor had prescribed sedatives, and she went to sleep quietly.

John knew how to make an impression when he had to. He presented a tall, neatly dressed, nice-looking appearance when he went on an interview. He knew how to smile and say the right things. He knew how to appear in control. When he answered an ad for a staff accountant position in the costs division of the Sutherland Paper Company, his meeting with the personnel manager went extremely well. The note made on his application read:

A very good appearance. Seems to be well adjusted. A very capable person with a good personality.

When offered, he took the new accounting job with the Sutherland Paper Co. at a salary of $7,000 a year. John was pleased. His career was apparently on the rise. But the job was in Kalamazoo, which was located in the southwestern part of Michigan, and the family had to relocate.

Helen looked at him pathetically when he told her the news. She didn't want to move again. Since their marriage in Newport News, Virginia, they had moved to San Francisco, to Highland Park, and to Inkster. This would be the fourth time in five years. The only good thing about it, she thought wistfully, was that it was farther away and more difficult to get to Kalamazoo from Bay City.

"I don't feel well," she said, genuinely ill.

"I'll do it all," John promised. "I'll pack the boxes."

"There's so much pressure . . . in my back and . . . in my head."

"Just don't . . ." He stopped.

"Don't what?"

"Don't drink. For the baby's sake. . . ."

She became hysterical. She wanted to go home. She wanted to go where it was warm. She wanted to see her family. She didn't want this baby. Why couldn't they move south to Virginia?

John called Dr. Schumann to ask him to recommend a doctor for Helen in Kalamazoo; but before he could tell him of the family's imminent move, the doctor told him he wanted to discuss Helen with him privately.

Sitting opposite him in his office, John was stunned when Dr. Schumann said, "I think you should seriously consider psychiatric intervention for Helen."

"But why?" John stammered.

"Because she won't agree to neurological testing."

"No . . . she won't."

"She's not handling this pregnancy well. And I'm sure she's drinking."

"But a psychiatrist . . ."

"Perhaps a psychiatrist may be able to help her out of her depression and persuade her to have some preliminary tests done."

"We have never gone to a psychiatrist in my family," John replied, setting his jaw grimly. "It's unheard of."

"Mr. List," the doctor said, measuring his words carefully. "I think your wife may be on her way to a serious illness."

"What?"

"She is seriously depressed," he began.

John nodded. "I know that. She's just not happy about the baby," he tried to explain.

"She seems to be inattentive when I speak to her. Even apathetic."

How could John tell the doctor that Helen didn't like him?

"There is an apparent poverty of thought," Dr. Schumann continued.

"Can't you give her something?"

The doctor sighed. He wasn't getting through to the man. "I've already prescribed a sedative. Tranquilizers can help, but only transiently, and I hesitate to give them to her in her condition."

"Perhaps our pastor might be able to help."

"Perhaps," the doctor said doubtfully. "But I think the problem is physical, not spiritual."

John didn't like the sound of it all. "Can you tell me what's wrong with her?" he asked, and the doctor noticed that the man's already deep bass voice took on a special resonancy with emotional provocation. "Specifically?"

"It's hard to say. It could be a simple depression brought on by the pregnancy. It could be more. Tests would have to be done. . . ."

"We can't," he said evasively. "We're moving. To Kalamazoo."

"Is that necessary? A change in environment might not be good for her in her present condition."

"It's not by choice. I have a new job. I must go."

"I strongly urge you to take what I'm saying seriously."

"When we get to Kalamazoo we'll go to the pastor," John concluded, even though he was pretty certain that Helen would refuse to go, especially to a new pastor. Maybe when they became familiar with their new church, she would consider it. He did not think he was ignoring the potential seriousness of his wife's illness when he said, "I will take care of it, doctor. Thank you."

The doctor nodded and wrote out a prescription for a mild tranquilizer.

14 | Lovers Lane

Ironically, in Kalamazoo the Lists moved into a house on a street called Lovers Lane. This time they bought instead of renting. The red house was a neat, conventional split level on a slight incline with a wide driveway, well-tended grounds, and enough room that they would be able to keep out of each other's way if they so desired. And keeping out of each other's way was much desired. Their home was hardly a Lovers Lane. Life had deteriorated into a tangle of trouble, from daily arguments over little things to angry fights over little things. For Brenda, the bloom of her new family had worn off long ago. Now, pushed to extremes by Helen's growing irrationality, John ignored advice from his doctor and his mother and began fighting back. He didn't have to hold his tongue all the time just because she was pregnant.

He was trying, he thought rigidly. Every penny spent was carefully recorded in his Budget Book and worried over obsessively. And he worked—not only on the job, but at home as well. He took care of the outside of the house, and he did it the "right way," too. In a very detailed chart, he carefully cataloged even the seeds he planted. The mowing never seemed good enough; he got down on his hands and knees and trimmed the edges of the grass by hand. He did more than his share of the work inside, too, both in taking care of the cleaning and in taking care of the children. He relentlessly picked up after Helen and the children, compulsively straightening up to the point of taking the extra time to stack silverware in the kitchen drawer with all of the handles pointing neatly in the same direction. He did not recognize the pattern of an obsessive-compulsive personality manifesting itself in the mass of details and perfectionism he demanded of himself. That was simply the way he had always been, the way things were done. He rationalized his behavior as necessary since Helen did practically nothing. All she did was criticize him both in and out of their bedroom. He was getting sick of it! Especially the comparisons with her first husband, first subtle, then overt. He didn't care that she was ill. She should start pulling her weight. She should have more discipline. She should go to church more. She should pray to God for guidance and assistance in her times of trial. *He was trying*! But everything about her behavior was foreign to him. He could not understand her.

And she should stop drinking! That was the biggest sin of all.

It seemed to Brenda that all her parents ever did lately was fight. The arguments fed on each other, one stemming from another, and when John became angry, his rage was awesome. When he shouted, the sound of his booming voice was frightening. The children cried. Brenda tried to hide. Finally she started spending more and more time away from home, finding with friends she had made in her new school the comfort she lacked at home. She yearned for companionship, for nurturing, for stroking. Her thirst made her audacious in her needs, and even though John fiercely objected to her late nights out, Helen openly encouraged her. "Let her!"

"What does she do out at ten o'clock at night at her age!" he demanded.

"She's *my* daughter."

"Do you think that's right!"

"And I say it's okay for her to have a little fun," Helen defended. "God knows there's little of that around here. What's she supposed to do at home all day long? Pray?"

One night Helen was particularly demanding at dinner. Patty's antics at the table bothered her. She didn't like what John had prepared. She was uncomfortable. Her back hurt; and when Patty began to cry, Helen got up and roughly picked the baby up out of her high chair. "Take her!" she said, handing the screaming child to Brenda. "Take her. Put her to bed. Do something with her. She's driving me crazy!"

Brenda clasped the struggling infant in her arms and took her to her crib.

Later, when Brenda was washing the dishes, John came into the kitchen holding a still quietly sobbing Patty in his arms. "We have to be very patient," he said.

"About what?" the girl asked dejectedly.

"Just be patient with your mother," he repeated softly, trying to convince himself as well. "She goes through some bad times sometimes, and we must try to be very understanding."

Brenda didn't understand at all. "You, too, Daddy?"

"Yes," he said, ashamed at the fights the girl had witnessed. "Me too."

He was extremely sorry about the arguments. He would pray for control.

* * *

On October 21, 1956, Helen gave birth to a boy.

Blessedly, the birth had gone fairly quickly and well, and immediately afterward Helen felt decidedly better. Most important, the baby was healthy. All prenatal anxieties about her secret had finally come to rest. In the hospital, as she held her new son in her arms, she seemed at peace and even happy. "We'll have to call your grandmother in North Carolina," she murmured softly to the sleeping infant.

John stood at the side of the bed and looked down at his firstborn son. He prayed silently while Helen touched the child's tiny hands, caressed his cheek, pressed her lips to his warm temples.

"His name will be John Frederick," John said.

"Why?" she asked softly.

"It's a family tradition to have a son called John, and Frederick was—"

"I don't care about family traditions," she interrupted.

But he became rigid. "There is no discussing this matter."

Even in her partially drug-induced euphoric state, Helen suddenly flared up. "Who are you? Hitler?"

John gritted his teeth. "He is my firstborn son."

"He's my firstborn son, too!"

"His name will be John Frederick after my father. That's final!"

Somehow Helen knew when to stop. John's eyes were scary when he stood his ground like this.

"I don't care," she acquiesced with a shrug. "Call him whatever you like."

John Frederick began to cry. Helen called for the nurse to take him away.

When they brought the newborn infant home from the hospital, Patty was a twenty-month-old toddler and into everything.

When Patty was two years ten months and John Frederick was thirteen months old, Helen became pregnant for the tenth time in her life. She was not quite thirty-three years old. By this time, with one stressful pregnancy after another and the physical illnesses that had never been adequately diagnosed, Helen demonstrated clear signs of the neurosis that would darken the remaining years of her life. Not only was she relentlessly demanding and domineering, but she continued to drink to excess despite the fact that drinking was strictly against the doctor's orders. Her addiction was a constant source of friction with John. He hid the liquor. She tried to sneak a drink. He hid it again. They fought. She hated him for trying to deny what was one of her few sources of comfort in a pitiless life. He lost patience despite all good resolves.

And then they discovered Brenda's secret. She could no longer hide it: she was pregnant, too. She had just turned fifteen.

John's sense of moral rectitude was severely offended by the teenager's revelation. An unwed mother in his own family. He could recall very clearly how unwed mothers were treated when he was a boy in Bay City. Theirs was a shunning offense, just as divorce was. He remembered the rigid codes taught at the Sunday schools when he'd attended the Zion Lutheran School, ones that he himself was teaching in the Kalamazoo Zion Lutheran Church's Sunday school, where he acted also as the church's treasurer. He knew the teachings were right. Morality is not situationally conditional. Either the rules are obeyed, or the consequences must be suffered. Punishment and reward were deeply ingrained into his psyche.

And now it had come to this. An unwed mother in his own home. The only saving grace was that she was still a child, only fifteen. But even at fifteen he himself had always observed the laws of the church. Age was not really an excuse for this kind of misbehavior. He thought with some bitterness at the harvest of leniency. "That's what comes of not putting my foot down even though I knew I was right. That's what comes of her staying out late at night. I was right!"

"Who's the father?" he asked quietly as he towered over the girl seated at the kitchen table. As usual, he hid the true depth of his feelings, keeping the internal rage always under tight control.

"Wayne Herndon," Brenda answered in a small voice.

"What are people going to think?" Helen demanded.

Brenda looked up. Incredibly, Helen was siding with John. For once Helen wasn't disagreeing with him. "How could you do this, Brenda?" she continued. "How? Don't we have enough problems without you bringing shame on us all as well?"

"I want to marry him." Brenda buried her face in the crook of her arm across the kitchen table.

"You're a baby!"

"You married when you were my age," she said, raising a tear-streaked face. "Why should I be different?"

"Because Wayne Herndon isn't Marvin Taylor, that's why!"

John gritted his teeth at still another comparison with the incomparable Marvin.

"You will not marry, and you cannot keep this child," John said quietly. "That's all there is to it. You must give it up for adoption."

"Adoption?" she sobbed.

Helen stepped in. "Do you want everyone to know?"

"I don't care."

"Do you want to go to a home for unwed mothers?"

Brenda looked up in confusion. "I . . ."

"That's the only thing to do to keep it quiet. I will find a place," John said.

"Go away?" the child asked.

"In this you have to listen to John," Helen continued. "For once he's right. You can't keep the baby. We have enough children around here, and you're not going to keep a child out of wedlock."

"I'll marry Wayne!"

"No!" Helen began fiercely. Then she caught herself when she saw her daughter's genuine distress, and her tone took on a more nurturing, a more understanding, quality. "Oh, honey, can't you see how concerned we are? You're so young. You've already made one mistake, don't make another, one right after the other. Wayne's just a boy. He can't take care of you. He can't support you. You have to finish school. And we've always had big plans for you."

"There will be no discussing it further," John stated categorically.

"I don't want the baby anyway. Maybe it will die!" Brenda sobbed.

John was shocked. Blood rushed to his face. His anger was frightening. "Don't ever say such a thing again!" Brenda got up so fast, she bruised her thigh as she backed against the kitchen counter. "Never!" he repeated.

All Brenda could see was that they cared more about what other people thought than about what she felt. She ran from the room.

Later that night, when it was quiet and dark and John had gone to a council meeting, Helen came into her daughter's bedroom. She sat on the bed next to the tearful child. "Why?" she asked gently.

"I was lonely," the child replied, bursting into fresh tears. "You and Daddy are always fighting."

Helen cuddled her sobbing child. She knew she was not as nurturing as she should be. "It's just that I feel so sick all the time," she tried to explain.

"I wanted to get away," Brenda said, clinging desperately to her mother. It had been so long since they had touched. "And I love Wayne."

Love, Helen thought. Could the child actually be in love? *She* had been with Marvin when she was her daughter's age, she remembered with deep longing as she stared into the darkness of the untidy room. But Brenda seemed so much younger than she had been. "You like John, don't you?" she asked her daughter with a quietly bitter edge.

"He's okay."

"Oh, I know you like him, but he's not your real father. Your real father, Marvin. Now he was something," she whispered softly as she stroked Brenda's damp cheeks. "He was a man. Not like John, stuck to his mother's apron strings like a baby. He's a sissy compared with your real father. Do you remember him, Brenda?" she asked wistfully.

"Not too much."

"Oh, don't you ever forget him, honey," Helen insisted with an air of urgency. "He was handsome and sexy and strong. Brenda, don't ever forget your real father. John can't hold a candle to him! In anything. Not in anything at all."

Brenda tried to remember what Marvin Taylor looked like.

Helen's pregnancy was just as difficult as all the others had been. Brenda's was not. Because she carried well, Brenda found she had the responsibility for taking care of both Patty and Johnny while her mother was under strict doctor's orders not to endure any strenuous activities or any stressful situations of any kind.

A family truce was called. It was a desperately welcome respite.

When it became obvious that Brenda's sinful secret could no longer be kept, she was sent to the Florence Crittenton Home for Unwed Mothers in Jackson, Michigan. Wayne Herndon wasn't consulted. Daddy visited her twice. Mommy never came. When Brenda's child was born it was immediately given away for adoption. She never saw it. She didn't really want a child at this point in her life, but she never forgave either of her parents for applying force toward the decision to do "what was best for all concerned."

John softened a little toward her after it was over. He tried to be kind to her. And she realized that she still loved her daddy. He might be strict, but he was always there for her, and as long as the truce remained intact, life wasn't bad on Lovers Lane. Mommy was too sick to get involved in her postpartum grief.

Finally, Mommy's child was born on August 26, 1958. He, too, was healthy. The secret preventive medication had worked again. John named him Frederick Michael. This time Helen didn't care about the name.

At the time Freddie was born, Patty was three years eight months old and John was twenty two months old. They were a handful. It wasn't long before the fragile family truce corroded under the added weight of tensions brought on by a houseful of babies. Now the family wars began in earnest. All early marital pretenses and attempts to get along were over. Brenda, often in the middle, found herself frequently siding with Daddy because by now Mom was really "boozing it up" all the time.

It got so bad that Reverend Louis Grother of Kalamazoo Zion Lutheran Church became aware of the family's problems despite all of John's attempts to keep them private. As treasurer of the church, John spent a great deal of time with the pastor. The children were small—two were in diapers—but he brought them to services frequently. Helen came only sporadically, and when she did attend services, she was withdrawn and shy and made a point of ignoring her fellow parishioners.

"Helen," Reverend Grother tried many times, "we would be so pleased if you would join some of the ladies of the parish to—"

"No." She mumbled an excuse.

No matter how the pastor tried to encourage her participation in church-related activities, she refused. He took it to be her natural shyness and retiring nature that kept her from participating. John was a very retiring sort of person, too. He never does much talking, either, Reverend Grother thought—certainly not about the family's problems, which he was sure had to do with the woman's drinking. It was too bad John couldn't confide in him. The church was there to offer support. It was the first line of defense in serious family problems. All ministers were trained in counseling, and, of course, if necessary, they often referred serious problems to outside professional help. Reverend Grother wanted desperately to help them. He liked the family, John particularly. Such a devout student of the Holy Bible. So thoughtful and considerate all the time. Never forgot to send a Christmas card.

At Reverend Grother's request, many of the ladies of the church tried to make Helen feel welcome. Reverend Grother could sense that John welcomed their efforts, even though he never said anything about it. That's the kind of guy he was, the pastor thought. The ladies visited Helen at home. They welcomed her. They tried to get her to join the Ultra Guild, a ladies group that met in the evenings, so that she could "feel a part" of the church. They tried to get her to participate in volunteer work. But nothing worked. Despite the little smile and the shy exterior she presented to the ladies, she was able to make one point very clear: she didn't want to be a part of the group.

"I don't know what's at the core of her unhappiness," Mrs. Putnam came back to tell Reverend Grother after visiting Lovers Lane. "She surely is a very unhappy woman, but she's not eager to get out of her shell, Pastor."

"What was her reaction to your visit?"

"She said . . . well, it was very much a 'Thanks, but no thanks' kind of response."

"I'm so sorry to hear that," he said, shaking his head.

"We really tried."

"I'm sure you did. And I appreciate your efforts." He shook her hand warmly. "It's just that . . . I really want to help that poor woman. And John."

"Pastor," Mrs. Putnam said slowly, "are you aware that she drinks?"

He hesitated before answering, "I've suspected as much."

He thought about the situation later when he was alone in his office sitting behind his desk. He had the feeling that John was the type of person who stayed in the shadows of life. You felt he was there, and that he was a good guy, that he was one of those faithful guys who was there to do whatever he could for you—not in an intrusive manner—and he never asked for anything in return. Grother wasn't the first person who thought John should probably have been a pastor, but then he didn't have the personality even for that. In many ways a pastor had to be not only ready to serve, but outgoing, a good listener, a good speaker. John was . . . well . . . he didn't like to think so . . . he really liked John . . . but . . . he was dominated by her. He felt sorry for him. He knew that John often got in debt way over his head buying things for her . . . to please her, but he could never seem to please her. The more she tossed around insults, the more he tossed around money. When she did come to services, she was always exquisitely dressed, as were the children. The best of everything. He had frequently noticed that her behavior toward her husband was not shy at all, that even though she spoke quietly to him, her words always had a hard, brittle edge to them. To all outward appearances, Helen was beginning to show signs of severe mental illness, and John was the hapless victim of her neurosis.

The day would come when Reverend Grother would say, with great sadness:

A part of him could have snapped and all the rest stayed constant.

Since neither of the Lists ever spoke about their problems, there was no way the pastor could know the extent of Helen's physical illnesses: the headaches she tried to suppress with liquor, the weakness she felt all the time, the physical jolts her frail body withstood under the strain of pregnancy, the terrible tiredness that overcame her nearly every time she stood up. Nor did the pastor know that John had finally given in to the shame of psychiatric intervention when he could no longer control his wife through prayer. Psychiatry did little good. Except for the litany of complaints against John, Helen did not participate well in her therapy. She was secretive about her drinking, evasive about her medical history, impatient with her children, and uncommunicative about her needs. It wasn't long before the psychiatrist put her on heavy doses of tranquilizers. The problems were swept under a cloud of pharmaceutical opiates; life on Lovers Lane became more peaceful, but Helen's dependency on drugs had taken a giant jump forward.

15 | First Signs of Violence

On a particularly warm, muggy evening, the three children had already been put to bed. Soon Freddie would be up for a bottle, but at the moment the house was quiet and, on the surface, serene. The kitchen table was set for a late dinner. John sat in his place at the table, reading. Helen sat opposite him with a glass of seltzer in her hand, staring at him as he read. She was having one of her good days, but it was Brenda who stood at the stove waiting for the spaghetti to be completely cooked.

"The sauce smells good," Helen said, closing her eyes and

breathing in the aroma deeply. At least it wasn't something German. "Doesn't the sauce smell good, John?"

He didn't answer.

She opened up her eyes. "I don't know what you're so quiet about. It's only seltzer," she said, shaking the ice in her glass. All he could think of was there was always a glass of *some* kind in her hand.

Brenda tried to give her mother a high sign not to start anything, but Helen ignored her. "Look at him," she said to Brenda. "He never changes. He's looked the same since the day I met him."

Brenda hated when her mother teased Daddy. It made her feel terribly uncomfortable.

John's eyes didn't leave the page.

Helen got up slowly and walked behind his chair. She deliberately made a face behind his back that Brenda could see.

"Why don't you get one of those butch haircuts?" she said suddenly.

"Oh, Ma," Brenda said, glancing at her stepfather.

"Like all the other men have," Helen continued, undaunted by her daughter's pleading look. "That's what the men are wearing these days, isn't it, Brenda?"

John continued reading silently.

"Those butch haircuts?" She turned to her daughter. "Brenda, I'm talking to you."

"Ma, cut it out."

"I'm talking to you." Her eyes were glazed, and Brenda realized there was more in the glass than seltzer. Or was it the medication? She couldn't even tell anymore.

"I asked you a question," her mother persisted. "Isn't that what all the men are wearing these days?"

"I dunno," she said sullenly. "I guess."

Helen circled the table and faced John. "That might actually be an improvement. You'd look . . . I don't know . . . different. Why don't you try it?"

He didn't respond.

"Oh, come on." She laughed. "Don't be such a fuddy-duddy. Why don't you try it? Something different for a change. You might like it."

Brenda could feel her nerves jumping. John's eyes were fixed upon the book. She didn't think he was reading anymore. The back of his neck was bright red. She wished dinner were over so that she could get out of the kitchen and out of the house to meet Wayne.

"Johnny," Helen teased, "c'mon. Try it, you might like it. *I* might like it. Wouldn't that be something? I might even like it, a manly butch look. Johnnnnnnny . . .''

Finally he stood up slowly. His face was textured with red blotches of anger. He held his book in his left hand and took the edge of the table with his right. One fierce flip of his huge wrist, and he over-turned the table, spewing all the dishes onto the floor with crashing force. Brenda cried out in terror.

Helen was caught unawares and was silent for a moment as she looked at the broken dishes strewn in shards all over the kitchen floor by the force of his fury. Then she looked up at him as he stood staring at her, trembling with rage. She opened her mouth to persist but suddenly was quiet. There was a look in his eye she had never seen before. He had never been violent before.

Both stood breathing heavily while the child, paralyzed with tension, stared at them. Then Helen said, "I'm not picking that stuff up," and left the room.

Brenda looked at Daddy until his breathing began to ease down.

"I'll help you," the girl said softly as John got down to one knee and began picking up the debris from his sudden explosion of rage.

In the other room, the baby started to cry.

The next day the entire left side of John's face became paralyzed. This time he could not move it at all. He found it terrifying to look in a mirror and realize that the left side of his mouth did not respond to the command of a smile. His speech was forced out through the right side. He kept to himself as much as possible at work, hoping that it would go away by itself. When it didn't, he sought the help of a doctor. It was the most frightening thing he had ever experienced. He thought he had suffered a stroke, but the doctor told him it was caused by nerves. It took three months for it to clear up completely.

The paralysis even frightened Helen, so much so that she finally agreed to John's repeated requests that she visit with Reverend Grother.

"Just once," she said.

Dressed neatly in an expensive pale gray suit that accentuated the delicate texture of her skin, she sat stiffly in the pastor's office at church. She had combed her hair and applied her makeup carefully. She knew she had lost a good deal of her attractiveness because of her illnesses. It took longer now for her to make herself presentable. She hated to face the fact.

"What can we do for you, Helen?" Reverend Grother said to her. "Surely there's something we can do to help."

"Nothing. It was John who insisted I come."

As far as Helen could tell, the pastor and the church could never help her out of her depressions or her prolonged grief over the loss of Marvin. All she had in his place was John. He was unsatisfying; he was not wealthy, as he had led her to believe. He was such a goody-two shoes. He was too religious, too pious, too boring. And as she stubbornly thought through the litany of complaints she had no intention of sharing with John's pastor—for she never felt Grother was hers—she stopped just short of blurting outright to him that one of his "favorite parishioners" was a terrible lover.

She was polite with the pastor, but just as uncommunicative as she was with her psychiatrist. It was almost as though she had a tiny self-destruct mechanism somewhere deep within her unhappy psyche that would ensure nothing could help her out of her condition, her ravaging, self-perpetuating cycle of behavior.

In his usual stoic response to his own unhappiness, John focused his attention on other things. There was a new son in the household. From the moment Frederick was born, John began to push for a promotion at Sutherland Paper Corporation. Not only did he feel he was entitled to a position commensurate with his abilities, but he needed the extra income and the boost to his ego. Money seemed to be the only way to suppress the vaunted specter of Marvin Taylor.

But there was a resistance on the part of management. Something about John List put people off. He was too . . . what was the word? Straitlaced. Too . . . stiff. Too tense. Too . . . And words failed. On the other hand, he was a whiz with figures and extremely competent in his own work, to the point of obsession with every minute detail of the job—not necessarily a bad trait in an accountant. Eventually resistance waned, and in light of John's subtle but persistent pressure for advancement, management decided to give him a try.

In January of 1959, when Freddie was five months old, John was finally promoted to a management position. Not only did he supervise many of the staff accountants who worked in the areas of taxes and internal auditing, but the position was one in which his friend Peter Schneider, the supervisor of general accounting at Sutherland Paper Company, had to report to him.

"Wonderful," Helen said dully. Her head had been aching violently all day. All she wanted to do was put it down on a pillow. What was he talking about?

"It's a big increase."

"How big?"

"Two thousand three hundred dollars more," he said, hoping the raise would stimulate some kind of happy response out of her. "That's ninety-three hundred a year, Helen. More than a thirty two percent increase."

"Wonderful," she repeated dully. "Maybe now we can buy new rugs."

She went to lie down. He was terribly disappointed in her lack of enthusiasm, but that night, when he called Alma, the response was quite different.

"Yes," he said. "It's about time. I've finally gotten the raise I deserve."

"*Ja*," she agreed.

"The others are not as good as I am, *Mutter*. They aren't as intelligent."

"I'm not surprised."

"It's time for me to move up."

"This is only right."

"*Ja*," he agreed enthusiastically. He finally felt the power of his new supervisory capacity. With over seven thousand employees, Sutherland was Kalamazoo's second-largest company. He believed sincerely that his promotion was justified.

Then came Alma's inevitable questions. "How are the children? Fine . . . fine. And Helen?"

"The same," he admitted.

Alma decided not to pursue the subject over the phone. It would only spoil the joy of her son's good news. Instead she asked, "Do you like it in Kalamazoo?"

"It's all right. It rains a lot."

"*Ach. Vergiss deinen Schirm nicht.*"

And he reassured her that he wouldn't forget his umbrella.

"*Zieh deine Ueberschule an mein Lieber.*"

Nor his galoshes.

And then, "*Du bist ein sehr guter junger Mann.*"

Yes, he thought to himself with the intense pleasure of achievement, "I *am* a fine young man." His mother understood.

Sixty-nine-year-old Selma White was their next-door neighbor on Lovers Lane. She wasn't spying on the young couple, but she couldn't help noticing things—particularly the difference in the way young Mr. and Mrs. List handled their children. Mr. List was so attentive. He took them for walks, he played with them when he came home from work; but the mother!

Mrs. White could see from her window. There she was again, parking the boys in their carriages outside the house early in the morning.

At noontime they were still there. In the broiling sun! Mrs. White thought with stern disapproval. Sometimes Mr. List brought them in at noon. Once or twice Mrs. White was positive those children had been left outdoors all day until either the teenage daughter came home from school or the father came home from work to bring them indoors.

She tried to befriend the young woman who always looked so pale. There were times when the older woman's heart went out to the frail young mother who invariably felt ill. Maybe there was something she could do to help.

Mrs. List, however, was not receptive to small talk. She was very retiring and shy. The only time she had ever invited Mrs. White into her home was when they had new carpeting installed and she wanted to show it to her.

Mrs. White walked into the split level and saw that the entire living room had been carpeted in white rugs. "Oh," she murmured, not knowing what to say. "How . . . lovely!" What she really thought was that Mrs. List's choice of colors was foolish, extremely extravagant. You can't let little children play on white rugs, she thought. Helen sensed her disapproval. The visit did not last long. She did not even offer her neighbor a cup of coffee.

Helen wanted white! She wanted its brightness, its purity. There was little enough joy in her life. Why couldn't she have white carpeting if she wanted it? The children didn't have to play in the living room, did they? There were other places to play. The living room could be for the adults. She found herself crying for no reason. An overwhelming sadness gripped her. Postpartum blues, she thought, but too much time had passed to blame the blues on the hormonal changes in her body after her delivery. The pregnancies, one right after another, kept her body in a constant state of hormonal flux. She was not well. She felt ill all the time. She felt achy. She cried. She wanted the white rugs. She wanted her own way. For once she wanted the happiness that white rugs would bring.

"She's not the kind of mother that your son is a father," Mrs. White whispered to the older Mrs. List when she came to visit the young family. "He's always very kind and polite to me."

Alma smiled.

Mrs. White surmised that he was used to being kind to older

ladies. She wasn't surprised. He was like that with his mother.

Seventy-two-year-old Alma visited frequently. She and Mrs. White became immediate friends. What a lovely woman, Mrs. White thought. Tall. Beautiful stature. Erect. Held herself like a queen with a crown of white hair and a sweet, generous smile. Her son looked a little like her, same-shaped face and eyes, same glasses, same stature. How could she know that Helen List hated the frequent visits, or that Brenda felt rejected when Alma insisted that she call her "Mother List" while the other children were taught to call her "Grandma"?

A roll of the dice, and the Civil War was about to be fought again on Lovers Lane. This time the opposing generals were John List and Peter Schneider. John and Peter had been fellow staff accountants at Sutherland until Peter was made supervisor of general accounting. Now, with the promotion, List had become his boss. Peter knew others thought List was a bit peculiar, but he rather liked him. He also had respect for the man's brains and the precision of his planning and methodology. Together they had devised a system to computerize many of the company's accounting functions that proved to be quite innovative and effective. John's input and expertise had been essential to its success. During the process of development they had become friends. When John began inviting him to his house to play "war games," he willingly agreed.

It was always the same. Slices of homemade cherry pie to the right, a dice roll to the left, and the battle began. Sometimes they switched wars and it was the Battle of Anzio Beach. Tonight it was the Battle of Bull Run.

Peter always assumed List's wife, Helen, had baked the cherry pies John served at the onset of the games, although he was never sure. She was a phantom-like figure in the background. He saw her move in the hallway across from the table where they had the board set up. She rarely came in to say hello. Invariably the children were already in bed.

But suddenly, in the middle of one of the games, three-year-old John junior came into the room. He looked as though he'd just wakened from a bad dream. His eyes were puffy, and he looked unhappy.

"Where's your mother?" John asked.

"Sleeping," the child said.

John excused himself to Peter and took the boy up the half flight of steps in the split level to the bedroom floor and disappeared for a few moments.

He put John junior to bed.

He looked in on Helen.

She was lying on her back, stretched out across the foot of their bed.

He could tell by the puffy look on her face that the sleep had been induced by drink rather than by natural fatigue.

While John was upstairs, Peter took the time to plan his next move. John was three steps ahead of him again. He was such a brilliant strategist. Peter imagined that was the reason he invited him home to play the game, since he didn't seem to have much of a social life. After Peter was reasonably sure of his next move, he went into the kitchen to get a drink of water while John was upstairs with the youngster. The kitchen table showed remnants of dinner, and the sink was stacked high with dishes and soiled pots. He felt a bit uncomfortable. It was not the first time he'd had the distinct feeling that Helen left a good many domestic chores for John to do.

He heard a footstep behind him and turned to see List standing in the doorway looking at him. His expression was inscrutable. "More pie?" John asked as he cut another slice of warm pie from the pie plate on the counter next to the stove.

"Yeah, sure. Some mess with kids, huh?" Peter joked, referring to the piled-up sink.

"I'll get to them after the game," John said as he led the way into the dining room where the board was set up. "Let's finish."

"Sure."

"I believe it was your move."

"I think you got me again," Peter said, shaking his head.

There was a sense of power behind the apparently mild smile List projected. And Peter became aware of the suddenly transparent coexisting images of the henpecked husband, the brilliant strategist in board games, the religious zealot, and the ambitious executive he presented at Sutherland.

Who is John List? he thought to himself. He wondered what he was like when something disturbed the careful balance he had structured for himself.

"Your move," John urged again.

Peter rolled the dice and concentrated on the board. He couldn't get over it. The man was an absolute genius when it came to strategy. In all the times they had played together, he had never been able to win even one game from his quiet co-worker. List had to win. He might put the children to bed. He might wash the dishes after the game. He might even get down on his hands and knees and scrub the floor. But he had to win. He had to prove himself on the board. With a sudden flash of insight, Peter realized that it was one way for John to be in control of his life, in "command." John would have made a great general, Peter thought, at least in the area of strategic planning. He wasn't too terrific at handling people, it seemed to him, either on the job or at home.

The more difficult Helen became, the more John turned to the comfort of his church. By now Helen had stopped attending church altogether. John's constant presence at the church made her lack of attendance even more noticeable. People never saw much of Helen unless they went to the house, which they continued to do at the pastor's urging.

"It doesn't work, Pastor," Mrs. Putnam said with a sigh, frankly tired of trying.

But Grother couldn't give up. He continued to try desperately to involve Helen. She continually refused.

Within the congregation, many phrases were used to describe her, ranging from "withdrawn" to "extravagant" to a guiltily whispered, "Someone who drinks too much."

John knew that everyone knew. The rumors even spread to his job.

In the office one day, Peter was standing at John's desk listening to his newly appointed boss give him instructions about figures needed on one of the company accounts when the phone on John's desk rang.

"Get that, will you?" John said, absorbed in jotting down some numbers.

Peter picked up the phone. "Mr. List's office."

"Let me talk to him, please," came a woman's voice. A thin film of hysteria was layered over the demand.

"It's your wife," Peter said to John.

John took the receiver Peter handed to him. "Hello . . ."

And Peter could hear the woman's voice on the other end of the line raised so loudly that he could almost make out the words. John glanced at him in embarrassment. Peter quickly lowered his eyes and busied himself with some papers on the desk.

"Calm down, dear," John said quietly into the phone. "What's the problem?"

He listened for a moment. Then he replaced the receiver in its cradle.

"I'm going to have to leave for a while."

"Is something wrong?"

John hesitated. He didn't have a car. He was a part of a carpool the two of them had begun. "May I borrow your car for a little while?" he asked. "I have to run home for a few minutes."

"What's the matter?"

"Helen is upset. . . ." John's face turned crimson. He couldn't look into Peter's face as he said, "Our son . . . the baby . . . has soiled his diaper." Suddenly his face changed. Now his face turned bright red with rage. "She doesn't want to change it! She'll leave him like that all day if I don't go home to do it!"

Peter had never seen him so heated. The intensity of his sudden fury was frightening. For the first time, Peter became consciously aware of John's physical size, as though in anger, his broadness and large head loomed to their full proportions.

Peter stared at him. "You're kidding," he said, backing away unconsciously.

As suddenly as the rage had erupted, it subsided. He watched as John composed himself and went to get his coat. The weather had turned misty and damp. There was a stiff, businesslike demeanor in his quick movements as he sat to pull on his rubbers over his shoes. He stood up and with a quick jerk of his broad shoulders shrugged himself into his heavy overcoat. Then he wrapped his scarf around his neck and glanced at Peter.

Peter quickly reached into his pocket and pulled out a large ring of keys. John stood silently by the edge of the cluttered desk as Peter struggled clumsily to release the car keys from the ring. John's face was beginning to puff with red splotches. It seemed to take forever to release the keys. Finally he handed John the ignition key of his car.

"Thank you."

"The car is parked by—"

"I know where it is."

"What should I say if . . ." He hesitated. "If anyone asks where you are?"

"Tell them I had an emergency at home and that I'll be back shortly," he said in a clipped voice.

An emergency, John thought with some rancor as he left the room. "He messed in his pants again," she had said. "I'm not changing him!" she had said. "If you want him changed, *you* come home and do it!" she had said.

The moment the door closed behind him, Peter got up and walked to the desk of a fellow accountant. "You are not going to believe this!" he said.

So many people knew. John was aware that they knew. That was the worst part for him. When he returned, everyone's eyes turned to look at him as he retraced his steps back to his office.

The incident did not bode well for John on his job. Eventually the story got back to his superiors. Peter should not have said anything. After all, John was a friend as well as his superior. But the incident had been so bizarre that he'd found himself blurting it out before he had stopped to consider how much damage it could do to John's already tenuous image to have it known that he went home to change his son's diaper in the middle of the day on the outrageous demand of a wife who was obviously suffering serious mental disturbances.

"That's what he chose to do," Peter said, suddenly indignant for John's sake. "I certainly wouldn't handle it that way, but . . . he chose to go home."

He shook his head, still finding the incident difficult to comprehend.

"Helen," John said, "there's going to be a party."

She stopped what she was doing. She seemed confused, in pain.

"I thought you didn't like parties. You never want to go out," she said, bewildered.

"I thought you'd like to go."

"But you always say 'no.' You always—"

"Just this once," he said gently. "It might do you good. We'll buy you a new dress and we'll go. Would you like that?"

He knew he was spending too much money. Marvin had never had money. Army men didn't usually have much. It was the one area in which, on a comparative level, he could do better than Helen's first husband. Sometimes it seemed to work, at least for a while.

"Go, Mommy," Brenda said. "You always look so pretty when you get dressed."

Helen smiled a melancholy smile. "You come shopping with me, Brenda. Okay?"

* * *

The party was at Peter's house. When they arrived, Helen made quite an impression. She looked stunning in the new dress that accentuated the slender beauty of her long neck. She smiled shyly. She moved about gracefully. She sat with her ankles crossed. She accepted every cocktail that was offered to her. John worried.

She got drunk.

She started flirting outrageously with Peter. She started telling him about Marvin, how in some ways Peter reminded her of her first husband. Then, when she started comparing John with Marvin, her voice grew louder. As usual, the comparison was unfavorable. Everyone was embarrassed. John knew she was talking through a film of alcohol. "John isn't at all like Marvin," she said. "He died a hero's death in Korea, charging up a hill, saving his men..." She turned to John while others in the room stared at the floor in embarrassment.

Peter thought, Why doesn't he shut her up!

But John didn't know how.

"All you did was push a pencil." She laughed. "Easy to fight a paper war behind a desk, isn't it. Let the other guys die for their country. Not you!"

Peter immediately filled in the awkward silence that followed by starting a loud conversation with someone standing next to him. He turned his back on the Lists to stop them from being the center of attention and to try to save face for John; the man was literally twitching. But Peter was not really paying attention to his own conversation. He let the other fellow do the talking while he found himself thinking again, Who is John List? Seeing the couple in action, he was beginning to be able to insert the hidden ingredients into the formula. List was obviously trying to measure up to this woman's idealized vision of her dead-hero first husband, he thought. By becoming a big-shot executive. By throwing money around. But if anyone should know, *he* should know that approach was poor strategy. If he were a powerhouse kind of guy instead of the quiet bookworm he really was, he would have handled it differently. He would have been able to confront the ghost hero head on. He would have forced Helen into serious psychiatric care.

The Lists left the party early. Helen knew that the wonderful impression she had initially made when they'd entered the room had changed dramatically by the time they left. She berated John for having brought her to the party. She cried all the way home. He didn't say a word.

* * *

In 1960, when Brenda was seventeen, she ran away with Wayne Herndon. They drove south across the state line to Indiana, where they tried to get married. However, when the justice of the peace realized they were both underage, he refused to perform the ceremony and urged them both to return to their homes.

"We'll go somewhere else," the boy told her in angry frustration as he stepped on the accelerator of his car. They didn't get very far. An automobile accident hospitalized Wayne with minor injuries, and Brenda was forced to give the hospital their names and addresses upon admittance. Doctors at the hospital called both sets of parents.

John and Helen List showed up immediately. This time they calmly lectured the two teenagers on the folly of their attempted elopement.

"There's plenty of time for marriage," Helen said. "Don't rush into things. Don't be in such a hurry."

All Brenda could think of was that Mom had three children, whom she, Brenda, spent most of her spare time taking care of. If she had to take care of children, they might as well be her own. With Patty, John, and Freddie, she had all of the responsibility of watching over them but none of the say in how to do it. She just followed instructions. Sometimes she would have liked to do things differently. And besides, she loved Wayne.

"I just don't want to live at home anymore," Brenda said rebelliously, and then felt a little contrite when Daddy looked at her with his large sad eyes, not asking why because he already understood why.

He never cuts me down if I do something wrong, she thought guiltily. Not even about the baby. Not really. It was just that he cares what happens to me, she thought, rewriting the history of her own feelings at the time. But he really *was* always there for her if she needed him. She sincerely felt that, too. Yet aloud she said, "We don't want to wait anymore."

"Brenda, you're both too young," her mother insisted.

"You got married at fifteen."

"That was different."

"Don't argue with your mother," John said quietly, not wanting to hear again why it had been "different" with Marvin. "You have to think of your future. We have plans to send you to college." He turned to Wayne. "And you, young man, before you take such a step, you have to think of your own future and of how you will support a wife.''

''I'll be able to take care of her,'' Wayne said with boyish confidence.

''Not now,'' Helen said softly. ''We can't give our consent. College first. I want Brenda to make something of herself.''

Brenda had other plans. Soon she would turn eighteen. Then there would be no way anyone could stop her from getting married and playing house on her own, without all of the tension and the sickness and the fighting.

When Sutherland Paper merged with Kalamazoo Vegetable Parchment in 1961 and became K.V.P. Sutherland Paper Co., John's professional problems began to match his personal ones. He was sure that the merger would mean another promotion for him, and he readily asked for one. But List got a bad job performance rating when executives found he had difficulty managing people. Not only was he such a perfectionist that he was unable to delegate responsibility—he had to do everything himself—but he couldn't seem to assert himself when dealing with subordinates.

George Vandem was the corporate compensation manager of the newly merged company. He was young, aggressive, and tough, and he wasn't happy.

''Look, List,'' he said after having called John into his office for a private conference, ''I'm going to give it to you straight. We don't think you handle your people well. A supervisor loses his effectiveness if his people take advantage of him. I'm sorry, but we're simply going to have to ask you for your resignation.'' The message was blunt and to the point. John was fired.

John had never been fired before. His cheeks burned with embarrassment. How had he ''lost his effectiveness'' as a supervisor? How would he tell Helen? What would she say? What would people think when they found out he had been fired?

''We suggest you begin looking elsewhere,'' Vandem continued. These things were better done quickly. No sense in dragging it out. ''Some of your time with us has been more than adequate. Good, in fact. We'll be glad to give you a recommendation if you need one.''

List stood up to his full height and loomed over the desk. Vandem instinctively tensed his muscles in a preparatory response to an unexpected surge of intimidation, but List turned and left the office, striding swiftly with the erect posture of a military man.

After the initial shock of dismissal, John became rigid with anger. How could this be happening to him? So many of the other men on the job were *stupid* compared with him. How could this be happening? He was filled with righteous indignation. But he immediately repressed his true feelings and began to make plans for his next step.

Peter Schneider was shocked at List's dismissal. He even tried to come to his defense. He knew Vandem liked him, and he could speak frankly. "I know he comes across like a bumbling numbers cruncher," he said passionately. "But he's not like that at all. Not really. He's got a will of iron in some things. And I happen to think he's brilliant in his work."

"Not in a managerial capacity, Peter."

"The man has a lot of problems at home, too."

"You know I can't take that into consideration. It's better all around if he goes. People don't take to him."

"I do."

"That makes one."

Peter had to accept the inevitable finality of management's decision. He was overwhelmed with sadness for his friend and for the irony of life. From the time of the merger, he knew List had kept looking up the ranks. He wanted to be moved up, and the jobs he aspired to were filled by people not much older than himself. There was little chance of promotion through attrition. Peter told him so, but List kept trying. And now, instead of the promotion he so desperately yearned for, he'd been fired.

John did not tell Helen. He decided to get a new job first.

In his indignation at having been terminated, he did not acknowledge the desperation behind the methodical approach he took to looking for new employment:

1) List each company in his private ledger.
2) Categorize all the possibilities.
3) List the pros and cons of each position.
4) Match his abilities with the needs of each company.
5) Write a cover letter.
6) Send his résumé.
7) Mark it in his book.
8) Acknowledge all responses in one column.
9) Select companies for interviews in another column.
10) Mark down impressions of each one in a third.

And under each category, the pattern of rigid preoccupation with trivial procedural details that had always marked his life persisted. Each category had dozens of careful notations. The perfectionism he imposed upon his approach shielded him from dealing with the broader picture, the fact that he was unemployed and looking for a job. In a way, the conscientious attention to each facet of his applications became a comfort to him.

On his résumé, he listed only three children. Brenda did not know that in a sense he had already cut her and her sins out of his life simply by not acknowledging her existence on his job applications.

On July 14, 1961, he was hired as general supervisor of accounting with a relatively unknown company in Rochester, N.Y., called Xerox Corporation.

He told Peter that he had also received one other job offer from a more established firm, but he was going to try Xerox. "I'm taking a calculated risk in going with them," he said. "A roll of the dice. They're smaller, but I think they have a future." He did not realize that the roll of the dice on this board game was making him a winner again. Xerox indeed had a future. Its copy machines were to revolutionize office procedures forever.

"We'll miss you."

Peter thought List looked at him strangely, as though he couldn't believe anyone would say that to him. "I'll miss you, too," John said.

"And our games," Peter said with a gentle smile. "I'll find someone else. Maybe I'll be able to win once in a while since I learned the game from you."

He could tell John was pleased. He had a warm smile. He really was such a sweet guy.

Peter watched as List went into Vandem's office to say goodbye.

"Xerox, eh," Vandem said.

"It's a small company. I think it has a future."

"What made you pick Rochester?"

"I didn't really pick it. It was just one of the ads I answered."

"Well, good luck. I'm glad you came up with something so quickly, List."

"I answered between ninety and ninety five ads in *The Wall Street Journal* before I took the job with Xerox."

Vandam thought it strange that anyone would be that methodical. Ninety to ninety five ads! But aloud he said, "Nice town. You'll like it there."

16 | Breaking Down

It was not going to be easy to pick up the family and move it to Rochester.

"Not again," Helen had cried. "Oh, please, not again."

She had nagged him constantly about money, about his lack of competence in every major and important aspect of their lives. And now this. She absolutely hated the thought of moving again. Since their marriage this would make the fifth time they would have packed up their entire household. The emotional dislocation became more difficult with each move. And now with all the children it was even worse.

"We'll *have* to move," he said in his controlled, deep-toned voice. "There's nothing to discuss."

"I don't want to."

"The job calls for—"

"Why in the world did you have to go and look for another job, anyway?"

"It was necessary."

She grasped the back of her head to try to squeeze away the tension. She was sure she had been having frequent recurrences of malaria lately, the last one less than six months ago. She was already flushed with the onset of fever, and even though the force of the argument was giving her the strength to fight the accompanying chills, pretty soon she would be forced to her bed again. "At least when I moved around with Marvin we went to interesting places all over the world," she said. "That's the military for you. Where does *accounting* take you? Rochester! I hate the North. It's too cold!" she complained bitterly.

He grimaced and swallowed the angry response he felt . . . and instead quietly repeated, "We'll have to move." The effort to control himself gave his voice even more resonance than usual.

"You think it's good for the kids to move so much?" she persisted. "They can never get settled anywhere. You think you're

such a terrific father! You think it's good for them? Well, it's not.
And it's not good for me.''

"That's where the job is!" he murmured.

"What was the matter mater with the old one?"

She wouldn't stop. And he finally had to tell her that the move
had been necessary.

"Why!"

Because he had been terminated from his job. . . .

She stared at him. Her eyes filled with tears of frustration. "I
might have known," she said. "Why'd you have to get fired?"

"I don't know."

"What did you do?"

"Nothing."

"That's probably the point," she said bitterly, and burst into
tears. All of a sudden her head felt as though it would explode with
pain. She desperately needed a drink.

Brenda heard it all.

"Oh, dear," she heard her mother say, suddenly giggling through
her tears. "We'll have to join a new church again. My, my . . . what
will Reverend Grother think? And the dear ladies from the Ultra
Guild?"

Brenda watched her mother reach for the bottle the moment her
furious stepfather left the room. Helen took it with her into her
bedroom.

The girl found herself terribly torn between them. On the one
hand, she knew the instability of her mother's condition. Even if
she didn't always know what was the matter with her, she knew
her mother frequently felt violently ill. Sometimes the drinking
seemed to overwhelm her afflictions and keep her calm. Other times
the drinking either provoked her illness or magnified her pains.
Moving again would be a desperate hardship for her. On the other
hand, Brenda felt sorry for her stepfather, too. He was doing the
best he could to support the family. Maybe people didn't always
like him—she'd always known that—but he was good at his job.
She was sure of that, too. And Mom didn't make it any easier on
him.

Mom had been drinking a lot lately, she thought. And Daddy . . .
he still jumped every time she demanded anything. Even Aunt Jean
made fun of him. "Doesn't he have a brain of his own?" she'd
always say. Brenda didn't know for whom she felt sorrier. They
were both so pathetic, she thought.

She knew Mom wasn't going to be very helpful or cooperative
during the transition. Her own resentment had built up considerably

by the time she was in the kitchen preparing dinner for the family again. Patty was six, John junior was about five, and Freddie was only three. Most of the packing would fall to Daddy and to her, Brenda thought resentfully. Helen sat at the kitchen table watching as Brenda pressed hamburger patties. She sipped a drink, gently slipping backward in time into her idealized memories of her first love.

"When the time comes," Helen said to Brenda through the growing serenity of an alcoholic haze, "make sure you marry the right one. Someone like your father. Your real father. John isn't good, not like your daddy. With your daddy," she said dreamily, "the walls would shake and the earth would move. . . ."

Brenda felt uncomfortable hearing about her father's sexual prowess again and about Daddy's poor sexual performance by comparison. She didn't want to hear about their sex life. It embarrassed her. She slapped the patties harder than necessary. She wouldn't listen. Besides, she had Wayne to think of.

And she was thinking about him as she lay in bed later that night. Then she heard them.

Mom was berating Daddy again, loudly enough for Brenda to hear through the closed doors. It was so clear to her what the problem was. He was trying to appease her, to make her feel better, but he wasn't performing up to expectations again. It's impotence, Brenda thought to herself. That's one of the problems. I'm sure of it.

She jumped out of bed at the sound of the yelling. She went to her door, opened it quietly, and peeked out into the dimness of the hallway. She saw John run out of his bedroom, tears actually streaming from his eyes. She could hear her mother crying in the room behind him. He stood uncertainly for a moment, then he tiptoed to the room across the hall shared by John junior and Freddie. He retreated inside, where he would spend the remainder of the night.

Maybe she had to go to Rochester with them right now, Brenda resolved as she quietly closed her bedroom door against the pitiable scene she had witnessed, but as soon as she could, she would leave them and return to Kalamazoo, where she had made friends, where Wayne was.

The family moved to a rented three-story house at 140 Clearbrook Drive in Rondequoit, a suburb of Rochester. The year was 1962. John was thirty-five at the time, Helen was thirty-four, and Brenda was nearly eighteen. The moment she passed her eighteenth birthday, true to her promise to herself, she immediately left home to return to Kalamazoo, where she married her boyfriend, Wayne Herndon.

Although Helen had scarcely had anything to do with Brenda since the time of the child's pregnancy, never having been able to forgive her completely, once Brenda was gone Helen missed her desperately.

But then she began to feel a bit better in Rochester after they had settled into their new home. She stopped drinking. Removal of alcohol from her system created a marked improvement in her well-being. She wasn't taking as many sedatives, either, so she couldn't explain the strange incident when she was certain that she had blacked out. She found herself on the bedroom floor with at least an hour of time unaccounted for. When she awoke, she had a terrible black-and-blue mark on her arm as though she had fallen. Since she hadn't been drinking, it must be a recurrence of the malaria, she rationalized, brushing away her fears.

She joined the Faith Lutheran Church with John; and when their new neighbor, Connie Anderson, asked her to join in raising funds for a local cancer drive, she readily agreed.

Helen liked Connie Anderson. Connie had a way of making people feel comfortable and easy. She had an infectious smile and a wonderful sense of humor, making the time they spent together raising funds for the Cancer Crusade a lot of fun. Without the burden of pregnancy or illness or drink, some of Helen's natural personality began to reappear for the first time in a long spell; she was attractive, even bubbly, and she was always very well dressed.

Her husband lets her buy so many clothes, Connie thought, more than she could ever wear, but she did look pretty, and he seemed to want to please her so much. It was nice to see them smile at each other since Connie had the feeling that under the veneer of the pleasant, close-knit family that they always presented to the outside world—going to church together, going to the park with the children—they were really a troubled couple. There always seemed to be a discernible edge of tension when they were together that she couldn't help sensing, but she could be wrong. They were nice neighbors, enjoyable people, she thought. Mr. List was not as outgoing as his wife, but he was very polite, and their young daughter was a delightful little girl, so grown-up for six years.

"I'm going to help Mommy cook dinner tonight," she said proudly. She had beautiful dark brown eyes.

"Why, Patty, what a big girl you are," Connie smiled.

Little by little Helen's strength revived in Rochester. She was feeling so much better that she even accompanied John to Mexico for a company convention. She hadn't suffered with a bout of depression in weeks. The irritability that dominated her waking hours had eased. Only intense displeasure could swing her moods to extremes of rage and despair. Nothing seemed to bother her too much lately. I'm getting better, she thought hopefully. Better. Not that there was anything seriously wrong with her anymore. That was all in the past. Almost fifteen years ago. There *was* that one time a few weeks ago when she was sure she had passed out, but she didn't like to think about it. When John told her about the convention, she was excited about accompanying him to Mexico, where it would be fun, and it would be a welcome change, and it would be warm. Sometimes, on her shopping expeditions for the right clothes to bring, she felt dizzy, but she wouldn't let the minor "spells" interfere with the joy of shopping.

In Mexico her illness began again. The insidious depression crept up like fog on a warm morning clashing with a chilly night, the characteristic irritability she had always demonstrated dominating their every waking moment together. John responded with impatience at her mood swings, rigid determination that she should "pull herself together." She reacted with vengeful attacks on his manhood to get even for his lack of understanding and insight.

On the way back from Mexico, silence settled in between them, giving them both some merciful peace.

When they stopped in Kalamazoo to visit Brenda, John left Helen with her while he went to visit his friend, Peter Schneider. Not only did he want to get away from Helen for a while—a brief, necessary respite—but he wanted to discuss with Peter matters he could not share with his wife.

Peter was delighted to see how well his old friend was doing. "You like it at Xerox, then?"

"*Like* it? I was right. There is where the future is," John said enthusiastically. "This is a period of phenomenal growth for the company. Right now. Have you heard of its '914 Copier'?"

"Yes, as a matter of fact. Who hasn't?"

"It was only introduced on the market in 1959, but it has launched us as a major corporation. Xerox is even listed on the New York Stock Exchange."

"That's wonderful," Peter said, sincerely pleased that his friend had made the right choice when he'd accepted employment with the young company. "And you? You're doing well there?"

"Yes." List knew that management thought of him as a mild-mannered gentleman and a devoted family man. He also knew he was building up an outstanding record with the company. Management had made that abundantly clear to him. "Peter," he said with pride, "I've helped the company to implement a billing procedure that allows it to assess a 'per copy' fee along with the normal rental fees for its machines.''—not an altogether revolutionary concept, but an important contribution nevertheless.

A very subtle arrogance in his demeanor as he talked to Peter showed that John's aspirations were once again making him set his gaze higher up in the ranks of the corporation, something that had not boded well for him in his previous job with Sutherland. But then again, Peter had always thought John List was brilliant; and if he continued to show his strengths with innovative billing procedures as well as new cost-effective accounting programs, there was no telling how high he could rise with an internationally growing company that had such a luminous financial future.

Still, something inside Peter made him think. John's best bet would be to work alone, a private think tank kind of thing. He shouldn't be involved too closely with people. Aloud, Peter asked carefully, "And your wife? How are things going with you two these days? And the children?"

"Fine," John said with grim good humor, too proud to reveal the truth to a friend who was looking at him with admiration. "Everything is fine. The children, too. All problems solved."

Helen pretended no such fanciful scenario with her daughter. When Brenda asked her mother how Mexico had been, her reply made it clear that it hadn't been a good trip. Being in such close proximity, with no one but each other to depend on for company, was bound to create further rupturing in the already delicate fabric of their relationship. They had returned more apart than when they'd started, and Mom looked pale and frail. The journey had obviously tired her greatly.

Not long after returning to Rochester, Helen began drinking and taking pills again to calm the stresses of her life. She no longer had Brenda's help. She now had full responsibility for all three children, and it was more than she could handle. She was beginning to feel sick again, practically all the time. Drinking dulled the headaches. Medication dulled the after-effects of the drinking. The vicious cycle was in full swing. Her depressions were severe and oppressive again.

She was a very sick woman. John saw it only as sinfulness.

Meanwhile, John was actually in his creative prime. He kept up an intense pace on the job with a methodology and precision that enhanced his workload capacity, while at the same time he took on many of the burdens at home that Helen's illness imposed upon him. His energy was bolstered by the certitude of his righteous approach to life. His daily prayers at the table became more resolute and longer. He refused to acknowledge the possibility that Helen's illness was anything other than self-imposed. He still believed that willpower and prayer were all that were necessary, while she still felt that this insistence of his was not only nonsupportive, but a moral reproach. Frequent back-and-forth phone calls with *Mutter* only reinforced the rigidity of his position.

No matter how hard he worked, John still had his worries on the job. Xerox Corporation was growing at an unprecedented rate. Even the most prophetic of its managerial personnel could not have foreseen the true magnitude of the "era of mass copying" when it first announced its revolutionary 914 Copier. They were always too conservative in their projections of actual revenue and progress. "Xeroxing" became the generic word for copying, just as Kleenex had become the generic word for tissue. *Fortune* magazine called the 914 "the most successful product ever manufactured in America."

Xerox's phenomenal success proved a mixed blessing for John List. Although he had risen steadily in position within the ranks, now, with the tremendous growth of the company, he was deeply worried that he might get left behind in the swell when it came time for promotions. He tried to discuss his job-related uncertainties with Helen, but her immediate expression of disdain made him withdraw.

"Are you in trouble again?" she asked.

"No."

"Please don't lie to me, John," she begged. "Are you in trouble with the company?"

"No!"

She couldn't stand it. Every time she felt even a little comfortable, or settled, or secure, something happened to disrupt everything. The last thing she wanted to contemplate was another change. Another move. She told herself she actually liked it in Rochester. She had made friends—not his stuffed-shirt church friends, but genuine neighbors, she told herself. She hadn't felt so at home anyplace since she had left Newport News, Virginia, over ten years earlier. In the daily daze of her illness, she didn't know that her friends were aware of her solitary drinking and spoke of it in hushed whispers among themselves. Connie Anderson tried to defend Helen, but the other neighbors noticed the slurred speech, the slight mist in the eyes, and wondered about the children.

To John, Helen's problems were always emotionally related, never physical, except as related to the after-effects of her drinking. He reproached himself for bringing up his concerns about Xerox. He could tell she was genuinely worried about moving again and decided it would not be good to communicate his anxieties to her.

Instead he went to his own source of comfort, his church.

This time he felt free to seek pastoral intervention, perhaps because this time he was not as close to the pastor as he had been in his other parishes. He was not serving on any church committees at Faith Lutheran Church because he didn't have time. These were the busy years, both at home and on the job. He was sure the pastor understood. His job responsibilities were growing. The pressures were intensifying under the weight of the competition he perceived all about him. His children were growing . . . Helen was . . .

But John was the kind of individual who couldn't really reach out for help openly. He actually spent much of his time with the pastor reassuring him that everything was fine. Only the most astute professional would have recognized the great need underneath the pride. The more desperate he became internally, the more self-assured he appeared externally. He conveyed an aura of confidence that was difficult to penetrate. Reverend Saresky thought he might be having problems, but it was easy to completely miss the great need through the self-assured picture he presented.

"When it comes time for promotions," John told the pastor, "some people could be left behind." His voice was steady.

"Why, John?"

"The company is still hiring," he continued. "They want to hire people who already have experience at large established corporations."

"Why should that matter to you?"

"It doesn't, really." His eyes never wavered.

"You certainly have experience. And you certainly have demonstrated your worth to the company."

"Yes, of course. I'm not worried. Some of my colleagues are." He was staring with steady eyes directly at the pastor as he spoke. "With management, it's always 'What have you done for me lately?' 'What can you do for me this minute?' 'What are you going to contribute tomorrow?' " he said. "So they worry."

Seeing through the shyness the pastor believed was an integral part of John's personality structure, he felt John seemed bright, secure, indestructible, in complete control. Reverend Saresky could tell that John wasn't seriously troubled by the expansion of the company, although he was actually talking more than usual. Ordinarily the man was shy to the point of being almost totally noncommunicative.

"There are constant shifts in personnel," he continued. "Constant. Changes every day."

Reverend Saresky knew all too well what he meant. Faith Lutheran Church was in the neighboring community. Many Xerox employees were members of his congregation. He knew that the stress level at this time was almost beyond endurance for many of them. People who had worked for the company for twenty-five years would suddenly find an executive and security officer at their sides, and they would be told to empty out their desks and turn in their badges, and they would then be escorted to the door. He knew it was due to the sudden rise in Japanese firms and Xerox's need, as management saw it, to clean house. Personally, he thought they did it ruthlessly. He knew that no one's job was secure and that the lack of security often had something to do with destabilizing home life. He also knew that John List's home life was already unstable. He would never forget his pastoral visit to their home when they'd first joined the congregation. There was no question in his mind that there was love in the home, but they were obviously also going through some very stressful times. He couldn't believe it when Helen had told him in front of John about her former marriage to a Green Beret officer and made a comment that if John were half the man that her husband was, they wouldn't have the troubles they were having. It was very painful for the pastor to hear. Nor was it an isolated incident. In all three times he visited the family in their home, Helen made the same unfavorable comparison. John never reacted, a point the pastor thought was unnatural.

"The personnel shifts," Reverend Saresky said, looking for clues to the change in John's behavior. Was he actually asking for help now? "Are they affecting your job?"

"No," John said noncommittally, even though he was sure that they were. "The company has enormous expectations of everyone. We're expanding at such a tremendous rate, mushrooming internationally. Some of the others are going to be left behind. Unable to measure up."

John couldn't bring himself to confide that the pressures were enormous for him, too. He couldn't tell the pastor that he was beginning to perceive the first shadows of the handwriting on the wall for himself, faint but indelible. That *he* might get left behind. And then what? The family had obviously come to depend on the salary he was bringing home. Helen was extremely careless in her budgeting, and he himself was overspending constantly to improve her view of him.

"Maybe they'll shift me around, too. Send me to another department that is not in my area of expertise. Or maybe—" the unthinkable—"I could lose my job altogether."

The pastor showed genuine concern. It already had happened to many of his congregants. "Is that a possibility?"

Suddenly John smiled shyly. "No. I'm just projecting the worst possible scenario. The paranoia of my colleagues is catching. I'm very secure in my position." His eyes were steady again. "Actually, I've implemented some very important new procedures. They know that."

The pastor was happy things were going so well for the man he had always respected as a devout husband, a kind father, and an excellent provider for his young family. He wished all of his parishioners were like John List. He was a regular churchgoer. Every week, without fail, he and his children were sitting in their usual pew for Sunday worship. They were an inspiration to the rest of the congregation. But Helen rarely accompanied them. The fly in the ointment, he thought sadly. He knew Helen's lack of participation was a great source of pain to John. "How *is* Helen?" he asked.

"Oh, she's much better," he lied to the pastor. "Much. One thing, though . . ." He hesitated. "I wish I could spend more time at home. Mostly, I'm on the job twelve hours a day. I wish I had more time to spend with the children. They're usually asleep when I get home, and they like it so much when I can get down on the floor with them and play games."

"You won't always be so busy, John." But he could see the man was exhausted.

"No . . ."

"And God will bless you with the serenity you deserve."

John smiled. "Yes, I know."

After he left, the pastor couldn't help wondering why List had to spend so much time on the job. Despite his denials, even in light of job insecurity, twelve hours a day seemed excessive to him. He shook his head and wondered whether the man was even in the right profession.

Katie De Maio pulled up into her driveway. She could see Patty, Johnny, and Freddie List in their own driveway next door. The boys were seated on the edge of the lawn playing a quiet game with a series of miniature toy trucks. Patty was seated on her front doorstep nearby, watching them.

"Hi, kids," Katie called over.

The boys looked up, smiled, and went back to their game, moving their trucks up and down the grooves they had worn into the edge of the grass.

Patty got up, said something to them, and walked across to the De Maio driveway as Katie pulled two loaded grocery bags out of her car. "How you doing?" Katie asked cheerfully as she slammed her car door shut with her knee.

"Mom isn't feeling good today," Patty said to her.

"What's the matter?" Katie asked, immediately surmising that Helen was alcoholically under the weather again.

"She's in bed," the seven-year-old child said.

"Is there something I can do to help?"

"On, no. Daddy does it."

And Katie realized that was true. She'd often seen John List at the supermarket doing the family shopping. Straight from work. In his suit and tie. Piling the cart full. Once when they happened to be standing on line together at the checkout counter, he'd asked her, "How do you usually prepare Campbell's tomato soup? With water or milk?"

"Usually with water. Unless I want it to be cream of tomato."

"Isn't it more nutritious with milk?"

"Oh, yes, of course."

"I'll make it with milk," he'd murmured almost to himself.

And Katie knew that this tall, heavy-boned man with the deep voice and large hands was going to go home and cook dinner for his family.

Another time she and her husband ran into him and the three children at the July 4th Community Fair held on the high school grounds. Helen wasn't with them.

"No," she said to her husband, Neil, as they watched the family move away from them toward the merry-go-round. "Connie Anderson can defend Helen List all she wants; she's a good, loyal friend. But that woman doesn't take care of those kids. He does it all. Even this. Taking them to the fair alone."

"Aw, c'mon." Neil De Maio grinned. "She's always rubbed you the wrong way."

"That's not it."

"Hey, it's okay by me. You don't have to like her just 'cause she's a neighbor. No law says you do." Neil watched John's retreating figure. "I'm not into him, either. He's pretty dull if you ask me."

"He's not so bad. He's shy, that's all."

"Well, he sure as hell doesn't live in the fast lane," Neil said. "I can't get two words out of him. In my book, he's dull."

The day after the July 4th fair, Katie tried to get the truth about the family situation out of Patty. But the little girl demonstrated a very protective attitude toward her mother. "There's nothing to tell," she said.

"Well, you're not taking care of your brothers again this afternoon, are you?"

"I don't mind."

"Would you like to come over this afternoon and play with Janie and Melissa?" Katie offered.

"Not today, thank you," she said. "I'm going to clean house today to help Daddy."

"What about your mother?"

"She's not feeling good today. I hope she feels better."

"So do I," Katie said solemnly.

Patty had assumed Brenda's position as a girl living at home. Now Patty tended to herself and the two remaining children and helped with the cooking and cleaning. She was not quite eight years old.

"I need your help," Daddy had said to her. "Do you think you can do it?"

"Yes, Daddy," the child said proudly. "I can do it."

"Not all the time," he reassured her. "Just when Mommy doesn't feel well. God punishes bad little girls, but by the same token, He rewards good little girls who are helpful to their parents."

At this point in time John was finding it easier to cope with Helen and the extra burdens of family life than to cope with the pressures at Xerox. He couldn't stop worrying, yet the enormous job-related pressures he was feeling were mostly self-inflicted, for he was promoted right along within the ranks as the opportunities for advancement presented themselves. The vice-president of the company, Richard Tobias, found List to be quiet, even a bit reticent in his communication skills, but more than efficient as long as he was working with extroverted people who initiated much of the necessary conversation.

Eight months after John first began worrying about the security of his position with the company, he was made assistant manager of accounting. By 1963 he had been promoted to director of accounting services under Richard Tobias's direct supervision, both times with concomitant raises in salary.

John was making more money than he had ever made in his life. In less than two years with Xerox, he had almost doubled his salary. Still, he worried.

* * *

Things were not going well financially for the newly married Brenda and Wayne Herndon.

"Come stay with us," Helen said enthusiastically on the long-distance telephone call from Rochester to Kalamazoo.

John looked up from his reading as he heard her speak into the receiver. Stay here? he thought, deeply concerned at such a prospect. Brenda and Wayne?

"Sure," he heard her continue. "Daddy's a big shot with his company. He can get Wayne a job here in Rochester, and then we can be together again. Oh, I've missed you so, honey."

A "big shot," she had called him. She'd never said that before. Now, when it suited her . . .

"No, no, there's plenty of room," Helen said, answering the obvious question. "And the kids miss you, too."

John waited as Helen paused in her breathless enthusiasm to listen to something Brenda was saying on the other end of the line. "Of course he can," Helen finally answered. "He tells me his company's growing like crazy. They can always use more help." Her eyes reached across the room to his. "Right?" And John knew that she expected him not only to try to get Wayne Herndon a job, but to succeed in doing so, or he would never hear the end of it.

John was not happy at the prospect of using his hard-earned influence to secure a position for Wayne. Wayne was a stranger to him. He was too young. He didn't have the necessary skills for a company like Xerox. But at Helen's insistence, John pulled as many strings as he could and managed to get the young man an entry-level training job in the maintenance department.

Wayne didn't like the work. Six months later, deeply entrenched within the troubled structure of the List family, Wayne Herndon was vehemently objecting to Brenda about the life-style they endured while under the same roof with her parents. Every night, at his mother-in-law's insistence, he slept on a cot in the basement while Brenda slept with Patty upstairs. Every morning he drove off to the offices of Xerox Corporation with John while Brenda remained at home taking care of the three children, all the housework, the shopping, the cleaning, *and* her mother as well. Despite Helen's sincere joy at having Brenda back home, her condition had deteriorated even further.

"Listen," Wayne finally said to Brenda one night when they were alone, "this just isn't going to work."

"We're saving money, Wayne," Brenda protested, knowing what was coming.

"You're doing all the work around here. I'm tired of it. She don't lift a finger."

"Mom just can't seem to stop drinking."

"I'll say," Wayne said unsympathetically.

"And she keeps making Daddy buy her all these clothes all the time."

"Look!" he said, cutting her short. He didn't want to hear any more about "Mommy" and "Daddy." "He can do whatever he wants, but I'm tired of sleeping in the basement."

"Don't get mad. . . ."

"Mad!" He almost laughed. "I didn't marry you to sleep in no basement."

"She's got these crazy attitudes about sex."

"Brenda, it's not like before. We're married now. She can't object to it now. Maybe *she* don't like sex."

"No, that's not it," Brenda protested. "She likes it all right. *You* see the marriage manuals she leaves all over for Daddy. *You* see them, don't you? And she talks about it enough."

"Well, I'm getting pretty tired of this whole sick scene."

Brenda was positive Mom kept them separated because she couldn't tolerate the idea of anyone enjoying sex in the house while she herself felt so deprived. She hoped John might read the manuals and learn to open up a little, perhaps be more spontaneous. "But he'd rather spend an hour reading the Bible," Helen had complained to Brenda, "than take a few moments to read something" that might improve their fading marital relations.

"And I hate the job," Wayne continued. "I hate going to work with John. He's a stuffed shirt. And I really hate all the stupid praying around here."

"Wayne. . . ."

"And your mom's a lush!"

"Don't talk like that!" Brenda cried defensively.

"And I'll be damned if I'm gonna sleep in the basement alone anymore. It's been six months, and I've had it! I'm going back to Kalamazoo," he said firmly. He looked at her. "You coming?"

He stared at her defiantly until she lowered her eyes.

"You know I'll come," she murmured. "I just wish there was something I could do to help here."

"There ain't."

* * *

John was glad they were gone. Wayne had not measured up to company expectations, and he was sure it reflected upon him. Helen, on the other hand, was desolate at the loss of Brenda. More than anything else, she missed her daughter's company. Brenda was the only one she could talk to, the only one who understood. John had no patience with her tears.

With Brenda gone back to Kalamazoo with Wayne, many of the responsibilities she had reassumed when she and Wayne moved in fell back onto Patty's young shoulders.

Helen was so despondent that John finally agreed to her repeated requests to get ''those films'' to spice up their troubled sex life. His own rigid moralistic code at the very thought of them finally caved in under the pressure of the relentlessness of her demands. Embarrassment at the thought of buying them in person forced him to send away for them and have them mailed to a post office box. He gritted his teeth in desperate discomfort as he and Helen watched the erotic films in the deep privacy of their bedroom after the children were asleep. He hated them even as he watched them. But they did help.

On a warm summer evening, Patty, John junior, and Freddie stood by the barbecue in the De Maio backyard as Neil De Maio poured bottled barbecue sauce over the chicken legs he was grilling for his family. The De Maio girls, Janie and Melissa, were swinging high on the new circus-colored swing set their father had erected for them in the backyard after an entire Saturday morning of bruised fingers and swearing. He wasn't much of a handyman, and he hated lawn work. List's carefully tended lawn made his look like a jungle. It didn't bother him as long as he didn't lose the kids in the grass, he said with a laugh.

''Come on,'' Melissa called. ''Come swing. . . .''

''I don't feel like it right now,'' Patty called back, watching Mr. De Maio at the grill.

Neil felt a bit uncomfortable as the child's eyes never left the barbecue. ''Where's your mother?'' he asked the child.

''Sleeping.''

"And your father?"

"Working late."

The man's heart went out to the three children who were obviously looking outside their home and beyond their parents for comfort and companionship. Maybe even for food, he thought. He looked over at his own two little girls and resented the inattention the List youngsters were enduring. The boys were normal enough, although he thought they were too quiet for their age. Maybe a little too well behaved, too controlled—especially John junior. The little girl was so pretty, so bright. She had too many responsibilities for a child her age. He knew that the three children spent practically every day at his house playing with Janie and Melissa. Katie told him so. That meant they usually stayed over for lunch. Now here they were, watching him cook dinner, activating a guilt he resented feeling, and tugging at his heartstrings with their conspicuous needs.

It was almost time to eat. He poked the chicken legs with a long fork to determine if any pinkness was left. He hated undercooked chicken. A gentle probing thrust, a twist of the end of the fork, revealed the interior of the meat, and he was satisfied; they were cooked through. The barbecue sauce had darkened. The aroma was delicious.

Katie came out of the back kitchen door with a plate full of steaming hot corn on the cob and bowls of salads. She set the tray in the middle of the redwood picnic table.

"Bring out some more plates," he said to his wife.

Katie looked at the three children and nodded. "There's enough paper plates out already," she said. Then as she passed by him, he heard her whisper teasingly, "Softie."

Neil turned to the Lists. "Would you like to stay for dinner?"

Patty hesitated.

"There's enough for everybody," he said jovially. "Come on, sit down. Janie, Melissa, Time to eat," he called. "Let's go!"

"Thank you," Patty said, and they all took a place at the table.

Having the children over was getting to be a habit. The De Maios didn't mind. They really liked them. They were better behaved than their own children, who practically upset the long redwood bench as they fought for positioning.

"Move over, Patty," Janie said. "That's my seat."

Patty moved over.

* * *

John found a chess partner in one of his subordinate staff accountants at work. John was an excellent chess player, and he enjoyed it, but his passion for strategy board games like Anzio Beach and Civil War never abated. Through the games he continued to demonstrate the superb skills he had to plan ahead, to categorize, to remember details. He even played occasionally with his superior, Richard Tobias.

"It's impressive," Tobias told his wife, Laura. "He wins every damned battle. He's really a superb strategist."

What Tobias could not fully appreciate, although he sensed it, was that they were more than just games to him. John *had* to win. Through the games he became a general, a winner, a man. As a man of God he found solace in his church. As a man of war he found solace in winning board games. Religion and war games. There lay the only peace.

The office party was a disaster. John should have known better than to suggest to Helen that she attend. "Just to get out of the house, Helen," he had said. "It will do you good." He would live to regret his moment of weakness.

And again, the melancholy expression on his wife's face as she stared at him through the lull after his suggestion. She disconsolately thought of the possibility of a party . . . of having a little fun. Helen turned her eyes down. She stopped to think a moment through the mist of confusion. She thought she felt better. Yes, she thought. I'm much better. Her head didn't feel so muddled all the time, and there was no denying that she was sick to death of her bedroom walls. Maybe . . . it would be nice. . . .

"But I won't know anyone there, John," she worried.

"None of the wives will know anyone."

At the party Laura Tobias turned to her husband and whispered over the rim of her cocktail, "That woman is really into drinking, isn't she?"

Richard Tobias turned to look at Helen List. Lovely woman, he thought. A bit frail-looking, but very pretty with full lips, warm brown eyes, and such a lovely, long neck. But by this time she was extremely drunk and making a spectacle of herself. He didn't like to see drunkenness at office parties. Bad enough with a man, but when it was a woman, the wife of one of his executives . . . Most unpleasant. He grimaced and tried to turn his attention away.

But Helen List was talking loudly to one of John's co-workers, who was doing his best to maintain a polite attention. He tried not to notice the slur in her southern drawl, a drawl that became more pronounced when she drank. "My first husband was a war hero," she said. "He got killed charging up a hill in Korea saving twelve of his buddies."

John took her elbow. She shook him off. The shy Helen was in good form. The liquor had oiled her tongue to the point where words were pouring out indiscriminately, wildly, all barbed at John. "Now John, here"—she laughed—"he charged a desk in San Francisco the whole time."

The man tried to move away.

"No, wait." She caught on to his arm. "Let me tell you. Let me ask you something. John, here, says he was in the Second World War," she drawled. "Now I'm not denying that. Okay. He was in Europe. Okay, honey! I'll buy that much. But listen to this. You tell me if you can believe this. He says . . . he says that he was a prisoner of war, and then the Germans let him go because he spoke German and they mistook him for being a Nazi. One of *them*." She burst out laughing. "Now can you buy that?"

The man tried to pull away again. "Mrs. List," he began.

"No, wait!" she insisted a bit aggressively. "Listen to what I'm saying! I'm telling you something."

Richard Tobias looked at John. His cheeks were patchworked with blood that had pressured to the surface in blotches as he listened to his wife bludgeon his manhood. He looked as though he were gritting his teeth, but the man was silent, immobilized with humiliation. He certainly wasn't handling his wife very well, Tobias thought in annoyance at his ineptitude. *He* certainly wouldn't let Laura get away with anything like this. All of a sudden he looked at List in a new light. Quiet? No problem. Shy? It didn't matter. But now he was clearly getting the image of an extraordinary wimp. And he didn't like it.

"He says," Helen continued. "He says . . . that . . . then he fought in the Pacific sector, *too* ! Now, I was in the military with my first husband for *ten years* and I know something about the military. Oh, honey, you bet. But the European theater and the Pacific theater? *Both?*" she asked incredulously. "Do you believe that? I mean, don't they always discharge a soldier after being a prisoner of war. . . . I mean a prisoner? Isn't that the way, usually? *You* tell me. . . ."

"I really don't know. . . ."

Richard Tobias had found himself listening to the woman's ravings despite his intense antipathy for the scene she was creating. Suddenly he found himself thinking that there was something to what she was saying. He began wondering. It really doesn't add up, he thought. He knew about John's war record. It had been part of his personnel file when he had been hired: "Prisoner of war." "Fought in both theaters of war during W.W.II." Now that he thought of it, it was highly unlikely that he would have seen combat in both sectors, especially if he had been released as a prisoner from the Germans.

"Are prisoners of war usually retired?" he found himself asking John.

John's cheeks burned. "Not necessarily," he answered.

Laura Tobias nudged her husband. He was immediately sorry he had asked the question. Perhaps John *had* augmented some of his heroics, Tobias thought sympathetically. After all, how could his record compare with that of her first husband, who had died a hero in battle? And with the lethal way that woman used the comparisons to belittle John, it would be understandable if he resorted to some embellishment.

But John could only think that his veracity had been called into question in front of his boss. He gritted his teeth so hard, his jaw hurt. He finally managed to take Helen by the arm and steer her away. The man she had cornered looked tremendously relieved.

No one noticed when they left.

On the way home Helen fell asleep in the car. John's teeth hurt. He was enraged.

John had started out at Xerox Corporation at $9,000 per year. By now, 1964, he had nearly tripled his income. He was earning approximately $25,000 annually, including $7,900 in bonuses. But it wasn't enough. He began to lobby seriously for advancement, for a vice-presidency in the company. The money was for Helen. The title was for him. He wasn't consciously aware of how much he needed the sense of identity a title would give him.

But Richard Tobias was beginning to be troubled not only by the new "wimp" image he had of List, but by the extreme nervousness List displayed when he was in a stressful situation. Last week's conference was a case in point. Under the pressure of speaking publicly to the assembled group at the conference table, List appeared to discolor right in front of their eyes.

They must be hives, Tobias thought in some embarrassment at the man's obvious discomfort. List's face was always a little pale and blotchy, but this time it had literally broken out into large red welts across his puffy cheeks.

"This fiscal year's end," he was saying, "will demonstrate . . ."

Tobias watched him with growing concern.

"An increase . . . of . . ."

Now he was twitching. Everyone noticed. There was an uncomfortable shuffling of feet under the huge highly polished oval table.

John was aware that his face was burning. Try as he might, he couldn't control the twitching of his cheek. He put his hand to his face. "The new revenues," he continued.

Tobias looked up grimly from the papers in front of him. He studied the man. List's head had fallen a little forward. He shifted his body from side to side on his chair as he spoke. Like a kid giving an answer at a spelling bee on television, Tobias thought grimly. The more List had to deal with people in his capacity as director of accounting services, the more pronounced his nervous afflictions seemed to become. Tobias couldn't help thinking they were worse since the debacle at the office party. Or was that his imagination? Was it that now he simply perceived him differently and noticed the man's shortcomings more?

Finally the conference ended.

John had managed to give his report. It was over. He could retreat to the seclusion of his office.

Helen knew that John was making big money for 1965. She wanted to live in a style commensurate with his salary. What else was he good for if not, at least, material comforts? God knew there was little else, but she couldn't get out often. She never felt well enough. When she did manage to go shopping, she was very extravagant. It drove John to distraction. There were many references in Proverbs regarding thrift, he thought, about being satisfied with what one was already blessed with, rejoicing in the blessings that God gave, not coveting or desiring what others had.

But even though she knew it drove him crazy, she bought whatever suited her fancy. One thing, she smiled to herself, she had nice taste. She'd always had nice taste. Now she tried to cover all of her depression, her feelings of inadequacy, her pent-up feelings of deprivation, her very real fears about her health, through reckless buying and spending, and through her drinking, and through her abuse of John. She kept pushing him for more and more. John couldn't control either her excesses in spending or her excesses in drinking.

In August of 1965 John made an appointment to speak with

Richard Tobias. When he walked into his office, his superior was seated comfortably behind his desk waiting for him to speak. List noticed the windowed, executive office with its rich mahogany desk and warmly leathered swivel chair behind it.

As John stood over his desk, Tobias, once again, was impressed with the size of the man. He was only six feet one, but he seemed larger. It must be the size of his head. It's a large head, he thought to himself. "Have a seat," he said aloud. He didn't want to have List towering over him.

"Thank you."

John sat down opposite him in the soft brown leather chair reserved for guests. He repositioned his glasses on the bridge of his nose. The glare of the desk fixture opaqued the lenses so that Tobias could not see his eyes clearly. But he knew this was a serious call by the way List leaned forward on his chair.

"What's on your mind, List?" he asked comfortably.

John looked at him steadily. "I've been here almost four years."

"That long? Yes, I guess so."

"And I've done well."

"Yes, you have," Tobias agreed. "And I believe the company has rewarded you well for your services."

"It's not enough."

"What would be 'enough'?" he asked after a brief pause in which Tobias looked at him carefully.

"I'd like a promotion."

"Well, there aren't any right now. I told you that the last time you asked for one."

"There is a vice-presidency opening up."

Tobias smiled thinly. "You've heard." Can't keep anything secret around here, he thought, annoyed.

"I've heard," John said in a deep, steady voice.

Tobias was surprised. He had rarely seen the man in such control.

"Well, management has decided to look outside the company to fill the position."

"It's a position that I'm suited for."

"I don't think you are," Tobias said bluntly.

John hesitated. He blinked behind his glasses. "I believe my work is sufficiently—"

"Oh, you're very capable, John. But it's more than that. More than capability."

"What?"

Tobias leaned forward. "Look, I'm going to talk to you like a Dutch uncle," he said gently. "Drop it. A vice-presidency calls for more than capability. It calls for interaction with people. For the ability to control decisions and to lead people. It means knowing how to deal with people. A kind of personality that—''

''I know how to deal with people.'' John seemed to swell in size on the chair right in front of him. Tobias had never seen him so resolute. ''I'm entitled to advancement.''

''Let it go, John,'' Tobias tried again. ''You've advanced a great deal since you've been with us. You're doing fine where you are. Don't reach for anything else yet. Maybe in time. But not now. . . .''

''In time? . . .''

''I'm telling you to drop it right now and stay where you are.''

''I'm entitled to a promotion,'' John repeated doggedly.

''You're not going to get one, List,'' Tobias's voice had hardened.

''What if I say I can no longer stay under these circumstances . . . while . . . while others are being promoted beyond me,'' he stammered, ''others who don't have my . . . capabilities?''

''Then I'd have to tell you to look for another job.'' Bluntly.

John's face turned crimson. ''Is that your final . . . answer?'' he asked.

''It is. As a matter of fact, it's absolute,'' Tobias said grimly. There it was.

''We'll be very sorry to see you go,'' Tobias concluded.

John had seriously miscalculated.

Tobias leaned back in his chair, looking at List with resolve and sadness. If the man had dropped it, he might not have fired him. Yet his confidence in List had been eroding for a long time.

John got up. Tobias watched him leave the office. Better to get it over with, he thought. Yet . . . he was truly sorry.

The meeting had not gone as planned. Fired again. . . . What was happening? Where was God? Why was he being so unjustly punished? ''Things will be different around here from now on,'' he raged when he returned home. ''Different!'' He was mean with anger. The children cowered in their beds, listening to his booming voice resonate throughout the house. When he yelled he was very frightening.

''It's not my fault,'' Helen cried.

''You make a fool of me every chance you get. You embarrass me in front of my subordinates and my boss. Now they say I can't handle people. I'll handle you! I'll handle you.''

The children could hear their mother crying. Daddy didn't usually yell. They didn't know what was happening. They were terrified. They heard the crash of glass.

''I'm a man!''

The sound of sobbing . . .

"And now I have to find another job. Another one! Again."

"You'll get another one . . . you'll be able to . . . get. . . ."

"I've been fired!"

"Stop yelling at me!"

"And I don't want to hear about Marvin again. Never again!"

"Don't talk about him. Don't . . . you dare!"

"Helen, I'm warning you."

"I hate you. *Hate you* !"

"Do you think I care anymore? After what you did? What do you think they thought about me when you got drunk like that? What do you think they thought about *you* ? Do you think you presented a pretty picture? *Do you* ?"

"It's not my fault!" she screamed. "You'll get another job. What are you doing? What . . ."

They listened.

"Oh, sure. Go ahead. Call your mother!" she screamed with bitter sarcasm. "I might have known. Go ahead! 'Mommy, Mommy, I've been fired. Again! What should I do?' "

There was another sound of glass breaking, then the slam of their mother's bedroom door.

Then silence.

Patty sat up in bed, staring into the darkness. John junior and Freddie looked at each other solemnly and lay back down in their beds, pulling the covers up. Patty listened in the darkness. She could hear the soft rumble of her father's voice. He was speaking in German.

The next night when Jean called up from Oklahoma, John told her very bluntly, "You can't talk to her."

"Why not?" Jean asked incredulously.

"Because she's drunk, that's why," he said with uncharacteristically vehement bluntness.

"What in the world is going on, John?"

"Your sister is an alcoholic, Jean. Didn't you know that?"

"No, I didn't, and I don't believe it."

Now John did something he rarely did: he complained out loud to someone. "And she has made me lose my job. She got so drunk at an office party that . . . she made me lose respect in the eyes of my employers."

"You lost your job?"

"Yes."

"And you're telling me it's Helen's fault?"

"Yes!"

"Oh, don't give me that!" Jean said angrily.

Jean was well aware of the curious pattern of John's employment record. She and Gene had certainly discussed it often enough. He would start off great, reach a certain level, and then something would happen—they'd get "on to him," Gene would say. But this was the first time he had ever blamed Helen.

"My sister is a sick woman," she began.

"She'd be less sick if she didn't drink so much!"

She'd never heard John so angry. So on the offensive. What was happening?

"Stop it!" Jean demanded. "What's the matter with you? Stop blaming her! Don't you have a brain? Can't you handle your wife's problems?" She expected him to fight back. "Can't you think of solutions?" she pushed on.

But he didn't fight back. Instead he backed off. "I'm sorry," he said.

"I want to talk to my sister," she demanded.

"She can't come to the phone," he said quietly. "That's God's truth." And then after a pause, he said, "Jean . . ."

"What?"

"I'm going to have to leave town. There's a job prospect. . . . a good one, but it's in New Jersey. Do you think you might be able to come for a visit while I'm away?"

Jean said she would. She wanted to see her sister for herself.

What was going wrong? he thought. His life was beginning to fall apart at the seams. He was a member of the church body. He had already gone through the process of "Who is this man, Jesus?" Long ago. And he had deeply accepted and believed the faith. The Lord has always been his point of reference for his entire life because he knew that He had his finger on the pulse of everything. Was He trying to tell him something? A desperation was beginning to set in on the edge of John's very controlled nerves.

He had waited until after everyone had left the steps of the church before approaching the pastor himself. He told the children to wait for him by the car. They watched from a distance as their father spoke quietly to the pastor under the arch of the church's front door.

"Is it Helen?" Reverend Saresky asked.

"Helen? No. I have to find a new job."

So John was going to be another casualty of Xerox's personnel policy, the pastor thought sadly. He waited while John hesitated. It was very difficult to tell the pastor that he had been fired. But after a long silence he said, "They let me go."

"I'm sorry to hear that," Saresky said sincerely. Another life disrupted. "But you'll find another position. A man of your abilities."

"There's nothing around here. It might mean another move. . . ." He looked off into the distance of such a prospect.

Reverend Saresky touched his arm gently. "We would miss you terribly if that proved to be a necessity, John."

"I don't understand it," John said suddenly. "Is God testing me?"

"Perhaps."

"I pray all the time. I read the Bible. . . ." His words were a comment of fact—not a plea for help. "I perform my daily devotions every morning. Before anything else." Suddenly his deep voice choked with passion. It embarrassed him. He immediately pulled back. But he thought to himself, Where is my reward?

Then again, who could understand the mysterious ways of God?

He can't handle the pain of failure, Saresky realized as he looked at the man he had come to regard as a friend as well as a parishioner. It's more than he can bear, "John," the pastor asked solemnly, "let me help you if I can. How serious is the trouble you're in?"

"Not serious at all," John said. "Nothing I can't manage."

Pride before fall, the pastor suddenly found himself thinking, and he tried to warn the man standing before him.

But John said, "I can handle it."

It was the summer of 1965.

His room at the Hotel Plaza in Jersey City was plain but comfortable and clean, all that he required as he got ready to go on what could be the most important interview of his career. He prepared carefully—what he would say, what he would ask for, how he would dress, how he would explain his current unemployment.

He spent the entire evening before the morning of his interview in quiet contemplation and prayer. By the time his 10:00 A.M. appointment arrived, he was ready to apply for the job he craved.

When he returned to Rochester, he was flushed with the excitement of victory. God had heard his prayers. Not only had he landed the best job of his career, but Helen looked better than she had in months. Having Jean stay with her a few days had done wonders. She wasn't drinking. Jean even took away her sedatives and talked her to sleep instead. Jean was loving and nurturing, supportive and patient. She supplied all the emotional nourishment Helen so desperately needed after so many years of emotional deprivation under what she rightly perceived as a steady stream of sermonizing in place of human understanding.

Now, as they listened to him tell his wonderful news, both so obviously delighted that he had landed such a prestigious position, John could see that Helen was combed and dressed. And she was joyous, and gay, like a little girl, as though she were on a manic high.

Jean was pleased to see her smiling . . . but she worried, even as John continued.

He had arrived at last. He had landed a position with the First National Bank of New Jersey in Jersey City as a vice-president and comptroller. He had his title at last: "vice-president."

"Vice-president?" Helen asked incredulously.

"Yes." he beamed.

"Vice-president of a *bank* !"

The children stared at their mother, wondering whether or not this was a happy moment. "Jean," Helen said. Her eyes were shining luminously, perhaps a little too brightly, too extended. But she was so happy. "Oh, honey, did you hear?"

"That's wonderful," Jean said sincerely.

Patty hugged her mommy. Jean hugged little Freddie. Johnny sat at the table smiling shyly. "You see, John?" Helen continued. "All your worries were for nothing. It was a blessing in disguise, your being fired."

"God does move in mysterious ways, after all," John said.

All recent angers receded into the background.

Helen burst out laughing. "Vice-president. Did you hear that children? Your father is going to be vice-president of a *bank* ! And the salary? John, what about the salary?"

"Twenty-five thousand dollars a year," he announced proudly.

Both women responded appreciatively. The children took their cue from them and oohed happily.

"But that's just the beginning," he said grandly. "There's no telling how far it can go."

Even Jean was impressed.

"What's a comptroller?" Helen asked, sitting down at the table eagerly.

"A top business executive," he said. "Someone who supervises financial affairs." He had his title and the salary to go with it. And Helen finally seemed proud of him. "The only thing is . . ."

"What?" she asked, staring at him anxiously.

"We'll have to move again. . . ."

Both John and Jean watched her closely to see what her reaction would be, but Helen didn't even seem to mind that. "I hate Rochester," she declared impulsively. "Why, I'll bet New Jersey is warmer than here."

"Sure, honey," Jean said, relieved.

"But this time," Helen insisted, "This time, we'll have to buy a house that goes with your new position as vice-president," she said grandly. "No more middle-class neighborhoods for us."

Suddenly weakness seemed to overwhelm her. "I declare," she said, deliberately putting on her best southern accent, "I do believe all this good news has tired me out. Just a little." She laughed lightly.

"Why don't you go lie down, Helen," Jean said. "I'll put the children to bed."

"You sure you don't mind?"

"Not a bit. Go ahead, honey."

"Well, all right. If you're sure you don't mind."

But as soon as she had put the children to bed, Jean took John aside when Helen was still "resting." She knew that Helen would be in bed for the night.

"John, listen," she began. "I'm worried."

"About what?" he said in that remote way he had. "It's a good job. And I didn't tell Helen yet, but I've selected a good area to buy a house in New Jersey. It's called Union County. I spent an entire day driving through all of it. Scotch Plains, Westfield, Mountainside. She'll like it there. Westfield in particular has a wonderful Lutheran church."

"It's not that. I'm sure it's a good job. And a good area. . . . It's Helen."

He paused in annoyance and exhaled a deep breath. "What about Helen?"

"There's something wrong, and I don't think it's the drinking. I think it's something else."

"What?"

"She's really sick. I think that's why she drinks," Jean went on. "She gets confused, and she's getting so paranoid, even with me. One minute she accuses me of spying on her, for *you* of all things, running to tell you things about her. Next thing she's hugging me and asking me never to go away. And she's so depressed all the time. I'm really worried."

He stared at her and stoically remembered what that doctor had said to him in Kalamazoo, what he had disregarded. "She's willful, Jean." he said rigidly, "and godless. That's the main problem."

"No, it isn't."

"We'll pray for her tonight."

"Oh, John, stop it! Pray!" she snapped impatiently, not catching the sternness that immediately pinched his mouth. "She needs more than prayers."

They were alike, he thought. Neither one of them had the right faith in Christ. To their family, church was merely a social organization. They weren't truly part of the body of believers who had a supernatural connection with each other and with God. If they had been, there would be less devine wrath served into their lives. "There are prescribed ways to behave," he said without blinking, "if one doesn't want to suffer the wrath of God."

"I don't believe you. Are you telling me she's being *punished*?" Jean was getting angry.

"For her lack of belief. For her weaknesses . . ."

"*She needs a doctor!*"

"She's been to doctors."

"Well, then another kind of doctor. There is something definitely wrong."

"No one in my family has ever gone to a psychiatrist," he said firmly.

She was stunned. "I wasn't talking about a psychiatrist. I was talking about a medical doctor."

"Medical?"

"Are you aware that she thinks she has a brain tumor?"

"Don't be silly," he scoffed.

"Well, she does. That's what she thinks sometimes. And she's always in a state of confusion. Maybe you don't even notice it anymore, you're so used to it; but I see a tremendous change, and to me it's frightening."

He thought carefully about what Jean was saying. A medical problem . . . that was different. "When we move to New Jersey, I will see to it that she goes to a doctor."

"Not just a doctor. A neurologist, John. Promise me."

"I promise."

"You're not just saying that?"

He was offended. "I always keep my promises."

* * *

John had looked first for a town with a good Lutheran church. Helen didn't really care as long as the house was what she wanted. Of the three towns in the area he had scouted, Westfield seemed to have all of the qualifications the family wanted. And it had the Lutheran Church of the Redeemer on Clark Street and Cowperthwaite Place in the heart of town. It was a beautiful building with a good elementary Lutheran school. He had already stopped in to introduce himself to Reverend Eugene Rehwinkel, its pastor. He liked him.

Then they found the house Helen wanted. It was one of the grandest houses on one of the grandest streets in Westfield. On top of a hill on a street appropriately named Hillside Avenue. It was a huge old Victorian structure, with a thirty-seven-foot-long ballroom!

"This is the one," Helen said from the middle of the ballroom, looking at the stained-glass windows stretching over her head across the ceiling. "This one."

And John looked at the stained-glass windows overhead and also stretching across a windowed wall opposite the fireplace. It looked like a church.

He agreed. This was the one.

The real estate agent was eager to make the sale, but he could tell from the responses to a few questions that John List was not going to be able to afford the house. It was the grandest house on the block—nineteen rooms in all, with the enormous ballroom in the rear of the first floor, plus two living rooms, a formal dining room, a huge eat-in kitchen, butler's pantry, a full laundry room, and many closets hidden away among the hallways. There were two staircases. The central staircase was splendidly ornate. It led to five large bedrooms and baths on the second floor. The back staircase led not only to the second floor, but to the maid's quarters on the third floor, which had been converted into a sizable two-bedroom apartment with a living room, kitchen, and plenty of storage area. Because the house was old and in a state of disrepair, the price had come down from $80,000 to $50,000. So what! These people didn't even have any money in the bank.

"Look," said the agent. "I don't want to tell you your business, but frankly, I don't think you can . . . well, let me put it this way. The house may be beyond your means."

Helen turned her gaze to John. "That's for my husband . . . to decide," she said with a very quiet determination.

"There's no point in going for something too high," the agent said reasonably. "You'll be turned down by the bank, and everybody's time will have been spent for nothing."

The couple sat silently in front of him.

"What about those two houses I showed you in Elizabeth?" he tried.

Helen shook her head.

"Or even that one in Scotch Plains. . . ."

"Westfield," Helen said under her breath. "This house."

"But Mrs. List . . ."

Suddenly she was emboldened by her desire to own this particular house and none other. "Besides being a certified public accountant," she said almost arrogantly, "my husband is the vice-president of the First National Bank in Jersey City. I think he should know his own finances."

"Let's go, Helen," John murmured, getting up.

"That tree," Helen said, ignoring him. "The one in the front. The magnolia tree. You see," she explained to the agent, "it reminds me of my home in North Carolina. I haven't lived in my home state for fifteen years. That tree . . . it's like home. That's what it reminds me of. My childhood home."

People always buy with their hearts instead of their pocketbooks, the agent thought. Never fails! He leaned back. "Your standards may be a bit higher than your husband's income."

John had already walked out of the sales office.

When Helen joined him outside, her eyes were full of tears. "Why did you leave?"

"We'll go to another real estate agent," he reassured her. "The house is on multiple listing."

They went to another real estate agent. They bought the house. Now all John had to do was find a way to pay for it.

He knew that the first agent had been right; he could not afford the house on his own. With his mother's financial help, however, he felt he would be able to manage it if they were careful about their expenditures.

"Has she ever been careful yet about such things?" his mother asked over the phone in her usual quiet voice, but John couldn't help catching the strong edge of acrimony.

"She has her burdens."

"You must stop her from spending all your money. She is not an industrious woman. That's doubly sinful." There was no challenging the admonition. It was absolute. " *Sie ist eine schlechte Ehefrau und Mutter. Sie ist eine Gottlose Sündige Frau.*"

"Don't," he begged. "She is not well. You know that."

Alma sniffed with heavy disapproval. She had already said more than usual. It was not usually her wont to criticize, at least not so openly.

Alma hung up the phone after speaking with John for about a half hour. She turned to her good friend Mrs. Hollister who had been visiting, and spoke to her about John's problems with his wife. "She drinks, Mrs. Hollister."

Mrs. Hollister shook her head in condemnation.

Helen, not understanding the telephone conversation, which was in German, waited impatiently for John to get off the phone. She wanted to call Jean, who was back in North Carolina visiting with the family.

"There's so much room, Jean," she said happily after making the connection to Elkin. "You'll be able to visit and stay over. And Mama, too, and nobody will get into anybody's way, either."

Jean was thrilled to hear how well Helen sounded. Maybe her sister was finally on her way to recovery. Or better yet, maybe there wasn't anything seriously wrong with her after all.

"Oh, Jean, it's so beautiful!" Patty, John junior, and Freddie crowded around their mother to absorb her gaiety.

"It's like Tara," she said. "Honest. I'm not joking." She laughed. "I'll feel like Scarlett O' Hara in that house. I'm not kidding, Jean. Wait 'til you see it. And John is even going to restore it. . . ." Her joy became infectious. Patty started to laugh, too. They were finally going to move to a big house of their own and they were going to be happy and they were going to be a family, and life was looking up.

Patty couldn't wait to tell the De Maios next door that "my father plans to restore the house." She had dragged John junior and Freddie with her.

"Does he now?" Katie asked a bit skeptically.

"My mommy said it's one of the showplaces of Westfield," Patty boasted.

" *Is* it? How nice."

"Don't you believe us?"

"Of course I do," Katie said kindly. "I'm really happy for you. For all of you. Where did you say this 'mansion' is?"

"Westfield," Patty said happily. "That's in the state of New Jersey."

"Does that mean you're moving away?" little Janie asked. And Patty nodded.

"Well, we'll miss you," said Katie. She looked at the three children who had spent so much time at her house playing and eating with her own children, and she realized with a sudden ache behind her eyes that she meant it.

When Helen called Brenda in Kalamazoo to tell her the good news and spoke just as enthusiastically about the beauty and grandeur of the new house—"one of the showplaces of Westfield!"—Brenda knew that again Daddy simply could not say "no" to her mother.

But seeing the situation with a mother's eyes, Alma List could tell from as far away as Bay City, Michigan, that despite all the surface ebullience, all was not well with her boy. Christina Worman had come to visit Alma, as was her custom. Once again, sitting on the front porch catching the cool summer breezes as they both crocheted with expert precision, they spoke away most of the evening. Alma told of John's prestigious promotion. She was so proud of him—not surprised at his achievement, she always knew he was blessed—just deeply proud, but eventually they always got around to discussing his problems with his wife.

"You haven't told me yet," Christina said.

"What?"

"How they're getting along."

Alma hesitated. She stopped crocheting and looked across the porch of the house that held so many memories for her.

"I have made a decision," she told her friend.

"What?"

"I am going to sell the house, and I am going to live with John," she said solemnly.

"But . . ." Christina was appalled at the idea. She knew how intensely the two Mrs. Lists disliked each other. "Do you think that's wise?"

"Maybe I can help them. He wants to buy a house. He will need my help."

"But to live together . . ."

"I understand there is a beautiful large apartment on the third floor. I could still have my privacy, and it's not good for me to be alone so much now that I'm getting on in years."

"The third floor?" Christina said, thinking that her friend had never before had to deal with steps. Was it a good idea to start now? At her age? "But Mrs. List," she began again.

"They are a very troubled family, Mrs. *Vor*man."

"I know. But to sell your home . . ."

"I will need the money."

"Mrs. List," Christina said kindly, "I don't want to interfere. Have I ever interfered? In all the years we've known each other? But there will be no turning back once you sell your home."

"I know." Alma paused as she stared for a long moment across the familiar expanse of South Wenona Street, once again reliving her memories . . . memories of the time when she'd nursed Anna Marie as she lay so helplessly on her deathbed, the time when she'd moved in as a bride to keep house for her cousin, J. F., the arrival of her only child, and rearing her beloved son all those close happy years before he had joined the military. How she wished they could return to those days. "The decision is made," she said. "John and I have talked about it for a very long time. I'll have a place to live for the rest of my life."

Once she sold her home and moved, she would put all her finances into her son's hands. As vice-president of a bank, he would know best how to handle her money. They had spoken about giving him power of attorney so as not to have to bother her with all the details that she did not always understand anyway. He was the expert.

The decision was irrevocable.

In Rochester, Helen was beside herself with desolation at the thought of her mother-in-law moving in with them. She was so upset, she couldn't hold down her dinner. "I don't want her living with us," she said weakly after a total stomach purge in the bathroom.

"She won't be living with us," John said, "She'll have her own private place upstairs."

"She'll be with us. . . ."

"She's getting old."

"I don't want her with us!" she suddenly screamed with approaching hysteria. "Not in my house!"

"It's done," he said quietly. "The decision has been made."

"Why wasn't I told?" Her eyes were so swollen, she could hardly see. "Why wasn't I consulted? Why do you two always talk behind my back in German so I can't understand what you're saying?"

"She's giving us the money for the down payment."

"I don't want her money. Not even after she's dead."

"Don't be ungrateful."

"I don't want anything of hers!"

"You wanted the house," he suddenly stormed in a voice that rang through the closed windows in the living room onto the lawn, where the children silently listened. "We wouldn't be able to buy the house if it wasn't for her," he yelled. "I managed to get a forty-thousand dollar mortgage only with the use of her bank account. She put everything she has in my hands.''

"I don't care."

"And the down payment! Where do you think I got that?''

" *I don't care* !" she screamed, totally out of control.

"It's the ten thousand dollars she's giving us. *Giving* us, not lending. *Giving* us. . . .''

John gritted his teeth as Helen burst into renewed tears. "I'd rather live in a hovel,'' she sobbed.

"It's done!'' he raged. "You wanted that house. And it's done. She's already sold her house. There's no turning back!''

Another fatal turning point had been reached. The two women would now be under the same roof—in separate quarters, but they would both be very aware of each other's presence from now on.

Later that night Helen called Jean to tell her the news, how her dreams of a new life had been shattered with the coming of her mother-in-law. She was desperately ill with a combination of sharply extended emotions, heavy medication, and the strong nightcap in her clenched palm. She had even thrown up the light snack Patty had insisted she force down after John retreated into the basement to commune silently with his God about his problems. Her head felt as though it had been clamped in a vise that was tightening . . . tightening . . . as though by an invisible force she couldn't control, until she could barely see straight or think clearly. "I don't care if that woman lives or dies,'' she whispered, still crying painfully. Her throat ached with the abuse of so much uncontrollable sobbing.

"Please, honey, calm down,'' Jean said. Helen sounded terrible, she thought, worse than ever before. Her phone calls were getting more and more painful to handle with each new crisis.

Helen closed her eyes as she spoke into the phone. "I'm going to want mom to come visit.'' Her words were beginning to slur together. "To live with us, too . . . as much as possible. And you . . .'' The sobbing finally stopped as the sedation began to take effect. "You've got to come visit all the time, Jean,'' she murmured. "I feel so alone. You've got to come. Do you think . . . that. . . . Mom would stay with me for a while?'' she asked plaintively.

All the fragile joy was gone.

That night, as John sat on the edge of the bed solemnly reviewing his decision, Helen walked toward him from the bathroom. He looked up at her, anticipating that the argument would continue. Instead he noticed that she was walking peculiarly—her gait seemed disjointed, uneven. He looked into her face, her eyes, even the blind right eye, were moving in all directions in brief, rapid movements.

"Helen," he began, frowning.

But before he could get up, she pitched forward suddenly, crashing into the floor almost onto her face. He jumped up, terrified. She was unconscious. What was it! An overreaction to drugs? Alcohol? He had no idea. He managed to get her dead weight onto the bed. By the time he returned from the bathroom with a wet washcloth, she was staring up at the ceiling.

He came to the bed carefully and stared down at her.

"I passed out, didn't I?" she asked in quiet confusion, pressing the palm of her hand against the rising welt on her forehead.

He couldn't speak as he gave her the washcloth. "When we get to Westfield," he began shakily, "we'll . . ."

She closed her eyes and turned her head into her pillow.

"We'll get help. We'll find out what . . ."

"I know," she mumbled. "I know what it is."

"What?"

"Malaria," she said almost inaudibly. She was so frightened at having passed out that she even forgot what they had been arguing about. "Keeps . . . coming back." He listened carefully, trying to make out what she was rambling about. "Tried to cure me," she said thickly. "And they did . . . oh, they . . . they . . ." Her voice faded into incoherent words for a moment. "But they left me with the malaria instead." She tried to raise her head. Her blind eye seemed to be looking in another direction as though it had lost all muscular control. "At least it's not fatal," she rasped, "but . . . keeps coming back and . . ." Tears were streaming from her eyes when she turned to look at him again. "It's the syphilis," she whispered.

He looked at her dumbly. He couldn't focus on what she was saying. Syphilis?

Finally it was out, after all these years. "It was nothing," she said, trying to minimize the impact of the dreaded word. She had never told anyone about it, not even Jean. "A mild case. From Marvin." She coughed. She wiped her eyes. She coughed again. "But they had to give me malaria at the hospital to cure it. . . . That's how they did it."

As he listened incredulously, the whole story poured out of her in disjointed bits, fear having finally loosened the resolve made so many years ago never to tell a living soul her shameful secret. In her confused, almost lethargic state, she wasn't very clear about what had happened. Her eyes kept shutting as though she were drifting off, but he managed to puzzle together the pieces of her story. In 1948 she had contracted syphilis from Marvin. She was sent to Walter Reed Army Hospital for treatment. Although penicillin was available as early as 1943, it was kept for the military. There was very little available for laymen, nor was it known at the time whether penicillin would even be an effective treatment; it was still being tested for effectiveness in the cure for syphilis of the brain as late as 1956. In 1948, when Helen contracted the disease, the standard treatment was rather primitive by today's standards: the patient was injected with malaria through the blood of another patient who had it or from another syphilitic patient—just as if a mosquito were transferring the blood from one person to another. Every three days or so the patient's temperature would rise. It was very . . . difficult . . . Helen drifted off.

"Were you cured?" John asked, trying not to deal with the immoral impact of one having such a dread social disease.

"Oh, yes," she murmured.

"And . . . contagion," he stammered. Syphilis . . . How to deal with the social condemnations?

"I'm not contagious," she said, her voice rising a bit hysterically. "I was cured. You're okay."

"But the children . . ."

"No, no," she said, leaning in to him almost conspiratorially. "I took gamma globulin every time. It was preventive . . . they don't have it."

Even though by nature John was excessively conscientious, moralistic, scrupulous, and judgmental of others as well as of himself, and as she spoke he had fleeting bitter thoughts about Marvin, the man who had always been held up to him as a paragon of manhood he could never match—*he gave her syphilis!*—he expressed gratitude to Helen instead. "I'm very grateful to you for taking preventive measures for the children," he said softly. He did not recognize the process of rationalization at work, that he was developing logical reasons for not having the myriad disturbing feelings he would rather not have. But it was all there: the pain getting close to the surface, harder and harder to bury the feelings deep enough so as not to hurt.

Helen smiled faintly, leaned back into her pillow, and closed her eyes, as though now that she had finally relieved herself of the terrible secret she had carried alone all these years, everything would be all right. She actually felt close to John. "Stay with me," she murmured groggily, "until I fall asleep. . . ."

He did. She fell asleep almost immediately. He sat rigidly at her side, thanking God that he and the children, in particular, had not been infected. He didn't recognize his own coping mechanism at work in his flat acceptance of Helen's confession—that if he didn't acknowledge the moral condemnations implicit in such a disease, if he didn't deal with it, if he pretended that it wasn't there, it *wasn't* there. The process was in keeping with the lifelong history of a man who spent his life praying his problems and his feelings under a rug.

17 | Westfield, New Jersey—1965

The "mansion" in Westfield had a big wraparound porch, large rooms, and high ceilings. Actually it had been a big, comfortable farmhouse, built in 1896 by John Samuel Augustus Wittke in the Victorian style of architecture that was so popular at the turn of the century. His grandson, John Wittke, still lived in a cottage behind the house that had once served as a guest house.

Now John Wittke stood on the front lawn with the new owners and gazed up at the old house. "It was something in its day," he told the Lists as he showed them photographs of the beautifully furnished interior of his grandfather's home and farm as it had appeared in its prime.

"When were these pictures taken?" John asked.

"Oh, somewhere in the twenties or thirties," Wittke said, rubbing his cheek. "Not sure, exactly. Bit of a mess now, though. Place like this needs care."

John and Helen looked at the photos eagerly.

"When you moving in?" Wittke asked.

"At the end of the month," John answered. "When the financing . . . when everything goes through the bank."

"John," Helen said dreamily, "we have to restore the mansion to what it used to be. Wouldn't that be wonderful if we could do that?"

"Just needs money," Wittke said. "Could be done, I guess. . . . Just needs money."

"May I borrow these photographs?" John asked.

"Sure. Go ahead."

"I'd like to study them."

"I guess it would be nice to see the old place shining again. Keep the photos as long as you like."

Uncharacteristically, John was also intoxicated by Helen's vaporous daydreams and began to make paper plans to restore the house. The porch of the house, with its squared roof held up by white Doric columns, was very reminiscent of the front portico of his boyhood home in Bay City. But it was much grander, like the baronial mansions on the eastern side of the Saginaw River. Once they fixed it up, it would fit in with all the other grand houses on Hillside Avenue, all of which were expertly restored and well maintained.

When they moved in, John was forty-one, Helen was forty, Pat was eleven, John junior was ten, Freddie was seven, and Alma was eighty years old. To all outward appearances it seemed as though another well-to-do ambitious young executive had moved into the neighborhood with his extended family. Nice. A young man who takes care of his aging mother.

Only John Wittke saw through the facade. When the moving van from Rochester delivered the Lists' furniture the day they moved in, he couldn't help noticing that the van was practically empty, and what little furnishings they did possess were old and of cheap quality. When he saw that no new furniture was ever delivered, he quickly assessed the truth of the Lists' financial status. No way, he thought. They'll never restore that house. No way. Maybe the wife's got big dreams, but there doesn't seem to be any money. Nope. He was positive that the lofty plans John List talked about for restoring his grandfather's aging mansion would never come to fruition.

Michael and Diana Ryan were a middle-aged couple with seven children who had lived on Hillside Avenue for twenty years. Their home was directly next door to the new List family. Traditionally, the Ryans always welcomed a new family in the neighborhood by bringing over a home-baked apple pie. Five days had passed, enough time for the family to settle in a bit, Ryan thought. His wife, Diana, was busy so this time, he went alone, apple pie poised in the palm of his hand.

He went around to the back of the house and knocked on the kitchen door. After a few moments the door opened, and there was his new neighbor, John List, standing in the doorway, large enough to fill the door frame; yet he could see that standing behind him were his wife and their three young children.

"Hi," he said. "I'm Mike Ryan from next door."

"Yes?"

It was strange, Ryan found himself thinking. They'd been in the house almost a week, and it looked as if all their furniture were still piled in the kitchen. John moved a little as though deliberately barring Ryan's view to the interior, but not before Ryan saw that the children were crawling around inside the furniture. I don't think he wants me to see the disarray, he thought.

"Well," he said aloud, "we always welcome new families with an apple pie," he said, holding it out awkwardly.

"Thank you," List said. He did not offer to move aside or ask his new neighbor into the house.

"Uh . . . if there's anything you ever need, I'm an artist, so I often work at home."

The dour look that crossed List's face gave Ryan the impression that his being an artist immediately precluded any possibility of communication.

"Thank you for the pie," Mr. List said as politely as he could, "but I must tell you that we value our privacy and we're not really interested in encouraging friendships."

"Oh," Ryan murmured, taken aback.

"I hope you understand."

"Uh . . . certainly . . ."

"Once again," John said as he slowly began to close the door, "thank you for the pie. I'm sure the children will enjoy it."

"You're welcome."

Ryan walked back to his own home slowly, in mild shock. That was the first time something like that had ever happened.

"I got that pie right in the face," he told Diana when he got home.

A few days later Hank and Joyce O'Malley also wanted to introduce themselves to their new neighbors. The O'Malleys had lived on Hillside Avenue in Westfield since 1954. It had always been a fairly gregarious neighborhood, even though the houses were set a good distance from one another so that there was little opportunity for leaning over fences to chat with neighbors. The children set the pace for neighborhood socializing. There were seventeen children just between the Ryans, the O'Malleys, and the Vandermeres, all a few houses apart from one another.

Freddie opened the back door. "Hi there, young man," Hank O'Malley said warmly.

They were a bit surprised as they heard the deep, gruff male voice from within demanding, "Who's that? What are you doing?"

The boy seemed frightened as he glanced over his shoulder. He faded quickly to the side, as Mr. and Mrs. O'Malley had already entered and come through the laundry room into the kitchen. John List immediately pulled back when he saw them. They were obviously very friendly people as they introduced themselves and began a steady stream of welcoming conversation. Mr. and Mrs. List listened quietly.

"The kids are the catalyst in the neighborhood," Hank O'Malley was saying as he and his wife stood just inside the kitchen, cake in hand. "Everybody's kids are in everybody's houses all the time."

He was not getting much of a reaction. Both Mr. and Mrs. List seemed reticent, shy almost, about speaking. "It's a neighborhood with a lot of kids," he continued. "The street's like a playground. I see you have three children of your own."

"Yes."

"Well, I'm sure they'll fit right in," Mrs. O'Malley said kindly. She turned to the serious, wide-eyed little girl standing by the sink. "What's your name?"

"Patty."

"Well, you'll all have to come over and play with my children—"

"They'll be pretty busy adjusting to their new school," John interrupted.

"Of course, but as soon as you do . . ."

"Thank you," Patty said.

"Sure," O'Malley said, moving into the room just enough to be able to place the cake on the kitchen table. "All the people in the neighborhood know one another well, circulate a lot, cocktail parties, barbecues . . ."

"I don't think we'll have much time for that sort of thing," Mr. List said softly but deliberately.

"Well . . ." O'Malley hesitated. "Let us know if you need anything."

"Thank you. We're fine."

"Okay. . . ."

"And thank you for the cake," Mr. List said politely.

"Not at all," Mrs. O'Malley said, getting a clear picture of the intrusion their visit presented to the family that had just moved in. Their visit was clearly expected to be brief and to the point. They hadn't been invited to sit down.

Neither the Ryans nor the O'Malleys consciously avoided the Lists after these incidents. The Lists simply weren't part of what O'Malley liked to refer to as "the neighborhood show." After their initial contact with them, there really wasn't any reason to seek them out further.

To all outward appearances, the List family continued to live the withdrawn life-style that had marked their manner everywhere they lived. Within the family structure itself, however, their lives became more restricted than ever before.

These people were strangers, John thought to himself after meeting his neighbors. They seemed un-Christian to him. That was only one of the reasons he chose to remain aloof. There were others. He wanted to hide Helen from scrutiny. He wanted to protect his own image. He wanted to hide the fact that underneath his external austerity, he felt out of place with all the affluence that surrounded him. Artists, doctors, engineers. Successful people. Well-to-do. Monied. Being friendly would only mean exchanging visits, and John knew there was no possibility of socializing with any of them. First of all, Helen was ill. Second, not only was there no money to buy furniture, but the house itself, seen now in the light of reality, was in a terrible state of disrepair. Part of the ceilings in the kitchen and dining room had actually collapsed. For the time being, until they settled in with all the new and much heavier expenses of the house—until his Budget Book balanced—he did not have the money to do anything other than sweep up the debris.

In the face of such insecurity, John began to demonstrate the full force of his rigid, Germanic upbringing in raising his own children. He had to keep them within the family fold, to ensure their safety from the evils of the world, to imbue them with the faith, the word of God. The prayers after meals became longer. Not only would he thank the Lord for the food they had received and for the many blessings He had bestowed upon them, that day—"Thank you, Lord, for the blessings of this new life. Keep us secure from an encroaching sinful world"—but he added as many sermonettes to the children's spiritual diet that he could: "Fear the Lord your God. Walk in all His ways. Love Him. Serve the Lord your God with all your heart and with all your soul."

The children silently kept their heads bowed during the scriptural recitations and obediently murmured, "Amen."

The only friendship John cultivated was that of the Reverend Eugene A. Rehwinkel of the Lutheran Church of the Redeemer. As usual, church was the only place he felt thoroughly comfortable. Partly to thank the Lord for the good fortune of his new position and partly because it was the only comfort he himself had, John offered to teach Sunday school again. He volunteered to lead the church Boy Scout troop. Shades of army drills and discipline slipped into his leadership as he often made the young troop march through Westfield in military-style precision, much to the amusement of those who stood to the side and watched. He even participated in Little League as an assistant coach. Baseball and soccer were the only activities in which he permitted John junior and Freddie to participate outside of church-related ones.

At first, to compensate for the fact that John didn't want his family to mingle with the neighbors, he tried to fill the emptiness by suggesting family excursions whenever it seemed Helen was up to it, but the children soon began to lack enthusiasm for such outings. It was Patricia who articulated to her aunt Jean how they all hated them because "all Mommy and Daddy do is fight." And she told of one such trip to Coney Island, where they'd fought so hard and long that Mommy got violently sick to her stomach and threw up. "Then I begged her to eat something 'cause I thought she was going to faint," she told Aunt Jean. "And she did eat, but she just got sick again. And Aunt Jean," Patty said sadly, "you know how it is. It lasts for days. Mommy was sick to her stomach for days."

She didn't confide to Aunt Jean how much she hated what she was beginning to perceive as her mother's weaknesses. Sometimes she'd find her mother lying across the kitchen table passed out with a little saliva drooling out of the corner of her mouth. John junior would just look and leave the room. Freddie never said anything. If Helen was aware of the unhappiness of her children, it didn't matter. Nothing mattered anymore. All she knew was that she felt violently ill all the time and that all of her pathetically happy dreams for a new life crumbled as her health deteriorated further. She even hated the house. There was no restoration, no joy, in the empty rooms. It was just another house, bigger than the others, emptier. And with it had come John's mother, Alma. She settled into the upstairs apartment, the only part of the house that resembled a home. *She* had furniture in her living room. The two living rooms on the first floor as well as the huge ballroom were practically barren. What little furniture they had brought with them seemed to disappear in the large rooms. John took over the front living room as an office, moving in a gray metal four-drawer filing cabinet, a black three-drawer metal cabinet, and a desk. It was the only room on the main floor that had draperies—ugly, floral things, but draperies.

The children's bedrooms didn't even have dressers, Helen thought bitterly. Their clothes were actually piled up on the floor. To have all of the disappointments in her life buoyed with the hope of a new life in Westfield, only to have her dreams crushed again, was more than she could bear. She spent a great deal of time in deep depressions. She drank to forget, to hide, to disguise her loneliness, her utter sense of emotional deprivation. That woman upstairs now, in her own home, over her head, a constant presence whether she could actually see her or not, was the final blow. She knew John went upstairs to spend hour after hour, night after night, with her. Helen took more and more to her bed. She was drinking at least five or six scotches a day and taking as many as five Doriden sleeping tablets a day. And always the worry. She knew something was wrong inside her head.

John increasingly found himself playing both father and mother to his three growing children. Helen seemed to have become incapable even of the most perfunctory household tasks. The house was too big for her. It overwhelmed her. He knew buying it had been a mistake; and every time his mother came down the stairs to try to help, Helen became almost hysterical with hostility. Soon Alma spent most of her time on the third floor except to go shopping and to church. She hardly mingled with the family.

John too was changing. Gone was the quiet sweetness of character and acquiescent personality that had characterized his youth. With the societal disintegration he saw all around him, compliments of the sixties, his religion was becoming even more important than ever. He saw demons everywhere.

He had to watch his children with even greater scrutiny—Patty in particular. She was beginning to blossom into a lovely young girl. The only people John encouraged his sons to associate with were the Baeder family, who were fellow parishioners of the Lutheran Church of the Redeemer. Their sons, Rick and David, were approximately the same ages as John junior and Freddie. Although there was school bus service—Hillside Avenue was quite a hike from school—he didn't want his children riding the school buses with the other children. He made arrangements with their mother, Barbara Baeder, to take turns driving the children to and from school.

John and Helen were becoming shadows in their own lives. It was a great surprise to everyone in the neighborhood when they accepted the Vandermeres' invitation. Despite their standoffish behavior, Mr. and Mrs. Vandermere, who lived directly across the street, decided to ask them to their yearly Christmas cocktail party. "I'd like you to think of this as a belated welcome-to-the-neighborhood party."

Their neighbors wouldn't give up, John thought. For some strange reason he couldn't adequately explain to himself, he felt obliged to accept.

"Well, how nice that you came," Hank O'Malley said. "Mrs.

List, glad to see you. How do you like your new home?"

"It's very nice," John answered for her.

"Well, I'm sure you'll be very happy here."

Helen smiled a bit reservedly.

"You know, I always liked that house," O'Malley continued in his friendly fashion. He'd long ago gotten over the initial rebuff suffered at the hands of the Lists several months earlier. "I know it very well. Me and my wife were very close to the Youngs, you know, the family that lived there before you people bought it. Tom Young, now he was something. A tremendous do-it-yourselfer. He was all over that house doing things all the time."

John and Helen listened politely but made no comment.

"And he was vice-president of a small independent company down here. You're a vice-president, too, aren't you? Of a bank, right?"

"Yes. Of First National Bank in Jersey City."

Hank waited a bit awkwardly for him to go on. When he didn't, he continued, "Tom liked to cook, and do things with his hands. Of course they moved." He smiled. "Tom thought his kids were getting contaminated with too much civilization. He wanted to take them off into the wild to live a clean life up in Vermont."

"He may have had a point," John commented.

Hank didn't know what else to say. He was rescued by Michael Ryan, who came over to greet the new arrivals.

"You've met the Lists," he said.

"Sure," Ryan said. "We live right across the street. Remember?"

"Yes," John said shyly. "Nice to see you again."

Ryan was glad his wife wasn't at the party. He knew she wouldn't feel like being too friendly. She was miffed, not only because of the "apple pie" incident, but because when two of her younger children had recently cut across List's lawn, he had chased them off, and she felt he was much more ferocious than he should have been toward young children.

This was the first time Joyce O'Malley had seen Mrs. List since their initial meeting at her back door. In all the months since they'd moved in, Mrs. List never seemed to be around. Now she turned to Mrs. List. She had entered wearing a mink coat, and she still had not taken it off.

"What a lovely coat," Joyce said.

"Thank you," Helen murmured. "Christmas . . ."

"Would you like me to take it for you?"

"No," John said. "We can't stay long."

"Oh."

"The children are home waiting for us," he explained.

"Can I get you a drink, then?" Joyce offered.

"No, thank you," Helen replied.

Across the room, Edith Reader eyed the new arrivals with mild interest. She and her husband, Jack, lived several houses away from the Lists.

"What's the matter?" her husband asked.

"Not a thing," Edith answered. "I'm just surprised to see them here, that's all."

"I don't think I've ever set eyes on her," Jack mused as he studied his new neighbors across the room.

"All I can say," Edith whispered to her husband, "is they're strange people. He's terribly unfriendly. It seems like they never want anybody around."

"This is Dr. Cunnick," Hank O'Malley said, making the introductions. "They live across the street from you."

John looked at him with interest. "Do you practice in Westfield, doctor?"

"No," he answered. "I'm a corporate medical director. I don't have a practice per se."

Dr. Cunnick thought Mr. List was a pleasant enough individual, although he perceived a lessening of interest when informed that he was not in practice. But the woman . . . she didn't look well, he thought. Extremely pale, hands shaking a bit, eyes too bright. She was demonstrating a highly medicated affect he thought, as though she had been heavily sedated before entering the room.

"How long have you lived here?" John asked.

"Since 1967."

"Perhaps you might recommend a doctor in the area."

They left the cocktail party early. It was the first and last time they would participate in any neighborhood social activity. The general consensus among the neighbors over the next few years was that the Lists were never overtly hostile in any way, just terribly private.

"If I'm out cutting my grass and he's cutting his, I'll wave," Ryan told O'Malley several months later. "But that's about it."

"Does he wave back?" O'Malley asked curiously.

"Oh, sure. He'll do that much."

"Strange duck," O'Malley mused. "Their house is very quiet all the time. I never notice any visitors. You?"

"No. Well, like he says," Ryan concluded, "they like their privacy. So, if that's what he wants, its okay by me."

It was Alma who baked cookies and brought them over for the children. The neighbors immediately took a liking to the friendly, gracious old lady.

And then the rumor quickly spread that Helen List had suffered "some kind of nervous breakdown." Several of the neighbors would have liked to express their concern and caring, but the opportunity never quite presented itself. It wasn't long before the invisible Mrs. List's condition ceased to be an active cause for concern.

18 | Is God Dead?

John couldn't believe it. He had found Patty with a copy of *Lady Chatterley's Lover* in her possession. She was only twelve years old! "Where did you get this?" he demanded sternly.

"It belongs to a friend of mine," she stammered. "In school...."

"Who!"

"A girl in school...."

"Do you know what this is?"

She was afraid to answer. Instead she shook her head.

"Do you have any idea how pornographic this book is?"

"My English teacher said," the girl began tentatively, "that it was ruled..."

"What!"

"'Not obscene,' Daddy, by a... by a court of appeals."

"You seem to know an awful lot about a book you say you don't know anything about," he said, slamming the book on the kitchen table.

Having *Lady Chatterley's Lover* in her possession opened up a floodgate of recriminations on Patty's head, and for John it was an internal recapping of the emotional violence he saw closing in on his world. It was like a warning. Even though he hated the thought of the Vietnam War, he hated even more to see that Patty had the peace symbol stenciled onto the cover of her looseleaf notebook. To him the peace symbol denoted a decade of disobedience and social violence of all sorts rather than peace. The mounting tally of violence was frightening. First the immolation of little black girls in a church bombing in the South; even churches were not held inviolate by a contemptuous world gone mad. Then the murder of President Kennedy. Then the murder of civil rights workers. The world *had* gone mad, driven to madness by its own godlessness, he thought in rigid despair. Look what his children were witnessing week after week. The chronology of violence done to the individual as well as to the national psyche was staggering. It was almost inevitable that someone would eventually try to profit by the horror infiltrating into everyday society by asking the question of whether God had finally abandoned man.

And there it was on the April 18, 1966 cover of *Time* magazine:

Is God Dead?

It was not a surprise to John, nor was the turnaround implied by the question. It wasn't God who was dead. Morality was dead. Virtue was dead. Ethics were dead. It wasn't God who had abandoned man. It was man who had abandoned God for the earthly rewards of greed, the blood lust of violence, and the sating of animalistic sensuality. John felt he was witnessing the beginning of the Apocalypse brought about by moral decay. Irreverence and godlessness had taken a serious toll. Man was paying for the sins of man. The price was heavy, but just. How does one protect one's children?

To the accompaniment of Patty's tears, he confiscated the offensive book.

"What am I going to tell my friend?" Patty cried.

"She's not your friend!" he said solemnly.

"But . . . it's not mine. She'll want it back."

"Tell her to come talk to me."

And then, suddenly, there were other things to think about.

Helen took a bad fall during another blackout incident, in which she seriously bruised her left ear and hip. This time John took her to Overlook Hospital in Summit, New Jersey, where, on January 29, 1966, she was immediately admitted. She walked with her eyes closed and her body and knees bent. She needed support. Although she was obviously suffering the distress of confusion, lethargy, and a violent headache, Helen was not cooperative. She hated being in the hospital and refused to talk to the doctors.

"I hate doctors. I want to go home," she complained to John. And then she said, "There's flowers on the windowsill." The non sequitur frightened him.

When Dr. Eugene Loeser, a neurologist, saw the patient on the day of admission, he immediately noted a profusion of nonsequential, irrelevant statements and requested that she have constant observation; he was worried that she might harm herself.

The history as recorded showed that the patient was:

Unable to walk without assistance because of imbalance and stiffness of the legs. Decreased vision in the left eye. One week and four days of headache. One week of gait disturbance. Two days ago she had fallen. Uncooperative. Dehydrated. She moaned and mumbled concerning her medical experiences twenty years ago. In 1948, the patient began losing vision in the right eye associated with pain in that eye. After three years, vision was completely lost. Visual difficulties started prior to the malaria.

Since Helen wouldn't talk to Dr. Loeser, it became necessary to obtain her history from John. There were further consultations with Dr. Arnold Rose, an ophthalmologist, and Dr. Richard Taylor, a psychiatrist. John told them that while Helen was in Korea twenty years ago she had contracted malaria, which was treated at Walter Reed Hospital. "She still has fairly frequent episodes of chills and fever," he said. He had already put the syphilis from his mind.

"When was the last episode?"

"Six months ago."

John had to admit that in Rochester Helen had had a neurological evaluation and had been advised to see a psychiatrist. "She did so for several months and then stopped." He didn't like to admit the need for psychiatric intervention, no matter how short the duration. "Just tell her it's not a brain tumor," he urged the doctor quietly. "She's very worried about that."

"Why should she think that?"

"Because her father died of cancer," he said.

It was Dr. Loeser's impression that:

Patient had head trauma and a possible fracture at the base of the skull. Possible drug toxicity. An overreaction to medicine causing general overall mental picture and gait disturbance. Acute mental syndrome.

He ruled out a lesion or any sort of pathology next to the pituitary gland of the brain.

On January 30, 1966, he wrote:

Patient about the same, but she was in a better mental
state. Examination of x-rays did not show any fracture of
the skull.

On January 31, 1966, he wrote:

The patient remains relatively uncommunicative.

Helen really didn't want to talk to him, yet she accused Dr. Loeser
of being in a hurry even though she persisted in long periods of
silence. Throughout Dr. Loeser's examination she made odd movements of her face: grimacing, lip-smacking responses without talking
or answering his questions.

Her most vigorous conversation was when the doctor rose to leave,
"I'll be all right," she said, "if someone will only read the editorial
page to me."

He felt there might be a physical reason for her mental unbalance.
He wrote:

Psychotic behavior. But continue organic workup.

On February 1, 1966:

The patient was found to be a bit more spontaneous in
speech and more rational. Her urine tested positive for
phenobarbitol, certainly not a medicine that had been
ordered during the hospital stay.

Dr. Loeser urged that she have a psychiatric examination as well
as an eye consultation.

Dr. Arnold Rose, the ophthalmologist, noted the two-week history
of Mrs. List's complaints of poor vision in the left eye:

Falling more often.
   Very disoriented.
   Often doesn't know where she is.
   Pupils are very dilated and respond only sluggishly.

February 2, 1966:

Patient fell out of bed but voiced no complaints.
Nurses noted she was having headaches.
Patient seemed confused and tended to lose her balance
easily.
Poor appetite.
Talking constantly of various subjects—wigs, war
experience.

On February 3, 1966 Dr. Rose noted:

20/20 vision on the left. Nearly normal affect in her
psychological responses. Answers questions and gives a
cogent history. Diagnosis: No active eye pathology.
Possible drug reaction. Possible hysteria

On February 4, 1966, Dr. Taylor did the psychiatric examination.
He found Helen in bed alert, talking, and cooperative despite her
obvious dislike of seeing a psychiatrist. He noted:

Her speech was excessive and fast, with little pause.
Defensive and clinging quality. Her orientation was vague
although her memory did not appear as though it was
impaired, except she really couldn't tell very much about
her blackouts. She seemed bright as far as her IQ, but her
judgment was impulsive and emotional.
Content of thought revealed no delusions or hallucinations,
but there is a slight tinge of paranoia.

Dr. Taylor found her quite guarded. She was swinging quickly
back and forth in how she approached him with a rather shallow,
moderately dramatic quality. "I was mildly depressed back in
1961," she said, "but it was gone—relieved, you might say, by a
little more recreation and a little more attention from my husband,"
she said. "Now, who knows what." Her attention wandered from
the point. "Where is the cafeteria?"

"How do you feel right now?" he asked.

"I'm new in town," she answered quickly. "I don't know anybody, and I don't know any doctors, and of course, I'm a little
anxious, it's such a big house, what do you expect, and the
neighbors, they don't like me because our house is very grand, you
know. Planting, planting, children, who cares. My husband has
every intention of doing it up good. I'm exhausted with all the work.

No wonder I get confused sometimes and frustrated. You ain't gonna blame me for that."

He noted that her story was very poorly organized and scattered with a "grandiosity. A bragging of social and financial status despite occasional bad English."

"And she's here all the time now," she went on breathlessly. "My mother-in-law. Upstairs. That's when my headaches started. When she moved in. Over my head. And I can't sleep. Can you prescribe some sleeping pills for me? Of course, I'm not depressed now. Our house is a mansion. And I don't take any drugs, I never take pills, not even sleeping pills. I wouldn't take any. Not even bromides for when I have headaches. Except for a rare pep pill, I don't take anything at all. Certainly nothing to drink. We don't do that down south."

He noted that her associations were loose and often irrelevant to what they were talking about, but she couldn't stop talking.

"My legs feel week sometimes, nothing really, and sometimes, it's the funniest thing, my coordination is out of line. And my eyes. You know sometimes I'm afraid I'm going to go completely blind. And I love to read. What would I do if I went blind in my left eye, too?" He could sense a very real underlying panic. "Have you looked at that carefully?" she demanded. "Down by the other side of the wall. I don't trust you guys to do the right thing. You've never done the right thing by me! Nobody ever does. Those sweat boxes, do you know what that feels like!"

"Do you remember falling?"

"No," she said sullenly, and then just as suddenly demanded, "What are today's headlines?"

"Do you remember the blackouts?"

She was quiet for a long time as though she were trying to focus in on his question. Finally she answered, "No. I can't remember anything afterward. But both times my vision is much worse for a spell, but I recall the trip to the hospital and the blackouts. Is John here? He's never around when I need him."

Impression: Latent schizophrenia, pseudoneurotic with inconsistent personality including depressive, compulsive, and hysterical features. No signs of overt psychosis.

He added:

I believe the major psychiatric effect here is hysterical aggravation of symptoms due to panic about her eye. This is not to say that organic causes do not have to be ruled out. A brain tumor or a stroke. Recommendation: Librium 3 times a day. And much reassurance. Doubt advisability of involving her in psychotherapy and stirring up her confused unconscious mind.

The x-rays of the hip and skulls did not show a fracture or abnormality. An electroencephalogram was mildly abnormal, especially in the left temporal region of the brain.

The front sheet of Helen's hospital record read:

Latent schizophrenia and headache. Secondary diagnosis: History of malaria, chorioretinitis, with blindness of the right eye.

There was no treatment. Helen gradually improved to the point that she could go home, and she was released on February 5, 1966. It was to be only the first of many hospital admissions for her.

While Helen's condition gave John a great deal to worry about, other problems continued to mount. There was another overshadowing crisis that suddenly demanded the major portion of concentration from John's troubled mind. Within one year's time of the move to Westfield, his career as a vice-president of the First National Bank in Jersey City was over. He had been unceremoniously fired.

Again.

He was stunned.

He didn't want to recognize that, by this time, termination had become the pattern of his career. The initial personable "good impressions" he gave on interviews quickly disintegrated on the job. As long as he was working alone he handled himself fairly well, but every time he was in a position where he had to deal with people on a one-to-one basis, he fell short of company expectations. He still couldn't bring himself to delegate responsibilities since he was sure that only *he* could do things the right way; he would soon became overwhelmed by the steady rise in his workload brought about by the perfection he demanded of himself.

He worked without pause. What in God's blessed name did they want from him? he thought. He was told by management that he had sixty days to find another job. He came into the bank every morning as usual. Part of him couldn't accept the fact of his dismissal. The naïve part of him hoped that if he didn't bring too much attention to himself and simply sat quietly at his desk doing his work, they would forget about having told him to find another job . . . that it would all blow over. But they hadn't forgotten.

After ten days of avoidance, of not even giving the slightest indication of a job search, he was called into the office of his direct superior.

"Look, List," his boss said without ceremony, "we don't think it's a good idea for you to stay any longer. Your termination is common knowledge. That makes your position . . . well . . . lame duck. It's not good for morale."

He cleared his throat as List's eyes pierced into his with a sudden surge of repressed fury, but he continued. "We feel it's best for all concerned if you take your vacation time and leave right away," he concluded quickly and firmly. He kept his own eyes fixed on List until the man lowered his gaze.

As John quietly cleaned out his desk, he kept his eyes glued to the papers he was gathering. Most of the employees who knew he had been fired had disappeared on "errands." Of the few left, no one looked his way as he walked out until he had passed them; then eyes bored into his retreating back.

All of his dreams for prosperity were shattered. This time he didn't tell his family he was fired. Instead, he dressed in suit and tie every day as though he were going to work as usual. Then he sat in the railroad station reading the classified section of *The New York Times* until there were no more ads to read. Afterward, with no place to go, he sat in a corner of the waiting room and read until it was time to go home again—a newspaper, a magazine. The Bible.

Every morning he played the same charade. There was no reason for anyone at home to suspect he was not going to work every morning as usual. Every day he sat in a corner of the waiting room, afraid to go home, not knowing where to get a job, afraid to face Helen, worrying about his mounting bills. He did not even tell *Mutter*. He was frozen, inert, unable to make a decision.

A month passed. He continued to read the want ads every day religiously. He prayed. For a few guilty moments he even thought that God was abandoning him. There was nothing in the want ads. Occasionally he would go on what he perceived might be a suitable interview. More often than not he sat and read in order to bury the growing anxieties he was experiencing, and when he couldn't concentrate on his reading, he spent the time thinking about the fraying fabric of his life. A failing career, no job prospects, a new home in desperate need of repair, heavy mortgage payments, an unsupportive wife who drank . . . . "Teach the young women to be sober," it was written in Paul's Epistle to Titus. Worse still, he had a wife who was drifting away from the church and a daughter who was drifting away from parental control. It wasn't just that damnable book Patty had been reading. She was becoming positively rebellious, beginning to show resentment about the weekly attendance at church he insisted upon. Oh, she didn't protest openly. She wouldn't dare, but he could sense her withdrawal. The questions she raised as she unconsciously weighed the strict values of the church against the growing permissive values shared by her peers. Unthinkable insurrectionary questions like "How can anyone be sure of all this?" as she was forced to bow her head while he prayed over their daily meals. None of her friends at school did things like that. Unfortunately, she was too old for the Lutheran Redeemer School. She was now attending public school, being exposed every day to new values, new thinking.

A second month passed spent in self-imposed isolation at the railroad station. Daily he watched the swell of commuters crowding through the rush hours, envying them their destinations. Daily he sat in lonely contemplation.

Patty was almost thirteen, he brooded. A dangerous age. Of the three children, she was his biggest worry. How could he make her understand how important it was to be soundly grounded theologically? With the conspicuous moral degeneration of the young, *making* her understand was becoming more important than ever before. He didn't want another Brenda on his hands.

Remember what Thomas said, he thought as yet another commuter train rumbled through on its way to New York City. When Thomas finally came face to face with the Lord after the Resurrection, he said, "Know that I have this evidence. I believe."

And the Lord said, "Only if you could believe without having to put your fingers in my side."

He couldn't seem to make Patty realize that what He was saying was there was enough evidence to begin with without physical proof. But some people need it, he couldn't deny that. Patty was becoming one of the doubting Thomases. She seemed fascinated with good and evil. He would give her a book to read, he thought. The Scriptures tell us that the foremost student of the Bible is the evil one himself. One had to arm oneself early.

A third month passed, and then a fourth. His depression was worsening.

He bought himself a container of coffee and made his way back to the privacy of his corner in the littered waiting room, which every day seemed a little grungier. He passed a man asleep on one of the hardwood benches. He was dressed in filthy military fatigues. His hair was long and unkempt. His face was unshaved. His mouth hung partially open . . . he was dead drunk and sleeping it off in a public place. He appeared to be in his early twenties. The sight sickened John.

He found his quiet spot away from the surrounding contamination and the rest of reality and sipped from his container of coffee.

And Helen? he thought. He didn't want to think of her physical disintegration or the staggering medical bills piling up. Rather he focused on what he perceived as her moral disintegration. Not only did she demonstrate the same undisciplined immorality as Patty, Helen continually *challenged* everything about Lutheranism. She was even sorry that she had converted. She'd actually said as much. How could he make her understand that there was no other way? The Book, the Word, the true Church. He had always been interested in theology. But then he thought, No, it was more than interest; he must continue to study the Word as a form of protection against the whirlpools of sin in which the world was slowly sinking.

As he sat in the corner of a hostile world month after month, he was stringently reinforcing the already deeply ingrained doctrines learned at his mother's knee. Time gave him the luxury to secure himself even more firmly in the rigidity of his beliefs. He knew no other way to think.

Despite all that had gone wrong, he continued to play the dutiful husband. It was almost a form of self-punishment, self-flagellation.

"Anything Helen wants, he jumps up and runs around like a child," Jean said to Gene in mild disgust after talking long distance to her mother, who had just returned home to North Carolina from another joyless visit to Helen. "Doesn't he have a mind of his own? And Helen likes only the best things. Whatever she wants, he buys. They're living way beyond their means in that stupid house they bought!" And Jean didn't even know he was unemployed.

"I'm really surprised at the way they live, Jean," Mom had said on the phone.

"Why?" Jean asked. "What do you mean?"

"I cut my visit a little short," she said a bit apologetically. "it's just so . . . dark all the time."

"Mom," Jean insisted, "c'mon, tell me. . . ."

"John's still quite a Mama's boy," Eva Morris said with a sigh. "You should see. She still tells him to put on his galoshes and take his umbrella in the morning when he goes out. Lord's truth! Even mittens. Things like that.''

"I don't believe it."

"I've heard her with my own two ears," she insisted. "The man is in his forties, for heaven's sake. You'd think that sort of stuff would have stopped by now, wouldn't you?"

"You bet," Jean declared emphatically.

"I used to think it was nice," her mother went on. "I always thought, A man will treat his wife the way he treats his mother. But it's not good."

"Yes! Go on."

"And then when he comes home at night after work, he goes right upstairs to his mother's apartment," Mrs. Morris confided in hushed tones. "Jean, I declare, he stays up there two hours or more every night."

"Why? What do they talk about?"

"Who knows? Mrs. List hardly ever comes downstairs anymore when Helen's around. Eats by herself all the time. Cooks everything up there in her white kitchen. Even the kids don't go up to visit her much anymore."

"Why not?"

"I'm not sure. They don't say much," she continued sadly, "but I think it's because she criticizes them. Tries to make them do things . . . behave . . . pray all the time, like *they* do. . . . Oh, I don't know, Jean." She sighed. "I think she's a very controlling woman. Which gets me back to the point, honey. He's a real Mama's boy, torn between his mother and his wife."

"Who's winning?"

"Oh, the mother," Mrs. Morris said without hesitating. "I don't think there's any doubt about that. They're so much alike, how could it be any other way? Anyway, I had to leave. I haven't been feeling well myself lately," she said a bit defensively, almost as though she felt she had to apologize for leaving her daughter in such an unhappy state. "But it was just so depressing. Like there was a big black cloud hanging over everyone, right inside the house. I don't think they've been happy there for a minute."

Jean was heartsick at the news but not surprised. This was not the first time she'd experienced a sense of foreboding for her sister's future.

"I don't like to stay there anymore, although Helen keeps telling me I have to come again and again," Mrs. Morris continued on and on, as though purging herself of all her own unhappy feelings brought about by her latest visit. "And even though Patty and Johnny tell me that all Helen and John do is fight, with me there, they kind of slow it down some, I guess. I felt so bad, honey, about leaving sooner than I'd planned. Little Freddie begged me to stay some more, not to leave. It was the most he said the entire time I was there. Never said much at all, just kind of hung close to me all the time. But I don't know. He's such a cutie, that child, but I'm really worried about him. He's the quietest of all. Jean, honey, he's such a loner, it isn't natural. All he does is spend time with that silly little Pekingese dog of his, you know, Tinkerbell, the one that snaps at you every chance he gets. Little beast. And all I ever see is John praying. It drives me kinda crazy, though, you know? I think it's excessive," she said a bit guiltily. "Y'know what I mean, honey? I think the kids are beginning to resent it, too. 'Specially Patty and Johnny, though they don't say much, Lord knows."

"And Helen?" Jean asked, her concerns over Helen's welfare only deepening with her mother's sad recitation. "How is she, Mom? How does she feel?"

"Oh, Jean," Eva Morris said. "She just never seems to get any better."

Jean's premonitions of some kind of impending disaster intensified. She made up her mind to write to Helen immediately.

Helen didn't know John was out of work, but she did know there was little money and that John had ordered the liquor store to stop deliveries again. She was merciless in her scorn of his inability to support them. She refused to consider cutting back on expenses.

In the meantime, while he spent days of desperation at the railroad station, the financial deterioration was worsening. Bills for fuel, electricity, food, and clothing were piling up. Every night he came home and after spending his usual time talking with Alma—he knew with a mounting sense of guilt that these were the only moments she lived for—he marked everything down in his Budget Book. It was a meticulous recording of his financial ruin, almost penny by penny. He could see, in black and white, that his life was careening out of control.

Secretly he began to borrow from his mother's account in order to keep the snarling wolf at bay. He promised himself he would replace the amounts he withdrew as soon as he got a job again.

During the six months of his self-imposed isolation, when he would not share his anxieties with anyone except God, he became uncharacteristically harsh at home, even verbally abusive with the children. They reacted nervously and even with fear when they saw him twitching with anger. They had no idea what was behind the inexplicable violent mood swings. Freddie, in particular, was terrified and tried to fade into the background when he saw his father's anger rising; it was easy enough to spot, for it was always accompanied by nervous facial tics and red cheeks. When List lost his temper, his deep voice reverberated through the huge, empty rooms. His eyes bulged fiercely. To the children, his anger, usually slow to develop, was an awesome and frightening thing.

There were times when they could see he was sorry. He'd cook a special meal or offer to play baseball with them on the lawn even though he was obviously exhausted. But, try as he would, John couldn't really control his mercurial disposition. He finally got a job with the American Photographic Co. as a staff accountant for $12,000 a year, half of what he had been making when he'd moved his family to New Jersey; but the way he outwardly perceived the world had permanently changed. Despair was now a constant, brooding companion.

On February 3, 1968, Helen was admitted to Overlook Hospital again. She had slipped in the bedroom against the bedpost and had a fractured dislocation of her left collarbone. John was angry this time. He was sure she hadn't blacked out for any reason other than alcohol. Once again he stopped liquor deliveries; they stopped talking to each other.

Dr. Brady, an orthopedic surgeon in Westfield, noted that she had fallen about four weeks before admission to the hospital. It took that long for John to get her to the doctor. She couldn't lift her left arm, and she was still swollen and black and blue when Dr. Brady saw her. On February 9 he excised the last inch of her clavicle running from the breastbone out to the shoulder in order to relieve her of her limitation of movement and distress. Shortly thereafter she went home.

She and John did not discuss the fall that had caused the injury.

"What kind of trees?" Hank O'Malley asked in a friendly tone when he saw John planting a long series of tiny trees along both sides of his property from front to back.

"Trees for privacy," List replied cryptically.

As O'Malley walked away he thought to himself, Those things are so scrawny that even if they do survive, it'll be years before they give him any "privacy."

But John was trying to build even higher the wall of isolation from the outside world.

By May of 1968 Helen was taking increased dosages of prescribed medication. Physically she was often completely off-balance. It was getting to the point where many days she could scarcely get out of bed. The doctors weren't sure what was wrong with her. Besides her drinking, which she wouldn't admit, there seemed to be an insidious degeneration of all of her normal capabilities to function.

The same month, Jean and Gene Syfert came to visit before leaving for Germany, where Gene was about to serve a two-year tour with the air force.

It had been a long drive from Oklahoma. It was their first visit to Westfield, and when they finally pulled up into the long driveway, they were duly impressed by the house's grandeur; Jean thought the big old house very beautiful on the outside, everything Helen had said it was, even though she was sure they couldn't afford it.

They knocked on the front door. There was no response. They went around to the rear of the house and knocked on the back door. Still there was no response. John was probably at work, and the children were most likely at school, but the Syferts had expected to find Helen home. They retraced their steps back to the front porch, and this time they knocked as hard as they could. By now Alma, who had heard the knocking, had come down from the third floor. She opened the door and let them in. After friendly but brief greetings, Alma explained to them where they could find Helen, then retreated to her apartment on the third floor.

Left alone to find their way, Jean and Gene had time to look around. They were immediately aware that the inside of the house was in need of many repairs.

"Look," Jean said, pointing.

As they ascended the staircase, they could see that water had been leaking through to the first floor from one of the upstairs bathrooms. They could tell it had been leaking for a long time.

"Looks like the roof may be leaking, too."

They found Helen in bed on the second floor. When she saw them, it was obvious that she was very happy to see them. As they spoke quickly, excitedly, Jean noticed that Helen was in a nightgown and that the bedroom was very unkempt, as was she. It appeared to Jean that Helen had not bathed. The first thing Jean noticed was that her sister's feet were quite dirty. Helen had always been so meticulous about her personal hygiene; now her body, her hair, her face, were actually unclean.

The bed linens are not clean, either, she thought, making a quick survey of the scene. The floor's not clean. The bathroom to this room's not clean.

She also noticed a great number of medicine bottles on the night table. She wondered how Helen could know which medication to take. "You know, sometimes I forget to take mine," she said, expressing her concerns carefully, sensing that Helen's emotional state was precarious. "Sometimes I can't remember if I took it in the morning or in the evening."

Helen shrugged away her sister's concerns, but Jean didn't like it. She didn't feel it was safe.

There was also an open can of peanuts and a jar of peanut butter sitting on the bedside table, which seemed odd to her. It looked as if it didn't belong there.

"That's what I had for lunch," Helen said, noticing Jean's searching look. Then she sat herself up stiffly in bed. "I'll call John." She reached for the bedside phone. "To tell him you're here."

The dresser was packed with worn, soiled books, the kind that Helen loved to read—love stories, mostly.

When Helen hung up the receiver she told them that John said he would be home in a little while.

"From the bank?"

"Oh, no, he doesn't work there anymore. He has another job. Didn't I tell you that?" They could see a sudden thought flash across her face. "Wait," she said, reaching for the phone again. They waited while she redialed John's number. "It's me," she said. "Listen, bring home some chicken and things for dinner tonight." It sounded like an order.

As usual, Jean thought, it was clear who was the dominant personality in the relationship.

After the second call, Helen got up from her bed. "I want to take you downstairs to show you something."

As they went downstairs to the dining room area, Jean could see that Helen was walking unsteadily, but she didn't ask for assistance. Once in the dining room, Helen removed several pieces of Waterford crystal from the china closet that they had bought when they were in Ireland. "Look," she said. "Do you like it?"

"It's beautiful!"

"I'm really very proud of it," Helen said. "It's very expensive. Do you like the house?"

"Oh, yes. . . ."

"Come," she said almost gaily. "I have to show you the ball-room."

Helen eagerly watched for their reaction as they walked into the huge room.

"You could fit our whole house in here," Jean said, and she could tell that their "impressed" response made Helen happy. Then Helen insisted on taking them down to the basement.

"But Helen," Jean began to protest.

"You have to come," Helen insisted. "I want to show you a sink down there that's very old. You'll love it. It's white with little red roses on it, and I want you to have it." Helen's happiness at seeing Jean had unleashed all of her generosity. She knew her sister loved antiques. "You must have it."

"But, honey, we're going to Germany in a few days"—Jean smiled—"and there's no way that I could take it now."

Helen looked terribly disappointed.

"But if you still want me to have it when I come back," Jean continued, "I'll take it then, okay?"

Helen smiled brightly. "One other thing," she said. "Upstairs."

She took them all the way upstairs to show them a hall tree that was in the hallway. It was very, very old. "I want you to have it. If you'd like to have it, at some point," she said, "you can take it home with you."

"Sure," Jean said. "Thanks, honey."

By this time Helen was exhausted. Jean and Gene walked her to her bedroom, where she went back to bed. As they left her lying quietly in her room, they looked at each other; Helen's condition had changed markedly from the last time they'd seen her in Rochester. She looked terrible.

John came home at five-thirty with bags of groceries for dinner. He, too, was genuinely happy to see them.

Jean watched as he unloaded the groceries on the kitchen counter. It seemed he had taken on more of the household duties: father, mother, cook, dishwasher, she thought sympathetically. He was fulfilling most of Helen's roles, even though he had a full-time job. She didn't realize that, as on the job, he didn't delegate much responsibility to the children. There was a deep part of him that resented the extra work, that felt Helen should try to pull her weight more despite her illnesses, but there was also a part of him that told him he had to do it all himself.

As usual, Jean wasn't surprised that he didn't complain or protest his homemaker role. In all the years she had known him, she had never seen him angry. It was as though the man were incapable of anger.

Gene spent time with the children while Jean helped John with the cooking. The Syferts were a warm, loving family when they were with their own three sons. Knowing the kind of interaction she and Gene had with their children, Jean thought she noticed a subtle change in John's interaction with Patty, Johnny, and Freddie. He seemed imperceptibly harsher with them than she remembered. But no, not he, she thought; she was wrong. He was still the sweet, gentle, soft-spoken man she had first met in Newport News, Virginia, almost eighteen years earlier. His demeanor hadn't changed. It was the children who had changed. Patty was a bit sullen and withdrawn, John junior was a shadow of his father, quiet, alone, reserved. Freddie, sweet, shy, little Freddie in particular, showed subtle signs of depression. Was it any wonder? It was obvious that they were on their own a good deal with John away at work all day and Helen bedridden most of the time. Jean would have to discuss with Gene the possibility of taking the children home with them for a while after they got back from Germany.

When it was time to eat, Helen didn't feel well enough to join them. John carried a tray up to her, but she was asleep. He carried it back down.

"It's a nice house," Gene said to John when he returned and joined them at the table, "but it needs a lot of work."

"I haven't gotten to all of it yet," John replied.

"The kitchen could use a painting, to my way of thinking," Jean said.

"Yes," he agreed.

"John," she began, "all those pills Helen has upstairs . . ."

"They're prescribed," he reassured her.

The next morning the children got themselves off to school as usual. John and Gene decided to go for a drive so that John could show him the town of Westfield.

They left Jean cleaning up. She washed some clothes in the laundry room after breakfast and began tidying up in general. John had already been to the store and purchased a roast for dinner that night, and Jean had suggested to him that he invite his mother down to join them for dinner.

"We'll see," he said noncommittally.

While Jean stood at the kitchen sink washing the breakfast dishes, she heard a series of dull sounds behind her. She went to the side of the kitchen where the spiral back staircase came down into the butler's pantry. There was Helen coming down the stairs. She had gotten out of bed and dressed herself in a yellow shirt with yellow shorts to match. To Jean's astonishment, she was coming down the steps on her fanny one step at a time. Jean reached her about five or six steps from the bottom.

"Honey, wait!"

Helen smiled wanly as Jean helped her into the kitchen. Jean was too startled to question why Helen was coming down the stairs in such a strange manner. She had no earthly idea what was going on with her sister or with the home or anything else. She only knew it scared the daylights out of her.

She made Helen sit down. "Will you drink some coffee if I make it?" she asked carefully.

"Yes," Helen answered weakly. "Don't worry, Jean," she said, looking up into her sister's concerned eyes. "It's just that sometimes I'm afraid of falling down the stairs."

"Why, for heaven's sake?"

"Sometimes I feel a little unsteady," she answered evasively.

Jean made the coffee. The two sisters sat and spoke quietly for a long time, capturing memories from the past. And then Jean found herself becoming silent and listening as Helen talked and talked, quickly, excitedly, jumping from one thing to another, telling her little secrets from her past. Talking about Marvin. Not once did she mention John or the children. It was as though they didn't exist.

Then a shadow seemed to cross Helen's face. She leaned toward her sister. "The doctor thinks," she whispered, "that I may have something called. . . . I don't know, exactly . . . brain atrophy."

"What's that?"

"Shrinking," Helen said, her eyes bulging in fear. "A shrinking of the brain."

"What?"

"Of the brain tissues, Jean." Helen held her sister's hand tightly. "My brain is shrinking. Atrophying." Suddenly she burst out laughing at such a ludicrous thought, but just as quickly she stopped. "Oh, God, I'm scared, honey. But they don't know anything for sure, the doctors."

The phone rang in the butler's pantry. Jean went to the corner of the pantry to answer it. It was the secretary at Roosevelt School. Freddie wasn't feeling well and needed to be picked up. As Jean was explaining to the school secretary that he would have to wait until his father returned, she heard a heavy thump behind her. She turned around. Helen had obviously gotten up and had fallen by the sink, she was lying on the floor unconscious. Blood was gushing from her chin where she had hit the edge of the counter on her way down as she'd pitched forward.

With a startled cry, Jean slammed down the receiver and hurried to her sister. "Helen!" She got a washcloth and tried to stop the blood gushing from the gash on her chin. She could see that she was not going to be able to do it; the cut was long and deep. Quickly she ran up the back stairs in the butler's pantry to Alma's apartment. She remembered that the old lady had been a nurse. There was no one else to ask.

Together, they managed to stop the bleeding and get Helen back to her bedroom. She offered no protestations.

Later that night, after Helen was safely in bed and the house was quiet, Jean confronted John with her worries. "What's going on, John? What?"

"She falls sometimes," he said quietly.

"Why!"

"I don't know."

"What's all this about brain atrophy?" she demanded, deeply worried.

"No, no," John reassured her. "Nothing definite has been diagnosed. It was just mentioned as a possibility. No one knows for sure."

"She should be hospitalized."

"I will take care of her."

"John . . ." Jean could no longer hide her anxiety. "She's terribly sick. I think she may be dying."

"No," John said quietly. "The doctor says all we have to do is keep her quiet for a while and keep her on medication."

"She should have a nurse," Jean insisted.

"You know that's very expensive."

"But . . ."

She saw his jaw tighten ever so slightly. "I will take care of her."

On the last night of the Syferts' two-and-a-half-day visit, the two sisters shared deep, melancholy thoughts together in the privacy of Helen's bedroom. To Jean, Helen seemed desperately ill.

"I'm not going to make it," Helen said softly.

"Oh, of course you are," Jean tried to reassure her.

"I get tired all the time," Helen insisted plaintively. "And then I have to lie down. And . . . and sometimes . . . Oh Jean, it's so awful! Sometimes I have a hard time breathing. You have no idea how frightening that is . . . to think you're not getting enough air."

That's why John moved out of the bedroom, she explained to her sister.

"I can't breathe," she had said to him. "I can't . . . you're making me nervous."

"What do you want me to do?" John had asked.

"You make me nervous in here," she'd cried, grabbing at her head. "I hear you breathing, and then I can't breathe. I feel like I'm suffocating." She had sounded as though she were having an anxiety attack. "I can't . . ."

John had moved his belongings to a spare bedroom down the hall. There was plenty of room in the old house.

How could things have deteriorated to such a point? Jean asked herself sadly.

Downstairs, John was showing Gene all of the records of his clients and taking him into the dank basement, telling him how easy it would be to disappear. Explaining how easy it would be to take on a new identity. . . .

Upstairs, Helen feverishly told her sister that she didn't think she would survive the length of their separation. "I wish you weren't going."

"Well, you know we have to."

"I know. . . ." Helen fell back onto her pillow and closed her eyes. "But this time, I have a feeling, Jean. Two years is a long time. I know I'll never see you again."

"Don't be silly." Jean was deeply worried.

"No, I mean it," Helen said, looking at her seriously. "I don't think we'll ever see each other again."

"You're just feeling depressed, honey."

"Maybe," Helen said, tears spilling out of eyes that bulged unnaturally in her thin face.

"I'll write," Jean promised. "Often. And you write to me. And don't worry," she reassured her unhappy sister. "We'll be together again soon. Two years isn't so long."

As she kissed her sister good-bye, Helen clung to Jean for a long moment. "Good-bye," she said. Her eyes glistened, and there was a catch in her throat, but she managed a little smile as Jean walked from the room.

Helen's health worsened steadily. John listened with rigid anxiety at the collection of ailments. For weeks she had been complaining of dizziness and fainting spells and frequent falling with no warning and no preceding grogginess. Several times John had to clean the floor next to her bed where she had vomited. When she got up she was so unsteady that she was in a constant panic about falling. Her injuries during her falls had gotten progressively more severe.

Between bouts she was all right, even able to run her home after a fashion, but in the last two and a half months the episodes had occurred so frequently that she was afraid to get out of bed. At her insistence, John even got her a wheelchair to go to and from the bathroom. Not accustomed to intimate communication, they didn't like to discuss their fears, but since the diagnosis of atrophy of the brain had been given to them, they were each privately convinced that she had a progressively fatal neurological disease.

On June 6, 1968, she was admitted to Overlook Hospital again.

When her physician, Dr. Mueller, visited her at her bedside for an examination, he noted that Helen had created a general air of untidiness and disorder around her bed and her person. She was having great difficulty in concentration during his examination.

"It's the Dramamine," she said defensively, "I take it for . . . I don't feel steady. I feel like throwing up." Her speech was slow, with reasonable content, the doctor thought, but with an erratic cadence and some slurring of speech. "That's why I get groggy."

"Do you take anything to drink?"

"No," she lied. "Never."

"Any other medication?"

"No," she lied again.

"Any convulsions?"

Her eyes had closed. She looked as though she had fallen asleep.

"Mrs. List," he called gently several times before she responded. She smiled at him. It looked as though it were a forced smile. He noted that her face was not symmetrical—more spastic on the right than on the left side.

"Any convulsions?" he asked again.

She was having difficulty concentrating. "No," she answered finally.

He found some weakness in her arms. Reflexes and sensory testing were normal. He questioned whether her grogginess was drug induced. His impression was

Widespread organic brain disease with personality change, lethargy and ataxia (staggering gait).
Possible middle ear problem, or chronic brain syndrome, or a tumor of the brain.

When John came to visit her the next day, she was asleep. He was told by the nurses that she had fallen out of bed and was incoherent when they found her. He sat quietly by her side during the visiting hour and looked at her as she slept. She seemed frail and pale against the white hospital sheets.

When he got home he told the children that she had sent her regards. Why tell them she had fallen out of bed? They were worried enough as it was.

On June 9 Dr. Zazanis saw the patient in consultation.

When he entered the hospital room, she was speaking softly to an imaginary person next to her. "Why don't you?" he heard her say. "That's fine. A wonderful idea. Come . . . sit by me."

She stopped when Dr. Zazanis came into her line of vision. "Good morning," he said.

"Good morning." She smiled.

She was more alert than she had been during Dr. Mueller's examination and was better able to bring her thoughts together; but even though she was more cooperative, she looked over her shoulder continuously as if she were having a visual hallucination.

After a lengthy examination, Dr. Zazanis offered an impression of

Schizophrenic reaction vs. a chronic brain syndrome due to a degenerative disease.

He thought that the cause of the degeneration was obscure at this point. He wanted to rule out the possibility of a blood clot pressing on the brain and recommended that a pneumoencephalogram be done. The x-rays showed a marked wasting away in the frontal lobes of the brain. A great deal of air was seen over the right side of the brain, but there was no filling of the hollow spaces. She still had some headache, which the doctor thought was due to the air spaces.

It was only one of many tests that would be administered.

This time Helen's stay at Overlook was to be fairly lengthy. While she was away, Alma began to make her presence felt at home. Now without Helen's knowledge, Alma did all of the laundry and all of the mending and often cooked for the family. She wanted to help; it was one of the original reasons she had moved in with the family. The work now eased some of the old lady's loneliness. She even helped Patricia make many of her clothes. Even so, Patricia always looked a little dowdy next to her more affluent classmates, who did their serious shopping in places like Bloomingdale's.

On June 14 the radiologist at Overlook Hospital did an arteriogram on Helen. Through the injected dye the arteries of the brain came out white, and he could see the pattern of the arteries. He felt that they were entirely normal except for a slight constriction of the internal carotid artery.

With each test, Helen became more terrified and more isolated in her fears.

A spinal tap was ordered and studied. The spinal fluid was essentially normal except for the relationship between the gamma globulin and the protein in the fluid, which was higher than one would expect to see in a normal patient. It suggested that something was going on in the brain. But unfortunately, because the spinal tap had been traumatized with blood, no special test of the spinal fluid was carried out for one of the several possibilities for her condition.

In a perverse twist, life had became more peaceful at home while Helen was suffering through one test after another at the hospital. John did all the shopping, Alma did all of the cooking, and fourteen-year-old Patricia did most of the cleaning. Patty wrote to her aunt Jean overseas that while Mom was in the hospital, her doctor made her throw away her medicines, and she "began to get better."

At Overlook Hospital, Dr. Mueller put a label on the front of Helen's chart:

Patient 43 years old.
Chronic Brain Syndrome. Atrophy of the brain.

After slowly improving on her own, Helen was discharged from the hospital on June 22. Once again, without a clear-cut diagnosis as to the cause of the brain atrophy, there had been no treatment. This time the hospital stay had been seventeen days long.

One night in mid-August of 1968, Helen was lying in bed reading when she suddenly screamed and lost consciousness. By this time John was used to Helen's episodes; and although it bothered him, he was too preoccupied with the bills he couldn't seem to catch up on to give the incident much thought.

Shortly afterward Helen, in her loneliness at being in her room all the time, managed to come down to the kitchen, where the children were having a dinner that Patty had prepared. John wasn't home. Although she didn't feel she could eat, she sat with them. They seemed happy to see her, she thought vaguely, although she could never tell things like that anymore. Within a few minutes she realized it had been a mistake to come down the stairs. She couldn't think of anything to say to them.

"I'm going back up," she murmured.

Suddenly she couldn't breathe. The children watched as her eyes seemed to bug out of her head while she gasped for air. They were terrified.

"Do something!" Johnny said frantically to Patty as Freddie backed away.

Patty ran to the phone in the butler's pantry and called the Westfield police. "Hurry," she cried. "My mother can't breathe. She's having an attack. Hurry!"

When the police came to the house, they recognized the passive, gray look that often followed the hyperventilation of an anxiety attack. Although the attack seemed to be over, the woman was very listless. She made no protest as they took her to Overlook Hospital in the police car.

John was desolate. More hospital bills. Why had Patty called the police? The "spell" would have passed on its own. It always did. Five more days of tests in the hospital with no accompanying treatment.

Three and a half months later, on December 10, 1968, Helen was admitted to the New York Neurological Institute for what would be a forty-four-day stay and a very thorough workup. She was admitted complaining of severe headaches in the forehead that would last for four or five hours at a time.

Dr. Vitalli, the admitting senior neurologist, found her to be pleasant, moderately anxious, but cooperative. He found her memory to be fuzzy, particularly with dates, and she was deceptively matter-of-fact about what she believed to be a fatal disease. Actually she was quite depressed and trying to hide the hostility she felt at being examined again.

Gait grossly. Feels steadier without shoes. Cannot walk heel-to-toe along a straight line. Unable to balance or hop on the right foot. Eyes do not move conjugately. Rapid alternating movements.

She was seen by a number of the house staff in training as well as a number of fully trained specialists. Several doctors listed a whole series of physical reasons in the brain that ought to be examined, such as toxoplasmosis, syphilis, tuberculosis, multiple sclerosis, along with a number of tests that should be administered.

Despite her protestations at having to undergo another lengthy series of tests, they were done.

The brain wave tests varied; some were positive, some negative. The skin test for TB was positive; she had had it at some time in the past, and she tested positive for venereal disease.

While life was always a little easier when Helen was not at home, John did not enjoy even a deceptive semblance of calm for very long. Not only was he still strapped for money and still surreptitiously borrowing from his mother's account, but after only a little over a year at American Photographic Co. he was informed that the company was going to move its base of operation out west. This was a serious blow to the already financially hampered head of the household. After the six months he had suffered out of work and now earning only half of his previous salary, he hadn't even begun to catch up, especially with Helen in the hospital again. The doctors had told him to anticipate a lengthy stay this time while they searched for the cause of her illness.

He quietly began worrying again.

On December 17, 1968, as a result of the extensive testing done, Dr. Maxilind, who was the head of the New York Neurological Institute, held a group medical conference.

"Since Mrs. List tested positive on the VDRL and the FTA absorption, and with the changes in the back of the eye," he said, "I can suggest that the two possibilities for her problems are syphilis of the brain or drug toxicity."

"We also found that some tests suggested minimal liver disease. Possibly due to alcohol consumption," added one of the consultants.

"That might support the drug toxicity possibility."

Helen had already had one fall in the hospital bathroom, but when confronted with the results of the tests, she was adamant in her defensive denials. "Absolutely not!" she stated emphatically. "I don't drink, and I have never had any venereal disease. And . . . and I've never taken any tranquillizers except Miltown in February of 1968, I think. It was prescribed, one pill four times a day."

She was shown the results of the tests.

"I smoke. That's all," she persisted in her denials. "About a pack a day . . . for eighteen years. I had malaria once. That's all."

They couldn't shake her, even though it had become patently clear that the patient was not giving the doctors the full story. By January 10, 1969, the nurses discovered hidden supplies of Doriden in several different places in her room. Each time she went out of the room, they counted how many she had left.

When the doctors confronted Helen again, this time with clear evidence of her lying, she finally conceded that she had been taking the Doriden even while she was in the hospital. She was transferred to the psychiatric ward, where, between hysterical sobs, she finally admitted that her time at Walter Reed Army Hospital back in 1947–48 had not been for malaria, but for syphilis of the brain, and that the doctors had used the malaria to treat the syphilis. Under persistent questioning, Helen subsequently admitted the "five or six" daily Scotches and the "four or five" daily Doridens that she had been consuming for years. Even without syphilis, that combination alone would have severely affected her balance.

They had finally achieved a breakthrough in the patient's thick wall of defenses. But it was too late. Tertiary syphilis of the brain; it was in its final stages.

Dr. Cunnick was in his yard. The late winter weather was invigorating. Much of Hillside Avenue was flourishing with the activity of aggressive snow shoveling after a thick snowfall. He turned as a shadow crossed between his shovel and the small drift of snow he was attempting to clear away from in front of his garage door. And there was John List standing to his side with a little smile on his face. Cunnick put aside the shovel when he realized the man wanted to talk. He didn't mind. He never thought of List as "strange" as some of the other people on the block did. Just quiet and private. But he did think it odd when List suddenly began confiding in him about the fact that he might be out of a job soon.

"This house is big enough for the whole family," List was saying. "I have to keep that in mind."

Cunnick imagined that the man was so troubled, he simply had to talk to someone. He didn't mind taking the place of a friend, so he listened with a sympathetic nodding of his head as List told him that his firm was moving away and that he had made the decision against relocating with the company. Having his own family to support, Cunnick could well imagine how it must feel to have the welfare of your life balanced between a job and a corporate whim.

"It's difficult for a family to move," List said. "The children have settled in here."

Cunnick noticed that List was gazing into space as he spoke. He felt he had become almost invisible to List.

Now he had *Mutter* to think about, too, John thought. There was no place for her to go. She had sold her house in Bay City. For him to move the entire family to a smaller house where they would be forced to live in closer quarters was unthinkable with the way Helen and his mother felt about each other. He supposed *Mutter* could go back to Frankenmuth. She still had relatives there, but it had been almost fifty years since she had lived there. No. They would all have to remain in Westfield. He would have to do something. With a sense of dread, he vividly remembered his agonizing days sitting at the railroad station when hope had grown paler and despair deeper as he'd listened to each passing train carrying thousands upon thousands of men who were supporting their families.

"What are you going to do?" Dr. Cunnick asked.

"Oh, I'll come up with something," John said.

"She had an extensive series of psychological testing done as well," the doctor said, going over his notes while John sat stiffly on the other side of the cluttered desk, listening. "The projective testing confirmed the previous impression of organic interference and also suggested severe emotional distress. It's also apparent in her handwriting that there are faulty word separations, wrong letters, letter omissions."

"What does it mean?" he asked.

"Well, Mrs. List gives an initial impression of intactness which is quickly dissipated, exposing severe difficulties in judgment and reason. She can't think clearly," he said, reading from his notes.

He knew that much himself, John thought cryptically.

"Reality testing is quite poor," the doctor continued. "Her thinking is vague, fragmented, arbitrary, tangential. She tends to think around a problem without concentrating on it. Everything she does is overpersonalized in relation to herself."

John nodded with what the doctor perceived as apparent intense interest.

"She's very dependent and yet quite isolated and detached, so that she has very little sense of closeness in her interpersonal relations. She really doesn't warm up to people around her. And . . ." He read on quickly. "Yes. This is borne out by nurses around her. So my impression is one of organic interference, which is exacerbated by anxiety and depression related to her strong dependency needs. She has to lean on someone for everyday life. This interferes with her functioning."

John nodded again.

Now the doctor looked at him closely. The man seemed in control. "She's very much preoccupied with her physical difficulties," he said, putting aside his notes, "and with life-and-death issues. She feels an intense need for external support and direction."

John waited.

"A great many physical tests were done as well as psychological ones."

"Do you have a final diagnosis, doctor?" John asked.

"Yes," he said distinctly. "Two of them. One: recurrent Doriden intoxication with minor addiction. Two: syphilitic encephalitis. And a reactive anxiety depression to diagnosis one and two."

John blinked uncomprehendingly. "Syphilitic encephalitis?"

"She is in the tertiary stages of syphilis," the doctor told him quietly.

John made no movement as he looked at the doctor stoically, waiting for him to go on.

"Syphilis of the brain causes such a collection of complaints that it varies from patient to patient, and it takes a long time to diagnose," he explained. "Even today it's not thought of, although it still exists. Hospitals rarely do tests for syphilis because we don't think of it as something that still exists in our community, but it was the contagious social disease before World War Two."

John listened quietly, with little emotion. The doctor had no way of telling what he was feeling inside: the shame, the despair, the hopelessness of it all. And no money. What was all this going to cost? Would his insurance cover all the testing?

"Why didn't you find out about this sooner?" John asked steadily.

"The tests to determine syphilis weren't done because there was no history given to support the possibility of syphilis," he said distinctly. "She never told us the truth until yesterday."

"Can she be cured?"

"It's pretty advanced."

"Could she have been cured if it had been diagnosed as syphilis sooner?"

"Very likely."

John himself had never even considered the possibility that her chronic illness might be caused by the syphilis she had contracted from Marvin. First, she had told him she was cured; and second, he had made himself forget the disease he didn't like to think of.

"Thank you," John said simply.

"Dr. Vitalli, one of our senior neurologists, suggests that your wife should return to have her neurological condition reevaluated after several months when she is completely off her tranquillizers."

"Thank you," he said again.

Helen was discharged from the hospital on January 22, 1969. It had been a forty-four-day stay.

The American Photographic Co. relocated in late spring of 1969. John was out of work again.

June went by. Then July stretched into August. In his jobless despair, John read Deuteronomy 28:67 over and over again. "In the morning thou shalt say,'Would God it were even!' and at even thou shalt say, 'Would God it were morning!'" How deeply he felt the weight of loneliness. How true the despair of that one simple Bible verse. If he could only die to escape the growing burdens... but it didn't seem that God would grant him that fervent wish. Could he do it himself? No, that would damn his soul eternally—sin without grace; suicide was not even a remote consideration. What then? What? And even if he were to die, wouldn't that be cowardly? Who would take care of the needs of his family? Would they be put out into the streets? Thrown upon the mercilessness of welfare? Already Helen was getting worse again, barely functioning under the lull of medication—or was it alcohol? Many times he wasn't even sure anymore. One thing he was certain of—she was dying of syphilis of the brain. And his children. What of them? Could he abandon them? Could he abandon his two young sons to fend for themselves in such a malevolent world full of societal upheavals? John junior was so much like himself—quiet, withdrawn, a loner. His life was going to be a carbon copy of his own—good grades, good mind, good potential, and none of the subtle requirements necessary to succeed in a world that favored superficiality over substance, personality over character. Freddie, too, was becoming even more of a loner than he himself had been at his age. He knew that both boys were often the butt of teasing and jokes in school, as he had been. What could possibly be in store for them if he were gone?

And Patty? Patty was headed down the path of perdition, he was certain of that. All the clues were there to be seen by the observant. She was beginning to go to one "party" after another with her new friends from the Westfield Recreation Center and to attend Friday night dances at the "dungeon" in the basement of the church. She was too young for such things, he thought, even if the dances were sponsored by the church. But Helen had always encouraged Patty's youthful, burgeoning sexuality... low-cut dresses, heavy makeup. Hadn't Helen learned her lesson when Brenda got in trouble?

Besides, a father could not abandon his family, he thought. That would be worse than death. He couldn't keep after them all as much as he would have liked. He had to concentrate on getting a job. This time he would be less particular and a little more aggressive in his search. This time he would take anything that was offered to him.

John began to ride the train. Often he ran into Dr. Cunnick as they rode into New York. Occasionally he would sit down next to him, and once again, Dr. Cunnick was surprised when List used the time to confide in him, talking again about the problem with his business moving away. "I could have gone with them. They asked me to, but as I see it, I have this large house where my mother has private quarters, apart from the family. . . ."

"Yes, I've met her. A charming lady."

"Yes . . . and the idea of starting out to look for something like this all over again . . . Plus my children seem to be . . . happy in the school system. My daughter is in plays." He frowned.

"So you've decided not to relocate with your company. I can understand that."

"Yes. I've decided to take my chances in the marketplace, and not have to go through searching for a home big enough for everyone."

There were a lot of men who would have made the same decision, Cunnick thought. "Do you have prospects in mind?" he asked.

"Not yet. But I saw an ad about earning sixty thousand dollars in the first year as a researcher for a writer. . . . I might look into something like that."

Cunnick thought that a bit naïve. Most of those ads were for marketing jobs.

"There's another one," List continued. "In insurance."

"Accounting?"

"Sales."

Dr. Cunnick thought sales would be the last kind of job List might succeed in, but it was really none of his business. He didn't know List well enough to be completely open about his reservations. He thought the shy, uptight Mr. List had made a bad business decision and selected a role for which he was unsuited. But then people did that every day.

In late August of 1969 John started selling insurance and mutual funds for State Mutual Life Assurance Co. of America out of its East Orange, N.J., office. From the $12,000 he had been earning with American Photographic Co. he went on straight commissions.

The first year alone his income dropped at least another $3,000 while the bills kept mounting.

John continued to borrow money from his mother's account. This time he told himself he didn't tell her because the money was for Helen's doctor bills and all of her prescriptions, and he knew how seriously *Mutter* disapproved of Helen. *"Sie ist eine Gottlose, sündige Frau."* Besides, he would put the money back as soon as things got a little better, and she would never have to know. No harm done. He had power of attorney, so he could make decisions like that if he thought it was necessary.

Weighed down by his worries, John was becoming even more of a recluse, more quiet, more compulsive. The greater the outside pressures, the more he tended to consolidate and resort to the security of familiar patterns of behavior; the behavior of an obsessive-compulsive personality never changes. Except for monitoring the children's activities, he participated little in the family's daily routines. Instead he spent hours meticulously cataloging the growth of every seed he had planted in his garden.

On March 16, 1970, John sold himself a life insurance policy on each of his three children in the amount of $5,000 each. For their future, he told himself. Even though he was thinking more about solutions, even drastic ones, he still denied his own thoughts to himself.

After he switched to his new job, he began to ride the train going to Newark and New York. Now he ran into Dr. Cunnick often.

Sometimes—not always, but sometimes—he sat next to his neighbor.

"How do you like your new work?" Cunnick asked.

"Oh, yes, fine. Well, it's difficult to get started in something new."

Cunnick knew the man was struggling in his new job. He even tried to help him with a few contacts for potential insurance sales. List thanked him for the contacts and began to talk of some of the evils of easy credit. "As an accountant, I see it every day," he said. "People making bad business decisions, bad investments, or getting in too deep."

"Credit is very easy in our society," Dr. Cunnick agreed.

"Oh, yes."

"It's very easy to get addicted to credit and put your finances out of whack. And people get desperate," he added.

"Yes. . . ."

"And where do you turn when you're desperate?"

"Of course, there's no desperation," List replied steadily. "There were merely logistical complexities that would have come up if I'd been forced to move them all."

Dr. Cunnick was surprised. He hadn't been talking about List; he'd been making a general comment.

"Fortunately moving turned out not to be necessary," List said.

19 | The Children

In 1970, during her sophomore year in high school, Patty found her niche as a teenager in Westfield. In the Westfield Drama Club, where she realized she had some theatrical talent, she began to blossom. Friendly and outgoing, sparked by a desire to grow and participate, she easily assimilated into the "cool" hippie-type crowd that hung around Shades, the soda parlor, on Elm Street. Patty's neat skirts and cardigans were soon replaced by grungy jeans and boots and tie-dyed shirts. Not only was she falling in line with the current, easily recognizable hippie mode of dress, the casual clothes were also a cover-up for her lack of up-to-date fashionwear. She grew her hair long, parted it down the middle, wore hip-huggers. The other kids had been dressing like that for the past two or three years, but for Patty it was a major transition. She had seized the freedom of choice in fashion. Her best friend, Alice, was delighted. Patty was finally changing from Daddy's little girl to being a person of her own.

Once Patty changed her appearance to fit in with the "age of Aquarius," she decided that she was going to "start doing things." She moved her possessions to one of the empty bedrooms near the back staircase. Now, slipping out of the house at night without being noticed was easier. She was attractive in her new image. She was tall, pretty, and developing a full-bosomed figure. Boys were beginning to notice.

Besides Shades, she began to hang out at the local deli with Alice and Elaine and Billy and Gary. For the first time in her life she had the sense that she belonged, that there even could be happiness "out there" away from home. Her newfound freedom gave her an infectious gaiety, but only when she was outside the house. At home she kept a low profile.

John List stopped the car in front of Bob Canfield's house on Raymond Street, three blocks away from Hillside Avenue. He and John junior waited for the gangling young athlete to bound down his driveway to the waiting Impala. Bob Canfield had gone to Wilson Grammar School while Johnny had been attending his early grades in the Redeemer Lutheran School. Now they both attended Roosevelt Jr. High, which serviced the north side of town. Although they shared classes together, the boys had first met through the Westfield Township–sponsored Little League baseball team when they were both still in their separate elementary schools. Currently, Johnny and Bob were on the same team. Bob was the pitcher, and Johnny, more heavy-set and taller than the average boy his age, was the catcher.

Johnny opened the car door to let the lanky youth into the back.

"Hi," Bob said as he tossed his baseball gear and gym bag onto the backseat before piling in himself. "Hi, Mr. List." In his haste, he seemed to fall into the backseat.

John nodded pleasantly and headed the car toward the field, where he was driving the boys to their baseball practice. In the car, he left the boys to their talk, but although his mind was elsewhere, he also listened as they spoke about the two big-time baseball leagues they hoped to qualify for, the International and the Major. No time, List thought. No time. . . .

Bob Canfield glanced at Mr. List as he and Johnny talked. He never initiated any conversation, he thought to himself. Not like *his* old man. Mr. List always seemed friendly enough, but a real quiet, meticulous type of guy. Mr. List tried to catch most of the games. He obviously liked baseball. He even offered to help sometimes, not that he actually coached, but sometimes he helped out. Not just dropping the kid off and running like his old man would do when it was his turn to drive.

Once, Bob had heard one of the kids on the team taunt John junior on the field about how he was scared of his old man and about how his old man was a religious fanatic making him go to church every week. It annoyed Canfield, who had a really ingrained sense of fair play. He never got the impression that Johnny was very religious. When you're a kid, you're not really religious, he thought. And scared of this quiet guy? Naw, he thought. No way! Bob couldn't even see Mr. List as any disciplinarian. He just seemed too meek, the sort you could never picture even yelling. Now *his* old man! That was a different story.

"I'm trying real hard to get my batting average up," Johnny was saying.

"You'd need a magic bat!" Bob joked, and Johnny laughed, his big teeth sparkling.

"You too!" Johnny added, pointing a finger.

"Me! I'd need a fairy godmother."

And Johnny laughed some more. And then he stopped and said seriously, "I really mean it, though. It's the only way we'll get into the big leagues. We'll have to practice and practice."

Mr. List pulled the car to a stop at the baseball field. Most of the team were already there warming up.

"Thanks, Mr. List," Bob called as they got out of the car. "My dad's gonna pick us up later."

"Fine. . . ."

As the two boys walked onto the field at Roosevelt Jr. High, all of the greetings thrown their way were from friends of Bob. Bob knew that Johnny didn't "hang" with the gangs in school, that his only extracurricular activities were baseball and soccer. Sometimes he thought he was Johnny's only friend. For some reason the kids made fun of Johnny and his kid brother, mostly for always carrying stacks of books. He never saw Johnny eating lunch with anyone at school. Usually he'd read or do homework and eat lunch at the same time. A lot of the kids thought he was a real bookworm. The funny thing was, Johnny never fought back. Once he stuck up for him himself. "Leave him alone, will ya? He ain't hurting nobody!" So they were kind of strange-looking kids! So what. Bushy hair, sticking out ears. So what! He liked Johnny. I'm sure he doesn't have a best friend, he thought as Johnny continued to talk about how he hoped to qualify for one of the big leagues.

Bob didn't think he'd ever make it.

Freddie often played baseball with his father and brother when the season was right, but he didn't join Little League. He didn't try to "break out" like Patty was doing. He didn't try to conform like Johnny, either. At school his teachers thought he had an impish, mischievous quality that was hidden under a cover of perfect behavior. Someday, they thought, if he permitted it to emerge, he would be fun. Mostly he avoided trouble and spent his time alone with the family Pekingese, Tinkerbell. He loved that silly-looking little dog, even though it was skittish in temperament and often snapped at strangers. To the little boy, he was a loyal friend and companion. His thoughts were like a little boy's song of love.

Stay with me while I do my homework. . . .

Then we'll go for a long walk. . . .

Someday I'll buy you a big steak. . . .

Sleep in my room. . . .

Someday we'll go swimming together. . . .

We're pals forever. . . .

Someday I'll get you a bell. A little bell on the collar for little Tinkerbell. . . .

Don't snap at people. They won't like you. . . .

Stay with me. . . .

Watch me feed the fish. . . .

Tinkerbell. . . .

The summer before they were all murdered, Patty went away to Camp Speers-Eljabar in Dingman's Ferry, Pennsylvania, for a two-week program in counselor training. Paula Hudson, twenty-four, was the head of the program. She was bright, cheerful, and particularly fond of Patty List, whom she was sure would, one day, make a fine counselor—once she got rid of some of her crazy ideas, she thought.

One night she found herself drawn to the teenager, who appeared unusually thoughtful and solemn. Something was obviously bothering her.

"I keep getting these feelings that something's not right," Patty said.

"Like what?" the counselor asked.

"I don't know. I can't put my finger on it . . . feelings," the girl said with the utmost seriousness. "Like something's going to happen. Like I'm going to die."

"Patty, don't be silly. . . ."

"Soon."

Paula Hudson studied the girl's lovely young face for a moment. "Patty," she finally asked, "did you draw that pentagram on the floor of the hall?"

"Yes."

"Why?"

"It's a symbol."

"For what?"

"Witches."

"Oh, come on. . . ."

"I mean it," Patty insisted. "The world is going in the wrong direction." She was so tired of all the sham beliefs. The hypocrisy was suffocating. She hated the necessity of prayers before meals, prayers after meals, church every Sunday. Either comply or suffer the consequences of his admonitions and rages. "Too much attention's given to the wrong things," she told Paula, "and not enough to what it all means. Well, there's a dark side to religion, too. It has to do with Satan and witchcraft."

"That's crazy, Patty, and you know it," Paula said firmly.

"No, it isn't. I read it in a book."

"What book?"

"A book my dad gave me all about the devil and things," she said. "And then I got another one out of the library. Look."

Patricia pulled a book out of a satchel she always carried with her. Paula leafed through the book and could quickly see what it was about. It had to do with devil worship, malefice; witch's covens, and initiation rites in which nude virgins were deflowered in orgies and then sacrificed in blood.

"Here's the other one," Patty offered. "The one my father gave me."

It was a book about the devil.

"Your *father* gave you this?" Paula asked incredulously.

"Yes."

"But it's about Satan."

"He told me one can't believe in God without believing in Satan, the fallen angel." Patty said, "and he's right. It's all there in the book."

Paula looked through the second book a little more carefully. "But it looks to me like this is a warning to take care, to be on guard, not to play around with the devil. Now that's quite a different matter from devil worship."

"Is devil worship the same as witchcraft?" Patty asked suddenly.

"What?"

"You know, calling upon the darkness."

"Patty, this is a lot of garbage, and you know it," Paula said, closing the books with what she hoped was a slam of finality.

"No, it's not. I belong to a Lutheran church group . . ."

"Okay, that's great. . . ."

"And there's a coven of witches in Elizabeth," Patty said solemnly.

The counselor sighed. Teenagers and their cockamamie ideas. "Believe me . . ." She smiled. "You'll outgrow all of this stuff."

"Will I?" Patty looked at her with her large brown eyes. "I do have that feeling, Miss Hudson," she said quietly. "About dying, I mean."

You'll outgrow that, too, Paula thought as she hugged the girl.

As John worked quietly in his garden, all he could think about were his diminishing options. What was he going to do? His constant, fervent prayers were not being answered. Why had God chosen not to respond to his silent cries for help?

He looked up at all the sudden commotion behind his house. It looked like there was some kind of a brush fire at the Wittke house, and all the neighbors were making a big thing out of it. He went on with his gardening.

Diana Ryan went over to help with the fire. She thought it odd that Mr. List was outside at the time and showed no curiosity at all. He was closer to the fire than anyone else, other than Wittke, but he was gardening, and he didn't move to the brush fire as most of the other neighbors did. Maybe he didn't view it as a problem, Diana thought, but to her it looked as if the fire could get out of hand.

Diana forgot about John List until she saw him again on the way back home after the brush fire had been brought under control. There he was, still working in his garden. She remembered the year before last he'd had a garden on the other side of the house. In the middle of it he had set up a huge red scarecrow. No one had ever seen an all-red scarecrow. One of her sons took a picture of it. They jokingly called it the List Witch. She was about to pass him with just a nod when she thought. This is ridiculous. I just can't walk by. He's a neighbor. "Hi," she said, stopping next to him. "I don't think we've ever really met. You're John List, aren't you?"

"Yes."

It was the first time that she'd ever spoken to him. "I'm Diana Ryan."

"How do you do?"

"How's the garden?" she asked.

"Fine," he said very pleasantly. "Everything's going well this year." As he was talking, John junior came out from the back of the house and whispered something to his father. John turned around with an exasperated look.

"Oh, listen, you're busy," Diana said, suddenly sorry that she had stopped. "So, I'll say good-bye."

"Good-bye," he said with a very sweet, gentle smile. She imagined she felt his eyes following her steadily until she was off his property.

When she got back home from camp at the end of the summer, Patty found herself feeling even more rebellious than before. Freddy caught her sneaking out of their mother's bedroom with one of her best summer sweaters in hand.

"She's asleep," Patty said when she realized he'd caught her.

He nodded.

"Don't tell," she whispered.

"I won't," Freddie whispered back.

Patty turned to leave him standing in the hallway, then turned back to look at his wide eyes. "She won't know," she explained a bit defensively. "And she never wears them anyway."

"It's . . . I won't say anything, Patty."

"Okay. Thanks." She smiled at her brother.

Freddie watched as she quietly closed her bedroom door behind her.

He knew that Patty often sneaked out at night. Sometimes she would merely throw a coat over her nightgown and hurry down the back staircase to meet her boyfriend at the Dollhouse, a little mansion outbuilding. Other times she would sneak out to meet Alice or Elaine.

At two o'clock in the morning the phone rang. "Who did you say this is?" John List asked.

"Sergeant Scutti of the Westfield Police Department."

"There must be some mistake," he said incredulously.

"I'm afraid not, Mr. List. She says she's your daughter. A Patricia Marie List from 431 Hillside Avenue."

There was a long pause as John allowed that to sink in. Then he finally said, "And you are telling me she was 'picked up'?"

"Yes, sir."

"For what?"

"For roaming the streets in the middle of the night," Sergeant Scutti said. "Not a good idea. Would you care to come down to the station to pick up your daughter?"

"I'll be right down," he said, and replaced the receiver. Without even putting on slippers, he hurried down the hall to Patty's room and saw that the bed was indeed empty and showed signs of not having been slept in at all. Picked up by the police! It was two o'clock in the morning. She obviously had sneaked down the back staircase to go traipsing about in the middle of the night. Now he realized why she had changed rooms.

Helen was asleep.

Although he dressed hurriedly, John dressed with care. He put on a business suit, shirt, and tie. By the time he arrived at the police station it was two-thirty in the morning.

The desk sergeant was behind a high counter surrounded by radio equipment and circulars. Two girls were seated on chairs to the left of the entrance. Over their heads on a huge bulletin board hung Wanted posters of a wide assortment of burglars, assaulters, and murderers.

When Patty saw John, she began to tremble. His eyes were burning with anger. He looked at the girl seated with her. "Did you do this!" he demanded. "Did you get my daughter in trouble with the police?"

A man who had been standing at the desk speaking to the desk sergeant turned to him. "I beg your pardon." The man wasn't friendly. "Who are you?"

"I'm this girl's father."

"Well, I'm *her* father!" he said, pointing to Elaine. "And frankly, I don't like your tone."

"I . . . I can't have my daughter picked up by the police," John stammered angrily.

"Maybe it's your daughter who's corrupting mine," the angry man said.

Sergeant Scutti tried to intervene as the two men faced each other. The difference between them was stark. One, incredibly, was dressed in a suit and tie—at two-thirty in the morning!—and the other looked as though he had hurriedly thrown on a light sweat shirt and a pair of pants over his pajamas.

Patty and Elaine started to cry.

"Daddy, please," begged Elaine.

"You be quiet! We'll talk about this at home."

"My daughter has never been in trouble like this before," John continued, trying to suppress his rage.

"Well, neither has mine!"

"Okay, okay," said Scutti. "Let's try not to act crazy. Let's just everyone calm down and sign them out."

John was shaking. His daughter, accused of corrupting. Patty was a good girl. What was she doing out at night? Who was this "girlfriend" with whom she had been picked up? What were they doing out in the middle of the night?

And finally, as they walked to the car, he said, "You will never see that girl again."

"It's not her fault, Daddy," Patty said, still wiping her swollen red eyes.

"Then whose is it?" he demanded. "Yours?"

Patty was silent.

"We will talk to the pastor this Sunday about this." He opened the door on her side. "Get in!" Patty shrank into the seat. John came around to the other side, got in, and started the engine. "Maybe he can make you see. Maybe he can open your eyes as to what's going on in the world right now."

"Can't we handle it ourselves?"

"These are dangerous times. There is a great deal of temptation around you," he said, trying to calm down. "You must be strong. But first, you have to recognize it."

Patty sank deeper into the front seat of the car.

As he pulled out of the driveway and made a right turn onto East Broad Street, John noticed Gray's Funeral Home almost directly across the street. They drove in silence.

I was right, he thought to himself. He had not really let on to Reverend Rehwinkel how upset he was when the pastor showed him the book he had confiscated from Patty when she baby-sat for the Rehwinkels, *The Treasury of Witchcraft*. Obviously the pastor was concerned enough to think it warranted parental attention, and now this incident with the police in the middle of the night. Youth was on a rampage far beyond the usual adolescent passions. It was almost beyond their control. They were being bombarded on all sides with dangerous stimuli. He hated the times he lived in. He hated the news—the Vietnam War, hippies, flower children, civil rights, bra-burning, draft card burning, protest marches, marihuana, LSD, assassinations, rioting in the streets. It was all blasphemous to him. Why read about it any longer? He preferred the solace and comfort of the Bible, his constant companion. It had the answers.

He also tried to unravel with prayer the tangled net of credit that was binding his thoughts into knots. *"The Lord shall give thee rest from thy sorrow, and from thy fear." Isaiah 14:3.* But when? he thought dolefully. How could he rest when every day the mailman was the messenger heralding his growing financial downfall? Even the small bills added up—water, milk, newspaper. So far this year his gross income had added up to less than $3,000. How could he not "sorrow" when *Mutter* was beginning to talk more and more of how much she missed Bay City? What if she suddenly decided to cash in her savings that had been dwindling monthly since they'd first moved to Westfield in 1965 and return to her home? How would he tell her that what started out as a little borrowing from her account that he always meant to pay back had become a frequent occurrence that, so far, he had never been able to repay? *"The Lord shall give thee rest from sorrow, and from thy fear," Isaiah said,* but the fear was constant. He had to find a way out.

At home, John was getting darker and darker. It was as though desperately black shadows were coming closer to engulf him. Trying to turn his attention away from his worries about money, he twisted them into exaggerated worries about the family's moral disintegration. He was beginning to feel great anger at them. It's their fault, he thought. They are deliberately trying to hurt me. And before they destroyed him, he had to do something. He denied his own violent thoughts to himself.

He evaluated and calculated and reevaluated and recalculated all the figures in his Budget Book. So many thoughts nagged in the back of his head, trying to hatch themselves out as actual "plans" for a drastic course of action. He rejected them all. But in March of 1971, he secretly borrowed more money out of his mother's account to buy a $225,000 life insurance policy on himself.

When thirteen-year-old Rick Baeder's parents went away on vacation for a week during the summer of 1971, Rick stayed with the List family. He was one of the few children who was always welcome at the List home. He even used to cut through the woods behind the List property to get to his house on Roanoke Road, and Mr. List never objected. Rick and his older brother, David, who was Patty's age, and the List children had all attended Redeemer Lutheran School together full-time when the Lists first moved to Westfield. Mr. List and Barbara Baeder, Rick's mother, took turns driving the children to school. He knew Mrs. List never participated in the driving because his mother told him she was "somewhat of an invalid."

Rick and Freddie had begun in the second grade together. John was one grade ahead of them, but at that time Redeemer had two grades per classroom, which meant that every other year Rick and Freddie shared the same classroom with the older John junior. Rick enjoyed playing with the List boys. Of the two, Fred was more of a loner than Johnny. Johnny was more into athletics, more outgoing, had more friends. Rick's mother said Johnny was more normal, getting into a little trouble now and then, like not letting his mother know where he was.

The week Rick stayed with the Lists was a busy one. Outside, they played baseball and football on the lawn. Inside, they played whiffle ball in the ballroom. Their shouts actually echoed in the large empty room. It was a great place to play, running around with Tinkerbell snapping at their heels, without fear of damaging anything worthwhile. When they weren't exercising their energies in ball games, they played board games. The List boys were very good at board games. Occasionally even Patty would join them for a game.

Rick couldn't help noticing that Mrs. List was like a shadow in the house. She stayed in bed watching TV nearly the entire time he was there. She was very odd, with her one eye bugged out like that. He'd heard a lot of stories about her "drinking problem," but he didn't see any signs of it while he was there. He did see a lot of pills, though. He told his mother later when she asked him. A lot of medication. In all the time he'd known Mrs. List, he'd seen her dressed only half a dozen times. Even now, when she got up once in a while to go to the kitchen to get something to drink, she'd be in a house robe. "I want you to be happy here, Rick, honey," she told him once. Then she was gone again back to her room.

One night when the boys were alone, Patty joined them in a game of Monopoly at the kitchen table.

"I'm going to ask Daddy to let me have a party," she said in the middle of the game.

"A party," Johnny said. "You've got to be kidding."

"A Halloween party."

"He'll never agree."

"Then I'll ask Mom," she said with a quick flare of her feisty temper.

"Don't, Patty. They'll just fight again."

"So what else is new?" Patty demanded. "I'm sick and tired of the way we live."

"Don't be so selfish!" Johnny's own temper flared.

Rick had never seen Johnny so angry in all the time he'd known him.

"I'm not selfish," Patty protested. "I'm normal."

"What's normal?" he asked wretchedly.

"Not this," she answered firmly. "That's for sure."

Johnny watched as Patty lit up a Marlboro.

"You shouldn't smoke. It's bad for you."

"Okay!" She crushed out the cigarette and pulled a thinly rolled cigarette out of her pocket. "How about this?" she said defiantly.

"Crimminy! Is that a joint?" Rick whispered excitedly.

The three boys crowded around. Even Johnny was interested. They watched as she held it firmly between her lips and lit the pointed, rolled tip. She took a deep drag, held it, and exhaled it slowly.

"Ever try one?" she asked.

The three boys shook their heads.

"Want to try?"

Rick grinned. "I do."

"Not you." She laughed. "You're just a kid." She held it out to Johnny.

He shook his head. "No, I don't think so."

But she could tell he was curious. "C'mon," she urged. "You gotta loosen up a little. You're wound too tight. Like Dad." She took another drag and held it out to him, a bold challenge in her eyes. He took the joint between his fingers carefully. The younger boys giggled as they watched the big kids experimenting with the forbidden. Johnny took a deep drag the way he'd seen others do it in the boy's room at school.

"Whattaya feel?" Rick asked. "What?"

"Anything?" Freddie joined in.

"Tell us what it's like."

By the time Patty and Johnny finished the joint, they too were giggling.

"It feels . . ." Johnny began.

"It feels . . ." Patty tried.

"Like heaven," Johnny concluded.

"Like the devil, you mean." Patty laughed and tossed her head.

They burst out laughing. Then they heard their father's car pulling up in the driveway.

"Quick!"

"Hurry!"

All four quickly waved arms, towels, anything they could get their hands on to dispel the sweet, telltale smell.

Yes, Rick thought, it was fun staying at the Lists' house.

As John List unloaded the groceries from the car, he brooded as he had all the way home. The family had become parasites eating away his meager earnings, eating away at all of his beliefs. The nightly "talks" with *Mutter* only reinforced the strength of his beliefs, and the longing to return to simpler times. He looked with loathing on everything about the past twenty years. If he could just cut them out, sever the past, smite it, return to the peace of daily communion with God without the destructive interferences of Helen and the immoral attitudes of the children. His children were being raised in a heathen world, without the strength of faith to sustain them through the mire. The world was collapsing with immorality. He repeated the familiar litany of complaints: Sex—war—pills—60's—drugs—marijuana. And the bills kept piling up. What could he do? He had secretly taken out two more mortgages on the house. One for $7,000 and another for $1,800.

Then, on October 14, 1971, he went to the Westfield Police Department to apply for a gun permit. Sergeant William Muth did the necessary fingerprinting and told him to return in two weeks. He never did. Instead he remembered his father's guns packed away in a box in the basement. He didn't need permits for them.

20 | The Turning Point

The last three months, working out of his home in telephoning potential clients, were fruitless. Even Dr. Cunnick's leads didn't work out, not one. A godless world had cheated him.

John opened the official-looking letter from the bank. It was a notice of impending foreclosure if he didn't make a payment on his mortgage immediately.

"Defaulted payments" leapt out at him from the page.

His face burned in shame as he held the paper in his hand. He thought of his mother's bank account. The money had just about run out. She didn't know yet. He had even depleted the $10,000 in stocks and bonds Alma had deposited with the Wall Street brokerage house on his advice. It had been good advice, he thought.

Defaulted payments . . .

It seemed that he had less than $1,000 equity in the house he had lived in for six years. And his income to date this year had only reached a little over $5,000. His financial affairs had finally come to a head.

They wanted to repossess this house.

Late at night he walked through the house from room to room. Every place he looked he could see the signs of deterioration. There were exposed beams in the ceilings in the kitchen and dining rooms where they spent most of their time. Almost all of the ceiling had fallen down from plumbing problems that he had never been able to afford to fix. He'd tried to do it himself; but he was no plumber, and the replacement parts were expensive. Nine bathrooms. Almost two per person. He smiled at the excess.

But outward appearances must be kept up, he thought. Neat grounds, neat lawn. He raked the leaves on his lawn . . . one last time. Outward appearances were neat, orderly, in control. Within John, there was chaos. Helen's emotional breakdown was externally visible, obvious. John's emotional breakdown—for without question he was having one—was internal. It was not obvious to anyone.

It was all intertwined—family failure, professional failure, wife, children, career, foreclosure, money gone. *Mutter*. Trying to twist reality to conform to a religious code, he could no longer separate one from the other. As protector he had let the family down. Their welfare seemed best served through death. If they couldn't live by the faith, they would die by it. He would have to see to that. Would anyone understand? Even *Mutter* might not understand the necessity of what he had to do. She would have to be sacrificed.

Financial ruin was only a few more weeks away. It was time to implement the decision that had been forming in his head for such a long time despite his many attempts at denial. It wouldn't be difficult to do. With his compulsive passion for order, the design had already crystallized in great detail in the back of his mind. Now all he had to do was accept the necessity of implementing it. He knew it was wrong, but accepted the necessity.

Once the decision was made, a calm began to set in. He would finally be able to shed the dragon he had been carrying around on his shoulders. There was no other way. He would have to do Christ's work, he rationalized. He would have to cut his moral losses, secure in the conviction that God's justice had prevailed as it always would in eternity, if not always in the present. The inner turmoil was suddenly in control.

The guns were an American .22 Colt revolver that his father used to take with him when he was carrying large sums of money from the store, and an Austrian military, semiautomatic 9-mm Steyr dating back to World War I. John hadn't fired a gun in a long time.

He took the time to go to a target range. Not only did he want to practice, but he wanted to make sure the guns still functioned properly. The Steyr had the year 1918 stamped into the black metal.

Let Patty have the party, he thought. He didn't have the heart to refuse her this. Not now. What difference could one party make?

"He's gonna let me have a Halloween party," Patty told her boyfriend as the gang from the drama department sat at the deli hangout.

"Hey! Progress!"

"He didn't want to," she said happily. "He was reluctant at first, but he did agree. You have to come." She turned to her friends. "All of you. A costume party. It's the first time he's ever let me have a party at home, and I want it to be terrific."

"What are you going to wear?" one of her girlfriends asked.

"I don't know." She laughed. "Maybe I'll come like a little angel. Or maybe I'll be a witch!"

"Woooo . . ."

"And everybody bring something," she shouted over the laughter.

"I'll bring the grass."

"No," she said, suddenly serious. "Hey, c'mon, guys. No fooling around when my dad's around. Okay?"

"Okay, don't worry about it."

"Promise me!" she said fiercely.

"Okay, *okay*."

She told John junior about the party.

"I don't want to come."

"Why not, Johnny? It'll be *here*. Daddy said yes. The first time. It's the first party we've ever been able to have in this house."

The age difference is vast between fifteen and sixteen, but that wasn't what bothered Johnny. "They're your friends," he protested.

"I'll introduce you around."

"I'll probably have soccer practice."

"Johnny," she begged softly, "don't be like him."

"There's nothing wrong with him," Johnny said, feeling he had to defend his father every time Patty intimated that he was too strict or too unbending. "He just cares too much, that's all."

"Don't hold back."

"I'm not. But sometimes I think you don't understand Dad," he said. "He has a lot of things on his mind all the time. And he cares too much about what happens to us all. And it's all up to him all the time. Maybe when I grow up I can help, but right now it's all up to him."

Patty sighed. "Okay. But it's now, not later. Please come to the party. I'll introduce you around," she repeated.

"I don't know," he murmured.

Patty knew he was very shy socially. And sometimes she worried about him. A few weeks ago she had run into a teammate of his at the deli hangout and asked him how Johnny was at soccer. "He's got a lot of heart," the boy had said.

"Is that good for the game?"

"Oh, yeah, sure. But he's not very good."

"Oh." She was disappointed. Somehow she had hoped that he would say Johnny was a real star athlete or something like that.

"But he gives it all he's got. That counts for a lot. And he's big."

"Do the kids pick on him?" she asked unhappily.

"Well . . . you know . . . sometimes."

On Halloween night, less than two weeks before they were murdered, Patty had her party. She deliberately celebrated the witch element of Halloween, with the witch's hat, the mask, the costume . . . the *fun* of it all!

Three of the Vandermere teenagers, Mitch, Mary, and Pam, had been invited to the party. Of the three, Patty was friendliest with Mitch. Pam was surprised that she and Mary were included. Mary was several years older, and she had her own circle of friends who weren't such oddballs. After a few initial attempts when the Lists had first moved in, she had never really tried to become friends with Patty. Now walking into the barren ballroom suddenly crowded with costumed teenagers, she remembered that when they were both little, Patty couldn't come out to play because she was always busy doing things in the house. This is probably the closest she's come to being a kid, Pam thought. Pathetic, she thought with sudden sympathy. She'd always had the impression that Patty played the mother role to her two younger brothers . . . cooked dinner and everything. "I don't even know why I was invited," she told her sister. "I hardly know Patty."

"What about ме?" Mary said. "The last time I was in this house was when they first moved in and I baby-sat for them once. Now that was weird," she said, remembering. "The first thing Mrs. List did was take me up to her bedroom to show me all of her clothes. There was hardly any furniture in the room, but her closet was full of clothes, and she had all these sweaters. I mean dozens of them."

"They're all weird."

"C'mon," Mitch said. "Patty's okay. She's real cool."

"Hey, no wonder there's all this devil stuff here. Halloween is great for that kind of stuff."

"I suppose."

"Y'know what Patty said to me once?"

"What?"

"Are you ready for this one?" he teased.

"What?" She laughed. "Tell me!"

"Well, last week, Patty told me that the devil lived in Scotch Plains and that everyone should make love with the devil."

Mary and Pam looked at their brother wide-eyed for a moment before they all burst out laughing. "Was she serious?"

"Wooooo. I'd like to try that," Pam joked.

At least fifty masked teenagers showed up at the ballroom party. They wore appropriate Halloween costumes—ghosts, devils, angels, goblins, witches. The majority were from the Westfield Drama Department and demonstrated a marked lack of inhibition. For most the party was a huge success. They danced, they played, they cavorted, they unmasked, they ate, they drank.

Patty was thrilled with the success of the evening. Even Mom enjoyed herself, suddenly appearing out of nowhere, it seemed, in the middle of the party. How long had it been since Patty had seen her mother smiling? Actually laughing? Actually participating in the festivities? She had put on a silly mask that belonged to one of the Vandermeres and had burst out laughing through the cardboard disguise. Patricia had felt a momentary bubble of hope for . . . what? For a possible change?

Then just as suddenly her mother disappeared upstairs, retreating once again to the solitude of her bed. Most of Patty's friends had not even been aware of her brief appearance. It had not lasted more than two minutes.

Of course, Patty could feel her father's presence everywhere. His disapproval had dampened the spirit of the party even before it began. Then Alice told her that he had kicked one of the boys for trying to make out with one of the girls, actually kicked him and asked him to leave. "I warned everybody to behave," Patty cried to her friend.

John was sorry he had agreed to the party. It didn't pay to be soft. Advantage was always taken. He hadn't expected so many people to show up. Patty hadn't told him how many people she'd invited, but he chose not to make an issue of it with her.

Freddie and Johnny remained in their rooms. Freddie kept Tinkerbell locked up with him so that he couldn't circulate among the guests and snap at them. Johnny spent most of the time studying, but every once in a while, he opened his door to listen to the sound of the music drifting up the stairs from the ballroom.

Two days later Tinkerbell disappeared. Rick had come over to play Monopoly, but Freddie was too upset to concentrate on the game.

"Tinkerbell's gone," he said.

"Where?" Rick asked.

"He disappeared," Freddie said. "Just gone. Like that. We can't find him anyplace."

"Have you asked around the neighborhood?"

"Oh, yeah," he said anxiously. "We looked and looked."

"He probably just ran away," Johnny said.

"No, he wouldn't do that," Freddie insisted. "He was too scared all the time. That's why he snapped. 'Cause he was scared."

"He was just mean," Rick said, remembering the last time the little dog had nipped his hand when he'd bent down to pet the top of his head.

"No," Freddie defended the missing little dog. "He only bit when he got scared about something."

"Well, he'll probably show up," Rick offered, seeing how upset Freddie was.

Johnny looked off into his thoughts. "He probably ran away," he said quietly. "From here. And then maybe he got picked up by someone."

"You think so?" Freddie asked a bit hopefully.

"Sure," his brother reassured him. "He's probably living with a nice family that'll treat him good."

"But I'm gonna keep right on looking," Freddie said, trying not to cry.

"Sure."

Except that Dad had told them they were all going to North Carolina to visit Grandma Morris, who was sick. He was excited about the trip. But how would they ever find Tinkerbell if they were away ?

* * *

John felt compelled to try one more time with Helen, to point the way. It was a moral obligation.

She looked up at John from her pillow. It had been a long while since he had sat on her bed. "Helen," he said softly.

"What?"

"Do you remember when we were first married and went to Washington?"

"What is it, John?" she asked a bit impatiently.

"When we started off our marriage with such high hopes," he said, his eyes focused deeply in the past. "I had such high hopes."

"That was a long time ago," she said, suddenly feeling desperately sad.

They looked at each other, both momentarily lost in the memories of long ago. How they had changed. It was almost twenty years. Not such a long time, but it had ravaged them. She had changed more physically. The lovely young lady had been vanquished by illness and drink. Nostalgia only made reality more devastating.

"Helen . . . I should like very much for you," he began again, "for us . . . to visit with the church elders."

"Oh, John, don't start," she begged.

"Please, Helen. Listen to me," he urged softly. "Let's not fight . . ."

"I don't want to fight anymore," she said, her eyes suddenly glistening with tears. "I don't even have the strength left for that. I don't want to fight." Her voice trailed off.

He waited a moment before going on with his mission. "Only good could come from pastoral counseling at this time," he persisted quietly.

"No."

He took her frail hand on the bedsheet and held it gently within his large hand. It had been a long time since they had touched. She looked at him plaintively. They both remembered how they had held hands so lovingly all those years ago. How could things have deteriorated so badly? He waited a long moment before he spoke again. "You're not well, dear. It would be beneficial."

"No!" She pulled her hand away. The contact had not lasted long.

"Just a short consultation . . ."

She shook her head on the pillow and turned it away from him.

"Helen . . ."

She looked at him again. Her eyes burned almost feverishly. When she spoke, her voice was soft but firm. "No, John. I can't."

"Don't reject God, Helen."

"It's not God I'm rejecting."

"Me?"

"Not even that," she said, suddenly overcome with great weariness. "It's just . . . your idea of God, maybe."

"I've already spoken to the pastor. He says he would be glad to come here."

"You had no right," she said, suddenly flaring up with anger. "No right to talk to him about me."

"He wants to help."

"He's your pastor, not mine."

"Helen . . ."

"I should have stayed with my own kind," she cried. "What's wrong with being a Baptist? But I don't want even them. You're all a bunch of hypocrites. Bible-belching hypocrites! There isn't a man among you. Not one! I want out! Out of it all!" She was getting hysterical.

"Helen, don't blaspheme," he stammered.

"I'll bring the sham of our lives out in the open if you keep this up!"

He rose from the bed in agitation. His cheeks were flaming now with panic at the thought.

"I will, John," she threatened. "I will if you don't leave me alone. And I want my name formally dropped from the rolls of the church."

"Oh, my God," he said, backing away.

"I don't want to be a Lutheran anymore!" she screamed. "Or anything. . . ."

He left the room.

The time had come.

21 | Thou Shalt Not Kill

November 9, 1971

7:30 A.M.

The day was just beginning for the List family.

John glanced out the window. The morning was bright with sunshine, but he knew it was cold outside. The weather report had predicted freezing temperatures the night before. He could feel a chill in the air of the large, rambling old house. The heating bills were enormous, he thought distractedly.

He was already dressed neatly in a suit and tie as though preparing for the start of a normal business day. He waited. He could hear that his family was beginning to stir. He had spent the night before in the easy chair in his front office contemplating the chain of events he was about to set in motion. The sequence was very important in order to ensure the orderly and systematic success of his plan.

In her third-floor apartment, Alma awakened. She slipped into her warm house robe and went to her bathroom.

Downstairs on the main floor in the kitchen, John waited while Patty, John junior, and Freddie picked listlessly at the breakfasts set before them. They were seated around the cheap Formica-topped table with its cold tubular metal legs. Not one of the chairs matched, John thought. Some were metal with plastic seats, others were banged-up wooden hand-me-downs he'd collected somewhere.

He checked the laundry room through the open door of the kitchen. The mops for cleaning up were all there, next to the washer and dryer.

As he placed the coffeepot on the white metal electric stove that hadn't been scrubbed in months, he stared briefly at the salad bowls and spices printed on the fading kitchen wallpaper. He'd never noticed them before. He poured himself a cup of coffee and distractedly noted that the rough-surfaced brick fireplace wall behind the stove was covered with layers of dust. Not very healthy, he thought. The kitchen, which was large to begin with, seemed even larger with the little furniture they had. Helen was never there in the morning to prepare breakfast for the children or to see them off to school, and although Patty did the best she could, they never ate properly. And breakfast was the most important meal of the day.

Freddie started to chatter about something. What was he saying? List forced his attention to his young son.

"What is it?" he said gruffly.

"I was just talking to Patty."

"What?" he demanded.

"I said that . . . that I'll see her there after school," he stammered. "At work."

"I'll be there," she answered, observing her father's dour expression.

Freddie and his sister both worked after school at part-time clerical jobs at KMV Associates, a local real estate firm. List approved of the fact that they kept their spare time occupied.

"You'll all have to take the school bus or walk," he said. "I can't drive you today."

The children nodded.

"Zip up your coat," John said to Freddie more sternly than the order warranted as young Freddie pulled a heavy winter coat over his sweater. The boy dutifully zipped it all the way up to his collar.

"You have too much makeup on," he said, turning to Patty.

She tossed her head in the rebelliously impatient manner she had adopted lately. "All the kids wear this much," she murmured.

"You're not 'all the kids,' " he said.

She lowered her eyes at his tone. She knew when not to argue back. What is the *matter* with him today? she thought. But then again, is today any different from any other day lately?

"Wipe it off, Patty."

She and Johnny exchanged furtive glances. His eyes were begging her not to push too hard. They knew Dad balanced on the razor's edge of fury lately. He was frightening when he got like that. Always saying strange things, such as "This family must be stopped from going to hell" or "I can't support you any longer" or "God understands"—things like that. You couldn't take him literally, but still, it was scary. Patty obediently pressed a paper napkin to her lips and got up from the table to get her heavy winter parka before he could say anything further. With a brief "Bye," she left by the back entrance, closing the latched-together Dutch doors behind her. She couldn't wait to get to North Carolina, anything for a change.

List turned to Johnny. "Will you be home right after school?"

"No," the boy said quietly.

"Soccer practice today?"

"Yes. Until six."

"Fine."

John suddenly looked closely at his older son. So much like me, he thought. As he studied his namesake, his mind wandered back to the moment of selection. November 1 is All Saints Day, he had thought, the Christian holiday when the faithful pray for all those whose spirits have reached heaven after the trials of their earthly sojourn. That would have been a good day. But then again, November 2 was All Souls Day, a day of prayer set aside for the souls of all who had died and who might not have reached heaven, yet, who, in fact, might be still suffering through the penance of purgatory. Maybe that would have been a more appropriate time, but since his travel plans had fallen through, he had to change the date anyway. He could not see that, perhaps, there was an unquenchable force of evil present in his consuming need to save his family mercifully from the sin of living or the curse of welfare. Nor could he know that the decision to change his plans from November 1 to November 9 would one day factor into decisions regarding his own fate.

John junior and Freddie left the house together by the back door as Patty had done. List went through the kitchen, down the long hallway to the front of the house. By the time he drew aside the edge of the curtains hanging limply across his front office windows, his sons had already come around the side of the house and were crossing the front lawn. He watched them disappear down Hillside Avenue together. They had missed the bus and were walking. It was a good hike, but they didn't mind. They had been eager to leave.

8:20 A.M.

All three children were gone. Only three people remained in the house: John, Alma, and Helen.

He turned his face away from the window slowly and looked up toward the second floor. He listened intently. There was no sound. He concentrated for a moment on the deep silence. Then he looked out of the window again and remembered that he had not picked up yesterday's mail. There was still time.

The mailbox was one hundred feet from the front entrance of the house, standing near the sidewalk of the broad, tree-lined thoroughfare. He walked down to it. As usual, the contents were predominantly bills. One return address showed an official-looking letter from the First Federal Savings and Loan Bank. He stared at the envelope without opening it. He knew it was another notification of the forthcoming foreclosure on his house. He looked up at the imposing structure standing in the distance like a malediction on the serenity he was trying to maintain for himself. He shouldn't have bought the house. Even if he had not lost his job shortly after signing the heavy mortgage note, he probably would not have been able to keep up the payments. He never should have listened to Helen. But she was so insistent.

John suppressed the inner rage again. December first of this year, 1971, would be their twentieth anniversary and she was still displaying Marvin's medals, still keeping the American flag that had draped his casket as though it were a sacred talisman.

He put yesterday's mail on his desk and waited patiently. Lately Helen had been having one of her relatively good spells and had been coming downstairs for breakfast. He was grateful for that. He didn't want to have to do it in the bedroom. That was too close to *Mutter*. While he waited, he wrote a note to the milkman to stop deliveries. He put it in the refrigerator in the butler's pantry, where the milkman always placed the family's order. It worried John that the man would be coming into the house. Timing was important. As long as the milkman came before Helen came downstairs, it would be all right.

John sat in the privacy of his front office. He hefted the black Steyr and clasped the wooden handgrip firmly in the palm of his hand. He took aim at a spot on the wall and squeezed the trigger. The empty gun clicked! It had a five-inch barrel. The longer the barrel, the more accurate it was. He picked up the tiny .22-caliber Colt revolver. It held eight shells. It wasn't as accurate as the Steyr. Too small, so small he could close his hand over it and actually hide it from sight within his palm—useful as a surprise factor, but firing at a moving target could be a problem. Yet a small bullet penetrated because of its smaller circumference . . . the velocity of it . . . a bigger bullet might hit bone and bounce off. But he was sure he could be accurate and quick. The quarters were tight. There would be little room for error. He had been a good shot in the army. Target practice had proved that he still was. He would fire several times, in quick succession. One bullet was sure to hit its mark. Then there was the rifling in the .22, he thought, gently spinning the cylinder with his left thumb as he inserted eight tiny shells into their chambers. With rifling in the barrel, the bullet came out spinning, which caused it to go straight.

But, no. The Austrian gun, the semiautomatic 9-mm Steyr, was the better weapon for his purposes. He would keep the Colt as a backup. The barrel of the Steyr held one bullet while the grip could hold a nine-shell magazine. He didn't have a loading clip, so he had to insert each bullet individually. He pulled the slide back, locked it, inserted the steel-cased cartridges one at a time from the top, pushing each down, feeling the tension of the internal spring. One in the barrel, nine in the clip. Ten bullets. That was eighteen in all.

Loaded. Safety off. Ready to go.

The plans had been made carefully, methodically. There must be nothing left to chance, no opportunity for mistakes. Once he began, there would be no turning back. The very finality of pulling the trigger the first time guaranteed the necessity of completing the tasks he had set for himself.

All of them.

In the deep silence of the house he could hear the back door open. Had one of the children come back unexpectedly? His heart lurched. He slipped the gun back in the desk drawer as he heard heavy footsteps going through the kitchen and coming to a stop in the butler's pantry. It was the milkman. Good, the timing was working out.

Herbert Argast always walked right into the house. As usual, no one was around. He was hoping there would be a check for him this morning. The Lists had accumulated quite a hefty bill—$184. Instead he found Mr. List's note. Mrs. List usually scribbled on a scrap of paper. This was on a memo pad with List's name at the top. Argast sighed in disappointment and left.

John silently made his way to the back of the house and locked the door. Then he went back to his office, opened the desk drawer, and resumed his waiting.

8:40 A.M.

On the second floor Helen groggily pushed aside the chenille bedspread and blankets and left her bed. She wasn't as unsteady as usual. Perhaps she would be able to go downstairs for breakfast this morning. She reached for the bottle of pills next to her on the night table. In the bathroom, she took water to force the pills past her swollen tongue and swallowed them.

She glanced up briefly at the medicine cabinet and away again. She didn't want to look at her reflection in the mirror. Her eyes always looked swollen when she wasn't feeling well. Air spaces. She touched her forehead lightly, not wanting to think of the reason for the headaches.

She rubbed her long neck. The pills seemed lodged in her throat.

She took another swallow of water before going back into her bedroom, where she put on a dressing gown. Losing her balance momentarily, she reached out and steadied herself on the edge of the table, knocking over the Zippo lighter next to the glass ashtray and the pack of Raleigh cigarettes. Maybe if she ate something. Dulled with medication, she managed to make her way carefully down the long flight of back stairs to the kitchen. When she walked in, she could see that butter and milk were still on the table, left over from the children's breakfast. She didn't know where John was. She didn't care. Since he had begun selling insurance from the house, it seemed as though he was always around.

Mercifully, today he didn't seem to be home. Maybe he hadn't come back from driving the children to school, she thought. With a shaky hand she poured herself a cup of tepid coffee before painfully sitting down at the table. Her legs were unsteady again, and she worried about making the ascent back to her bedroom. She took a bite out of a piece of leftover dried toast.

The last thing she heard was a soft shuffling sound behind her. But before she could turn around, John shot her once in the back of the head with the 9-mm Steyr pistol. She fell forward, hit the table, and then slipped backward onto the floor. Her head hit the dirty linoleum floor with a thud. Some of the toast she had been eating flew out of her mouth. Some lodged in the back of her throat.

It was over very quickly. It had been so simple. An instant explosion and it was done. The bullet entered through the base of the skull, fractured the occipital bone and lacerated the structure which connects the stem of the brain to the spinal cord connecting all the vital centers. John worried about the noise. The sound reverberated more than he had anticipated. Gunshots always sound louder indoors, he thought. Immediately he went through the butler's pantry and stood in the arch cutting the main center hall from the back hall. He hid behind the arch and looked up toward the main stairs for any indication that the noise might have aroused *Mutter* on the third floor. Slowly he moved to the foot of the staircase and listened for a long time. He knew from past habit that unless she had heard the gunshot and had become alarmed, she would not come down the stairs if there was even a remote possibility of running into Helen.

All was silent. It was safe to go back into the kitchen.

From this point on he felt as though he were on automatic pilot. There was no stopping himself. He had found his final solution. His intellect no longer served him.

John looked at Helen lying awkwardly on her back, permanently silenced in her sudden death. She was out of pain now. He took a moment to examine his feelings. He thought he might feel bad despite the absolute necessity of his action, but he didn't. There wasn't even the slightest doubt that this had to be done. It was best to get it over with as quickly as possible, to put it behind him.

He went to the downstairs closet where the children had stored their rolled-up deep blue sleeping bags. He pulled one out and took it to the large ballroom in the back of the house. He thought for a moment where to place it. The room was almost empty, except for a desk to the left of the entrance with Patty's guitar and some sheet music on top, one old tattered leather stuffed chair, and a miniature pool table to the right of the fireplace. There were some toys on top of the pool table—a baseball bat, a toy house, a small vase of artificial flowers.

He unrolled the sleeping bag on the floor next to the pool table and placed it perpendicular to the wall. The inside layer of the sleeping bags had a deep red background with tiny delicate white, blue, and gray flowers strewn across the soft padding.

Satisfied that it was ready for her, he went back to where his wife lay next to the knotty pine kitchen cabinets while her blood discolored the striped linoleum floor. He looked at her curiously and stopped a moment to watch the expanding pool of blood spreading about her head. Somehow he hadn't anticipated so much blood from one bullet, even though he knew from his combat experience that head wounds bleed excessively. He had known he would have to clean it all up. He just hadn't expected so much.

He stooped over and took her by her ankles. Inch by inch, her nightgown slowly rode up to her thighs as he dragged her body past the little elephant doorstop he had placed on the floor to hold the kitchen door open. He dragged her down the back hallway past the main staircase, through the main living room, and into the ballroom. Helen's arms were sprawled above her head, trailing behind, gathering the leaking spillage of blood from her head wound. Her arms and hands were streaked with dark red stains as she bled onto herself during the slow journey to the ballroom. List looked at the long, streaky trail of blood Helen was leaving behind. More to do, he thought.

He drag-lifted her, face up, onto the sleeping bag. Lifeless, her frail body seemed heavy. His hands became sticky wet. They left splotches of her own blood on her exposed thighs as he stretched her legs on top of the field of flowers. The heels of her bare feet, slightly apart and tipping outward, touched the intricate design of the hardwood parquet floor. Her mouth was open, but silent. He didn't bother to cover up her exposed legs.

By now the colors in the skylight stretching high overhead across the ceiling were gleaming brilliantly in the cold morning sun. They sparkled across the hardwood parquet floors. They looked celestial, like colors from the stained-glass windows in church: a fitting place for his dead family. Even empty as it was, by far the most beautiful room in the house. He remembered how Helen's insistence on buying the house began the moment she'd walked into the ballroom and looked up at the beauty of the stained-glass ceiling. It was only fitting that she should repose beneath it. She would decay while the colors through the skylight changed daily with sunrise, sunset, rain, clouds, and brilliant sunshine. The colors danced. Even the pine trees on the faded wall mural looked fresh.

The blood was still oozing out of Helen's head. At least now it was being absorbed by the soft padding of the sleeping bag she lay upon. He went to get the other sleeping bags from the storage closet, set them on the floor, and placed them side by side in a neat row at a right angle to Helen's body, directly in front of three unburned logs by the ornate metal fireplace grill.

He prayed.

Now to clean up. Wads of newspapers and paper toweling. A pail. A mop . . .

9:25 A.M.

Alma's short, gently waved hair was completely white now. She didn't really feel like having breakfast. Except for occasional painful bouts with arthritis, she was in good health, but her usual morning headache throbbed with dull repetition at the base of her skull. She knew she had to eat in order to start up her metabolism. As a nurse she recognized the importance of schedules, routines, precise planning. At the waist of her print housedress she tied a short apron. She was now ready for the day. She always dressed as soon as she rose and had her morning bath. Her routine had been the same for decades. She did not approve of women who went about the house all morning in robe and slippers. Helen was always . . . She pursed her lips in a thin line. She didn't really want to think of her daughter-in-law right now.

In her growing loneliness, Alma had continued to write cheerful little notes to her friends Mrs. *Vor*man and Mrs. Hollister in Bay City, which in her heart she still considered her home. They were all about how much she enjoyed being near her grandchildren. The notes, written carefully and periodically, were just as much to cheer herself as to send greetings to her friends. How could she tell them that even her beloved John was changing? Troubled. Quiet. So deeply involved in thought that often when he came for his nightly visits, he could do no more than stare into space. At times like these it was always a comfort to read the Bible together. That always helped. But she was worried.

But when Mrs. Hollister called her only the other day, Alma could no longer keep up the pretense of contentment she tried to convey in her notes. She told her that she had come to regret her decision, that she was sorry she had ever come to Westfield.

"This is a sad house," Alma said. "A very sad house."

How sorry Mrs. Hollister was to hear that. "Does she still drink?"

"Yes," Alma confirmed. "And she stays in bed most of the time. They think I don't know, but I know. I see everything."

"I miss you here, Mumma."

"And I miss my home in Bay City," she said, tears suddenly springing to her eyes. "And all my friends at the society." She was getting older. She had her own needs to think about. Life was getting shorter, and she spent quite a bit of time in sadness lately, thinking how the end of her life was being spent cooped up on the third floor of a house filled with hostility toward her. She no longer smiled as easily as she used to. She knew how much pain her beloved son was in all the time, but she longed to go back to Bay City and all of the friends she had made over the past fifty years there. She longed to visit Frankenmuth again. There were things she felt she would like to do before she died.

Even the children seemed to distance themselves from her. She knew that Helen had poisoned their minds against her a long time ago. There were times when she felt completely helpless in the face of the family's problems, when she felt desperately alone. But John needed her. He too felt alone. She could tell. He never smiled anymore, not even when they spent their quiet times together.

Johann, Johann, she thought quietly. I knew it was a mistake to marry that girl. I knew it right from the very first moment. A mother knows these things. You should have married one of your own kind. . . .

"Does John know how you feel?" her friend asked her.

"Oh, yes," she had sighed. "I tell him all the time. There should always be honesty between mother and son."

She slipped a slice of toast into the toaster and waited. She lifted her head when she heard what to her seemed like a small explosion. She couldn't really tell where the sound came from.

The main staircase in the house was still impressive with its panels of dark-stained mahogany wood, dark bannister over spiraled white posts, only a few of which were missing. Strange, John thought, he was noticing little things now, as though seeing them for the first time. The steps were carpeted with what once had been a rich gold rug. Now the rug was worn, stained, and so faded that it was difficult to determine what the original color had been. However, it was still padded enough to absorb the sound of his footsteps. They were muted as he walked with careful, precise, very quietly placed steps, up the two flights of stairs leading to his mother's third-floor apartment.

He walked past the old wooden bedroom doors on the second floor—layer upon layer of peeling, cracked paint—a clothes rack in the hallway outside Patty's door—the main upstairs landing—windowed, nicely curtained. *Mutter* had put up those curtains. They were soft and pretty.

John knocked on the door and waited patiently before entering to her soft response: "*Herein.*"

He could smell the crisp odor of fresh toast penetrating the stuffy kitchen air. She rarely opened a window, a habit held over from the bitterly cold windy days back in Bay City. His mother was surprised to see him. John didn't usually visit so early in the morning. They usually had their time in the evenings.

"*Guten morgen, Johann.*"

"*Guten morgen, Mutter.*"

"What was that noise before, John?" she asked in German.

"Nothing, *Mutter.*"

She noticed that he was holding his right hand slightly behind his back but thought little of it. Memories of times when he was a child and would try to hide something from her—a toy, a book—fluttered vaguely in her sleep-dulled morning consciousness. She had never needed to press him, and she did not press him now. He eventually told her everything. That was the kind of relationship they had always had. Close. Loving. Full of mutually shared confidences. John was her reason for existence. The hours they had spent together last night had been particularly close. John had wanted to talk, not of Helen, or finances, or the problems with raising children in these perilous times, but of life and of God and the kingdom of heaven.

A glass of milk was on the table, a quarter pound of sweet butter with a small butter knife. The little dish with roses imprinted in the center was ready for the single slice of bread that had been pushed down into the toaster. She liked her toast dark.

She managed a broad smile for her son, wondering vaguely if

something was wrong, if Helen was all right, if the children had gotten off to school on time. Well, if something were wrong, John would tell her soon enough.

He looked serene, though.

"*Herein, herein,*" she encouraged. He had remained across the room by the door.

She stood by the stove, next to the open door to the large storage room off the kitchen, waiting for the toast to pop. A movement to her side caught her eye, and she turned to look at him. She looked surprised and even curious when she saw the gun pointed at her head from across the room. She recognized the gun. She hadn't seen it in years, certainly never in her son's hands. The thought of John with a gun was inconceivable to her. She did not fully comprehend this last moment of her life.

"*Was ist los?*"

"Don't be afraid."

"John, put that down."

"*Nein, Mutter.*"

He pulled the trigger, but she had moved. It's hard to hit someone from five feet away, he thought. On television they always make it look so easy, but the slightest move, there's really only a margin of four inches to hit someone in the head. It wasn't an easy shot. The bullet missed and crashed through the open door into the far wall of the storage room.

Alma screamed, "Are you crazy?" But now she was terrified. She ran into the storage room to escape. She turned to the right of the water tank standing in the middle of the room. "*Was ist los mit dir?*" She moved around the walkway surrounding the high-walled enclosure to the water tank, trying to hide behind it. Her son advanced to the door. In her fear, thinking that he was following her around the tank, she completed the turn around the walkway and was running back toward the kitchen door when she came face to face with him. She saw it coming. This time he fired at close range several times in rapid succession. A single fatal bullet hit her just above the left eyebrow. The other imbedded itself high in the wall behind her.

She fell to her knees with the solid thud of dead weight as her body crumpled under the shock of such sudden violence. Her brittle knee bones broke with a cracking sound as she fell backward, almost sitting on the backs of her legs. John watched with silent concentration. Her face became swollen with gushing blood as her life oozed out of the dime-size hole created by the bullet that had penetrated her skull and lodged in her brain.

He jumped as the darkened bread popped up in the toaster behind him, breaking the silence of her death.

She lay just a few feet away from her scrubbed white stove and her spotless white metal kitchen cabinets. Her legs were severely bent at her broken knees. Her knees were wide apart and thrust upward slightly off the floor, pointing toward the kitchen door. Her feet were spread so far apart that her buttocks touched the floor between the two-inch heels of her sensible white walking shoes. Her head was thrown back, her mouth agape, her eyes wide open and staring wildly at the ceiling behind her.

He went behind her and tried to lift her up by her shoulders. He wanted to bring her down to the ballroom, although it would not be right to place her next to Helen. The two women had not liked each other. But she was too heavy to carry all the way down the stairs, through the halls, and to the back of the house. It would also mean cleaning her blood off the gold rug down two full flights, which would be difficult to do. He would have to leave her where she had fallen.

Suddenly John felt physically exhausted.

He sat for a moment, deeply breathing in the smell of his mother's blood. He looked about. It had splattered as far as the back wall. He disliked the mess. It made him uncomfortable.

He picked up some of the newspapers that were lying on the floor next to the brown paper grocery bag from Big Buy filled with neatly folded bags, and he sponged up some of the blood. Her eyes were staring at him. He got a towel from the kitchen and covered her face with it before he continued the cleanup. Fortunately she wasn't bleeding as much as Helen had, but he wanted to get the blood before it soaked into the wooden floor beneath her head. His leg bumped into the low wooden half barrel also filled with neatly folded-up brown bags. Finally he finished cleaning and stood up. He covered his eyes with his hand for a moment to hide his mother's body from view as she lay in such an unladylike position and said a silent prayer for her soul.

Right next to her was an erect grocery bag full of more folded brown bags. On the side in big bold letters was the printed inscription, "The best for less. O'Conner's Finest Quality Meats." He shut the closet door on her corpse.

10:00 A.M.

List worked out of the East Orange, New Jersey, office of State Mutual Life Assurance Company. On this morning, however, he had a scheduled conference with his boss, Burton Goldstein, manager of the company in the home office in Jericho, New York.

He looked up the number and dialed Mr. Goldstein.

State Mutual's answering service responded to his telephone call. "Who?"

"Mr. List. Mr. John List," he answered.

"No, Mr. Goldstein is not in yet. Any message?"

"Yes. Tell him that I am not feeling well and will not be able to make our scheduled meeting today."

"Not be able to make meeting," the girl repeated as she jotted down the message. "Got it. Anything else?"

"And that I will call him to make another appointment."

"You'll call him to reschedule?"

"Yes."

She disconnected almost before he had gotten the word out.

11:30 A.M.

John caught a glimpse of himself in a mirror. There were bloodstains on the front of his shirt and on his wrists and sleeves. He sat on Helen's bed as he took off his shoes, leaving small stains of blood on the sheets. As he disrobed, washed himself, and put on a fresh change of clothes, he prayed silently.

Satisfied that he was presentable again, he made a mental note to take care of his stained clothing as he went into his study and began to tick off the items on the list of things to do that he had burned into his mind during all of his careful preparations.

Item number 1:
   Kill Helen. Done.
Item number 2:
   Kill mother. Done.
Item number 3:
   Cancel conference with Burt Goldstein. Done.
Item number 4:
   Telephone Reverend Rehwinkel.

John dialed the number of Reverend Eugene Rehwinkel, pastor of the Redeemer Lutheran Church in Westfield.

"I've just put the family on a plane to North Carolina," he lied.

"Is something wrong, John?" the minister asked.

"Helen's mother is very ill. In fact, she may be dying."

"I'm very sorry to hear that."

"Thank you. They will all be gone for a few weeks."

"I see."

THE MANY FACES OF JOHN LIST

John Emil List in 1971 at the age of 46, shortly before murdering his family.
The Westfield Leader

An FBI computerized updated image of what he might look like at the age of 63 in 1988.

A New Jersey State police sketch of what he might look like in 1988.

Forensic sculpture of List created by Frank Bender for TV's *America's Most Wanted.*
AP/Wide World Photos

Robert P. Clark as he appeared on June 1, 1989 after his arrest in Richmond, VA.
AP/Wide World Photos

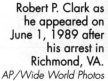

THE MURDER VICTIMS

On the night their father murdered them, he wrote to his pastor: "I know that many will only look at the additional years that they could have lived but if finally they were no longer Christians what would be gained."

Helen List, 46 wife of the murderer

Alma M. List, 84 mother of the murderer

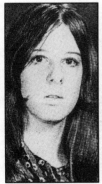

Patricia Marie, 16

Frederick Michael, 13

John Frederick, 15

BEFORE AND AFTER

The beautiful ballroom in its glory days. In the 1920-30's when this photo was taken, it was known as the "gallery." It displayed rich furnishings and objets d'arts.
John Wittke

Almost 50 years later, the same view. Now almost barren, it served as a family morgue for the murdered Helen and her three children. A policeman looks forlornly at the bloodied sleeping bags. The bodies had been removed one month after they had been killed. Patty's guitar rests on the small desk in the corner. *New York Daily News*

In 1971, on the steps of the church after the funeral, Gene Syfert escorts his mother-in-law, Eva Morris, mother and grandmother of the murdered family, with the help of Reverend Eugene Rehwinkel. *New York Daily News*

FIRST FLOOR

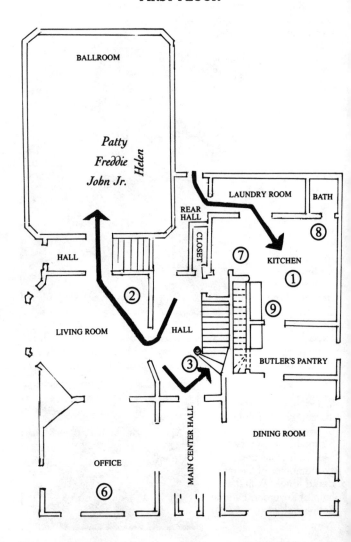

MURDER PATH OF JOHN LIST

1. Shot Helen in kitchen – once in back of head.
2. Dragged her into the ballroom.
3. Went upstairs to the third floor.
4. Alma ran around water tank trying to escape.
5. Shot her once above the left eye from the doorway.
6. Ran errands outside the house, wrote notes.
7. Shot Patty as she walked through kitchen door, dragged her to the ballroom.
8. Shot Freddie in kitchen, dragged him to the ballroom.
9. Shot John Jr. as he tried to escape.

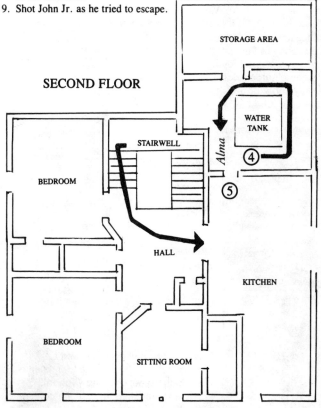

THIRD FLOOR
APARTMENT

STORAGE AREA

SECOND FLOOR

WATER TANK

Alma

④

⑤

STAIRWELL

BEDROOM

HALL

KITCHEN

BEDROOM

SITTING ROOM

AS THEY KNEW HIM

Reverend Robert A. West in his study at St. Paul's Lutheran Church in Denver, Colorado. To this day he still maintains a quiet loyalty to the church elder, Bob Clark. "I only know Bob Clark. I do not know John List."

Wanda Flanery, neighbor and friend in Denver, who identified List as Clark after seeing *America's Most Wanted* episode.

Sandra Silbermann, who worked closely with Bobby Clark at Maddrea, Joyner, Kirkham & Woody, felt she had lost her best friend when the FBI arrested him at their office on June 1.

Co-worker, CPA Les Wingfield, also present at the time of Clark's arrest.

Ellen Scott Brandt and Kathleen L. Gardner of *The Westfield Leader*. Ellen ran into the street shouting "Yahoo!" when word reached them of the capture of the town "Bogeyman."

BROUGHT TO JUSTICE

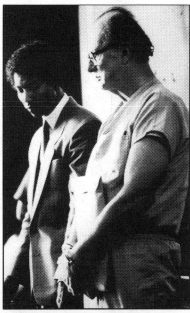

John Emil List at his arraignment on five counts of murder in Elizabeth, N.J. He still maintained he was Robert Clark. With him is Public Defender Elijah Miller, Jr.
AP/Worldwide Photos

Lieutenant Detective Bernard "Barney" Tracy often visited the gravesite on important anniversary dates in the vain hope that the killer, prompted by sentiment, might return.

Officer Haller who, with Officer George Zhelesnik, Edwin Illiano and Barbara Sheridan, discovered the bodies.

LEFT WITH MEMORIES

Delores Miller Clark— the 6th "victim" who married Robert P. Clark in November of 1985 thinking him a dedicated man of God and woke one morning to discover he was a mass murderer.
The Courier News

Robin Kampf, Freddie's age at the time of the murders, with the diary in which she recorded her reactions to the crimes.

Author, Mary Ryzuk, in her library surrounded by notated newspaper photos of some of the major participants in the List murders. Intensifying the tragedies for her are photos of her own two sons, Regan and Mitchell (lower right hand corner) who were the same age as Patty and Freddie at the time of their deaths. It was a major reason for her interest in writing their story.

On February 16, 1990, Robert P. Clark finally admitted that he was John Emil List. On February 18, 1990, author Ryzuk visited the gravesite once again. She found one fresh chrysanthemum in a small green vase, and, taped to the stone, a hand-written note in red ink that read: "Finally, you can all rest in peace . God bless." By the end of the week the note had blown away.

"And I'll be joining them as soon as I clear up a few things here."

"Of course." The pastor was sorry to hear that the family was approaching a sad time in their lives. "And John?"

"Yes?"

"I'll pray for her."

There was a short beat before John answered, "Thank you."

It wasn't a total fabrication, John told himself. There was some truth in this explanation. There *was* an ailing family member in North Carolina: Eva Morris, Helen's mother.

Item number 5:
     Notes to school authorities and other important loose ends.

John sealed the notes to the schools and to KVM. He would have to hand-deliver them after the children had already left school and work. He would slip the notes into mail slots when no one was around.

Next, cancel the daily newspaper. He called the Westfield Home News Service and left a message on the answering machine to stop deliveries "until further notice."

He had decided not to cancel either his phone or his utilities. He didn't want anyone calling and having suspicions aroused by being told the phone had been disconnected. And he had to make sure that the lights he left on throughout the three floors of the house would burn long into the days and nights after he was gone.

Next, quick notes to his neighbor, John Wittke, to Goldstein, and to "The Finder"—all before lunch. There wasn't much in the house to eat, a can of tuna, some toast. No use going shopping. No one had questioned the barren cupboard since they believed they were going on vacation. He sat at the kitchen table where shortly before he had wiped up Helen's splattered blood. He bent his head over his food in prayer. Already the veil was lowering between him and the events he had set in motion.

1:20 P.M.

John left by the back door, making sure that he locked it behind himself. First, he went to the Suburban Trust Co. on the triangular corner of Elm and E. Broad streets in the center of Westfield. It seemed to him in his well-disguised inner anxiety that the community bank was surprisingly busy for a weekday afternoon. At exactly 1:37 P.M. he entered the privacy of the vault, where he withdrew all of his mother's remaining bonds from their safety deposit box. The bonds totaled a little over $2,000. He was stamped out of the vault at 1:57 P.M. It took nearly a half hour to sign all the necessary documentation before he could cash her bonds. When John was satisfied that the interest due was calculated to the exact penny, Mrs. Gay Jacobus counted out the $2,000 plus interest in small bills and change and placed them in an envelope.

"Would you please seal the envelope and put your initials on it," he requested, "so that my mother won't think I took any of the money?"

He watched as Mrs. Jacobus sealed and initialed the envelope.

"Thank you," he said.

He filled out a withdrawal slip and emptied his own checking account. Next he did the same for his mother's checking account. Now she would never know that all that was left of her fortune was the $7.94 he decided to leave in her account so he would not have to close it. By the time he left the Suburban Trust, he had a little over $2,800 in cash.

Item number 6:
    Go to post office.

At the Westfield Post Office, he posted the sealed envelope with the key to his cabinet. He marked it "Special Delivery" and had it mailed to himself at the Hillside Avenue address. This was done very deliberately so that the authorities wouldn't have to damage the door when entering the house.

While at the Westfield post office, he asked the postmistress on duty to please stop delivering the mail to 431 Hillside Avenue, including any for Mrs. Alma List, while he and his family vacationed. He was handed an official form to fill out. He looked it over carefully and filled in the answers to all the questions as precisely as he could.

"When would you like deliveries to be resumed?" she asked.

"I wrote, 'until further notice,' " he answered quietly, pointing at his words on the printed form.

"Certainly, Mr. List. We'll keep it all here for you."

"Fine."

"Don't worry about a thing."

"No."

"Have a good trip," she said cheerfully.

"Thank you."

2:30 P.M.

He was home again. His outside afternoon errands had been methodically completed. He looked at the bloodstains that he hadn't been able to wash away on the linoleum next to the kitchen cabinets. The linoleum had become deeply porous with age. He would try to clean it up better, but first he sat down at the desk in his study. He had letters to write.

Item number 7:

What could he write to Helen's sister, Jean Syfert? Or to her mother, Eva Morris? Or even to his mother's sister, Lydia Meyers? Best to keep it simple, he thought. They would never understand the rightness of what he was doing. *"Dear Jean . . ."* *"Dear Mother Morris . . ."* *"Dear Aunt Lydia . . ."* He sat back at the desk in his study. So far he had covered everything, precisely as planned.

He held the Steyr, the gun of choice, between the palms of his hands in a prayerful position, touched his forehead to the cold metal of the telescoping barrel, and silently prayed to his God. The prayers, always a comfort, came to him a bit sporadically at the moment. He still had many things on his mind, many details to sort out, many last-minute arrangements to make. He had to make sure he didn't forget anything. He had to be careful; it wasn't over yet.

Systematically he finished mopping up the blood that had drenched through the sleeping bag onto the floor behind Helen's head.

The telephone rang.

It startled him. He went to the ringing phone in the butler's pantry and stared at it for a long moment. It was almost as though he were afraid that if he picked up the receiver, the person on the other end would be able to see through the line directly into the scene of death.

The sound of the ringing was penetrating and insistent. Finally he reached for the receiver. "Hello," he said.

"Dad?"

"Oh . . . yes. Patricia. Where are you?"

"I'm in town."

He blinked. "Is something wrong?"

"No, but . . . could you pick me up today?"

He looked at the blood-soaked towel in his hand. "What's the matter?"

"It's just that I don't feel too good, and I'd like to leave a little early," she said.

"Are you sick?"

"Nothing serious. But I'd like to come home. Can you come get me? I'm at Duke's Sub Shop."

"Get you?" he asked, almost not comprehending.

"Please, Dad?"

"Come get you?" he repeated. He hated the local teen hangout.

Patty hesitated a moment. Dad sounded so strange. "What's the matter, Dad? Is everything all right?"

"Did you get permission to leave school early?" he asked, ignoring her query.

"Oh, yes."

"Because it wouldn't be right to just walk out. Without permission, I mean."

"I know. It's okay," she reassured him.

"Fine."

"I'll be waiting in front of the sub shop, okay?"

Patricia heard a slight pause on the other end of the line. "Wait for me," he said so softly that she barely made out her father's words. John replaced the receiver very quietly as though he were afraid of disturbing the deep silence around him.

Item number 8:
    Patty.

3:17 P.M.

He buttoned up his jacket against the deep chill in the air as he unlocked the door on the driver's side of the Chevy Impala. He always kept the blue four-door sedan locked. One could never be too careful. The motor hummed steadily the moment he turned the key in the ignition. He liked the car. He would miss it.

He drove carefully, making sure that he obeyed the speed limits. It wouldn't do to be stopped now.

Disturbing thoughts suddenly flashed through his head. He heard the sound of the gunshots again. He saw the blood spurting again. He rigidly shook the sounds and images away. He must continue with his plan. He was delivering his loved ones into God's hands. Although Patty went to church, he told himself, she no longer received holy communion. That was a disaster, part of his own failure in his most important role—protector of the family. Now he finally had it all under control. He was putting a brake on all the failures before the matter deteriorated further.

It was a short ride to the center of town. He saw Patty standing in front of Duke's Sub Shop with one of those friends of hers from the Westfield Recreation Center. Probably one of those "actresses" who encouraged Patty's participation in the drama group. Patty looked very young with her parka tightly closed at her chin against the cold and her long hair blowing in the wind. He heard her say good-bye to the girl as he pulled the Impala to a stop at the curb and leaned over to unlock the door. She opened it and slid onto the seat beside him.

"Bye, Patty. See you tomorrow," the girl called.

"Tomorrow!" Patty waved.

The ride home began silently.

Patricia turned to look at her father's profile as he waited for a red light to turn green. His cheeks looked fleshy—wet. John felt her gaze. He turned to smile at her.

"Is Mom all right?" Patricia asked.

"Yes," he answered. "She's fine."

Looking out of the window, Patty slipped into the solitude of her own thoughts. It was a habit long ago born of a need for emotional evasions.

Despite the serenely rigid exterior her father always presented, she knew that he was worried. She knew he was having money problems. Did they really need such a huge house? she wondered. It certainly had not brought them happiness. There was simply more room between them now. There were more physical avenues of escape. And they could not keep the house up the way most houses in Westfield were kept. The paint was peeling off the family relations just as the paint was peeling off the walls. She glanced at her father again.

He was wrong! Patricia felt strongly about it. They couldn't just live day after day with nothing but religious expectations, duties, and constant gloom. She believed Daddy's approach in his perception of the world was too rigid and narrow, that he overemphasized certain aspects of life to the exclusion of others. He certainly didn't take much pleasure in life. She wanted to live a normal life with people and friends and a bit of the gaiety she had found in her associations with her new friends. Well, at least he'd allowed her to have the Halloween party. People had a right to joy in life. Not only responsibility. Not only duty. Not only God.

She stopped herself short; she felt guilty thinking that. She tried to think instead of her boyfriend. He was her major preoccupation these days. She could overlook the awkwardness of their first time together and think instead of what the relationship meant in terms of belonging to someone. Of being taken care of. Of being loved. Of being needed. Of being so intimate a part of another human being's life. She was in love with him. She was so sure of it and had even told her friend Alice about it. She felt whole, clean, and pure at the same time that she felt excited and breathless, although sometimes she felt the sharp edges of sin cutting away and damaging her sense of discovery and joy.

Her father turned the car onto Hillside Avenue.

The silence between her parents had become more bitter. Sometimes Patty wished they would scream and yell at each other as they used to, rather than live in this endless silence.

She glanced across at her father. He seemed angry about something again. His face was red and blotchy.

She had to get out of the house. Going to college would just mean prolonging her dependency at home. The work-study program she had switched to would get her out sooner, she thought as they drove the remaining short distance home to her death.

He got out of the car first. By the time she had gathered her sub sandwich and her school belongings spread across the front seat between them, John had already unlocked the back door to the kitchen and entered. She got out of the car and followed him into the kitchen. He stood a little to the side as though waiting for her to enter.

The moment she turned her back to him to put her books on the counter, he raised the Steyr and, practically touching her, pointed it straight at the back of her head. He wasn't taking any chances this time. He squeezed the trigger only once. But at that precise moment, Patty began to turn around. The bullet caught her in her left cheek. It hit the foramen magnum, ricocheted off the temporal bone, and exited the same side of her face. Still dressed in her winter parka, Patty dropped to the floor, crumpling like a rag doll.

John looked at her for a long, silent, unemotional moment before he grabbed the ankles of her jeans. Then he dragged her into the ballroom, her sneakered feet dangling loosely past his hands, along the same path he had taken with her mother. He had to place her carefully in order to roll her limp body onto the fully opened sleeping bag closest to the fireplace just under the little pool table. He had only three sleeping bags—he remembered when he'd bought one for each of the children. This one would have to do for two. He placed her head very close to Helen—only inches away in a T angle to her mother's naked left calf. Patty looked a little like a baby, sort of curled up with her left cheek pressed deeply into the flowers on the blanket.

As he repressed the tender thought, he bumped against the pool table. The vase of artificial flowers tipped over onto its side.

He prayed for the soul of his lovely young daughter as he began to mop up her blood. Newspapers acted better as a blotter, although he used paper towels, too. Then the mop, the wiping down with water, rinsing it in the deep sink in the laundry room next to the kitchen. He had to be as thorough as possible lest the others see the blood when they got home. He stuffed the soaked toweling into another brown bag. The first one had leaked through. There was a long, thin red stream oozing out of its saturated bottom, spreading slowly across the floor.

The phone in the pantry rang.

John jumped at the intruding sound. He picked up the receiver quickly.

"Hello, Dad." It was Freddie. "Do you know where Patty is? She was supposed to come to work this afternoon."

"Didn't Miss Gilmartin tell you I called?"

"No."

"We had a little family problem. Stay right there, son. I'll come and get you at five when you're finished."

"You don't have to, Dad. I'll walk."

"Stay there. I'll get you."

John put down the phone. He couldn't take the chance that his young son might dawdle on the way home and run into John junior. Johnny's soccer practice ended at 6:00 P.M., and two, together, might be too much to handle at the same time.

4:20 P.M.

Item number 9:
Edwin Illiano and Barbara Sheridan.

That Illiano! He'd been filling his Patty's head with nonsense, telling her she was a "natural, very talented." She already wasted enough time playing her guitar lately without adding the hours of rehearsal that being involved in school plays demanded. Now she was understudy for the lead role in *A Streetcar Named Desire*. Illiano would probably phone when she didn't show up for rehearsals; he might even stop by the house.

John made a call to take care of the matter. "Patricia won't be able to participate," he said a bit coolly to the drama coach.

"I'm sorry to hear that," Illiano said.

"The family is going to visit relatives in North Carolina," John continued.

"We'll miss her."

The call to Barbara Sheridan was even more brief. Family emergency . . . ailing mother-in-law . . . extended vacation . . . North Carolina . . .

On November 20 the curtain on the school play would go up. The production would proceed without Patricia. No one would know that she had been lying dead on the floor of her home since November 9.

4:55 P.M.

Item number 10:
    Freddie.

The drive to KMV on Elm Street to pick up the boy only took a few moments.

Freddie had finished cleaning out the ashtrays and wastepaper baskets, the last of his chores, and he was seated at the front desk waiting. He was worried about the unit test he was going to be missing in his first class period at school, even though his teacher, Marvin Marr, had told him he could make it up when he returned from North Carolina. Still, he couldn't help worrying. When he saw his father's car pull up outside, he said good-bye to Margaret Koleszar, the stenographer, and quickly left the office.

Once again, the ride home was short and silent. The boy sneezed once. Even though he could feel he was coming down with a cold, he would have preferred walking home from KMV. He was still hoping to find Tinkerbell. During the entire ride home, he kept his eyes open for the little dog. Maybe he was wandering around lost . . . looking for home . . . trying to find his way back. Freddie kept a can of dog food ready for the moment Tinkerbell reappeared. Please, God, please. . . . And the fish. He had forgotten to feed the fish yesterday. He had to go to the bathroom. And he was hungry. And he had a stupid head cold that was giving him a headache.

John unlocked the back door, but this time instead of going directly through the laundry room into the kitchen, as was his habit, Freddie dashed straight ahead toward the main center hallway. His hard-soled shoes thundered on the bare floor. He didn't notice the splotches made by his mother's and sister's blood in the back hallway that his father had unsuccessfully tried so hard to wipe away.

"Freddie, wait," John called out.

"I have to feed the fish," he called back, turning into the dining room where the fish tanks were lined up.

John waited silently by the closet in the back hallway to head him off in the event Freddie came back the same way he had run. If the boy turned left through the living room and into the ballroom instead of going into the back kitchen . . .

Freddie looked at the fish in the dining room. The house felt cold as usual. He dipped his finger into the water. It was chilly, but the fish didn't seem to mind. Although no one had reprimanded him, he felt guilty about forgetting to feed them. As he poured fish food into the four tropical fish tanks lined up in the dining room, he looked at the wallpaper. Patty hated it. Old and ugly, she always said, but he thought it was elegant, kind of Chinese. Freddie poured extra food into each tank to make up for yesterday. The fish belonged to his mother, but she never remembered to take care of them.

He did not go back into the hallway. Instead, schoolbooks still in hand, he walked through the butler's pantry toward the kitchen. He glanced at the cake bin on top of the refrigerator in the pantry. It was empty. John heard him and backed up through the rear hall, through the laundry room, and entered the kitchen from the opposite end. Freddie saw his father standing at the table waiting for him. He passed him and went into the little back bathroom. He lifted up the cover of the gray bowl with its pink shag covering and studied the wallpaper as he always did when he relieved himself. He didn't like this one as much as the dining room. It had people in old-fashioned clothes dancing, like romantic stuff.

He zipped up his dark corduroy pants and returned to the kitchen. His father was still there waiting for him.

"I'm hungry," he said, and turned to drop his schoolbooks on the table.

He heard the silence of the house. It was not unusual. But where was Patty? How come she hadn't started dinner yet? Dad had said "a little family problem." He hoped it wouldn't delay dinner. He hadn't had anything since noon, and he was really hungry. Maybe if he ate, his headache would go away.

It took less than thirty seconds for all of these final thoughts to race through his mind when he dropped his books on the table and said, "I'm hungry."

He didn't notice his father raising the reloaded Steyr.

This time John's hand shook a bit—Freddie was his baby.

Freddie didn't see the barrel of the gun pointed at the back of his head. He hardly heard the sound of the shot as his father pulled the trigger and the 9-mm bullet crashed into the back of his skull at the precise spot where moments before the little boy had felt the throb of pain.

The pain was gone. He was killed instantaneously.

Freddie was the lightest of all, a mere ninety pounds, but it was easier to drag his body than to lift it. John pulled him over so that his head lay near Helen's waist. John looked down at his youngest son lying on his stomach to the right of his dead sister on the same sleeping bag, facing her. Their winter jackets would absorb some of the blood, John thought, less to clean up. This time he brought the brown paper bag right into the ballroom and stuffed it with all the sopping toweling. But he had plenty of time for the mop-up. John junior was still at soccer practice.

He rested and prayed.

John didn't know that the Roosevelt Junior High School Warriors had decided to practice indoors because of the dipping temperatures. Half of the forty-man team had been told to go home. John junior was one of those who had been excused.

Rick Baeder didn't seem to care much about being sent home early, but to Johnny it was terribly disappointing to be singled out so clearly as second string. Was that going to be the story of his life? Second string?

"C'mon," Rick said. "I already called my mom to come pick us up."

They went into the locker room to change out of their uniforms.

In the car, Johnny hardly heard his friend's running conversation. The depression that grasped at his subconscious every time he approached his home had begun to set in.

His favorite times were when he was away from home on the soccer field, where all of the energies pent up by unidentified inner angers could be expended into legitimate athletic activities: flying at the ball . . . kicking it across the field. His game was very aggressive and very strong, and by the time he finished banging that ball around, he always felt better, even well enough to face going back home. Oh, well, he could go up to his room to read, and he had homework to do.

What his father had never mentioned was that working was also an escape. John List, Jr., had a secret hiding place: the inner world of his work.

List was not ready for John junior, his "item number 11."

He was startled when he heard the wheels of Mrs. Baeder's car crunching on the gravel driveway outside, then the slam of a car door. Why was the boy home so early? He had said soccer practice would take until six. List hurried to get the gun where he had set it down. He hadn't even reloaded. With a sharp movement, he pulled back the slide and inserted additional cartridges into the pistol.

"Pick you up tomorrow morning," he heard Barbara Baeder call out. Tomorrow was her turn to drive the boys to school.

5:45 P.M.

Johnny knew immediately that something was wrong when he set his blue-and-white "Westfield" gym bag on the counter next to the fire extinguisher and the blender. In a split second he noticed the stains on the floor next to the table and remembered his father's implied threats over the past weeks, threats he hadn't wanted to believe.

He felt something behind his right shoulder and turned abruptly to where List was standing in the corner of the room. He saw the gun in his father's hand and reflexively grabbed his arm. "Dad, what are you doing?" he screamed.

Johnny was strong, and instinctively he grasped the fact that this struggle was one of life and death. His father's eyes were wide but stoic with determination. His face was flushed and determined. List hadn't anticipated a struggle. It infuriated him.

"Dad!"

The gun in his father's hand went off. The bullet pierced the ceiling. As List and his son slipped to the floor in their struggle, two more shots were fired, both imbedding in the laundry room door. Reflexively the boy struck out, landing a wild blow. As another bullet crashed into the pantry wall on the opposite side of the room, he managed to pull himself to his feet. List fired at him again and missed. The bullet crashed through a kitchen cabinet door. List fired again, and the bullet missed again, going through the pantry and lodging high in the frame of the dining room window on the opposite side of the house. The boy started to run. His father pulled himself together, took steady aim at the fleeing youngster, and fired again twice in rapid succession. One bullet pierced the back of Johnny's neck behind his left ear. The impact twisted him around. The second hit him in the right side of the head.

John List, Jr., fell. His jaw broke in the fall.

The boy moved, tried to get to his knees, moaned softly, crawled toward the small hallway that led to the main part of the house, and stopped. He could go no farther.

List was enraged. He walked over to his son and stood over his body, trembling. He could see, even at this angle, that Johnny's eyes fluttered open. The boy rolled over onto his back and looked up at his father. List fired again, directly between his son's eyes. John junior's eyes closed but continued to flutter. He wouldn't die. His father fired again into his heart until the Steyr was empty. List's face was pink and blotchy with welts. He took the .22-caliber revolver out of his pocket and fired into the motionless, dead body of his son again . . .

and again . . .

and again . . .

and again . . .

and again . . .

and again . . .

and again . . .

. . . mutilating his son's flesh through the opening of his winter jacket, until the second weapon, too, was empty. The boy had been hit ten times.

The hivelike splotches on List's face felt hot and alive. His face was burning up. The boy should not have fought him like that. He should not have been so disrespectful. The struggle had unleashed the overkill reaction of all his pent-up rage. He had forced him to lose his temper, to lose control. He took his son violently by the ankles and dragged him unceremoniously to the growing family morgue in the ballroom.

List pushed him onto the remaining sleeping bag. His son's right hand hung off the side. It was still wearing a now bloodied woolen glove where his right ring finger had deflected one of the bullets. List picked up the hand and tossed it over his stomach. His shirt had turned red as the blood seeped out of the chest wounds. List grabbed the lower part of the sleeping bag to position him closer to Freddie, at the level of his mother's head. The maneuvering left the lower sides of the sleeping bag slightly turned up, covering his left hand and part of his lower body. The boy's head was turned to his right, his chin almost to his right shoulder. His bushy hair was messed and matted with blood. His face was almost entirely covered with blood. He faced his younger brother.

The family morgue was complete.

It took a long time for List to calm down. Finally, breathing normally, he looked around. There was so much blood this time. He cleaned up again, with more haste and less care. First the kitchen, where blood had poured out of his son's body in gushing spurts; then the hallway and living room again, where the trail left by Johnny was greater than any of the others. Now there were three brown paper bags of bloodied paper toweling. List crammed the newspapers he used to absorb John junior's blood into the third bag and went again to get a wet mop. He tried to wipe up some of the blood that had been splattered on the walls and woodwork during all the killings.

The job was impossible, and he finally gave up. No one was left to come home and become alarmed at the sight of blood. They were all dead, all in a row. List spread a cloth kitchen towel over Helen's face, screening her from his sight for the last time. He need never look upon her again. It quickly took on the dark stains of her blood. He was annoyed at its persistence in leaking through the thin covering, thereby continuing the testimony to him of the violence of her death even now that it was over. He left the children as they were, dressed in the winter coats they were wearing when they had been caught by surprise seconds before their murders. But he did not want to look at their dead faces anymore. They were beginning to appear grotesque to him. He covered each young face with cloth towels that he found in a kitchen drawer.

After a final quick mop-up, he dropped the mop in the laundry room sink. The floor was wet, so he placed a small oscillating fan on the floor opposite the fireplace and turned it on. It sent cool waves of air across the room, drying the floor and the bodies as he went to complete his tasks.

All of the preparations had been made after weeks of studying the current family daily routine, so there would be no slip-ups. He even called Barbara Baeder and told her about a sudden change in plans; she need not bother picking up the boys. They would be leaving for the South early in the morning. She wasn't there. He left the message with Rick.

6:45 P.M.

Item number 12:
 The letter to Reverend Rehwinkel.

A few more things first. List dialed the Westfield Police Department.

"Sergeant Howser, here," came the quick response.

"My name is John List. I live at 431 Hillside Avenue, Westfield."

"What can I do for you?"

"My family and I are going to be away on vacation, and I was wondering if you would be good enough to keep an eye on my house during our absence.''

"How long will you be gone?"

"I'm not exactly sure. Quite some time, I think."

7:10 P.M.

He left the house and drove to the darkened schools, Westfield High and Roosevelt Jr. High, where he deposited in mail slots the notes to the principals. The temperature had dipped from its forty-degree high of the day. It was now twenty degrees. He returned to the house, worrying about how much heating oil he had left.

Before he wrote the most important letter of all, the one to his pastor, he thought very intensely to determine if he had forgotten anything. He reexamined all of the details of the murders without once reconsidering the enormity of what he had just done. No, he had forgotten nothing. He had tied up all the loose ends. He had balanced the books. All that remained to be done was to write the letter.

But first it was time for dinner.

8:15 P.M.

Back to item number 12.

Finally, List sat down with a pad of yellow paper to write the most important letter of all, the one to his pastor, Reverend Rehwinkel. In his neat script, he carefully and reasonably explained the reasons for what he had done. Then he breathed more easily. He knew that he was free of blame for his day's work. He believed that in the Lutheran religion, the confession of a sin automatically absolved the sinner; the letter to his pastor was very important for the good of his soul as well as for the pragmatic necessity of final instructions.

He reread all five pages of the letter. Satisfied that he had explained his situation well, he placed the letter in the filing cabinet with a little note labeling the drawer: "Letter to Reverend Rehwinkel."

Now he could go to bed.

He slept fitfully.

On the morning of November 10, after a light breakfast, List was ready to leave. He moved the thermostat in the house to its lowest setting—fifty degrees; things kept better at lower temperatures. Besides, he didn't want to risk running out of fuel and having the pipes burst. The bank would be losing enough; why should it take the additional loss of that kind of water damage? It didn't strike him that his sense of priorities was totally confused, that he had just murdered his mother, his wife, and his three children, and he was concerned about things such as frozen pipes, and bank interest, and preventing the front door from being broken down.

Two final things remained to be done before he left. He carefully selected appropriate music for the solemnity of the occasion, liturgical music to play softly and continuously on an automatic record player in the back hall closet. Right, he nodded, as the melody resounded throughout the huge, still house over an intercom and speaker system. Then he silently went about the house and turned on lights on each of the three floors, so that they would burn into the nights long after he was gone.

He went back into the ballroom one last time to touch his knees to the parquet floor next to his dead family and pray fervently for their souls and for their speedy entrance into the kingdom of God. He'd had a job to do, and it was done. He had performed God's work. "And now they've 'Passed from death unto life,'" John said. "'He that is dead is freed from sin.'" Those words from Romans 6:7 had always brought him comfort in his daily melancholy before he had clearly seen his way out. He felt no pain or remorse. He was calm, relieved, and even quietly content in the rightness of his acts. It was all for the best. In simplifying his life, he had saved them all.

He gathered up his Bible, a few of his personal belongings, all of his war games, the money he had withdrawn from the bank, and the brown paper with his bloodstained clothes—to be deposited deep into a garbage bin in Queens on his way to Kennedy Airport, where he would abandon his car and take a bus to Penn Station in New York City. As he left the house by the back door, the sound of gunshots dimly reverberated in his head. They would soon be still. He finally had taken full control of his life.

And so, on the morning of November 10, 1971, all preparations having been made, not only to conceal the obviously premeditated murders, but to afford himself ample time to escape, John Emil List left, for the last time, the home he had shared with his family for six years, leaving behind not only his dead family, but also his class ring, his driver's license, his umbrella, his galoshes, his raincoat, and his muffler. He unlocked the door of his 1963 Chevy Impala sedan, got in, started the engine, and slowly drove out of the long circular driveway. The last thing he had done was to burn his passport and every photograph of himself that he could find.

From the moment he left the house on Hillside Avenue, John Emil List existed no longer.

PART III | AFTER THE KILL

22 | Fugitive At Large

Where is John List?

That question would haunt friends, neighbors, the residents of Westfield, the Westfield Police Department, the Union County Prosecutor's Office, and twenty-four agencies of the Federal Bureau of Investigation for the next 17½ years.

Why had he killed his mother, his wife, and his children?

That question would haunt the remaining members of John's and Helen's families forever. Mrs. Fred List, wife of one of John's nephews, who still lived in Bay City, Michigan, and one of the few Lists who attended the funeral, said sadly, "We don't see how he could go on living if he'd done something like this."

List had made Westfield, New Jersey, famous. The faces of the slain family were splashed across newspapers and shown over and over again on TV. The faces were beautiful, young, vulnerable, and full of hope. Capped with photos of the lone "suspect," the headlines in local newspapers screamed the death story for days:

FOUR STATES CENTER OF HUNT FOR MASS KILLER
> *Daily Record* —12/9/71

FIVE IN FAMILY FOUND SLAIN; 50-STATE ALARM SEEKS DAD
> *The Westfield Leader* —12/9/71

WESTFIELD TRAGEDY—HUSBAND HUNTED IN MASS SLAYING
> *The Star Ledger* —12/9/71

5 IN JERSEY FAMILY ARE FOUND SLAIN
> *The New York Times* —12/9/71

FIND SLAIN FAMILY FATHER'S CAR AT KENNEDY
> *Daily Record* —12/10/71

LIST'S CAR FOUND AT JFK; COPS CHECK FLIGHT RECORDS
> *The Star Ledger* —12/10/71

MURDERED LIST FAMILY BURIED; SEARCH STILL ON
> *Daily Record* —12/11/71

LIST'S LETTER INDICATES INTENTION TO STAY ALIVE
> *The Star Ledger* —12/11/71

Pastor Makes Appeal to Man Being Sought in Murder of 5 in Jersey
The New York Times —12/12/71
"Daddy, you're all I have left . . ."
The Star Ledger —12/12/71

But by December 13, less than a week after the hideous discovery of the five decaying bodies was made, the story slipped off the front pages. Even a major local New Jersey paper like *The Star Ledger*, whose daily editions had been keeping the sensational story hot and alive, slipped it to page thirteen with a brief announcement: MURDER CASE AGAINST LIST GOING TO UNION GRAND JURY. Now on the front page of *The Star Ledger* was an ironic story by Herb Jaffe— JERSEYANS RESTRICTED ON HANDGUNS PERMIT —and one by Linda Lamendola saying that the "holiday sales are very merry."

Only the local newspaper, *The Westfield Leader*, was still headlining the story on its front page, on December 16,1971. It stated, HUNT WIDENS FOR LIST, SUSPECT IN FAMILY KILLING. *The Westfield Leader* would be instrumental in keeping the case alive for the local populace for years, as though people on the paper could not rest until "their" murderer had been captured and brought to justice. Too many in the community had been touched by the tragedy. Police Lieutenant Bernard Marmelo, for one, shook his head in disbelief. He was one of the policemen who, at the "owner's request," had been assigned the responsibility to make sure the house on Hillside Avenue was kept under surveillance while the family was away on their "trip."

The List home was called the "murder house," the "ghost house," the "death house." Everyone wanted to see it. The beautiful old mansion became Westfield's major tourist attraction. Not only did thrill-seeking teenagers dare each other to go up to the empty "ghost" house, but literally hundreds of people came by to look, to stare, to imagine, to pray, to hope for justice. In essence they were each paying a form of condolence call to the murdered family. In the process of exhausting all the interest, both ghoulish and sincere, the local streets often became virtually impassable.

The recurrent question on everyone's mind was, "Why did he do it?"

While the neighbors shut their doors against the intrusion of "tourists" waiting for it to "all go away," the discussions among themselves were endless. Their conjectures ranged the full spectrum: It was because he loved them too much. It was because he hated them. Because he was broke. A religious fanatic. A lunatic. A sadist.

A mental defective. A professional failure. A total misfit.

"I really think it had more to do with his finances and his professional failures," said Dr. Cunnick, who had been sitting quietly at a local gathering listening to others analyze and reanalyze the murderer's motives. "Religion plays a part, I'm sure, and I think we have to look deeply into his interpretation of the Lutheran doctrines for some of his reasons, but that's not enough. We have to go further."

"You may be right, doc. He was in real financial difficulties, and he had been stealing from his mother for so long. I understand it was a considerable sum."

"I heard something like two hundred thousand dollars," Joyce O'Malley offered.

"God, that's a lot of money...."

"To the point where at the time he blew her brains out, she only had seven dollars and ninety-four cents left in her checking account," Edith Raeder added.

"Is that what they said? All of it was gone?"

"So I hear."

"I wish we had more facts," sighed Diana Ryan.

"The exact amount doesn't matter. The fact is that it was a *lot* of money."

"Where'd the old lady get it all?"

"I read she sold a house in Michigan and that her husband left her pretty well set with some kind of business that she also sold. Banked it all, probably. And then she gave him power of attorney."

"Christ! If you can't trust your own son . . ."

"It's a lot of money. . . ."

Voices trailed off into visions of betrayal.

"Don't forget," Dr. Cunnick added, "the man was failing in his job. He was a proud man. I don't think he could handle it. The failure . . ."

"You know, I read in one of the papers," ventured Diana Ryan. "You think Helen List put pressure on him to lead a life-style he couldn't afford?"

"But they didn't lead a grand life-style," Ellen Vandermere disagreed. "They were recluses. This enormous house sitting there empty, and they were recluses. Moving into a big mansion. Why that whole dynamic there? Why did they do that?"

"Doc, what do you think?" Hank Ryan asked, turning to him again.

Dr. Cunnick shrugged noncommittally. "I don't know," he said, unwilling to give in to wild speculation. It wasn't his style. "But there's a strange inconsistency," he admitted.

"It's interesting that he brought them to the ballroom," Ellen Vandermere offered, "almost like the scene of the crime. Halloween, I mean, where they'd had a good time. My kids said it was a good time, the party."

"Okay, look." Dr. Cunnick finally gave in, too emotionally involved to retreat totally from the discussion despite his professional reservations. "We can go in a couple of different directions with this thing. Again it's all speculation," he disclaimed before proceeding, "because we don't know all the facts. But it could be that he had paranoid religious delusions of some sort. Maybe he killed the family because God told him to."

"Could that sort of thing be instantaneous and then stop?" asked Edith Raeder.

"No, it doesn't just start and stop. He may have been delusional for years. He may still be delusional if he's alive," he said. "The preoccupation with religion could be a couple of things. It could be that he was simply a religious person, but it looks like, with all the stuff that's been coming out, that he had an obsession with religion. It may have served some kind of psychological purpose. Religion may organize him in some way. It's certainly one of the possibilities."

"What are some of the others, in your opinion?"

"Okay, let's speculate," he said after a moment, giving in completely now, verbalizing his own thinking. "He could be some sort of savior. He had to start again and try to save the world. His wife became ill, and Patty represented evil people, and he had to free himself of this family and move on. That's all possible, but not likely because he's never had any treatment. It doesn't look like he ever came to the attention of any psychologist before. So although the delusional theory is possible, it's probably not likely. Someone with delusions of that kind, well, it would show up in some way. From what I understand, people who worked with him didn't notice anything abnormal about him. Neither did any of us, either, except that he was a very quiet guy who went about his business. Rigid, reserved, withdrawn. But he wasn't bizarre. He wasn't having explosive outbursts, he wasn't talking to himself. Other signs that would suggest a more florid psychosis would have to have been noticed by someone. So the delusional theory, while possible, is probably not likely."

They all waited for him to continue. He didn't particularly like being the center of attention, but he went on with his theorizing, too engrossed himself to stop now.

"I still think," he continued, "that the professional and financial pressure was the deciding factor. He was in a job that I always knew he was not suited for—sales, but he never asked for my opinion, and I never gave it."

"He sure didn't know how to put people at ease," O'Malley offered with a bit of a grin.

"Exactly."

"Sure," Jack Raeder said. "Making just a little money, while getting deeper and deeper into debt. He may have taken out loans, but it looked like it was all a house of cards; it was only a matter of time before it was going to fall down."

"It sounds like that point was reached when his mother's money ran out," Hank Ryan added. "There are just so many loans one can take out on a house."

"Right," Dr. Cunnick agreed. "There comes a point when the bank says 'no' without some money back. I tried to give him a couple of contacts for insurance when I realized how bad things were getting for him, but I really think he was completely trapped there. A lot of people become trapped. This whole economic thing is a very serious matter these days. It's no news that the desperation of poverty often leads directly to crime. The question is, why did List solve his problem the way he did?"

"He could have just walked out."

"He could have done a lot of things. Except that he may have been experiencing such humiliation that the only way out from *his* perspective was not a logical solution, but it was *his* solution. Sounds like what he might have done was rationalize his behavior. Don't underestimate the ability to rationalize something. Human beings can rationalize anything, especially if it's in the name of religion. Religion will help anyone rationalize anything. Throughout history people have killed other people . . . crusades, inquisitions, terrorism. Even today in this country, you can be for or against things all in the name of religion. It legitimizes things. Religion probably had to be a part of it, but I think more important than that is that he had the ability to encapsulate all this and keep it separate from everything else in his life. That's a very important psychological mechanism. We all do it to some degree. Some people have an extraordinary ability to encapsulate parts of their life."

"What's that?"

"Separate it out. Until it doesn't bother them."

"I know what you mean," O'Hara said. "A lot of soldiers who've killed in Vietnam can't do that. So that the nightmares of the killings keep coming back.''

"And they have posttraumatic stress reaction,'' Cunnick continued. "That type of thing. Or even someone who has not killed but been in a car accident, for instance. Some people can get over it very quickly; they simply encapsulate it and move on with their lives, while others have recurrent thoughts and fears and can't even drive anymore. List appears to be a compulsive personality, neat, rigid, overcontrolled, orderly, methodical. He could also be a paranoid personality or both.''

"I never really got a sense of paranoia,'' Diana Ryan said. "Just isolation.''

"Paranoia fits with the religiosity,'' Dr. Cunnick said with a shake of his head. "The overcontrol.''

"Well,'' Ralph Vandermere said dryly, "he obviously had an exceptional ability to 'encapsulate' his behavior, as you call it. It sounds like after he did this, he had it all rationalized and encapsulated emotionally, and now he'll go on with the rest of his life in a very typical way.''

"Go on! Go on where?'' Diana Ryan said. "I think he's going to kill himself.''

"Maybe,'' Vandermere said. "But if he were going to do that, why didn't he do it at the same time he killed his family? That's more the pattern of mass family murderers. They shoot everybody and save the last bullet for themselves.''

A long pause followed as everyone thought about it.

"You know,'' Dr. Cunnick said with quiet passion, "it really bothers me that no one caught on just how desperate he was. In our society, where admitting loss of control of finances carries such a stigma, people in all the helping professions—clergy, physicians, psychiatrists—should recognize the destructive power of financial stress on a family. They have to *dig* for information, especially when the causes for the distress seem hidden or don't ring true. And they should make sure that people have access to credit counseling services.''

"Can you imagine this happening again?'' Diana Ryan said softly. "Him doing something like this again?''

Dr. Cunnick sighed heavily. "Understand, I'm a medical doctor. I'm not a psychiatrist. But it seems to me,'' he said thoughtfully, "that if he did it once, he could do it again.''

* * *

While the adults had the benefit of logic and reasoning and psychological analysis at their disposal to aid in the catharsis of their emotions, the children in the neighborhood had no such sophisticated means to purge their fears. They had to deal with the situation mostly through their imaginations.

Soon after the murders were publicized, fourteen-year-old Robin Kampf developed an obsessive interest in Mr. List, her private bogeyman, that would last for years and even affect her professional life when she grew up. She cut out every article she could find that had anything to do with the case and began a private scrapbook, her own collection of information about the man who had disappeared but who would not go away.

Little Rick Baeder, an intimate acquaintance of the slain children, also had nightmares after the murders. At the time, an addition was being built onto the Baeder home. Rick had a recurrent dream: Underneath the new addition, growing daily with its two-by-fours and plywood amid the smell of fresh sawdust, spackle, sheetrock, and paint, he saw John List, Sr., quietly and simultaneously building a secret hiding place. He was always there, somewhere deep under the house, concealed beneath the new oak floorboards, far away from the arm of capture, but close enough to be a constant presence. It would be a long time before Rick's nightmare ceased to haunt his sleep at night.

23 | Manhunt

While the neighbors speculated about the motives for the killings and the newspapers headlined the sensational story, the police initiated the systematic apparatus for a nationwide manhunt.

The search was being conducted by the Westfield Police Department and investigators from the Union County Prosecutor's Office. However, late in the day of December 9, when List's car was found across the state line in New York by the Port of New York Authority Police, the Federal Bureau of Investigation was permitted to join in the investigation under the "Fugitive Felon Act for unlawful flight to avoid prosecution."

After identifying the Chevrolet Impala by its New Jersey license plate, the head of the Port of New York Authority Police turned it over to his old friend, Westfield Chief of Police James F. Moran. The two of them had grown up together in the same neighborhood in Jersey City.

"Jimmy, the voucher on the windshield was stamped November tenth," he told his old buddy.

"No time on it?"

"Nope."

"Half-ass, if you ask me."

"I don't. Hey," he joked, "who's gonna pay the parking? It's been here over a month."

"Take it up with Governor Rockefeller," Moran joked back.

The car had obviously been parked either after midnight on the night of November 9, shortly after the killings, or on the morning of the 10. It was still not certain when the murderer had actually departed the scene of the crime.

Apparently List's family had been sent on the "extended vacation" without him, Chief Moran thought wryly, while he himself had disappeared into the friendly skies somewhere with what was left of his family's money. But Moran believed that leaving the car at JFK could have been "a drop." He probably left it and took off another way. After all, Newark International Airport was much closer. Why he had driven across the state line to JFK was anybody's guess.

While checking with all the major airlines to see if anyone remembered a forty-six-year-old accountant answering to List's general description—"Not likely, but do it anyway!"—the police went over the Impala with the proverbial fine-tooth comb. "Make sure you don't miss a thing!" ordered Moran. Nothing of evidential interest was found during the inch-by-inch scrutiny, except for the handwritten letters and the two weapons left behind by the killer. The car was the last concrete trace of John Emil List, mass murderer.

Robert J. Bell was Westfield's chief detective at the time and would handle most of the investigation. It was quickly determined that neither of the suspected murder weapons had ever been registered with the Westfield Police Department despite the fact that the suspect had applied for a gun permit. Bell had the two weapons sent to Trenton, N. J., police labs to be tested for ballistics.

"The Steyr's a 1918 model," he speculated to the chief. "Very old. It might have been in his family for years."

"Do they check?" Moran asked.

"Oh, yeah. They're the ones all right. Both of them."

"Well, that's something, anyway," he said a bit impatiently. He wanted to get this guy. Now!

Bell, in his thirties, was clean-cut and well dressed—usually in white shirt and tie with a firearm strapped under his arm. Chief Moran was less formal in appearance. In his late forties, he still sported a tight-bristle crew cut, a leftover from his military days as an infantryman. He had been in active combat in France during World War II, where in 1944 his outfit was almost completely wiped out during the Battle of the Bulge. He certainly was no stranger to violent death. But in combat, he said to himself, you can shoot back. As a police officer he had seen death many times as well. Even as a youth, the product of what could certainly be called a "rough childhood," Moran was often intimately involved with violence. He himself was stabbed twice in street fights before he'd hit his teens. But you don't expect to see this kind of violence in this kind of neighborhood. You don't expect to find an entire family slaughtered by the man of the house, who is supposed to protect them.

It angered him professionally—The numbers alone! he kept thinking—and the sight of the boy shot so many times by his own father bothered him on a deep personal level.

On December 9, 1971, after an extensive and comprehensive search of the once elegant mansion on Hillside Avenue, Westfield police issued a nationwide murder warrant for the arrest of John Emil List, Sr., in the killings of his family, officially branding him for the first time as a "mass murderer."

On the same date List also had the distinction of being placed on the "Most Wanted" list of the Federal Bureau of Investigation.

Besides the murder warrant, thousands of copies of the FBI poster "Wanted Bulletin" were circulated to every post office for display and to every law enforcement agency, police department, and sheriff's office in all fifty states.

On December 10, a 1:30 P.M. meeting was held at Westfield Police Department Headquarters on East Broad Street supervised by Chief Moran and Chief Inspector Bell. In addition to participating local detectives, present at the meeting were all of the law enforcement agencies involved in the hunt—FBI officials and detectives and assistant prosecutors of the Union County Prosecutor's Office.

It was an evaluation meeting in order to go over all the evidence already obtained, such as List's "confessionary letters," and to sift through all the potentially evidentiary records that had been legally ordered released by the United States Attorney's Office in Newark—

The bulletin—FBI No. 213 305 J4—read:

INTERSTATE FLIGHT - MURDER

WANTED BY FBI

JOHN EMIL LIST

DESCRIPTION
AGE: 46, born September 17, 1925, Bay City, Michigan
HEIGHT: 6'   EYES: brown
WEIGHT: 180 pounds   COMPLEXION: fair
BUILD: medium   RACE: white
HAIR: black, graying   NATIONALITY: American
OCCUPATION: Accountant, bank vice-president, comptroller,
             insurance salesman
SCARS AND MARKS: mastoidectomy scar behind right ear,
herniotomy scars both sides of abdomen
REMARKS: reportedly a neat dresser
SOCIAL SECURITY NUMBER USED: 365-24-4674

CAUTION
LIST, WHO IS CHARGED IN NEW JERSEY WITH MULTIPLE
MURDERS INVOLVING MEMBERS OF HIS FAMILY, MAY BE
ARMED AND SHOULD BE CONSIDERED VERY DANGEROUS

A federal warrant was issued on December 9, 1971, at Newark, New
Jersey, charging List with unlawful flight to avoid prosecution for murder
(Title 10. U.S. Code, Section 1073)

IF YOU HAVE INFORMATION CONCERNING THIS PERSON, PLEASE
CONTACT YOUR LOCAL FBI OFFICE.
TELEPHONE NUMBERS AND ADDRESSES OF ALL FBI OFFICES
LISTED ON BACK.

Signed by the Director
Federal Bureau of Investigation

J. Edgar Hoover

Director
Federal Bureau of Investigation
Washington, D. C.   20535

bank accounts, records of investments, personal documents, and the List family mail that had been held under postal regulations by the local U.S. Post Office.

The order was issued by Judge Jerome Switzer in Newark, one of the detectives reported.

"Anything important there?"

"One hundred sixty-two pieces of mail. Nothing particularly significant."

"What about his safety deposit box at Suburban Trust?"

"Nothing. A few pieces of jewelry. Nothing of any great value."

"And the avenues of escape?"

"We're fairly certain he didn't leave Kennedy by plane."

"Other routes?"

"Not normal ones. At least not under his own identity."

"Helen List's passport was found in the filing cabinet. Last entry . . . Mexico."

"What about his passport?"

"Missing."

"Wouldn't do him much good."

"Maybe he wants us to think he used it."

"He could have bought himself a phony one. He had enough money left over for that. What's the going rate these days for a phony passport?"

"Five hundred dollars or so."

"A foreign country would give him a little more breathing space."

"Naw. He'd stand out."

"Not if he spoke the language."

"We know he took a ten-day tour through Europe in 1963."

"Where?"

"Germany, Ireland, England."

"You think he might have been setting this whole thing up that long ago? In 1963?"

"Who knows with a mentality like that. He wasn't such a gung ho, macho type, you know what I mean? He may have started thinking about it years ago before he finally got the guts to see it through."

"Without going into details, or giving anything away, the one thing we're pretty sure about is that we believe he began planning his escape at least ten days to two weeks before the actual killings."

"You don't think he might have done himself in somewhere?"

Many murmurs of disagreement on that point.

"Why go through all the hassle, then? It was a pretty elaborate system of alibis."

"Right down to a note in the milk bottle. . . ."

The meeting lasted all afternoon.

"The search'll center in New Jersey, New York State," Chief Moran told the group, "where we know for a fact the suspect had an employment record. It'll also extensively cover Michigan, his home state, as well as North Carolina and Arizona. This is where we'll concentrate. . . ."

"Why North Carolina and Arizona in particular?"

"We know that's where there are some family members still living."

The Teletype and radio alarms that were first extended from state police headquarters in West Trenton, New Jersey, to police departments in all fifty states now branched out to international agencies as well. Interpol and police departments in all countries having diplomatic relations with the United States joined in the search for the fugitive. The alarm indicated that the wanted man might still be armed and should be considered dangerous.

Armed service lists were inspected.

Death lists were examined.

FBI fingerprint files were run through a comprehensive check. List's army fingerprints were on record. If he were ever fingerprinted for anything else, even a misdemeanor, he would be immediately apprehended.

By December 16, ten days after discovering the bodies, Union County Assistant Prosecutor Mike Mitzner was happy to report to the newspapers that through the combined efforts of the Union County Prosecutor's Office and the Westfield Police Department they had pieced together what they considered to be a substantial case against the fugitive and that all evidence indicated that List had committed the murders with "care, dispatch, and neatness." Union County Prosecutor Karl Asch, who, along with the Westfield police and his assistant, Michael Mitzner, had been conducting the local investigation and was now reputedly leading a worldwide search for List, told reporters that the contents of List's letter to Reverend Rehwinkel would be kept secret until the time List was brought to trial.

The Westfield Leader still featured major articles about List with inconclusive progress reports:

Local and county police reportedly have exhausted almost all leads in the search for List, who has not been seen since about 11/9/71. . . .

Meanwhile, the official investigation proceeded. With not much else to report, Karl Asch said he believed List would eventually be discovered or make his own decision to explain to society his version of what occurred.

In Westfield, the town's four detectives collected massive files of evidence all held in replenishable looseleaf notebooks: a file on List's fingerprints and handwriting with samples of both; a file on ballistics alone; one on personal family biographies; there were even separate comprehensive files categorizing, in detail, how the evidence in the other files had been collected.

On December 17, 1971, Union County Prosecutor Karl Asch went before a Union County grand jury to seek five murder indictments against List, charging him with the fatal shooting of his family. And without much ado, in the crisp, perfunctory manner of undisputed arraignments, the grand jury indicted John List on charges of having murdered "with premeditation" his mother, wife, and three children.

On November 9, 1971, John List's disappearance was so successfully thought out and so thoroughly planned that policemen now searching over half the world were not even sure on which continent he was. Agents from twenty-three FBI offices meticulously followed wild-goose chases in cities all over the country as well as in Europe and South America.

It was only the beginning of a 17½-year odyssey as dozens of tantalizing leads took detectives from New Jersey across oceans and continents. All ended in cold trails. Thousands of man-hours were spent and hundreds upon hundreds of files eventually accumulated in large plastic blue bins at the Westfield Police Department.

On December 31, 1971, an article appeared in the *New York Daily News* by William Sherman with a blazing headline that read PSYCHIATRIST: HE'S A PROBABLE SUICIDE. In it Dr. Henry Davidson, of East Orange, N.J., a leading clinical forensic psychiatrist, made some interesting assumptions based upon what was known of the missing major participant: "A man so obviously bound up in notions of religious duty would probably kill himself through remorse. He may have conceived a death for himself as an unclaimed body in a flophouse somewhere." Davidson speculated that the suicide would be a form of catharsis from the "tortures he suffered as family head in his Westfield, N.J., home." He went on to explain that suicide was usually committed by a man who was "totally alienated from family and community or totally 'boxed in,' as List felt himself to be." The psychiatrist went on to comment upon the police belief that List was still alive; even an escape under an assumed name was a form of "identity destruction." From all Davidson could surmise without actual examination, John List was an "alienated, introverted figure who had suffered serious setbacks to his ego through his professional failures." If he chose a different life instead of suicide, a new identity could greatly assist his need for a complete emotional release from his entire past.

Although the analysis was highly speculative, it might be close to the truth. If "John List" no longer existed, if he had become another person, perhaps he *had* committed a form of psychological, if not actual, suicide.

Not only did no one know which continent he was on, no one knew, in fact, whether he was even alive or dead.

If this were a game board, there would be no doubt as to who had won the battle.

24 | Fire, Fire, Burning Bright In the Middle of the Night

Almost nine months after the murders, at 10:00 P.M. on the night of August 29, 1972, at the Westfield Fire Station on North Avenue, Fireman J. Brennan relieved Fireman T. Gary. He checked the water pressure, which read 58 pounds, and the air pressure, which read 150 pounds.

It was a typical evening in the Westfield Fire Department with eleven people on duty, ten paid personnel and one dispatcher.

At 11:00 P.M. Fireman Larkin relieved Fireman Brennan. He checked the water pressure in at 58 pounds and the air pressure at 147 pounds. At midnight he placed a type #8 in service. Nothing else occurred during the silent hour before midnight when Deputy Chief G. Breitfeller relieved Fireman L. Larkin.

The quietude continued past midnight into the earliest morning hours of August 30. The center of Westfield was deserted and silent. Across the street from the closed post office, Wyatt & Koss's clothing store for men and boys, where List had purchased clothing, was shut tight. The owner of the liquor store on East Broad Street where Helen ordered her liquor had long since gone home. Ferrara's Restaurant, where occasionally the List children stopped off to buy a pizza, was also shut down for the night. Even those on duty at the police station in the municipal building were experiencing an uneventful night.

Less than ten blocks away, at approximately 1:50 A.M. on the morning of August 30, two shadowy figures moved through the deserted rooms of the boarded-up house at 431 Hillside. They spoke in furtive whispers.

"Will they be able to find these trailers?" one anxiously questioned the other, who was in charge. "I hear they can find out anything in an investigation."

"That's why we're using rolls of toilet paper for trailers. They'll burn. We've got to connect all the points that way. With trailers."

Skulking through the preparatory process before the first match was lit, they trembled with anticipation of the moment of ignition as well as with the thought of possible detection. It was as though they were already feeling the shame of discovery—reputations were at stake—and the accompanying legal problems that could develop.

"Why do we have to set it in so many different places?"

"So that it'll go up all at once and then there'll be no way they can save it," said the arsonist in charge, although neither thought of himself as an arsonist. They tried not to think of the lawlessness of the incineration they were about to set in motion. "There have to be points of origin all the way down from the third floor to the first," he said with assurance.

"Okay."

"It has to all go up at once."

"I know."

"Make sure you don't miss a spot. See that the trailers touch. No gaps." Rolls and rolls of toilet tissue were unwound in long strips between the heavy spills of gasoline. That's the way to do it, to have that many starts, the leader thought. A good way to make sure. "Be careful with that gasoline," he continued. "Don't get any on yourself . . ."

The smell of fumes as the gasoline poured out of the cans was almost as intoxicating as the excitement.

"Will they be able to tell if it was gasoline we used?"

"Stop asking so many questions!"

"I want to know!"

"They won't be able to pinpoint it."

"But lab tests—"

"You asked me, now listen! If the police send any samples to the lab . . ."

"The police . . ." The follower froze in his tracks as he listened.

"The test will just be able to pick out the ingredient that's in gasoline and determine that it's part of a flammable liquid. That's all."

"It can't be traced?"

"No."

"I've never done anything like this before."

"Neither have I. Hurry, so we can get out of here."

They carefully set points of origin for the fire all the way down from the third floor to the first, curling through the upstairs rooms, the hallways, winding down the staircases. The preparations took longer than either of them had anticipated, but they were finally ready. Before the leader lit the match they looked at each other one more time, eyes wide. This was a felony, the kind of thing that goons and hooligans did. Not people like themselves. They were both surprised at how caught up they had become in the exhilaration of the moment.

"Okay?" asked the leader, matches poised. "It's not too late to back out now. . . ."

"Do it."

"You're sure."

"Yes."

The matches were tossed. Breathing heavily with excitement and fear, they made it out safely as the first flare rose behind them, singeing the air, scorching the walls, burning the memories. It would all be over soon. Finally. Once and for all.

About 3:00 A.M. Mrs. Emerson awakened her husband at 6220 Birch Avenue, three blocks below Hillside Avenue in a low-lying area of Westfield.

"Do you smell smoke?" she asked.

He was immediately alert. "I sure do," he said as they both got out of bed and turned on the lights.

A quick but thorough check assured them that the source of the smoke was not within the walls of their own home. Mr. Emerson opened his front door and stepped out onto the porch.

"It's stronger out here."

"Can you see anything?" his wife asked.

"Nope. But *something's* burning. Seems like it's coming from up the hill."

"God, I hate that smell. I'm calling the fire department . . ."

And as she dialed, she thought, Somebody's got real trouble tonight.

The fire horn rang in Box 15, the system used to call the general alarm. It blared insistently into the night, over and over again, a deep, groaning, melancholy sound. At the station the call was recorded as "Alarm #484: House fire." Because it was a humid night and the air was very heavy, the smoke did not billow up. Engine number one, which responded to the call to investigate the smell of smoke on Birch Avenue, reported that even though the smell of smoke was downhill from the source—low—they saw a glow in the sky up at the top of the hill. When they followed the glow up Highland Avenue, they found the fire.

Within moments a ladder truck was at the scene, and four pumpers were relaying water to the top of the hill. Also within moments, the commotion had awakened the entire neighborhood. The residents, aroused from their sleep by the persistent spine-tingling sound of the fire horn, knew something was happening at the List house again.

O'Malley looked out of his window. His bedroom was unnaturally illuminated from the fire glare outside. He could see a huge fire truck parked in his driveway. "Joyce," he called to his wife in bed. "Hurry. . . ."

Their first thought was that the friendly neighborhood vandals had gotten the house. It had already been vandalized several times.

"Well," he said quietly. "Finally. There it goes. . . ."

When the phone rang in Frederick Poppy's bedroom in Mountainside in the middle of the night, both he and Mrs. Poppy knew instinctively it had something to do with the Lists. It wasn't the first time they had been aroused from sleep. When Mrs. Cunnick, wife of Dr. Cunnick, their next-door neighbor, found out Poppy was the administrator of the estate, she used to call him frequently.

"Mr. Poppy, there's somebody in there again. . . ."

His wife would go through the roof. "Not again!"

She wasn't surprised when her husband had accepted the responsibility as administrator. He'd done it before with old man Bamford. He had buried Mr. Bamford's wife and gained the old man's trust to the point that he'd asked her husband if he would be a coexecutor of his estate. Fred never made any money out of it, she remembered, just as he would never make any money out of the List estate. He might not even recoup his expenditures. But the List estate was different. Not like Bamford's. There were fears involved. She had always been deeply concerned that the murderer would come back to kill them too if he found out about Fred's involvement. But Fred always said, "Look after your fellow man," and had taken on the task.

Now, at quarter to four in the morning, Reverend Rehwinkel was calling.

"You'd better come down," he said. "The List house is going up."

"Fire?" Mr. Poppy asked incredulously. He had had it all boarded up tightly. Again and again.

"Yes."

"I'll be right down," he said, and quietly replaced the receiver.

He told his wife as he dressed. There was a sense of relief that it might soon be over, but she knew he was also upset. If he could have held on, he might have been able to sell the house and maybe pay back some of the creditors, including Gray's Funeral Home, where he worked.

Maybe the house won't be a total loss, she thought as she got up to make a quick pot of coffee as he prepared to leave.

She tried to remember back to the details of the funerals, but some of it was a little hazy in her mind. It had been such an emotional time for everyone. It was one of the children, she thought, one of the boys. There was one small policy on one of the children for about $2,000. Fred had taken that money, plus the $500 or $600 he had received from the sale of the furniture, and with that money he'd paid the funeral home in Michigan for Alma List, paid for the opening of the grave in Michigan, paid for the transportation there, paid Gray's Funeral Home for their merchandise, and that was it. As far as the plots in Fairfield Cemetery were concerned, that was vague in her mind. She didn't see how he could have paid for them. Four plots. At least $2,500 to do it and to rent hearses. He'd had to do that, too. And the people from whom he'd bought the caskets had had to be paid. She remembered the conversation he'd had at the time with the owner of Gray's Funeral Home.

"We're not going to get our normal service charges on this," he had said, and the man was distraught about it. But then her husband tried to reassure him. "Forget it," he had said. "You're getting publicity here that's worth a hundred thousand dollars."

And then the man had said, "Okay." He had little choice. There was a job that had to be done. The victims had to be buried.

Now she remembered. The church paid for the plots. That was

it. And for the opening of the graves. And when it came to the tombstone, the marker, Fred had suggested the Lamperty Brothers to Mrs. Syfert and to the minister. They were monument people in Plainfield. He had even gone so far as to tell the Lamperty boys about the circumstances, and they'd graciously given the stones at their cost. But he still had four concrete vaults at $250 each.

She sighed at the memory. Fred never once complained, even though she felt he had been sucked into it all. The List tragedy had had an impact on a lot of lives, she thought. Now this. A fire in the middle of the night.

There were a lot of people watching as the house burned down, one hundred, a hundred and fifty, two hundred. Difficult to count; they were all over. Fire Chief Ruerup knew the trucks had a hard time getting up Hillside Avenue because of the amount of spectators. Once at the scene, the fire was hard to get to and difficult to control. It was an old house with dry, hard wood that burned real hot once everything got going in there, Ruerup thought. A very hot fire.

At headquarters, Captain Ridge kept in contact with the fire scene. Mountainside Fire Department assisted. Plainfield was on standby with their number six engine already waiting at Westfield headquarters. Cranford had their truck on standby in their own quarters.

A three-alarmer. All our trucks are out there, Ridge thought. If we need another truck, Cranford will send theirs up.

Fire Chief Ruerup looked up at the blaze with a professional eye. The structure was totally involved. No electricity, empty house, barricaded, and still such total involvement. He shook his head. This was torched. No doubt about it. Somebody burned it down. He wondered whether it was burned just to get it out of there. It certainly hadn't been burned for profit. No one stood to gain by the fire. Someone just poured some flammable liquid all around the house—saturating all the flammable material, floors, what-have-you. He was positive the house—the "death house"—being there was a sore spot with all the neighbors.

He looked over at some of them watching the fire and wondered. He wished he could hear what they were saying.

Rumors were everywhere.

Some believed List returned to Westfield to set fire to the house so that it could not be sold and turned into the "List Museum."

"I'm sure he's been back. I've seen activity there," said one.

"It's kids," said another.

"No. List came back, I just know it."

"What for?"

"To find something. To conceal something."

"No, it doesn't make sense," O'Malley said, always trying to keep a clear sense of perspective. "If he were going to burn it, he would have done it when he killed them."

"But that wouldn't have given him enough time to get away. He needed that time."

"But why come back now?"

"Maybe he had to see the place again. And then seeing it again brought it all back."

"Guilt?"

"And so he had to burn it down to get rid of it."

"Maybe. . . ."

Driving to the scene of the fire, Fred Poppy couldn't help thinking about the many hours he'd spent at the property after the funeral, actually standing security guard at the house at night, in his station wagon with his German shepherd. His boss hadn't wanted him spending much time on the matter of the List estate, but he had anyhow. He had a strong sense of responsibility. And Mrs. Cunnick kept calling, "Mr. Poppy, somebody's in there again," with candles, having "seances." Candlelight could be seen through the thin cracks in the plywood boards barricading the windows and doors. He wondered if that was how the fire got started. Candles. What he couldn't figure out was how they'd managed to get in when he felt that he had had the house completely secured. He never saw anyone come or go, not even the police, who had promised they'd survey the place all the time. One time he had run a light string across the driveway from one end to the other. Then the next time he went up for a security check he found that the string had not been broken. Yet whenever he went inside, he could tell people had been there. Mattresses, writings on the wall. Devil stuff. Something was going on all right.

One Saturday morning when he wasn't too busy he had decided to sit down there for an hour or so before going to Gray's. And lo and behold! there were some kids inside. He parked out of sight and quickly circled the house. There! He'd found the mode of entry—an open cellar window. Poppy had run his station wagon right up against the cellar window, barring it shut. Once the intruders were trapped inside, he'd gone next door to Mrs. Cunnick's house to call the police. He had felt pretty good at finally having caught the vandals.

Chief Moran was one of the policemen who'd responded to his call.

"They're inside," Poppy had told him as he'd unlocked the door.

Inside they'd found three boys and one girl. One of the boys, from Roselle Park, was eighteen; the other three were minors from Westfield. They seemed genuinely frightened at being apprehended, Poppy thought distastefully, but there they were with the mattresses on the floors and rubbing shaving cream all over each other's bodies so they could slide around easier in their sex play. It was amazing how the memories of the dead and the violence with which they had met their death had added to the titillation at furtive teenage sex parties.

"I want them booked," Poppy had said grimly.

Moran was pensive for a long moment. Then he had quietly pulled him aside. "Fred, let me talk to you," he'd said. "All those children came from good families. . . ."

"I don't care," Poppy had said angrily. "They've caused me a lot of problems."

"These are prominent people in the neighborhood," Moran had said, ending his plea for withdrawing the complaint with, "This will be bad news for your business, Fred. Think about it."

Now, arriving at the scene of the fire, Poppy was again annoyed that he had let himself be talked out of pursuing the matter. Just the thought of the kind of climate in Westfield at that time, heads turned the other way at the misdemeanors of affluent people, still made him angry.

Because of crowds and fire trucks and hoses crisscrossed every which way on the streets, he had to park his station wagon some distance away and walk the rest of the way to the house. The smell of the thick black smoke was everywhere. His eyes watered.

"Fred," Reverend Rehwinkel called when he reached the house. "Over here."

He picked his way through puddles across the tangled maze of hose, until he reached Rehwinkel's side.

"My God," Fred said, staring up at the crimson flames shooting at least twenty feet out of the entire upper story of the house into a hot humid sky. It was worse than he'd imagined.

"Yes," Reverend Rehwinkel said quietly. "One thing after another. I'm sorry I ever got you involved, Fred."

"You did what you had to do," Poppy answered, but he knew what the pastor meant. There was absolutely no opportunity at all of Poppy's recouping the money he had spent on the funerals and as administrator of the estate. Nothing would be salvaged. The fumes were noxious. The smell was acrid. The glow was brilliant. The flames were spectacular. The loss was total.

He wondered whether or not anyone would ever be prosecuted for burning down this house—his nightmare responsibility.

"At least I managed to sell the furniture," Poppy told Rehwinkel. "What little there was. . . ."

"Thank goodness for that much."

A beam crashed through the floor of one of the upper-story rooms, sending gasps through the crowd and showers of sparks throughout the charring interior. "I met with two or three bidders," he continued steadily, his eyes never leaving the blaze, "and finally a fellow in Plainfield gave me the best offer, and I said okay."

The beam had crashed through to the main floor.

"So that following Saturday, he and his men came in and took the furniture out. There wasn't much, but there was a beautiful new stove in the kitchen. I'm talking about a big chef's stove that was worth about fifteen or eighteen hundred dollars."

Poppy could see the chandelier that hung from the third floor right down into the center hall. It was worth a couple of thousand dollars. "Everything in the house needed work," he continued as he kept his eye on the chandelier, "but the house was clean. I felt that they did with the house what they could, that they appreciated it."

The staircase went around and around. Now it was completely engulfed in flames.

"Even the billiard room below the ballroom had its own lavatories," Poppy said. "I think there were two in there, and a huge walk-in fireplace."

"I didn't know there was a billiard room, too," Reverend Rehwinkel said quietly.

The chandelier swayed, hanging by a chain from a burning beam high on the third floor.

"You could walk right into those fireplaces. And there were eight or nine bathrooms."

"That many. . . ."

The chandelier finally gave way and fell. Poppy didn't skip a beat as they watched it crash down into the consuming fire below. "He was in the process of putting new fixtures in there." Sparks, splintering glass, billowing smoke . . . "And that's where he was starting to make improvements." He cleared his throat. "That's where List was starting. In the bathrooms."

* * *

Another theory popped out among the tight-knit group of neighbors who were still huddled together, standing apart from the other spectators, as though this were their private tragedy and the rest of the onlookers were intruders.

"I think it was burned down by the neighbors."

"Teenagers?"

"No. The neighbors." This was said quietly, thoughtfully, and with great solemnity.

"What are you saying?"

Shock.

"It was a horror. A death house. A tourist attraction. A nuisance," said the onlooker as though going through a litany of charges against the structure. "Right?"

"A real stigma," someone said in agreement.

"I think somebody wanted to get rid of the stench and the tourists."

"Oh, my God. Do you really think so?"

"I think so."

Old Westfield families owned the homes in the area. Expensive. Tasteful. Rich.

"I hope not. I'd hate to think of someone we know getting arrested for arson."

"Won't this nightmare ever stop?"

Looking up at the house. "Maybe that's what they were trying to do. Stop the nightmare. Put an end to it."

"Burn it out."

Arson was on everyone's mind now. Poppy could sense it. He too was sure that was the cause of the fire. Remembering how the police didn't want to prosecute the kids he wanted to book for trespassing, he was also sure this arson would probably be swept under the carpet of bureaucracy and benign acceptance. "They're not going to prosecute anybody," he thought. He was absolutely right.

The theory that some of the neighbors had deliberately tried to blot out the horror of the murders by removing the scene of the crime itself was shared by the police and the fire department. Although an investigation followed any fire of undetermined origin with such total burnout, nothing ever came of it.

You could see that trailers had been set going all the way up, so you would know someone had been there, Fire Chief Ruerup thought to himself. That's where six or seven samples of charred floor were picked up and sent in to the state lab. There was no doubt that a flammable liquid had been used . . . gasoline, turpentine . . . and according to the officer who first came on the scene, it was all over the place. Ten, twelve, fourteen starts. But not one step was ever taken to either prove or disprove what to the trained eye was more than a theory. Arson. It was quietly decided to let the matter rest— drop it—not pursue it. The fire would remain an open file. Just another one of the many active files connected with the List case.

The neighbors were almost ashamed to admit it as they looked up at what was beginning to look like only the charred skeleton of a house: but there was a hidden sense of relief as well. Even though they preferred to think it had been set by kids, by vandals, not by adults, no one would ever know for sure.

And then came the final spectacular collapse.

The roar of almost two hundred people vied with the sound of the violent implosion as the interior of the structure could no longer sustain itself against the consuming flames. The two upper stories crashed through the ballroom floor, bringing the entire interior— Alma's apartment, all of the bedrooms, and the ballroom itself— hurtling down with a deafening crash. All that was left was a tangled mass of snapped and splintered charred beams, which had fallen down into the cellar. Thick smoke spread in ground-swell waves, forced by the impact to billow up into the heavy air, blackening the sky further. The roof had caved in. The ballroom roof collapsed. The center hall, total chaos. Black, charred, completely gutted. The devastation was total.

There were tears in John Wittke's eyes as he and his wife, Dorothy, watched what to them was the end of an era. "I remember when we used to trim my grandfather's thirty-five-foot tree from the third-floor balcony," he said quietly.

Shortly after the fire, Police Chief Jim Moran called Frederick Poppy at Gray's Funeral Home. "Now that it's burned down," he said, "you have to demolish it."

"Sorry," Poppy said candidly. "Not me. I don't have five cents."

"As administrator of the estate . . ."

"The estate doesn't have five cents in it, either, you know that."

"Well, it can't stay like that. It's a hazard."

"Jim," Poppy said evenly, "I think you'd better get in touch with the bank and have them do it."

He didn't know if the bank paid for the demolition or if the town wound up paying for it. At this point, he didn't even want to know, just as long as the responsibility for hiring a wrecking crew didn't fall to him.

Three weeks later, on September 19, 1972, the remains of the burnt-out house gave way to the heavy, indifferent thumping ball of a wrecking crew as the property, now condemned as dangerous, was demolished.

Perhaps it would end with the demolition, thought the neighbors. But once again crowds of spectators stood about. With each thud of the wrecking ball, the house crumbled a little more, as though it were being beaten right into the ground. The stench of charred wood still permeated the air. Each crumbling wall released more of the stench.

Finally, it was done. Now all that remained after the razing was the huge heap of debris to be hauled away. And still the curious came to stare at the mound of rubble. They couldn't seem to stay away. They watched even as the chunks of debris were being hauled away—bits and pieces of a once-beautiful mansion in a string of dump trucks.

On November 22, 1972, Union County Sheriff Ralph Oriscello announced that he would conduct an auction sale of the John E. List land at 2:00 P.M. on December 6 at the county courthouse in Elizabeth, N.J. The sale had been ordered by the First National Savings and Loan Association, which held the first and second of the three mortgages on the property for a total of $41,446.89 and $6,513.16, plus interest up to and including September 21. The third mortgage for $1,562 with $916.71 interest was held by the Suburban Trust Co., in Westfield. The notice was posted and printed in *The Westfield Leader*.

Shortly after 2:00 P.M. on the afternoon of the auction, Irving B. Johnston, Jr., the attorney for the First National Savings and Loan Association, began the bid with a call of $500.

Almost immediately, James O'Brien of 86 Forest Road, Fanwood, N.J., called out, "Five thousand dollars."

"Ten thousand." Benjamin Bontempo put in his bid. He was from Lincoln Avenue in Cranford and had heard about the auction through friends. He liked the location of the property and didn't mind what had "happened" there. Like O'Brien, he was looking for a good buy in a good neighborhood.

"Fifteen thousand," said O'Brien.

"Twenty thousand."

A man by the name of Calzone upped it, "Twenty-five thousand dollars."

"Twenty-seven thousand."

"Thirty thousand," Bontempo countered. The amount was getting close to the limit he had set for himself.

The bidding continued to alternate between Bontempo and Calzone, O'Brien having dropped out. The bids were getting tighter—$31,100, $32,300, $32,800—until Bontempo bid, "Thirty-five thousand five hundred dollars," and Calzone raised it to $36,000.

There was a pause in the bidding.

That was it. Bontempo had reached his limit. Calzone knew that he was alone in the bidding.

Then a new voice offered, "Thirty-six thousand one hundred dollars."

Calzone remained quiet. There were no other bids; the block was pounded, and the 314-by-166.67-foot property was sold to Kurt C. Bauer of 416 Wells Street, the editor and publisher of *The Rahway News-Record*.

Sitting together in the back of the room where the public auction was being held were the Reverend Eugene Rehwinkel and C. Frederick Poppy. They watched the proceedings quietly and unemotionally. Although the press attended and attempted to interview them, both men remained silent. Even Johnston refused to say how the proceeds of the sale would be divided.

25 | Just an Ordinary Guy

"How do you do. My name is Robert P. Clark."

The man who applied for the job was six feet, one inch tall, about 180 pounds, and wore glasses. His complexion was light, and his hair, which he wore long and combed straight back, was dark brown.

There was a touch of gray at the hairline that revealed, to the discerning eye, the fact that his hair was dyed. He wore a mustache.

"Clark?"

"Yes."

The job had been advertised on a thin piece of cardboard tacked to the right of the entrance.

"Where do you live?"

"Across the street."

The manager looked outside the front of the door of the Holiday Inn West Motel. It was one of a chain, in Golden, Colorado, a sun-baked town, caked with dried dirt but comfortably nestled at the foot of the Rocky Mountains under intense gray-blue skies. The old silver-gray trailer across the street in the cheap trailer park was small and modest and not in great repair. It was usually occupied by migrants. This guy don't look like no migrant, he thought. Not the usual kind, anyways. He talks good, and those glasses make him look like a schoolteacher. The manager glanced over at Frank Moreland, who was wringing out a heavy, charcoal-colored mop. Now that's what transients usually look like. Poorly dressed, stubbled, wearing old clothes that don't fit right and usually look slept in. This guy had on a suit and tie. No, he didn't look like no transient. He certainly didn't look like no cook, either.

"That trailer over there?"

"Yes."

Frank Moreland pushed the dirty mop lazily back and forth across the lobby floor as he listened to the manager at the front desk interviewing the guy who wanted the job as a cook. Frank had seen him the day before at the trailer park, where he too had been bunking down recently.

"How old are you, anyway?" the manager asked Clark.

"Just over forty," the man lied.

The manager would have taken him for older. "Where you from?"

"Pittsburgh."

"East, huh?"

Bob Clark hesitated for just a fraction of a beat. "A long time ago."

"Well, don't matter none as long as you can cook."

"Oh, I've been doing the cooking all my life," Bob Clark said.

"You just passing through?"

"I haven't decided yet."

"You want the job?"

"Yes."

"I'll need your social security number."

"It's 523-90-7630."

On November 22, 1971, only twelve days after the killings in Westfield, Clark had already applied for a new Social Security number. He knew that anyone under fifty years of age could get a Social Security number without question. It was issued to Robert Peter Clark, residing at the Motel Deville, 650 W. Paltax St., Denver, Colorado. On the application he had written:

> Mother: Ruth Ann Clark
> Father: James Peter Clark
> D.O.B.: 4/26/31

He had created a new identity with a new set of parents and a new birthdate, but not a new personality. Camouflaging himself by hiding in plain sight, he blended in well with the background. However, when Bob Clark saw a local newspaper article about the murders, he expected to be caught; a week or two at the most, he thought. Fears of discovery and of a prolonged jail term forced him to retreat even further into the background of life, making unrelenting solitude almost a certainty for him. Life was deserted, like an abandoned train station with neither train nor passenger ever passing through. He was a stranger to everyone, even to himself. But not a stranger to prayer, his great strength and sustainer. He'd had to arrange his life so that he could control every aspect of it. He'd had to eliminate things that he couldn't control. Yet, ultimately, he had to work.

"Job don't pay much. And it's paid by the hour. You get paid only if you work."

"That's fine."

Frank Moreland chuckled to himself. He knew why they only paid by the hour. Too many guys would take a job and not show up. That's what it was like when so much of the work was done by transients like himself. This fella, now he didn't look like no skid. But then you could never tell. The guy might just be down on his luck. Or he might be a straight-looking kind of skid. He'd seen them before, too.

Now, Clark took the job as the night cook and was glad to get it.

For the first time in months he was in a position where interaction with others was necessary. He would handle that, too, as he had handled everything else.

Frank Moreland cleaned the kitchen at the Holiday Inn. He was an old-timer who had seen better days, but he was friendly and talkative, and for Bob Clark, who was on the taciturn side, he was good company. At fifty-five he was actually about ten years older than Clark, and he looked like a derelict as he sat drinking scalding hot black coffee one night, he told of the time he'd mopped up the floor of an old saloon in the dry country of Arizona and had nearly been shot when two old codgers decided to relive the days of the Old West and settle a minor dispute with live ammunition.

As he listened, Clark thought about his own well-planned circuitous route—West Philadelphia, Detroit, Jackson, Ft. Wayne, and ultimately his true destination, Denver . . . because he had a desire to see the Rocky Mountains. He had read articles about Denver before he had arrived that said Denver was reputed to be the West's most wicked city. It was filled with bordellos and gambling dens and was considered a con man's paradise, but to Clark it seemed peaceful. He remembered looking out the bus window at the huge freeway system and the little communities with vast miles between. The entire locale seemed to have a built-in anonymity. You could come to the Denver area and get lost, he thought as Moreland finished his story. "Hell," Moreland was saying with a chuckle, "you took your life in your hands just mopping up a floor."

It was late at night, and Bob and Frank were alone in the back kitchen of the motel. Clark was packing up some leftovers he was going to take home with him to his trailer across the street.

"I been to just about every skid town this side of the Rockies and west of the Mississippi, every skid alley and backdrop you could think of. I know the backside of more towns than you could ever know the front end of," Moreland said. He had come in from the mountains "a while back" looking for something to do when he had come upon the same run-down trailer park Clark found.

"Where you from, anyway?"

"Michigan," Clark said, instinctively going back to roots. It was a rare moment of candor. Then he got up and busied himself at the sink with his back to Moreland.

Moreland was full of stories from his travels across the country. But their discussions rarely went anywhere after a half hour or so. He sensed their lives didn't run on the same track. Clark was a little boring, actually. He never had any yarns to tell. He listened, but he didn't give much. Moreland sighed as he put aside his coffee and began scrubbing down the stove. The moon was high. Moreland could see it through the back window of the kitchen. It was full and round and voluptuous and brought out memories of heady nights on the town. Which town in particular he wouldn't be able to tell. Not that it mattered. After a while they were all the same.

"Hey, Bob," Moreland called out softly across the blackened stovetop he was scrubbing down with steel wool as he looked up from his thankless task. "Got a girl?"

"What?"

"A girl. Y'know." He winked. "Any romantic interests? Sometimes it gets pretty lonely round these parts at night."

"There's no one!" came the quick response.

There was something about the manner in which Clark had snapped the answer back that made Moreland decide to drop the subject. Fast. Silently he went back to the scrubbing, thinking that a scraper would be more appropriate than steel wool to do the job right but not caring enough about the outcome to be that conscientious. The grease was gonna just pile on again anyway.

He glanced up sideways at his new friend. Hell, he thought to himself, you just don't go on with something like that if a guy makes it that clear he ain't willing to talk about it none.

Clark pressed the thin hamburgers flat against the sizzling grill with the huge spatula . . . sunny-side-over light . . . letting the French fries drip off some of the reheated oil. The brainless repetitiveness of the work gave his mind the chance to rest. In the effortless days, free of stress, he reinforced the strength of his convictions. Through confession, as the Scriptures advised, he had given his guilt to Jesus. Confession absolves guilt. But then, pride does not really feel guilt. He was riding the beast at a manageable pace . . . down to a trot . . . to a walk. The beast was grazing.

He hadn't heard anything further, but he hadn't been reading the papers. It didn't matter. Perhaps the murders would be kept a local issue. It was not vitally important. And it wasn't as if the people were there. The body is just a shell without the soul. Death releases the soul to its eternal salvation. There was a sense of serene joy in the thought. He willingly endured the numbing trials of remaining completely alone nights. The peaceful country managed to calm the occasional troubled edges of his spirit. How vast and quiet everything seemed in the West. He couldn't get over that. Even during the greatest moments of kitchen rush, there seemed to be a lack of pressure. No consuming passions. No monumental debts.

But even so, money was thinning out. That side of life always intruded on the serenity, and when he was suddenly fired for not being fast enough at the grill, not only did the familiar humiliation of failure hit hard in its unexpectedness, but he was forced to look for a job again.

When he managed to get a job as a cook at the Piney Country Club in Parker, Colorado—to "upgrade," he told himself with an ironic little smile—he helped Frank Moreland get a job there as a cleaning man.

"Now that was a nice thing to do," Moreland said, thinking Clark was a good enough friend despite the fact that he wasn't much of a cook or a conversationalist.

"It's nothing. . . ."

"Helping a fellow skid like that."

Clark looked at him strangely for a moment. "We'll both upgrade," he said finally. "Besides, that's what life is all about. Helping one another."

"Hey. Yeah. Right," Frank agreed, although that wasn't the way he looked at it. To him it had always been more in the line of, "Stay out of the other guy's way." You never know who you're dealing with.

Bob Clark had a place to sleep, a job, food. Life had taken on a monastic simplicity that was spiritual in its minimal material comfort. He wanted to enjoy it for as long as possible. What more did anyone need? Except, perhaps, just a little more money, he thought, looking up at the clear sky that stretched unbroken in all directions as far as the shaded eye could see. He had to keep pushing his glasses back on top of the bridge of his nose as they slowly slid down every time he lowered his head in the numbing heat. He wasn't used to this kind of heat yet. He would have to tighten the little screws to clamp the glasses tighter onto his temples.

While looking for a new job, he researched the Denver area again. This time when he drove on the freeway, he missed the exit. He didn't mind. It gave him the opportunity to see some of the surrounding area close up. It again struck him as a more relaxed, easier place to live than the New York Metropolitan area. On the drive north toward the airport, there were mountains in the background. He liked that. It was a perfect backdrop for a quiet contemplative life. Denver itself seemed very easy to miss. He liked that, too. There was a downtown area, and then there were a great many outlying areas that came up very quickly and disappeared just as fast; it seemed like a lot of small, nondescript communities slipping away into obscurity. Parker, Colorado, was just southeast of Denver. The Piney Country Club in Parker catered to a better class of people than the Holiday Inn West. The pay was a little better. He was going to move out of the trailer into a small furnished apartment.

Things were looking up. The period of intense concealment was abating; staying out of sight . . . going out only when it was dark . . . eating in the privacy of a small out-of-the-way room . . . keeping to himself . . . spending quiet time alone in a dark church, seated isolated in a shadowed pew. He hadn't anticipated that it would be quite so simple. He was beginning to feel more secure about slowly coming out. Anxieties about capture were beginning to abate; he felt rather like a long-distance runner finally breathing easier after a period of rest. He was now ready to expand horizons toward the convenience of a better job with better pay. Moreland helped him move to a small apartment on South Columbine Avenue in Denver.

"That's it?" Moreland asked as he looked past Bob Clark into the interior of the trailer. "That's all of your possessions?"

"That's all."

"Why, that's only one pickup truck's worth of stuff. Hell, even I got more'n that," he joked.

"I like to travel light," Bob quipped back.

"All those cartons. Betcha they're full of books."

"Not all."

Moreland lifted each one slowly. They seemed heavy enough to him to be filled with full-size dictionaries. He was beginning to have nagging back problems with severe aches right at the base of his spine. He straightened up painfully after loading one of the heavier cartons in the pickup and groaned loudly.

"I can do it," Clark said quickly when he realized the man was in some distress.

"Naw, naw," Moreland said, pushing him aside. "I'll do it. I can do it." It seemed to him that everything Clark owned was neatly stored in boxes, including a couple marked "Files" and "Records." There was a box marked "Tax Books," another marked "Tax Records," another marked "War Games." There was a box for clothes, a box for kitchen items, everything neat and orderly and carefully itemized and compartmentalized. Some of the items looked as though they had never even been removed from the boxes. One of the open boxes had a light layer of dust attesting to the fact that they had not been recently packed. Funny, Moreland thought as they loaded the last of them. The guy lives outta boxes. That's worse than me.

"What's all the tax stuff for?" he couldn't help asking.

"Oh," Clark offered easily, "I'm going to take a few courses at H and R Block so I can earn extra money doing taxes."

"Well, you sure got the brains for it." Moreland chuckled.

"Never could figure out why a guy with your brains is slinging hash."

"The free meals," Clark answered.

Moreland burst out laughing. "Yeah, but they could kill you!"

At this point, almost three years after the murders, Bob Clark felt safe enough to take small risks. Although he would stick to a series of small obscure companies, for the first time since running away he listed himself in a Denver telephone directory. Now he was eager to get back to his own profession as an accountant and was beginning to feel that perhaps enough time had passed to take the chance.

But slowly, slowly. There was really no rush. He had all the time in the world. His background in Colorado was as a cook. When he switched jobs again, his third since coming west, it was to a restaurant in a Denver department store that offered a little more money to a man with his culinary experience.

The boys were playing baseball in a wide-open area with no parameters to entrap a flying ball. It took him a moment to realize he had developed a facial tic as he watched. From this distance, their faces were indistinguishable. They looked familiar.

He felt uncomfortable.

He moved on. Back to the welcome cell of solitude.

Night slipped into day, day into night, with a repetitive calm. The dramatic difference in locale made his former life seem far, far away, off in remote corners of the world. He encouraged himself to keep the past completely hidden from the present. He was basically a man without a past. He was almost amnesiac in its absence. Except, perhaps, for the occasional maverick dream.

The year was 1974.

26 | They Won't Forget

On the East Coast, the murder was resurrected.

On June 2, 1974, the Sunday *New York Times* ran a two-paragraph filler blurb on page thirty-seven titled, JERSEY MURDERS, in which J. Wallace LaPrade, special agent in charge of the FBI in New Jersey, said that although they had no idea where the fugitive was, they would not close the case until he was found or proven not to be findable. "And not findable means we find his bones."

While time could never dissipate the memory of the "ballroom murders" for those who were intimately involved with the case, even those who were innocent bystanders and had not been privy to the carnage inside the house on Hillside Avenue always described their feelings in passionate terminology.

"I'm really angry about this, that it keeps coming up!" said one nearby resident who never wanted to give her name to the press. She'd never heard of any of the Lists until the murders but that didn't soften the heat of her anger, "that he hasn't been found! Why not?" she demanded.

Reading *The New York Times* brought it all back for Hank and Diana Ryan. The odd thing about the whole story, Hank thought, was that at the time the police chief talked so much about what a tremendously thorough job they had done, "left no stones unturned," and yet the Westfield police never came to the house to talk to him. The FBI, however, was very thorough. He remembered when the FBI agent had knocked on the door about a year after the murders, a really nice young agent, who'd talked as much as he'd questioned. Hank and Diana reminisced about the interesting thing he'd told them. First he'd wanted to know if they'd heard any rumors . . . anything that might help the FBI in their investigation.

"No," they had replied honestly. "What about you people? Has anything turned up?"

"Not yet," the FBI agent had said, "but there's one thing we know. A kinda of funny thing. John List went to a hardware store on Elm Street right here in Westfield and bought a lot of chicken

322

wire fencing, and a rather expensive post hole digger.''

"Really?" Diana had said.

"All the elements to make a rather large enclosure. And we weren't able to find any of it in the house.''

"What would he need that for?"

"Well, we don't know yet," the agent had said. "We speculated, since he had a good deal of time on his hands . . . you know, not working too much and all . . . that he had a lot of time to roam around just before he disappeared, that he might have established an identity someplace else before the murders—let's say, in Vineland—and started a chicken farm there. In other words, he created another identity in Vineland, and had a chance to begin again by just walking right into it. . . . Of course this is speculation. . . .''

Diana thought it made an interesting story, but she was quite certain that List had killed himself.

Little Robin Kampf, who had been only 13½ at the time of the murders, was becoming obsessed with the thought that he was "still out there," and over her mother's objection, she was still amassing a rather large collection of everything she could find in the newspapers about him. Robin thought it was very strange as she read *The New York Times* article. Bright and inquisitive and impressionable as ever, she analyzed her own reactions to the murders, which she cataloged in her diary:

It's been on my mind constantly for a good seven or eight months. I still have the same thirst for information on it, although it's not as intense as time goes on. Lots of other things to think about too. It subsided somewhat. But then things would stir it up, like when the house caught on fire, there would be press on it and anytime that would happen, like when the property was sold at the auction, it would kick up all these feelings again and I'd check under my bed for a couple of days and then forget about it again. But I always want to know where he is. That never changes.

I always wonder.

I have this little game I play. I go into malls and look around and try and see if "this man" resembled him or if "that man" looked like him with a possible disguise or something. . . .

And then, after a while, Robin would pretty much forget about List—"Lots of other things to think about, too"—until the press recalled the whole story again with some kind of memorial article. There would be another clipping for her collection and another entry in her diary.

By this time, Hank O'Malley, while still interested, found the constant reactivation of the tragedy by the press to be a nuisance. Everybody would come around again, "gawking." He resented it. It angered him. He found it to be an intrusion.

Chief Investigator Robert Bell of the Westfield police continued to shadow the gravesite at Fairview Cemetery in the hope that List would turn up on some anniversary and Patty List's schoolmate, Terry Henderson, called the Westfield Police Station with the first of her many calls to ask if Mr. List had "been caught yet."

The desk sergeant had to tell her, "No. Not yet."

"Oh." She sounded disappointed. "I hope you don't mind that I called," she said. "I was just wondering. . . ."

"We don't mind," he answered.

Chief of Police James Moran changed the FBI bulletin in his breast pocket. He had fingered it so many times in the last three years that the edges had become frayed and illegible, even though he knew it by heart:

If you have any information concerning this person . . .

Hope does spring eternal.

He couldn't know that when he went to a national police convention in Denver, Colorado, in 1975 and stayed at the Brown Palace, he was a mere three blocks away from where Bob Clark would eventually reside.

"And I'm even angrier at the Lutheran church," the same angry neighbor who didn't know the Lists personally cried vehemently to anyone who would listen. "The police are total incompetents, but the church won't even try to cooperate! They may be helping to hide a mass murderer!"

The neighbors had tried to get the Missouri Council of Lutheran Churches to circulate a flyer with List's photo to all of its churches in the country. The Lutheran Council is the cooperative umbrella organization under which Lutherans from the various denominations cooperate with one another. The neighbors were sure that if the fugitive were alive, he would eventually show up in a Lutheran church somewhere, considering the extent of his "religious fanaticism"; but the church council had denied the request to distribute the flyer throughout its nationwide parishes.

Barney Tracy, who had just started with the Westfield Police Department, had a deep well of compassion, not only for victims of crimes, but for the guilty as well. He was about six feet tall, mild-mannered, soft-spoken, and very handsome, with short, spiked blond hair, piercing blue eyes, and a keen wit. He became one of the Westfield police officers who would "stay with the List case" for years.

Barney knew about the List flyer. He could understand the heat of the neighbors' feelings upon being rejected by the Lutheran Church Council, but on a professional level he couldn't really find fault with the council's response. The registrar of the Lutheran Council had been contacted directly through the prosecutor's office as well, explaining the need to apprehend List. Like the neighbors, the authorities always felt that List would eventually be associated with a Lutheran church somewhere. From a professional standpoint, Barney agreed. He's not going to change, he thought. Zebras don't change their stripes. But the council wrote back with a response that, in essence, stated, "You have your job and we have ours."

At first, Barney thought, Oh, why wouldn't they do it? but the more he pondered the issue, the more he understood. I kind of agree with them, he finally thought to himself. He could understand what they were saying, despite the help the council might have given the authorities in apprehending the fugitive suspect. The neighbors wanted List's Most Wanted photo printed in the Lutheran Church of Missouri Synod newspaper. Should the church turn informer on any parishioner seeking comfort within its sanctuary, even if he was a murderer? What was its role? And what about the readers of a religious newspaper? Something like that could be a serious intrusion and a frightening thing. Barney was Catholic; he could understand the need for privacy within the confines of a church, like the seal of the confessional.

He sighed.

Yes, he could understand how they felt. Everybody. Both sides. That was the wellspring of his compassionate nature—being able to see both sides. But he was twenty-four and impatient, too. He had been involved in the case only a short time, and already he felt terribly dissatisfied. Going through all the files amassed over the past three years, he still felt frustrated at how much more he would like to know. He pored over every piece of evidence, studied the graphic bloody photographs of the victims, and spent hours theorizing with fellow officers about the crime and the criminal. They did a very good job in the initial investigation, he thought, but the way they had examined evidence—autopsy reports and so on—added to his frustration. Gathering evidence was so much more efficient now than it had been even just a short three years ago. There wasn't even anything conclusive in any of the reports about such elementary things as entry wounds or exit wounds, other than that the victims all had been shot.

It *would* have been easier if the council had cooperated, he thought again out of his frustration. Then again, the other side: there's no way of knowing whether the flyer would have paid off.

"I guess you can't put Wanted posters on an altar, can you!"

27 | Welcome to the Fold

On June 19, 1975, Reverend Robert West, pastor of St. Paul's Lutheran Church on Grant Street in downtown Denver, Colorado, welcomed a new parishioner into its membership. There was the usual official ceremony in which Robert P. Clark pledged to become part of the church family, but when it came to the customary transference of records from one church to another, Clark made it clear that he was starting fresh. There were no records to send for.

West couldn't remember how many times Clark had attended services before he finally came to him and said he was interested in joining. The pastor never made new people feel guilty if they didn't join. He always told them, "Even if you're not a member, I will serve as your pastor if you have a crisis or illness in the family."

It was not unusual for a prospective member to study the parish before joining.

"We're what we call an Anglican Lutheran church," Reverend West told Clark when it was obvious that he was visiting the pastor at St. Paul's to study the church, its concerns, its activities, its membership.

"Our concern is the nurture and strengthening of people in the faith and not necessarily probing into their lives,'' Reverend West always told prospective new congregants. ''As they become faithful members, very often people will ask for counseling and we'll work with them, but we don't bring them in that way.''

Reverend West sat at his large, cluttered mahogany desk in his parish study. Behind him was a wall of books in dark-stained, heavy wooden bookshelves—theology, philosophy, psychology. They were lying at many different angles, denoting that the books were in constant use rather than placed for show as a backdrop to a minister's authoritative presence. There were coffee mugs and candlesticks and bookends interspersed with the volumes. The study was warm, homey, and friendly, just like the man himself. Most people who met him walked away feeling embraced by the genuine warmth of his presence. Those who knew him well said he was a ''wonderful'' human being.

Bob Clark studied him closely as he spoke. He didn't even realize it on a conscious level, but what he was searching for was a very nurturing church affiliation; what he really needed was a protective, sheltered environment, one that was almost parental in the security of its embrace.

''There is something here,'' Bob Clark began tentatively, ''that might be just what I'm looking for.''

Reverend West did not press Clark to tell him what he was looking for in a church. He just continued to talk quietly to the gentle man seated opposite him in his study.

''Yes, I hope that's true,'' the pastor said. ''Perhaps that's because you can sense that we're not automatically suspicious.''

''Suspicious?''

''We're a very diverse community here. Our parish includes the highly educated, and the uneducated; it's really a cross section of humanity. Over the years our membership has tried to be hospitable to all people. The way we treat each other is very important to us all. I even talk with the ushers and say, 'Now if people don't want to give a name, don't force it.' ''

''You believe people should have the right of anonymity?''

''Absolutely,'' West replied with conviction. ''And especially since people come downtown to our parish sometimes for that very reason. We don't know where they come from, and we've had people come for as long as six months before they finally felt secure enough to sign a visitors card and ask me to call them. A lot of people need that kind of anonymity.''

He looked at Clark carefully. The man didn't seem to be the least bit threatened by their conversation, even though he fit the classic pattern West was describing. In fact, Clark was nodding pleasantly, which made the pastor feel free to go on. "Very often they're coming out of jail, or divorce, or a nervous breakdown, and they want to be nurtured and still want to have privacy at the same time. You know, I think some of our members are probably like children in a sandbox. They want to sit near each other, but they don't want to play together."

"I guess some adults are like that, too," Bob Clark agreed with a smile.

Reverend West laughed. It was a rich, warm sound. "Yes, I guess," he said. "When we do bring in members, we use the party room in our condo to welcome them." He stood up behind his desk. "Let me show you around."

Clark could see that the pastor standing at his full height was younger than he, thinner, but just as tall.

"When I went back to California to complete my studies," Reverend West said as he walked with Bob Clark toward one of St. Paul's meeting rooms, "I talked with a new generation of ministers who call themselves 'Wounded Healers' because they've been around. They've typically had struggles with drugs and alcohol and broken lives before they entered the ministry. They didn't enter it right out of college. They are certainly dedicated in their own way, but, still, I see them as people who really only want to work nine to five. Whatever you do,"—he laughed,—"don't die at night."

Yes. Wounded healers, Clark thought. And wounded parishioners, too.

Reverend West noticed Bob Clark glance particularly at one of the flyers pinned to a bulletin board. It offered group-help. "That's always interesting," he encouraged.

"No." Clark smiled. "That sort of thing is not my style."

"That's all right. No need to join anything, but these groups are different from the kind where you analyze everything and delve into everyone's lives. These people are very religious; they don't want to delve into anything. They just want acceptance and care, with no questions asked, and they want quiet help because, very often, their lives are just so terribly sad. The group is simply for support, nothing more."

Clark nodded again noncommittally.

Finally, after many long months of visits and service attendance, Robert Clark made up his mind to become an active member of St. Paul's congregation.

Seated in the party room with many established congregants and one other new member, Clark listened, outwardly very composed, inwardly a bit nervous, as the other man spoke about himself. Clark knew introducing yourself to the others in the active membership was the customary thing to do.

"Well, I've been a shoe salesman all my life," the round little man said a bit sheepishly. "It seems that all my life I've been dealing with looking at the bottom-most part of people."

Everyone laughed good-naturedly.

Encouraged, he added, "I like feet."

Then Reverend West made another introduction. "Our newest member, Bob Clark, who has been visiting us for some time." All eyes turned to the large man, whose eyes were hidden by the glare of the overhead light across his spectacles.

"Everybody usually tells what his background is," Reverend West hinted gently.

Visibly, Bob Clark didn't seem to mind, although there was a hint of supplication behind his slightly tremulous smile. "Nothing unusual or shocking," he began. "I was brought up Lutheran. My whole life. From the earliest days, including elementary school. And I came to St. Paul's because it was on the bus line."

Everybody laughed and thought this was a great reason to have joined their church community. "The bus line!"

"Oh, that's wonderful."

"How lucky for us."

"Fate was calling you here."

"Are you married, Bob?"

"No," he answered easily. "Not anymore, that is. My wife died. . . ."

Immediate murmurs of condolences.

"Of cancer," he added.

The outpouring of sympathy was so sincere and so profuse that there was no need to go on with any further explanations. His heart swelled with tenderness. So, whether or not St. Paul's was on the bus line, he knew he had hit the right congregation. Support? Yes. Prying? No.

Clark was generally very closemouthed about himself but he said that he was an accountant. Immediately, knowing how working within the structure of the group often broke the ice with many people, Reverend West asked Clark if he wanted to be on the finance committee.

Clark agreed.

"I used to teach Sunday school," he added, looking off into the distance.

"Would you like to do that here? We have children who—"

"No," he said quickly. "That was a long time ago." He seemed uncomfortable with the thought.

"No problem," West reassured him.

Although Bob Clark generally kept to himself and to those in the congregation appeared to be a genuine introvert, he became an active church member. Reverend West would later realize he knew absolutely nothing of Bob Clark's past: where he came from, what he had been, what he had done. He knew only that the man appeared to be at total peace with himself.

And he was.

The boy nestled in between them on the davenport— warmly protected against the world. The three of them had their heads bowed as they quietly read from the Bible.

As a church member again, quiet, peaceful, contemplative, he was at home on his own inner davenport. Protected.

Taking on the outward appearance of contentment, he began to feel an inner security. Tension had subsided here in the mountains, where men seemed insignificant contrasted with the vastness of God's world. Wide spaces, mountains, sky, sky, sky, sky . . . God's heaven was in the sky. God was all around, hovering about like an embracing protector. Clark felt warm and comfortable, at peace.

Sometimes the night could still be treacherous, but less and less. He had prayer—the great healer—to keep anxiety deep below the surface. Robert P. Clark had found his refuge.

By 1976, five years had taken enough of the edge off the pain of the murders to permit a bit of black humor to be exchanged between people in the two New Jersey departments that were involved in the long-term investigation. Sergeant Joseph Simmons of the prosecutor's office enjoyed nothing more than to tease Captain James Moran, better known to them as Mugsy, who he knew still carried John List's FBI flyer in his pocket.

"You're going *where?*" Simmons asked an associate, Jake O'Hara, who was leaving on vacation in a couple of days.

"Japan, for two whole weeks," his friend answered.

"Japan. Terrific!" Simmons cried, practically clapping his hands in anticipation. "That's great. Look, do me a favor . . ."

"What?"

But Simmons was already at his desk writing on one of the postcards he kept in the top drawer of his desk for just such an occasion. In the most careful script he could manage, he wrote:

Wish you were here,
Yours truly, John E. List.

"Now when you get to Japan,"—he laughed—"mail this to Moran. . . ."

"I'll be stopping in San Francisco first." Jake grinned, going along with the barb. "Want to send him one from there, too?"

"Great! Yes!" And Simmons carefully wrote another postcard addressed to Moran:

Having a swell time. Miss you,
Sincerely, John E. List.

When Moran received the cards, he was a good sport about the joke. This wasn't the first time he had been teased by his friends about the case. Usually the good-natured barbs arrived at his office as little notes on memo slips headed, "From the Desk of John E. List, Career-Builder."

In 1977, a headline over Allen J. Zullo's story in *The National Enquirer* read:

AFTER 6-YEAR SEARCH, WORLD'S POLICE CAN'T FIND MAN THEY SAY KILLED WIFE, MOTHER & CHILDREN.

Commenting on how List was an ordinary man who had committed an extraordinary crime, Zullo's few paragraphs went on to rehash the entire story again, from the killings to the discovery of the bodies to the disappearance of the murderer. Under List's 1971 photo was the caption:

WHERE IS HE?

The story, no longer front-page news, was featured on page forty-one; even the sensation-seeking *National Enquirer* buried this article.

28 | Back to Numbers

Lying in bed in his cheap apartment, Bob Clark stirred restlessly. His brain felt numbed by drawn-out inactivity. His eyes burned with the rigidity of prolonged staring at ceilings.

It was now a full six years since the murders, and he was tired of living the life of a cook, one step above poverty, wearing clothes that didn't match, barely eking out a living doing part-time bookkeeping work. He was tired of living hand to mouth, of never having enough money even to buy a new jacket.

It was time to take the chance of finding full-time employment in his own field.

Numbers.

Sheldon Thorn, an executive with the accounting firm of Glass, Whiteman and Baker, interviewed him for one of their clients, Roberto Distributing Company.

"Robert P. Clark." The man said his name slowly, softly, almost under his breath. Very bright, but what an introvert! Sherman thought. Smart enough when he did speak, if you could hear the guy! But he looked as if he had fallen onto hard times, doing odd jobs and some bookkeeping work.

Thorn sighed. He didn't think the guy was right for the job at Roberto Distributing.

Clark seemed to understand a rejection was coming, and before Thorn could discard his application, he said with sudden surprising strength, "I need a full-time job. I'm an accountant. I'm good at what I do."

The manner in which the quiet man spoke up suggested the existence of a strong backbone beneath the soft, passive exterior.

Thorn made one or two inconsequential notations on the card in front of him on his desk, glancing up at the man in between notations. He was a little old to be looking for an entry-level position . . . but then again, so what? he suddenly found himself thinking. A man goes into debt, has a difficult time financially, and just gets down on his luck. Thorn felt an unexpected surge of sympathy. It could happen to anyone. People could become trapped by economic hardship. Sometimes all they needed was another chance.

Thorn hesitated for a moment longer and then realized he couldn't come up with a reason to say no to the man. "Roberto Distributing in Denver," he said, handing Bob Clark a card. "They're a carpet wholesaler. Go see Mr. Jim Roberto. He's the general manager."

Jim Roberto found Robert Clark to be a bit strange when he came for his interview. He couldn't put his finger on what it was that made him feel that: the way he tilted his head when he talked, the intense look in his eyes as he searched into Roberto's face while waiting for an answer, the way he was dressed? Still, Thorn had sent him, and Thorn's judgment was usually sound.

Roberto hired Bob Clark for his fourth job since coming to Denver. His starting salary was $900 per month. He was now in his own field again.

The Newgate Apartments at 10400 W. 44th Street were in Wheat Ridge, Colorado, a small suburb west of Denver proper. The pseudo-Tudor designed complex was neat, clean, and inexpensive. The furnished apartment Bob Clark rented overlooked a large expanse of grassy lawn. Newgate itself boasted a "country atmosphere," spacious floorplans, central laundry, clubhouse, jogging, pools, playground, spa, sauna, and tennis courts. It was definitely a step up from the South Colombine apartment house Bob Clark had moved into with Frank Moreland's help. He had since accumulated a few more possessions than the cartons of boxes they had loaded onto the back of a pickup truck at the time, but he still remained reclusive.

Eating lunch alone, usually in the secondhand orange Volkswagen he bought for himself, with the windows rolled up and classical music playing on the radio, Clark struck everyone as "a little strange," but harmless.

What seemed an innocent pastime—listening to music—was a part of his calculated self-healing process. The music anesthetized his conscience against any unwanted nostalgic ruminations—pushed them ever farther into the recesses of his subconscious mind. He could ease into a suspension of conscience through prayer, meditation, and, now, glorious music. His mind no longer had to concentrate actively on "things" and could simply surrender to being washed over with rich, fulfilling sounds ... Mozart, Bach, Beethoven. Joyous screens against the past.

Those who watched his isolation felt a little sorry for him and made overtures toward him. His employer, Jim Roberto, in particular, tried befriending him, even to the extent of discussing his own marital problems with him.

"I've been through that," Clark responded sympathetically. "I know what you mean."

"Married?" Roberto asked.

"Once. A long time ago."

"Did you have any kids?"

Bob Clark shook his head. "No," he said. "We never had any children."

"I'm never going to get into that kind of mess again." Roberto sighed.

"Neither will I. It had not been ..." Bob Clark hesitated.

"Problems?"

"Yes."

"Bad?"

"I'll never marry again. That much I know."

29 | Delores

Bob met Delores through an adult singles group at a monthly supper program held by another church. He decided to attend the program at the last minute. Again fate had set the inevitable in motion. . . .

"Let's go bowling in Newport News," Gerhard Herrmann had said to his army buddy, John.

"Let's go bowling in Newport News," Jean Syfert had said to her widowed sister, Helen.

Fate intervened for Delores Miller, too. Had she looked closely, she would have seen that fate was wearing a black dress.

Delores, somewhere in her forties, was thin and tall, standing erectly at about five feet ten inches. Her blond hair was short-cropped and curly. The dark dress she wore to the church social set off the color of her hair and her pale blue eyes, giving them an extra luster. She was not a beautiful woman; in fact, some people thought her plain. But she was attractive enough when she took the time to dress up for church services or exerted a little extra effort for a church social. To Bob Clark, her coloring gave her a familiar Aryan quality, but minus the pride and austerity usually associated with it. Nice in a woman, he thought.

She was timid and very quiet, too, just like Bob, and they immediately seemed to get along together: two quiet people, neither one threatening the other. Her voice was low, soft, gentle, very much in keeping with her innate shyness. But Delores Miller was a divorcée.

He remembered when he waited outside the room as his father sat on the church council to determine the fate of the young divorcée in Bay City. As an adult, he now thought with a slightly self-serving edge, the rules were too strict. His position was changing; rules could be broken; they were not meant for everybody.

"And you?" she asked. "No family?"

"No one."

"Parents?"

"Both dead."

"I'm sorry," she said sincerely.

"That's all right," he assured her with a smile. "They both lived long lives."

"My mother lives in Maryland," she said.

"Maryland?"

"Baltimore."

"I've never been there," he said, summarily dismissing the marriage ceremony that had taken place on December 1, 1951, in Baltimore.

"I miss Baltimore," she said.

It wasn't long before she told Bob Clark about her first husband with whom she had lived in Baltimore. She didn't say much—it seemed a painful subject—only that they had lived in a big house, they had wanted for nothing materially, and that there had been another woman. Delores had been terribly disappointed and broken up over the collapse of their marriage vows. She escaped to Denver after the divorce.

Finding a job hadn't been easy; unemployment was a perennial problem in the area. The position she managed to get at the commissary of Fitzsimmons Army Hospital was little more than a warehouse job, one step above that of a common laborer. The work was physically very difficult—lifting and hauling boxes and crates—and the woman in charge treated her little better than a slave. Power in the hands of the unscrupulous who enjoyed wielding authority could easily create unhappy working conditions and workers.

The only good thing about the job was that it was at the end of Peoria Street, a few minutes north from where she lived in Aurora, a southwestern suburb of Denver.

Finding living accommodations hadn't been easy, either. The condominium apartment she'd bought when she first came west was in Somerset Village, the first turn after Auburn Street at the other end of Peoria Street. It was a lower-middle-class unit in one of those low-slung complexes that were usually advertised in the kind of glowing terms that make them seem one step above country-club living. The entrances—staircases edged between narrow brick corridors—were hidden from open view and created built-in security problems. She locked her gate all the time, but that didn't stop her apartment from being robbed shortly after she'd moved in. It had been such a violation, such a personal intrusion, and very frightening. It wasn't long before Delores realized she had bought a condo in a crime-ridden area nestled between Stapleton International Airport, Lowry Air Force Base, and Buckley Field, all of which contributed an incessant roar of jet engines overhead.

The only thing Bob Clark told Delores about himself was that he had been married once before and his wife had died of cancer.

Reverend West was glad to see that his parishioner Bob Clark had found a companion. The man had always been alone. To the congregation, he was a withdrawn bachelor type, involved with his own concerns. When a picnic or special event was announced—some intergenerational, some strictly adult—he would usually attend alone. Now he took Delores Miller everywhere. She was a member of another church at the time they met, but they always came as a couple to the social events at St. Paul's. They particularly liked the music programs.

Reverend West noticed that Bob was somewhat protective of Delores, who appeared to be very fragile and childlike. Like Bob, she was also very shy and retiring by nature. When they were together, they remained close. Reverend West could tell they related very well, almost softly, *sotto voce*, as though they were on another plane of sound than the normal world. It was also obvious that she was deeply devoted to the Word of God, a point that he knew was important to Bob.

After meeting Delores, Bob suddenly felt he could do better socially than he had been. A different kind of pride was beginning to assert itself. He realized he was a little tired of the sparsity of a reclusive life.

Perhaps he could turn over a new leaf.

There was no limit to the attention Bob paid to Delores's needs.

It bothered him to know how hard she worked at Fitzsimmons Army Hospital—actual physical labor, hauling boxes. How difficult for someone so frail. She never complained, at least not to him, but she looked tired and undernourished.

A little good German cooking would help, he thought. A hearty soup. She worked very hard. He looked at her. Perhaps she was too thin.

She accepted the sweetness of his attention. There was an indulgent parental quality in his wanting to take care of her. She smiled at the ministerings he took so seriously. "Make sure you have a good breakfast before you start such a day. A tall glass of milk for energy," he would say, not hearing the echo from his own childhood.

Come have a tall glass of milk for *enerchee*. . . .

In September of 1978 he decided to move to Aurora, closer to her, as though by being nearer he could help to protect her against the dangers of the crime he perceived all around her.

"Aurora means a new dawn," he told her. "A new beginning." It seemed prophetic, he thought.

He moved into "Brentwood on the Park" at 12707 E. Mississippi Avenue, Aurora, a few blocks south of Delores's condominium, Somerset Village. Brentwood was a 285-unit rental complex that had, according to the rental brochure, a swimming pool, volleyball court, spacious closets, controlled-access entry, laundry facilities, volleyball, and even jogging. The 560-square-foot apartment was unfurnished but air-conditioned, fully carpeted, and it came with a stove, refrigerator, draperies and storage. It was on the bus line right off Interstate 225.

When he moved in, the rent was $158 per month.

Brentwood on the Park was what was known as an adult community. There was a fair housing law in March 1989 that made adults-only properties illegal, but in 1978 when he moved in, it was restricted. There were no tenants' committees or activities in the complex. Bob Clark felt these restrictions—no tenants' organizations and no children—suited his needs perfectly.

Cindy Taylor, the manager, collected the $100 security deposit required. She had been in the business long enough to judge that Mr. Clark was going to be an excellent tenant. He had an abundance of credit references: Sears, Wards, Visa, and Mastercard.

On the application, he wrote that he had a 1974 Volkswagen, license SA9 129, and a driver's license, K57092. He also wrote down a Social Security number and a bank account number.

Under Employment, he listed: Accountant, Roberto Distributing Inc., 1½ years, salary: $900 a month. Under Emergency Phone, he requested that Miss Delores Miller be notified. Under Previous Employment, he wrote: R. C. Miller Co. No such business was ever registered with the Colorado Secretary of State's office. He had to invent himself as he went along. If he needed to be younger, he took five years off his age. If he needed previous employment records, he manufactured them. "R. C." for Robert Clark. "Miller" for Delores—R. C. Miller Co. Brentwood on the Park did not check references. He moved in with only a few boxes of personal belongings, all of his tax files, his war games, and a waterbed.

"Well, you'll have to get waterbed insurance," Cindy Taylor told him. "We've had problems before with flooding from those things."

"No problem," he said. "I already have waterbed insurance."

Interesting, the manager thought. He didn't look like the waterbed type to her. But then, you can never tell.

There were many sides to Delores's thinking regarding the relationship that was growing between her and Bob. Most of the time, she liked having him close by, but there were other times when she thought he was meddling in her life too much. He was full of admonitions and cautionary advice and suggestions about everything from diet to shopping to finances. He was a very careful planner. Maybe it was good. He was teaching her to be methodical in her life plans, too, which could only be beneficial. It was comforting to be under the umbrella of such parental-like scrutiny and dedicated ministerings to her every need. Her own mother was two thousand miles away in Maryland. Bob was more attentive than she had ever been. He watched over her with a devotion usually reserved only for the most dearly loved ones.

It was flattering and comforting, but then—the other side again— there were many times she wondered where it was all going to lead.

They had spoken of marriage shortly after they met, but both had shelved the idea quickly, each with his own private reasons for deep hesitation at the prospect of a legal union.

Then again, she was tired of working. She wanted to rest. The work was very arduous. She often felt cold. She could feel her strength slipping away, waning, sometimes to the point where lifting up another box weighed more heavily in her dreary anticipation than in reality. She was no longer young.

Prayers and devotions always added to her physical as well as her spiritual health, and somehow she would go on. In this Bob was a great source of power and strength. She had never before known a layperson to be so devoted to God. Now here was a man who would never stray. Here was a man she could trust. . . . *Here was a man who would never break God's commandments* as her first husband, Don, had done.

She welcomed Bob's lack of desire to pursue the relationship to a natural coupling between man and woman. She wasn't ready for that. She might never be. Disappointment at her husband's rejection had made her steel herself against her own natural instincts. Better to feel nothing than to yearn and suffer the frustration of unfulfillment. Marriage was not brought up again. She was content with the status quo.

For Bob Clark, however, life had taken a dramatic and unexpected new turn. He often worked at Roberto's all day Saturday and Sunday doing whatever had to be done; he was intensely conscientious. But all of his spare time was now spent either with Delores Miller or doing volunteer work at St. Paul's. There was still peace, solitude, and quiet in his life, even happiness. Delores was the great comfort he'd never anticipated having. He needed to take care of her. He had found a devotional refuge in his church. Now he found an emotional refuge in Delores Miller.

He never once recognized that John Emil List, who became Robert P. Clark, had subconsciously begun the transition back to the model image of John List. Ironically, it was as Bob Clark that he was finally beginning to live the true life he had been reared to live as John List.

The twenty years he had spent in his former life had been anathema to him. They held everything he hated—drugs, alcohol, uncontrollable self-indulgence, un-Christian behavior. It was wrong. He had had to cut them out. He had had to bring life back to a clear path of sobriety and devotion to God. He believed it implicitly. Most of the time, however, he didn't think of what he had done at all. Except perhaps, on the anniversary of their deaths.

What he did do, was create the kind of life he had always wanted: passions spent, nights filled with solemn calm, prayers filled with joyous freedom. Now, finally, for the first time in his life since he had become a man, he was living the true Word. In the body of Bob Clark, he had become the incarnate John List—man of God.

Delores fit into this perfect pattern with a naturalness and a beauty that was almost ordained. There was actually the possibility of a new life. It was exhilarating. At the same time it created ripples in the serenity of the life he had invented for himself when he'd first come to Colorado.

The possibility of a new life—or was it the promise of one?—shone like a beacon from God to the faithful, offering hope. Could Delores be for him the human embodiment of the beacon so far off in the distance? He stared deeply into the possibilities. Should he dare to try? After all, he was still a man. It would be comforting to feel like a man again. Such thoughts came as disturbing intrusions. Alone at night, the pulse behind his eyes beat like a drum. Blood was rushing to his head, intensifying the pounding.

His mother would have liked Delores, a voice within him insisted. She was quiet, industrious, a very hard worker. She took care of the house, she was deeply devoted to God and to Lutheranism, in particular. True, she had been divorced, but after his first wife, *Mutter* would have appreciated Delores. She even cooked for the church socials.

30 | Troubled Legacies Left Behind

October 6, 1979—Union County, New Jersey

Superior Court Judge Bryant W. Griffin sat in court trying to unravel some of the legal debris left behind by John List's disappearance. There were four insurance policies in question: a $225,000 life insurance policy on List himself, and three $5,000 life insurance policies he had taken out on each of the children a year and a half before he had killed them. Present at the pretrial hearing were Richard Eittreim, representing State Mutual Life Assurance Co., and David J. Meeker, the lawyer for C. Frederick Poppy of Gray's Funeral Home, the administrator of Helen List's estate, who handled all of the funeral arrangements for the murdered family in December of 1971. Mr. Poppy had never been reimbursed for the five-family-member funeral. He was hoping for some kind of reimbursement now, even if it was only partial. Conspicuous by her absence was Helen's daughter, Brenda, who, by virtue of having been adopted by List, was the only living heir. No one had heard much from her since the funeral. Poppy had found it difficult to get in touch with her. But somehow she'd heard of the move to declare List legally dead and had immediately telephoned State Mutual. It was Brenda who would stand to benefit if her stepfather was declared legally dead and the insurance claim could be proven valid.

Both Meeker and Eittreim agreed at the pretrial session that the two issues of insurance validity and legally declaring the fugitive dead were so intertwined that it would best serve all parties concerned to have them settled simultaneously by Judge Griffin.

David Meeker was on his feet as he made his plea on behalf of List's estate. "We feel that Mr. List should be declared legally dead under the New Jersey statute that says a person may be so declared if he disappears and is not heard from again for a period of five years. Mr. John Emil List has indeed disappeared as of November of 1971, and has not been seen or heard from for a period of over eight years. Under the circumstances, Your Honor," he concluded, "we should like to make a motion to have the aforesaid Mr. List declared legally dead so that we may then proceed to the matter of the $225,000 insurance policies he bought and whether or not they are still in effect."

Richard Eittreim, the lawyer for State Mutual Assurance Co., for whom List had sold insurance, was quick to disagree. "Your Honor," he posed, "obviously a man who murders his family is going to 'disappear.' He had a very good reason to go: apprehension and jail. He should therefore not be declared legally dead. All presumption must be that he is 'out there' hiding from the authorities."

The proceedings were handled quickly, unemotionally, and in a very businesslike manner. On the question of whether the policies had lapsed, Mr. Meeker called Benjamin Peterson to the stand.

After being duly sworn in, Mr. Meeker asked him, "Please state your name."

"Benjamin Peterson."

"By whom are you employed?"

"State Mutual Assurance Company, home-based in Jericho, New York."

"And what is your position at State Mutual?"

"I am supervisor of premium records for State Mutual."

"When were the two policies in question taken out?"

"One was taken out on March 16, 1970, and one was taken out exactly one year later, on March 16, 1971."

"How much has been paid in premiums?"

"The premiums were prepaid only up to August of 1972."

"In the amount of?"

"Six thousand dollars."

Mr. Meeker argued, "Your Honor, it is my contention that if the policies are declared void, then the premiums have been paid in vain."

"Well," said Judge Griffin, "that is what we are here to decide. I will set a date for the decision to be after the February 8 deadline when all pertinent material is to be presented. And when I have reviewed it all—"

"Your Honor," Mr. Eittreim said.

"Yes?"

"I would hope even if you decide that, under the extenuating circumstances of this case, John List should not be presumed dead, that you will at this time . . . now . . . also settle the issue of whether or not these two policies have lapsed. This request is made in order to avoid another legal tangle in the event he should be found to be dead sometime in the future."

"Noted."

On Tuesday, April 12, 1980, Superior Court Judge Bryant Griffin ruled that the $225,000 insurance purchased by J. Emil List had lapsed. His ruling was based on the fact that the premiums had been prepaid only until August of 1972, approximately nine months after the discovery of the murders, which made the policies no longer valid in 1980 when the proceedings were brought to contest.

With this decision of invalidity, the judge no longer was forced to consider the question of whether or not the fugitive was legally dead. If the policies had been valid, then he would have had to decide whether or not the insurance money should be paid and to whom.

David Meeker was out of state at the time of Judge Griffin's decision. He could not be reached for comment on the ruling or on whether he would appeal the decision.

Richard Eittreim smiled. "Of course, I'm naturally pleased by the decision," he told the ever-ready waiting press.

Mr. C. Frederick Poppy, who had been present at all the proceedings, shook his head in disappointment. It didn't seem that he would be able to get even a small portion of the $225,000 insurance money as reimbursement for the heavy costs of the family funerals. Of course there was still the matter of the three $5,000 life insurance policies List had taken out on the children. The judge's ruling had not addressed their validity, so there was still a chance.

When he spoke to David Meeker, Poppy told him he still wanted to try for reimbursement out of those policies. The policies had been paid up at the time of the deaths of the insured. Validity was not really a question. Nor was the legality of List's death. The question was to whom should the monies be paid.

"We'll bring it up to the judge in a separate hearing," Meeker said. The hearing was set to take place four months later in August 1980.

Mr. Poppy had waited this long. He would continue to wait until then.

On August 28, 1980, the newspaper headline over Mary Epperson's byline in *The Star Journal* read:

INSURANCE FIGHT IN LIST KILLINGS

Decision was reserved after a hearing before Superior Court Judge Griffin Wednesday on whether an insurance company should pay death benefits for 3 children thought to have been murdered by their father more than 8 years ago....

The matter of the three $5,000 policies was once again brought to the attention of Judge Griffin by Richard Eittreim for State Mutual Assurance Co. and C. Frederick Poppy, administrator of the estates of List's three children and wife.

Before hearing the attorneys' statements, Judge Griffin said, "For the sake of clarity in this matter, we will assume that Mr. List murdered his family."

Interesting, thought Mr. Poppy, who was present. He knew it

was an unusual case. The court still had not decided whether List was legally dead, even after all this time. Judge Griffin had said in last Wednesday's hearing that whether List was alive or dead had no bearing on the insurance case. That was interesting, too, and he hoped it would weigh in his favor in the case now before the court.

"Your Honor," Richard Eittreim argued for State Mutual Assurance Co., "under the law, a wrongdoer may not benefit from a crime. Since Mr. List has not been heard of since the murders, and since we can assume that he is still alive, any insurance monies would go into his estate. In a sense he would then be benefiting from his crime."

David Meeker agreed but added, "Your Honor, someone who kills his family is, under a New Jersey statute, ineligible for insurance benefits. The monies would therefore go under the direction of a trustee, who would pay the debts of the family—in this case, the appointed administrator of the estate, Mr. C. Frederick Poppy."

Mr. Poppy listened patiently.

"Although the law was passed in 1978, seven years after the murders," Meeker continued, "the introductory statement of the statute says it is merely a restatement of a previous law. It would therefore apply in this case."

"Very well, I'll review the case again," Judge Griffin said, "before making a final decision."

"Can you give us an approximate time on when your decision would be forthcoming?" Meeker asked, noting that Mr. Poppy had already waited a long time.

"Let's say in approximately two weeks," the judge concluded. Poppy could wait the additional two weeks.

But the matter was not decided until October 8, 1980. The headline over Mary Epperson's October 9 article in the *Journal* read,
        JUDGE RULES INSURANCE VOID IN LIST KILLINGS.

    RICHARD EITTREIM, ATTORNEY FOR THE INSURANCE
COMPANY, CONTENDED THROUGHOUT THE HEARINGS THAT THE
COMPANY IS NOT LIABLE TO PAY PROCEEDS ON A POLICY WHEN
THE BENEFICIARY OF THAT POLICY HAS KILLED THE
INSURED. . . .
    IN THE RULING, JUDGE GRIFFIN EXPLAINED THAT IN SIMILAR
CASES, SOME PERSON OTHER THAN THE MURDERER HAS SOME
INTEREST IN THE POLICY. HOWEVER, IN THIS CASE, ONLY LIST
WAS NAMED AS A BENEFICIARY.

Superior Court Judge Bryant Griffin, therefore, ruled that State Mutual Assurance Company was relieved of its obligation to pay the $15,000 death benefits on the insurance policies purchased by John List in March 1970 on the lives of his three murdered children.

C. Frederick Poppy's long wait was over. Gray's Funeral Home would continue to bear the entire cost of the funeral arrangements Poppy had so carefully made for John List's family almost nine years earlier.

None of it was any concern of Bobby Clark of Aurora, Colorado.

31 | Echoes

The years went by very quickly with monotonous similarity, like pages turning on a calendar in an old movie. If Clark had been unsettled when he arrived in Colorado, he stabilized in Denver once he joined the church. Stabilization meant peace and calm, wonderful days in the bosom of St. Paul's—work, volunteerism, privacy. All very serene as well as very busy and useful: serving in elected, unpaid positions on the church council, serving on St. Paul's visiting committee for sick parishioners. He liked old people; he felt very protective and solicitous toward them. They in turn depended on him, confided in him, and grew to love him.

In 1984 he was elected treasurer of the church. It seemed so natural. He was at home.

Someday he, too, would serve on the church board... the boy thought. Someday he, too, would follow in the familiar pattern of his grandfather, father, uncles...

Reverend Robert A. West was very fond of Bob Clark. He was a model parishioner. West knew that working with other people was not one of Bob's strong points. Yet he, personally, had no problems along those lines. Together they worked closely and well on the finance committee, monitoring the flow of dollars, planning budgets, and executing them. Bob was very thorough and precise. He was willing to take direction from the finance committee. Occasionally he even made a few suggestions himself.

Reverend West had worked with a number of other treasurers over the years. Robert Clark's distinction was that he was, first and foremost, an accountant. His response was always typically the response of an accountant: to him, the bottom line was always money, the facts, and the figures. There was a certain rigidity in this black-and-white approach. If he thought he had the facts and the figures, he would not back off, by God, no matter how you reasoned. It took some getting used to. The previous treasurer had not been an accountant, and he had been more able to blend together the human needs of the church's programs with the financial needs; but with accountants, like Bob, it was all money, or the lack of it. The human element never entered into the equation at all. On the plus side, however, Clark was just as good with the "history" of things as he was with numbers, a matter with which the committee was seriously trying to keep in touch. St. Paul's had to rely on outside resources because the membership could not afford the full ministry without some external support. Clark helped develop the "history of giving." Also, he did not get as frustrated over financial setbacks as some of the previous treasurers. When disbursements exceeded income and the books weren't balancing, he would simply go back to the recent history and say, "Well, for the last three years this is what has been happening..." not this panicky thing that, "We're going to go broke." He was cool in analyzing the financial problems. But in the end, the books had to balance. The big joke around Bob Clark was, "They say accountants never die, they just lose their balance."

Occasionally the pastor thought Bob seemed restless, that he was taking on too much. If anything, he was a perfect portrayal of the old "work ethic," but no matter how hard he worked he always seemed to be playing financial catch-up by virtue of the sweat of his brow: eight hours at Roberto Distributing, if not longer, then the overtime with H&R Block, a few private accounts on weekends. He even helped several church members analyze their stocks and personal finances, gratis.

Even so, if he felt pressured, he never said so to his minister.

That was all right, Reverend West thought. Lots of people have reversals, and you don't necessarily question it. Many of the people at St. Paul were very private. They wanted to keep quiet about their past. It was characteristic of St. Paul's Church that members of the congregation did not probe into each other's lives. Sometimes people laughed at what sounded like a contradiction, he thought. We say that we're a caring community, but we know so little about one another, about someone like Bob Clark, for instance. Yet part of being a caring community included the obligation not to intrude. As pastor, you walked a thin line. You waited for the request, the invitation into your congregant's little world. Sometimes it happened, sometimes it didn't. Sometimes, they'd come to church for a year or two before they'd say, "You know, Pastor, I have something to tell you." But it was never that way with Bob Clark.

A fellow council member, Bill Sauter, was a lawyer who worked for a very large firm doing corporate litigation work. Bill never knew what to talk about with Bob outside of church concerns— "The music sounds nice in church today. . . ." "The finance committee is meeting on Tuesday. . . ." "Are you going to the annual dinner meeting on Saturday?"

He tried discussing the current problems about drugs, a particular concern of his since he had growing children, but Clark backed off. He tried talking about children; but Bob didn't have children of his own, and he obviously didn't know how to communicate with them. Bill knew that there were a lot of single people in the church community who were not used to being with children. He had seen Clark talk to his own two daughters on occasion, but it was all superficial talk, and he always got the impression that Bob felt extremely uncomfortable around them.

He thought he'd hit upon a topic of mutual interest when he mentioned to Bob that he had graduated from the University of Michigan, and Bob had looked up with something akin to the delight of recognition, saying, "I've spent time in Michigan."

"At the university?"

But Bob had backed off just as quickly. "No. Just Michigan."

"Whereabouts?" Bill asked. "That's my home state."

"I just passed through once. Beautiful country."

Then, after listening to Clark wheeze consistently during one of the meetings, Bill finally found a subject that Bob was willing to talk about at length. Allergies. They both had allergies, and they often compared notes. No—he was a nice enough guy, Bill thought, but allergies weren't much of a basis for a steady friendship. Actually Clark was boring, if you came right down to it. His lady friend, Delores, whom he brought to all the meetings and dinners, was just as quiet and withdrawn as he. At the next dinner, Bill thought, he would make sure he found a seat next to someone else.

One of Bob's functions as treasurer of the church was to make

public treasury reports to 120 fellow congregants at regularly scheduled luncheon meetings. Speaking at the luncheon, List subconsciously felt a surge of power similar to the one he'd felt in his
golden days with Xerox Corporation when he was in control of his
destiny—forging ahead, caught up in the excitement of a new,
progressive company with new ideas. Now all eyes turned to Clark
as he spoke about that which he knew and felt the most comfortable
with—numbers.

Bill was surprised that Clark handled himself so well in front of
the membership. He was articulate and self-assured while speaking.
Where was the shy man he usually presented? Standing before the
membership, he suddenly took on an assurance that gave him the
unfamiliar aura of being in complete control. Bill Sauter was impressed and a bit puzzled. Sometimes the man seemed so weak, so
much—well, he hated to say it, but yes, so much of a wimp. At
other times he demonstrated a backbone of steel that was totally out
of character. It made Bill think to himself, Will the real Bobby
Clark please stand up?

Reverend West was aware that some of the council members
thought Bob was boring, but he found him endlessly fascinating.
Despite Bob's obvious financial problems, the pastor noticed that
when Bob was on the board, he stayed out of all the discussions
regarding the poor and indigent. There were many people on welfare
in Denver. St. Paul's was very socially oriented. It ministered to
street people who came in constantly. It even supported a homeless
shelter. Bob didn't have a condescending attitude toward them for
being on welfare; in fact, he tried to help them, but there was a
reticence in his attitude that West noticed. There seemed to be a
double side to his personality. On the one hand he was so considerate
and helpful to the poor. On the other hand, there was a proud edge
to him that seemed to say, "Not me. I will never be in that position."
It was almost as though poverty were a taboo subject with him.

The Office of Government Ministry, which monitored all legis-
lation on economic issues and social concerns and then translated
them to the parishes, was housed at St. Paul's. A great deal of board
time was spent analyzing the ministry's findings. Bob was never
critical of its function, although there were many board members
who were.

"The church has got to be an arena big enough for all of us,"
Reverend West said in the middle of one heated debate. "We do
disagree, but we disagree with an understanding. We have to be big
enough to know nobody always has the right answer."

"We can't afford that welfare program," said one council member. He turned to Bob Clark. "Right?"

West looked at Clark, who had no expression on his face. Clark was a whiz with his little calculator during finance meetings. Now, as he pulled out figures, multiplied, divided, percentaged them out, the man felt comfortable, at home. Reverend West smiled.

The same kind of comfortable monotony and calm colored Bob Clark's life on the job. Long, tranquil days at Roberto Distributing with classical music playing softly on a radio in the background as he worked. Nothing personal decorated his office, no photographs or family memorabilia. Certificates from a deceased staff accountant that had been on the wall behind his desk when he'd moved into his office remained untouched. He'd never bothered to take them down.

Clark's refuge at St. Paul's gave him the security he needed to begin to look for improvements in his professional life-style. He wanted to move up in the job market. On October 4, 1979, with an excellent reference from Jim Roberto, he was hired at a salary of $300 a week by Alfred Logan, vice-president of All-Packaging Co., an Aurora manufacturer of folding boxes that were used in supermarkets. His position was that of an office manager-comptroller. He also did accounting and bookkeeping and supervised three clerks.

As usual, he was a very conscientious worker. No one had to ask him to work overtime. Many were the times he worked weekends on his own, just as he had at Roberto Distributing. It was little wonder that Logan liked him. By 1980 Bob Clark's job was upgraded to comptroller of the company. This major improvement gave him the responsibility of handling all the financial affairs of the company, including its banking and the payroll for thirty-two employees. He had a title again; the raise in salary to $490 per week was commensurate with the added responsibilities with which he had been entrusted. Now his desire for a more normal life, one that would include a full relationship with Delores, suddenly became possible. With obvious calculation he began to set the stage for such a new life. He carefully passed comments on the job that finally led Mr. Logan to ask, "You were married once, weren't you?"

Logan had always thought Bob a somewhat sad-looking man, but now his face took on a tragic aura. "Yes," he said.

"Divorced?"

"No. It wasn't a good marriage, but she died."

"Oh."

"A long terminal illness. I took care of her. It took years for her to die."

"Sorry to hear that. What was the matter with her?"

"Cancer."

"Oh," Logan said again. He could tell that it was a painful experience, and he decided to back off; you don't force those kinds of memories on a person. But Clark seemed to want to talk about it all of a sudden.

"It was a long illness," he said again.

Logan waited for him to go on.

"It practically wiped me out. There were all of these tremendous hospital bills, but I took care of her."

"Well, if anyone deserves better, it's you," Logan said sincerely.

Logan waited a moment and then changed the subject. "About Sunday. You make sure you take Sunday off."

"Yes. I have plans after church."

And Logan knew that meant he had plans with Delores Miller.

So he had been married and his wife had died, Logan thought. He supposed there had been no children. He didn't ask. He was surprised that Bob had revealed so much, since he rarely spoke about himself. Well, as long as he didn't talk about church matters again, Logan thought. He could get pretty monotonous on the subject. He was such a quiet, unassuming man, good with figures and, in Logan's estimation, great with people. He hoped the man could get the second chance he so richly deserved.

Wanda Flanery was originally from Kansas City, Missouri. A woman in her late fifties, she was of average height and a little overweight, with short cropped hair and an open, friendly Irish face. One of the first people she met after she moved into her small condominium on Peoria Street was her neighbor, Delores Miller. They began their relationship casually at first over a shared fence, but soon they got to talking regularly. Wanda was warm, simple, observant, religious, and poor. "You have to be religious when life is so tough," she said philosophically.

Delores agreed that God was a great comfort.

"We're Irish Catholic," she said, coughing.

"Lutheran," Delores offered.

Wanda noticed that Delores's casual daily attire of slacks, usually worn when she went to work, changed to skirts when she went to church. Wanda believed in dressing properly for worship too. The two women related well. Both had had difficult lives, and both did a great deal of physical work: Delores handling boxes at Fitzsimmons Army Hospital, Wanda cleaning houses and apartments in the area.

Delores noted that Wanda's apartment was sparsely furnished. Wanda sat on the one easy chair in the room, while Delores sat on the couch facing the TV, on top of which were framed pictures of her grandchildren. Between the door and her chair there were bags on the floor full of books. "I like to read," she explained. There was a chinese figurine on a side table next to the sofa, and some inexpensive flower baskets hung on the wall on the L-shaped part of the living room that led into the dining room.

Wanda felt that Delores had been through a lot emotionally. And she's only in her forties, she thought sympathetically. "Wait till you get to be my age," Wanda laughed. "Fifty-seven. I hope things ease up for you before that."

"You don't look fifty-seven," Delores said kindly.

"Sure I do," Wanda said with simple acceptance. "It's okay."

As they spoke Wanda nodded and smiled a great deal. She was very forthcoming with stories about herself, and she clearly liked to talk.

"You see, my husband is disabled," she offered.

"Oh, I'm sorry."

"That's okay. He's been like that for years," she said, coughing again.

"Like what?" Delores asked, noticing that Wanda coughed a great deal.

"My husband is a paranoid schizophrenic."

Delores was immediately sympathetic. "And you take care of him?"

"Oh, yes, sure," Wanda said easily. "He's got a doctor here, but I take care of everything. We've been married since 1951. Thirty-four years." She sighed. "You don't live with someone who's got that kind of sickness without learning something about the mind. I know about those things."

She prided herself on being able to understand people. To "see through them," as she liked to put it. "I really like to sit back, to watch, to take things in. I've got three children and six grandchildren. You don't go through life without learning about people. Not if you look at things squarely. Are you married?"

"No, not anymore," Delores said a bit sadly. "I was once. We're divorced. . . ." Her voice trailed off.

So that was where the pain came from, Wanda thought to herself. From her ex-husband.

It was Cindy Taylor's responsibility as manager to check on Bob Clark when he told her he was moving. He had lived at Brentwood on the Park from September 1978 until now, November 1985, she noted as she checked his file. Every month she posted his rent, which he always paid on time by money order or by check. She sighed. She was sorry he was moving, even though he had kept such a low profile. She hardly remembered ever seeing the man. It was just that now she'd have to rent the apartment again, and that was a hassle. Only ten percent of all rentable apartments in Denver were occupied.

Suddenly she remembered him. The waterbed! Of course. He hadn't looked like the waterbed type, she thought, laughing quietly to herself. Waterbeds were pretty common in Denver, but him? Well, you can never tell about people. Who knew what kinds of currents ran under even the stillest of waters?

There was nothing in his file that would have called attention to himself. The average tenant file was thick with complaints and work orders about leaky faucets or stopped-up toilets. Some of the letters were quite angry, but there was nothing like that in Mr. Clark's file. It was the cleanest file she had ever seen—not a thing in it that would call attention to himself. It was as though no one had lived there at all. He didn't even have any magazine or newspaper subscriptions that would keep coming after he'd gone. That was always such a nuisance when tenants didn't cancel subscriptions or leave forwarding addresses.

Mr. Clark had given the required thirty days notice. There was no reason she could see not to return the security he had deposited when he first took the apartment. She returned $56.93 of his security deposit, keeping the remaining $43.07 for cleaning and utilities. When he moved he took no personal possessions with him other than the waterbed and boxes of tax files.

Wanda Flanery was very surprised when Delores called her over one day to introduce her to a man named Bob Clark. She hadn't the slightest idea that Delores had even been dating. Bob Clark seemed like a really nice guy, Wanda thought after the introductions had been made, but Delores seemed a little embarrassed. "He's . . ." she stammered, and hesitated.

"Something wrong?" Wanda asked.

"No, not at all. It's just that Bob is moving in with me . . . here."

"Well, hey!" Wanda teased with a big grin washing her face with delight. "What's going on here?"

"We're going to get married," Delores said quickly.

Wanda was immediately sorry, seeing how distressed they both seemed at her teasing. "Listen," she amended quickly, "like I always say, it's none of my business."

"No," Delores continued, "you should know. We've been going together for eight years, and now we've decided to get married. . . ."

Eight years, Wanda thought, trying not to smile. Nothing like rushing into things.

"And we wanted to get him moved in and settled with his things," Delores explained, "before we go to Maryland to get married." Delores didn't feel like adding that they had opted for the cheaper monthly payment; her condo was only $250, while his rent had risen from $158 a month to $315 in the seven years he'd lived at Brentwood.

"Maryland." Wanda nodded with a pleasant smile.

"Where my mother lives."

"How wonderful. Well, all the luck to you both," she said with warm sincerity. She liked Delores and really wished her well.

Marrying again. Well, that was terrific, she thought.

Although memories are our true possessions, in Bob Clark's case unshareable, it takes a great deal of strength of conviction and calculation to categorize and separate the memories one wishes not to deal with even when alone—to forget, to destroy—a true form of psychological encapsulation. Don't think of it. Don't deal with it. But the time capsule can never be totally sealed forever. Bob Clark found himself unconsciously comparing wealthy suburbs in which one had doctors and engineers for neighbors to Somerset Village with someone like Wanda Flanery as a neighbor. Wanda was a woman whose entire life had been spent dealing with desperations, who cleaned other people's houses for a living, who he felt was uneducated. It was such a completely different life. These were disturbing thoughts to be put aside again, this time forever. Forget it. This was not the time for pride. Wanda Flanery, in her simplicity, was no threat, which actually made her the perfect neighbor.

There was no doubt in his mind any longer. He had the longing and now the job to financially substructure the need. The bottom line was money. Now they would have enough, never suffer the humiliation of financial hardship. Clark finally felt that he was ready to marry again, to attempt a new life, to start over. The past was past. It had not caught up with him. He could put it forever behind him. He was sixty years old.

Later, when Delores and Wanda were alone, Wanda teased Delores gently about the man she was about to marry. "He says he's fifty-seven years old. Now, come on." Wanda grinned. "I just turned fifty-seven myself, and he looks a lot older than that."

"Oh, no," Delores insisted. "He was just fifty-eight. He just had a birthday."

"He's a lot older than you."

"No, he isn't."

"Not that it matters, but why does he dye his hair, then?"

"Oh, I shouldn't have told you."

Wanda laughed warmly. "So what? It doesn't matter."

"It's better for him on his job not to have gray hair," she rationalized. "So I tint it brown for him."

But on a more serious level, Wanda knew Delores had her problems about the marriage. She kept saying, "I don't know if I should marry him or not. I'm simply not sure about it." One day it was "yes," and the next day it was "no." And Wanda realized that Delores didn't love Bob the way she had loved her first husband.

Neither one of them heard the echoes from a past life, echoes with a prophetic pounding that would have been frightening if Clark had heard them himself.

Delores seemed to Wanda to be someone who had been so deeply hurt by her first husband's infidelity that in a second marriage she was ready to settle for a man who was a Christian and calm and stable.

But, "Look, Delores," Wanda finally asked bluntly, "if you're not sure, why get married at all?"

And Delores told her, after a long hesitation, that she was tired and that Bob was the most saintly man she had ever met.

Even Wanda, who was Catholic, felt the strength of Clark's spiritual abundance. And she had to admit, he really was such a likable man, too. There was even a passivity about him that might make him easy to control. All men should be controlled to a certain degree, she thought with humor. Otherwise the natural tendency would be for the man to assume the role of a dictator. She sighed. Most men were like that. But not Bobby Clark. Delores could do worse. Wanda helped Delores select her wedding dress, a simple, traditional beige satin, trimmed with lace.

Lying about his age, claiming to be only fifty-three years old, Robert P. Clark married Delores Miller in November of 1985, almost fourteen years to the day of the savage murders of John List's mother, Alma, his wife, Helen, his daughter, Patricia, and his sons, John List, Jr., and little Freddie.

Without paying conscious heed to any developing patterns, Bob agreed to go to Baltimore, Maryland, where Delores's mother lived, for the simple Lutheran ceremony that would join them together for better or worse. Bob simply did not allow himself to think of the time when another marriage took place in Baltimore between a lanky young soldier and a pretty young widow thirty-four long years before. At least this time they weren't going to Maryland to avoid the results of a blood test.

And, of course, Delores could not possibly know that the marriage ceremony was like presenting her throat to the knife. She was an intensely private person herself and rarely asked questions. She accepted whatever Bob told her. When Wanda asked Bob if any of his family would attend, he said they were all dead. Delores's lack of probing unwittingly made her a ready accomplice in her own destiny.

But life, tranquil on the outside, refused to continue without problems.

"Sorry to see him go," Logan said to Mr. Morrow, the president of All-Packaging.

"I thought he was a model employee," Morrow said, surprised at Logan's decision.

"In most ways."

"I'm not questioning your decision, Alfred," Morrow continued, "but I would like to understand. I thought you felt he was an asset to the company."

Logan cleared his throat. "But he insisted on still doing everything by hand."

"By hand?"

"It was a slow thing . . . gradual . . . but he became less and less of an asset as time went on," Logan said. "His job grew, but he didn't."

Logan felt terribly guilty about it even as he said it. The man worked on weekends repeatedly without having to be asked, but even that was peculiar. It placed a terrible imposition on the other workers. They often mumbled resentment about his "over-dedication," which they felt made them look bad. And Logan had completely changed his entire evaluation. He just doesn't know how to interact with other people, he now thought. But aloud he said, "He couldn't implement the computer mode that we need now. He did everything by hand."

Morrow was well aware that, very often, when a company wanted to let an employee go for whatever reason—personality, inade-quacy—management would often give a job-related reason for doing so. "Inability to adapt to new trends" could serve as a reason. On the other hand, the man was getting on in years. He looked to be some-where in his sixties, and perhaps he really was beginning to slow down.

"You know best," Morrow said. It didn't really matter to him. "I barely knew the man anyway. John Clark?"

"Bob Clark."

"Hmm." Morrow nodded and changed the subject.

Fired! It was a terrible emotional blow to Clark. What had hap-pened? He and Delores had been married only four months. He had a throbbing sense of *déjà-vu*.

But he *was* slowing down. In his honest private moments he admitted it. Sometimes he found it difficult to concentrate. He didn't want to try to learn anything new. He remembered the time he had set up an entire computer program. That seemed like an eternity ago. Doing the work manually was safer, surer.

Fired . . . dear God. . . .

Without telling anyone, Clark went to the filing cabinets that held the company's personnel records and removed his folder before leaving All-Packaging Company for the last time.

Bob sat opposite Reverend West in the pastor's office at St. Paul's Church and told him that he had been "laid off again."

"What will you do now?" the pastor asked with genuine concern.

"Well, I'm working out of my home now, and Delores is still working in the commissary at Fitzsimmons."

Reverend West knew Bob saw everything as facts and figures. Bottom line: money. No human element. And now the human element was a part of the equation after all. Bob had been laid off, and the man was obviously feeling, at the very least, frustrated. The fact that he had finally spoken about a personal matter for the first time in eleven years was indication enough of his anxiety. The pastor could tell he was genuinely distressed about losing his job. He had just married, and now he wasn't bringing home a salary. He had even said laid off "again."

"Again?" the pastor asked.

But Bob would not elucidate. "I'm doing some marketing out of my home . . . 'Robert Clark Services,' " he said evasively.

When Clark explained that he was using those advertising inserts that went to private homes to offer his accounting services, the pastor worried. Not only was the Denver economy depressed right now, but, "Bob," he said, "that's so far from what you were doing. . . ."

"It's only temporary," Clark said, suddenly shifting into a calm mode. "Until I can get going."

West studied him carefully. Bob demonstrated no desperation in the discussion.

"I've applied to a number of places," he continued easily.

Not only had Bob Clark created a new life that was a replica of the one he had escaped, but another pattern was repeating. Bob had talked to Reverend West but covered up his true feelings, as he had in a similar conversation with a pastor in Kalamazoo. He had been fired again—echoes of Sutherland Paper, and Xerox Corp., and the First National Bank. He had even been fired as a cook. He was now working out of his home, as he had in Westfield, N.J., futilely trying to create a viable business selling out of his office at home—"A Memo from the Desk of John E. List, Career-Builder."

Echoes of the history of his entire work life continued to reverberate as he slid backward in his professional life.

The fried chicken and potato salad for lunch were neatly packed in a hamper. Packing a lunch would save money on the little afternoon excursion they had planned to distance themselves from their growing problems. Delores prepared the lunch, but Bob was the one who planned everything, right to a T, Wanda thought. Organized, I guess you'd call it. Delores wasn't that way before he'd moved in with her, but she kind of fit in with the "organization" of their lives. Obviously, Wanda reasoned, Delores didn't mind.

Bob and Delores had taken Wanda with them to Heritage Square to spend the afternoon window-shopping at all the quaint little shops. Delores did stop in one of the shops to buy miniature figures just like the ones she had bought at the church bazaar the last time they'd gone. Delores loved the church bazaars. One of Bob and Delores's hobbies was classical music. They had a nice collection of albums. Delores's other hobby was miniatures in a shadow box. She had shown Wanda the little church she'd built in it. Now she was filling it with little miniatures. "It's not very expensive," she said as she made a selection. "We have to be careful now," she said, "about expenses."

As Bob lagged behind them, he didn't hear Delores complain to Wanda that she was tired of working. "My salary isn't enough to support the two of us," she said, obviously beginning to worry at the situation she unexpectedly found herself in now that Bob had been fired. It was a little too soon to be overly pessimistic about their financial outlook, but Wanda knew by now that Delores was a bit of a worrier by nature. She also knew too well how easy it was to fall behind in payments.

The picture now had changed to one of Delores supporting Bob. He cooked dinner. She complained. He gardened. She was sickly and showing it more. Echoes. He didn't let on to anyone that he was again beginning to feel the familiar edge of desperation closing in on him. That, in itself, was the most fearful echo of all. Maybe marriage wasn't lucky for him. Only four months married, and already stress was beginning to pile up.

Could it happen again? Given the right set of circumstances?

If he had done it once, he could do it again.

He didn't want to think about it. He pushed it back deeply into the now crowded hidden parts of his mind.

32 | A Fifteenth Anniversary

A call came into the precinct in Westfield.

"I'd like to talk to someone in charge of the List murder case."

"Maybe I can help you," said the desk sergeant.

"No, it has to be someone in charge," said the voice with a definite air of urgency.

"Okay. That would be Chief Moran. Hold on a minute."

The man identified himself as Samuel Hilz of Pleasantville, New York, when Moran picked up the line. "You're going to think I'm crazy," he began as so many others before him had begun, "but I think my neighbor is John List, the man you're looking for in connection with those murders."

There was a call from San Bernardino, California. "You're going to think I'm out of my mind, but I think I know where John List is. He has a scar, right? Behind his ear?"

Then a caller from Atlantic City reported, "There's no doubt in my mind at all. It's the guy. He's an accountant. Well, I think he is. He's wonderful with numbers. And I saw what looked like the scar behind his ear. And he's about five seven."

The call from Laurelton, N.J., seemed like a good lead. "I've never made a call like this, and I know you probably are going to think I'm nuts . . ." Tall, 180 pounds, quiet, the right age, spoke with a German accent—that didn't ring quite right—but, as in all the hundreds of tips before, Chief Moran patiently had each and every one checked out. Contact the local police departments. Ask for assistance. Look up the people who called. Check with the FBI. Check out the suspect. Hundreds of calls. Hundreds of dead ends.

Tired little newspaper articles had periodically resurrected the killings on the inside pages of local New Jersey newspapers—THIRTEEN YEARS AND NO LIST, read one update. POLICE STILL PURSUE MASS KILLER, read another. And then the obligatory repetition of the grisly details: "Dragged them from the kitchen . . . mopped up the floor . . . wiped up the blood . . . blood-soaked towels." Now some of the details were getting confused and distorted, like a story that is repeated too many times and takes on new directions. Now the two women had been found in "upstairs bedrooms." Now everyone who knew him always considered him a "brilliant loner." Now his features had become so "typically American" that he would most likely not be in Europe, where he would be easy to spot. Now he had told the post office to stop his mail for "only a month."

The tips or sightings of the fugitive numbered somewhere over three hundred. Tracing them was like trying to track a UFO: San Bernardino, California; Puerto Rico; Tulsa, Oklahoma; New Jersey; Europe; Asia; Latin America. Taxpayer dollars were disappearing in the search. Many of the leads had to be ruled out immediately— wrong height, no scar, wrong age—but the patience of law enforcement personnel ran deep. There was no giving up in a case like this. The search continued. Somewhere, John List was hiding. Every law enforcement agent who worked on the case was sure that, someday, John List would be apprehended. No one wanted to give up the hunt.

Chief Moran had pretty good reason to feel confident. In 1980 only two of the twenty-six murders committed in the county remained unsolved. In 1981 the stats were even better: thirty murders—thirty murderers apprehended. In 1983 there were thirty-six murders—only six unsolved. That wasn't a bad record. Every single unsolved case was still open. John List's headed the list. So he's keeping a low profile. So he's a nondescript kind of guy. So he doesn't stand out in a crowd. So he's not doing anything to attract attention to himself. So what! *Someday* he'll make a mistake. And when he does, Moran thought, someone will be waiting to snap the cuffs on his wrists. Me!

Union County clerk Roger Halpern was on the dais in charge of the program. He noticed that, as usual, Chief James Moran of the Westfield police was in the audience seated at a table surrounded by local police officials. Moran never missed the annual Horns dinner held for hundreds of employees of the Union County government.

Halpern mischievously nudged a fellow organizer who was standing on the platform with him when he saw the chief. "Watch this," he whispered. Then he took the microphone in his hand and yelled, "Hey, Moran!"

Conversation diminished immediately as all eyes turned to Mugsy, the well-known chief of police, whose face broke into a wide grin. He knew what was coming. "Will you look at this?" he said, elbowing a fellow law enforcer seated next to him. "They're not gonna let us off the hook."

"Did you solve the List murders yet?" Halpern shouted at him from the dais.

Moran jumped to his feet. "I've solved it!" he shouted back, flushed with good-natured humor. "I've solved it all right. John List did it. Now we just have to catch him!"

The room rang with good-natured laughter.

* * *

Robin Kampf was on assignment. No one was more aware of the fifteenth anniversary of the murders than Robin. She had never forgotten John List, but she had pretty much outgrown her childhood obsession with him. Over the years there had been a great many other things to occupy her mind: growing up, school, friends, boyfriends. At Seton Hall University in New Jersey she had majored in journalism and television with a minor in sociology. After graduating with a communications degree, she spent important time looking for the kind of job that would fit in with all the imaginative aspects of her personality that needed expression. New Jersey's Suburban Cable Television Company suited her needs perfectly. She had interned at the station during her senior year at Seton Hall and ambitiously worked the graveyard shift on WMTR and WDHA radio at night as well. She was twenty-three years old now and a very pretty five-foot-one-inch young lady, with deep chestnut-colored hair, blue eyes, and a round face placed on an angular jaw that gave her a distinctive look.

Her initial job as a technician was to insert commercials and run programs out of master control. Soon she had interested her station manager in a proposal for a news magazine program she called *INFO New Jersey's Magazine*. Beginning with five-minute filler pieces, which she focused on local news feature stories, the enterprising Robin had worked to increase the show to a half-hour format. In her capacity as writer-producer, she produced short feature documentaries for the program. By 1984 *INFO* had won its first ACE Award, the cable television industry's equivalent of the Emmy. It won again in 1985 and 1986 and then again in 1987, the fifteenth-anniversary year of the List murders.

Robin had often thought about doing a piece on the "Ballroom Murders" even though it wasn't the type of story *INFO* usually did, and she didn't know if she should pursue it, not only because she knew it would occupy a lot of her time, but because she could never quite forget how consumed she had been with the case when she was a child. It had been a very strange period in her life. For a good seven or eight months, the murders had been constantly on her mind. She had a great thirst for information about them. As time went on the intense need subsided somewhat, but then something would happen, such as the house fire or the auction, to stir it up again. The stories in the papers would kick up all the old feelings again, and she would check under her bed for a couple of days as she used to do. Then, when she picked up *The Westfield Leader* and read the story about the fifteenth-anniversary year, she realized that she had found the perfect angle for her TV magazine show.

She went back to all of the newspaper files she had accumulated on the case from the time she'd first heard about it, and she began reviewing all the pertinent entries she had written into her diary over the years. In rereading her nervous young teenage entries, she realized that, in many ways, she was representative of all the vulnerable children who had been so emotionally affected by the murders.

Now the story was crying out to be done. Robin no longer had any doubts. She knew she was the natural person to resurrect it and write the documentary for *INFO Magazine*. She could feel herself getting excited at the prospect, though just the thought of it had already begun to color her private moments with the edge of anxiety that would engulf her again when she became intimately involved with the project. The thought that List, the bogeyman, was unpunished, unrepentant, but most of all "still out there somewhere" was a deep spur in her preparations. She realized that the obsession that had begun so many years ago had not really ebbed over the years; it had merely temporarily gone undercover. No backing out now. The commitment was already made. John List, mass murderer, on *INFO Magazine*. Okay. Go for it.

The Westfield police and the FBI were extremely receptive to the documentary. Except for what appeared in the local newspaper, *The Westfield Leader*, they hadn't received any press coverage on the murders in a long time. They felt that if the media reminded people that "this guy was still at large," it could aid them in their continuing search.

One of the first people Robin met with in her initial research was the handsome young Barney Tracy, who was now a lieutenant detective on the police force. It was 8:15 P.M. at night when they sat at his desk in the detective bureau located in the back of police headquarters. He was casually dressed in sneakers and sweats after coming from a football practice with his son. He was extremely friendly and willing to discuss the List case in detail.

At Robin's first question, "What time did the call come in to police headquarters?" he grinned, stood up, and walked over to a closet that was recessed into the wall. He stood on his toes to reach a closed storage space above the closet and opened the double doors to reveal a blue plastic storage bin about 2 feet long, 1½ feet wide, and about 2 feet deep. In it were the List files, including the police report, ballistic reports, and murder scene pictures as well as many other photos.

He brought the bin over and placed it on his desk. After each question Robin asked in reviewing the history of the case, Barney consulted the files to verify the information he gave her. He was very congenial, eager to give his personal views on John List. He explained to Robin that if there was one thing he thought he did well, it was "character-studying" a person. "List had a Nazi mentality," he said, summing up his opinion of the fugitive. "In his head, the murders were justified. Maybe *we* don't understand, but that doesn't matter to him. There's no weight of guilt on this guy. No remorse. He thinks he was right."

Robin realized that over the years the case had taken on legendary proportions in Union County. List himself had almost become mythical. Not a folk hero, certainly, she thought, but he had become like D. B. Cooper, the skyjacker who was never found. Some still thought the two fugitives were one and the same. Preposterous, she thought. But many had come to think of the murders as the perfect crime. Some admired the "genius" List applied to his disappearance, so reminiscent of the "brilliant" strategy that he applied to his board games. And some felt intrigued by the aura of horror fiction that continued to cling to the story—the house that burned down, the ghosts of the dead family, the ghost of the living List.

She remembered that one Union County assistant prosecutor was even quoted in one of the papers as saying that in a small church somewhere in America, an old sexton was slowly sweeping the aisles. "He wandered into town years ago, and no one asks his name anymore. He is doing penance. His name is John List." It was a highly romanticized view of a man who had murdered and was sadly living out his life in penance to God and his church. After years of menial servitude he might already have died quietly somewhere and been buried under an assumed name. "Somebody may even be putting flowers on his grave, not knowing they were flowering a mass murderer."

Many believed these scenarios to be close to the truth. Others did not. When Robin went to the Westfield Police Department, to the FBI, and to the Union County Prosecutor's Office with her TV crew to set up for the raw footage, she realized that the views of these people, who had been discussing their most famous unsolved crime for the past fifteen years, were far from romantic in their assessment of the killer.

"There's no such thing as a perfect crime! Does that get me! Perfect crime!"

"It's not a solve-the-crime case, it's a find-the-killer case. This List is one cold fish. Don't forget how he asked the bank teller to put her initials on the cash envelope when he took the last of his mother's money."

"Look," Lieutenant Bell summed up, "it's easy enough to disappear, but it's hard to stay hidden forever."

The more Robin discovered about the List case, the more she wanted to know; yet when Chief Moran opened up a very large album of photographs taken at the murder scene, Robin immediately felt edgy. She glanced at the upside-down album on his desk.

"I don't want to see any gruesome, gory pictures," she said quickly, trying not to reveal her unease. "That's not what I'm looking for. I don't want to sensationalize the case. I'd like to do a more informative type of approach."

"Sure," Moran said as he turned the pages one at a time—slowly—remembering the events, reliving them in the process of review. He answered all of Robin's questions willingly. He was soft-spoken, knowledgeable, and completely at ease, but when he pulled out some of the glossy colored photos of the murder scene and turned them around for her to see, Robin found herself thinking, I'm in over my head.

She instinctively squinted her eyes so as not to be able to focus on the photos. I want to get out of this, she thought. I've heard enough. I've seen enough. My thirst for knowledge about the murders has been fulfilled. No more. . . .

Later that night she wrote another entry about List in her diary, the first one in years:

The most gruesome photo I could stand was the bloodstained paper towels stuffed into the brown paper bags in the kitchen. You see those photos in the newspaper in black and white, and it certainly is not as effective as when you see them in 8 × 10 glossy in color. That was horrifying.

I got as far as those pictures and the pictures of the ballroom with the bloodstains on the hardwood floors, that was about all I could take. But as he was flipping through the photo album, he stopped for some reason at one photograph, and I looked down quickly, I don't know why, and I saw a very, very gruesome photo which will stay with me for the rest of my life. It was a close-up of one of the victims, just rotted to the point of blackness and decay. It was something out of Night of the Living Dead—*it was horrifying.*

Robin felt a wave of terror run from the top of her body all the way down to her toes. She thought she was going to pass out. "Look," she said uneasily to Moran, "I have to stop for a minute for a breather here."

As she collected herself, she tried to think of other interviews she had conducted. Why have I pursued this? she wondered. The *INFO* programs she had produced and written to date had never been like this. She and her crew had never handled anything like a simple single murder, let alone mass murders. Why am I going from doing pieces on wine making in New Jersey to recounting the List tragedy? And looking at those pictures!

By the time the story was in the can, and Robin had the raw footage, she felt that she didn't want to do it anymore. The ironic part of her growing dilemma was that the List story was the first one she was going to work on entirely by herself. Ordinarily she had an editor with her, but this time her editor was working on another job. Now she would have to do the editing alone, and she was spooked—completely, obsessively spooked. She kept putting off editing the story. She repeatedly sat down to write the script and simply couldn't do it. The words didn't come. The legal-size yellow pad remained blank in front of her.

She found herself trying to legitimize the necessity of doing the story by telling herself, "I'm helping these poor, innocent victims out. By putting this story together, I'm going to be a savior of some sort, and maybe, as a result of my story he'll be found."

She convinced herself that now she had a mission and a duty to complete the story. She knew she wasn't the only one who hoped to be instrumental in cracking the case, but that was the spur that set her to work.

Robin spent at least nine hours in the editing room putting the fifteen-minute story together. She was very happy with the result. She had a few more days of editing time scheduled, but she would not stay overtime tonight. She had often stayed at work as late as eleven o'clock at night all alone in the building. But not this time. There was no way she was going to put this story together once everybody had gone home—and she didn't, no matter how much she wanted the "star" of her show to be caught.

Robin sat in her apartment and waited for the program to air on its premiere night. She had watched the show at least fifty times at the studio during the process of editing, but sitting all alone at night, she found that it still had the ability to spook her. She wished she had invited a friend over to see it with her.

Robin's face appeared on the screen as she told the story of the List murders with honesty and integrity, minimizing the sensational aspects of the case while maximizing the potential of television to aid in the capture of fugitives. The program, replete with the interviews Robin had conducted with police and FBI personnel, offered information and insight, accurate details, and visual corroboration through police photos of List, the family, and the house where the murders occurred. Chief Moran would one day say it was the best piece he had ever seen done on the List case. During the month of March 1987 the program aired on local New Jersey cable Channel 3 every Tuesday at 7:30 P.M. It told the story well and asked for help in apprehending the fugitive. If *INFO* had aired nationally, it might have led to List's capture.

As soon as the show was over, Robin's phone rang. The sudden blare of sound startled her. When she answered, a male voice said, "Is this Robin?"

The deep voice was unfamiliar. She couldn't place it. "Who is this?" she asked.

"Is this Robin Kampf?" the voice asked.

"Yes, who is this?" she repeated.

"I saw your story," he said, "I thought it was great."

By then she was really frightened. "Who is this?" she demanded.

"It's David, from work." She sighed in relief. Her immediate thought when she picked up the telephone had been that it was John List calling her to tell her he liked the story and to "keep up the good work."

The *INFO* program and the fifteenth anniversary of the murders created a new impetus to go after the fugitive with vigor. A computerized sketch of what he might look like after fifteen years was released. It showed List, who would now be sixty-one years old, with age lines, slightly sagging jowls, and grayed thinning hair to fit in with the receding hairline he had had even at age forty-six. But it was still the same man with the same mild, expressionless, bespectacled face, wearing a suit and a tie.

The past finally began to creep up on Bobby Clark early in 1987. Wanda Flanery bought *World Weekly*, one of the sensational tabloid newspapers commonly sold in supermarkets, the kind that specialized in gossip and exposé and featured weekly cures for cancer, crash diets, and the latest stories on UFO contacts. When she opened it up to one of the lead stories, a two-page spread about a mass murder that had happened in 1971 in New Jersey, she found herself staring at a sixteen-year-old photo of John List and the updated computerized photo alongside of it. It was her neighbor, Bob Clark, she thought with a surge of shocked recognition.

There he was. The suit and tie, the sweet, soft expression of the mouth, the eyeglasses, even the ears that stuck out. But there was more than a physical resemblance. She read the article swiftly—the man was Lutheran and an accountant. It all fell into place. That's what trips him up, she thought as she read about the man who had "slaughtered" his entire family. That he even went back to his church and his numbers was a dead giveaway. He must be the same man.

She looked out of her window across the patio. There he was, getting out of his white Toyota with grocery bags in his arms, meticulously dressed, as usual, in a suit and tie. Him? He killed his three children? And his mother? And his wife? Wanda couldn't get over it. In this community you sometimes took your life in your hands when you stepped outside your door. *That* she could understand. *That* was normal. But having a sweet-faced mass murderer for a neighbor was hard to believe.

Holding the tabloid in her hand and staring at the photo, she found herself remembering how only the other day, Delores had told her that he was driving her crazy. She knew Delores was a worrier, and she kept saying over and over again, "I don't know what I'm going to do." Bob had been unemployed for a long time and was "loafing" around a lot. He was inside the house, and Delores and Wanda were out on the patio having a cigarette at the time. Delores often went outdoors to smoke when Bob was home out of consideration for the fact that he was asthmatic.

Wanda was surprised when all of a sudden Delores deliberately raised her voice and said loud enough for him to hear, "If Bobby doesn't hurry up and get a job instead of hanging around the house all the time, I'm leaving him."

Wanda was certain he heard her. How could he not? She knew working at Fitzsimmons was hard on Delores. When Delores just as suddenly said something about how it used to be different the last time she was married, Wanda impulsively asked her, "You still love him, don't you? Your first husband?"

Delores was quiet for a moment. Then she answered very softly, "Yes."

Hadn't Wanda just read something similar about the murderer's first wife's feelings in the article?

Life sure wasn't easy on her friend. Sometimes Delores seemed to be content. All the time Bob was out of work, he fixed dinner and waited on her. Yes, he was good to her, very attentive, Wanda thought. It was like having a mother taking care of her. There were some compensations, but stress was beginning to pile up. Wanda knew that they had already taken out a second mortgage on the condominium and that they had joined eleven other owners in a dispute with the management of Somerset Village. Now they had defaulted on some of their payments. Were they sliding toward poverty like that other poor family in New Jersey? Reading about how financial hardship had led John List to murder gave Wanda grave cause for concern. Maybe she should call the police.

No.

She would show the newspaper to Delores. She waited until later in the evening when she saw Bob get into his car and drive off again before going next door.

Delores was on the patio. ''Hi,'' she welcomed her with a smile.

''You busy?''

''No.''

''I want to show you something.''

''What?''

Wanda held out the newspaper to her friend. It was folded back to the page with the photos of John List. ''Look,'' she said. ''Is this your husband?''

Delores looked at it and said, ''Oh, my God! What did he do?''

''Well, it says here he murdered his whole family.''

Delores turned pale. While she read the article, she kept shaking her head and looking back at the photos, saying, ''Oh, my! Oh, my!''

''It looks just like him,'' Wanda said.

Delores finally rejected the comparisons, summarily dismissing the idea as absolutely impossible. The more she looked at the photos, the more convinced she became that the two men were not even remotely alike.

''No,'' she said finally, and folded up the newspaper. ''I don't think it's him.''

Wanda wasn't convinced. ''Well, keep it,'' she said, ''and show it to him.''

A week or so later, when Wanda saw Delores again, she asked, ''What did you do with my paper?''

''Oh, that,'' Delores said. ''I threw it away. It was nothing.''

Well, she must know her own husband, Wanda thought uneasily. If Delores didn't think it was him, she wasn't going to push it any further. Still, a woman's intuition was important. She couldn't help wondering. She didn't know if she was psychic or what, but, no, she wouldn't push it. He does my income tax for nothing, she thought, and tried to bury her troublesome intuition.

Still, Wanda couldn't completely forget it. She went out to buy another copy of the tabloid. A serious question had been raised in her mind; the likeness between the two men in looks and life-style was too startling to be completely coincidental. She found that she was afraid to show the picture to Bobby, just "in case" he really was John List. From that point on, despite Delores's absolute faith in her husband, Wanda found herself exercising restraint, and even caution, when she was with Bobby. The seeds of suspicion had been firmly planted. It suddenly occurred to her that Bob never spoke about himself or his past. In fact, she couldn't remember his ever mentioning anything at all about where he came from. Now, in light of the article, the omission struck her as significant. Then she remembered that when he and Delores were married, he had told her his family was dead.

She watched him carefully. Sometimes she felt a little afraid, even though Delores was so sure it wasn't that other man. Then again, what else could she let herself think? Wanda could understand her dilemma. People don't like to face unpleasant things, she thought. They sweep them under the carpet. That's why so many people live on lumpy carpets. Eventually, though, she concluded with a certain amount of homespun philosophy, if you live on lumpy carpets too long, you can trip and break your neck. That suddenly became a concern. Was Delores living on lumpy carpets? Wanda thought of going to the police with her suspicions. But "you just don't go to the police about a friend."

He brought Wanda flowers from his garden.

"What's this for?" she asked, surprised.

"It's because you're so good to Delores. You're always watching out for her."

"Only because I know this area," she said, "and I'm all around cleaning apartments and things."

"I know you always lock the gate."

"It's nothing. Delores likes to keep people out since she had that robbery." She looked at the flowers. "You don't have to do that."

"I want to."

"Well, thanks, Bob."

Much as she tried, Wanda couldn't help worrying about Delores's safety. They were having so much financial trouble. Wanda thought he might kill her, too. After all, he'd killed his family when they were in financial difficulty. But then, she reasoned to herself, they were slipping back from the Lord, too, and he'd killed them so they'd go to heaven. If he was the guy the police were looking for, she hoped that Delores's protective shield was the fact that they prayed together. She consoled herself by telling herself it was a very major difference from the "last time."

All thoughts about the Bob Clark/John List resemblance flew into the background of her life when Wanda was suddenly struck with a heart attack.

It was Bob and Delores Clark who took her to General Hospital, where her condition turned out to be serious enough to warrant a heart bypass operation.

Shortly afterward, Clark answered a newspaper ad in a local Denver paper placed by an employment agency in Richmond, Virginia. He had hesitated for a moment. Virginia . . . Why not? It was less economically deprived than Denver, less crime ridden than where they were living now. It might be good to get away from Denver. He answered the ad. It was late in 1987.

After making the initial contact by letter and then by phone, Bob flew to Richmond at his own expense for an interview with the Richmond Professional Placement Agency. The vice-president of the agency was Richard Severeid.

"I'd like to work in a more vibrant economy," Bob told him. "Denver is economically depressed at this time."

"You're willing to relocate?"

"My wife has relatives in Maryland; we'd be a lot closer than we are in Denver. She misses the East. Actually, we'd welcome a change at this time in our lives."

"All we have are entry-level positions."

"That's all right."

"Well, let's see what we can do for you."

Severeid sent Clark on several interviews in the Richmond area before finally putting him in touch with Mr. Charles S. Joyner, one of the two partners in the accounting firm of Maddrea, Joyner, Kirkham & Woody in Richmond. The firm was located on the second floor of a two-story brick building in a little shopping mall facing a large J. C. Penney department store.

In order to get the position for which he was now a bit desperate, Clark had shaved six years off his age and taken a major risk; he'd told Mr. Joyner that he, Robert Clark, had a BA degree in accounting, and a master's degree in finance from the University of Michigan. Mr. Joyner relied on the employment agency to verify his résumé, but no attempt was made by the agency to check out "Mr.

Clark's'' academic background. That he obviously had academic credentials seemed to be enough.

"The tax season's coming up," Mr. Joyner said.

"Yes, I know."

"And we need somebody right away."

"I'll come out first. My wife will join me once I get settled."

"You know, of course, that the job is for an entry-level staff accountant."

"Mr. Severeid told me the details."

He never told Joyner that he had an advanced degree or that he was a certified public accountant. Joyner might have thought he was overqualified for an entry-level position. He accepted the staff accountant job at a salary of $24,000.

It was over twenty-two years since John List had accepted a position with the First National Bank in Jersey City at a salary of $25,000. The sum had seemed huge then. Inflation had reduced its buying power.

Delores was very happy when he received the offer of employment in Virginia, even though, at the moment, they could neither rent nor sell the condominium she had bought ten years earlier. She was lonely for the East, tired of the dry heat of Colorado, and hungry for the smell of moisture in the air.

When Delores visited Wanda in the hospital to tell her they were going to move, Wanda was full of stories about all of her medical problems. She hadn't been doing well. A staph infection had taken over her body. "Then they took me in and cut up each square like this, left me open," she told Delores painfully. "And then they turned around and closed it up, and I didn't heal, 'cause, you know, being a diabetic. But since they cut down here, they cut part of my backbone, and so I've got osteoporosis now."

Delores didn't know what she was talking about. It didn't sound right to her, but she didn't want to challenge her. Just telling the story made Wanda tired.

"But I'll be fine and I'll come out and I'll go back to work," Wanda finished. "It's just another one of those things you have to get through. I'm telling you, I've become even more religious since I'm in here. I know I don't look it when I'm smoking." She laughed. She was making Delores laugh. "I'm serious," Wanda continued, always willing to enjoy a moment even in the midst of discomfort. "You too. We shouldn't smoke."

"I know."

"We're defiling our bodies," she said, and burst out laughing again.

Delores laughed with her. Wanda was really so dear to her. They had been close. She would miss her when they moved away.

"But you know," Wanda went on, "back in Arkansas where I come from, my son is an evangelist."

"I didn't know that," Delores said. "Your son. How wonderful."

"Oh, yes," Wanda went on, nodding. "Not Catholic, but a man of God. And there wasn't a day that went by that we didn't have prayer. Usually in the morning. I really do believe in God, in Jesus Christ."

"Of course."

"Frankly," she said in her simple pragmatic manner, "I don't know how anyone can have problems and not be religious."

Delores agreed wholeheartedly.

"Really, where would they get help from?" Wanda asked. "I trust in Him. Thirty-eight years with my sick husband He's been right there for me. By my side and my poor husband's. He doesn't leave."

"You're a good soul," Delores said, smiling at her gently.

Wanda shifted her aching body to another position. "Listen to me go on. You should have stopped me."

"I wanted to hear everything."

"But how about you?" she asked, smiling up at her friend. "Tell me about you. How you doing?"

"Well, I have something to tell you," Delores began quietly. "We've decided to move."

"Move?" This came as a total surprise to Wanda. "That's pretty sudden."

"You know Bob has been sending his résumé everyplace, even out of state."

"Yeah, I know."

"And he hasn't had any luck."

"And now he's got a job?"

"An offer of a good position . . . in Richmond."

All of the old suspicions were suddenly resurrected in the sick woman.

Wanda's mind wandered while she listened. "An accounting job. . . ." Had Delores told Bob about his look-alike, John List? "I'll be so happy to go back east. . . ." Had she ever shown him the tabloid photo of the fugitive? "It's so much closer to my mother. . . ." All of a sudden they're going cross-country like that. "I don't know what we're going to do about the apartment. . . ."

Wanda tried to focus in on what Delores was saying. The apartment . . . They both knew this was a high-risk area. People didn't want to move in.

"And then with all the problems with the FDIC," Delores went on.

He's playing a part, Wanda thought as she tried to concentrate on what Delores was saying. That's probably the whole thing of it. He not only changed his name to Bob Clark, he became Bob Clark, and he no longer thinks he's John List. That's what it is, she thought. It's possible he's not the same person, but if he did commit those murders. . . . well, you can't change into another person. Maybe that's what he's been trying to do. Take on a different name, become a totally different person. But what if the thoughts that led to murder once aren't different? Wanda had never known anyone who could do that, who could change like that and be another person. We all have so many sides to our personalities, she thought, but this is different.

No! she suddenly said to herself, negating her own insights as she smiled up at Delores from her sickbed. It can't be true.

Still, no matter how Wanda tried to talk herself out of thinking that Bob was the fugitive from New Jersey, she couldn't help wondering if the Clarks decided to move so suddenly because of the tabloid photo, if, perhaps, things were closing in.

But Wanda Flanery was alone in her suspicions of Bobby Clark. Delores never asked questions. When they moved, his life in Virginia, as usual, centered around his work, his wife, his garden, his church. He presented himself as a very average man. He was much too ordinary to attract any notice. His very ordinariness was the best cloak to hide the fugitive. He became part of the background, the wallpaper, the scenery. He did not stand out in any way at all. As a fugitive from justice, Robert P. Clark was the opposite of the accepted notions of evil or sin. To all outward appearances he was the quintessential soul of respectability.

33 | Closing In

Richmond, Virginia

You could set your clock by when he went to the john. That's how regular his habits were, Sandra mused to herself.

Sandra Silbermann was the secretary/receptionist for the Virginia accounting firm of Maddrea, Joyner, Kirkham & Woody. She worked in the front office. Just behind her was a wall separating the reception area from the offices of her two bosses, Mr. Joyner and Mr. Kirkham, and the offices of the two staff accountants, young Les Wingfield and the new man, Bob Clark.

Les Wingfield was a CPA. Fast and bright but easygoing, he spoke with the slow, soft drawl of a southern accent that Sandra, who still had a distinctive New York accent, liked so much. Bob Clark was something else. He had a midwestern accent and a deep bass voice with a nasal, stuffed-up quality. And he talked loudly. But it wasn't the sound of his voice that set him apart. He's peculiar, Sandra thought, when she first met him. You could also set your clock by what she thought of as his "watering habits." Every hour on the button, Bob would come out of his office and fill up his Thermos with water at the cooler. When she heard he was fifty-seven years old, younger than she was, she thought he looked older. He might have been very bright once, but she had the feeling "right off the bat" that he was going downhill.

Sandra looked over to where he sat as she passed his office. He was reading again. He was so quiet all the time, she began to wonder if he were on tranquilizers.

She didn't know it was simply that time was passing. He was getting older, and he was beginning to feel it, the aging process only reinforced by the tiredness that overcame him even when he sat at his desk reading something interesting like *Money* magazine.

"You know, those certificates on the wall belonged to the guy who used to be here," she stopped to tell him. "He's dead now."

He glanced up at them and nodded pleasantly.

"You could take them down, put up your own," she suggested.

"That's okay."

"I could do it for you, if you'd like."

"Don't bother. It doesn't matter."

She shrugged and continued on to her desk on the other side of the wall.

Bob Clark had nothing personal in his office.

The man never changed. The same habits flipped through his life as though he were trapped in a time warp. He was methodical, predictable, routine, clean. He saw to it that the bathroom was full of towels and toilet paper, though taking care of such matters was part of the building cleaning service. He became anxious if supplies were low, and he'd ask her to call the supplier to reorder the necessary toilet articles.

She couldn't put her finger on what, exactly, made him seem strange to her. He just didn't seem like a regular guy, not a "with it" guy, as she thought of it. He didn't seem contemporary, that's what it was—not contemporary. Sandra was a Depression child whose husband lost his family at Auschwitz. She was a bit stocky, with short, thinning, tinted red hair, crooked teeth, and a quick laugh that demonstrated an easy ability to enjoy life no matter what hardships came her way. Born and raised in the Tremont and Grand Concourse sections of the Bronx in New York City, Sandra was definitely a "with it" lady with a typical New York Jewish sense of humor. She had three children, all of whom were college graduates with multiple degrees. Whenever she talked of her children and realized she was bragging too much, she added the often repeated but obligatory punch line, "The dumb one only has *two* degrees," and she would burst out laughing.

But despite the fact that she thought Bob Clark a bit strange, Sandra Silbermann grew to like him. Not only did she find him to be thoughtful, considerate, and kind, he was interested in the same things that interested her—gardening, flowers, and health. They both subscribed to *Prevention* magazine, and they often talked about what to eat to avoid getting cancer or heart trouble. He even turned out to be helpful enough to take the postage meter to the post office for her when she hurt her wrist, and they would answer the phone for each other and take each other's messages.

"I like the Jane Fonda exercises," she said to him one day.

"Well, I'm not going to do that," he replied.

"No, but you know what we *can* do?" she suggested. "We can start using the stairs instead of the elevator all the time. It's only one flight."

Les Wingfield shook his head as the two of them began to use the staircase every day. Tall and handsome, only in his late twenties, Les was too young to worry about health. He continued to use the elevator.

In Bob Clark, Sandra had found a co-worker with whom she'd "hit it off," while Bob had found a comfortable working niche in which he developed a warm friendship with the fun-loving Jewish lady from the Bronx.

Sandra knew he was having difficulty running his new home on his salary. She also knew he had bought it with the understanding that his wife would help by getting a job once she joined him from Colorado, but somehow that never seemed to materialize. Two weeks after Bob had come to Virginia to start his job, his wife followed. She couldn't decide what kind of job she wanted. Sandra thought she took her sweet time thinking about it—three or four months, at least—while poor Bob was struggling to the point where he took a part-time job with H&R Block in the evenings to make ends meet. His wife certainly wasn't helping him, Sandra thought, and she found herself giving Delores a quick assessment: she's a nice, gentle woman, very religious and very fragile, but not too swift. "She likes to sit at home and let Bob do everything." Whether it was because Delores was helpless or because Bob was controlling, Sandra never quite knew. It was probably a combination of both. Eventually she came to think that a significant part of their marital style had to do with the fact that he had to plan and control everything.

But Bob was worried about money, Sandra could tell. He had confided to her that he wanted to wait until his wife found steady work before buying the house so he could figure out exactly how much they could afford. Meanwhile, he wanted them to live with Jonah Folger, the man he had been staying with to date, at least until Delores steadied herself into a permanent job. He liked the man. They had become friends. But Delores needed and valued her privacy too much to live with a stranger and insisted they buy their own house immediately. She took a part-time job as a cosmetologist until she had a car accident in which she hurt her finger. The finger required minor surgery, and she was forced to give up her job.

They bought the house she wanted anyway. Sandra knew it was because Bob wanted to please his wife.

In February of 1988, Bob and Delores set up house again. They moved to Midlothian, a suburb fifteen miles southwest of Richmond. They selected a $76,500 three-bedroom, ranch-style house in the development of Brandermill. It was slate blue with a brightly painted red front door. Brandermill was a combination country club–bedroom community where the houses ranged in price from $70,000 to $359,000. There were golf courses, tennis courts, swimming pools, and a beautiful restaurant overlooking the Swift Creek Reservoir. Their house, on the lower economic spectrum of the development, was situated on a tiny wedge-shaped piece of property at the curved end of a cul-de-sac. It was very private and set deep within the development off the main roads.

Bob and Delores could not afford to join Brandermill's clubs even if they had been predisposed to do so. Instead, cloaked in obscurity, they joined the Lutheran Church of Our Savior in Chesterfield County under the ministership of the young Reverend Joseph Vought. Once again they began to lead the very ordinary, prosaic existence that had always marked both of their lives.

Delores stood on the modest porch before the bright red front door upon which hung a heart-shaped wreath of colorful cloth scraps and an Amish plaque reading, "Bless This House." A series of cowbells imbedded in a leather strap were hung from a nail to the left of the door. With a cup of coffee in hand, Delores waved goodbye to Bob every morning as he departed for work. She heard him exchange "good mornings" with the Fergusons next door. Eight-thirty was starting time at Maddrea, Joyner, Kirkham & Woody. He would arrive between eight-ten and eight-fifteen A.M. with the brown paper-bagged lunch Delores prepared for him. Sometimes he ate at his desk. More echoes resounded from the past as he more often sat in his car in the parking lot and ate his lunch to the accompaniment of soft classical music on the radio.

Les Wingfield couldn't help overhearing Bob when he spoke on the phone with his wife, first of all because the offices were close together, and second because Bob spoke very loudly on the phone.

"Did you nap, dear?"

Hard of hearing, Les thought as he passed Bob's office to bring some papers to Sandra at the front desk. Les had a warm, friendly smile, which he flashed at Sandra as they both heard Bob say, "What did you have for lunch?"

Les couldn't help rolling his eyes a bit at Sandra as they unwillingly continued to be privy to Bob's private conversations with his wife.

Sandra nudged Les. "I think it's nice."

"Make sure you eat enough," Bob was saying. "A good nourishing lunch. . . ."

"Listen and learn," Sandra joked in a whisper to the young man towering over her desk. "Did you know he brings her flowers every day?"

"No."

"Well, he does."

"That's nice."

"It looks like rain today, dear," they heard. "Make sure you take your umbrella if you go out."

"Listen," Sandra whispered, "I hold him up to my husband as a model husband because he's so affectionate and so good and understanding and loving to his wife."

"I love you," Bob said before hanging up the receiver.

"You see." She grinned up at Les.

"Well, if you ask me . . ." Les began.

"I don't." Sandra laughed.

"If you ask me," Les persisted, "he should spend less time on the phone with his wife and more time paying attention to his work."

Sandra looked up at him, sobered. "Bad?"

"Pretty sloppy, if you ask me. Take a look at it sometime. Just between you and me," Les finished, "I certainly wouldn't let on to Mr. Joyner, but frankly, I think Bob's overstating his credentials. He makes a lot of mistakes."

Sandra sighed. She hoped it wasn't true. She'd have to pay close attention to the work Bob handed in to determine for herself if Les's harsh assessment were true or merely a mild form of youthful professional jealousy.

The first time Delores stopped in at the office, Sandra and Les couldn't help thinking she was sort of pretty, well kept, kind of nice, very quiet, and much younger than Bob. Maybe it's a father-daughter type relationship, Sandra thought to herself. He seems very protective of her.

Not bad. Les grinned to himself. Bob's doing better than I thought.

Wanda was on the phone calling from Colorado. Delores sighed. She knew what was coming. "So they don't want to rent it?"

Before she and Bob moved to Richmond, there had been talk of Wanda's daughter and her husband renting her empty condo. She was still hopeful that they would take it, but now Wanda told her, "They can't afford it, Delores."

"I don't know what we're going to do," Delores said, beginning once again the litany of familiar complaints. "You know I hurt my finger in that automobile accident and I have to have surgery, and then I'll have to wait until it heals before I can get another job."

"I know."

"And when I first came here I got a job in an army depot just like in Colorado, but it was too far to drive back and forth every day and I had to quit. Now with this surgery coming up and the insurance claims Bob is putting in for, which we don't know if we'll get . . ."

Delores sounded depressed. Wanda knew that Delores was a bit of a complainer, but she got the impression that tensions had seriously mounted. It had been "one thing after another," always having to do with money. Sometimes she even got the feeling Delores was beginning to think that perhaps she had hitched her star to a loser.

"I had two thousand dollars in my savings account," Delores continued, "and we had to use that to move to Virginia. It's just about all gone. And you know my grandmother's clock?"

"Yes."

"Well, it broke en route to Virginia."

"Oh, I'm so sorry to hear that," Wanda said sincerely. "I know how much you loved it."

"I just feel that everything is going wrong," Delores cried softly, "and that our problems have gotten so out of hand, and now the apartment is still unrented . . ."

Wanda hesitated. She didn't want to give Delores any more bad news, but she had to tell her what happened.

"About the apartment," Wanda began.

"Yes?"

"My daughter's kind of glad they didn't agree to take it."

"Why?"

"Well, first because of the money. You know my son-in-law and my daughter and I, we clean private homes. We don't make much, and it's beginning to get too hard for me."

"Oh, Wanda," Delores quickly sympathized, "I know. Especially after your operation."

"We're trying to do better." Wanda sighed. "My daughter, she looks like a kid right now, but she's got a job with a friend as assistant manager in a boutique."

"That sounds easier and like it has more future."

"Not really. It's not much of a boutique." Wanda paused. "Anyway . . ."

Delores waited.

"There was a flood."

"A flood?"

"Well, that's what I really called to tell you about," Wanda explained sadly. "You know the swimming pool above the apartment? Well, something happened when they emptied it, and it flooded your apartment. It was a mess. The kids would have lost just about everything if they had rented it. . . .'' She stopped.

Delores felt as though she would cry. More problems, one right after another. Finally she pulled herself together enough to tell Wanda, ''We still owe about four thousand dollars in back payments.''

Wanda didn't know what to say. ''Look,'' she comforted, ''it'll all work out somehow.'' She thought Delores might be crying. ''Delores? . . .''

''Yes?'' Delores whispered.

''Did you rent a place down there in Virginia?''

''Yes, we did,'' she replied. ''Actually, we bought it. It's very nice.''

That doesn't fit, Wanda thought. Where did they get the money? And then, as usual, she found herself thinking, Hey, it's none of my business.

''We bought the house in my name,'' Delores said, adding to the mystery.

If they could afford to buy a house, why didn't they buy it in both their names? No, something was wrong. There they were again—those nagging doubts still in the back of her head waving the red flag for attention. Wanda wished she didn't feel so uneasy about it, but the doubts refused to dissipate no matter how hard she tried to rationalize them away.

Les was punching numbers into his calculator. He was aware in the deep inattentive recesses of his mind that Bob was on his daily lunchtime call to Delores.

''How can I get it through your head!'' Bob suddenly yelled uncharacteristically into the phone. He sounded very angry.

Les's ears perked up in astonishment. He had never heard Bob speak that way to his wife. What happened to ''dear,'' and ''I love you''? Bob's voice, now controlled to the level of softly whispered words Les could no longer distinguish, had boomed in unchecked rage with a deep-throated resonance that filled the office. Les had never heard him angry before. It was intimidating. He actually found himself thinking a bit uneasily, I'd hate to have him mad at me.

Les remembered that he had often tried to get closer to Bob but had never been able to manage it. They had gone out to lunch a couple of times to the restaurant in the deteriorating Executive Inn around the corner. Bob said scarcely a word as they ate. He always looked as though a part of him were lost somewhere in time, on a plane that didn't exist in the present.

"I used to have an Impala once," he suddenly said one day.

Les waited for him to go on, but he didn't. That was strange. Something's wrong, he thought. An Impala. Where did that come from? He wanted to ask him how he had fallen onto hard times. Why was he an entry-level accountant? A man his age should be a lot further along in his career. He wanted to ask him if he had been in the army, if he had been in World War II or in Korea. He even wanted to ask him if he had ever "taken out a bunch of guys" in the war, because there was something about him, as if he were harboring this deep, dark, secret . . . something! But Bob never talked about guns or war; it was always flowers, weather, food. And Les found that he could never bring himself to ask anything personal no matter how intense the curiosity. There was something about Bob that suggested he believed his personal life was nobody's business but his own.

As they ate in virtual silence, Les found himself looking at the man out of the corner of his eye. Physically there wasn't any reason for him to be afraid of Bob. He was just as tall, and younger, in better shape. But there was that certain indefinable "something" about him.

Les dismissed his own ambiguous unease by telling himself, forget it. He's just a tax preparer.

34 | His Favorite TV Program

The new life List managed to create, imitating so closely the rather wimpy image of his former self, was about to crumble in a most ironic and amazing manner. It would happen with the aid of television itself, through one of Clark's favorite programs, *America's Most Wanted*.

* * *

Early in 1989 Frank Marranca, captain of investigators in the Union County Prosecutor's Office, was feeling particularly frustrated that no progress had been made on the List case after so many dead-end leads had been pursued. In April of 1988 he happened to catch a new program on Fox television, *America's Most Wanted*, which focused attention on what the producers described as America's most notorious fugitive criminal cases. In the hope that List might still be alive, Marranca wanted to enlist the help of the program in finding List.

"You've got to be kidding," an associate of his said. "That's nothing but trash television for the couch potatoes."

"What do I care?" Marranca asserted calmly. "We aren't doing so hot. It's been eighteen years. I'll take whatever help we can get, whether it's trash television, media-inspired vigilantism, or somebody standing on the street corner waving a sign, saying, 'This way to John List.'"

His direct superior, Prosecutor John Stamler, thought the idea was worth following through. He gave Marranca official clearance to send *America's Most Wanted* all the information the office had on the case. The producers sent back a letter saying that until they could see how well their show was airing, they weren't sure they could take such an old case.

Six months later, in January of 1989, Captain Marranca learned that Michael Lindner, one of the executive producers of *America's Most Wanted*, was going to be a speaker at the Eastern Regional Armed Robbery Conference in Delaware. Once again Marranca spoke to Stamler, who again gave him and Sergeant Jeffrey Hummel the go-ahead to take the List file to the conference and meet the representatives from the show.

After Michael Lindner gave his presentation at the conference, Marranca and Hummel brought Lindner up to their room, sat down with him, and explained the case with the entire bulging file of police reports, photographs, and newspaper clippings spread out across the beds.

"We feel that List's still alive," Marranca told Lindner, "living somewhere in the Midwest under an assumed name, probably remarried, probably working as either an insurance salesman or accountant. We also think that without the help of a program like *America's Most Wanted*, we probably won't be in the position to apprehend him."

"We feel sure he's had no more police contact since the actual homicides," Hummel added.

America's Most Wanted, which weekly reenacted two or three true crime stories on its Sunday night slot, was viewed by a nationwide audience of at least twenty million people. There was no other way the FBI could have reached that many people so directly. Often the crimes depicted were brutal. Hundreds of viewers, eager to have a direct participation in the manhunts for these notorious fugitives, became virtual bloodhounds. They willingly responded to the dramatized reenactments of the crimes and called the hotline with "tips" and "leads" based on the "mug shots" shown on the air.

"These pictures are old," Lindner said, shaking his head. "From 1971. Even the New Jersey State police composite dates back to 1983."

"It's all we have," Marranca said.

"I'll get back to you."

Margaret Roberts, managing editor of *America's Most Wanted*, thought the most notorious crime in New Jersey's history was a perfect candidate for dramatization on the program. Even with the problem of not having a recent photo, it was a go.

America's Most Wanted dealt with the big crimes. The little crimes that created such desperation in the lives of the affected victims still often went unnoticed. When Delores called Wanda to wish her a happy Mother's Day, she added that she was still very depressed about the condo. "We're very desperate for money," she told her old friend. "The apartment is going to rob us of everything we own. Bob gets annoyed with me, I know," she added, "but I've been very depressed over all this. I can't help it. It's ruining us."

Financial trouble had continued to follow and plague the Clarks. Delores, always the worrier, was becoming more vocal to Bob about her depression over the apartment. He usually said nothing, not even when he knew she kept calling and writing to Wanda Flanery. He would have preferred to cut Wanda out of their lives completely.

"You're lucky to be out of here," Wanda told her. "Things are worse than ever."

"What do you mean?" What could possibly be worse than the flood? she wondered.

Wanda spoke with a resignation that was astonishing considering the continual despair of her own life. "You remember my daughter, Anne?" she asked.

"Yes. Of course."

"Anne was assaulted by two guys and then strangled."

"Oh, my God."

"They left her there, thought she was dead. Why she ever went out at that time of night I don't know."

"Oh, Wanda," Delores said, suddenly ashamed that she was so worried about money in the face of the tragedy Wanda was recounting.

"This man who had lived next door to them over here in the same complex," Wanda continued, almost emotionless. "His girlfriend was still there, and they had a little boy. The boyfriend didn't live there, but he'd come in at night and beat her, and the baby would be crying. Finally Anne got tired of all the screaming, and she called the police. He knew it was Anne who called them. He still had that on his mind."

"So you think that's who did it?" Delores asked, appalled at what Wanda was telling her.

"Oh, we know," Wanda said. "They got him. But since it's this area, they blamed it on drugs. And Anne couldn't prove anything, and she didn't report it right away, anyway."

"I don't know what to say," Delores said, her own problems considerably subdued in the wake of Wanda's. She felt ashamed talking about money when things were so terrible for Wanda and her daughter.

"That's okay. She's starting to come around now," Wanda sighed. "All kinds of problems, and everyone has them, I know that. I understand. We never walk in each other's shoes, so we all think our problems are the worst. We just have to make the best of it."

"Bless you," was all Delores could think to say in the wake of such a sad story. And then, "Wanda? . . ."

"Yes?"

"I love you."

"I love you, too, Delores. And don't worry. Things will work out fine."

"What's the rate of success?" Captain Marranca asked Margaret Roberts of *America's Most Wanted* as they went over all the information on the fugitive.

"It's been pretty good," she said proudly. "We started airing only fifteen months ago. Since then, we've dramatized and profiled something like a hundred and fifty fugitives, give or take a couple. More than half have been caught. About eighty. And almost fifty of them were a direct result of tips that came into our hotline."

"That's a pretty good average," Marranca commented.

"We like to think so." Ms. Roberts smiled. "Then there was the guy who escaped from a California jail for kidnapping and jewel theft. Our hotlines got him in May in Rapid City, South Dakota. And do you remember the suspect who was accused of torturing and killing twelve people in Mexico?"

"Rings a bell."

"It was all drug-related. He was apprehended in Arizona just this past April."

"I'm impressed," Marranca said.

"But we've got a problem with this List case, not having an updated photo of him."

The murders were almost eighteen years old. The precious few photos of John List were at least twenty years old. "Our show hinges on the indelible image of the human face," she said. "Or to put it another way, the mug shot."

"So now what?"

Then Michael Lindner came up with the idea of a bust. Deciding on a daring experiment, he turned to Frank Bender, an artist and forensic sculptor from Philadelphia, Pennsylvania, to make a life-size bust of the wanted man, using old photographs and attempting to depict what List might look like today.

"Do you think it will work?" Marranca asked with an excited grin at the prospect.

Lindner shrugged. "Never know 'til we try it. We've never done it quite like this before. But it's worth a shot."

Frank Bender was a forty-seven-year-old commercial photographer and sculptor who specialized in creating busts of fugitives for authorities. He had a finely shaped goatee that always pointed toward his work and thick eyebrows that pointed upward. His eyes were sharp, piercing, and testified to good humor. Bender remembered the case only vaguely.

"Think you can sculpt a likeness of him as he would look today, twenty years after the last photograph," Ms. Roberts asked him, "if we give you all the information we've received from the police?"

"Sure," he said easily, privately feeling the weight of responsibility. All he had to work with was a 1971 photograph, a computerized "update," and a police description. "It's a challenge," he told her, "but I've worked on harder projects."

Forensic sculpture was a sideline to his chosen profession as a commercial photographer and painter. The unusual avocation had started quite by accident in 1977. He had accompanied a friend's girlfriend on a tour through the Philadelphia Medical Examiner's Office and the Philadelphia morgue while she fingerprinted unidentified bodies. One body waiting for identification was that of a murdered woman who had been shot three times through the head at point-blank range. Because of advanced decomposition, identification was virtually impossible. More in the line of "artistic" experimentation at the time than any devotion to civic duty, Bender offered to sculpt a bust based on his own conception of the woman's features. A circulated photograph of the completed bust led to identification of the victim by a New Jersey detective who had her "Missing Person" on file.

The newly born physiognomic reconstructionist suddenly found his services in greater demand than he ever would have anticipated. He earned only between $100 and $200 per sculpture; but he was eager and enthusiastic about this part of his work, knowing that it frequently helped, not only in capturing fugitives, but in identifying murder victims as well. He often worked directly with human skulls on his kitchen table in Philadelphia, a slightly ghoulish touch. Now another one. Mr. John Emil List. Good.

Bender turned to a friend, Richard D. Walter, a criminal psychologist from Michigan, for help in fleshing out the psychological puzzle of List.

Walter came to Philadelphia, and while the two men walked through the city, stopped for coffee, and wandered in and out of antique shops, they tried to reconstruct a man who would kill his family. All psychological indications supported an assumption that since the fugitive was so rigid in his approach to life, he would not be likely to have had plastic surgery. He would probably continue his life pretty much as before—even the same occupation, the same kinds of clothes, similar eyeglasses; would probably remain the simple, meat-and-potatoes guy he had always been; would not be a likely prospect for health foods, jogging, working out in a gym, or any of the activities that might keep him looking young. They knew List was a worrier and often reacted to stress with twitching and red flushes. Nerves, tension, and stress were strong aging factors. It was obvious from the photo supplied by Ms. Roberts that List's hairline had already begun to recede when he was forty-six. The loss of hair would have progressed farther back, leaving a very high forehead and a partially bald cranium. He would have sagging jowls and a downturned, saddened look. The two men even tried to decide what color socks List might wear. "Dark," said Walter.

Working the bust on a well-used, waist-high bench stained with the drippings from years of earlier works, Bender had no certainty that the psychological profile was accurate, but he had a gut feeling it was pretty close. He stared again at the face of John List. He had to keep reminding himself that this sweet-faced, gentle-looking Mr. Nice Guy had pumped bullets into the brains of his three children. What kind of a guy would do something as rotten as that? Bender's jaw set in determination. The clay in his hands was like a mold into which to pour the truth; the sculpting tool was like the sword of an avenging angel; the developing model was balanced on the scale of Justice. He was going to get this guy!

John List's two-dimensional smiling face watched from his photograph as the reconstruction slowly progressed and the model, set on a turntable stand only inches away, took on a third dimension. The artist worked skillfully with all the tools of his art—clay, form, erasers, brushes, paint—but mostly with perception, intuition, sensitivity, and creative fervor, all the intangible qualities that have their roots deep within the soul of the artist.

Standing at her living room window, Wanda had a clear view of the patio where she and Delores used to go to smoke when Bob's asthma drove them outdoors. She held Delores's latest letter in her hand. Obviously things hadn't gotten any better for the Clarks. Wanda shook her head sadly and shared the contents of Delores's letter with her other daughter, Eva, who was sitting on the couch staring at the television. "All their money problems just won't go away," Wanda told her. "She's lost everything, Eva. And she doesn't know what she's going to do."

"What do you mean, lost everything?" Eva asked, glancing up from the TV news.

"The bank foreclosed on the apartment."

"Oh, wow. That's too bad."

"You know what gets me?" Wanda said softly, the same old suspicions haunting her thoughts about her friend.

"What?"

"You know she'd been working here at Fitzsimmons for ten years."

"Yeah."

"And she only had a couple more years to go before retiring and getting a pension from them," she continued, quietly building up her case.

"So?"

"So why'd she quit before it came due? She even lost her pension by leaving so sudden. Now that don't make sense for working people to give up a pension like that and move halfway across the United States. Does it?"

There was no compelling evidence of any crime besides a look-alike photo in a cheap newspaper. There was just the compelling nagging of her own troubling intuition.

"You know, Eva," she mused, "I've always thought I was a little psychic."

Eva grimaced with the memory of teenage years under her mother's watchful eye. "Well, you always knew what *I* was up to."

No one ever sat on that patio anymore, Wanda thought, staring out of the window. She missed Delores.

"I wish I wasn't," she said. "Psychic, I mean. . . ."

Here he was in Virginia again, and still he was free. The disquieting possibility of his being apprehended had long since ceased to be a major worry. Coming back to Virginia just cinched his sense of security. So Bob didn't look upon it as getting careless when he told Sandra Silbermann he had originally come from Michigan. He even told her in the course of their many discussions about health, "There was a time when I had Bell's palsy."

"Really?" she said. "That's awful. How'd that happen?"

"I don't know. One doctor told me it was nerves."

"Whenever they don't know what causes something," she scoffed, "they blame it on nerves."

"It left me partially paralyzed on the side of my face."

"That would scare me to death," Sandra sympathized. "Could you still talk?"

"Yes. A bit distorted."

"How long did it last? The paralysis, I mean."

"Oh . . ." He tried to think. He couldn't remember exactly. "A while."

Sandra Silbermann frequently confided in him, too. She told him her personal problems, especially those that involved her three children. She had a girl and two boys who were the same age John List's children would have been had they lived to maturity. He never avoided the topic. In fact, he offered advice.

"You know, if you have children, you have problems," he said.
"You never had any?"

"No," he said easily. "Not even with my first wife."

"I didn't know you were married before," she said, surprised.

"Yes," he said, suddenly changing the story he had been telling everyone up to now—even Delores—that his wife had died of cancer. "I'm divorced," he said. "I adopted the daughter of my first wife, but that was a long time ago." For the first time in years Bob felt completely safe. He even told Sandra, in passing, that he had lived in New Jersey once.

Completely safe. What he didn't know was that he was in jeopardy of losing his job.

Again.

The progress of Frank Bender's work came through a series of trials and errors. There were no guidelines or rules to follow. There were no textbooks with charts. He tacked up enlarged photos of John List's face and lived daily with the face of the murderer. It continued to smile gently at him as he worked on his reconstruction.

Frank had achieved what he considered to be the right skin thickness by pressing and gluing erasers onto the raw skull model of the face. Then, using the photograph as a guideline, he filled in the spaces of the face around the erasers with the soft, pliable gray clay. He impressed the character of the man into the image as he pressed the pliable gray clay into the spaces around the erasers. A meat-and-potatoes man . . . not an exercise freak . . . let's sag those jowls.

He was closing in on the likeness of an aging John List. He was sure he had it: the long scar from the mastoid operation running behind the right ear all the way down to the collar line; the left ear protruding from the head farther than the right ear; grayed hair and the consistently worn suit and tie; the heaviness of the eyelids of a sixty-three-year-old man; the horn-rimmed glasses he always wore; the sweet-soft shape of his mouth turned down at the corners with age; the sagging jowls. After the head was finished, Bender made a plaster mold that he filled with fiberglass. Finally he smoothed the rough parts of the face with sandpaper and carefully painted it with human tones.

* * *

By now Les Wingfield had lost respect for Clark's abilities as an accountant. Les felt you could really tell what people were like when you worked with them day in and day out. You could really see them for what they were. He went over Bob's work. It was full of errors and sloppy. It convinced him that the man was lying about his credentials. Clients had to be billed based on the amount of time spent on their accounts, so it was all right there, he thought. He'd be in his office working away on his calculator while Bob would be at his desk reading a book.

Les didn't feel about Bob as Sandra did and wouldn't have minded if the company let him go, but he didn't think the company had a firm policy regarding the firing of an employee. They might ice him out. He tried to warn Bob, but Bob laughed when Les commented on the way he wrote. He looked over his shoulder and said, "This handwriting of yours," Les drawled, "why, it could be that of a mass murderer."

"Really?" Bob asked, looking up.

"I swear"—Les laughed with him—"but what do I know?"

Sandra knew Les was right. Bob's work wasn't always accurate. Not only were there lots of mistakes, but it was messy and frequently smudged besides. She had to make corrections to fix it up. She tried to cover up for him.

Les only suspected the bosses wanted to get rid of Bob; she knew it for a fact. She knew they had already started the process of freezing him out by giving him less and less work to do. It wasn't long before Bob got the message that something was wrong, and he seriously began to worry about losing his job . . . again.

Sandra noticed that his insecurity began to manifest itself in blotchy cheeks and an occasional twitching of his lower lip. She knew it would be a devastating financial blow. Even with his salary, he couldn't make ends meet. Last year, when the time came for company raises, he wasn't given one.

"Do you think I should go in and ask them about it?" he asked her anxiously.

She didn't know how to tell him. "I don't know," she said, pained that she had to be so evasive with her friend. "Maybe not. If they had been able to give you a raise . . ."

"They never seem to be around."

How could she tell him that his employers were avoiding him because they were not happy with his work, that they weren't talking to him because they were freezing him out, that they were hoping their quiet strategy would force him to quit?

He tried very hard. He was so anxious to make sure his work

was right that he often shared it with Sandra for advice and corrections. But despite his anxieties, he still nodded and dozed off at his
desk. His eyes were taking on the bleached look of advancing years.
He couldn't control the slowing-down process. Then he stopped by
her desk one day. He had a faraway look in his eyes as he told her
the bank in Colorado had sent a notification that they had foreclosed
on the condominium he and his wife owned.

I'd be desperate, she thought. He seems so removed, almost as
though it were happening to someone else.

Frank Bender was finally satisfied with the bust. He turned it over
to Michael Lindner of *America's Most Wanted*. It was very gratifying
to see that everyone seemed extremely pleased with it.

"Here we go," Lindner said.

The script had already been researched and written. They began
preparations to air the program. It had taken five months from the
first concept to the actual airing.

35 | Unmasked

Sunday Night—May 21, 1989

The show had all the components for good, sensational television,
beginning with the man himself—a man who would slaughter his
own family. He was a wife killer, a mother killer, and a multiple
child killer. The story had sharp elements of the unexpected—the
killer was not a wild-eyed Manson-type killer who had spent more
than half his life in and out of reform schools and jails; he was an
accountant and Sunday-school teacher who had led an unmemorable
existence and who had, throughout his lifetime, given every indication of being a wimp. It had the melancholy drama of sincere
religiosity gone awry—fanatically warped Christian beliefs that had
put the deadly sword of self-righteous punishment in the hands of
a professed man of God. It had a contemporary morality lesson in
the story of a man who had reached too high up the financial ladder,

way beyond his capabilities, and wound up reaching only the level of his own incompetence.

The story even had an exciting background against which to play: that of the late sixties with hippies, the hippie movement, drugs, Vietnam, long hair, tie-dyes, and death with the peace symbol hovering in the background. Finally, it had the incredible mystery of a disappearance that had frustrated law enforcement agencies throughout the country and world for eighteen long years. "The oldest case we've ever pursued on *America's Most Wanted*," the announcer said.

It had everything! It even offered the sense of having the fugitive right there in the studio, as the announcer stood over Bender's thirteen-inch, ten-pound plaster bust, saying, "There's a scar behind his right ear from a mastoid operation that runs right down to his collar line. . . ."

No one who was connected with the show could possibly know, as the image was projected over the air, that Bender's reconstruction was incredibly accurate in its likeness. The only difference was in the expression of the man's mouth. The real John List of 1989 was even more forlorn and morose in expression than the bust Bender had created.

Although there were inaccuracies in the scenario of the killings, the segment on John Emil List made a great show.

The important thing was—would it work.

Frank Bender watched the program with anxious excitement. The dichotomy of a man who had always been a deeply religious, community-oriented man turning killer had not escaped him. He had struggled hard to get the "Mr. Nice Guy" component in his plaster depiction of the killer. His work would have to be "right on" in order to lead to any positive identification. He knew that if his reconstruction had depicted a real "sleaze bag," more people would probably have called in to the TV program's hotline. But Mr. Nice Guy here . . . Bender was afraid they'd say, "It looks a lot like a guy I know, but it couldn't possibly be."

He was wrong. Over three hundred people called in after the Sunday night reenactment of the five murders. Two hundred of the calls received were substantive enough to warrant investigation. One of the callers was from an anonymous viewer in the Richmond, Virginia, area who said the bust looked very much like an accountant in Midlothian, Virginia. The correct occupation . . .

Now they just had to wait.

* * *

America's Most Wanted was one of Bob Clark's favorite television programs. He watched it every Sunday night. He told his neighbors, the Stefanos, to watch it. Sometimes Bob and Delores viewed it together with the Stefanos. Bob liked to make deductions on the crimes brought to view. The strategies were sometimes similar to those used in the Civil War board games that Bob had introduced to his neighbor as a way of spending a pleasant evening.

As luck would have it—luck finally favoring the side of justice—Bob and Delores went to a church social the Sunday evening of May 21 and missed the airing of the show that featured the List family killings. Bob had no idea that the story depicting the dark underbelly of his life had been aired on 129 Fox network stations that went into the homes of twenty-two million viewers. One of the homes was a little one-bedroom condo on Peoria Street, a crime-ridden section of Aurora, Colorado. It would generate the "tip" that tipped the scale.

Wanda Flanery, her daughter, Eva, and her son-in-law, Randy Mitchell, sat in the little living room on the sofa facing the TV. When the man on television started talking about John List, Wanda's ears perked up. "That's the guy I saw in the newspaper!" she exclaimed. "The same guy! Just like Bob Clark."

"You must be kidding," Randy said with a distasteful twist of his mouth. "It can't be the same guy. . . ."

"Shh . . ."

"John had a devout religious upbringing as an only child, in a very strong religious family," the announcer on television was saying.

"Just like Bob!" Wanda said.

"It was not a phony. It was a practicing faith. . . ."

"Yes . . . that's right. Yes . . ."

"Mom," Eva said, wide-eyed, "you really think it could be? The picture they showed *does* look a little like him. . . ."

"Shh. Watch."

"List couldn't keep up with his financial failures," the man continued.

"Well, that sure repeats a pattern," Wanda commented in a quick whisper. "Bob's the same way. And they're both accountants."

All three of them continued to watch with avid interest as the five murders were slowly reenacted for the benefit of the television audience.

"Wow, that's pretty gruesome," Eva said. "You think Bob Clark could have really done something as awful as that? Bob Clark?" Suddenly she found her eyes tearing.

"I don't know," Wanda said, shaking her head. "It all seems so impossible, but . . ."

Then the picture of the Bender bust came onto the screen.

"That's Bob!" both Wanda and Eva yelled at the same time. Eva burst into tears. Wanda's heart was pounding, and she felt chilled.

"These photos show how List appeared in 1970," the announcer was summing up. "Naturally List has aged quite a bit. He'll be sixty-four years old this September."

"That's about right." Wanda nodded vehemently.

"Forensic sculptor Frank Bender has reconstructed this bust based on List's cranial structure. We've progressed his balding pattern, and we believe he's gray. . . ."

"No! She colored his hair!" Wanda blurted out to the face on the screen.

"There's a scar behind his right ear from a mastoid operation, runs right down to the collar line. . . ."

"Did you ever see that?" Randy demanded, unconvinced. Things didn't happen like that. Not to people like them. This guy everyone's looking for living next door and going to church all the time? Come on! He thought the program was probably a phony, anyway.

"Yes. I'm positive I have. Eva?"

"I don't know," she said with uncertainty. She wasn't sure about the scar, but she was sure that it was the same man, anyway.

"If you know anything about John List, call 1-800-CRIME89," came the final appeal. "It's a free and confidential call."

Wanda got up and walked over to the television, thinking. Slowly she clicked it off. "We've got to call," she said thoughtfully. "It's Bob. I've always known it."

"It can't be," Randy insisted.

"I know it's Bob," Wanda insisted with equal vigor. "We've go to call up."

"What if you're wrong?"

"They'll know it."

"It don't seem right, turning in someone you know," Eva said unhappily. "And Delores . . . what about Delores?"

"What if I'm right?" Wanda asked, searching into their faces.

They looked at each other as their minds raced quickly over the gruesome details of the program they had just seen.

"I'm sad and scared for Delores," Wanda said. "But if it is Bob

...I don't say people can't change, and maybe God will forgive Bob. But he has to pay for what he did."

Randy looked at their sad, worried faces, and thought he'd better do something. He picked up the phone. "She's right, Eva," he said. "What was that number?"

"Uh . . . 1-800-CRIME89."

They watched him as he dialed.

"I'm calling about the List thing you just had on the air," he said into the receiver.

He listened for a moment.

"Well, we think we know the guy. Is there any reward?"

He listened and began shuffling his feet back and forth in irritation. Wanda and Eva looked at each other. They could tell that Randy was getting miffed. "Is there?" he demanded over the phone.

"What is it?" Wanda whispered anxiously. "What are they saying?"

"Well," Randy said, his voice raised a notch with the anger of disappointment. "You don't really want to know where he is, do you?" And he hung up.

"Randy, what happened?"

"They're not talking about any reward or anything. Why should I stick my neck out for nothing?"

"Randy, will you call back!" Wanda insisted.

"If you don't, I will," Eva added.

Reluctantly Randy Mitchell called the hotline number on the TV screen again. He gave them the telephone number and address of the Robert Clarks in Midlothian, Virginia, which Wanda read out to him from the back of the envelope of Delores's last letter.

The phone call cost them the privacy of their little world. From that moment on they became unwilling celebrities. Channel 9 called. Channel 7 came by. Newspaper people with photographers popped in, reporters and writers called to ask for interviews. Everyone wanted to know Wanda's story about her relationship with the Clarks and, in particular, about her friendship with Delores.

36 | Gotcha!

It was approximately ten o'clock on the morning of Thursday, June 1, 1989.

Kevin August headed the team of four FBI agents from the Richmond office of the FBI. Acting on the tip generated by the *America's Most Wanted* program, the four went to the little slate blue ranch at 13919 Sagewood Trace, deep in the Brandermill development in Midlothian, Virginia, home of Mr. and Mrs. Robert P. Clark.

They were greeted at the door by Delores.

"My name is Kevin August," the young black man with the thin mustache said as he showed her an identifying badge. "These are my associates. We're from the Federal Bureau of Investigation."

Delores's heart began to pound. The FBI. At her door.

"What can I do for you?" she murmured.

"We're looking for a Mr. Robert Clark."

"My husband."

"Is he here?"

"No. He's working. Is something wrong?" she asked, turning pale.

August wanted to break the news to her gently. When they informed her they were looking for a man who had murdered his family in New Jersey, her thoughts flashed to an image of the tabloid Wanda Flanery had shown her before they'd left Colorado. This again. It had come back to haunt her. She had not wanted to deal with it the last time the specter of this crime had penetrated her simple life, when Wanda had shown her the awful story about "that man" in New Jersey. Why was this happening again? It sent her fleeing through the memories of the past as though chased by demons screaming at her, "Now you *have* to stop here. Now you *have* to look at what happened."

She opened the door wider to admit them into her home—into her modest little world that was about to collapse.

"There can't possibly be any connection between my husband and this man," she said weakly. "Look, I'll show you...."

Silence followed her as she went to get their framed wedding photograph.

She had waved to Bob from the front porch only a few hours earlier. When they spoke on the phone a half hour ago, he had said nothing. No warning. Nothing different. "I'm getting all the papers together for the insurance claim," he had said. Their lives were the same that morning as they had been yesterday morning and every morning since she could remember. She was momentarily soothed by the familiar territory of habit as the memory of this day, begun like every other with the ritual of devotions after breakfast, swept over her. She picked up the photograph, looked at it deeply for a moment, and then went back to the waiting agents.

She showed the wedding picture to them. "This is my husband," she said, her eyes begging Mr. August to tell her it was all a dreadful mistake. Her heart pounded. She waited for him to tell her about the mistake.

"It was taken in 1985. November. When we married."

But the photo merely reinforced Mr. August's conviction that the two men—John List and Robert Clark—were one and the same. Some investigators had quietly believed he would never be found or that, at the very least, they would have to wait for some old guy to come up with a deathbed confession saying that he was John List. Now, as they passed the photograph among them, they nodded their heads. The same mouth, the same eyes, the same jawline, the same-shaped head, the same glasses, and, of course, the same profession. Mr. August was already beginning to relish the sense of discovery. The agents were certain that they had finally found their man, that they were the ones who were going to bring in the fugitive who had been on the FBI's "Ten Most Wanted" list for almost eighteen years. It was a tremendous coup. Mr. August repressed the surging sense of excitement as he pulled out the FBI flyer with the 1971 John List photos and the police description. He showed it to the woman.

That was when Delores Clark began to tremble. She looked at the FBI flyer. She denied the unwanted surge of recognition. Was this the man she'd married? No. It isn't, she told herself, but aloud she said weakly, "It could be him."

"Calm down, calm down," Mr. August told her gently, suddenly feeling sorry for the distraught woman. "This is only an inquiry. These identifications are usually mistakes."

Although Delores reacted with disbelief, she tried to overcome her shock and be as cooperative as possible. She wanted to be helpful in resolving questions about Bob's identity, if only to prove they were wrong.

"Where does he work?" Mr. August asked.

There was only the briefest hesitation before she gave them the address of Maddrea, Joyner, Kirkham & Woody.

"I'll call to tell him . . . ," she began.

"No," he said gently.

Leaving one agent with Delores to ensure that she would not call her husband before they reached the accounting firm, Mr. August and his partners went to find the man they were convinced was John List.

When the front door closed behind them, Delores sat down. As she gripped the imprisoning arms of an easy chair, she wondered fleetingly whether Bob would ever walk through the front door of their home again. She realized it was premature to ruminate along such lines. She tried to keep her thoughts in the middle of the road, straying neither toward wild despair on one side nor toward total negation on the other. She began quietly to pray.

The agent who remained behind kept himself unobtrusive as he waited with her.

It was ten minutes after eleven in the morning. The two owners, Joyner and Kirkham, had just left for Charlotte. The only people in the office were Sandra Silbermann, Les Wingfield, and Bob Clark. Sandra sat alone at the front desk, Les was in his office, and Bob was in the back photocopying some papers for his insurance claims.

Sitting in his office, Les heard the door open. He didn't pay attention.

"Who's in charge?"

"I'm the secretary," Sandra said. "Can I help you?"

"We're from the Federal Bureau of Investigation."

Les looked up when he heard the male voice identifying himself as FBI. Maybe they want my prints or something, Les found himself thinking. Or maybe they don't want to talk to me. Maybe Bob.

"Does Robert Clark work here?" he heard.

"Yes. Shall I get him for you?" Sandra asked, rising. Had Bob committed some little white-collar crime or something? He had some money problems, she knew.

"Where is he?" the agent asked.

"In the back running off some copies. I'll get him."

"No." He stopped her. "Is there a back exit?"

"No," she answered, frowning. This kind of precaution for a white-collar crime?

Les knew something unusual was going on. He stood up, waited, and listened. Something cautioned him not to go outside his office to investigate. Surprisingly, he found himself thinking, I don't want to get shot.

"Can I ask what's going on?" he heard Sandra say.

"Where is the copier?"

Sandra gave the agent a puzzled glance before turning her head toward the shuffling sound coming down the hallway. She knew Bob was on his way back from the copier. "That's him."

They heard approaching footsteps in the hallway. The three of them separated, spreading out in the small reception room. Kevin August gently moved Sandra out of the way.

Bob entered.

He became immediately alert when he saw the men. He looked at them and instinctively braced himself against the truth. Reality was seductive even to those who wished to bury it in denial. He found himself waiting. Before they could say anything, he held out the piece of paper he had been holding toward Sandra. She reached for it. One of the agents took it out of his hand and handed it to Sandra, once again moving her away.

Thoughts were racing through her mind. She couldn't get over it. They behaved as though they thought Bob were dangerous. She tried to catch Bob's eyes, but they were now focused on Kevin August.

"Are you John List?" he asked.

He blinked. It had taken him a moment to realize the full significance of the question. "Are you John List?"

"No, I'm not," said Bob.

Then it all happened very quickly. The three agents grabbed him and turned him toward the wall dividing the reception area from the rest of the offices.

Sandra gasped.

Bob didn't really seem surprised. He didn't say a word. A melancholy look of defeat clouded his eyes as his wrists were pulled behind his back and clamped with the cold steel of handcuffs.

Les leaned forward to listen. When he heard the click of handcuffs, he came out of his office. He saw that they had Bob up against the wall right outside his office with his hands behind him. He looked wide-eyed at the black man. The man looked back at him before turning back to Bob.

"Do you have a mastoid scar?"

"Yes."

"Have you had a hernia operation?"

"Yes." That was all he said.

"The scars match up," Kevin said to one of the other agents.

While one of the other FBI agents took Sandra into Mr. Joyner's office, another remained behind to check out the top of Bob's desk. The hurry to get to Maddrea was over. The hurry to leave was over. They wanted to make sure they had overlooked nothing. Les stood in the door and watched as the man scanned Bob's desk.

"What'd he do?" Les asked

"Murdered five people."

"Bob?"

Les realized the FBI agents were looking for a copy of Clark's handwriting, his résumé, documents . . . anything. He didn't know if they had a search warrant, but he didn't really care. Not if the guy had committed murder. He looked back again at Bob standing up against the wall. It surprised Les that Bob offered no negation of the charges against him. Les half expected Bob to be telling everyone that none of it was true, that he didn't know why this nightmare was happening to him, but he remained mute and malleable. Les turned to follow Sandra into Joyner's office. He suddenly wanted to talk to her very badly, but he stayed at the door while the agent showed her the FBI printout about a man called List who had murdered five people. He could see she was in a state of shock. Les didn't know what *he* was in as he stared at them through the door.

Sandra almost fell over as she read the flyer. She read it several times. It wasn't sinking in even though the words jumped off the page at her:

> *List, who is charged with multiple murders involving members of his family, may be armed and should be considered very dangerous.*

Dangerous? Bob? She was completely astonished. So *that*'s why they had moved her aside, she realized. They must have thought he had a gun. She couldn't get that to register, either. Bob with a gun? It was almost laughable.

When she came out into the reception area again, Bob was still against the wall. She looked at him, trying to catch his eye. He was subdued. No protest. She realized he was just doing whatever they told him to do. He didn't look at her.

"We'll be taking him out now."

"Wait," Sandra said. "His hands . . . he's got handcuffs on. He can't put his coat on."

Les realized she was worried about Bob.

"What?" one of the agents asked.

"Can you take his jacket?" Sandra said. "It may be cool."

"If it's not him, he'll be back for his jacket before lunch."

She was standing close to Bob as they began to usher him to the door. As the FBI agents led him out of the office, he stopped a moment to turn and look at Sandra. It was a look she had never seen before on Clark's face. His expression was full of rage. She found herself actually thinking it was like "the look of murder." Was he angry at her? Did he think she had turned him in? Or was it that he didn't have his glasses on and she'd never seen him without his glasses? Why doesn't he have his glasses on? she wondered.

As the FBI agents took him out to the small elevator, she and Les stood in the doorway and watched. She found herself thinking, He'll never step through the door of this office again.

The Symphonie Mélancolique sounded softly in the background from a corner of Bob's office as the elevator door slowly closed.

Les went back into his office to look out of the window facing the parking lot downstairs while Sandra dialed her desk phone to try to get in touch with the bosses in Charlotte. She knew it was too soon; they wouldn't be there yet, but that didn't stop her from trying. It was something to do.

Holding on to his elbows, the agents walked Bob past the "No Soliciting" sign on the wide double-glass door entrance . . . flanked by evergreens . . . three broad concrete steps down . . . a final look at Circuit City Stores to the left . . . the Maryland Building straight across the parking lot.

"My car," he said softly. "It's in parking spot number thirty-seven."

They didn't respond.

Bob glanced at the cream-colored, low-slung J. C. Penney building just across the street at the far end of the mall as they led him underneath the deck where they had parked their own cars. He was supposed to stop there on the way home to buy some mulch. They had the best price of all the places he had checked.

They put him in the backseat with one agent while Mr. August got in front. The other agent stepped into the second car parked directly behind the first.

August looked in the rearview mirror as he turned the key in the ignition. He could see a tear sliding down the face of the man in the backseat.

This is the guy, he thought. He's crying already. He's caught, and he knows it. The man never even asked what the charge was. The first thing an innocent man does is ask what the charge is. An innocent man doesn't usually cry. He may get plenty scared, but he's usually outraged at a false arrest, and he damn well wants to know why!

From his window on the first floor, Les couldn't see Clark and the agents get into the cars, but he saw them pull out as they finally left the shelter underneath the building and slowly wound past the automatic newspaper dispensers and the Federal Express and U.S. postal drops at the end of the mall on the right. It was only a fifteen-minute car ride to Grace Street, where the local FBI offices were located.

Bob Clark had two options—to admit to being John List or to deny it. Confronted with the truth for the first time in eighteen years, he chose to dig his heels in and deny. "My name is Robert Clark," he suddenly asserted from the backseat of the car.

"We'll put it to the test of fingerprints," August said quietly. "It won't take long."

"I ought to know who I am," he insisted doggedly.

Then he became quiet again as the car headed toward the center of town.

Fingerprints! All of the debris from his past was about to bury him. He was inwardly surprised that the arrest had come as such a jolt to him. He had eluded apprehension for so long, he had almost convinced himself he was invincible. He had been able to stage a total disappearance. It gave him a sense of power that he couldn't share, a sense of power that the reality of his life had always denied him.

Now everyone was going to know, or think they knew, and they were forcing him to review, at least to himself, the lamentable failure of his life and the dramatic termination of his own human mortality. He had kept it buried for a long time. The familiar old voice of righteousness tugged at the back of his head. There had been no other way.

His hair clung to his head in dampened little gray wisps. Another tear slid down his cheek. What would Delores think of all this?

"My name is Robert P. Clark," he said to himself as he looked out the window.

* * *

Sandra and Les turned to look at each other in the silence that followed the departure of the FBI with Bob.

"The odds of something like this happening," Les began.

"It's a crock!" Sandra said.

"I think it's a good possibility that he's that man."

"You never liked him," she accused immediately.

"That's not true. But stop and think," the young man said quickly in the face of Sandra's mounting defensiveness. "The signs were there. The whole time he was here . . ."

"No!"

"I know, it's such an unbelievable thing to have happened, and the odds of working with someone like that . . ."

Sandra got up angrily.

"Stop and think," he said.

"I don't want to." Suddenly the wind left her sails. "I don't want to believe he could do something like that," she said softly.

"Well, we've got to consider the possibility," Les insisted. "I can't believe the normalcy of the man's life. The guy's getting married, buying houses; he's going to court; he's got a driver's license. . . ." He didn't share with Sandra the fact that Bob had always intimidated him. He didn't know why. He had never been able to figure it out. But now . . . he guessed somebody who had escaped the law for eighteen years . . . It's got to be an incredible sense of power. To have done it and escaped it.

"Well, I don't believe it!" Sandra said with sudden decisiveness.

She left the office to go to the lawyers in the next-door office to tell them about it.

Alone, Les walked into Bob's office. He picked up Bob's last time sheet for the month of May. It showed how much work he really did. Twelve billing hours for the whole month. That's not that much, he thought.

Less than a half hour later, the phone rang. Les picked it up.

"This is Kevin August from the FBI."

"Yes."

"Is Sandra Silbermann there, please?"

"No. She's next door . . . at the lawyer's office."

"Is this Lester Wingfield?"

"Les," he corrected a bit inanely.

"Well, Les, the fingerprints match. We have a winner."

"Oh . . ." He couldn't think of anything else to say.

"You can tell Miss Silbermann that Bob Clark will not be coming back to work today."

"Thank you very much." ·

"We'll be back to pick up his things."

"Sure. . . ."

"Samples of handwriting, things like that."

"I think there's a letter he wrote when he got the job. But it might have been typed. . . ."

Les sat in his office waiting for Sandra to return. He did a few little things on his calculator, but he couldn't concentrate. He knew he was in a state of shock. He could have gone to get Sandra next door, but he waited instead . . . thinking.

When she finally did return, Sandra took one look at his face and knew he had heard something. And he told her, "They said he's not coming back. They said they've got a 'winner.'"

Her eyes clouded over with tears.

"You know, Sandra," Les said slowly, "I've been sitting here thinking. I know I've seen his 'Wanted' flyer in the post office."

She stared at him.

"I used to want to be an FBI man. And every time I had a few minutes to spare, I'd look around at the posters. I know I've seen his picture. I remember thinking, Man! they'll never catch this guy; he must be in South America or something," he said, shaking his head in wonderment at the craziness of life. "I remember the time I went in there, I was looking at the whole wall. I looked at oc- cupations. Most of the guys who were wanted were carpenters, fast- food workers, and here was an accountant. It struck me."

"You didn't recognize him?" she asked.

"He looked different. The picture was taken when he was forty- five."

"Don't you see him as a victim at all?" Sandra asked with a touch of melancholy.

"Maybe I feel sorry for the guy in a way. I guess he snapped. Thoughts like that may run through your mind, but, Sandra," he said, suddenly feeling the horror of it, "you just don't do it. And the guy did."

"What do you think they'll do to him?" she asked, looking back toward his office.

"I don't know. But the things that he did, if he did them . . ."

"He tried to live a good life since he was here. . . ."

"If you ask me, he was too nice to be true!" Les said with emphatic rejection. "He even had a Fraternal Order of Police sticker on his car. Did you ever see it? That's real gall if he really is the guy.'' Les shook his head in amazement. "The chances of working with a guy like that . . . a mass murderer . . . What's the mathematical probability of that?''

Sandra remembered holding Bob up to her husband as a paragon of virtue and consideration. When her husband heard the story of Bob's arrest, he laughed. "This is the man my wife wants me to emulate.'' He told everyone he could about it until he realized that Sandra couldn't eat or sleep for days. "This has really bothered you, hasn't it?'' he finally asked gently.

"I feel as though I've lost my best friend.''

The Union County Prosecutor's Office in New Jersey received a letter from Wanda Flanery asking about a reward. She was informed that neither the TV show nor the prosecutor's office was offering one.

37 | The Merry Month of June

June 1, 1989

In Westfield, New Jersey, senior editor Kathleen L. Gardner and assistant editor Ellen Scott Brandt of *The Westfield Leader* returned from a quick lunch at the Bagel Stop around the corner. Both had startlingly clear blue-green eyes and were young, eager, and lovely. Ellen stood at least five foot nine inches in flats with long, straight, dark hair; Kathleen was almost as tall with short-cropped blond hair. Since early that morning they had been dealing with the results of the past Tuesday's primary results. The election was already set as the next edition's lead story when the phone on Kathleen's desk rang.

She picked up the incoming call. *"Westfield Leader,"* she said.

"Hi. Who's this?'' asked a female voice.

"This is Kathleen Gardner.''

"Are you the editor?''

"Yes I am. Who's calling?''

"Well," the woman hesitated. "I'd rather not say, if you don't mind. . . ."

"Not at all," Kathleen said, poising her pencil for what was probably going to be some juicy bit of gossip she wouldn't print anyway. "How may I help you?"

"Well, I was just wondering . . . Is it true that John List has been caught?"

Kathleen's heart skipped a beat. "I'm sorry. Would you repeat that?"

"Well, a friend of mine just called me . . ."

"Are you from Westfield?" Kathleen asked calmly as she gesticulated wildly to Ellen Brandt to come over.

"Yes."

"Go on," Kathleen urged. "What have you heard?"

"She said . . ." The woman's voice went on, "This friend of mine. She's also from Westfield. She said that she heard a radio report just now, no more than twenty minutes ago, that John List was taken into custody."

"We haven't heard anything to that effect yet. Hold on one minute."

Kathleen put her hand over the receiver and whispered to Ellen, "Get on the phone to Barney. This woman says they caught John List."

"What!" Ellen exclaimed, and immediately dialed the Westfield police headquarters.

Kathleen went back to the caller on the phone. "We're checking out the story now. If you'd like to hold on . . ."

"Oh, yes. I'd like to know if it's true or not," said the unidentified woman. "I've often thought about him over the years. I always figured he was dead."

Kathy remained on the line with the woman, who was recounting how many times she had thought of the murders that happened on Hillside Avenue so many years ago. Meanwhile Ellen was immediately connected with Detective Lieutenant Bernard Tracy. "Barney," she said quickly, "this is Ellen from the *Leader*. . . ."

"So you've heard," he said with dry amusement.

"It's true?"

"You bet it is," he confirmed.

And Ellen screamed an ear-splitting, "Yahoo!!" into the receiver. Pandemonium broke loose in the office of the local newspaper.

"It's true!" Kathy exploded into the receiver, where the unidentified woman was waiting for confirmation of her friend's report. "It's true! They got him!"

"Where?" Ellen asked Barney excitedly. "When?"

Barney laughed at the lovely young girl's enthusiasm. "Down in Virginia. Under an alias. Now calm down."

"I can't!"

"Look," Barney said calmly, "there's going to be an FBI press conference at their headquarters in Newark. Now why don't you girls get out your press cards and go join in on the news firsthand."

"Oh, you bet we will." She slammed down the receiver, then realized that she had hung up on her friend—picked it up again and shouted, "Thanks!" into the dead receiver and slammed it down again.

The office of the little local Westfield newspaper was in a state of elation. The entire staff joined in instantaneous celebration that overwhelmed the usually tranquil atmosphere. Almost like VJ Day!

"We'll go," Kathleen said. "Right now. To Newark. The FBI...."

But Ellen had run out of the office into the street. She went immediately next door into the Jarvis Pharmacy, which shared the building with the *Leader*, and told Kitty Duncan, owner of the pharmacy. "They got him. They got John List!"

"What?" Kitty exclaimed.

But Ellen was already out in the street stopping every passerby she saw on Elm Street. "They captured John List... List... They've got him!"

Kitty Duncan ran into the *Leader* and listened as Kathleen joyously thanked the unidentified woman on the phone who had been the first one to apprise them of the great news.

Ellen, flushed with excitement, returned to the office again after completing her self-appointed task as town crier.

"Come on," Kathleen exclaimed to her. "We've got to get to that press conference!"

And as they hurried out of the office, Ellen turned to the rest of the staff and called out, "Stop the press!"

Laughter followed the young ladies as they departed.

The overflowing jubilation was understandable. John List had been the town bogeyman for 17½ years. He had become a sour legend. His capture would put an end to the night fears of many of the more imaginative town residents and would cap off the careers of so many who had been involved in the long search.

Westfield Chief of Police Anthony Scutti and ex–Chief of Police James Moran were seated at a diner in East Windsor, New Jersey. June 1 was the third anniversary of Moran's retirement. It was exactly three years to the day since he had retired from the police force and Scutti had taken over the reins as Westfield's chief of police. Still close friends, they had just returned from attending a meeting for the New Jersey State Police Chiefs Association when they decided to pull off for a quick late lunch at the diner. After ordering from the slightly stained, oversize menu, Scutti's beeper went off.

Moran grinned as Scutti put down his hamburger and got up from the booth with a groaning sigh. "Hey, better you than me," Moran called out, picking up his coffee cup with a playful flourish as Scutti went to phone headquarters. "I'm a retired man!"

Chief Scutti wasn't gone long. When he returned to the table he was smiling from ear to ear. "Congratulations!" he cried, holding out his hand to Moran.

"What's this?" Moran asked as he obligingly shook the extended hand. "Did my wife have a baby I don't know about or something?"

Scutti shook Moran's hand hard as though to cement the news he was about to impart. "They got John List."

"Oh, my God!" Moran exclaimed. "They got him?"

"Yep."

"Where? Who got him?"

"The FBI in Richmond, Virginia," Scutti replied. "We just got the word."

"Because of that TV show?"

"Looks like it."

Moran couldn't believe it. Just like that? After two decades of searching, it almost seemed too simple. "It's him?" he repeated, having difficulty in allowing himself to be convinced that the manhunt was finally over. "They're sure?"

"Fingerprints match," Scutti replied with a satisfied sigh. "Scars, mastoid, hernia. The works."

Moran finally leaned back with a huge smile. "This is the best thing that has ever happened to me. That bum should never get away with what he did. What an anniversary gift!"

The two large men grinned at each other like mischievous little boys and shook hands again.

Several miles away, in Newark, FBI Agent Barry Martino, who had been working on the case on and off for some time, returned from lunch to be greeted with the news of List's capture. "Yeah, sure," he said, and went on about his business.

But despite understandable skepticism, the manhunt was indeed finally over after almost eighteen years of frustrating dead ends. Now, egged on by excited media glitz in the spectacular aftermath of *America's Most Wanted*, the John Emil List case was suddenly about to propel forward with lightning speed as though trying to make up for all the lost time.

Kathleen Gardner and Ellen Brandt were among the first to arrive at the Gateway I Building, where the hurriedly called press conference was to take place. The room was filled with some of the best-known reporters from some of the largest metropolitan dailies in the country, including *The New York Times* itself. Not many small-town newspaper editors get the opportunity to participate first-hand in a story as big as this one, the girls thought excitedly. Of course they had a proprietary feeling about the List case; it was their story, their killer, their bogeyman, and many of the national reporters and news agencies would acknowledge as much by turning to *The Westfield Leader* to request fillers, color, and additional information to round out their own stories.

The girls recognized many familiar faces from the New Jersey entourage: Chief of Police Anthony Scutti, Deputy Chief Inspector Robert Bell, and their old friend Detective Tracy, to whom they waved specially, mouthing, "Thanks," over heads in the crowded room. Then there was John C. McGinley, special agent in charge of the Newark FBI office, Union County Prosecutor John Stamler, other unidentified officials from Union County, and, of course, ex–Police Chief James Moran, displaying the frayed FBI flyer of the fugitive that he had carried in his breast pocket from the beginning. For the first time since he'd first set foot in the death house on Hillside Avenue years ago, he was just about ready to discard it.

"Gladly . . . now." He grinned. "Catching List is the best thing that ever happened to me. How can a guy murder five people and just walk away from it? That's bothered me a long time."

The air in the room was celebratory with much handshaking and backslapping.

"Made my day," came one retort.

"I knew he couldn't disappear forever," came another.

"It was only a matter of time," came still a third.

Kathleen and Ellen managed to corner Lieutenant Tracy and Union County Prosecutor David Hancock before the press conference began. "I'm looking forward to meeting the guy," Tracy said to them cheerfully. "He's had eighteen years of freedom. It's time the prosecution started and he paid for his crimes."

They turned eagerly to Hancock to urge a statement.

"It's gratifying as a prosecutor when someone who has intentionally been eluding you for so long is finally apprehended and can be brought back," he offered. "It kind of brings a close to a chapter in one of the most notorious murder cases in Union County history."

At the conference Kathleen and Ellen sat at the long press table crowded with national newspaper and media personnel and took notes avidly until it was almost over. Then Ellen Brandt stood up to ask, "Will List be up for the death penalty?"

A hesitant breath.

Ex–Chief Moran spoke up. Ever the consummate professional, he did not display his own feelings as he said, "There was no death penalty in 1971 at the time of the murders. If convicted, the most Mr. List could expect would be life imprisonment."

A loud contentious murmur swept through the press corps.

Now David Hancock of the Union County Prosecutor's Office spoke above the murmurings. "I should like to point out that things are moving along quickly. FBI fugitive charges have been dropped in order to speed the extradition process to New Jersey. The FBI had only a fugitive warrant. The murder warrant is held here in Union County. Paperwork is currently underway to have List, alias Robert P. Clark, brought to Union County. He has not waived extradition, and, of course, no one knows if he will."

The thought of having List back in New Jersey created another stir of excitement and expectation among the assembled press corps.

"Another point of interest," Hancock continued. "No bail can be set in Virginia for a suspect who faces either life in prison with no chance of parole or the death penalty. However, a bail of one million dollars was set for him simply to take a one-minute walk from federal custody to state custody."

While the press conference was in progress at FBI headquarters in New Jersey, Robert P. Clark appeared before United States Magistrate David G. Lowe in the district courthouse in Richmond, Virginia.

He was escorted into court under heavy guard. He wore a short-sleeved white shirt open at the collar. Necks craned to see in public the pariah whose hands, cuffed in front of him, held a book. The man who had made such a point throughout his entire life of treasuring his privacy stood tall, erect, almost proud in bearing. But he appeared sad, and his eyes, behind dark-rimmed glasses, avoided contact with all those who stared.

Referring to him as "John List, also known as Robert Clark,"

Judge Lowe authorized federal officials to release the prisoner into Virginia custody. He was arraigned on Virginia state fugitive charges and charged with five counts of first-degree murder.

Throughout the session Bob sat stone-faced. Still very calm and self-contained, he insisted, "I am not John List."

"Your denial is duly noted," replied Judge Lowe.

"I should like to request a court-appointed lawyer," Bob Clark added.

Judge Lowe glanced down at the quickly assembled file on the bench before him. "According to my records here," he said in a clear, even voice, "you've been earning two thousand dollars a month at your present place of employment, and you have a balance in the amount of twelve hundred dollars in a savings account. Request denied!"

A preliminary hearing was set for June 8, when it would be decided if Mr. List/Clark should be extradited to New Jersey. Held without bail, the suspect was remanded to Henrico County Jail in Richmond, where corrections officers were instructed that he was not permitted to talk to anyone except his attorney.

He was given the name of Joel G. Clarke, a local attorney.

June 2, 1989

The story of the fugitive's capture broke across the nation in a spectacular spree of jubilant headlines.

CAPTURE STUNS NEIGHBORS
Elizabeth Daily Journal—6/2/89

MASS MURDER SUSPECT NABBED 18 YEARS LATER
New York Post—6/2/89

INSIDE THE JERSEY HOUSE OF HORRORS
New York Post—6/2/89

HE WAS TOO NICE TO BE TRUE
Elizabeth Daily Journal—6/2/89

CAUGHT BY THE FBI AND A TV POSSE
People—6/19/89

SUSPECT IN 5 KILLINGS IN 1971 CAUGHT WITH AID OF TV SHOW
The New York Times—6/2/89

Westfield, New Jersey, was buzzing. Now there were cameramen and newsmen everywhere—on Hillside Avenue, on Elm Street, in front of *The Westfield Leader*, set up at the triangular corner where John Emil List made his last withdrawal from the bank. Relief, even joy, was expressed by residents at the arrest of their most notorious former neighbor. Mrs. Bennett, who had seen the lights go out in the murder house on the night of December 7, 1971, said, "I really thought all these years he must be dead. My husband and I watched the television show and said to ourselves that 'ten to one nobody will call.'"

Jack J. Camillo, a sixty-eight-year-old lawyer who grew up in Westfield and remembered the murders vividly, said, "I don't think anything ever moved the spirit of the people in this town as those murders did."

"I'm glad he was caught," added former neighbor Hank O'Malley. "He's got a big debt to pay."

Other residents were having "List parties." Staff members of The Leader received bizarre invitations in the shape of guns and confetti. The current residents of the beautiful red brick house way up on the hill of 431 Hillside Avenue, the property where the murders took place, almost gleefully planned to throw a party to celebrate List's capture.

Someone suggested making up T-shirts captioned, "List Busters!" Others jokingly suggested changing the name of the town from Westfield to Listfield.

While Westfield residents rejoiced, others mourned. Despite the revelation of the crime once again recounted in great horrific detail, John List had somehow managed to elicit loyalty and a deep sense of caring from those who had known him as Bobby Clark.

Mr. and Mrs. Joseph Stefano, who lived next door to the Clarks, were probably the closest friends the Clarks had on Sagebrook Trace in Midlothian. Joe Stefano spoke quietly and reservedly about the man who had introduced him to Civil War and World War II board games. "It's impossible for anyone to believe that he is the person who committed this crime." He pointed across his lawn. "You see that American flag over there? It was a gift to me and my wife from Bob."

"I don't know John List. I only know Bobby Clark," Jonah Folger said passionately. It was with Folger that Bob had lived when he first came to Virginia alone. "If he was the last man on earth, he still wouldn't be alone. You understand what I'm saying? He was a religious man. A devout Christian. If he says, 'God bless you,' he's not just saying it. He means it!"

Pat Ferguson, who lived on the other side of the Clarks, stood over his barbecue, grilling chicken legs for his family. "I don't know what a guy who's killed five people is supposed to look like, but he's not that person. He worked hard in his yard, went to church every Sunday."

Mrs. Arndt, who sat on the church council in Denver with Clark for four years, said he was a very private person "who displayed great kindness and helped the seniors."

"He was well liked," said Reverend Robert West, pastor of St. Paul's in Denver, where Bob, whom he called a devout church leader, had worshiped for over ten years. "He had gained the respect of the parish," Reverend West said sadly. "There was nothing to cause us to be suspicious of his demeanor or credibility. If this is true, then somehow, some way, he was able to stabilize himself here."

"Oh, that's John," said the Reverend Louis W. Grother with a smile of recognition as he looked at a photo of Bob Clark taken in 1989. "How can anyone believe otherwise?" Grother had been the List family minister for seven troubled years in Kalamazoo. Then he shook his head sadly and made a statement epitomizing the kind of loyalty John List had always aroused in fellow congregants. "No matter what he's done, I still love the man."

It proved to be a very busy week for editors Kathleen Gardner and Ellen Brandt and the rest of the staff at *The Westfield Leader*. The phone rang constantly. They resurrected all the past issues from their archives that had dealt with the story from day one, answered all inquiries, and with journalistic exultation attacked what was to be the story of a lifetime for them.

Anyone who has doubted that the local newspaper is in fact the center of community activities should have been in our office last week when the news broke that John List had been arrested.

The word spread rapidly by way of news networks throughout the country, spurred by a TV broadcast of "Most Wanted" persons. Just as rapidly, searchers of more details, to round out their stories, found that Westfield, scene of the crime, had its own newspaper.

At the same time, the FBI offices in Newark were barraged with questions from newsmen. Drucilla Wells, acting as a spokeswoman for the bureau, said that List was scheduled to appear in a U.S. District Court in Richmond, Virginia, on Monday morning, June 5, for a bail hearing. "The suspect will also be evaluated on his degree of dangerousness and risk of flight," she added.

The American Civil Liberties Union immediately raised questions about the fairness of the television program *America's Most Wanted*. Colleen O'Connor, national director of public education, was quick to issue a statement to the press: "Our worry is that the program portrays the actual crime prior to an indictment or conviction in a way that suggests guilt," she said. "It has the effect of validating the accusation. That could preempt the right to a fair trial in some cases." That was certainly an important point, but no one in the Union County Prosecutor's Office paid much attention. They were too busy rubbing their hands in anticipation of activating a long delayed prosecution. Eleanor Clark, Union County's assistant prosecutor, said to the press, "I anticipate having no trouble identifying him and bringing him to trial."

While the journalistic drama unfolded with speedy reportorial elation, and various interested factions jockeyed for prominent positions, the human drama behind the headlines was being lived in solemn despair.

In Midwest City, Oklahoma, Jean Seyfert sat at her kitchen table spread out with dozens of family photographs from the past—Helen and John in Virginia when he was a lanky young soldier stationed at Ft. Eustis, when they had just begun dating. How beautiful they looked to her—so young, so fresh, and seemingly so in love. The beautiful faces of the children. It was almost too painful to look at them again. The family portrait that had been reprinted by just about every news agency at the time of the murders was, once again, spread out all over the front pages. Why had that picture been taken? she had always wondered. The family had sat for the portrait just before he'd killed them. Whose idea was it to have it taken? Was it supposed to be some sort of memorial? Some sort of record? It was never explained . . . never understood.

Tears streamed down her face. "We used to get along well, John and I," she said to her husband, who sat down next to her and carefully fingered some of the photos himself.

"Everybody wants to talk to you about it," he said. He had been acting as the screen between her and the incessant requests for interviews.

"I guess I'd like to see him," she said, staring at the mild, sweet face of the man she had been responsible for introducing to her sister at a bowling alley in Newport News. "But what would I say to him?"

"Do you want to talk to anyone?"

"Not now," she cried, turning John's picture over vehemently. "Not now. I don't think I could go through it all, all over again."

"Okay, I'll keep them away," he said gently. "But they're terribly insistent."

"Later," she said weakly as she looked at the beautiful portrait of her sister when she had been in her prime—beautiful long, slender neck, the lovely full lips. "I don't want Helen to be maligned," she said suddenly. "Like she was back then, making her out to be nothing but an alcoholic and a nag. She was a sick woman. That's what they have to understand."

"Yes," he agreed. "It's up to you and Brenda to set the record straight, Jean. Eventually you'll have to talk to them."

"I will. I just have to catch my breath first."

"I know."

Jean picked up a photo of Patty, wide-eyed, as though looking toward what she hoped would be a bright future. "I'm glad my mother isn't alive to have to go through all of this again," she whispered, wiping her eyes and remembering how desperately her mother had reacted to the murders. Although Mrs. Morris had been sick, there was little question in Jean's mind that the heartache and depression brought on by the massacre had pushed her over the edge as though there had been little left to live for. Now she was gone; she had died in August of 1988. She'd never lived to see the day her son-in-law was arrested, but she had received a posthumous birthday gift. June 1 was her birthday.

Brenda Herndon De Young went into complete seclusion with her children when the story of her stepfather's capture broke. Having lived a desperate life of financial deprivation, a broken marriage, and recurring depression since the tragedy, she didn't want to resurrect it all again. She felt the need to "set the record straight," especially about her mother, but she didn't know if she was up to it. She tried desperately to repress in her own mind the enforced memory of the entire tragedy again. So Mom drank, but she wasn't all that bad. She was a very sick woman. Brenda didn't think Daddy had ever felt very passionate toward her. He was looking for her to fail, so he could say, "I'm perfect and she's imperfect," she thought bitterly. It wasn't a loving relationship. Who knew that better than she, who had suffered through so many of the arguments? That's what disturbed her the most when she read all those reports that people made up about her mom. Mom was sick! she wanted to scream at all those horrible reporters. She was medicated! Hardly functioning! It was deeply disturbing that Mom takes the rap that she takes. . . . Now, when she is written about in the papers all over again, she'll be portrayed more as someone who drank, a floozie. In reality, she was just an emotionally and physically sick person. Life had gotten beyond her control.

Brenda couldn't stop brooding. Every detail was emblazoned now not only in her head, but in the headlines again. She tried to shut it out. She couldn't. The faces of Patty, Johnny, and Freddie were still as clear and fresh in her mind as the faces of her own children. She wanted to hide.

And then there was the latest victim, Delores H. Miller Clark.

As a pastor, what do you say to people who are going through such trauma and crisis? wondered Reverend Joseph Vought. Fair-haired and blue-eyed with a dark mustache flecked with gray, the handsome young pastor was in his early thirties. The Lutheran Church of Our Savior in Richmond was not his first pastorship, but he had been in Virginia only since 1984 and had known Bob and Delores Clark for a little over a year. In the short time they had been members of his congregation, he had grown very fond of them. Now he found himself driving a deeply shaken Delores to the Henrico County Jail to visit her husband, who, astoundingly, was being held for multiple murder.

Reverend Vought did the best he could under the circumstances, not knowing that he would suffer migraines for months afterward. It had been a real baptism by fire for him, dealing with the media and suddenly being thrust into the national limelight. He had such mixed feelings. He shared with his entire congregation a lot of hurt for Bob and Delores. He shook his head to clear it as he turned the wheel into the parking lot of the jail where Bob was being held. He wanted to be completely "there" for both Bob and Delores without dealing with his own intrusive inner thoughts at the moment.

Disregarding the turned white collar over his deep blue shirt, the authorities at the jail asked him for identification before permitting him to visit the incarcerated suspect.

"I'll go in first," he said to Delores.

Sitting in tense stunned anticipation, she nodded. He patted her shoulder gently. The woman seemed to have aged twenty years overnight.

When Bob was escorted into the cinder-block walled room where the pastor waited, Vought saw that he was not in civilian clothes. He looked disheveled and unnatural in his creased prison issue. Although Bob was obviously relieved that he was finally with someone he knew and felt comfortable with, he still appeared bewildered. All Vought could do was reassure him that God was still there.

Bob's eyes were sorrowful and swollen with crying. He had suffered the injury of discovery. There was no blush of shame, only the shadow of sadness. He brushed a huge hand across his eyes. He appeared shell-shocked as he glanced with empty, unseeing eyes around the gray room that held him prisoner.

"Delores is here, Bob."

"Here?" He looked at his pastor blankly.

"In the other room. She's waiting to see you."

Bob started to shake as he tried to control the onset of renewed sobs.

"Why doesn't she come in?"

"They won't permit it." The pastor choked a bit, caught up in the man's trauma. "As your pastor, they'll permit me a contact visit with you, but you'll only be able to see her—"

"Through a partition," Bob interrupted. "That's it, isn't it? Through a glass wall." He broke into renewed tears at the thought. "My God . . ."

Reverend Vought went out to where Delores awaited his return.

"How is he?" she asked anxiously.

"They're bringing him into another room where you'll be able to see him." He couldn't bring himself to say, "Through the glass partition," but she knew. The guard led them into a gray, cold, antiseptic-looking room. The glass partition had light hand stains on it where others before them had tried to reach each other through the icy barrier. There was a connecting telephone on each side.

The door at the far end of the room opened. Bob came through. Reverend Vought thought Delores looked faint when she saw him dressed in prison garb, but she grasped the receiver in her hand and waited for her husband to pick up on the other end of the line.

The guard who ushered Bob in had been assigned to the first shift in a twenty-four-hour suicide watch over the prisoner. Now he retreated to the far side of the room from where he watched his charge. There were enough tears between the two of them to drown the fires of hell, the guard thought uncomfortably. Better keep a close eye on this guy.

Reverend Vought sat to the side away from Delores, trying to remain unobtrusive. He looked at her as she kept her eyes on the face of the man she had married. In many ways she was very fragile, he thought as he watched the tearful interaction. In other ways she was one of the strongest people he'd ever met. The young minister turned his head away from their mutual despair.

The guard, on the other hand, strained his ears to catch what they were saying to each other. Had the chilling secret been kept from her? It was out of curiosity more than anything else that he tried to hear what they were saying. He heard, "Westfield . . . wife . . . the children . . . so ill . . ."

He watched as the wife listened to her husband with the receiver pressed tightly to her ear and her eyes glued to his face through the Plexiglas that separated them. He couldn't really hear their conversation, only bits and snatches. But he found himself shaking his head. So he's finally telling her, he thought. It's about time. Poor woman. Then again, Clark might just as well have been talking about how he never heard of these people they had accused him of murdering. The officer shifted his feet and tried to turn his attention away. He was having a difficult time dealing with the woman's obvious agony at their conversation. Clark, List—whatever the hell his name was—was crying, too.

Reverend Vought looked back as Delores stood up.

Only ten or twelve minutes had passed. He could tell they were dealing with some of the basic things now—make sure you do this, don't forget to do that. He knew that trying to take care of business was helping to keep her stress level down to a minimum.

Then Vought and Delores left, with Bob forlornly watching them as they walked out of the room. Before leaving the building, she checked on visiting and was told she would be able to visit her husband twice a week.

They left the jail by a side door, but the press was already waiting for them. It was only the beginning of Delores's harassment by the press. Quick to notice "her face red and blotchy with tears and dark rings under her eyes . . ." they were to hound her mercilessly for weeks, angling for a photo, begging for an interview. It took a great deal of maneuvering on Reverend Vought's part to be able to escape them. He drove away at a speed uncommon for him, crossed the James River, and pulled into the rear of a Burger King parking lot. Satisfied that they hadn't been followed, Delores slipped on her sunglasses before they entered the establishment. She was too upset to think of food, but it was a way to break the tension of the press chase. Meeting Bob had been a beautiful event in her life, she thought as they found an isolated booth, and through the church their contact was even more special. "Bob is not that man," she said as she sat deep in a corner of the booth.

In Salzburg, Michigan, Harold List was shown a recent photograph of Bob Clark. "That is a picture of my cousin, John

Emil,'' he said. "I don't see why there should be any question about it.''

Vought knew Delores had been married once before, but he didn't know much about her first marriage. He knew only that her first husband had given her a great deal of heartache. He tightened his jaw at the irony. As he watched her nibble on a burger, he found himself wondering absently if Delores had ever been in any danger. Delores and Bob had always seemed very loving and affectionate. He knew they suffered frustrations and anxiety about their financial situation. But he was positive their concern for each other was genuine.

There were so many things he wanted to discuss with Delores, questions that plagued him. According to New York's *Daily News*, one of the reasons John List had killed his family was his financial failures. He didn't know what to think about that. He knew there were people who thought that their financial conditions translated into their ultimate status before God. A flourishing vocation could be interpreted as being blessed by God, to a certain extent a validation of one's faith. He wanted to ask Delores if Bob ever talked of such matters with her. But he did not ask. To do so could have demonstrated a doubt as to Bob's real identity, and at this moment in time he didn't wish to share any nagging doubts with Delores. He wanted to present a believing front upon which she could lean, at least for the time being. There was no proof of anything yet. Then he found himself thinking of the FBI fingerprints and wondered if fingerprints could be mistaken.

When she said, "Bob is very committed to his faith and his church," it was almost as though she heard his thoughts and felt she had to defend him against any doubt.

"I know."

Beyond regular worship attendance, Bob had not been involved in anything else. His attendance was faithful and committed to the liturgy; the pastor could see that, but Delores was the one who came to the Bible study. When Vought visited them in their modest home in Midlothian and they spoke about doing their devotions together, they seemed to be totally in sync with each other. Every morning they read their Bibles regularly after breakfast. Their faith wasn't a fake. He had seen evidence of it himself . . . Bibles, religious materials . . .

"Do you have brothers or sisters?" he asked her.

"Yes. I have a sister up north," she replied distractedly. "A brother."

He knew that she was concerned about being called to testify publicly about her life with Robert. She was not happy at the prospect.

"If Bob isn't released soon, I'm going to have to sell the house," she said suddenly.

"Don't make any decisions now," he advised.

Maybe she would move to Maryland, although she was concerned about her mother. Would this follow her? she wondered, and then realized that it wasn't going to go away easily. She couldn't eat. Trying to swallow was painful. She pushed her plate aside. She didn't want to drag her family into this.

"Would you like to leave?" he asked.

She looked at his plate. "You haven't finished."

"That's all right. Let's go."

She slipped on her sunglasses.

As they drove away from the Burger King, he said "Delores, this must be hell for you."

And she said very quietly, "Well, I don't know how this is going to come out, but all things work for good for those who love God."

Reverend Vought almost drove off the road at the strength of her religious convictions, and he suddenly found himself thinking that she had never been in any serious danger even if Bob *was* John List. Religion was the one bond she had with Bob that List's wife never shared with John. It didn't occur to him that John List had shared an even stronger religious bond with his mother, Alma, and he had shot her in the head.

After a few moments of silence, as they drove toward Midlothian, he finally said, "I told him that as his pastor he was free to confess. And as his pastor at this point I'm here in a crisis situation for both of you. He shared what he shared."

She was silent for a moment. Then she said, "I know he's not John List," reinforcing the denial she had to believe.

When they arrived at the little ranch house at the end of the cul-de-sac in the Brandermill development, so lushly verdant with the onset of summer, the press was waiting for her in force, crushing the carefully tended green lawn with heavy feet. Her neighbors, also out in force at all the media attention their usually quiet little neighborhood was receiving, were craning their necks to look at her—as though they had never seen her before. She knew they had been speaking to the reporters. What could they possibly say? she wondered.

"Bob used to become so impassioned during board games that sometimes he would break out into a sweat." The Stefanos were the Clarks' best friends.

"The guy was so average," Pat Ferguson said, shaking his head in wonder. "You talk about an average neighborhood, this is it. This sort of thing just doesn't happen in my neighborhood."

"I remember one night, when they were visiting us," said Mrs. Stefano, "the subject of the past came up. Bobby, who heard us from another room, immediately came in and motioned to Delores, wide-eyed, as though indicating to her that she was to say nothing. I don't know what it meant. . . ."

What had they said? Delores wondered as she darted into the house past the neighborhood children, who were running about in a festive mood. She locked her door.

The newspapers continued to have a field day:

SLAY SUSPECT'S WIFE STANDS BY HER MAN
New York Post—6/3/89

I AM DEVOTED TO HIM
Elizabeth Daily Journal—6/3/89

PASTOR CALLS FOR COMPASSION IN LIST CASE
The Record—6/5/89

"I love my husband very deeply," Delores insisted in a brief statement she gave to the media through a family friend. "I have never known Bobby to be anything but a sweet and gentle man of good character. We have had a happy marriage filled with mutual love and respect."

Hounded by the media as her world crumbled, on the verge of a nervous breakdown, Delores went into seclusion and prayer to escape the sudden horror of her life and the barrage of requests for interviews.

In Richmond, Robert Clark waived a bond hearing. Joel G. Clarke, who had been hired to represent him on June 1, said his client would have no comment. Bob remained in prison awaiting a hearing to establish his true identity.

Forced to live in her own private prison, one not of her own making, Delores remained a shadow, avoiding all eyes, worried, wondering, trying not to think the unthinkable, praying for help and guidance by a God who suddenly seemed to have gone silent. She didn't know how she was ever going to be able to deal with it. She had given her life to her husband with all her trust. She had made a vow. She would stick to it. She was stuck with it. She held her position—turning to her minister, turning to her God, hiding from the media, hiding from herself.

In a dream that night, she was running as though freed from the ground, overcoming gravity in heightened leaps. She was startled into wakefulness. No, he did not do this terrible thing, she thought, breathing heavily. She prayed herself back to sleep.

A hearing was held, its business to show probable cause that the suspect had been in New Jersey at the time of the murders. There would also be another official comparison of Clark's fingerprints with those of the known killer. It was scheduled for Thursday, June 8, after which, if the prints matched, Robert Clark would be transferred to Newark, New Jersey, to be tried for mass murder.

On June 2, Clark's lawyer, Joel G. Clarke, suddenly dropped the case without explanation.

Another attorney, David P. Baugh, picked it up at Bob's request. Baugh was unavailable for comment to the press. To Delores he said, "Let's wait for the results on Thursday before we decide on any further steps."

Lonely and frightened, she told close friends she was at a complete loss. Hardly eating or sleeping since his arrest, she wanted to communicate only with her pastor, Reverend Joseph Vought.

As Clark was ushered out of the federal courthouse, he declined requests for comments. He was escorted by Virginia State Police Special Agent Glen Henelright and Henrico County investigator Ross Mise.

"Where you taking him?" called out one newsman as cameras clicked away busily.

"From the county jail's federal prisoner's area to the general population of state detainees," said Mise.

"He had threatened to kill them."

"Oh, come on," Lieutenant Detective Barney Tracy said.

"I'm serious," Edwin Illiano insisted. He sat in the detective's office telling the story. Illiano had aged considerably. He was much stockier than Barney remembered, and his hair had thinned, but the former drama teacher of the Westfield Recreation Center had the same intensity he remembered all too well. "Patty told me this wild story," he was saying, "about how her father sat them all around the dinner table and told them he'd have to kill them because he couldn't afford to support them anymore."

"She actually told you that?" Tracy said skeptically.

"Yes," Illiano said. "Of course, I didn't believe her. I told her people say things like that all the time. I've done it myself to my own kids. But John junior, too. Just before they left on vacation, he grabbed me by the arm and practically begged me to stop by the house, often. On any pretext I could think of."

"Why?"

"Because he thought his father might do something crazy. Like kill them all."

"Lots of people say 'I'll kill you,' but they don't mean it," Barney said, looking at him carefully.

"That's what I told the kids," Illiano said, demonstrating the reasonable air he had adopted with the children. "Still, they both said the same thing."

Tracy leaned back in his chair. "Well, you know how kids are," he said. "And I imagine Patty was very impressionable."

"I know. I sat with her in the car and told her exactly the same thing one night about a month before they were killed, when I drove her home from rehearsal."

"You gave her parts in your plays."

"Oh, yes. At the time she was killed she was understudying the part of Blanche DuBois in *Streetcar Named Desire*. She was very talented. Probably my most talented student. What a waste. . . ."

"How come she was only the understudy?"

Illiano hesitated.

"I mean," Tracy continued, "if she was your most talented?"

"Well, she needed experience."

"I see. Go on."

"I must tell you," Illiano said, getting back to his reason for visiting the detective, "I can still remember Patty's wide eyes staring at me in the dim light of the car as we sat in her driveway, and I can still feel the pressure of John junior's grip on my arm. Those kids looked scared."

"Why didn't you tell us this story before?" Tracy asked. "There's nothing about it in the records."

"I didn't remember then."

Detective Tracy didn't believe him. One of those "thespian" types with a flair for drama, he thought. If Illiano knew that the kids were frightened at the time of the killings, he certainly would have made an important issue of it back then. How come he's only remembering it now, after 17½ years? Just when the case breaks?

No, Tracy thought. He didn't believe Illiano's story.

He believed that the passage of years and the possible culmination of the sensational case were bringing about dramatic embellishments for some, unwanted revisits of horror for others.

Patricia Mozoki, who had been a child during the time of the murders, wrote to her hometown newspaper, *The Westfield Leader*, from her home in Nantucket, Massachusetts:

Editor, *Leader*:
  The CNN broadcast showing the arrest of John List took me off-guard and brought back a flood of memories—all filled with shock and horror. I can remember all too vividly having to check my closet and "crawlspace" before sleeping as an eight-year-old. I am not alone in rejoicing in his capture, but I am keenly aware that although this tragedy may end a story for many Westfield residents, the nightmare has only begun for those who came to know and care for a man who called himself Robert P. Clark— my heart goes out to them.

Wearing a scarf over her blond hair and sunglasses to hide eyes swollen with tears and darkened by lack of sleep, Delores finally ventured out of her home with a sympathetic friend from the Lutheran Church of Our Savior. Under the glare of flashing light bulbs and photographers invading what little was left of her privacy, she stepped into her maroon Toyota and drove to the home of her pastor.

"So many have asked for my story," she told her friend as they drove. "Writers, journalists . . ."

The woman friend knew that Bob was very interested in having Delores attain financial security. She'd even heard a rumor that . . . She hesitated uncomfortably. "What do you want to do about it?"

"I don't know," Delores murmured. "I'm very confused. I've already turned down *People* magazine. I'll have to discuss it with Bob."

"That's a good idea."

To her, it did not seem morally right to capitalize financially on so much pain. She hesitated for a long moment before she turned to her friend and asked, "What do you think?"

It was one of the few times since she had met Bob that she had aised a question of great import to someone other than Bob without discussing it with him first.

The friend began carefully. "There are arguments, pro and con . . ."

"I know."

"And you have to weigh the personal anguish that may come as a result of sharing your story, your marriage."

"Sharing my marriage with the press." She frowned in distaste.

"It might make sense telling it straight. It could be of value and benefit."

"To whom?"

"To you. And to Bob."

The unasked question lay between them like a heavy weight of separation.

Then there was that awful rumor the friend had heard—that Bob had said, "We have a story here. We can make money on it. . . ." Had he really said that? Delores would not corroborate the rumor, but it was obvious she felt very uncomfortable with the thought of "selling their story." Her friend didn't want to question her about it, but she couldn't help wondering if it were true that Bob had told Delores to hold out for the best offer. When they reached Reverend Vought's house, the pastor and Delores contemplated the sad events of the past few days and the suddenly uncertain future. Together, they prayed to God for strength.

June 4, 1989

Reverend Robert A. West, in Denver, Colorado, suddenly thrust into a national spotlight through the notoriety of one of his former parishioners, stood under the beautiful Gothic ceiling curved high over the altar of St. Paul's and quietly called upon his congregation to pray for the soul of the man he now realized they never really knew.

"Times of tragedy are times to cry out for God's mercy," he sermonized. "Our prayers reach out to Delores and Bob at this time of tragedy, mindful that they have different needs. Bob came to us and joined St. Paul's June 29, 1975. While with us he was faithful at worship, a good steward in support of our ministry, and generous in bringing homebound members to worship and church events."

Reverend West wanted desperately to understand what could possibly have happened. He, too, had been a victim of Clark's deceptions. He could not help wondering, knowing Bob had murdered, what could have been going through his mind every time he received Sunday communion, which began with the confessional:

If we have no sin, we deceive ourselves, and the truth is not in us. But if we confess our sins, God, who is faithful and just, will forgive our sins and cleanse us from all unrighteousness.

"As a parish family," he continued in a strong steady voice that belied his own inner turmoil, "we have been shocked and saddened by the tragic news about one of our former members and responsible leaders of our congregation. In a very real sense, what has befallen one of us has befallen us all."

The pastor had spent hours trying to sort it out, trying to recall anything that Bob might have said about his past, to no avail. Bob had been very private about his personal life. His life was his work, his church, and his wife. He never exhibited violence in all the years he was at St. Paul's. West found himself thinking even as he wrote his sermon, "Either he was able to be so cold and calculating and impersonal to develop a new life, or he had the ability to sublimate the murders so that the incident never existed for him. Or maybe it was a combination." He shook his head slowly as he paused over his typewriter. "He may have lived like a man standing on a trapdoor—with a mad dog underneath."

"Bob was arrested last Thursday in Virginia," he continued from the pulpit, "and charged with the murder of his mother and wife and three children in New Jersey, November 1971."

The pastor had taken much time to construct the sermon he hoped would bring, at least, the solace of understanding to the tragedy they, as a congregation, felt so close to.

"As a parish family, our shock is not that a person like this could be in our midst, for we all have a hidden and dark side in our lives. The church is not a gallery for saints, but a hospital for sinners. Our shock is that the man we came to know and respect in his eleven years as our partner in the ministry at St. Paul's could have committed such a heinous act of violence against his family.

"In my almost twenty-four years of ministry here at St. Paul's, I continue to be motivated by Dietrich Bonhoeffer's definition of a Christian: 'To be a Christian is not to be religious in a particular sort of way, but to be human.' Therefore my commitment to ministry at St. Paul's is to enable and equip people through the gospel of Jesus Christ to be human in a dehumanizing society."

He paused and looked deeply into the faces of his congregants.

"Pray God that Bob's eleven years among us enabled him to be more in touch with the person God intended him to be rather than who he was as the person charged with the murder of his entire family in 1971.''

Not a soul stirred in the church as they listened solemnly. Except for the sound of an occasional muffled sob, a deep silence surrounded the pastor's words.

"Our concern and prayers," continued Reverend West, "reach out to his wife, Delores, who loved and married him as the person we knew, and who now must come to terms with who he was as John List. Only God can know the anguish of Delores and Bob and the family and friends of those who were murdered. And only God can minister to each of their needs.

"As a parish, let us be true to our calling, and be careful not to be judgmental and self-righteous, but rather to reach out in Christian love to both Delores and Bob and all who have been touched by this tragedy. Let us pray. . . ."

Every head bowed silently.

In another church in Richmond, Virginia, fifteen hundred miles away, a much younger pastor, Reverend Vought, stood in the Lutheran Church of our Savior on the same Sunday morning. He looked down at all the anxious faces waiting for him to help them to understand what had happened. He knew the congregation was stunned. He knew they were all trying to reserve judgment. For them, the Clarks had been kind people.

He struggled for the words that would heal the shock of the parishioners who had worshiped side by side with the Clarks. At this moment in time, words were simply not adequate. "They have been faithful church members," he said, clearing his throat. "Tragedy can come into our lives unexpectedly, as it has with Bob and Delores. Even as people of faith, we live in a world where life is fragile and we are vulnerable."

He looked down into the earnest faces of so many of the children in the congregation, knowing that Bob, who had taught Sunday school at one time, was suspected of murdering his own children.

The children looked up at him, waiting for him to continue.

"There are lots of things that cause us to question the goodness of God," he said quietly. "A lot of them happened this week."

Their eyes were wide with unanswered questions.

June 5, 1989

Delores sat on her darkened porch at nine o'clock. The silence of the night was almost startling. There was only a hint of a whispering breeze stirring through what she had come to consider—hiding, alone—the "protective" shrubbery surrounding the porch.

Christopher Ferguson, the eleven-year-old boy who lived next door, was suddenly standing in front of her on the bottom step. From his own front porch, he had seen her shadow come through her front door as she had slipped out into the evening.

"Hello, Mrs. Clark," he said. She could see the flash of the boy's honey-colored eyes as he looked at her from the bottom step. He was big for his age.

She mumbled something. He strained forward to hear. She cleared her throat and repeated, "Hello, Christopher."

They used to speak frequently, but he hadn't spoken to her since all of "this stuff" had happened. Now he wondered about her. He'd heard his parents talk about the case. "I feel so sorry for Delores. . . ." He had seen how she couldn't even walk across her driveway without having reporters snapping photographs of her— "Mrs. Clark . . . Mrs. Clark . . . this way!" He had heard his father speak of justice—"The police don't arrest someone for nothing. . . ." He'd heard the neighbors—"We exchanged books and videotapes. . . ."

Tender in age as he was, Christopher didn't want to intrude on the woman, but instinctively he knew that his presence would not be a threat to her.

"How are you feeling?"

"Not too well."

"Is there anything I can do for you?"

"No. Thank you."

Her face slowly became clear as his eyes accustomed themselves to the dark. He had never seen anything so sad in all his young life. "What are you doing?" he asked innocently.

"Sitting."

The young boy sat down on the steps near her. He wasn't waiting for her to talk. He was simply there in case she needed him.

After a very long while, she said, "Your parents came over to offer help. It was nice of them."

He didn't know what to say. "It's dark," he offered.

"I like to sit in the dark," she said. There was another very long pause before Mrs. Clark said very softly, "I love God very much."

Again he didn't know what to say. So they sat together quietly, without awkwardness, listening to the hush of the night, breathing in the first scents of summer, feeling like friends in the harmony of their mutual silence. He made a wriggling motion of his hand against his ankle where he felt an ant beginning a slow ascent. Then he ran his toes slowly across an open crack on the wooden boards of the porch.

They could hear the telephone ring in Delores's living room.

She stood up. "I'll have to go in now."

He stood up with her. "Good night, Mrs. Clark."

As she turned he couldn't help seeing her face clearly in the interior light as she opened the bright red front door. Her cheeks were wet.

"I'll always be your friend," the boy whispered to her. She looked back at him with a gentle, appreciative smile before she disappeared within the house.

Within the living room, Delores was almost afraid to pick up the ringing phone. Reporters had so many ways of finding out things, even unlisted numbers. But the phone wouldn't stop ringing. Reluctantly she lifted the receiver out of its cradle.

"Hello," she ventured tentatively into the mouthpiece, ready to replace it quickly if it were an obtrusive caller.

"This is Jonah...."

"Who?" she asked, bewildered, not focusing in on the name.

"Jonah Folger."

"Oh, yes, of course. Jonah. I was going to call you."

"The reporters got a hold of my name somehow. They've been all over me with questions about Bobby."

"I'm sorry."

"They found out that I knew him when he first came to Richmond, and they wanted to know all about him. I didn't tell them a thing!" he said emphatically. "And they'd better not print my name in the paper, either!"

"I'm sorry about all the trouble," she repeated.

"Bobby called me," Jonah said after a moment.

"He did?"

"Yes. To apologize. Just like him to apologize for any embarrassment he may have put me through," he said, demonstrating the capacity Clark seemed to have to elicit loyalty from his friends, whatever the circumstances.

"Yes..."

"And he cried. Right there on the phone. He said it was all just terrible."

Delores brushed her hands over her swollen eyes as she listened.

"I don't know John List," Jonah was saying angrily. "I only know Bobby Clark. But even if it's all true..."

"It's not."

"I know... but even if it is, it still wouldn't be a man with a history of murder, but a man with a murder in his history. That's what I told them!"

"Jonah . . . do you think it's possible?" she asked at the same time she found herself thinking that what this loyal friend refused to acknowledge in his shock and pain for Bobby was that it was not just one murder, but *five* murders. It was not just one day in his history, but days, weeks, months, perhaps even years of thinking about it—that's what the police were saying—and then finally executing his plans. And an entire family was wiped out. *An entire family!*

"If it is possible," Jonah insisted, "then something snapped. That's what I'm saying. That's not the way he was. Hell, I know it. You know it. It was one day out of all these many, many years."

"Yes, just one day."

"He told me his first wife was an alcoholic and a spendthrift who had died of cancer, and he also told me he had a daughter who was uncontrollable."

"He told you that?" she asked, startled.

"Yes, he did," Jonah said emphatically, and then hesitated briefly at the possible significance of such an admission. "He never mentioned having any sons." He persisted in his picture of Clark despite his momentary hesitation. "He displayed no taste for violence. What he did like was Walter Cronkite . . ."

"Yes, yes," she agreed readily. "And documentaries."

"And the *National Geographic*."

"Yes."

"Does that sound like a violent man to you?" Jonah laughed quickly. "He didn't even like football!"

"No, that's right," she agreed again. "He liked baseball."

She listened greedily to the reassurances. The listening was so sweet, even though her restless brain was not stilled despite his persuasive convictions.

"Remember what he always said about football," Jonah said, trying to finish the point he was making. "Just a bunch of guys batting their heads together out there instead of using their brains."

"Did you know his father was German?" she asked suddenly.

"Yes. So what! He showed no particular sensitivity about his past that I could tell. His father was German, so he had an interest in things Germanic. That's all there was to all those stupid stories about his board games. I never saw him get excited or break out in a sweat about them."

She knew he was right. In fact, Bobby tended to be even-tempered.

"I've only seen him angry, really angry, only one time," Jonah continued, building up his case with determination. "Remember when I had that cataract operation?"

"Bobby mentioned something about it, I think," she said, trying to think back through all of the crowded confusion of her thoughts.

"And the doctor told me not to do any heavy work for a while?"

"Yes, I do remember that," she said, having retrieved the dim memory out of the past.

"And I picked up a typewriter, and Bobby saw me. And he yelled, 'Put that thing down before your eyeballs fall out.' And that's the only time he ever got mad. The only time!"

She felt better. Her breath had stopped gagging in her throat. "I'm so glad you called."

But Jonah was continuing over her breathless words, as though he had opened up a valve of memories, thoughts, and incidents all colored with so much outrage and indignation at his friend's plight that he had to spew them out nonstop. "He told me once that he had an undergraduate degree in accounting and a master's degree in finance, both from Michigan, and that he was a certified public accountant."

"Did he?" Delores found herself hesitating with doubt again and tightened her aching grip on the receiver. "But, Jonah, that coincides with what they say about that other man. . . ."

"Don't you go listening to all those stories, Delores!" Jonah exclaimed belligerently.

"But . . ." She could not completely reconcile herself to the controversy raging within her own thoughts. "Why did he have to take entry-level positions if he had such a heavy background in academic credentials from such a highly accredited university?"

"Don't let them sway you one bit. It makes for good press. That's all! Bobby is deeply religious and law-abiding."

"Yes, but—"

"No 'buts'! No 'buts'!" he insisted with fierce loyalty. "If the sign says 'thirty-five miles an hour,' his foot comes right off the damn accelerator."

"Perhaps he was exercising the talent they say he had for deflecting attention from himself," she ventured indecisively. "Not doing anything to stand out. . . ."

"Stop it. Shame on you!" he admonished her. "I suppose when he goes into a Burger King for a hamburger and bows his head to say grace to his God, he's not attracting attention to himself!"

"I'm sorry. It's all been so confusing."

"Of course." Jonah lowered his voice. He had called to reassure the woman, not to yell at her. But he was more tightly wound up about the whole thing himself than he had realized. "Just don't ever let them get to you, Delores," he begged in a suddenly softened tone. "Who knows Bobby better than we do, anyway?"

She smiled. "You're right, of course."

"And if you ever find yourself falling into the trap they're trying to build, well, you just pick up the phone and call me right up."

"Yes. Thank you. I will. It's just that I couldn't help reading all those stories."

"You stop reading all that garbage!"

"I'm glad you called."

"Now, is there anything you need?"

"No."

"You said you were going to call me."

"Oh, yes," she said. "Bob said that if anyone is going to write our story, he wants it to be you."

There was a long silence on the other end of the receiver. "What story?"

Delores hesitated in bewilderment again. "I guess . . . about an innocent man accused of something he didn't do. . . ."

"Oh. . . ."

Sandra picked up the incoming call. "Maddrea, Joyner, Kirkham and Woody," she answered automatically, her mind focused on the letter she was reading.

"I have a collect call from a Mr. Robert Clark," came the operator's drawling voice. "Will you accept the charges?"

Sandra dropped the letter on the desk.

"Clark?" Sandra's brain fast-forwarded. Should she accept the call or shouldn't she? What would her bosses think? Why was Bob calling here? She hadn't seen or heard anything since they had taken him away in handcuffs the other day. What would she say to him? "Yes. I will," she heard herself saying calmly.

"Go ahead with your party, sir," the operator said.

"Sandra?"

"Yes," she answered, recognizing the voice immediately.

"This is Bob Clark."

She was stunned. "Yes, I know. Bob! For heaven's sake. Where are you?"

Les Wingfield heard her raised voice. He came out of his office quickly and stood by her desk, his eyes questioning her. She nodded up at him. He watched her as she looked at him while listening to the sad voice on the other end of the line.

"I'm . . ." Bob hesitated. "Sandra, the reason I called is because I wanted to apologize."

"Bob . . . for what?"

"For being arrested at the office. I'm terribly sorry if it caused you any inconvenience."

She didn't know what to say. "I was . . . it was such a surprise. . . ."

"I'm truly sorry."

"Are you all right?"

"Yes, I'm fine."

"Thank you . . . for calling."

"And Sandra?"

"Yes?"

"There were a few personal items . . . a jacket . . . that I left behind."

"They came and took everything," she said.

"They?"

"The FBI."

"I see. Okay. Thank you."

"Take care of yourself," she said a bit inanely.

"You too. Good-bye, Sandra."

"Good-bye, Bob. . . ." She listened as the line disconnected. Then she hung up the phone and looked at Les. "He apologized for being taken here. He sounded very sad."

Les grimaced.

"It was very considerate of him to call."

Still Les didn't answer.

"And he wanted to know about some of the things he left behind."

"That's why he really called."

"No . . ."

"Look, Sandra," Les said in his deep slow drawl, "if he did what they said he did, well, I have to tell you, I don't think we should foot the bill for a bunch of criminals. I believe in the death penalty."

Sandra looked away sadly. "I always liked him."

June 6, 1989

Detective Lieutenant Bernard Tracy of the Westfield Police Department and Sergeant Edward Johnson of the Homicide Division of Union County—another handsome young detective with straight blond hair—left New Jersey on Tuesday morning, June 6, to do investigative work related to the List case in Virginia.

Upon arrival, Johnson went immediately to the FBI office on Grace Street while Barney went to the Henrico County Jail to speak to prison officials. A Virginia detective pointed to a man on the other side of the room speaking to jail personnel. "There's your man List and our man Clark." The detective grinned.

"That's him?" Barney asked, almost startled.

"None other than Mr. Two-Face in person."

They were obviously moving him from one place to another within the jail, and Barney was lucky enough to have happened to catch the transaction.

"Where do you want me to stand?" Barney heard List ask in a very deep, loud, masculine voice. "Where do you want me to go? Here?" List was cooperating, but then again, Barney found himself thinking quickly, he was in jail. What else could he do?

It was the first time he had ever set eyes on the fugitive. He had been expecting to see a shell of a man. Having heard all the stories about him over the last ten years, he had always thought of him as a wimpy accountant. Having seen all the newspaper photos of him since his June 1 capture, he expected to find a defeated old man with a bent head. Barney was a bit stunned at the flesh-and-blood reality of the man. He was physically big in stature, a big-boned man with a large head, and he appeared solid, in good physical shape.

List turned to Barney suddenly and stared at him. Barney could tell that List was measuring him up, wondering who he was. To Barney's surprise, his stare was somewhat intimidating. He appeared to be very confident of himself, in complete control. This guy knows what's going on, Barney thought, completely reevaluating his previous perceptions. *We're* the lesser people: that's what he thinks. And we, poor slobs that we are, just don't understand him. Barney's eyes narrowed and locked with List's. He suddenly perceived John List as someone different from other people, as an egotistical individual, somebody who thought that he was right and the rest of the world was wrong. Again he found himself equating with him a Nazi—someone who could stick somebody in an oven, take a sip of lemonade, and say, "Man, it's hot in here," without feeling any sorrow. Then he was able to go on with his life with very little emotion. Here was a man who was very intolerant of other people and their shortcomings as he perceived them. *His* way was the right way. Barney had come to Virginia believing that List was partially a victim himself, and that through circumstances beyond his control he had destroyed the people whom he loved. But now, looking at the arrogance in the man's demeanor, Barney didn't think he loved anyone as much as he loved himself. What could be more selfish than what he'd done? Barney found himself thinking almost angrily. List had relieved himself of all his burdens and gone on to live peacefully with himself. Ordinarily if a guy did something like that, he killed himself, too, because he couldn't live with what he'd done. So here was a guy who's bright, very sane, in the sense that he was aware of what he was doing and the probable consequences, but he had very little feeling about it. To Barney the fact that the accused did not really want to cooperate more than to stand where he was told and continued to insist on being called Robert Clark was revelatory and deeply disturbing. He's laughing at everybody, Barney thought. He's not a man who deserves our pity. This is a person who isn't ready to change and really thinks that he's right! He's an interesting personality, but a dangerous one.

Someone nudged List. He was forced to turn away.

June 7, 1989

When the FBI agent Kevin O'Hara was sent to All-Packaging Co., In Aurora, Colorado, to investigate the background of the man Alfred Logan knew as Robert Clark, but whom the FBI referred to as John List, Logan was very positive in his defense of the man he had fired. "I don't have anything bad to say about the man at all," he declared.

Agent O'Hara could tell that "Mr. Clark's" arrest had proven to be a very emotional experience for everyone at All Packaging, most particularly Alfred Logan.

"Don't ask me if Bob was 'strange' at times," Logan said. "All those stories they're writing about him. It's all a lot of bullshit, if you ask me. There was absolutely nothing suspicious or threatening about Bob at all," he said angrily. "Why, there were times when I came down heavy on him right here. Hard! There were even times when the president of the company came down on him, too."

"Can you tell me why?" O'Hara asked.

"No! What difference does it make? Office stuff."

"Okay."

"And all I know is, if Bob was capable of doing all those awful things he's been accused of doing, I think it would have happened here!"

O'Hara couldn't help wincing a bit at Logan's logic. Did he really think they could possibly have come down on him heavily enough for him to kill on the job? He decided not to challenge Logan. He was obviously too upset. Instead O'Hara asked politely, "Would you mind looking into your files and pulling out the records you have on Mr. Clark? Résumé, background, anything we might find useful in trying to secure his true identity.''

"Not at all," Logan said. "But you won't find anything unusual in them. He was a very straight kind of guy."

But when he searched through the filing cabinet for the folder marked "Robert P. Clark," Logan couldn't find it. "It's gone," he said. "I don't understand it."

"Who has access to these files?"

"Just us. The executives in the firm. Mr. Morrow, the president. Me, I'm vice-president. And Bob."

"Bob Clark had access to these files?"

"Well, yes, of course. As comptroller he would have."

"Do you have any idea where his file might be?"

"No," he said, perplexed.

"Any other place it might be?"

"No." Logan shook his head slowly. "Bob must have taken his file when he left the company. That's the only thing I can think of. I have no idea why."

"What can you tell us about him?"

"I liked him, that's what I can tell you I liked him!"

"Why did you fire him?"

Logan sat down and slumped on his chair. He didn't want to talk about this, but he realized he had to tell the FBI what they wanted to know. "Because he insisted on doing everything by hand," he began unwillingly. "The old-fashioned way. And we were switching over to computers, and he simply couldn't handle it." Now he warmed up to the memory, almost angry at Bob for forcing him to relive what for Logan—a genuinely kind man beneath a gruff exterior—had been a distasteful business necessity. "It slowed him down tremendously. He couldn't make the adjustment. He did everything in a methodical, precise manner. Very good at what he did, but slow!" He got up suddenly. "Look! I don't want to get involved. You don't know for sure this is the same guy who killed his family."

"We're pretty sure," Agent O'Hara said calmly.

"Well, I'm not convinced," Logan said, stubbornly going back to his original position of not wanting to cooperate with the whole unhappy situation. "Not Bob. Maybe I'll feel like saying more if it's proven that he's the same guy, but right now I'm not going to say anything against him. I was really sorry I had to let him go, especially since he had just gotten married, and that's about all I'm going to say."

"Do you feel guilty about that? Letting him go?"

"Look, I'm running a business here," he said defensively. "There's no place for those kinds of feelings. You do what's best for the company. I'm just sorry it had to be Bob, that's all."

June 8, 1989

Now the necessary detail investigative work began in earnest. Evidence that for years had been kept in plastic bins for the long-awaited prosecution included photographs, autopsy reports, ballistic reports, firearms believed to have been used in the murders, and all the notes and letters the thorough killer had written the night of the crime—including the only one that had never been made public, the long handwritten confessionary letter to his pastor, Reverend Eugene Rehwinkel. While Westfield detectives were collating, labeling, and preparing all the evidence that would be used by the office of the Union County prosecutor, Kathleen Gardner and Ellen Brandt went back to their desks at *The Westfield Leader* on Elm Street and wrote:

> It is one week since List's capture, and most of the news crews have packed up their equipment and left to cover other stories in other towns. The initial excitement is over for them, but Westfielders have 17½ years of pent-up emotions that they have only begun to release. There is still the question of John List returning to New Jersey to face prosecution.

On Thursday, June 8, 1989, United States Magistrate David G. Lowe in Richmond, Virginia, set an extradition hearing for July 6 and ordered the suspect, whom he referred to as "John List also known as Robert Clark," held without bail.

June 14, 1989

Delores spent the two weeks following Bob's arrest in seclusion and despair. She didn't eat. She didn't sleep. She was desperately worried about money. "How will I make ends meet now?" she asked her friend Anne, from church, who continued to visit her.

"Somehow it will work out," said Anne.

"But how?" she cried. "I don't understand what's happening. Or *why* this happened. It can't be true. None of it."

"He never gave a hint of . . . anything?"

"No!" Delores snapped. "He's not that man."

A man who would murder his wife, all three of his children—his own flesh and blood and his own mother. It was thoroughly inconceivable. At this point the crime was so heinous that she would not have been able to accept it even if she had seen him with his hand pointing the murder weapon at their heads. Not her Bobby.

She began to cry again. The friend held her in her arms. "How am I supposed to go on with my life," she sobbed, "after something like this? I feel so . . . lonely."

The first time Reverend Vought visited the jail with Delores, the sheriff had let him in on a one-time-only basis because he was the prisoner's pastor and the situation was one that called for immediate crisis intervention. Afterward the young pastor had to go through all the normal procedures for visitation. He had to bring his ordination certificate to the jail and fill out an application form in order to get himself registered and approved for further visitation rights. Because of the red tape, Reverend Vought had had no contact with Bob for two weeks.

By the time he came again, it seemed as though he were visiting a different person. When he entered the interview room, Bob waved to him from across the room. "How are you?" he called out. He seemed thoroughly at ease with himself and glad to see the pastor.

"I'm fine," the pastor said, overcoming his surprise at the change in Bob. "How are they treating you?"

"Very well," Bob said. "The conditions here are pretty good."

Reverend Vought had just had a phone conversation with Anne about Delores's condition.

"I'm in a dayroom with other prisoners now," Bob said, "reading books, talking with some of the brighter ones. . . ."

He seemed to have accepted his situation. Whether he'd become used to the circumstances, or whether he was realizing that finally he didn't have to put up a front anymore, the pastor couldn't tell, but there was a definite change in Bob from the day after his arrest, when he had been distraught enough to threaten suicide.

"I spend some time watching television," Bob said.

He almost told Reverend Vought that on one occasion, when America's Most Wanted came on the air, one of the inmates called out to him, "Hey, Bobby, your show is on. Want to watch? Come on, kid. You're the star!" Laughter had followed him as he'd retreated. He decided against mentioning the incident at the moment.

There were no more tears, Reverend Vought realized. It was all just something he had to get through now. The proud bearing had returned, the erect posture, the tilt of the head.

"And of course," Bob went on, "I spend a great deal of time with the Bible and in daily prayer. It's a great comfort to me and a source of strength."

Reverend Vought suddenly found himself thinking of the other man—John List. He didn't know John List, he only knew Bob Clark. . . .

"I'm adjusting well to the routine here," he heard Bob say.

But John, the man he did not know, intruded on his thoughts and fascinated him as he listened to Bob talk about his experiences as a prisoner and the strength and comfort he continued to glean from his daily devotions. He heard Bob ask him to perform the confession of forgiveness for him. Vought was beginning to believe that the reason John List had gravitated to the church was to try to "make it all square." Maybe that was the motivation. Here's the church with the body of Christ, who says, "Love," "Peace," "Grace"; and when something so dissonant had happened, he had to work on it and somehow make it square. At least that's what he thought John List would do.

Reverend Vought sighed to himself. There was a time when he hadn't wanted to be a pastor as his father had been before him. Pastorship had its challenges. Working with people could be difficult and strange and wonderful all at the same time. Then there had been a turnabout in his thinking when, as a youth, he was grasped by the gospel that said, "You are loved in spite of yourself." During the times in his own life when he felt he was most unlovable, he was reassured by knowing, "You are loved in spite of yourself." He found himself trying to relate this belief to his feelings about Bob. Bob, or John List, was loved in spite of himself. The confession of forgiveness. It was the last time the young pastor would see Bob Clark.

Later, when Delores asked him, Vought was able to report that they had had a good visit, a more normal one than the first time; but he couldn't help wishing that Delores was adjusting as well as Bob was.

June 15, 1989

Governor Thomas Kean of New Jersey signed a petition to Governor Gerald Bailles of Virginia requesting the extradition of "John Emil List, also known as Robert P. Clark." The governor of Virginia was expected to sign a similar document so that trial proceedings could take place in New Jersey's Union County, where the murders occurred.

When Delores finally agreed to hold a press conference, it was held in the office of her attorney, David Baugh, in Richmond. She was simply dressed in a short-sleeved, open-collared shirt and dark skirt. Her short-cropped blond hair was neatly coiffed. Her eyes were partially hidden behind plain wire spectacles. She wore practically no makeup, and her full, sensitive lips were moist and slightly parted as though she were having difficulty breathing. To no one's surprise, Delores had decided to stand by the man she loved and knew as Bob Clark. She had known him for over twelve years and was convinced he was everything a wife could hope for in a husband. Gentle, kind, devoted, a believer in God, and essentially a good provider despite the ordinary financial ups and down that many people at their socioeconomic level endured.

"That man in New Jersey is not the man I know," she said, standing next to Baugh. Her attorney, a soft-spoken black man with a round face, tightly knit black hair, and glasses perched lightly on top of a full nose, held her elbow protectively as she spoke. "The man I know is kind and loving, a devoted husband and dear friend. I hope somehow this is not true." She hesitated ever so slightly while memories of her phone conversation with Jonah Folger jumped into her consciousness. "And if it is," she murmured, "that he was so stressed out that something snapped. I am devoted to him. I hope that somehow God will see us through this."

"How long have you been married?"

She was startled by the question. She thought her statement spoke for itself. But she answered submissively. "Almost four years. In November it will be four years."

"What did you talk to him about when you first saw him in jail?" came the first intrusive question.

"When I was permitted to visit him, my husband was very distraught and upset." Her voice was getting softer.

"Did he tell you about the murders?"

"We did not discuss the case," she said so very quietly that they had to lean forward to hear. "We preferred, instead, to have a pleasant conversation."

"About what?" demanded one voice. Even the other newsmen glanced with distaste at the questioner as though they were saying, "Look, we have to be here, it's our job, but let's give her a chance, okay?"

Delores lowered her head a bit, trying to regain control of her turbulent emotions. David Baugh, noticing her distress, opened his mouth to speak for her. She shook her head at him and continued. Her voice shook a bit as she said slowly, "We preferred to reminisce about our life together."

Now there was a distinct hush in the room. Behind her glasses they could see that her eyes were moist. She lowered her head again, and her chin quivered almost imperceptibly. "The man I know as

Robert P. Clark," she continued, "is a sweet and gentle man of good character."

And when the reporters tried to press her further, David Baugh started gently to pull her back.

"Did you have any idea who he really was?"

"How do you feel now that you know?"

"When did you find out the truth?"

David Baugh squeezed her arm gently, his full lips set at her ordeal. Delores bowed her head under the assault of questions, but she tried to lift it as she said in a very soft but firm voice, "I do not believe it. I love my husband very deeply. I do not believe this is the same man."

"That's enough," Baugh whispered protectively.

"Didn't a friend of yours back in Colorado show you a picture of him in a paper that covered the killings?"

"Yes, she showed me a photo, but I dismissed it because I felt it wasn't true. It's still not true. I believe that," Delores insisted. "My life has been a nightmare since this began June first, when the FBI man told me his suspicions. We have had a happy marriage filled with mutual respect and love. That's all I can tell you. I don't believe he is the same man," she said adamantly.

David Baugh spoke up now. "You have to understand that my client, Robert Clark—" and he stressed the name ever so slightly to indicate that it was to be held separate from the name of John List "—maintains that he is not the killer who has been sought for the past eighteen years." At this point he terminated the press interview.

Delores sat back, relieved that the ordeal was over, and wondered what to do next.

June 22, 1989

Virginia Governor Gerald Bailles received a written request from Governor Thomas Kean of New Jersey to turn the fugitive over to New Jersey authorities. Only after such a request is made can an extradition hearing be held. The date for the hearing was moved back from July 6 to June 29.

June 28, 1989

Sheriff Ralph Froehlich and Deputy Sheriffs William Malcolm and William Malcolm, Jr., his son, flew with Peter Campanelli of the Sheriff's Office Fugitive Squad to Richmond to await the outcome of List's extradition hearing. No one knew what action Clark and his attorney would take in court the next morning, but they were ready in the event that things went smoothly. After an eighteen-year search, it was about time things went their way.

June 29, 1989

Air-conditioning had not yet been turned on. The Virginia court-room was already warm at 9:00 A.M., the time set for the extradition hearing. As they had from the moment of Clark's arrest, events continued to move rapidly. Judge Al Harris sat on the bench looking down at David Baugh and his infamous client, "Robert P. Clark," as the proceedings began. The suspect, looking every inch a re-spectable citizen, appeared attentive and very interested in the pro-ceedings. By prior agreement Judge Harris was not going to challenge the man's identity or even refer to him by either name, List or Clark, in open court. The extradition hearing, substantially braced with petition agreements signed by New Jersey Governor Kean and Virginia Governor Bailles, was over very quickly. Within ten minutes Clark was on his way back to Henrico County Jail, where the law enforcement contingent from New Jersey was waiting to whisk him away. Within fifteen minutes his attorney, David Baugh, was giving a statement to the ever-ready corps of newsmen waiting for the results of the hearing. Even they were surprised at the speed with which the hearing had proceeded.

"At exactly nine-ten this morning, my client, Robert Clark, waived extradition," David Baugh said to them.

"Why is that?" asked one.

"But he has a right to fight extradition if he so chooses, doesn't he?" asked another.

"Yes," Baugh responded. "It was a very brief court appearance. During the proceedings no one asked him what his name was."

"Was that intentional?"

"Yes, it was," he admitted, "so that the dispute over his true identity would not have to be resolved immediately, and the matter of extradition could be expedited."

"What's the story?" asked another reporter. "Can we say he waived his right because he wants to settle this?"

"Say whatever you like," Baugh said pleasantly.

"Wouldn't postponing extradition delay a trial in New Jersey?" asked another.

Baugh shrugged noncommittally.

"Is that the point?" another questioned. "As an innocent man, clearing his name is what's important to him? With as little delay as possible?''

The attorney smiled at the leading questions. "That's all, gentlemen."

"But the FBI said the fingerprints match."

"Of course that remains to be seen," Baugh said.

"What did he say? What kind of a mood was he in? How does he feel about returning to New Jersey?"

"You know better than to ask that." He smiled. "As far as I'm concerned, my legal obligations are over. As of this morning, Mr. Clark has no further legal matters pending in Virginia, but I still can't discuss anything my client may or may not have said to me."

He grinned as they groaned loudly. "Come on, come on. . . ."

He told them that he would remain as a "friendly adviser" to Delores Clark but did not mention that he would act as her broker in the matter of the many calls that continued to come in to his office from those who wanted to buy her story. "That's it, boys." He started to walk away.

"Come on, give us a break. . . ."

Baugh paused for a moment and turned back. "I will say only this much. . . ."

Everyone leaned forward attentively.

"Legally, my client, Robert Clark, has ten days to challenge the warrant and to mount a court fight to block the extradition. However, Mr. Clark has agreed on advice of counsel to return to New Jersey as long as he returns as Robert P. Clark, not as John List."

They all knew that extradition proceedings could have taken months. They also knew that by waiving extradition in the manner in which he had been advised, he was, in effect, agreeing to return to New Jersey to face prosecution for the five murders without conceding who he was or what he was alleged to have done.

Robert P. Clark was immediately transferred to the custody of the Union County officials, headed by Sheriff Ralph Froehlich, who had been waiting patiently for the extradition procedure to be over. Papers were signed. Forms were filled out—quickly. Let nothing interfere with getting him safely *home*. Reservations on Piedmont Airlines were already made and waiting. Clark was permitted to go back to his cell at the Henrico County Jail to pick up a few personal belongings and books before the flight to New Jersey.

Before leaving the jail, he had to be handcuffed. Sheriff Froehlich knew there was usually a cooperative relationship among sheriffs. We can always work things out, he thought as he went to the sheriff of Henrico County with a special request. "I have the retired Westfield chief of police with me in the other room," he told him. "Chief Moran's been looking for this guy for eighteen years. I know this request is unusual, but it's your jail, and you're the boss until the prisoner's turned over to me. We ourselves don't usually like to let someone else come in and steal our thunder," he said, "but would you mind if the chief comes in and hooks up the suspect? Out of courtesy."

"Hell, no! Glad to."

Great southern hospitality, Froehlich thought warmly, while the Virginia sheriff, in turn thought, That's mighty generous of Froehlich. Warm, good feelings were running high.

Chief Moran entered. He went to Clark with a pair of handcuffs and stood right in front of the prisoner, possibly a little closer than he had to stand in order to perform the hookup, Froehlich thought, hiding a smile. Moran, with his short-cropped white crew cut, was much shorter than Clark, but he was 100 percent policeman as, with great satisfaction, pride, and a slight tremor in his voice, he growled, "I'm Chief Moran. I'm your worst nightmare come true. Put your hands out."

Clark put out his hands. Moran hooked him up with a sharp snap. Then he stepped back. It was a good moment, Froehlich thought. Moran finally had the satisfaction he had been looking forward to for so long. Probably a high spot in his career, Froehlich thought, feeling good for old Mugsy.

Virginia State Police were relieved to see the prisoner taken out of Henrico County Jail by the contingent of New Jersey lawmen. The flurry of national publicity after Clark's June 1 arrest had been excessive in their opinion. "You'd think the guy was Manson," drawled one officer.

"Worse," said a Jersey lawman. "Manson killed strangers. This guy worked closer to home."

"Looks like a l'il ol' pussycat to me."

"Well," said Virginia State Police Major M. H. Bruce, stretching his legs out comfortably. "He's gone and we're happy."

Sheriff Froehlich looked at his handcuffed prisoner as he escorted him out through the basement of Henrico County Jail. Clark wore a light gray business suit, an open-necked shirt, and white sneakers. He was very pale and quiet but cooperative. He gave no reaction, demonstrated no resentment, showed no emotion at all. Froehlich looked about as they stepped into the waiting car and realized that there had been no sign of Mrs. Delores Clark anywhere. He had half anticipated a tearful farewell. When David Baugh, List's attorney, came over to Froehlich at the courthouse asking, "Sheriff,

I would appreciate it if you could make arrangements for Mr. Clark to call his wife from the airport before the flight," Froehlich knew that Delores was deliberately keeping out of sight. If he could arrange a private phone call for a minute or two, he would. Why not?

"I'll do the best I can for you," Froehlich said sincerely.

On the car trip to the airport in Virginia, he thought, What do you say to a guy like this with his Bible and his Michener books on his lap? Finally, looking out the window, Froehlich couldn't help remarking on the beauty of the Virginia countryside. "Wouldn't mind retiring to a place like this," he said. "I've always been interested in the Civil War."

"My wife and I just went to a Civil War reenactment," Bob said quietly. "They do it all the time in Virginia."

"Really?"

"We went recently."

"No kidding. Beautiful place."

Then Clark became quiet again. He turned his head and looked out of the window. Froehlich wondered what he was thinking. He probably knew he was seeing the last of Virginia on the way to the airport. It was doubtful he would ever return, but who knew what a guy like that thought about?

Henrico County personnel escorted them right to the Richmond airport, where security was waiting for them. The coordination was phenomenal, Froehlich thought. The move from the jail to the airport was done with the precision of a military maneuver.

Clark tensed up considerably when he saw all the news media waiting. Froehlich got out of the car to talk to them. "Look," he said reasonably, "I've got a job to perform, and I understand you've got yours, too. Let's work this out together, okay? In a full spirit of cooperation. Try not to get in our way, and don't stick those mikes in our faces, and we'll walk at a reasonable pace through the airport to give you a chance to take your pictures. Okay?"

Held by the arms, towering over the lawmen, Clark stared straight ahead stiffly as cameras, only a couple of feet away from his face, recorded his grim, stony departure from Virginia. In some of the photos snapped for the evening editions, his head and face were maintained in so rigid a posture, he appeared a living parody of the plaster bust on TV that had helped to bring about his downfall. Another layer of privacy was shredded away. The downturned mouth, the soulful eyes, the handcuffs restraining his wrists linked to the chain about his waist, further restraining his arm movements . . . it would all be in the newspapers. Front page. Headlines. But

Mr. Clark caused no one any problems as he was escorted slowly up the escalator.

Airport security had set aside a private room for the hour delay they were forced to endure. Bob Clark was permitted to make a phone call to his wife before boarding the plane.

The morning flight was booked to half capacity by civilian passengers. Sergeant Edward Johnson of the Union County Prosecutor's Office, Homicide Unit, and Lieutenant Detective Barney Tracy were also returning home after collecting additional evidential data from the FBI office in Virginia. The prisoner was surrounded front and back by lawmen. At one point after the door was sealed closed, the pilot came back and said to the sheriff, "I'm sorry. You'll have to take the handcuffs off."

Froehlich looked in his pocket for the key. "We've got a fugitive here."

"I know, sir. But regulations state—"

"I know, I know," Froehlich said, inserting the key in the lock.

"It's a common procedure," the pilot said as he looked at the fugitive. "In case of emergency all passengers must be able to move freely."

Froehlich unlocked the handcuffs.

"Thank you," said Mr. Clark.

"As soon as we land, they go right back on," Froehlich told his prisoner.

"I understand," said Mr. Clark.

It was only a one-hour flight to Newark Airport.

"Hey, John," Sergeant Johnson, sitting next to Barney, called to him. "Want a bagel?"

Mr. Clark looked up, with no reaction to having been called "John." Barney watched with narrow eyes as Johnson held up the bagel for List to see.

"No, thank you," the prisoner said.

"How about a soda?" Campanelli added.

"Whattaya say, John?" Froehlich asked. "Should I get it for you?"

"Thank you."

When Froehlich got up for a moment, Johnson stopped him and whispered, "He didn't seem to mind being called 'John.'"

"Hey," Froehlich said, "I could have called him 'Harry.' I could have called him 'Mandrake the Magician.' He could have corrected me if he wanted to. He didn't."

"How did he sign his extradition papers?"

"Robert P. Clark."

Barney shook his blond head in disbelief. "He's gonna stick to that?"

"Looks like. You have any doubts that he's List?"

"Not even a slight one," Barney said emphatically. "It all adds up. Proof positive."

"Well, he's a cool one. And a perfect gentleman," Froehlich said, and resumed his seat in the back of the plane next to the prisoner.

Johnson sat down next to Barney again and offered him a bagel. Barney waved it aside. "You know, there's a possibility that guy might get away with it," he said suddenly.

"No. I don't think so," Johnson answered, taking a large bite.

"The court and judicial system work in strange ways," Barney whispered insistently. "A defense attorney isn't looking for the truth. He's looking for ways to prevent the truth from being told."

"What else is new?" Johnson muttered through a full mouth.

"You'd have to live on another planet to believe that any defense attorney is looking for the truth, because the truth is what puts their guy in jail!"

Sergeant Johnson wasn't feeling as pessimistic. "What are you worried about? We got him. Our office has him nailed. Good. Solid."

But Barney wasn't about to be appeased. "The whole thing is backward."

"Don't let this get to you," Johnson said. "We got our man. Trust me. Trust the prosecutor's office. Trust Eleanor Clark. She's a real first-class hot shot. You think she'd let this character get away? No way! You can bet on it!"

They both laughed warmly. They knew Eleanor Clark well. She was the very dynamic Union County assistant prosecutor with a reputation for always getting her man.

Bob Clark paid no attention to the whispering up ahead. He mentioned to Froehlich that he liked Errol Flynn and some of the old war movies before he busied himself reading his book by James Michener during the flight north.

The Piedmont jet touched ground in Newark at exactly 12:30 P.M., less than three and a half hours after the extradition proceedings in Richmond.

The law enforcement agents waited until the cabin had emptied of regular passengers before preparing to remove their prisoner. As they waited, Froehlich looked out of the window. He saw Chief Moran going down the ladder carrying his bag. He seemed very much alone. Froehlich motioned Clark to stand up. "Have to cuff you again, buddy," he said as he wondered what was going through Moran's mind.

He looked out of the window again. What a mess. The word had gotten out. Every window in the airport was mobbed with TV cameras and still-camera reporters. It was havoc. Are we gonna get in trouble here? he thought. If we go through the normal exit into the waiting area, it'll be a circus. Fortunately I've got a good staff. His other detective, Yanusz, formerly with the federal marshal's office, had made arrangements to drive right onto the tarmac. When they exited the plane they went down the ladder directly into the cars and took off. They were never boxed into that damned near riot that was taking place. Great going, staff, he thought. Within moments of arrival, List was whisked off the tarmac at Newark Airport. He was taken to an unmarked car that was waiting to carry him straight to the Union County Jail in Elizabeth, N.J.

The maneuver may have fooled the media at the airport, but word of List's impending arrival spread quickly throughout the administration complex and the Union County Courthouse.

Dozens of county employees convened in small jubilant huddles to get a glimpse of the man who had eluded authorities for nearly two decades. County clerks, tax collectors, title searchers, secretaries from the engineering department, and clerks from the registrar's office all waited. Everyone wanted to see him.

All were disappointed, however. List's appearance was anticlimactic. He was seated in the back of the car flanked by two sheriff's officers. The car rounded the corner to the rear alley entrance of the jail garage.

"No fair!" shouted one employee out of a second-story window. Knowing the layout of the building, he realized they were taking the prisoner straight into the loading bay area at the rear entrance, where the electric door could be quickly lowered even before the prisoner emerged from the car. This not only gave him protection, but also effectively blocked him from view.

"No fair!" chimed a chorus of protests. There was genuine disappointment. They had been waiting a long time to get a glimpse of the notorious bogeyman from Westfield.

After Froehlich had fulfilled his responsibility in transferring the fugitive back to New Jersey, he shook his head in mild bewilderment. "You certainly don't get the idea that this man is the type who would commit the kind of crime he's accused of. Just goes to show you. External appearances mean nothing, right?"

Pending arraignment of the murder indictments returned by a grand jury nearly eighteen years before, Clark was put in a special observation area at the Union County Department of Corrections, where all defendants facing similar kinds of charges were kept. He was placed in a sequestered jail cell for his own protection, since other inmates, trying to gain a bizarre form of attention, will often attempt to harm notorious prisoners. This time Clark brought no books or magazines, only a Bible, to the isolated cell where two guards were, once again, assigned to him on a twenty-four-hour suicide watch.

Events continued to move speedily.

Union County Prosecutor David Hancock, who was supervisor of the Homicide Unit, announced that Mr. Clark's arraignment was set for July 10 before Judge William L. Wertheimer.

Elijah Miller, Jr., the deputy public defender, was assigned to represent the defendant in the case against him despite the fact that many private attorneys had offered to take his case for nothing, merely for the publicity. Bob thought Miller was a good choice; since, as a public defender, he didn't stand to make any extra money, the tendency would be to think of the client's welfare before his own.

Assistant Prosecutors Eleanor Clark and Brian D. Gillet, who were going to co-prosecute the case for the county, were already in the process of reviewing all the evidence that had been preserved since the murders occurred. Witnesses were being located. Subpoenas were being prepared. Eleanor Clark made it clear to the press that she was certain the prosecution could provide the requisite proof.

July 10, 1989

At one-thirty in the afternoon on the day of arraignment, the ornate seventh-floor courtroom in Elizabeth was crowded. More than 180 national and local newsmen, media personnel, and spectators were present. Kathleen Gardner and Ellen Scott Brandt from *The Westfield Leader* felt very lucky to have gotten seats immediately behind the defendant's table.

"Silence," called a Union County deputy sheriff. He looked toward the enormous brass door through which the mass murderer was to be escorted momentarily.

"Silence," he repeated.

First a breathless hush rushed through the room, then waves of whispers, as heads looked for a view of the tall killer. He entered manacled at the wrists, a large, heavy-looking manila envelope containing release papers from Virginia pressed to his stomach. As the court officers held on to his elbows and navigated their way through the stares, he kept his head lowered, his eyelids shutting out the humiliation.

Judge Wertheimer, coincidentally a Westfield resident himself, watched as the defendant was admitted before him. His own wife and three sons were among the interested spectators who attended the hearings. List appeared in traditional khaki prison issue; his shirt had "Union County Jail" printed across the back. The neatness he was so known for by all friends and neighbors had been abandoned and uncombed tufts of white hair sprang from his balding head.

He was led to a long table in front of the judge. Elijah Miller stood up and pointed him to a chair at his side.

It was the first time Kathleen and Ellen had ever seen "him." And here he was so close. It was weird. Clark/List was attentive. He seemed unafraid. When he talked to the soft-spoken Elijah Miller, they too, as so many before them, were surprised at the resonance of his voice. He continued to treat the entire arraignment procedure as something he just had to get through. They discerned a subtle air of annoyance in his demeanor they had not anticipated. He seemed to be totally oblivious of all the commotion around him, the sense of theatre, the excitement in the room. Seeing him did not dispel the mystery of Westfield's bogeyman for Kathleen and Ellen.

Judge Wertheimer looked up at the murmuring crowd of people and waited for the whispers to subside before proceeding to read List the five December 1971 indictments accusing him of the murders.

Now Clark and his attorney stood up to face the judge.

Judge Wertheimer's steady voice rang through the courtroom clearly as he read that the grand jury had charged that "one John Emil List did willfully, feloniously, and with malice aforethought" kill five members of his family on November 9, 1971.

Clark stood before the judge, swaying slightly, his head tilted to the side. Then he looked down with his eyes shut tight. Mild-mannered, quiet, meek, hands joined together with handcuffs, thumbs interlocked, held low below his stomach, wrists attached to the chain encircling his waist, he appeared to be a man at prayer, while inside himself quiet thoughts of rage at the indignities being perpetrated against him raced through his mind as he felt the stares and listened to the charges. He had settled the matter of internal justice a long time ago. Now he was faced with external justice, which understood nothing but bone facts stripped of the flesh of understanding human needs. The pitch dark of the confessional was in his own soul. Absolution was really only a matter between him and God. He was sure he'd left no footprints. At no time did he recognize the intense power of rationalization at work. He never suffered the fear of damnation. At the moment, he suffered only the strain of continual politeness.

Brian Gillet sat calmly at the prosecutor's table. He wiped his eyeglasses clean. Then he leaned back and, gently stroking his mustache, watched the defendant. Next to him, his co-prosecutor, Eleanor Clark, was a bundle of energy. Even seated she appeared vibrant, dynamic, with her short-cropped black hair, an Irish face that was probably freckled when she was an adolescent, white teeth, blue-green eyes, and bright red lipstick. Throughout the hearing she appeared to doodle on a white scratch pad, but it was more than doodling. She punctuated all of the spoken words with arrows, underlining her own thoughts with written accents. Many pages were covered, torn off, turned over, discarded. It was as though she were graphically outlining her own thoughts as well as everything that was said in the courtroom. Brian glanced at her doodlings and smiled. He knew Eleanor's dynamic style well.

"How do you plead?" the judge asked after he had completed reading the charges.

The defendant did not flinch as he entered a plea of "not guilty" to all five counts. "I am not John List," he said stonily. "My name is Robert P. Clark."

A deep murmur of indignation swept through the courtroom.

At her table, Eleanor Clark jabbed more doodles at the paper in front of her before she stood up.

"Your Honor," she said confidently, "we feel we will have no trouble identifying this man as John Emil List. We request that a five-million-dollar bail be set for the accused, one million dollars for each of the murders."

Elijah Miller was quick to protest above the appreciative clamor that greeted the request, but Judge Wertheimer waved away his protest. "I can think of seventeen and a half very good reasons why bail should be set at five million dollars," he said emphatically.

Robert Clark smiled for the first time as the courtroom once again burst into a roar of approval.

Before the hearing was concluded, Judge Wertheimer set December 4, 1989, as a tentative trial date.

Eleanor turned to Brian Gillet and whispered, "Let's get out of here before the circus really begins."

They were up and out of the courtroom even before the defendant was escorted back through the gilded doors. Gillet went in one direction, Eleanor in another, but Randall Pinkston of CNN Cable

TV sensed that they were on an evasive run and quickly followed. He caught up with her in the elevator. Her tiny pointed nose crinkled at the base as she laughed out loud at his maneuver.

"No comment," she said. She meant it.

Kathleen Gardner and Ellen Scott Brandt looked at each other as they sat back in the courtroom with satisfaction. "That woman, Eleanor Clark, looks like a human dynamo."

"I don't think List stands a chance!"

They crossed their fingers at each other in youthful exuberance.

38 | Brought to Justice

John List continued to maintain that he was Robert Peter Clark until Elijah Miller, his attorney, pointed out to him that his best defense lay in preventing the admission into evidence of the letters left behind at the scene of the murders. Clark finally agreed, and on February 16, 1990, Miller reported that his client had acknowledged he was in fact John Emil List.

Superior Court Judge Edward W. Beglin was expected to preside at the trial. But it was Judge William L'E. Wertheimer who sat on the bench instead, and it was to him on March 26, 27, and 28 that Miller presented pretrial motions to suppress all evidentiary material found on December 7, 1971, on the grounds that the murder house was entered without a search warrant.

At the time the crimes had been committed, New Jersey had had no death penalty, so, if convicted of first-degree murder, John List faced life imprisonment, not execution. Under the 1971 criminal code, to obtain a conviction of first-degree murder, the prosecution must prove that the defendant acted "willfully," "deliberately," and with "premeditation." A second-degree murder charge might be obtained if Elijah Miller could disprove any one of the qualifying conditions. If the defendant were found to have been functioning with "diminished mental capacity," the sentence for the crime could be less severe. There was also the possibility of "not guilty" by reason of mental defect.

The courtroom where the trial was held bespoke the weight of judicial authority from the high ceilings supported by gilded colonnades to the huge unpolished brass doors, from the judge's elevated mahogany bench, to the jury's stuffed brown leather chairs. Dominating the wall behind the judge's bench was Harienstein's mural, *Faith Leads the Way—June 23, 1780*, which depicted "Parson Caldwell" distributing hymnals to Revolutionary soldiers to use as wads for their rifles. Few in the room caught the irony that in the List case, also, the accoutrements of religion were subverted to the cause of killing. The doors had opened to the public at 8:30 A.M. By 8:33 the courtroom was packed to its 150-person capacity while some thirty disappointed spectators remained in the large lobby outside. Thirty-seven representatives of newspapers and other media were given priority seating in the first four rows.

The manacled defendant, John Emil List, was escorted into court by Sergeant Joan Spano's security force. Necks craned. It was the first time many in the courtroom had seen the prisoner in the flesh. Dressed in a brown suit that didn't fit well across the shoulders, he clutched large manila envelopes at his waist. Thin strands of gray and white hair were spread slightly askew over his shiny pink scalp. His chin was loose, his mouth a bit open, soft, and moist, almost sensuous-looking. He looked tired, old, pale, thin. He had lost twenty to thirty pounds since his arrest ten months earlier. List did not look at the press or pay attention to the rustle of their pads. He listened attentively to court personnel, moved where they told him to move, sat down, and offered his wrists to a security guard, who reached forward with the key to remove the cuffs. It would be an often repeated procedure, as every time the prisoner was escorted in or out of the room, handcuffs were secured over his wrists. Members of the press closest to him looked at the hand whose long delicate fingers had pulled the trigger. At one time, very early in his life, John List had played the violin.

Elijah Miller, Jr., entered carrying a stuffed leather briefcase. The forty-five-year-old attorney, known throughout the courthouse for his "spiffy" dress habits, wore a deep scarlet tie with his white shirt and blue pin-striped suit. He was tall, slim, and handsome, with beautifully rich chocolate-colored skin, hair cut in a modest Afro style; and when he was greeting people he knew, his ready smile lit up his usually serious face. List greeted him warmly.

Eleanor Clark, Union County assistant prosecutor, entered. Her loose-jacketed black suit and soft white blouse was accented with a single strand of pearls and button pearl earrings. With her short black hair, small, sharply tipped button nose, and iridescent blue eyes, she was very pretty, particularly when she smiled. She walked quickly, with determination. It was obvious she had been looking forward to this moment since List's arrest. At forty-six she was a picture of energetic confidence.

Moments later thirty-three-year-old Assistant Prosecutor Brian Gillet entered, followed by two men carrying huge cartons of carefully labeled black loose-leaf notebooks, evidentiary material, easels, and oversize blown-up photographs.

"All rise," Sergeant Spano said as she preceded the judge into the courtroom from his chambers. "Superior Court is now in session. The Honorable Judge Wertheimer presiding."

The judge entered and took the bench. "Please be seated."

There was an air of expectancy as the pretrial motions began. The issues being raised were important enough to determine the outcome of the trial. The final verdict could rest upon the judge's decision to grant or deny the motions Mr. Miller was about to present. First, since there was so much press coverage and public interest in the case, Mr. Miller asked Judge Wertheimer to sequester the jury.

The request was denied.

For the next three days Judge Wertheimer listened to a motion made by Elijah Miller to suppress all the evidentiary material that had been taken from the List home on the night of December 7, 1971, when the murders had been discovered. Miller contended the police had entered his client's home illegally, that they did not have a search warrant, and that his client's constitutional rights under the Fourth Amendment that ensured privacy and personal security rights had been violated. Among the evidence Mr. Miller wanted suppressed were all the notes List had written the day and night of the slayings and the two handguns that had been found in his desk when the police broke its lock.

Mr. Miller and Ms. Clark argued vehemently over the motions raised as conflicting witness testimony was presented. Mrs. Barbara Baeder testified she had been concerned because she "hadn't heard" from any of the Lists. Mrs. Cunnick reported phoning the police at nine-thirty about "a white Pontiac" that was in the List driveway. Captain Alfred Vardalis stated that he was concerned for the safety of Alma List, who might have been "alone in the house." Officers Zhelesnik and Haller entered the house first without direct instructions from Vardalis. Contradicting what he had said in 1971, Edwin Illiano stated that he was the first to enter the house by opening the window "in one fluid motion." Vardalis then testified he considered the entry "routine."

Amid the legal arguments about search warrants and illegal entry, ntriguing evidence was now being revealed for the first time in almost twenty years: the two guns, the ammunition, and the notes and letters marked: 1) "Please contact the proper authorities," 2) "The key to the desk is in an envelope addressed to myself," 3) "The keys to the files are in the desk."

Ms. Clark presented testimony from Captain Frank Marranca, head of the Union County Homicide Squad, that someone using the name Robert Peter Clark and who had a Denver motel address had applied for a Social Security number on November 22, 1971, only twelve days after List disappeared and two weeks before the bodies of his family were discovered.

But despite the reasons the witnesses offered, Mr. Miller argued, "Other than a few lights burning out, there was no apparent emergency to warrant entering the house illegally. Not one attempt was made to contact relatives. Just because a person does not pay his mortgage does not constitute abandonment. My client retained full possessive interest in his house. Being delinquent doesn't mean you lose your home."

Eleanor Clark was quick to interject impatiently. "Already on November 22, 1971, the defendant had engineered a new identity. So his argument that he had not abandoned that house is preposterous."

"Your Honor, a warrantless search is invalid," Miller insisted. He asserted that even after the bodies had been found, a warrant should have been obtained before breaking into Mr. List's desk.

Ms. Clark took a step behind her chair and grasped the back of it. "I remind the court that the police officers on the scene had now found five bullet-ridden bodies. A massacre in a suburban New Jersey town in 1971! I maintain that they had good reason to look inside Mr. List's desk!"

Judge Wertheimer ruled, "The police search was justified. It was inevitable that the bodies would have come to light." He cited many precedents in addition to the rule of inevitable discovery. He also maintained rather forcefully that anyone who saw the defendant being returned to New Jersey in handcuffs and leg irons knew that he had no intention of ever returning to the house. "There can be no clearer portrait of a person who had abandoned his past. The defendant not only abandoned his house, his car, his credentials, and mortgage payments, he abandoned his past life of John E. List," the judge said. "The notes were marked, 'To the finder,'" he continued. "They were right on top of the desk. 'Please contact the proper authorities.' It was an invitation to look. The police were there; they were the authorities. It was obvious List expected the

authorities to act upon the scenario he had left behind. John Li[
could not maintain a reasonable expectation of privacy to expect
search warrant, not after he had remained at large for 17½ year
without any claims. No fact is more conclusive of the abandonme[
than the way List lived under the alias of Robert P. Clark. Eightee
years, six months, and twenty-three days shouts that he intended t
flee. The house was proven to be abandoned in fact and in law. Th
Fourth Amendment of the Constitution does not protect abandone
property. Entering without a warrant and opening locked drawe[
was therefore permissible.'' The judge looked at Elijah Mille
calmly. ''Motion denied.''

The next item on Mr. Miller's agenda was the motion to hav
List's letter to Reverend Rehwinkel declared inadmissible becaus
it fell under the protection of the priest-penitent rule of confiden
tiality. Having lost two motions, Miller now argued passionatel
that New Jersey rules protected pastoral communication from bein
used against a congregation member in a court of law. He calle
Reverend Rehwinkel to the stand. The fifty-year-old pastor had snov
white hair and a bright pink round face. His voice was rich an
resonant as he solemnly declared he regarded the letter List ha[
written to him to be privileged. ''I assumed the letter was privat[
from the time I first saw it the night the bodies were discovered,''
he said, ''but the police had opened it first. I gave it back to ther
after reading it myself. I told Chief Moran that it was absolutel[
confidential and I hoped they'd treat it that way.''

Eleanor Clark challenged discrepancies in the pastor's logic
When, under cross-examination, Rehwinkel said, ''If I had receive[
the letter first, none of it would have come to light,'' she aske[
incredulously, ''You would have kept it from the police? What abou
the other letters he wrote that were in the same unsealed manil[
envelope?''

''I would not have revealed them, either.''

''But they were marked to other members of the family, and 'T[
the authorities.' ''

''I would not have revealed any of them.'' Rehwinkel explaine
he had been in a state of trauma when he identified the bodies. ''[
don't use the word lightly,'' he said. ''I had to walk away from
police officers to overcome my emotions as I read the letter. I neve
felt that John would hurt a flea.'' Under Ms. Clark's prodding, h[
went on to say that he had met with Mr. and Mrs. Gene Syfert an
Mr. Joseph Bivins, a cousin, to discuss certain items in the lette[
such as List's request for cremation and distribution of family pos
sessions. ''We did discuss why John had done it, but I spoke onl[

in general terms." He smiled. "That was my right as long as the pastoral comforting was helpful."

But ex–Chief Moran and Michael Mitzner, former Union County assistant prosecutor, testified that they considered the letter to be evidence from the moment they saw it.

"The reverend was at the police station practically every day for weeks," Moran said dryly. "He never said the letter was private."

"*I* was the one who told him to keep it confidential," Mitzner said bluntly. "There was no doubt that we were holding the letter as evidence."

"Did the pastor object?" Ms. Clark asked.

"It wouldn't have mattered."

"Did he?"

"He did not."

The arguments between prosecution and defense continued back and forth for almost a half hour before Judge Wertheimer gave his ruling. "After reviewing the legal arguments and the testimony, I find that the defendant's letter to Reverend Rehwinkel does not fall under the protection of the priest-penitent relationship. Nowhere in the five pages does the defendant seek forgiveness. The statements in the letter could just as easily have been made to a plumber friend as to a pastor. In a protected confession," Wertheimer continued, "privacy, secrecy, and request for confidentiality are important factors. This is not so much a confession as it is an explanation and a list of instructions," he said. "If Mr. List wanted to communicate with Rehwinkel in confidence, he could have gone to the church; he did not. He could have called him on the phone; he did not. He could have mailed him the letter; he did not. He could have marked the envelope 'confidential'; he did not. He could have sealed the envelope; he did not even do that. It could have been found by anyone. Having chosen not to mail the letter, List gained nearly a month's head start by the time police found the bodies," Wertheimer pointed out. "John Emil List was more interested in escape and anonymity than absolution. Nor has Reverend Rehwinkel once raised the priest-penitent issue in all of the eighteen years since Mr. List has been at large, nor even after his capture last June." The judge also noted that the pastor himself also waived any claim he might have had that the letter was to be considered confidential by disclosing portions of it to relatives of the deceased. "You cannot hold up the priest-penitent privilege as a sword in one hand and a shield in the other," he declared. "The letter is part of the State's search for the truth, and the jury should have an opportunity to read it. Motion denied."

John List showed no emotion. He stared down at the shiny surface of the defense table with his head cocked to one side, his left hand covering his mouth, but Elijah Miller frowned. He knew he had lost the most important battle of the trial.

The next day, he went before the N.J. State Supreme Court in an attempt to have the trial moved out of Union County and to have the jury sequestered. The state's highest court rejected his motions by a vote of seven to zero.

It was at this point that Mr. Miller revealed that his client would plead not guilty by reason of "mental defect." Court was adjourned until Monday, April 2, 1990. List went back to his cell in the county jail for the weekend.

When the main lights were turned on at 6:00 A.M., he usually woke up. He enjoyed the surprising silence of the early-morning hours. The twenty-two other inmates housed in the segregation area left him pretty much alone. Now, he arose and prepared his toilet articles—toothbrush, toothpaste, soap, towels, electric razor, clean underwear. The guard would be around at any moment to let him out of his cell for his daily shower. This morning, only half-asleep, he had heard the guard walking by on soft-soled shoes on his last half-hour round. Every thirty minutes they checked his cell. Oddly, he felt protected. He sat patiently on the edge of his bed and waited to be brought back to the courtroom.

As he was ushered to his seat at the defense table on the opening day of the trial, many in the courtroom wondered why John List didn't own up to what he had done and throw himself upon the mercy of the court rather than plead innocence by virtue of diminished mental capacity. After all, there was no death penalty; it wasn't as though Miller were fighting to save his client's life. It might even be good for the man's soul to take his punishment, serve his sentence, and not put the remaining family members through the horror of reliving the tragedy in all its cruel graphic details.

Fifteen jurors were quietly seated in the jury box. One of the final sixteen selected had asked to be excused because, on second thought, he didn't believe he could be impartial. Of those remaining, there were seven white men, two black men, three white women, and three black women. They looked on attentively as Brian Gillet stood up in front of them. In his hand he held List's five-page letter to Reverend Rehwinkel, which had been the object of so much controversy in the pretrial motions. The contents of the letter were to be revealed now for the first time in almost eighteen years. Gillet held himself to his full erect height, adjusted his glasses on the bridge of his nose, and began to read in a strong quiet voice.

(page 1)
Nov. 9, 1971

Dear Pastor Rehwinkel,

I'm very sorry to add this additional burden to your work. I know that what has been done is wrong from all that I have been taught and that any reasons that I might give will not make it right. But you are the one person that I know that while not condoning this will at least possibly understand why I felt that I had to do this.

1. I wasn't earning anywhere near enough to support us. Everything I tried seemed to fall to pieces. True we could have gone bankrupt and maybe gone on welfare.

2. But that brings me to my next point. Knowing the type of location that one would have to live in plus the environment for the children plus the effect on them knowing they were on welfare was just more than I thought they could & should endure. I know that they were willing to cut back but this involved a lot more than that.

3. With Pat being so determined to get into acting I was also fearful as to what this might do to her continuing to be a Christian. I'm sure it wouldn't have helped.

(2)

4. Also, with Helen not going to church I knew that this would harm the children eventually in their attendance. I had continued to hope that she would begin to come to church soon. But when I mentioned to her that Mr. Jutzi wanted to pay her an Elders call, she just blew up (This is not a criticism of Ed) & stated that she wanted her name taken off the church rolls. Again this could only have given an adverse result for the children's continued attendance.

So that is the sum of it. If any one of these had been the condition we might have pulled through but this was just too much. At least I'm certain that all have gone to heaven now. If things had gone on who knows if that would be the case.

Of course Mother got involved because doing what I did to my family would have been a tremendous shock to her at this age. Therefore, knowing that she is also a Christian I felt it best that she be relieved of the troubles of this world that would have hit her.

(3)

After it was all over I said some prayers for them all—from the hymn book. That was the least I could do.

Now for the final arrangements:

Helen & the children have all agreed that they would prefer to be cremated. Please see to it that the costs are kept low.

For Mother, she has a plot at the Frankenmuth Church cemetary [sic]. Please contact

     Mr. Herman Schellhas
     Rt 4
     Vassar, Mich. 41768.

He's married to a niece of Mothers & knows what arrangements are to be made. (She always wanted Rev. Herman Zehnder of Bay City to preach the sermon. But he's not well.)

Also I'm leaving some letters in your care. Please send them on & add whatever comments you think appropriate. The relationships are as follows:

Mrs. Lydia Leyer—Mothers sister
Mrs. Eva Morris—Helens mother
Jean ["& Gene" crossed out] Syfert—Helens sister
["Fred & Clara"—Johns sponsor—crossed out]
["Herb & Ruth"—Freds sponsor—crossed out]
["Marie"—Pat's sponsor]

(4)

Also I don't know what will happen to the books & other personal things. But to the extent possible I'd like for them to be distributed as you see fit. Some books might go in to the school or church library.

Originally I had planned for this Nov 1—All Saints Day. But travel arrangements were delayed. I thought it would be an appropriate day for them to get to heaven.

As for me please let me be dropped from the congregation rolls. I leave my-self in the hand of Gods *Justice* & *Mercy*. I don't doubt that he is able to help us, but apperently [sic] he saw fit not to answer my prayers they [sic] way I had hoped that they would be answered. This makes me think that perhaps it was for the best as far as the childrens souls are concerned. I know that many will only look at the additional years that they could have lived but if finally they were no longer Christians what would be gained.

Also, I'm sure many will say "How could anyone do such a horrible thing."—My only answer is it isn't easy and was only done after much thought.

(5)

Pastor Mrs. Morris may possibly be reached at
      802 Pleasant Hill Dr
    Elkin—Home of her sister.

One other thing. It may seem cowardly to have always shot from behind, but I didn't want any of them to know even at the last second that I had to do this to them.

John got hurt more because he seemed to struggle longer. The rest were immediately out of pain. John ["probably"—crossed out] didn't consciously feel anything either.

Please remember me in your prayers. I will need them whether or not the government does its duty as it see [sic] it. I'm only concerned with making my peace with God & of this I am assured because of Christ dying even for me.

P.S. Mother is in the hallway in the attic—3rd floor. She was too heavy to move.

John.

There was a long silence in the courtroom when Mr. Gillet finished. The letter itself, as read in an even, steady, unemotional, strong baritone, was to be the single most damning piece of evidence. At the defense table, while John List wiped his eyes and stared at his hands folded in front of him almost in a position of prayer, Elijah Miller sat listening with a deep frown. He knew he had his work cut out for him.

"Ladies and gentlemen," Mr. Gillet continued after a long moment in which the cold, calculating words of the killer sank in, "you'll note that the defendant, John List, expressed his concern about the government doing its duty as it sees it. Well, today, eighteen years, four months, and twenty-three days after a day of horror in Westfield, New Jersey, the State is bringing this indictment to trial!

"The evidence will show, ladies and gentlemen, that this defendant meticulously planned, not only the murders of these five members of his family, but also his escape . . . that the defendant *thought* about these killings before he did them. That he *considered* his options. That he *considered* the plan that he was going to use, the plan that he alone conceived, the plan which turned into a day of horror . . . the worst possible nightmare for any mother, child, or wife—their brutal, senseless killing at the hands of somebody they loved. Not only loved, but trusted and depended on. . . . The State will prove to you, ladies and gentlemen, that the defendant committed these murders of the five members of his family in a *premeditated, willful, and deliberate* manner. At the end of the case, the State will ask that you return a verdict of guilty of first-degree murder for the murder of Alma List, for the murder of Helen List, for the murder of Patricia List, for the murder of John List, and for the murder of Frederick List!" he said, pounding the counts home one at a time. "Thank you."

Brian Gillet sat down at the prosecution table in the silence that had followed his opening statement.

"Thank you, Mr. Gillet," said Judge Wertheimer. He looked over at the defense table. "Mr. Miller."

Miller got up and slowly approached the jury box. "Good morning, ladies and gentlemen of the jury," he said softly. Appropriately for a case where identities were confused, Miller began his opening statement by mistakenly attributing to Alice in *Alice in Wonderland* the observation made by Dorothy in *The Wizard of Oz*. "Like Alice in Wonderland," he said, "I've come to the conclusion that we're not in Kansas. Much like Alice, I kind of wish we were. But we're here, and we're about to begin an odyssey. The odyssey we're about to begin is an adversarial journey . . . but our system of justice is based on fundamental fairness, which means that we're judged by our peers by fair and impartial assessment. We do *not* enter with preconceived notions or hidden opinions. We give a fair shake to our people. We are not concerned with just form, but with substance. Unlike the European system, you're not assumed to be guilty. You are assumed, if not presumed, to be innocent unless and until the State has proven with a never-shifting burden, and proven each and every element of a crime or crimes charged beyond a reasonable doubt."

It was difficult to hear the soft-spoken defense attorney even in the silence of the room, but Elijah was not interested in the reaction of the spectators in the courtroom. The reason for his use of a colloquial style soon became clear as he spoke to each and every juror directly with an intimacy and a touch of deep sadness over the matter under consideration. "It's terribly, terribly important to strive to be fair because the issues in this case are inflammatory and they tend to polarize people. If that happens, the true facts and underlying motivations may never be found . . . and justice cannot be had. I represent John List, the man sitting at the table over there. Take a look at him," Miller said. "First, he's a human being. Second, he's an American citizen. Third, he's a veteran of World War Two and the Korean conflict," he said, attributing to his client as many standard elements of good and loyal citizenship as he could, "and it is he, John List, who is entitled to the constitutional protection that our nation provides. Nothing less. That's what our system of justice depends on. It depends upon fairness, when all is said and done. Fairness."

He went on to explain the agonizing rebelliousness of the sixties, John's rigid German Lutheran upbringing, and how, because of his ingrained work ethic, he "was *expected* to succeed. Success was the gauge of a man. Failure was never even thought of! But that was not to be. John List in November 1971 faced overwhelming choices, overwhelming problems, overwhelming pressures which might have been too much even for a normal person. But John List was not a normal person. He was simply not equipped to cope with the pressures and the times. And inevitably *he was forced to act as he did.*"

A murmur rose in the courtroom at the assumption behind Miller's statement, but he pressed on. He kept his voice soft, sad, and sincere. "He felt more and more depressed, helpless, hopeless, and desperate. He had always been taught that welfare was a sin. He felt trapped. He felt that because of his failures . . . *he no longer had any options*. He saw but one last horrific avenue that the concept of 'sin and grace,' as he had been taught, would allow: *to act as he did!* Lay witnesses and experts will tell you what he was like on that fateful day when he entered hell with his eyes open and he committed these acts with love in his heart for his mother, for his wife, and for his children. He acted as he did for the salvation of his family. The doctors will tell you that he truly believes he sent them to heaven and that he prevented them from eternal damnation. Ministers will tell about 'sin and grace,' that they taught John 'Thou shalt not kill,' but that all sins may be forgiven, even killing. Let there be no mistake. John List did this! But these killings were something other than murder."

Elijah's opening statement, for all of its sincerity and passion, was a blend of assumptions and conclusions. The newspapers would interpret his words as meaning that John List murdered his family with love in his heart—in essence that he had "loved them to death"!

The prosecution began to present its case. It was powerful in its evidentiary weight. Although Miller did not claim his client had not committed the murders, Eleanor Clark presented each of the 137 individual pieces of evidence—a bag containing wood chips and linoleum from the kitchen floor at Hillside Avenue, the bullets, the guns, the letters, the notes, bloodied towels, a vial containing bone fragments of one of the victims—as though she must refute an argument for innocence. It was a recitation calculated to bring home to the jury the enormity of the crimes, the killer's premeditation, and the meticulous planning not only of the ambush and execution of his family, but of his determination to escape detection.

Over the next three days the State called thirty-nine witnesses to support the physical evidence.

Barbara Baeder: Testified she last saw John junior when she drove him home the afternoon of 11/9/71.

Gay M. Jacobus: Suburban Trust: Redeemed Alma List's $2,000 in savings bonds for John List on 11/9/71.

Richard Baeder: Thirteen at the time of the killings: Mr. List called his home the night of 11/9/71 to inform Baeder's mother that the children would be absent from school indefinitely because they had to visit a sick grandmother in North Carolina.

Herbert Argast: The milkman: "No more milk until further notice."

Robert L. Scully: Suburban Trust teller at the drive-in window: Cashed a check for John List in the amount of $85.

Gene Syfert: Testified that his brother-in-law was obsessed with unsolved mysteries.

Carol Hollstein: Suburban Trust teller at the drive-in window: Cashed a check for John List made out to John List and Alma M. List in the amount of $200.

Mildred Kreger: Westfield High School attendance officer: Concerned about the children, she went to house and knocked on door while they were dead inside.

Eileen Gilmartin Jones: KVM Real Estate: List called her on 11/9/71 to tell her Patty was sick and wouldn't be in to work.

Margaret Koleszar: KVM Real Estate: Saw John List pick up his son Freddie after work on 11/9/71.

Warren T. Vliet: President of KVM Real Estate: Found note on the floor on the morning of 11/10/71 stating that the children would not be at work since they were going to North Carolina. When he heard of the murders, he remembered the note and gave it to the Westfield police.

Lorraine Eisenbach: Westfield Home Newspaper Service: Found a message from Mr. List on answering machine on the morning of 11/10/71 to cancel newspaper subscription.

Ann Sales: Secretary of Roosevelt Junior High School: Found Mr. List's note on her desk that the boys would be absent from school because of a sudden trip to visit a sick relative.

Captain Alfred Vardalis: Pried open desk in Mr. List's office at Lieutenant Bell's request. He found the 9-mm Steyr and the .22 Colt revolver, which he turned over to Lieutenant Bell.

Captain Frank Marranca: Gathered evidence in Virginia regarding Robert P. Clark.

Officer Stanley J. Cyran: Took Robert P. Clark's fingerprints.

Lieutenant Glenn Owens: Print and handwriting expert: Identified Clark's and List's fingerprints as being identical.

William Praesel: Patricia's friend from Duke's Sub Shop: "She believed in strange things. She believed in witchcraft. She told me she had an altar someplace."

Barbara Sheridan: Told of entering house the night the bodies were discovered.

Officer George A. Zhelesnik (ret.): Told of entering house with Officer Haller, Illiano, and Sheridan the night the bodies were discovered.

Lieutenant Robert J. Bell (ret.): Former Westfield police. Lieutenant Bell testified to all the physical evidence found at the scene of the crime, bullets, bags full of bloodied toweling, guns, ammunition, notes, letters, keys, and so on. The list was so extensive it took forty-five minutes to identify each and every item. Bullets were found on floors, windowsills, and cabinets. "It looked like he was shooting all over the place," he said.

Sergeant Earl Lambert: Drove List's abandoned car from JFK Airport to Westfield Police Department.

John Connelly: Had bloodied garbage bags x-rayed at Northport Hospital in Summit, N.J., then physically examined each.

Captain John Lintott: Firearms expert: Identified guns and demonstrated how to load.

Sergeant William Muth: Took John List's application for a gun permit in October 1971.

Edward Dross: Social Security administrator: Explained how anyone under fifty years of age could obtain a Social Security number on the spot or through the mail.

John Bakke: Custodian of records for First Fidelity Trust Bank: Presented John and Alma List's last bank statements in which accounts had been terminated.

Lieutenant Glenn Owens: Made chart at the scene of the crimes where each bullet and each spent bullet casing had been found.

Sergeant Edward Johnson: Investigator in the Union County Prosecutor's Office: Identified an application "Robert P. Clark" sent to an employment agency in Virginia in 1987.

Jean Syfert: Helen List's sister: Identified five photographs of Helen, Patricia, John junior, and Frederick; also identified a photo showing Helen with Brenda Taylor De Young, her daughter by her first marriage, and John List's mother, Alma.

Marvin Marr: Formerly a teacher at Westfield's Roosevelt Junior High School, where he taught all three List children: Testified that on the day of the killings, November 9, 1971, Frederick List told him he wouldn't be able to take a unit test the next day because the family was going to North Carolina until after Thanksgiving. He asked for advance assignments, and Marr told him to come in after school, but he never showed up.

Sergeant William Mello: Of the Union County Prosecutor's Office: Was present at the List autopsies, testified as to where the bullets had been found in the bodies of the victims.

Officer William Roeben: Hand-sifted through the four garbage bags found at the scene of the crime.

Dr. Maximilian Schoss: Former Union County assistant medical examiner: Performed autopsies on the List women, said all three were shot in the left side of the head. Alma List was shot above the left eyebrow.

Ex–Chief James A. Moran: Identified the note reading "Guns and Ammo" that had been taped to a drawer of List's desk and the two guns found in the drawer.

Detective Robert Kenny: Did a biography of Patricia and stated, "Patty believed strongly in witchcraft and felt she was a witch herself." He also identified a note he retrieved from Westfield High School saying that Patricia List would be "out for a few days," and a 11/9/71 stop-mail order signed by John List that had been retrieved from the Westfield Post Office.

Captain Richard Tidey: State police handwriting analyst: Testified that the same person wrote the five-page letter to Reverend Rehwinkel, the application for a gun permit in October of 1971, and the three letters to a Virginia employment agency in 1987 and 1988.

Andrew Nardelli: N.J. State forensic scientist: Testified regarding his 1971 findings in his analysis of bullets, linoleum, clothing, and hair samples taken from the scene of the crime. The blood found on five of the bullets was identified as human blood; human hair found on one bullet was identified as that of Fred List, and hair identified as that of John was found on another.

Kevin M. August: FBI special agent: Testified about the arrest made in Richmond, Virginia, when the suspect, who claimed to be Robert P. Clark, said he had never been in New Jersey.

The prosecution had completed the presentation of its case. Now Ms. Clark submitted into evidence all of the photographs of the murdered family that had been taken the night they were discovered. Mr. Miller objected vehemently at the inflammatory nature of the photos; they were grisly in their depiction of the massacre that had taken place, the deteriorating condition of the bodies when they were finally discovered was evidenced in vivid color.

While the photos were passed to the defense table for Elijah's scrutiny, John sat with seeming impassivity. He glanced only once at the colored photos lying on the table a few feet away from him while his attorney made valiant efforts to suppress them.

In the final ruling, most of them were admitted into evidence by Judge Wertheimer.

By the time the prosecution rested its case, there was little doubt in anyone's mind what had happened on November 9, 1971.

Now came the defense's turn. The only course left to Elijah Miller was to try to prove that John List had killed his family because, at the time of the killings, he was suffering from a serious mental defect compounded by a medically diagnosable obsessive-compulsive personality disorder, all of which was brought about by his overly rigid German Lutheran upbringing, his complete obedience to the dictates of his strict religious indoctrination, the overwhelming financial and societal pressures that he was ill equipped to handle, and the conviction that he was sending his family on to a better life in the hereafter.

Now began four days of witnesses for the defense.

To show how John had been reared by overly strict authoritarian parents, Elijah called on John's first cousin, Ralph List, from Frankenmuth, Michigan, who himself had been raised in the tradition as founded by the German Lutheran missionary community and adhered to by many of the List ancestors. Ralph List was a seventy-two-year-old gentleman with a full head of wavy white hair who appeared considerably younger than his years. He corroborated the picture Elijah had painted of the isolation in which John List had been raised. "John was a very nonathletic type of a boy," Ralph List said in a clear voice. "He'd hardly ever participate in a lot of sport activities that were always going on. The few times he did play, he'd perspire, and his mother would get very concerned about it. She was afraid he'd get hurt."

"She took extra care of him?"

"John's mother looked after him constantly," Ralph said with a mild shake of his head at the memory.

"In your view," Elijah asked, "would people brought up in the German tradition of Lutheranism, as practiced within the List family, look down upon anyone who would apply for welfare?"

"Oh, yes," Ralph List testified without hesitation. "That's the last thing they'd do. His father was very prosperous, even in the Depression. Always work, work, work. Even when he was retired, he still went around delivering noodles to different stores. Even at his age. That's the way he was."

The next thing Elijah wanted to demonstrate was the extent of Helen List's illness, since her deteriorating physical condition, he contended, was one of the overwhelming pressures on John List, not only the emotional stress List suffered as he watched his wife's progressive degeneration, but the fact that her condition presented continuous and extreme financial hardship. To this purpose Elijah called Dr. Henry M. Liss to the stand.

Dr. Liss was a diagnostic and records specialist with an impressive background of medical credits that took a full fifteen minutes to enumerate. Soft-spoken, calm, and very professional in his approach, Dr. Liss revealed for the first time the full extent of Helen's illnesses, her numerous hospital stays, her unwillingness to cooperate in her own diagnosis by hiding details about her medical history, and finally the fact that, at the time she was killed, she was suffering from the final stages of tertiary syphilis of the brain.

The revelation was an unexpected bombshell. It created the kind of stir Elijah had hoped for. He would actually welcome the sensational headlines the word *syphilis* would produce. Few in the courtroom were aware that Helen List had been suffering from such a socially unacceptable disease. Even Helen List's sister, Jean, did not know. Jean sat in the courtroom next to her husband. She had had to listen to all the detailed graphic descriptions of the murder scene, and now came the news that her sister had been suffering from syphilis. Jean sat stiffly, stonily, and listened.

"I always liked him," she said later on in her testimony for the defense, referring to John, who looked up at her appreciatively. "My sister was the domineering one." Her testimony even gave the impression that Helen might have manipulated John into marriage under the guise of being pregnant. Jean told of her last visit with her sister, where she found her physical condition to have deteriorated severely. She told how Helen remained in bed practically the entire duration of the Syferts' three-day stay, how John had been burdened with all the extra household duties Helen could not perform. She spoke of finding her sister unclean and unkempt. "The first thing I noticed were her dirty feet," she said. She described the morning Helen came down the stairs on her backside and had fallen over in a dead faint. She even told of Brenda's out-of-wedlock pregnancy at the age of sixteen and how it had affected John and Helen. "Helen never liked children much," she offered. It was John who went to visit Brenda in the home for unwed mothers. It was John who was supportive of Brenda. Helen wouldn't talk to the child. And then she said, "Helen began drinking after that." Eventually her testimony was interrupted by the judge as he himself began to question its relevancy. But a certain amount of damage had been done to the prosecutor's case when the murdered woman's own sister spoke of how overburdened her likable brother-in-law had been.

The next day Carole Agus, columnist for *New York Newsday*, wrote an article, headed "What a Difference a Deal Makes," in which she virtually accused Jean Syfert of testifying for the defense because she had made a deal with Republic Pictures for the List story, and Republic Pictures expected her to be in a position to get John List's personal version and full cooperation. She charged that Jean's testimony about what a "nice guy" he was had been given for the purpose of getting on John's good side. To corroborate her premise, Ms. Agus stated that Jean had earlier given her an extensive interview in which Jean told her that she had never liked John, that he was "sissified," "not outgoing," "standoffish," and "different-looking." She also said that he had never paid Brenda any attention. It was a sad allegation and a sad day for all concerned.

The question on everyone's mind was whether List would take the stand in his own defense. Now the reliability of any such testimony was discussed by Dr. Lionel Ehrenworth. Dr. Ehrenworth was called in by the defense to testify that John List seemed to be suffering from memory loss. The doctor, who examined List in the county jail on February 15, 1990, found that he had untreated diabetes mellitus.

"When not treated," Ehrenworth said, "it can lead to memory lapses."

He had been with List for approximately two hours, during which time he said List was rambling and unable to answer simple questions about his own background and family. "He couldn't even remember what college degrees he held, nor his own employment history, without some prompting."

"Preposterous," Eleanor Clark declared on cross-examination. "The man was tested with an IQ of one thirty-seven. During your examination, doctor, did you take it into account that he was in *jail?*"

"Yes," Dr. Ehrenworth said defensively.

"That 'memory loss' might be self-serving?"

"But I still believe the jail diet, which is not right for him, is making him worse."

Eleanor would eventually call her own diabetes specialist, Dr. Robert Matz, who asserted that there was absolutely nothing wrong with Mr. List's memory. Dr. Matz also emphasized that loss of memory in diabetics occurred only in the very final stages of the disease, which was certainly not the case with John List.

Next in line for the defense was a series of Lutheran pastors, gentle, white-haired old men who had ministered to John List throughout his lifetime. They had come from Bay City, Michigan; from the University of Michigan; from Kalamazoo, Michigan; from Rochester, New York; and from Westfield, New Jersey—all to help their former congregant, whom they had always admired and loved and who was now in such desperate trouble.

First on the stand was the Reverend Alfred T. Scheips, who had known John from 1961 to 1964 when he attended the University of Michigan. "His basic reliance was upon the God who created and redeemed him and whom he wanted to serve," he said.

"Does the phrase *sin and grace* have any particular significance to you?" Elijah asked.

"Well, I think that any Christian pastor would emphasize that biblical concept."

"Is there a sin that cannot be forgiven?"

"In the gospel our Lord said every sin could be forgiven except the sin against the Holy Ghost." It was obvious that Reverend Scheips, who spoke with a quiet dignity and grace, was being accepted by the jury. They liked him.

Now Elijah softly asked the crucial question. "What if someone commits suicide? Is it possible to attain grace after suicide?"

"Life's a precious thing," Reverend Scheips answered. "For-

nately, in some of these difficult cases, we are not in the judgment
at. But we have a judge that we know will do what is right. So,
vouldn't know how to answer that except that it's common practice
our congregations that if a person commits suicide, he would be
ven an honorable burial, and he would be placed in the just hands
God. I don't know if that answers what you—''

"What I'm asking is," Elijah persisted, "is it possible to have
ntrition after one commits suicide?"

"Well, suicide is pretty final. You can't have contrition after
at."

That's what Elijah wanted to hear. "A person is now dead. What
cet of that person do you take care of?" he asked.

"Well, I don't know," Reverend Scheips said, a bit confused by
e question. "Are you talking about Christian burial? The body?"

"And what else?" Elijah asked, gently waiting for him to mention
e soul.

"The belief of the average Christian, on the basis of Scriptures,
ould be that on the point of death, a person's soul goes to heaven
r hell."

Good. "Are there any teachings by the church in regard to sui-
de?"

"The taking of life is certainly wrong . . . The Church would, of
ourse, feel that suicide is never a recommended way out of any
roblem."

"Can someone be forgiven for killing?"

"Why, I would think so, surely," the reverend said, a bit trou-
led.

The religious difference between suicide and murder was estab-
shed.

"Is grace attainable after one kills?"

"Oh, yes," he said with certainty. "I think forgiveness, of
ourse, is part of the grace. Maybe it's the same thing. And I'm
ure that a person can be forgiven."

"Your Honor, I have no further questions."

Eleanor got up to cross-examine the likable pastor. "Reverend,
as the defendant a religious fanatic?"

"I wouldn't say so."

"Does the Lutheran church exclude poor people?"

Elijah jumped to his feet. "I object to the question," he said.
Poor people? Let her ask about welfare, not poor people. That's
different question."

"If someone were unable," Eleanor continued calmly, "to support his family because of personal tragedy and had to go on welfare does the Lutheran church consider that a sin?"

"No, not at all. There is nothing wrong that I know in any Lutheran or Christian ethic about accepting that kind of relief," Reverend Scheips answered.

Elijah now called the Reverend Louis Grother, List's pastor at Kalamazoo's Zion Lutheran Church from 1956–61.

"Are you familiar with the concept of sin and grace?" he asked

Reverend Grother laughed good-naturedly. "I'd better be, as a clergyman."

"Is there a sin that may not be be forgiven?"

"Well, deeply theological, there is the sin against the Holy Spirit which is rejection of God's grace to an individual. When and how that occurs is not easily defined, but at that particular stage, God sort of seems to give up the individual and that's the end."

"Does suicide fall into that stage?"

"Well, yes and no. In this respect we've always had a horror of suicide because you are immediately going into eternity and into judgment before God."

"Does that mean you would not be in a state of grace before you went for final judgment before God?"

"Well, you see, I don't consider myself a judge. I'm on the side of God's working group to spread grace and not give judgment."

"Are you saying that one should strive to attain grace before he met his Maker?"

"Well, my concept is that grace is chasing after us rather than we after it," he replied.

"And would suicide preclude someone from being able to face God without sins on his soul?"

"Oh, I guess it would be a terribly awesome thing to me if I knew somebody deliberately committed suicide. But at that stage I am no longer the judge."

"Can one attain a state of grace if he kills?"

"I would only think about the thief on the cross who was accepted by Christ and who, according to, at least, what we know of him, was a person who broke every law of God, including murder," he said, glancing over at John, seated with averted eyes.

"And he was forgiven?"

"That's right. In the last moment of his life."

"I have no further questions."

Reverend Grother waited patiently for Eleanor Clark to begin her cross-examination. "Christianity teaches that God will forgive if you're contrite, isn't that true?" she asked quietly.

Reverent Grother paused thoughtfully. He was obviously a sincere man who was trying to help John but who felt morally obligated only to give answers that came from beliefs rooted in fifty-three years of ministerial service. "God will forgive if the person is penitent."

"You would agree with me," she said, her voice becoming just a little strident, "that having the concept of killing and in the future being contrite and therefore being *saved* is sort of a contradiction of that repentance?"

It was obvious that the question troubled the good man. He frowned with deep consternation before he replied, "Well, it might be a distortion. Every sin is serious. But God always offers forgiveness to the penitent. But the penitent, of course, has to be completely sincere. In other words, not merely going through a ritual."

"Right," Eleanor persisted, sensing his ambivalence. "But if you *committed* killing with the idea that 'I will be forgiven in the future, but I can't commit suicide because I won't be forgiven,' is that consistent with a repentant person?"

Another long pause. Reverend Grother glanced over at John, who still had his eyes lowered. "I don't know if I can answer that question."

"Would you agree with me, Reverend," she pressed, "that the Lutheran church and the Christian religion believe in the concept of free will?"

"Very much so," he said sadly.

"So would you agree with me that it would be contrary to Lutheran teachings to kill your children to make sure their souls got to heaven?"

The man was having a great deal of trouble dealing with the implications of the question. He turned to the judge unhappily. "Must I answer that question?"

"If you can," the judge urged.

"I hesitate . . . in the present circumstance because I think I'd be acting as judge."

"I'm asking you what the Lutheran religion teaches," she said softly, knowing that to push the man too far might not sit well with the jury. "I'm not asking you to judge an individual."

Reverend Grother took a deep breath. "I don't believe I've ever been up against that situation, and I don't believe that there is a doctrinal rider regarding that kind of situation."

"So then you would agree with me," she jumped in quickly,

"that the Lutheran church would *frown* upon someone killing his daughter so that her soul would go to heaven?"

"Your Honor, I protest—" Elijah tried.

"It's an appropriate question," the judge interrupted him. "Let the witness answer it."

"I would say," Reverend Grother said slowly, aware that his words could only hurt a man he still loved, "that the Lutheran church and the Scripture would frown upon anybody deliberately killing anybody."

There. She had made him say it. In his own words. "No further questions."

As Reverend Grother stepped off the witness stand, his eyes sought out John's as if he hoped that John would look up at him. He didn't. The reverend's expression was troubled as he walked away. He wondered whether he had hurt or helped John, but there was nothing else he could do. He had answered honestly the questions put to him.

The next morning, Elijah called the Reverend Herman Mayer, former pastor at Bay City's Zion Lutheran Church. Reverend Mayer was John's first pastor; he had baptised List in 1925 and confirmed him in 1939. The old man's hand shook slightly as he took the oath on his own well-worn hand Bible, which he had brought with him. "My name is Herman Mayer. From St. Louis, Missouri, at the present time," he said in a deep baritone that had weakened a bit with age.

"How old are you, sir?" Elijah asked.

"I'm approaching ninety-four. I have been a pastor for seventy-plus years. Seventy-one years."

A murmur of appreciation spread through the courtroom. Reverend Mayer was a large man, imposing in stature, erect in bearing. Except for the mild quiver in his voice, brought on more by the gravity of the situation than his years, he was in full control.

After the preliminaries, in which Reverend Mayer said, "John received a thorough education in Christian doctrine, Christian practice, Christian living, and what a Christian is to do throughout his life," Elijah got around to the same question he had asked of the other pastors.

"Were there discussions about sin and grace?"

"Definitely so. Because that's the basic topic that comes up again and again. All have sinned and come short of the glory of God. We believe in universal sin, and at the same time, we also stress that all have been redeemed. Christ has redeemed and died for all people. We'll soon celebrate Easter again. All sins are forgiven, great and small. You know, some people have the idea that sins are only the big sins. They think only of the Ten Commandments: Thou shalt not kill, steal, commit adultery. But the Lord says, not only is it wrong to kill, but even to have anger and hatred and an unforgiving spirit in the heart.''

Eleanor doodled on her note pad.

Elijah took the same worn tack, the only one he had to go on, as he tried to build the case that his client had no recourse other than to do what he did. ''Can one be forgiven for one of the major sins? Killing, for instance.''

''Major? There is no difference between a major and a minor sin,'' Reverend Mayer corrected with resonant authority. ''All are sins,'' he stated clearly. ''Because the Lord says whether you commit adultery or whether you have lust in your heart, both are sins? We emphasize that all are sinners, and there is not a just man upon earth that doeth good and sinneth not. That is a scriptural verse.''

''Did you teach these doctrines to John List?''

''That was part of the instruction. We first teach the religious law from the Book of Leviticus, and we emphasize particularly the Ten Commandments. We were very specific in these things. We took each commandment one by one.''

''Did John List believe in sin and grace?''

''Objection.''

''Sustained.''

''I cannot say what he believed,'' the reverend insisted upon answering, ''but it was taught him, and I assume he accepted it. He gave his vow to that on the day when he was received into the church as a confirmed member.''

''Did you teach about suicide?''

''Definitely. Under the Fifth Commandment, 'Thou shalt not kill.' All forms of killing, hatred, animosity of any kind, all that comes in there. Also suicide. Murder, naturally.''

''Is there anything special about the connotation of suicide and grace or the ability to obtain grace?''

''Do you mean to say whether a murder can be forgiven?''

''That's another question.'' Elijah smiled. ''What I'm asking now is, is there any special significance to one's ability to obtain grace if one commits suicide?''

''Well, it all hangs together. A murderer is a sinner in a very high degree,'' he said forcefully. ''And whether it's murder of somebody else or murder of yourself.'' He stopped himself. ''Are you trying to ask me whether a suicidal person can be forgiven?''

''Sort of,'' the judge interjected.

"Well, I can only answer that I'm not the judge, Your Honor. God is after all the judge. The only sin that cannot be forgiven is the unrepentant attitude against God. Is a suicide a person who believes in God and trusts in God? I don't see how he can be." That wasn't exactly the way Elijah would have hoped Reverend Mayer would phrase it. "Nevertheless," he continued, "suicides are committed, and I would judge as a fellow believer that if this person was in his right mind, he has committed a sin which cannot be forgiven." *That's* what Elijah wanted to hear. "He is unfaithful to God's promise. He's unfaithful also to the Word, which says, 'Trust in God above all things.' He lacks trust in God! And therefore that cannot be forgiven. A lack of faith in the Holy Spirit to guide us in all our life." He looked around the courtroom and up at the judge. "I don't want to be a preacher here today."

That's fine, Elijah thought. He couldn't have said it better himself. And out of the mouth of this grand old man the words had an extra weight that he didn't think even Eleanor could budge. "No further questions, Your Honor."

"Reverend," Eleanor Clark began gently, "Christianity teaches that God will forgive all sins and forgive all sinners, but that means that the sinner has to be penitent!" she said emphatically. It wasn't a question.

"Right!"

"And the reason that suicide is such a sin in Christianity is because it signifies despair! Correct?"

"Correct."

"And it signifies a loss of belief in God!"

"That's the important thing. It's the attitude that you do not believe anymore, that there is no hope for you."

"So that it would be inconsistent to say that you believe in God and to commit suicide."

"That is correct. By Christian teachings, I'd say it's a perversion. You are doubting God's word and you have no faith and it's the lack of your faith which condemns you."

"But if you had lost your mind, wouldn't the Church say that, therefore, it isn't a sin?"

"The Devil has a way of deranging . . . of giving us deranged ideas, and I would say that may be the answer."

"How about this, Reverend?" she asked forcefully. "If you're in sound mind, and you commit suicide, then it's a sin, right?"

"I would say, yes."

"So the problem lies for a person who is of sound mind and kills five people, then of course, if he commits suicide, it *is* the most grievous sin, isn't it!''

In all honesty, he had to agree. ''Yes,'' he said clearly.

''No further questions.''

''There are two different questions here,'' Elijah said, trying to regain lost ground. ''One about suicide. One about murder. Committing suicide, is that a sin?''

''Yes.''

''Killing someone or family members, is that a sin?''

''Yes!'' he answered firmly. ''Strongly so!''

''Can you be forgiven for killing your family?''

''All sins can be forgiven. Even murder.''

''Thank you,'' Elijah said softly.

''If you are penitent!'' Eleanor said loud and clear.

''If you are penitent!'' he agreed just as strongly. ''But they can be forgiven.''

John List sank a bit lower on his seat as the aged pastor made his way from the witness box still holding his head high, despite the ordeal of testifying in a murder trial.

Next in the list of pastors was the Reverend Edward Saresky of Faith Lutheran church in Rochester, N.Y., where List had been a parishioner from 1961 to 1964. After Saresky had testified at length that he had known John and Helen List when they were going through some of their most troubling times in Rochester, Elijah got around to his most pressing issue.

''In regard to his religious principles of sin and grace . . .''

''I would have to say to you that just around the time John was a member of our congregation, there was a rather strong corruption of sin and grace,'' Saresky cautioned. ''You may have heard the term *situation ethics*, a view that was held at the time. A common illustration that was used was: If there was a plane that was crashing and the pilot was stuck in the seat and the plane was on fire, ending the suffering of that individual by killing him was an act of love, an act of grace. That's a corruption!'' he declared.

It was never clear why Elijah was spending so much time on the concept of sin and grace except to show why his client could not commit suicide, which was hardly the major issue in the case. Nothing was brought out to indicate that John's personal religious belief system supported even a warped reason to kill his entire family. It was not even clear that he could be sure at the time of their murders whether they were in the necessary state of grace to go to heaven themselves. In addition, each time one of the pastors reiterated the commandment ''Thou salt not kill,'' Miller's client was damaged. On the one hand, Elijah was asserting that John was so strict in his religious beliefs that he couldn't tolerate the occult, that he couldn't go on welfare—even though not one pastor said that welfare, or its equivalent, was a sin of any kind—that he couldn't commit suicide because if he did, he would die without being in a state of grace and would, therefore, go straight to hell, but each of his pastors testified that he had been strictly taught that killing was a sin. In fact, all of the testimony seemed graphically to show that List's concept of sin and grace was self-serving and convoluted. Few in the courtroom could help wondering what had been the point of all of the testimony by the pastors since not one had corroborated John's "beliefs." All had tried very hard to be supportive of their former congregant, for whom they obviously still had strong feelings, but in the final analysis they all had to agree with Eleanor Clark that John's concept of sin and grace was a "distortion," a "perversion," and a "corruption" of its true meaning.

Reverend Rehwinkel was called to the stand. He leaned into the microphone and answered questions in his rich, sonorous baritone.

"John spoke to you of his problems?" Elijah asked.

"Yes, he did, but of, course I cannot reveal—"

"Can you tell us this," Elijah interrupted. "Did they decrease or increase in severity before the fateful day?"

"They increased."

"Did the problems have any effect on him?"

"I really don't know how to quite answer that. He wasn't as active in the governing of the church . . . in the church council. He never missed church. Is that sufficient?"

"Could you tell us what you preached to John during that period of time, 1968 to 1971, in regard to sin and grace?"

"Well, that's just one of the tenets of the Christian faith. Basically we would probably use the Scripture passage from Ephesians two, verses eight and nine, 'for by grace are you saved through faith'"

"Did that have any special significance to John?"

"I think it has for every Christian. Sin and grace is a reality of life."

"Is there a special teaching that the Church has in regard to the concept of suicide?"

"Suicide would be quite outside of the state of grace."

"Why?"

"It's murder. Do you want me to put it another way, Your Honor?" Judge Wertheimer did not reply. "That's taking God into your own hands," the reverend continued. "That's playing God."

"How does suicide differ from killing someone else?" Elijah pressed.

"There really is no difference."

"They are both sins, is that correct?"

"Period!"

"Can one be forgiven for committing suicide?"

"Every sin is forgivable. Only when you tell the spirit to get out of your life, then you don't have a chance. But even that is forgivable upon repentance."

"Can you repent if you kill yourself?"

"Hardly."

"So what we're saying, then, committing suicide differs from murder in that facet."

"That you couldn't repent? Oh, yes."

"And if you can't repent, is grace attainable?"

"Well . . . I guess I have to revert to . . . I'm not God."

"Thank you. I have no further questions."

It still wasn't quite clear what Elijah had accomplished with Reverend Rehwinkel's testimony, except once again to state that John List felt murder could be forgiven but suicide could not. Eleanor Clark got up slowly. She approached the pastor for her cross-examination with her head lowered thoughtfully. "Reverend Rehwinkel, you knew the List family more than as pastor-parishioner. They were friends, were they not?"

"Yes, Mrs. Clark, they were friends, as I think I stated last time."

"On the videotape?"

"Yes. It was what we call 'chemistry' today. Patty was a babysitter for us. So in that sense the answer would be, 'Yes, they were parishioners, and yes, they were friends.' Is that all right?" he asked, looking for her approval.

"If you would have known that the defendant was near despair, you would have reached out and tried to help him, right?" she said, looking at him directly now.

"Oh, yes." He smiled.

"Would you agree that, if you had any idea that the defendant felt he had no place to turn, you would have tried to convince him otherwise, right?"

"Mrs. Clark," he asked, "do I 'agree'?"

"Do you agree," she insisted, "that if you had any idea that the defendant believed that he had no other place to turn, you would have reached out to him and shown him that wasn't true?"

"If I would have known that?" he asked. He seemed unwilling

to accept her statement without qualification, so Ms. Clark changed the direction of her question.

"You knew Alma List," she said, her voice getting louder. "You knew her, right?"

"Yes. I always referred to her, Mrs. Clark, as a great lady of the Lord."

"And you characterized her as being nonjudgmental."

"Nonjudgmental," he agreed. "Very kind and gentle."

"And you would agree with me that she was, in your words, 'healthy as a horse'?"

He smiled. "Yes."

"And because of your relationship with the defendant, you were aware of the presence of the Syferts in their lives? The type of people they were? That they were, in the finest sense of the word, good Christian people?"

"That's a good phrase."

"And you would agree with me that in the finest sense of the words *good Christian people*, they would have reached out to the defendant and helped him if they had known about his despondency and despair?"

"You're asking me," he asked carefully, "if they would have known, would they have done that? Yes, I believe they would, Mrs. Clark."

"Is it true that the notes that the defendent left at the scene"— a bit of sarcasm was beginning to creep into her voice now—"the note 'Guns and Ammo,' 'Insurance policy,' 'To Burt Goldstein,' 'To the Administrator' . . . they fit right into his personality, right? Accountant's personality as you knew it. So when you were asked about those notes, it didn't surprise you, right?"

"It doesn't surprise me." Then he tried to pull back a bit. "When you say 'notes,' you're referring to the other letters?"

"I'm referring to the fact that you weren't surprised that things were left in such an orderly fashion."

"I never saw them, but no, it doesn't surprise me."

"Now you would agree with me, Pastor Rehwinkel, that the defendant was never to your knowledge a religious fanatic."

"No way!"

"And you would also agree with me that a characterization of the defendant as being such a formal-type person that he would mow his lawn in a suit is inaccurate, right?"

The pastor took a deep breath. "I'm not sure where we're going," he said, demonstrating that he was trying to keep one step ahead of Mrs. Clark. "He might not be as casual as other people, but he wouldn't mow his lawn in his shirt and tie. Is that fair enough to respond?"

"But on another occasion, you said that you found the characterization of the defendant as being someone who would be so formal as to always be in a suit and tie inaccurate, right?"

"Inaccurate? On what occasion? Are we on the lawn again?" There was laughter in the courtroom. "No, really . . . I . . ."

Mrs. Clark smiled along with him. "Do you recall saying on a video interview given to the defense that you found it to be an inaccurate portrayal of the defendant that he would be mowing his lawn in a suit?"

"Oh, yes, I'd have trouble believing that."

"Would you agree with me that using the terms *recluse* and *withdrawn* in regard to John List would be inaccurate?"

He took a long pause before his answer. "That could be qualified a number of ways. He was a quiet, gentle person, but I would not see him that way. What the neighbors saw, what others saw . . ." He stopped.

"And you would agree with me," Eleanor persisted, coming on a little stronger now, "that if you had had *any* signs whatsoever that the defendant was despairing of his fate prior to these tragedies, you would have done something about it?"

"That's correct."

"And that you saw nothing to indicate to you that, either as a friend or as a pastor, you should give him solace. That right up until the time that you got the phone call to come to the List household on December 7, 1971, and saw the carnage, you had no idea that the defendant was suffering from any psychiatric problems or anything, right?"

"I'm not qualified to speak on psychiatry . . . but my observations, and I think my statement before was, 'He wouldn't hurt a flea.' So yes, I was shocked."

"And you would agree with me that the whole point of grace in Christianity is the concept of contrition. And that only *God* can determine if someone is contrite enough!"

"Unless if, before God, you confess to the pastor those things that are bothering you and the pastor can give absolution in person."

"Not through a letter?"

He didn't answer.

"Now, Pastor, would you agree with me that saying that you could kill five individuals and be forgiven, but that he couldn't kill himself because it wouldn't be forgiven, is a perversion of religion?"

"I wouldn't agree with that. I think the word *perversion* is wrong."

"Corruption?"

"I think the word *corrupt* is wrong."

"Distortion?"

"Very wrong."

"Incorrect concept?" she tried.

He smiled. "Outside of the grace? I guess today we'd call it 'doing your own thing,' " he said calmly.

She swirled and looked at him incredulously. "Killing five people is doing your own thing, Pastor?"

"Oh, well . . ." He tried to back away. "If you could just rephrase the question . . ."

"No further questions!"

Elijah was quick to jump to his feet, sensing the wave of disbelief that had rippled through the courtroom. Reverend Rehwinkel's face was so red to begin with that it was impossible to see whether or not the pastor had blushed under the gaffe into which Ms. Clark had led him.

"You used the euphemism 'doing your own thing,' " Elijah said. "What was that context?"

"Well, I think it wasn't a very good choice of words. The grace of God would be binding, and the grace of God can forgive until you play God yourself."

When Reverend Rehwinkel stepped down from the witness box, he had to pass before the defense table. With a broad friendly grin on his face, he nodded and winked at John List as he passed. Members of the press who were seated only feet away in the first row of the courtroom looked at each other with raised eyebrows.

"I guess all is forgiven," whispered one newsman.

"Christ Almighty!" said another in open disgust. "Five people, kids included, and his pastor's winking at him like a good ol' boy?!"

All that Elijah had left to present was the testimony of the psychiatric experts who he hoped would show that his client acted in a manner consistent with a diagnosable mental defect. To this end came the lengthly, detailed, and informed testimonies for the defense of Dr. Sheldon Miller and Dr. Alan Goldstein, both of whom diagnosed List as suffering from an obsessive-compulsive personality disorder, as outlined in *The Diagnostic and Statistical Manual of Mental Disease*. First to the stand was Dr. Sheldon Miller. There was no question in his mind as to the diagnosis; he was emphatic in his opinion.

"Could you go into the symptoms as described in the manual?" Elijah then asked Dr. Alan Goldstein.

"Certainly. I'll read the symptoms that I believe qualify List for this diagnosis," Dr. Goldstein said, reading from the manual. "One: 'Perfectionism interferes with task completion—inability to complete a project because one's own overtly strict standards are not met.' Two: 'Preoccupation with details, rules, lists, order, organization, or schedules, to the extent that the major point of the activity is lost.' Three: 'Unreasonable insistence that others submit to exactly his or her way of doing things—or unreasonable reluctance to allow others to do things because of the conviction that they will not do them correctly.' Four: 'Excessive devotion to work and productivity to the exclusion of leisure activities and friendships, not encountered for by obvious economic necessity.' Five: Overconscientiousness, scrupulousness, and inflexibility about matters of morality, ethics, or values, not accounted for by cultural or religious identification.' Six: 'Restricted expression of affect.' (Affect means emotion.) 'A difficult time showing or demonstrating emotion.' "

"Can you give an opinion, with a fair degree of medical certainty, whether John List meets the criteria you have just described?"

"He does," said Dr. Goldstein. "There are nine in all. I have read the six that I believe fit Mr. List. In layman's terms," he added, "I ought to mention that a personality disorder, according to the American Psychiatric Association, is not a symptom, in and of itself, of an emotional disturbance. It is a long-standing, enduring set of personality traits. The characteristics have their roots often early in adolescence, last basically throughout someone's lifetime, and are highly resistant to psychotherapy. They represent who the person is. They are a significant problem because personality disorders interfere with social relationships, with one's enjoyment of life, and, at times, with one's thinking and ability to evaluate situations. They may interfere with the ability to perform vocationally and maintain a job. So we're talking about a lifelong pattern of behavior. I would add, by the way, that the presence of a personality disorder, particularly this type, which I found when I interviewed and tested Mr. List, is consistent with all of the other information I was able to uncover about the defendant eighteen years ago. So that one can make certain inferences about his behavior eighteen years ago on the knowledge that he is this obsessive-compulsive personality. I believe it is the same diagnosis that Dr. Miller and Dr. Simring assigned to the defendant."

Dr. Steven Simring was the State's psychiatric expert who had also interviewed the defendant.

"Do both doctors agree with your diagnosis?" Elijah asked.

"As rare as that may seem if one listens to the media, all three experts, Dr. Miller, Dr. Simring, and I, were agreed that Mr. List suffered then and suffers now from an obsessive-compulsive personality disorder."

"Your diagnosis today squares with what happened back in 1971?"

"Couldn't be clearer. Mr. List left his fingerprints in the form of his notes and in terms of the clear impressions he left with just about everyone with whom he had contact. The diagnosis is a series of behavioral traits which were so marked that those who knew Mr. List had an indelible impression of him. And again, the same that he left on the three experts, myself included, who evaluated him."

"Do you recognize *The Diagnostic and Statistical Manual of Mental Disease* as an authority?"

"It's the only authority in terms of diagnosis. You had asked me for the symptoms of an obsessive-compulsive personality, and I think the description of that constellation of symptoms describes Mr. List and has some direct relevance to his behavior on November 9, 1971. Reading from P. 354 of the manual, 'The essential feature of this disorder is a pervasive pattern of perfectionism and inflexibility, beginning by early adulthood and present in a variety of contexts. No matter how good an accomplishment, it does not seem good enough. Preoccupation with rules, efficiency, trivial details, procedures, or form interferes with the ability to take a broad view of things.' And that's sort of a general description of an obsessive-compulsive personality disorder. They're described, again reading from it, 'People who tend to be excessively conscientious, moralistic, scrupulous, and judgmental of others as well as themselves.' "

"Does that apply to Mr. List?"

"It's a perfect fit," Dr. Goldstein said with absolute assurance. "Not only does he meet at least six of the nine diagnostic criteria described very clearly, it's interesting to note that in reviewing the two or three hundred pages of military records, three of his evaluations done by superior officers, from 1944 until he was discharged from the service, contain terms that point to his unquestioned degree of morality, the extreme diligence with which he approached tasks and fulfilled his responsibilities. Words almost lifted out of the manual, which was not published at that time, I might add."

Elijah then asked the most important question in terms of a possible lesser verdict than first-degree murder for his client. "Have you formed an opinion with a fair degree of medical certainty as to whether the patient's mental state affected his ability to act with willfulness, deliberateness, premeditation on 11/9/71?''

"I have formed such an opinion, yes."

"What is it?"

"My opinion is that on November 9, 1971, because of a variety of emotional problems, his thinking was grossly interfered with. Specifically his perceptions of his situation at the time led him to believe that life was hopeless and that he was helpless to change his situation. As he saw the situation, and as he told Dr. Simring in his videotaped interview, ruin was only a few more weeks away. Only a few hundred dollars left. The mortgage was due; the utilities were due. There was no money left. He saw his family falling apart, the walls closing in on him . . .''

No matter how she tried, Eleanor Clark couldn't shake either Dr. Miller's or Dr. Goldstein's testimony, that John List could not help what he did given the set of circumstances at the time of the murder and the rigid hold his religious beliefs and his psychological disorder imposed upon him. Both Dr. Miller and Dr. Goldstein were adamant in their professional assessment that John List was not emotionally accountable for his actions. Then she called her last witness, Dr. Steven Simring, the State's rebuttal psychiatrist.

Although all three doctors, Miller, Goldstein, and Simring, agreed that List met the necessary criteria to be clinically diagnosed as an obsessive-compulsive personality, Dr. Simring differed with Miller and Goldstein, saying List was suffering from obsessive-compulsive personality "traits" rather than "disorder."

Miller and Goldstein said List's obsessive-compulsivity put him on a collision course with the tragic events, that once he had come to the idea that he had to kill his family, there was absolutely no possibility of his deviating from the course; but Dr. Simring disagreed, saying that John had the capacity to deliberate and cover all of his options. The ability to deliberate was the point that both Eleanor Clark and Elijah Miller kept homing in upon, as that one point alone could be the deciding factor between a verdict of first- or second-degree murder.

Despite all the testimony given by the police, experts, neighbors, pastors, and doctors during the eight days of the trial, the one person everyone still hoped to hear from was John List himself. Now, with Dr. Simring's testimony, List did not need to take the stand because the doctor read to the court statement after statement List had made to him during the course of a four-hour interview. John had known the interview was not confidential, and, as was his usual habits with any authority figure, he cooperated. The courtroom listened closely as Dr. Simring read from his notes. It was almost like having John Emil List on the stand himself.

"I debated in my mind should I get married," Dr. Simring read from his notes. "I decided we should go ahead with it. We went to Baltimore in 1951. I found out about a marriage license and blood tests, which we didn't need in Baltimore. On Friday evening, November 30, 1951, we were preparing to marry. Her sister and her sister's husband were going to be part of the wedding party. Helen told me she was very happy she wasn't actually pregnant. In later years, I thought maybe I was getting married because I thought she was pregnant. I'm not sure to this day whether she was or was not. I went ahead with the wedding anyway. If I had had more time to consider it, I might have changed my mind.

"I met Delores six years after the 'incident,' but we didn't marry until 1985. We dated for almost six years. I jumped into it last time, and Delores, for her part, jumped into marriage, too, and both of us wanted to be pretty sure.

"By the time we moved to Inkster, Helen and I were having marital problems that translated into sexual problems, and she began drinking heavily. . . . I once hit a guy for overdoing it, for kissing Helen. . . . She suggested erotic movies which helped our sex life. It was pretty much straight sex. I don't believe in kinky sex. . . . Helen was always sick. But it got much worse when we moved to New Jersey. She was a major diagnostic problem. They couldn't tell what was wrong with her. I felt I was a burdened husband with a wife who was ill. I resented her because, even though she was ill, I felt she could have done more around the house. And I resented the tension between Helen and my mother. I felt squeezed between two strong-willed, domineering women.

"It wasn't Helen's fault that her husband gave her syphilis. She never told me when we got married. By the time I found out about it, it had already gone to the brain and it was too late. There was brain damage.

"Everything seemed to be going wrong. I couldn't do well on the job. I was unemployed. I was borrowing from my mother. Helen was getting worse. There didn't seem to be any way for her to get better. I didn't have person-to-person skills. I couldn't delegate authority well on the job. My children were getting into their teens. I was concerned about their friends and particularly about their friends' use of marijuana. I was worrying more and more. I was praying something would happen to give me the income to support my family.

"I was concerned about my problems. I was concerned about the ising of my children'. I always learned that I had to take care of y own problems. My mother and Helen knew there were problems, at I didn't really let them know how bad things were. I was con- rned about Patty. Patty didn't think that marijuana was so bad. I as concerned that the boys might get into marijuana and drift away om the church. Patty attended church, but she didn't take com- nunion on a regular basis.

"All these things built up in my mind. I saw no way out. I couldn't apport them. If I left, I thought, what would happen to my mother? he's getting old. She didn't have enough income. Helen couldn't ake care of herself. I didn't want the children to be sent to foster omes. I didn't know what kind of person would end up raising nem if that happened. If Helen was the problem and I shot her, ney would still have to go to a home, to go into poverty. I was aised in the Depression. I knew things were tough, that people ardly had enough to get by on. I didn't want to put them in that osition.

"Finally I broke and killed them.

"In the Lutheran religion suicide is not an option. If I committed uicide, I would go straight to hell. So I thought that if I did it this vay, my family would all go to heaven, and at least later on I would ave a chance to go to heaven myself. It was a horrible thing, but nce I started, I was like on auto or autodrive. I killed all of them o that no one would survive. No one would have to think about vhat happened and then it would be worse. It was almost with a igh of relief that I killed all of them, and there weren't one or two urvivors. Looking back, it was such a horrible thing. If I had to lo it over again, I'd find some way of getting help.

"It really began two or three weeks earlier, approximately in October 1971. I'd become despondent about taking care of my amily. I ran through my mind three possibilities. One: running way. Two: killing myself. Three: killing them. I've already told ou why I couldn't kill myself, and as far as running away, why, hey would be helpless and left to suffer. And that left only one ossibility. I kept debating the alternatives. I kept praying something good would happen. One or two weeks before the incident I was till going through my options."

At this point in Dr. Simring's testimony, he said it was important o rule out the possibility of hallucinations, if, in other words, the lefendant was delusional, if he had a belief that he was governed y some higher purpose to save the world or fight Satan. Or if he elt his actions were being impelled by radio forces or television.

Dr. Simring broke the flow of List's account and asked him, "We• you hearing any voices?"

"No, not at all," he had answered.

"Were you seeing any visions? Did God give you any instruc• tions?"

"No, nothing like that."

Dr. Simring had asked many questions in this regard, and hi• responses were uniformly negative. He went on reading List's ac• count:

"I had considered it before, but there was no final decisio• made," List had said. "I had considered the options and the alter• natives for about three weeks but had arrived at no final decisio• until the evening before the shootings themselves."

"What was the final straw?" Dr. Simring asked.

"I just decided that our financial position was so bad that ther• was no way I could save it. We were behind in our bills. My jo• was not in danger, but I wasn't really earning anything on that job I had no longer been getting the five-hundred-dollar salary."

"Did you make plans to carry out your decision?"

"Yes, two or three weeks before. In October. I found the guns Both of them were souvenir weapons. I went to a range to mak• certain the guns were working properly. I'm not a target practice• but I wanted to make sure they were functioning, and they were. bought ammunition for these two different kinds of weapons in gun shop."

Dr. Simring went on to explain the very elaborate plans List mad• to carry out the killings in a serial fashion. "I didn't want tw• members of the family present at the same time," List had said.

"How did you sleep the night before?"

"I slept well. Then I got up the next morning and got the childre• off to school. At about nine A.M. Helen was having toast and coffe• at the table in the kitchen. I killed her."

"Can you give me the details?" Dr. Simring had asked.

"She was at the table. I went up behind her and shot her. I didn'• want any of them to know, that's why I shot them from behind," he said, contradicting the actual autopsy reports, which indicate• that he had shot from the side. "It's not her fault," List had said "if she had atrophy of the brain. It's not her fault that she was • domineering person. She and my mother were domineering, bu• that's the way they were," he said simply, still denying the dee• resentment he felt.

"What did you do, precisely?" Dr. Simring asked again.

"Well," he had replied, "she was having breakfast, toast an•

offee. She may have said, 'Good morning,' I don't remember. I hot her in the back of the head, and she crumpled forward. Then went upstairs. I shot my mother in the back of the head," he said. Alma had been shot just above her left eyebrow. "It was in her kitchen storeroom. I shot her in the back of the head so they would not suffer. If there were any survivors, the survivors would suffer. I shot her at close range. I tried to drag her, but she was too heavy. I moved Helen to the ballroom. I cleaned up the mess."

"He remembered running errands to the bank and post office, although he was vague on some of the details," Dr. Simring said. "Then I asked him if he had lunch after he killed his wife and his mother."

"Yes, I did," List had replied. "Right after that."

"He was also a bit vague about the sequence in which he had killed each of the children, or even if he had picked them up."

"I remember seeing Patty in the entryway," List had recalled. "By the washer/dryer. I met her at the door. I came with her and I shot her in the back of the head."

"Once again," Simring corrected, "she was shot in the side of the face."

"Then Freddie, then John," List had said simply. "John was different. When he fell his body had some jerking movements. So I pulled out the .22 and I shot to hit him on the heart. I didn't want him to suffer," he said vaguely, trying to remember. "I think he was last . . ."

"I should point out," Dr. Simring said to the court, "that this was the only time the defendant appeared a little emotional. His eyes became a bit teary when he discussed this with me. During the rest of the interview, his demeanor was pleasant, very friendly. Not flat. Not businesslike. And at times, during the interview, he was able to chuckle a bit. Not about these facts, but when we talked about the irony of life, the irony of the case. It was like two professionals talking about a case." Dr. Simring looked down and continued to read from his notes. "These are direct quotes," he said.

"I wrote to some relatives," List had said. "I expressed some sympathy. I picked up some stuff, clothes, books. I had supper. I went to bed, but I didn't sleep very well that night. I got up on Wednesday morning about six or six thirty. I took some of my possessions, books other things, and I shipped them by Railway Express, a service at the time." The courtroom was deadly silent as people tried to envision the murderer sleeping upstairs while his slaughtered family was either in a storeroom overhead or laid out one floor below. "I knew I wanted to head west," he had continued to Dr. Simring, "because I always thought I'd like to see the mountains." The mountains . . . "I convinced myself," he said, "that *this is* the only way out, and I made up my mind I had to carry through with it. I didn't want to have anyone remaining."

Dr. Simring asked him at that point, "Did it ever occur to you that Patty might have had other ideas about her sixteen-year-old life, how she would want to live it? I mean, did you weigh that into your consideration?"

"No," he said. "I didn't foresee that or take anyone else into the plan. I did not consider how this would affect others. It's almost like I was looking in the wrong end of a set of binoculars."

"What does that mean?"

"I had gotten to the point that I had convinced myself that there was only one solution and that was it."

"Did you know that what you did was against the law?"

"I'm sure I did. It's just like I had no control over what I was doing. It's like some force, some force that made me move, something beyond my control, especially once it started. The control of my outside thinking ability, like some outside coercion. It compelled me to do it once it got started."

"He was trying to convey this," Dr. Simring told the court, "in repeating this metaphor, this figure of speech, that he had made the decision to kill all of them, but once the first one was killed, then there was the chain of events that led to two, three, four, and five. And that's why he continued to say, 'especially once it got started.'"

"Beforehand," List had said, "I finally convinced myself that there was no other solution and I had to go through with it. It was like I was on autodrive after I shot my wife. Autodrive, complete, shooting my whole family."

"Did you ever tell anyone about it?" Dr. Simring had asked him.

"No. Absolutely not."

"Are you aware that what you did is also against moral law?"

"Of course it's against the moral law," he said. "One should not kill. The Ten Commandments and the finer breakdowns of the commandments. I should not hurt other people. Not even verbally. As to the civil law, I know what I did was wrong. But when I got it into my mind . . . I knew that I would be punished. I didn't really think I would get away with it for more than a week or two. I was surprised that I was away for so long and nothing happened. Within a week or two, I was convinced that someone would come and catch me rapidly after that. By the time I got to Denver, I was convinced the police would recognize me, that there would be a 'Wanted' bulletin or something."

"Did you ever think of turning yourself in to the authorities?"

"No. I knew I had done wrong. I decided, though, to stay free as long as I could. I might have had it in my mind to turn myself in, but I gave it no serious consideration."

He was so honest! No matter how self-condemnatory his statements were.

"Why didn't you consider turning yourself in?" Simring asked.

"I was afraid of the consequences," he said candidly. "I was afraid of going to jail for a long time. I took a lot of steps to avoid detection. For a while I wore a mustache. In the late seventies I shaved it off. I kept a low profile. I wanted to make sure that I didn't get into any trouble. I made sure I never even got a parking ticket. I made sure to do nothing that would leave fingerprints anywhere, such as a situation in which I might be fingerprinted. For example, I didn't apply for a passport because I'd need a birth certificate or fingerprints or something for identification. You know, doc," he said with a gentle smile, "this is a big country, easy to lose yourself in."

"Did you ever unburden yourself to a minister in the confidence of his chambers?"

"No," he said honestly. "I was finally enjoying my life, and I didn't want to do anything that would disrupt it."

"Did you ever tell anyone? Anyone at all?"

"No. I didn't want to take the chance of anyone turning me in. Besides, I didn't want to burden anyone else with the knowledge of what I had done."

"Did you give any thought all these years about what you had done?" the doctor asked him.

"You know," he said thoughtfully, "what happened was always in the back of my mind. Especially the first year or two. Then I didn't really think about it on a daily basis. When I said my prayers, I would ask for forgiveness, but after a while I only thought about it when the anniversary of the deaths came up, essentially once a year. I made up my mind I'd live the best I could through the church. I became active again, and I tried to make up for what I had done. I went to St. Paul's in Denver and became active on the church council. I visited the sick, I wanted to contribute something worthwhile."

Concluding his recitation of List's own words, Dr. Simring offered his final diagnosis:

"The M'Naghten test is a standard test of legal insanity and criminal responsibility in cases of significant mental illness. The test works like this: In order not to be responsible, number one, you have to have a mental disease or mental defect. Number two, as a result of that mental disease or defect, a) you did not know the nature or quality of your act, or b) you did not know it was wrong. There is no disagreement between Dr. Goldstein, Dr. Miller, or me that, at all times, Mr. List had a clear mind. No clouding, confusion, fogging, in his mind. At no time was he hearing voices, seeing visions, hearing the Lord or the Devil giving instructions. At all times, whatever he did came from him and his own decision process. Everyone agrees at no time was he psychotic, meaning out of touch with reality. We know his intelligence is astoundingly high—an IQ of 137. He was not drunk, did not use drugs, not even prescription medication. The bottom line is, he had a clear mind. He did not suffer from a mental disease in the sense that is used in the M'Naghten test.

"While he had obsessive traits, he knew the nature and quality of his act. He knew it was a gun. He knew the gun could shoot and kill people. Finally, and most important, he knew at all times what he did was wrong, both morally by his own standards, and legally by the standards of the law. It is my opinion and that of the other two experts, that he does not meet the criteria for legal insanity."

Now Eleanor Clark began to set the foundation for a verdict of first-degree murder.

"Doctor," she asked, "are you able to reach an opinion as to the defendant's mental capacity to form 'malice' and intent to kill five individuals?"

"It was clear from the appellate decisions that I read that 'malice' has a very specific meaning. Under the criminal statutes, one or both of the following states of mind have to precede or coexist with the commission of a crime. One, An intention to cause death; two, the knowledge that the act to cause death will probably do so. It is my opinion Mr. List was able, and at all times capable, of acting with malice."

"Doctor," Clark asked, "did you reach any conclusions about the defendant's ability to form the mental element of 'premeditation'?"

"Yes. It is my opinion that at all times John List was capable of premeditating the acts which he carried out."

"Doctor," Ms. Clark continued, "as far as 'deliberate,' did you form an opinion as to the defendant's ability to 'deliberate'?"

"Yes. To 'deliberate' means, once you premeditate an act, can the individual then deliberate upon the pros and cons and the ups and downs. It is my opinion that, at all times, John List was capable of deliberating upon the deed which he had premeditated."

And finally, "Doctor," Ms. Clark asked in her sharp, clear voice, "did you form an opinion as to the defendant's ability to commit the crime willfully?"

"Yes, I did. According to the law, 'willful' means once you premeditate an act, once you deliberate upon it—that is, weigh the pros and cons—'willful' means that you then intentionally execute the plan to commit the act. He did."

"No further questions."

No matter how hard Elijah Miller tried to break Dr. Simring, he held on firmly to his opinion; he was unshakeable. "Once the pressures were taken off," Elijah said sarcastically, "he could function again, couldn't he?"

"He had fewer dependents," Simring replied cryptically.

"His believing he sent them to heaven, wasn't that delusional?"

"No!" Dr. Simring even went on to say that he believed List was a religious hypocrite. The words hit the courtroom very hard. "There is religious belief, and there is religious hypocrisy."

"Can *you* judge religious hypocrisy?" Elijah demanded.

"He says that he killed five people even though it was against his moral law, but as for killing himself, he couldn't commit a sin. That's religious hypocrisy!"

The damage was done.

All that was left were the closing statements to a jury that had listened to nine stunning days of testimony.

In his closing statement, Elijah Miller spent one hour and twenty minutes trying to get a reduced verdict for his client. He battled passionately, reiterating all the points he had raised in the trial: Helen's illness, John's mental state at the time, his obsessive-compulsive personality, his religious background, why he felt he had no recourse to do other than what he did, how he truly believed he was sending them to heaven. Over and over, Elijah tried to press home the point that John was a sick, desperate, fragmented man who could not help what he had done. He attacked Dr. Simring for not personally speaking to some of the witnesses in the case, for sitting in "an ivory tower," for being an "armchair intellectual," for Elijah knew only too well that Dr. Simring's testimony, in which he offered John's own assessment of his crimes in his own words, had been very damaging. He attacked the inflammatory nature of the photographs of the victims that had been submitted into evidence.

Elijah Miller's attempts on behalf of his client were heroic, but he had nothing concrete to go on but the hope of winning the jury's sympathy for his client as a sick, pathetic, warped creature who had been terribly put upon by life and who had been incapable of seeing any other manner of behaving.

Eleanor Clark wasn't buying any of it. "Ladies and gentlemen of the jury," she began almost angrily, "I can see why Mr. Miller invoked *Alice in Wonderland* in his opening and the theater of the absurd in his closing. The defendant acted as a hideous angel of death weighing the options right up until the night before killing his family. The State puts in forty-one witnesses, and all we've heard for the last five days, ad nauseam, was that he had two spankings, he had a wonderful, loving, strict parents, he came from a close family, and a religious community in Michigan. Must I go on?" she demanded. "Ladies and gentlemen, the reason you are the people who are going to decide this case, the twelve ordinary, commonsense members of society, is because that's what a criminal trial is about. When the judge gives you the law, what it comes down to is you're going to go into that room and you're going to decide on your own experiences, what you know about ordinary life, common sense, and you're going to say, 'Hey! That's Mr. Miller's job. He's an advocate, but *give me a break*!' "

In the brief twenty minutes of her closing statement, she continued to emphasize all the concrete evidence that had been amassed against the defendant, determined to enlist the jury's sympathies on behalf of the victims. "And let's get to the sick wife! Helen List certainly had her share of problems. Her first husband gives her syphilis. Her second husband kills her! Situational ethics? Kill her because she's like a pilot in pain? Well, was Alma List dying? Was Patricia List dying? Was Frederick List dying? Was John List dying?"

Then Eleanor Clark strode over to the defense table to stand almost directly in front of John List. "Forty years ago, when this country's sense of fair play was being held hostage to sly innuendo and half-truth, somebody stood up and said, 'Have you no shame?' " She pointed a finger directly at the defendant and shook it at him, then admonished him for using his wife's venereal disease as an excuse. "Well, the State says today, 'Have you no shame!! Helen List had to be smeared in the courtroom with half-truths and sly innuendoes. Why?' " she demanded.

Finally, in closing, she said in a voice crisp with conviction, "Ladies and gentlemen, there is a saying in the law. 'Justice delayed is justice denied.' Because this defendant was so successful in maintaining his fugitive status, don't deny the state of New Jersey, or Alma, Helen, Patricia, John, or Frederick, justice! The State asks of you, *demands* of you, based upon the evidence, to return a verdict of guilty for each of these victims in the first degree.''

It was a forceful performance.

The next morning a verdict had been reached. Sergeant Joan Spano's full security force lined the courtroom as the jury filed into the jury box.

Judge Wertheimer looked at the packed courtroom. "I do not want any demonstrations," he warned solemnly. Then he turned to the jury, "Have the members of the jury agreed upon a verdict?"

"We have, Your Honor," said Ronald Fain, the jury foreman, in a quiet voice.

"With regard to count one, Alma List," asked the judge in a clear, firm voice. "How do you find the defendant? Not guilty? Guilty of murder in the first degree? Guilty of murder in the second degree?"

John leaned his head forward slightly and tilted it to the side as he listened.

"Guilty of murder in the first degree," said Mr. Fain.

John's mouth tightened almost imperceptibly as he tilted his head back again, kneaded his long fingers together, and looked down sadly.

"Was that verdict unanimous?" the judge asked.

"Yes, it was."

"With regard to count two, Helen List? With regard to count three, Patricia List? With regard to count four, Frederick List? With regard to count five, John F. List?" The judge demanded a verdict for each member.

"Guilty of murder in the first degree," Ronald Fain repeated each time.

No sound broke the silence of the courtroom as each of the jurors was polled. Bail was revoked. Sentencing was set for May 1, 1990, two weeks later. Court was adjourned. The prisoner was led out in handcuffs. John had tears in his eyes.

The jury had taken nine hours to agree upon a verdict. That they deliberated that long was a testament to the fight Elijah Miller had waged on behalf of his client. Ultimately a single line from the five-page letter List wrote to Reverend Rehwinkel the night of the murders led the jury to find him guilty of first-degree murder instead of one of the lesser charges. One member of the jury held out for a day, but after they'd read and reread the passage in the letter, "Originally, I had planned this for Nov. 1, All Saints Day. But travel arrangements were delayed,'' all were in agreement. His change of plans to ensure his escape convinced the jury that List had deliberately and with malice committed the murders.

Cheers greeted Eleanor Clark and Brian Gillet on the crowded steps of the courthouse, where a huge press conference awaited them. ''Justice may have been delayed, but it was not denied!'' Eleanor Clark declared with a big smile as she and Brian Gillet acknowledged the congratulatory reception that awaited them.

John sat in jail for two weeks awaiting sentencing. The correction officers' area in the jail was known as the bullpen. John had to make all of his phone calls from the bullpen. He dialed the Richmond area code. Delores, John thought as he dialed the number where she was staying. She was like the children he didn't have—a substitute for the children he had destroyed.

Delores had never come to the Union County jail to see her husband, although Sheriff Froehlich had made all the necessary preparations for her if she had chosen to do so. It would have been too expensive—the traveling, the motel, the restaurant—but John called her frequently. ''Delores,'' he had said at the beginning, ''when this is all over, we'll get a new house and begin again.'' She determined then to stand by the man she'd married, not letting herself think of the barbarous things they said he had done . . . inhaling sadness for the rest of her days . . . until the time one of them died. Then the final day of judgment. She thought of the gospel. There were two parts: gospel law and gospel love. Had John held up the ''law'' part of the gospel as a guide for total obedience by his family while he'd used the ''love'' part of the gospel to forgive himself and rationalize away his deeds? It was all so confusing.

He dialed collect. It was a major worry. She didn't know how she would be able to pay the phone bills. The bills were not a realistic concern of his. He was no longer butting his head against the financial barriers in his life. He had never wanted his family to go on public assistance—that had been part of it—but what kind of a future was there for Delores? A life on welfare? . . . He didn't think of it. ''We'll start all over again. . . .'' She had wanted to believe him, but she knew it meant having to stop her own belief system altogether. She was always jumpy these days. She should get a job again. Tired and depressed as she was, it might be good; it would give her something to do. Sadly, she thought she was still in love with him. Delores never had enormous expectations of personal fulfillment. Now, living within the prison of private experience no one else could ever know or share, it no longer mattered.

She continued to sleep only fitfully. Darkness eventually seized everything, even the sun. Sometimes, when she woke for brief periods during those restless nights, did she ever think what her life might have been had the elders of the Lutheran church not refused to circulate the "Wanted" bulletins throughout their member churches? If they had agreed to that circulation, a man by the name of John List might have been captured as early as 1975, when he'd formally joined St. Paul's Church in Denver . . . before she'd ever met Bob Clark. Not only would thousands of man-hours in the search have been spared, not only would hundreds of thousands of dollars have been saved, but Delores might also have been spared the heartache of marrying a man who would one day force her to face the fact that she had been duped and had given her love to a multiple murderer, thereby adding her to the list of victims.

May 1, 1990

Judge Wertheimer sat on his bench before the mural of Parson Caldwell and the Revolutionaries. "Mr. List, is there anything you wish to say before sentencing?"

To everyone's surprise, John stood up. "Yes, I do have a short statement I would like to tell you," he said, clearing his throat. With his head bowed to the table from which he read, he said in a muted voice, "I wish to inform the court that I remain truly sorry for the tragedy that happened in 1971. I feel that due to my mental state at the time, I was unaccountable for what happened. I ask all those who were affected by this for their forgiveness, their understanding, and their prayers. Thank you." He sat down.

His brief statement angered rather than appeased. When Eleanor Clark said that sometimes being merciful to the cruel was being indifferent to the good and that Mr. List had already had eighteen years' worth of parole, she was voicing what many people, in their hearts, believed to be the truth. They felt that he *still* was not accepting the responsibility for his actions.

Now it was Judge Wertheimer's turn. He had tried to conduct the trial in a fair, impartial, strong, and thoroughly professional manner. At times he had broken the solemnity with a touch of levity. Now he was fiercely sober and serious as he looked squarely at John List.

"The defendant will please rise."

John List stood.

"This sixty-four-year-old defendant was convicted by a jury on April 12, 1990, on five counts of first-degree murder in the case that captivated widespread fascination in almost every facet of our society,'' Judge Wertheimer began quietly. "The defendant's name and his deeds in November 1971 have proven to be a specter that will not as easily be obliterated from the community's mind as they were from his own conscience. His acts stand as a permanent, pathetic, and profane example to the potential of man's inhumanity to man. They will not be soon or easily forgotten, and the name of John Emil List will be eternally synonymous with concepts of selfishness, horror, and evil. The defendant stands before this court as a stranger to all that his family held dear. He is an alien to his privileges and his potential. The question that attends this sentencing is how a man with all the defendant's advantages could become an aberration to his upbringing, his education, and his religion. Because of him, one must always fear that any person can do anything to any other person no matter how horrendous or vile. This fear is somewhat tempered, however, when one concludes that the man who stands before this court is a man without honor!'' he said forcefully.

John stared straight ahead.

"His attorney says the defendant was taught to be the protector and provider of his family, but that is no different than most of us are taught. To this court's knowledge, thankfully, it has never been used as an excuse for cold-blooded murder before! The defendant is a man without honor!'' he repeated. "When faced with a sick wife and one that probably became extremely difficult to live with, he neither remembered his wedding vows nor sought spiritual or professional counseling. He found death to be a more plausible alternative to divorce, because he is a man without honor! He killed his mother, who was neither harm nor burden to anyone. She was elderly but self-sufficient, loved and had friends and resources with which to live her remaining years comfortably, but John Emil List did not merely walk away, for he is a man without honor!''

Every time the judge pronounced the words *without honor*, John's gaze dropped further. The judge's public condemnation and rebuke were difficult to endure, but he never once altered the rigidity of his pose.

"He is a man who could coldly, calculatingly, and cunningly conceive and carry out a cowardly plan to assassinate each of his three children,'' the judge continued, his voice strong and clear. "Not only were they of his own flesh and blood, but they were innocents with their entire lives before them. John Emil List decided, however, that he was God! He decided to be jury, judge, and executioner, and discovery in this case has revealed that when it was all done, he did not even seek forgiveness from his church or his God. Rather, John Emil List abandoned the remains of his family, his name, and his past and evaporated into the country for almost eighteen years. He rejected the idea of surrender because he was, quote, 'enjoying himself too much,' end of quote. John Emil List is without remorse and without honor!

"After eighteen years, five months, and twenty-two days, it is now time for the voices of Helen, Alma, Patricia, Frederick, and John F. List to rise from the grave. For it is the criminal justice system, through its trial courts, that speaks for all victims of crime. It is easy to lose focus in criminal trials, particularly when victims cannot or do not appear, and particularly when faced with what appears to be a frail, quiet, benign, and elderly defendant. However, this court cannot be allowed to lose sight of the carnage of the victims, what was taken from them, and what was taken from the community. When I say the community, I indeed mean the community. It was brought to the court's attention that an entire generation of children grew up throughout the area, but primarily in Westfield, fearing that someday, somehow, some way, their father, their protector, their provider, would mindlessly murder them. Remember 1971 was well before counseling in the schools was recognized as a helpful tool in facing and overcoming tragedies such as this. So this man, without honor, deeply affected more than just his own family; and today there are those who live with very real, albeit hidden, fears and phobias, which are the direct product of the defendant's malevolent mind and evil hand!

"What, then, is the appropriate sentence for John Emil List? There was no case in 1971 and 1972 that addressed the philosophy of concurrent versus consecutive sentences, as our Supreme Court has now done in *State vs. Yarborough*. This court finds that holding, however, to be valid here as a compilation of criteria known but not compiled in the early 1970s. This court further agrees with Appellate Division Judge Warren Brody, who noted last November in *State vs. Rogers* that the same sentence can run partially concurrent and consecutive in the appropriate case. *This*, however, is not the appropriate case!

"This defendant has already escaped the bar of justice for more than eighteen years. We know from his trial that he still suffers from a compulsive-obsessive personality disorder, which his experts claim triggered these events. Thus, if he ever returns to the community, there is a very real risk that he could reprise these horrific acts; and that is not a risk this court is willing to assume. The defendant's crimes were directed at multiple victims, at different times of the day, and embodied separate acts of violence. By his own words, set forth in S–41 in evidence, they were carried out only after much thought. It is axiomatic that for what he did to his wife, his mother, his daughter, his two sons, and for how he traumatized an entire community, the defendant should have no hope of breathing the free air that graces the lives of law-abiding citizens.''

Finally, after recounting all of the aggravating and mitigating factors of the case, Judge Wertheimer was ready to pronounce his sentence.

''It is the sentence of this court on count one for the murder of Alma List that the defendant be remanded to the custody of the commissioner of the Department of Corrections for the remainder of his natural life and until released in accordance with law.

''It is the sentence of this court on count two for the murder of Helen List,'' he continued, ''that the defendant be remanded to the custody of the commissioner of the Department of Corrections for the remainder of his natural life until released in accordance with law, consecutive to count one.

''It is the sentence of this court on count three for the murder of Patricia List,'' he said without pause or change in intonation, ''that the defendant be remanded to the custody of the commissioner of the Department of Corrections for the remainder of his natural life and until released in accordance with law, consecutive to counts one and two.

''It is the sentence of this court on count four of the murder of Frederick List that the defendant be remanded to the custody of the commissioner of the Department of Corrections for the remainder of his natural life and until released in accordance with law, consecutive to counts one and two and three.''

And finally, ''It is the sentence of this court on count five for the murder of John F. List, that the defendant be remanded to the custody of the commissioner of the Department of Corrections for the remainder of his natural life and until released in accordance with law, consecutive to counts one and two, three and four.

''Mr. List,'' he said, looking directly at the John, who had not moved a muscle during the entire time the judge was speaking, ''you have forty-five days to appeal this sentence. You have a right to appeal as an indicant, pursuant to rule 3:21-4. You have a right to be represented by an attorney. If you can't afford one, one will be appointed for you. Do you understand your rights?''

''Yes, I do.''

''Good luck, Mr. List!'' Judge Wertheimer said tersely. ''Court is adjourned.''

The courtroom burst into thunderous cheers and spontaneous applause while John removed his glasses and rubbed his eyes.

They didn't understand! Nobody did! There was nothing else he could do at that time!

When the lights went out at 10 P.M., John List carefully placed his glasses on the small table near his pillow before he lay down in bed. It was warm and reasonably comfortable.

He would fare well in the solitude of prison. His instinct for survival had always been in full operation and still was. The pressure was finally off. The man who didn't want to go on welfare would now live at the public's expense for the rest of his life, a permanent guest of the state. The regimentation, along with constant pastoral aid, suited his personality and his needs.

The nights were very silent. He crooked his arm over his closed eyes and looked into the past once more . . . as an observer rather than a participant.

The twenty years of his marriage to Helen were an abnegation of the life in which he had been brought up. In the torment of that time with her, he had become more and more enraged, more and more desperate. He wasn't sure at which point exactly he'd decided that he had to cut those twenty years out. Like a cancer, every vestige had to be removed. In one day he had excised it all. All the blood relatives he would have had to leave behind, had he chosen simply to walk out the door, had been eliminated.

He had had to cut out *Mutter*. She in particular! He really didn't even know why himself. The surface reasons were easy enough: the pain she would feel at what her son had done, at the loss of her grandchildren, and the fact that all the money she would need was gone. But were these really the basic reasons? Killing *Mutter* may have been a subconscious admission that the familiar patterns with which he was now forever burdened were her fault, that her overprotectiveness had robbed him of his masculinity in some subtle but profound way, and he had never been able to retrieve it.

His eyes were feeling very heavy. As he began to fall asleep in the private darkness of his cell, he thought vaguely of the rest of it . . . as an observer . . . that, astonishingly, he had set about re-creating the exact life he had been headed for before his marriage to Helen. In a psychological sense, John List had committed a form of emotional suicide. Bobby Clark was an entirely new person, formed to lead the life John had been programmed for, with a set of rigid principles, a single austere life-style, and a religion that supported it. Life had become tranquil, serene, full of devotional duties, a love of God, services to the church. A bit unworldly but familiar, it had all the emotional comfort, support, and religious ambiance of Bay City, the "Salzburg" of his youth.

As Robert Peter Clark he had finally become the true John Emil List.

It's all *Mutter's* fault, John List thought drowsily. She should not have made him feel so special. She should have protected him against Helen.

John closed his eyes once more. He resented that he had to think of these things again. He didn't ever want to think of them again. And *Mutter* would forgive him. He felt certain of that.

* * *

Today approximately 3,500 people live in the little town of Frankenmuth, Michigan. Several hundred still carry the surname of List. They all point with pride to their common ancestor, Johann Adam List, John Emil's granduncle, who, with his brother, Johann List, John Emil's grandfather, were two of the first Lists to arrive in this country. They all point with pride to the first covered bridge and the beautiful tall white spire of St. Lorenz Church, which they had helped to build.

In the peaceful little graveyard to the side of the church is the final resting place of Alma List, interred next to her sister, Augusta, with one place remaining in the family plot. Everyone knew it had been reserved for Alma's beloved son, John Emil.

* * *

And on the silent edge of Westfield lies Fairview, a quiet little cemetery where about 24,000 people are buried. A nondescript, three-foot-high concrete slab marks the graves of Helen List and her three children. Two days after Bob Clark finally admitted he was John List, a small piece of paper was found glued to the center of the tombstone. It bore the handwritten inscription:

Finally you can rest in peace. God bless.

Bibliography

"Five in Family Found Slain; 50-State Alarm Seeks Dad," *The Westfield Leader*, December 9, 1971.

Cohen, Robert, "Westfield Tragedy, Husband Hunted in Mass Slaying," *The Star-Ledger*, December 9, 1971.

Bullock, Marilyn, and Bruce Baily. "A Churchgoer . . . But a Loner. The Lists Were a Neighborhood Mystery," *The Star-Ledger*, December 9, 1971.

"Four States Center of Hunt for Mass Killer," *The Daily Record*, December 9, 1971.

Johnston, Richard, J. H., "5 in Jersey Family Slain; Husband Sought, *The New York Times*, December 9, 1971.

"Murdered List Family Buried; Search Still On," *The Daily Record*, December 9, 1971.

"Find Slain Family Father's Car at Kennedy," *The Daily Record*, December 10, 1971.

Johnston, Richard, A., "Pastor Makes Appeal to Man Being Sought in Murder of 5 in Jersey," *The New York Times*, December 12, 1971.

Cohen, Robert, "List's Car Found at JFK; Cops Check Flight Records," *The Star-Ledger*, December 10, 1971.

———, "List's Letter Indicates Intention to Stay Alive," *The Star-Ledger*, December 11, 1971.

———, "Pleas for List's Return, 'Daddy, You're All I Have Left . . . '" *The Star-Ledger*, December 12, 1971.

Bailey, Bruce, "Murder Case Against List Going to Union Grand Jury," *The Star-Ledger*, December 13, 1971.

"Hunt Widens for List, Suspect in Family Killing," *The Westfield Leader*, December 16, 1971.

"Suspect Indicted in Killing of Five," *The New York Times*, December 17, 1971.

"The Ballroom Murders," *Newsweek*, December 20, 1971.

Fielder, Lore, "Wanted Poster Is Issued," *The Westfield Leader*, December 20, 1971.

"Search Continues for List," *The Westfield Leader*, December 23, 1971.

Sherman, William, "A Father's Torment: Inside Story of N.J. Murders, Money, Marital Woes Lay Behind Killings," *The Daily News*, December 28, 1971.

———, "When It Was Done, He Knelt and Prayed," *The Daily News*, December 29, 1971.

———, "Life Was Just Too Much for Him All the Way," *The Daily News*, December 30, 1971.

———, "List Is Out of Sight—But Not Out of Mind," *The Daily News*, December 31, 1971.

"Fire Guts List Home, Site of Mass Murders," *The Westfield Leader*, August 31, 1972.

"Fire Destroys Home of Man Sought in Slayings of Family," *The New York Times*, August 31, 1972.

"List House Leveled," *The Westfield Leader*, September 21, 1972.

"To Auction List Land," *The Westfield Leader*, November 22, 1972.

Johnston, Richard, J. H., "Auction of List Property Recalls 5 Westfield Slayings," *The New York Times*, December 6, 1972.

"List Property Sold at Auction," *The Westfield Leader*, December 14, 1972.

"Jersey Murders," *The New York Times*, June 2, 1974.

Zullo, Alan A. "After 6-Year Search, World's Police Can't Find Man They Say Killed Wife, Mother & Children," *National Enquirer*, 1977.

"Legal Decision Due on Fugitive Murderer," *The Daily Journal*, October 6, 1979.

Koppisch, John, "Judge Will Rule if John List is Legally Dead," *The Daily Journal*, January 29, 1980.

———, "$225,000 Policies Lapsed. Judge's Ruling in List Case," *The Daily Journal*, April 16, 1980.

Epperson, Mary, "Insurance Fight in List Killings," *The Daily Journal*, August 28, 1980.

———, "Judge Rules Insurance Void in List Killings," *The Daily Journal*, October 9, 1980.

"Insurance Ruled Void on List Relatives," *The Daily Journal*, October 13, 1980.

Longo, Kathleen, "List Slayings Top Mystery in County," *The Daily Journal*, September 19, 1983.

Emerson, Tony, "18 Years After Murders, Police Still Pursue List," *The Daily Journal*, December 7, 1984.

Hinmon, Derrick, "The Perfect Crime? List Still Missing 15 Years After Killing Family," *The Courier-News*, December 6, 1986.

"John List Still Missing 15 Years After Slayings," *The Westfield Leader*, December 11, 1986.

Gluck, Gabriel H., "15 Years Later, File Remains Open on Dad Who Killed Family and Fled," *The Star-Ledger*, December, 14, 1986.

"A Father and His Victims," *The Courier-News*, March 14, 1986.

"Local P.D. Deluged with List Leads After Program Airs," *The Westfield Leader*, May 25, 1989.

Bratt, Heidi Mae, "Capture Stuns Neighbors," *The Daily Journal*, June 2, 1989.

McDarrah, Timothy and Leo Standora, "Mass Murder Suspect Nabbed 18 Yrs. Later, Remarried and Living Quiet Life," *New York Post*, June 2, 1989.

Strupp, Joe, "He Was Too Nice to Be True," *The Daily Journal*, June 2, 1989.

Gross, Ken, Sellinger, Margie Bonnett, and Jack Kelley, "In Hiding for 18 Years, A Wanted Man Is Caught by the FBI and a TV Posse," *Crime*, June 1989.

McFadden, Robert D., "Suspect in 5 Killings in 1971 Caught with Aid of TV Show," *The New York Times*, June 2, 1989.

Spoto, Mary Ann, "Officer Recalls Grim Fall Day," *The Daily Journal*, June 2, 1989.

Hoffman, Bill, "Slay Suspect's Wife Stands by Her Man, Can't Believe he Killed Family," *New York Post*, June 3, 1989.

The Associated Press, "N.J. Slay Suspect is Latest Nab by TV's *Most Wanted*," *New York Post*, June 3, 1989.

Haywood, Karen, "I Am Devoted to Him," *The Daily Journal*, June 3, 1989.

Hopkins, Kathleen, "List Hunt on Minds of Editor, Reporter," *The Daily Journal*, June 3, 1989.

Hopkins, Kathleen, "List to Face Bail Hearing," *The Daily Journal*, June 3, 1989.

Hoffmann, Bill, "She Never Had a Clue," *New York Post*, June 5, 1989.

"Pastor Calls for Compassion in List Case," *The Record*, June 5, 1989.

"List Sculptor Struggled to Get 'Mr. Nice Guy,'" *The Star-Ledger*, June 5, 1989.

Haywood, Karen, "Compassion for 'Clark' is Called For," *The Daily Journal*, June 5, 1989.

Gluck, Gabriel H., "Suspect's Church Prays for Man It Never Knew," *The Star-Ledger*, June 5, 1989.

Hopkins, Kathleen, "List Waives Bail Hearing," *The Daily Journal*, June 6, 1989.

"Sculptor's Fulfillment: Art of Crime-Busting," *USA Today*, June 6, 1989.

Hopkins, Kathleen, "In-Law: List Would Tell Me Why," *The Daily Journal*, June 7, 1989.

Semler, H. Eric, "Old Crime Held Town in Thrall," *The New York Times*, June 7, 1989.

"John List's Children: Gone, But Not Forgotten," *The Westfield Leader*, June 8, 1989.

Gardner, Kathleen L., and Ellen Scott Brandt, "John List's Capture Ends 17 1/2 Years of Wondering," *The Westfield Leader*, June 8, 1989.

Appelman, Hilary, "Manhunt Is On, List Arrest Encourages Authorities in Other Long-Term Investigations," *The Daily Journal*, June 8, 1989.

"List Calls, Says Sorry," *The Daily Journal*, June 8, 1989.

Hopkins, Kathleen, "Cops Anxious to Return List," *The Daily Journal*, June 8, 1989.

Orr, J. Scott, "Wife of Accused Mass Killer Convinced He's Not John List," *The Star-Ledger*, June 9, 1989.

Appelman, Hilary, "Suspected Fugitive Awaits Extradition," *The Record*, June 9, 1989.

Appelman, Hilary, "List's Extradition Hearing Set for July 6," *The Record*, June 9, 1989.

May, Clifford D., "Prosaic Life of Suspect in '71 New Jersey Murders," *The New York Times*, June 9, 1989.

Spoto, Maryann, "List's Return Is Postponed," *The Daily Journal*, June 9, 1989.

Douthat, Strat, "John List Gave Self Away," *The Daily Journal*, June 10, 1989.

————, "Murder Suspect Created Disguise in His Own Image," *The Daily Journal*, June 12, 1989.

"After 18 Years, A Bust," *Time*, June 12, 1989.

Jacoby, Tamar, "Murder, They Broadcast," "America's *Most Wanted* Solves a Gory Mystery," *Newsweek*, June 12, 1989.

"Unsung Heroes" (to editor), *The Daily Journal*, June 15, 1989.

Livesey, Eileen (to editor), "Another Viewpoint," *The Westfield Leader*, June 15, 1989.

"Fugitive Charges Dropped, List Remains in Va. Custody," *The Westfield Leader*, June 15, 1989.

Douthat, Strat, "The Fugitive, In 18 Years on the Run, Slaying

Suspect's Life Comes to Resemble His Old One,'' *The Los Angeles Times*, June 18, 1989.

Ken Gross (N.Y.), Margie Sellinger (Va.), Jack Kelley (Colorado), "Crime," *People* magazine, June 19, 1989.

Gluck, Gabriel H., "List Back in Jersey to Face Charges He Murdered Family," *The Star-Ledger*, June 30, 1989.

"Murder Suspect Brought to N.J.," *The Daily Record*, June 30, 1989.

Saffron, Inga, "Multiple-Murder Suspect Is Returned to New Jersey," *The Philadelphia Inquirer*, June 30, 1989.

Moran, Thomas, "John List Is Returned to N.J.," *The Record*, June 30, 1989.

"D. B. or Not D. B.? N.J. Killer: Could He Be D. B. Cooper?" *New York Post*, July 1, 1989.

Esser, Doug, "Has FBI Landed D. B. Cooper?" *Herald Examiner*, July 1, 1989.

Brandt, Ellen Scott, "List Is Read Long-Awaited Charges," *The Westfield Leader*, July 6, 1989.

"John List Is Back in Union County," *The Westfield Leader*, July 6, 1989.

Richissin, Todd, "It's List's Day in Court," *The Daily Journal*, July 10, 1989.

Spoto, Maryann, "List Bail Set at $5 Million," *The Daily Journal*, July 11, 1989.

Sullivan, Joseph F., "Judge Sets Bail at $5 Million for Suspect in 1971 Killings," *The New York Times*, July 11, 1989.

Crabill, Steven, "Judge Sets $5 Million Bail for List," *The Record*, July 11, 1989.

Gluck, Gabriel H., "List Faces Trial on Anniversary of the Murders," *The Star-Ledger*, July 11, 1989.

Saffron, Inga, "$5 Million Bail Set in List Case," *The Philadelphia Inquirer*, July 11, 1989.

Diamond, Randy, "N.J. Slay Suspect: 5M Bail," *The Daily News*, July 11, 1989.

"Man Pleads Not Guilty to Murdering Family," *The Washington Times*, July 11, 1989.

Gritzan, Steve (Dear Editor), "Lasting Impressions of the List Murders," *The Star-Ledger*, Tuesday, July 18, 1989.

Vejnoska, Jill, and Mary Romano, "Mystery of John List, Piecing Together Life of a Mass-Murder Suspect," *The Courier-News*, August 13, 1989.

Vejnoska, Jill, "John List: The Deadly Puzzle, Under Her Thumb," *The Courier-News*, August 14, 1989.

Vejnoska, Jill, "John List: The Deadly Puzzle, An Honest Heart," *The Courier-News*, August 15, 1989.

Romano, Mary, "John List: The Deadly Puzzle, Love and Honor," *The Courier-News*, August 16, 1989.

Agus, Carole, "Who Is John List?" *Newsday*, August 16, 1989.

Vejnoska, Jill, "John List: The Deadly Puzzle, Trouble in Paradise," *The Courier-News*, August 17, 1989.

Romano, Mary, "John List: The Deadly Puzzle, Failure and Futility," *The Courier-News*, August 18, 1989.

Romano, Mary, "John List: The Deadly Puzzle, The Last List," *The Courier-News*, August 19, 1989.

Vejnoska, Jill, "John List: The Deadly Puzzle, New Lyrics, Old Tune," *The Courier-News*, August 20, 1989.

Romano, Mary, "John List: The Deadly Puzzle, The End of the Line," *The Courier-News*, August 21, 1989.

"Sculptor's Strategy Is Turning Heads," *The Daily Record*, September 17, 1989.

Gluck, Gabriel, "Quiet, Orderly Days for List As He Awaits Next Step Toward Murder Trial," *The Sunday Star-Ledger*, December 24, 1989.